THE COMPLETE BOOK OF
FORMULA ONE

MOTORBOOKS
INTERNATIONAL

First published in 2003 by Motorbooks International, an imprint of MBI Publishing Company, Galtier Plaza, Suite 200, 380 Jackson Street, St. Paul, MN 55101-3885 USA

Talk to the publisher about this book: rob@motorbooksinternational.co.uk

ISBN 0-7603-1688-0

Printed in Hong Kong

THE COMPLETE BOOK OF
FORMULA ONE

ALL CARS AND DRIVERS SINCE 1950 • 3685 PHOTOGRAPHS • COMPREHENSIVE DATA

SIMON ARRON AND MARK HUGHES

CONTENTS

1950s

1960s

1970s

1980s

1990s

2000s

INTRODUCTION

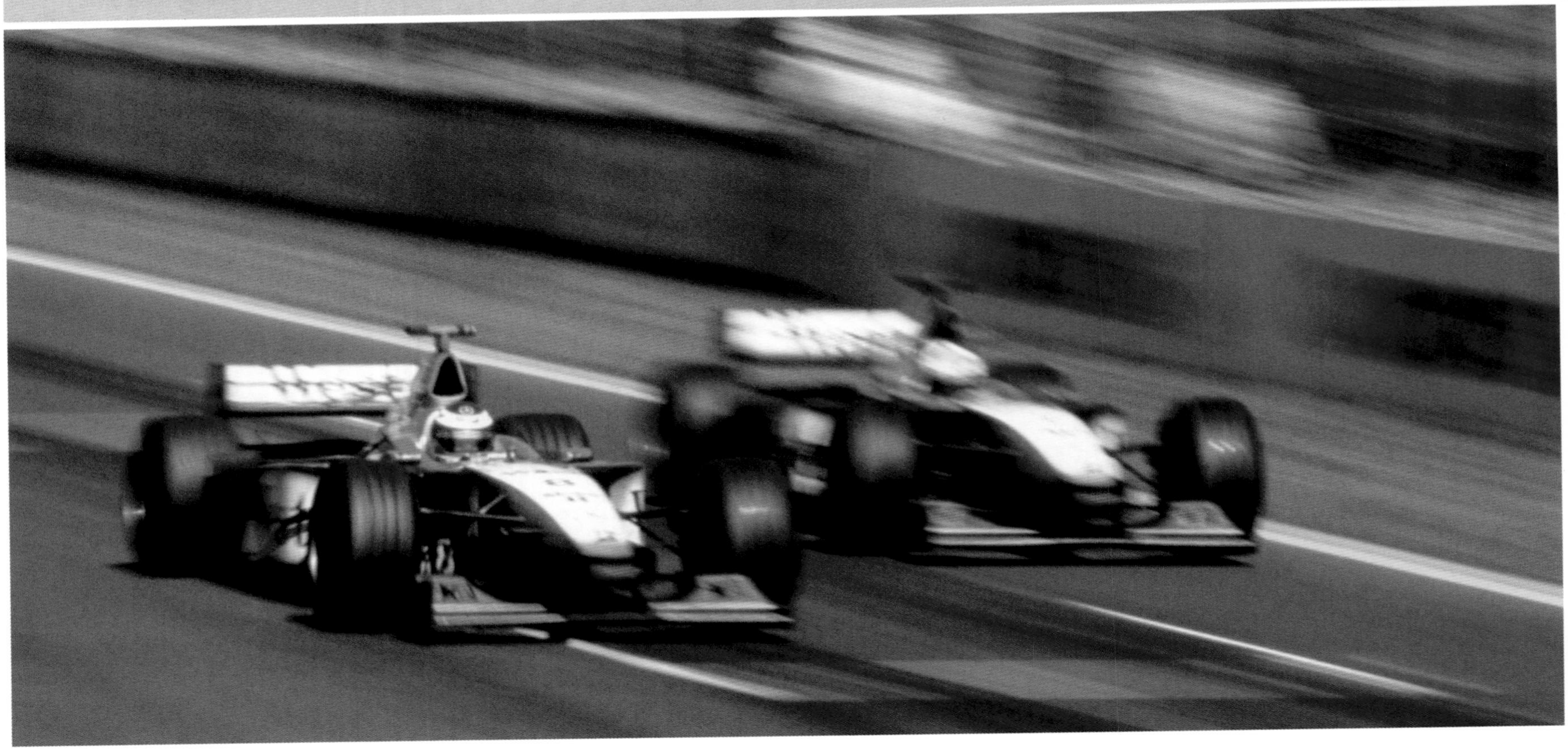

Want to know what the Stebro, Connew or the Eifelland looked like? Or what colour the first McLaren was? When did Team Lotus race a Maserati? Exactly how ugly was the colour scheme of Damon Hill's first F1 car?

The idea behind the *Complete Book of Formula One* is simple – to publish the most comprehensive photographic record of the drivers who have raced in the Formula 1 World Championship since it was inaugurated in 1950. Overviews of each season are complemented by a car-by-car guide to that season's competitors in championship order, showing each car they started a race in.

That was the challenge. We just needed to find the 2,765 pictures to fulfill the remit. Similar books already exist for single races such as the Le Mans 24 Hours and Indianapolis 500, but the sheer volume of photographs required to do justice to the whole F1 world championship (and the relative lack of coverage of the early years) have previously made an attempt to record all starters virtually impossible.

No single archive could contain all the images required, but LAT was ideally placed to be the backbone of this book. Formed in the mid-1960s by the publishers of *Motor Sport* and *Motorsport News*, LAT was acquired by Haymarket Publishing in 1996, and has since added the extensive archives of *Autosport*, *Motor* and *Autocar*. The estimated nine million images make LAT the largest collection of its kind in the world, covering the history of motor racing from 1895 to the present day.

Heading the research has been long-time LAT archive linchpin Kathy Ager. An unobstructed, in-focus action shot of the relevant car was obviously the aim (and normally the result), but every effort has been made to include the best reference possible. If this was taken in the pitlane, or during an unsuccessful attempt to qualify for a championship round during the season, or while racing the same car in a non-championship F1 race that year, then the picture has been included for completeness.

While the sport's leading photographic agencies now send up to seven photographers and digital technicians to every grand prix, coverage of the championship was much more haphazard in the 1950s. For instance, newly published motor racing weekly *Autosport* preferred to send its photographer to the Brighton Speed Trials in early September 1950 rather than to the first world championship grand prix the

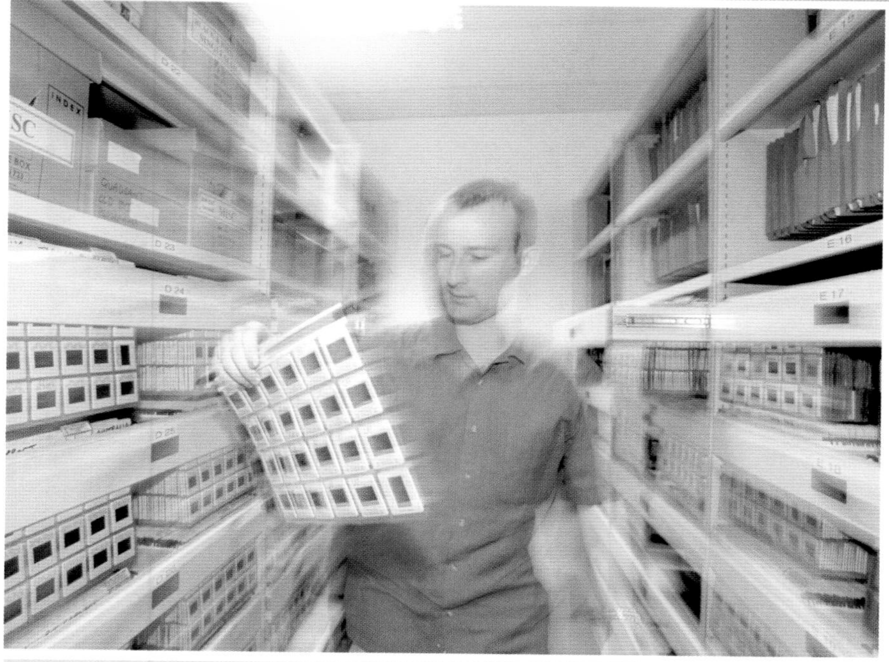

Far left
Melbourne domination: the triumphant McLarens of Mika Häkkinen and David Coulthard begin their successful 1998 season at the Australian Grand Prix

Above
The backbone of this book comes from the estimated nine million images held in the LAT archive – the largest collection of its kind in the world

COMPLETE F1 FACTS (to end of 2002 season)

- Red cars won every championship Grand Prix until Mercedes-Benz arrived in 1954
- Car number 1 won most races (16.47%) – 5 is the next most successful number
- Average age of drivers to start a race is 30.87 (it was 44.06 in 1950 but dropped to 29.99 by 2002)
- Jacques Laffite raced most with the same number (132 grands prix with 26), and for the same team (Ligier, also 132)
- Number 13 was used once – by Moises Solana in the 1963 Mexican GP
- The lowest number never raced in Formula 1 is 45
- Britons started in all bar four races
- Graham Hill's F1 career is the longest (16.69 years)
- The largest World Championship field is 34 starters (1953 German GP) – smallest is 10 (1958 Argentine GP)
- Eight drivers retired on the opening lap of their only grand prix – Marco Apicella is reputed to be the least successful, spinning before the first corner of the 1993 Italian GP

JOIN THE HUNT FOR THE MISSING PICTURES

Let us have one or more of the few missing pictures, and we will add your name to the Complete Book of Formula One Roll of Honour. We will also provide a free copy of the book for those who provide pictures in time for the next edition of the book.

Go to the website at www.MotorbooksInternational.co.uk and you will find a section dedicated to the search for the pictures. You will be able to download in the right dimensions to fill the slots.

magazine would cover, and the Italian GP report ran without illustration. Despite this, the LAT collection has coverage from all but a handful of championship races.

Seven months of research resulted in almost all the necessary images from these files, and other omissions have been filled with the valuable assistance of various archives, especially the GP Library, the Klemantaski Collection and Iacona & Bertschi Collection, Archives Serge Pozzoli, National Motor Museum and the William Green Motor Racing Library – a full list of credits can be found on page 480.

The result is the most comprehensive illustrated record of the cars and drivers to have competed in the championship – only 31 images are missing, and all before 1962.

But for instance, the search for Hans Herrmann at the 1959 British Grand Prix has ended in frustration. It was the only time the German started in a Scuderia Centro Sud Cooper T51, his engine failed to fire properly and he was slow away. He proceeded to trail the field for 21 laps before retiring – and the British photographers appear to have ignored his presence.

The 1953 German Grand Prix might have been the championship race with the most starters (34), but photographers appear not to have bothered with the local competitors because seven of these have not come to light. Someone, somewhere must have them…

However, these are isolated frustrations in the story. The *Complete Book of Formula 1* charts the changing shape of the sport – from the all-conquering Alfa Romeos at the start, through the transition from rear-engined continental marques to the front-engined British manufacturers in the late 1950s to the emergence of commercial sponsorship from 1968. The growing professionalism of the sport in the past two decades has now seen more stable grids (and therefore more compact car-by-car sections), and the competitive nature of Grand Prix racing has grown ever greater.

The 600 drivers who started a grand prix to the beginning of the 2003 season are featured in the comprehensive driver's section – complete with career statistics to the end of 2002. Portraits of many of the great and not-so-great drivers are featured.

This might have been a mammoth undertaking, but the result fills a void in previous coverage of the sport's top category.

Peter Higham
LAT Photographic

MOTORES
DIESEL

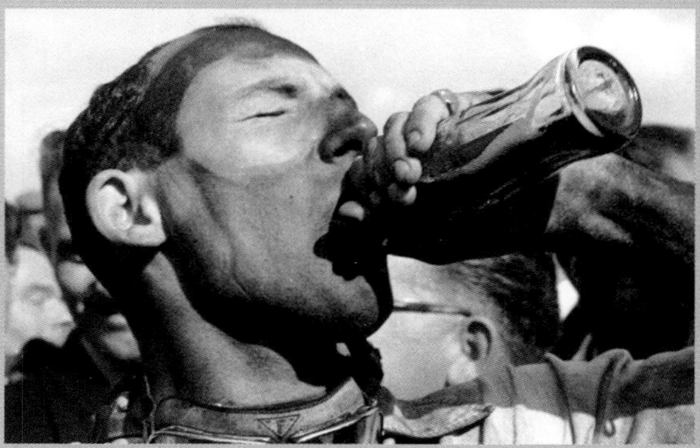

1950s

1950

FARINA MAKES HISTORY AS HIS SPORT'S FIRST WORLD CHAMPION

Above
May 13 1950: Giuseppe Farina is seldom regarded as one of the all-time greats – but he won the first world championship grand prix, at Silverstone, and went on to take the inaugural title

Left
Monochrome set: Fangio sprints ahead of Alfa Romeo team-mate Farina at Reims. The Argentine went on to win comfortably after fuel pump failure sidelined his rival

Right
Sip stop: Fangio takes a breather at Silverstone, before a broken oil pipe forced him to retire

Alfa Romeo had been forced, for financial reasons, to withdraw from grand prix racing the previous year, but the launch of a world championship in 1950 brought the Italians out of retirement. Still relying on the supercharged Alfetta – a car that had made its debut as a voiturette formula car in 1937 – the company felt confident that no one else had a car to challenge the old warhorse.

It was right and won all six championship grands prix. America's most famous race, the Indianapolis 500, also counted towards the title, as it would until 1960, but few Europe-based racers bothered taking part. Alfa's drivers fought among themselves for the honour of being the sport's first world champion and Giuseppe Farina won the inaugural race, which was held around the perimeter track at Silverstone – a wartime airfield in Northamptonshire, England.

Farina emerged victorious only after team-mate Juan Manuel Fangio's engine broke – and this defined a pattern for the season: Fangio was invariably faster but Farina had the better finishing record and duly became the sport's first world champion.

Enzo Ferrari had helped create the Alfetta when he was still working for Alfa Romeo before the war. Now he produced his own cars – and they had been successful the previous season, while Alfa was away from the sport. They were no match, however, for the returning Alfetta.

Raymond Sommer came closest to upsetting the formbook. At the wheel of an old-fashioned, unsupercharged Talbot, the Frenchman used driving skill and superior fuel economy to give Alfa a real fright during the Belgian Grand Prix, but then his engine broke. His spirited performance would have significant future consequences.

Above
Plus ça change: of all contemporary grand prix circuits, Monaco has altered least over the years. Froilan Gonzalez (Maserati 4CLT/48) and Luigi Villoresi (Ferrari 125) lead a gaggle through streets that were unprotected by barriers back in 1950

Below
Class act: Fangio was leading in Monaco when he noticed that fans had their heads turned away from him. Curious, he backed off – and was able to pick his way through the remains of a multiple pile-up ahead. He was more than a lap clear at the end

GIUSEPPE FARINA – WORLD CHAMPION 1950

1950

CHAMPIONSHIP CAR-BY-CAR

* Drivers who used an assumed name appear in quotation marks throughout.

1ST GIUSEPPE FARINA (ITA; AGE: 43) 30 PTS

Alfa Romeo 158 S8 sc
Alfa Corse
Races: GBR (car #2); MON (#32); SUI (#16); BEL (#8); FRA (#2); ITA (#10)

2ND JUAN MANUEL FANGIO (ARG; AGE: 39) 27 PTS

Alfa Romeo 158 S8 sc
Alfa Corse
Races: GBR (car #1); MON (#34); SUI (#14); BEL (#10); FRA (#6); ITA (#18 and #60)

3RD LUIGI FAGIOLI (ITA; AGE: 52) 24(+4) PTS

Alfa Romeo 158 S8 sc
Alfa Corse
Races: GBR (car #3); MON (#36); SUI (#12); BEL (#12); FRA (#4); ITA (#36)

4TH LOUIS ROSIER (FRA; AGE: 44) 13 PTS

Lago-Talbot T26C S6
Écurie Rosier/ Automobiles Talbot Darracq/Charles Pozzi
Races: GBR (car #15); MON (#16); SUI (#10); BEL (#14); FRA (#20 and #26); ITA (#58)

5TH ALBERTO ASCARI (ITA; AGE: 32) 11 PTS

Ferrari 125 V12 sc
Scuderia Ferrari
Races: MON (car #40); SUI (#18)

ALBERTO ASCARI (CONTD)

Ferrari 275 V12
Scuderia Ferrari
Races: BEL (car #4)

ALBERTO ASCARI (CONTD)

Ferrari 375 V12
Scuderia Ferrari
Races: ITA (car #16 and #48)

PICTURED AT NON-CHAMPIONSHIP RACE

6TH "B BIRA" (THA; AGE: 35) 5 PTS

Maserati 4CLT/48 S4
Enrico Plate
Races: GBR (car #21); MON (#50); SUI; ITA (both #30)

7TH= LOUIS CHIRON (MON; AGE: 50) 4 PTS

Maserati 4CLT/48 S4
Officine Alfieri Maserati
Races: GBR (car #19); MON (#48); SUI (#26); FRA (#30); ITA (#6)

7TH= REG PARNELL (GBR; AGE: 38) 4 PTS

Alfa Romeo 158 S8 sc
Alfa Corse
Races: GBR (car #4)

REG PARNELL (CONTD)

Maserati 4CLT/48 S4
Scuderia Ambrosiana
Races: FRA (car #32)

7TH= PETER WHITEHEAD (GBR; AGE: 35) 4 PTS

Ferrari 125 V12 sc
Driver
Races: FRA (car #14); ITA (#8)

10TH= PHILIPPE ÉTANÇELIN (FRA; AGE: 53) 3 PTS

Lago-Talbot T26C S6
Driver/Automobiles Talbot-Darracq
Races: GBR (car #16); MON (#14); SUI (#42); BEL; FRA (both #16); ITA (#24)

10TH= YVES GIRAUD-CABANTOUS (FRA; AGE: 45) 3 PTS

Lago-Talbot T26C S6
Automobiles Talbot-Darracq
Races: GBR (car #14); SUI (#6); BEL; FRA (both #18)

10TH= ROBERT MANZON (FRA; AGE: 33) 3 PTS

Simca-Gordini 15 S4
Équipe Simca Gordini
Races: MON (car #10); FRA; ITA (both #44)

1950

CHAMPIONSHIP CAR-BY-CAR

10TH= DORINO SERAFINI (ITA; AGE: 41) 3 PTS

Ferrari 375 V12
Scuderia Ferrari
Races: ITA (car #48)

10TH= RAYMOND SOMMER (FRA; AGE: 43) 3 PTS

Ferrari 125 V12 sc
Driver
Races: MON (car #42)

10TH= RAYMOND SOMMER (CONTD)

Ferrari 166/F2/50 V12
Driver
Races: SUI (car #20)

10TH= RAYMOND SOMMER (CONTD)

Lago-Talbot T26C S6
Driver/Automobiles Talbot-Darracq
Races: BEL (car #6); FRA; ITA (both #12)

15TH FELICE BONETTO (ITA; AGE: 47) 2 PTS

Maserati 4CLT/50-Milano S4
Scuderia Milano
Races: SUI (car #34); FRA (#40)

16TH EUGÈNE CHABOUD (FRA; AGE: 43) 1 PT

Lago-Talbot T26C S6
Écurie Lutetia/Philippe Étançelin
Races: BEL (car #20); FRA (#16)

CLEMENTE BIONDETTI (ITA; AGE: 52) 0 PTS

Ferrari 166I-Jaguar S6
Driver
Races: ITA (car #22)

ANTONIO BRANCA (SUI; AGE: 33) 0 PTS

Maserati 4CL S4
Scuderia Achille Varzi/Driver
Races: SUI (car #40); BEL (#30)

JOHNNY CLAES (BEL; AGE: 33) 0 PTS

Lago-Talbot T26C S6
Écurie Belge/Driver
Races: GBR (car #18); MON (#6); SUI (#4); BEL (#24); FRA (#42); ITA (#2)

GIANFRANCO COMOTTI (ITA; AGE: 44) 0 PTS

Maserati 4CLT/50-Milano S4
Scuderia Milano
Races: ITA (car #62)

CAR PICTURED AT NON-CHAMPIONSHIP RACE

GEOFFREY CROSSLEY (GBR; AGE: 29) 0 PTS

Alta GP S4 sc
Driver
Races: GBR (car #24); BEL (#26)

JOE FRY (GBR; AGE: 34) 0 PTS
BRIAN SHAWE-TAYLOR (GBR; AGE: 35)

(shared car)
Maserati 4CL S4
Joe Fry
Races: GBR (car #10)

BOB GERARD (GBR; AGE: 36) 0 PTS

ERA B-type S6 sc
Driver
Races: GBR (car #12)

BOB GERARD (CONTD)

ERA A-type S6 sc
Driver
Races: MON (#26)

JOSÉ FROILÁN GONZÁLEZ (ARG; AGE: 27) 0 PTS

Maserati 4CLT/48 S4
Scuderia Achille Varzi
Races: MON (car #2); FRA (#36)

1950

CHAMPIONSHIP CAR-BY-CAR

EMMANUEL DE GRAFFENRIED (SUI; AGE: 36) 0 PTS

Maserati 4CLT/48 S4
Enrico Plate
Races: GBR (car #20); MON (#52); SUI (#32); ITA (#38)

DAVID HAMPSHIRE (GBR; AGE: 32) 0 PTS

Maserati 4CLT/48 S4
Scuderia Ambrosiana
Races: GBR (car #6); FRA (#34)

CUTH HARRISON (GBR; AGE: 44) 0 PTS

ERA C-type S6 sc
Driver
Races: GBR (car #11); MON (#24); ITA (#32)

LESLIE JOHNSON (GBR; AGE: 38) 0 PTS

ERA E-type S6 sc
English Racing Automobiles
Races: GBR (car #8)

JOE KELLY (IRL; AGE: 37) 0 PTS

Alta GP S4 sc
Driver
Races: GBR (car #23)

"PIERRE LEVEGH" (FRA; AGE: 44) 0 PTS

Lago-Talbot T26C S6
Driver
Races: BEL; FRA (both car #22); ITA (#56)

HENRI LOUVEAU (FRA; AGE: 40) 0 PTS

Lago-Talbot T26C S6
Écurie Rosier
Races: ITA (car #64)

GUY MAIRESSE (FRA; AGE: 40) 0 PTS

Lago-Talbot T26C S6
Driver
Races: ITA (car #40)

PICTURED AT 1949 BEL

EUGÈNE MARTIN (FRA; AGE: 35) 0 PTS

Lago-Talbot T26C S6
Automobiles Talbot-Darracq
Races: GBR (car #17); SUI (#8)

DAVID MURRAY (GBR; AGE: 40) 0 PTS

Maserati 4CLT/48 S4
Scuderia Ambrosiana
Races: GBR (car #5); ITA (#50)

NELLO PAGANI (ITA; AGE: 38) 0 PTS

Maserati 4CLT/48 S4
Scuderia Achille Varzi
Races: SUI (car #2)

PAUL PIETSCH (GER; AGE: 39) 0 PTS

Maserati 4CLT/48 S4
Driver
Races: ITA (car #28)

CHARLES POZZI (FRA; AGE: 40) 0 PTS

Lago-Talbot T26C S6
Driver
Races: FRA (car #26)

FRANCO ROL (ITA; AGE: 42) 0 PTS

Maserati 4CLT/48 S4
Officine Alfieri Maserati
Races: MON (car #44); FRA (#28); ITA (#4)

TONY ROLT (GBR; AGE: 31) 0 PTS
PETER WALKER (GBR; AGE: 37)

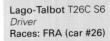

(shared car)
ERA E-type S6 sc
Peter Walker
Races: GBR (car #9)

1950

CHAMPIONSHIP CAR-BY-CAR

CONSALVO SANESI (ITA; AGE: 39) 0 PTS

Alfa Romeo 158 S8 sc
Alfa Corse
Races: ITA (car #46)

HARRY SCHELL (USA; AGE: 28) 0 PTS

Cooper T12-JAP twin
Horschell Racing Corporation
Races: MON (car #8)

HARRY SCHELL (CONTD)

Lago-Talbot T26C S6
Écurie Bleue
Races: SUI (car #44)

PIERO TARUFFI (ITA; AGE: 43) 0 PTS

Alfa Romeo 158 S8 sc
Alfa Corse
Races: ITA (car #60)

MAURICE TRINTIGNANT (FRA; AGE: 32) 0 PTS

Simca-Gordini 15 S4
Équipe Simca Gordini
Races: MON (car #12); ITA (#42)

LUIGI VILLORESI (ITA; AGE: 41) 0 PTS

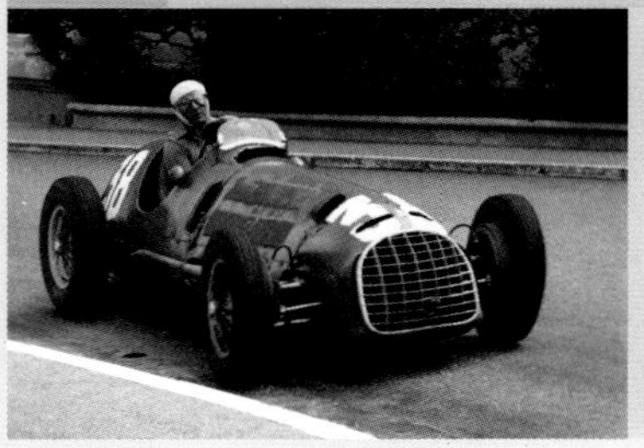

Ferrari 125 V12 sc
Scuderia Ferrari
Races: MON (car #38); SUI (#22); BEL (#2)

GRAND PRIX WINNERS 1950

	RACE (CIRCUIT)	WINNER (CAR)
GBR	BRITISH GRAND PRIX (SILVERSTONE)	GIUSEPPE FARINA (ALFA ROMEO 158 S8 SC)
MON	MONACO GRAND PRIX (MONTE CARLO)	JUAN MANUEL FANGIO (ALFA ROMEO 158 S8 SC)
SUI	SWISS GRAND PRIX (BREMGARTEN)	GIUSEPPE FARINA (ALFA ROMEO 158 S8 SC)
BEL	BELGIAN GRAND PRIX (SPA-FRANCORCHAMPS)	JUAN MANUEL FANGIO (ALFA ROMEO 158 S8 SC)
FRA	FRENCH GRAND PRIX (REIMS)	JUAN MANUEL FANGIO (ALFA ROMEO 158 S8 SC)
ITA	ITALIAN GRAND PRIX (MONZA)	GIUSEPPE FARINA (ALFA ROMEO 158 S8 SC)

1951

FANGIO LEAVES IT LATE

Far left
Juan step beyond: Fangio raises his hand in triumph after scoring a comfortable Spanish GP victory and securing his first world title. The writing was on the wall, though, for Alfa Romeo: its cars were outdated and the team quit the sport at the end of the season

Above
Spanish stroll: Alberto Ascari's Ferrari noses ahead at the start in Pedralbes, near Barcelona. The Catalan capital is the only city to have hosted world championship grands prix at three different venues

Left
Grime and reason: sporting the oily smears that were part and parcel of a grand prix driver's lot in the 1950s, Ascari (second right) prepares to celebrate victory at Monza

Although Alfa Romeo clung on to the world championship by the skin of its teeth, the result of the British Grand Prix hinted at an impending change in the grand prix hierarchy. It was here that Froilan Gonzalez used the new, unsupercharged Ferrari to beat Juan Manuel Fangio's Alfa into second place.

Enzo Ferrari and designer Aurelio Lampredi had been impressed the previous season that an unsupercharged Talbot could occasionally push the more powerful Alfas very hard over a race distance, because it spent less time refuelling in the pits. So Ferrari built a naturally-aspirated 4.5-litre V12 that was much more powerful than the Talbot. It was still some way short of the supercharged Alfetta, but impressive fuel economy was very much in its favour.

Once Gonzalez opened the floodgates the Ferrari was clearly the quicker car – and Alberto Ascari won the next race with it. On several occasions only Fangio's uncanny skill kept the Alfa ahead and he was able to fend off Ascari to take his first world title. The development potential of the 14-year-old Alfa design had come to an end, however, and the company withdrew from Formula One at the end of the year.

Farina, the previous year's champion, was this time overwhelmed by Fangio. Alfa Romeo's third driver Luigi Fagioli stormed out of F1 in a rage after being asked to hand his leading car over to Fangio during the French Grand Prix. The Italian had displayed a similarly short temper when he was a pre-war Mercedes driver. Now, like the Alfetta, he was consigned to history.

Above
Wherefore art thou, Alfa Romeo? At Silverstone Gonzalez signalled a shift in the balance of power by scoring Ferrari's first grand prix win

Below
Britain expects (albeit not too much): Reg Parnell put BRM on the world championship map in the British GP. He finished fifth, five laps in arrears

JUAN MANUEL FANGIO – WORLD CHAMPION 1951, 1954, 1955, 1956 & 1957

1951

CHAMPIONSHIP CAR-BY-CAR

1ST JUAN MANUEL FANGIO (ARG; AGE: 40) 31(+6) PTS

Alfa Romeo 159 S8 sc
Alfa Corse
Races: SUI (car #24); BEL (#2); FRA (#8 and #4); GBR (#2); GER (#75); ITA (#38); ESP (#22)

2ND ALBERTO ASCARI (ITA; AGE: 33) 25(+3) PTS

Ferrari 375 V12
Scuderia Ferrari
Races: SUI (car #20); BEL (#8); FRA (#12 and #14); GBR (#11); GER (#71); ITA; ESP (both #2)

3RD JOSÉ FROILÁN GONZÁLEZ (ARG; AGE: 28) 24(+3) PTS

Lago-Talbot T26C S6
Driver
Races: SUI (car #42)

JOSÉ FROILÁN GONZÁLEZ (CONTD)

Ferrari 375 V12
Scuderia Ferrari
Races: FRA (car #14); GBR (#12); GER (#74); ITA; ESP (both #6)

4TH GIUSEPPE FARINA (ITA; AGE: 44) 19(+3) PTS

Alfa Romeo 159 S8 sc
Alfa Corse
Races: SUI (car #22); BEL (#4); FRA (#2); GBR (#1); GER (#76); ITA (#34 and #40); ESP (#20)

5TH LUIGI VILLORESI (ITA; AGE: 42) 15(+3) PTS

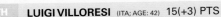

Ferrari 375 V12
Scuderia Ferrari
Races: SUI (car #18); BEL; FRA; GBR (all #10); GER (#72); ITA; ESP (both #4)

6TH PIERO TARUFFI (ITA; AGE: 44) 10 PTS

Ferrari 375 V12
Scuderia Ferrari
Races: SUI (car #44); BEL (#12); GER (#73); ITA; ESP (both #8)

7TH FELICE BONETTO (ITA; AGE: 48) 7 PTS

Alfa Romeo 159 S8 sc
Alfa Corse
Races: GBR (car #4); GER (#77); ITA (#40); ESP (#24)

8TH REG PARNELL (GBR; AGE: 40) 5 PTS

Ferrari 375 V12
Vandervell Products
Races: FRA (car #26)

REG PARNELL (CONTD)

BRM P15 V16 sc
British Racing Motors
Races: GBR (car #6)

9TH LUIGI FAGIOLI (ITA; AGE: 53) 4 PTS

Alfa Romeo 159 S8 sc
Alfa Corse
Races: FRA (car #8 and #4)

10TH= LOUIS ROSIER (FRA; AGE: 45) 3 PTS

Lago-Talbot T26C S6
Écurie Rosier
Races: SUI (car #8); BEL (#14); FRA (#40); GBR (#22); GER (#84); ITA (#18); ESP (#28)

10TH= CONSALVO SANESI (ITA; AGE: 40) 3 PTS

Alfa Romeo 159 S8 sc
Alfa Corse
Races: SUI (car #28); BEL; FRA (both #6); GBR (#3)

12TH= YVES GIRAUD-CABANTOUS (FRA; AGE: 46) 2 PTS

Lago-Talbot T26C S6
Driver
Races: SUI (car #6); BEL (#22); FRA (#46); GER (#87); ITA (#24); ESP (#32)

12TH= EMMANUEL DE GRAFFENRIED (SUI; AGE: 37) 2 PTS

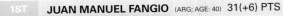

Alfa Romeo 159 S8 sc
Alfa Corse
Races: SUI (car #26); ITA (#36); ESP (#26)

1951

CHAMPIONSHIP CAR-BY-CAR

EMMANUEL DE GRAFFENRIED (CONTD)

Maserati 4CLT/48 S4
Enrico Plate
Races: FRA (car #18); GER (#79)

GEORGE ABECASSIS (GBR; AGE: 38) 0 PTS

HWM 51-Alta S4
Hersham & Walton Motors
Races: SUI (car #12)

"B BIRA" (THA; AGE: 37) 0 PTS

Maserati 4CLT/48-OSCA V12
Écurie Siam
Races: ESP (car #18)

PICTURED AT NON-CHAMPIONSHIP RACE

ANTONIO BRANCA (SUI; AGE: 34) 0 PTS

Maserati 4CLT/48 S4
Driver
Races: GER (car #92)

PICTURED AT NON-CHAMPIONSHIP RACE

EUGÈNE CHABOUD (FRA; AGE: 44) 0 PTS

Lago-Talbot T26C S6
Driver
Races: FRA (car #44)

LOUIS CHIRON (MON; AGE: 52) 0 PTS

Maserati 4CLT/48 S4
Enrico Plate
Races: SUI (car #30)

LOUIS CHIRON (CONTD)

Lago-Talbot T26C S6
Écurie Rosier/Écurie France
Races: BEL (car #18); FRA (#42); GBR (#23); GER (#85); ITA (#20); ESP (#30)

JOHNNY CLAES (BEL; AGE: 35) 0 PTS

Lago-Talbot T26C S6
Écurie Belge
Races: SUI (car #2); BEL (#16); FRA (#28); GBR (#25); GER (#94); ITA (#26); ESP (#36)

PHILIPPE ÉTANÇELIN (FRA; AGE: 54) 0 PTS

Lago-Talbot T26C S6
Driver
Races: SUI (car #4); BEL (#20); FRA (#38); GER (#86); ESP (#34)

RUDOLF FISCHER (SUI; AGE: 39) 0 PTS

Ferrari 212 S4
Écurie Espadon
Races: SUI (car #38); GER (#91)

PHILIP FOTHERINGHAM-PARKER (GBR; AGE: 43) 0 PTS

Maserati 4CL S4
Driver
Races: GBR (car #17)

BOB GERARD (GBR; AGE: 37) 0 PTS

ERA B-type S6 sc
Driver
Races: GBR (car #8)

CHICO GODIA-SALES (ESP; AGE: 30) 0 PTS

Maserati 4CLT/48 S4
Scuderia Milano
Races: ESP (car #44)

ALDO GORDINI (FRA; AGE: 30) 0 PTS

Simca-Gordini 11 S4
Équipe Simca Gordini
Races: FRA (car #36)

GEORGES GRIGNARD (FRA; AGE: 46) 0 PTS

Lago-Talbot T26C S6
Driver
Races: ESP (car #38)

1951

CHAMPIONSHIP CAR-BY-CAR

DUNCAN HAMILTON (GBR; AGE: 31) 0 PTS

Lago-Talbot T26C S6
Driver
Races: GBR (car #18); GER (#88)

PETER HIRT (SUI; AGE: 41) 0 PTS

Veritas Meteor S6
Écurie Espadon
Races: SUI (car #52)

JOHN JAMES (GBR; AGE: 37) 0 PTS

Maserati 4CLT/48 S4
Driver
Races: GBR (car #16)

JOE KELLY (IRL; AGE: 38) 0 PTS

Alta GP S4 sc
Driver
Races: GBR (car #5)

CHICO LANDI (BRA; AGE: 44) 0 PTS

Ferrari 375 V12
Scuderia Ferrari
Races: ITA (car #12)

"PIERRE LEVEGH" (FRA; AGE: 45) 0 PTS

Lago-Talbot T26C S6
Driver
Races: BEL (car #26); GER (#90); ITA (#22)

PICTURED AT NON-CHAMPIONSHIP RACE

HENRI LOUVEAU (FRA; AGE: 41) 0 PTS

Lago-Talbot T26C S6
Écurie Rosier
Races: SUI (car #10)

GUY MAIRESSE (FRA; AGE: 40) 0 PTS

Lago-Talbot T26C S6
Écurie Belgique
Races: SUI (car #40); FRA (#48)

ROBERT MANZON (FRA; AGE: 34) 0 PTS

Simca-Gordini 15 S4
Équipe Simca Gordini
Races: FRA (car #30); GER (#82); ITA (#46); ESP (#14)

ONOFRÉ MARIMON (ARG; AGE: 27) 0 PTS

Maserati 4CLT/50-Milano S4
Scuderia Milano
Races: FRA (car #50)

STIRLING MOSS (GBR; AGE: 21) 0 PTS

HWM 51-Alta S4
Hersham & Walton Motors
Races: SUI (car #14)

DAVID MURRAY (GBR; AGE: 41) 0 PTS

Maserati 4CLT/48 S4
Scuderia Ambrosiana
Races: GBR (car #15)

PAUL PIETSCH (GER; AGE: 40) 0 PTS

Alfa Romeo 159 S8 sc
Alfa Corse
Races: GER (car #78)

ANDRÉ PILETTE (BEL; AGE: 32) 0 PTS

Lago-Talbot T26C S6
Écurie Belgique
Races: BEL (car #24)

PICTURED AT NON-CHAMPIONSHIP RACE

FRANCO ROL (ITA; AGE: 43) 0 PTS

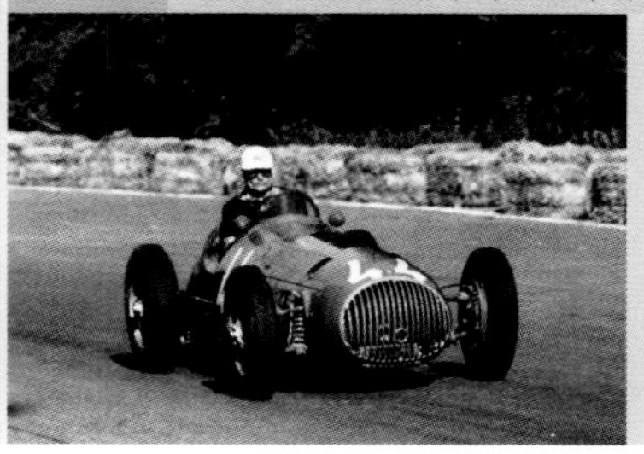

OSCA 4500G V12
Officine Specializate Costruzione Automobili
Races: ITA (car #44)

1951

CHAMPIONSHIP CAR-BY-CAR

HARRY SCHELL (USA; AGE: 30) 0 PTS

Maserati 4CLT/48 S4
Enrico Plate
Races: SUI (car #32); FRA (#20)

PICTURED AT NON-CHAMPIONSHIP RACE

BRIAN SHAWE-TAYLOR (GBR; AGE: 36) 0 PTS

ERA B-type S6 sc
Driver
Races: GBR (car #9)

ANDRÉ SIMON (FRA; AGE: 31) 0 PTS

Simca-Gordini 15 S4
Équipe Simca Gordini
Races: FRA (car #34); GER (#83); ITA (#48); ESP (#16)

JACQUES SWATERS (BEL; AGE: 24) 0 PTS

Lago-Talbot T26C S6
Écurie Belgique
Races: GER (car #93); ITA (#28)

MAURICE TRINTIGNANT (FRA; AGE: 33) 0 PTS

Simca-Gordini 15 S4
Équipe Simca Gordini
Races: FRA (car #32); GER (#81); ITA (#50); ESP (#12)

PETER WALKER (GBR; AGE: 38) 0 PTS

BRM P15 V16 sc
British Racing Motors
Races: GBR (car #7)

PETER WHITEHEAD (GBR; AGE: 36) 0 PTS

Ferrari 125 V12 sc
Driver/Graham Whitehead
Races: SUI (car #16); FRA (#24); ITA (#16)

PETER WHITEHEAD (CONTD)

Ferrari 375 V12
Vandervell Products
Races: GBR (car #14)

GRAND PRIX WINNERS 1951

	RACE (CIRCUIT)	**WINNER** (CAR)
SUI	SWISS GRAND PRIX (BREMGARTEN)	JUAN MANUEL FANGIO (ALFA ROMEO 159 S8 SC)
BEL	BELGIAN GRAND PRIX (SPA-FRANCORCHAMPS)	GIUSEPPE FARINA (ALFA ROMEO 159 S8 SC)
FRA	FRENCH GRAND PRIX (REIMS)	FAGIOLI/FANGIO (ALFA ROMEO 159 S8 SC)
GBR	BRITISH GRAND PRIX (SILVERSTONE)	JOSÉ FROILÁN GONZÁLEZ (FERRARI 375 V12)
GER	GERMAN GRAND PRIX (NÜRBURGRING)	ALBERTO ASCARI (FERRARI 375 V12)
ITA	ITALIAN GRAND PRIX (MONZA)	ALBERTO ASCARI (FERRARI 375 V12)
ESP	SPANISH GRAND PRIX (PEDRALBES)	JUAN MANUEL FANGIO (ALFA ROMEO 159 S8 SC)

1952

SIX OF THE BEST FOR ASCARI

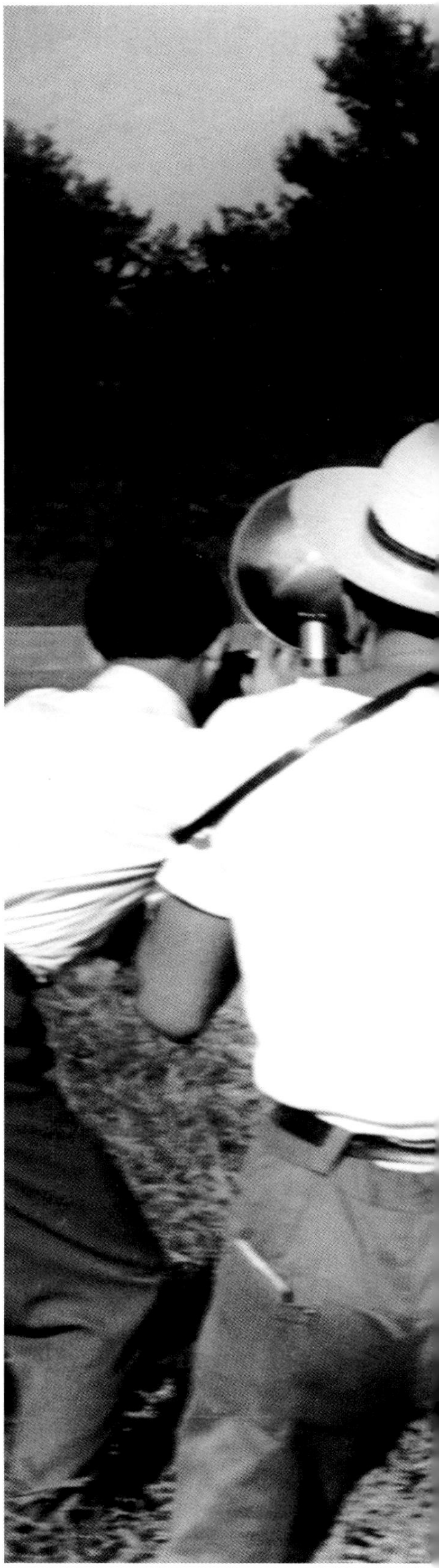

Above
Say it with flowers: sporting a natty line in inverted Tupperware, Alberto Ascari is congratulated on his French GP success at Rouen

Right
The joy of six: Ascari missed the season-opening Swiss Grand Prix to prepare for the Indianapolis 500, which counted towards the world championship, but he won all those he entered. He scored his sixth – and final – victory of the campaign at Monza

Left
Cooper-Bristol rover: young Englishman Mike Hawthorn made a name for himself with a string of promising drives. Familiar bow-tie firmly in place, he heads Lance Macklin's HWM en route to third place at Silverstone

Top
Sand and deliver: Ascari (left) and Hawthorn get the jump on fellow front-row qualifier Farina at the start of the Dutch GP, the first world championship race to take place amid Zandvoort's coastal dunes

Above
The class of '54: Hawthorn (white overalls, bow-tie, blond hair), Ascari (Chianti gut, hands on hips), a couple of roof-mounted loudhailers and another photographer's right arm are prominent features of this group shot, taken in the Monza paddock

Right
Walk on by: Gordini drivers Maurice Trintignant (left) and Robert Manzon prepare to start the British GP, which neither finished

RARELY HAS SUCH DOMINATION BEEN SEEN. IT WAS THE COMBINATION OF AN OVERWHELMINGLY SUPERIOR CAR AND ONE OF THE GREATEST DRIVERS IN HISTORY. THE REST DIDN'T STAND A CHANCE

Ferrari's Alberto Ascari took part in six of the season's seven grands prix and won every one of them. Rarely has such domination been seen in the sport. It was the combination of an overwhelmingly superior car and one of the greatest drivers in history. The rest didn't stand a chance. Ascari's only realistic opposition – Maserati star Juan Manuel Fangio – spent most of the season in hospital following a neck-breaking accident early in the year at Monza.

It was ironic that Ferrari's domination was so absolute. On the eve of the season the sport's governing body had announced that the 1952 and '53 world championships would be run to F2 regulations, rather than F1. The move was designed to increase competition, because it was felt that F1 would be a one-Prancing Horse race in the light of Alfa Romeo's with-drawal and BRM's persistent struggle to generate performance.

Jean Behra (Gordini) beat the Ferraris in a non-championship race but never came close to repeating the feat when it most counted. Maserati's challenge was hurt by Fangio's injury and for most of the year it didn't even enter a car. Froilan Gonzalez took a good second place in the final race of the season at Monza, however.

For upcoming young Brit Mike Hawthorn, the world championship's adoption of F2 regulations was an unexpected opportunity to shine on the big stage. He took full advantage with some great performances in his outclassed Cooper-Bristol, including third place in the British Grand Prix. His efforts earned him a Ferrari drive for the following season. Other young British talent such as Stirling Moss (Connaught, Cooper-Alta) and Peter Collins (HWM-Alta) didn't have the equipment to showcase their skills to the same extent.

1952

CHAMPIONSHIP CAR-BY-CAR

1ST **ALBERTO ASCARI** (ITA; AGE: 34) 36(+17.5) PTS

Ferrari 500 S4
Scuderia Ferrari
Races: BEL (car #4); FRA (#8); GBR (#15); GER (#101); NED (#2); ITA (#12)

2ND **GIUSEPPE FARINA** (ITA; AGE: 45) 24(+3) PTS

Ferrari 500 S4
Scuderia Ferrari
Races: SUI (car #28 and #32); BEL (#2); FRA (#10); GBR (#16); GER (#102); NED (#4); ITA (#10)

3RD **PIERO TARUFFI** (ITA; AGE: 45) 22 PTS

Ferrari 500 S4
Scuderia Ferrari
Races: SUI (car #30); BEL (#6); FRA (#12); GBR (#17); GER (#103); ITA (#14)

4TH= **RUDOLF FISCHER** (SUI; AGE: 40) 10 PTS

Ferrari 500 S4
Écurie Espadon
Races: SUI (car #42); GBR (#19); GER (#117); ITA (#18)

Also see Peter Hirt

4TH= **MIKE HAWTHORN** (GBR; AGE: 23) 10 PTS

Cooper T20-Bristol S6
LD Hawthorn/AHM Bryde
Races: BEL (car #8); FRA (#42); GBR (#9); NED (#32); ITA (#42)

6TH **ROBERT MANZON** (FRA; AGE: 35) 9 PTS

Gordini 16 S6
Équipe Gordini
Races: SUI (car #8); BEL (#14); FRA (#2); GBR (#24); GER (#107); NED (#10); ITA (#2)

7TH **LUIGI VILLORESI** (ITA; AGE: 43) 8 PTS

Ferrari 500 S4
Scuderia Ferrari
Races: NED (car #6); ITA (#16)

8TH **JOSÉ FROILÁN GONZÁLEZ** (ARG; AGE: 29) 6.5 PTS

Maserati A6GCM S6
Officine Alfieri Maserati
Races: ITA (car #26)

9TH **JEAN BEHRA** (FRA; AGE: 31) 6 PTS

Gordini 16 S6
Équipe Gordini
Races: SUI (car #6); BEL (#16); FRA (#4); GER (#108); NED (#8); ITA (#6)

10TH= **DENNIS POORE** (GBR; AGE: 36) 3 PTS

Connaught A-Lea-Francis S4
Connaught Engineering
Races: GBR (car #6); ITA (#30)

10TH= **KEN WHARTON** (GBR; AGE: 36) 3 PTS

Frazer-Nash FN48-Bristol S6
Scuderia Franera
Races: SUI (car #22); BEL (#36); NED (#34)

KEN WHARTON (CONTD)

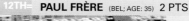

Cooper T20-Bristol S6
Écurie Ecosse
Races: ITA (car #40)

12TH= **FELICE BONETTO** (ITA; AGE: 49) 2 PTS

Maserati A6GCM S6
Officine Alfieri Maserati
Races: GER (car #105); ITA (#22)

12TH= **ALAN BROWN** (GBR; AGE: 32) 2 PTS

Cooper T20-Bristol S6
Écurie Richmond
Races: SUI (car #26); BEL (#10); GBR (#11); ITA (#38)

12TH= **PAUL FRÈRE** (BEL; AGE: 35) 2 PTS

HWM 51/52-Alta S4
Hersham & Walton Motors
Races: BEL (car #28); GER (#112)

1952

CHAMPIONSHIP CAR-BY-CAR

PAUL FRÈRE (CONTD)

Simca-Gordini 15 S4
Écurie Belge
Races: NED (car #14)

12TH= ERIC THOMPSON (GBR; AGE: 32) 2 PTS

Connaught A-Lea-Francis S4
Connaught Engineering
Races: GBR (car #5)

12TH= MAURICE TRINTIGNANT (FRA; AGE: 34) 2 PTS

Simca-Gordini 15 S4
Équipe Simca Gordini
Races: FRA (car #30)

MAURICE TRINTIGNANT (CONTD)

Gordini 16 S6
Équipe Gordini
Races: GBR (car #25); GER (#109); NED (#12); ITA (#4)

GEORGE ABECASSIS (GBR; AGE: 39) 0 PTS

HWM 52-Alta S4
Hersham & Walton Motors
Races: SUI (car #16)

BILL ASTON (GBR; AGE: 52) 0 PTS

Aston NB41-Butterworth F4
Driver
Races: GER (car #114)

PICTURED AT NON-CHAMPIONSHIP RACE

MARCEL BALSA (FRA; AGE: 43) 0 PTS

BMW Special S6
Driver
Races: GER (car #110)

ÉLIE BAYOL (FRA; AGE: 38) 0 PTS

OSCA 20 S6
Driver
Races: ITA (car #34)

GÜNTHER BECHEM (GER; AGE: 30) 0 PTS

BMW Special S6
Driver
Races: GER (car #130)

GINO BIANCO (BRA; AGE: 36) 0 PTS

Maserati A6GCM S6
Scuderia Bandeirantes
Races: GBR (car #34); GER (#115); NED (#18); ITA (#46)

"B BIRA" (THA; AGE: 37) 0 PTS

Simca-Gordini 15 S4
Équipe Simca Gordini
Races: SUI (car #10); BEL (#20)

"B BIRA" (CONTD)

Gordini 16 S6
Équipe Gordini
Races: FRA (car #6); GBR (#26)

ERIC BRANDON (GBR; AGE: 32) 0 PTS

Cooper T20-Bristol S6
Écurie Richmond
Races: SUI (car #24); BEL (#12); GBR (#10); ITA (#36)

ADOLF BRUDES (GER; AGE: 52) 0 PTS

Veritas RS-BMW S6
Driver
Races: GER (car #126)

HEITEL CANTONI (URU; AGE: 55) 0 PTS

Maserati A6GCM S6
Scuderia Bandeirantes
Races: GBR (car #35); GER (#116); ITA (#50)

1952

CHAMPIONSHIP CAR-BY-CAR

PIERO CARINI (ITA; AGE: 31) 0 PTS

Ferrari 166/F2 V12
Scuderia Marzotto
Races: FRA (car #40); GER (#104)

JOHNNY CLAES (BEL; AGE: 35) 0 PTS

Simca-Gordini 16S S6
Équipe Simca Gordini
Races: BEL (car #18)

JOHNNY CLAES (CONTD)

Simca-Gordini 15 S4
Écurie Belge
Races: FRA (car #32); GBR (#27)

JOHNNY CLAES (CONTD)

HWM 52-Alta S4
Hersham & Walton Motors
Races: GER (car #113)

PETER COLLINS (GBR; AGE: 20) 0 PTS

HWM 52-Alta S4
Hersham & Walton Motors
Races: SUI (car #18); BEL (#26); FRA (#22); GBR (#29)

GIANFRANCO COMOTTI (ITA; AGE: 46) 0 PTS

Ferrari 166/F2 V12
Scuderia Marzotto
Races: FRA (car #38)

TONY CROOK (GBR; AGE: 32) 0 PTS

Frazer-Nash 421-BMW S6
Driver
Races: GBR (car #23)

KEN DOWNING (GBR; AGE: 34) 0 PTS

Connaught A-Lea-Francis S4
Connaught Engineering/ Ken Downing
Races: GBR (car #4); NED (#22)

PHILIPPE ÉTANÇELIN (FRA; AGE: 55) 0 PTS

Maserati A6GCM S6
Scuderia Bandeirantes
Races: FRA (car #28)

JAN FLINTERMAN (NED; AGE: 32) 0 PTS

Maserati A6GCM S6
Scuderia Bandeirantes
Races: NED (car #20 and #16)

TONY GAZE (AUS; AGE: 32) 0 PTS

HWM 52-Alta S4
Driver
Races: BEL (car #42); GBR (#28); GER (#120)

YVES GIRAUD-CABANTOUS (FRA; AGE: 47) 0 PTS

HWM 52-Alta S4
Hersham & Walton Motors
Races: FRA (car #24)

EMMANUEL DE GRAFFENRIED (SUI; AGE: 38) 0 PTS

Maserati 4CLT/48-Plate S4
Enrico Plate
Races: SUI (car #38); FRA (#16); GBR (#32)

DUNCAN HAMILTON (GBR; AGE: 32) 0 PTS

HWM 52-Alta S4
Hersham & Walton Motors
Races: GBR (car #30); NED (#28)

WILLI HEEKS (GER; AGE: 30) 0 PTS

AFM 8-BMW S6
Driver
Races: GER (car #123)

1952

CHAMPIONSHIP CAR-BY-CAR

THEO HELFRICH (GER; AGE: 39) 0 PTS

Veritas RS-BMW S6
Driver
Races: GER (car #122)

PETER HIRT (SUI; AGE: 42) 0 PTS

Ferrari 212 V12
Écurie Espadon
Races: SUI (car #44); FRA (#36); GBR (#20)
Note: Rudolf Fischer (SUI; Age: 40) – shared car at FRA

HANS KLENK (GER; AGE: 32) 0 PTS

Veritas Meteor S6
Driver
Races: GER (car #128)

ERNST KLODWIG (DDR; AGE: 49) 0 PTS

Heck-BMW S6
Driver
Races: GER (car #135)

RUDOLF KRAUSE (DDR; AGE: 45) 0 PTS

Greifzu-BMW S6
Driver
Races: GER (car #136)

CHICO LANDI (BRA; AGE: 45) 0 PTS

Maserati A6GCM S6
Scuderia Bandeirantes
Races: NED (car #16); ITA (#48)

ROGER LAURENT (BEL; AGE: 39) 0 PTS

HWM 52-Alta S4
Hersham & Walton Motors
Races: BEL (car #30)

ROGER LAURENT (CONTD)

Ferrari 500 S4
Écurie Francorchamps
Races: GER (car #119)

ARTHUR LEGAT (BEL; AGE: 53) 0 PTS

Veritas Meteor S6
Driver
Races: BEL (car #38)

DRIES VAN DER LOF (NED; AGE: 33) 0 PTS

HWM 52-Alta S4
Hersham & Walton Motors
Races: NED (car #30)

LANCE MACKLIN (GBR; AGE: 32) 0 PTS

HWM 52-Alta S4
Hersham & Walton Motors
Races: SUI (car #20); BEL (#24); FRA (#20); GBR (#31); NED (#26)

KENNETH McALPINE (GBR; AGE: 31) 0 PTS

Connaught A-Lea-Francis S4
Connaught Engineering
Races: GBR (car #3); ITA (#28)

PICTURED AT NON-CHAMPIONSHIP RACE

ROBIN MONTGOMERIE-CHARRINGTON (USA; AGE: 37) 0 PTS

Aston NB41-Butterworth F4
WS Aston
Races: BEL (car #40)

STIRLING MOSS (GBR; AGE: 22) 0 PTS

HWM 52-Alta S4
Hersham & Walton Motors
Races: SUI (car #46)

STIRLING MOSS (CONTD)

ERA G-type-Bristol S6
English Racing Automobiles
Races: BEL (car #32); GBR (#12); NED (#36)

1952

CHAMPIONSHIP CAR-BY-CAR

STIRLING MOSS (CONTD)

Connaught A-Lea-Francis S4
Connaught Engineering
Races: ITA (car #32)

DAVID MURRAY (GBR; AGE: 42) 0 PTS

Cooper T20-Bristol S6
Écurie Ecosse
Races: GBR (car #7)

HELMUT NIEDERMAYR (GER; AGE: 36) 0 PTS

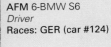

AFM 6-BMW S6
Driver
Races: GER (car #124)

ROBERT O'BRIEN (USA; AGE: 30) 0 PTS

Simca-Gordini 15 S4
Driver
Races: BEL (car #44)

REG PARNELL (GBR; AGE: 41) 0 PTS

Cooper T20-Bristol S6
AHM Bryde
Races: GBR (car #8)

JOSEF PETERS (GER; AGE: 37) 0 PTS

Veritas RS-BMW S6
Driver
Races: GER (car #129)

PAUL PIETSCH (GER; AGE: 41) 0 PTS

Veritas Meteor S6
Motor-Presse-Verlag
Races: GER (car #127)

PICTURED AT NON-CHAMPIONSHIP RACE

FRITZ RIESS (GER; AGE: 30) 0 PTS

Veritas RS-BMW S6
Driver
Races: GER (car #121)

FRANCO ROL (ITA; AGE: 44) 0 PTS

Maserati A6GCM S6
Officine Alfieri Maserati
Races: ITA (car #24)

SHOWN DRIVEN BY JOSÉ FROILÁN GONZÁLEZ IN PRACTICE

LOUIS ROSIER (FRA; AGE: 46) 0 PTS

Ferrari 500 S4
Écurie Rosier
Races: SUI (car #12); BEL (#22); FRA (#14); ITA (#62)

ROY SALVADORI (GBR; AGE: 30) 0 PTS

Ferrari 500 S4
G Caprara
Races: GBR (car #14)

HARRY SCHELL (USA; AGE: 31) 0 PTS

Maserati 4CLT/48-Plate S4
Enrico Plate
Races: SUI (car #40); FRA (#18 and #16); GBR (#33)

RUDOLF SCHOELLER (SUI; AGE: 50) 0 PTS

Ferrari 212 V12
Écurie Espadon
Races: GER (car #118)

ANDRÉ SIMON (FRA; AGE: 32) 0 PTS

Ferrari 500 S4
Scuderia Ferrari
Races: SUI (car #32); ITA (#8)

HANS STUCK (GER; AGE: 51) 0 PTS

AFM-Kuchen V8
Alex von Falkenhausen Motorenbau
Races: SUI (car #2)

1952

CHAMPIONSHIP CAR-BY-CAR

MAX DE TERRA (SUI; AGE: 33) 0 PTS

Simca-Gordini 11 S4
Alfred Dattner
Races: SUI (car #50)

CHARLES DE TORNACO (BEL; AGE: 25) 0 PTS

Ferrari 500 S4
Écurie Francorchamps
Races: BEL (car #34); NED (#24)

TONI ULMEN (GER; AGE: 46) 0 PTS

Veritas Meteor-BMW S6
Driver
Races: SUI (car #4); GER (#125)

GRAHAM WHITEHEAD (GBR; AGE: 30) 0 PTS

Alta F2 S4
Peter Whitehead
Races: GBR (car #1)

PETER WHITEHEAD (GBR; AGE: 37) 0 PTS

Alta F2 S4
Driver
Races: FRA (car #26)

PETER WHITEHEAD (CONTD)

Ferrari 125/F2 V12
Driver
Races: GBR (car #21)

GRAND PRIX WINNERS 1952

	RACE (CIRCUIT)	WINNER (CAR)
SUI	SWISS GRAND PRIX (BREMGARTEN)	PIERO TARUFFI (FERRARI 500 S4)
BEL	BELGIAN GRAND PRIX (SPA-FRANCORCHAMPS)	ALBERTO ASCARI (FERRARI 500 S4)
FRA	FRENCH GRAND PRIX (ROUEN-LES-ESSARTS)	ALBERTO ASCARI (FERRARI 500 S4)
GBR	BRITISH GRAND PRIX (SILVERSTONE)	ALBERTO ASCARI (FERRARI 500 S4)
GER	GERMAN GRAND PRIX (NÜRBURGRING)	ALBERTO ASCARI (FERRARI 500 S4)
NED	DUTCH GRAND PRIX (ZANDVOORT)	ALBERTO ASCARI (FERRARI 500 S4)
ITA	ITALIAN GRAND PRIX (MONZA)	ALBERTO ASCARI (FERRARI 500 S4)

1953

ASCARI EXTENDS RECORD RUN ON WAY TO TITLE NUMBER TWO

Above
Title deeds: Ascari gets the jump on Fangio as the season kicks off in Buenos Aires. Three wins at the start of the year laid the foundation for another title success – but in 2003 Italy was still be waiting for its next champion

Right
Parklife: Fangio, Ascari and Farina dispute the lead amid Monza's verdant surroundings. No, we don't know what that vacant chair is doing there, either

Left
Fattest lap: prior to finishing fourth at Silverstone, Froilan Gonzalez explains to his mechanics that he has been jogging – albeit not since 1936

Above
Thirst among equals: from the left, Farina, a token Ferrari team member, Ascari and Villoresi take on refreshments at Zandvoort

Top
Mike England: Hawthorn fends off Fangio at Reims, where he ended Ascari's winning streak and scored Britain's first GP success

The world championship catered for Formula Two cars for the second straight season and Alberto Ascari's Ferrari dominated just as surely as before. He triumphed in the first three grands prix of the season to extend his winning sequence to nine – an achievement that has never since been matched.

Despite that, however, the Maserati challenge increased notably. Coming back after spending most of the previous year recovering from a broken neck, Juan Manuel Fangio became Ascari's closest challenger. It helped, too, that Fangio's team-mate Froilan Gonzalez was a furiously fast driver: this gave the Maserati challenge added depth.

The breakthrough came at Monza during the final event of the season. The early stages of the race featured a slipstreaming four-car battle between two Ferraris (Ascari and Giuseppe Farina) and two Maseratis (Fangio and Onofre Marimon). Marimon was forced to pit with a damaged radiator and lost a lap to the leaders. Critically, though, he rejoined the battle even though he was out of contention.

At the last corner Farina tried a desperate lunge inside Ascari and the latter was forced to take extreme avoiding action. As Farina ran wide, Ascari began to spin and Marimon ran into him. All this enabled Fangio to nip by and claim victory. At the 11th hour, Ferrari was thus denied a clean sweep of the world championship's F2 era.

Earlier in the summer, Mike Hawthorn made history as the first British driver to win a world championship grand prix. In his first season with Ferrari, he narrowly fended off Fangio and Gonzalez in the French GP at Reims.

ALBERTO ASCARI – WORLD CHAMPION 1952 & 1953

1953

CHAMPIONSHIP CAR-BY-CAR

1ST ALBERTO ASCARI (ITA; AGE: 35) 34.5(+12.5) PTS

Ferrari 500 S4
Scuderia Ferrari
Races: ARG (car #10); NED (#2); BEL; FRA (both #10); GBR (#5); GER (#4 and #1); SUI (#46); ITA (#4)

2ND JUAN MANUEL FANGIO (ARG; AGE: 42) 27.5(+1.5) PTS

Maserati A6GCM S6
Officine Alfieri Maserati
Races: ARG (car #2); NED (#12); BEL (#4 and #6); FRA (#18); GBR (#23); GER (#5); SUI (#30 and #32); ITA (#50)

3RD GIUSEPPE FARINA (ITA; AGE: 46) 26(+6) PTS

Ferrari 500 S4
Scuderia Ferrari
Races: ARG (car #12); NED (#6); BEL (#12); FRA (#14); GBR (#6); GER (#2); SUI (#24); ITA (#6)

4TH MIKE HAWTHORN (GBR; AGE: 24) 19(+8) PTS

Ferrari 500 S4
Scuderia Ferrari
Races: ARG (car #16); NED (#8); BEL (#14); FRA (#16); GBR (#8); GER (#3); SUI (#26); ITA (#8)

5TH LUIGI VILLORESI (ITA; AGE: 44) 17 PTS

Ferrari 500 S4
Scuderia Ferrari
Races: ARG (car #14); NED (#4); BEL (#8); FRA (#12); GBR (#7); GER (#4 and #1); SUI (#28); ITA (#2)

6TH JOSÉ FROILÁN GONZÁLEZ (ARG; AGE: 30) 13.5(+1) PTS

Maserati A6GCM S6
Officine Alfieri Maserati
Races: ARG (car #4); NED (#14 and #16); BEL (#2); FRA (#20); GBR (#24)

7TH EMMANUEL DE GRAFFENRIED (SUI; AGE: 39) 7 PTS

Maserati A6GCM S6
Driver
Races: NED (car #18); BEL (#30); FRA (#46); GBR (#31); GER (#17); SUI (#42); ITA (#58)

8TH FELICE BONETTO (ITA; AGE: 50) 6.5 PTS

Maserati A6GCM S6
Officine Alfieri Maserati
Races: ARG (car #6); NED (#16); FRA (#24); GBR (#25); GER (#7); SUI (#30 and #32); ITA (#52)

9TH= ONOFRÉ MARIMON (ARG; AGE: 29) 4 PTS

Maserati A6GCM S6
Officine Alfieri Maserati
Races: BEL (car #28); FRA (#22); GBR (#26); GER (#8); SUI (#36); ITA (#54)

9TH= MAURICE TRINTIGNANT (FRA; AGE: 35) 4 PTS

Gordini 16 S6
Équipe Gordini
Races: ARG (car #28); NED (#24); BEL (#18); FRA (#4); GBR (#29); GER (#10); SUI (#8); ITA (#36)

11TH= OSCAR GÁLVEZ (ARG; AGE: 39) 2 PTS

Maserati A6GCM S6
Officine Alfieri Maserati
Races: ARG (car #8)

11TH= HERMANN LANG (GER; AGE: 44) 2 PTS

Maserati A6GCM S6
Officine Alfieri Maserati
Races: SUI (car #34)

KURT ADOLFF (GER; AGE: 31) 0 PTS

Ferrari 166C V12
Écurie Espadon
Races: GER (car #34)

JOHN BARBER (GBR; AGE: 23) 0 PTS

Cooper T23-Bristol S6
Cooper Car Co
Races: ARG (car #22)

EDGAR BARTH (DDR; AGE: 36) 0 PTS

EMW-BMW S6
Rennkollektiv EMW
Races: GER (car #35)

1953

CHAMPIONSHIP CAR-BY-CAR

ERWIN BAUER (GER; AGE: 41) 0 PTS

Veritas RS S6
Driver
Races: GER (car #32)

ÉLIE BAYOL (FRA; AGE: 39) 0 PTS

OSCA 20 S6
Driver
Races: FRA; ITA (both car #34)

GÜNTHER BECHEM (GER; AGE: 31) 0 PTS

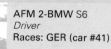

AFM 2-BMW S6
Driver
Races: GER (car #41)

JEAN BEHRA (FRA; AGE: 32) 0 PTS

Gordini 16 S6
Équipe Gordini
Races: ARG (car #30); BEL (#16); FRA (#2); GBR (#30); GER (#9); SUI (#6)

GEORGES BERGER (BEL; AGE: 34) 0 PTS

Simca-Gordini 15 S4
Driver
Races: BEL (car #34)

"B BIRA" (THA; AGE: 39) 0 PTS

Connaught A-Lea-Francis S4
Connaught Engineering
Races: FRA (car #42); GBR (#10); GER (#14)

"B BIRA" (CONTD)

Maserati A6GCM S6
Scuderia Milano
Races: ITA (car #44)

PABLO BIRGER (ARG; AGE: 29) 0 PTS

Simca-Gordini 15 S4
Équipe Simca Gordini
Races: ARG (car #34)

ALAN BROWN (GBR; AGE: 33) 0 PTS

Cooper T20-Bristol S6
Cooper Car Co/ Équipe Anglaise
Races: ARG (car #20); GER (#38)

ALAN BROWN (CONTD)

Cooper T23-Bristol S6
RJ Chase/ Équipe Anglaise
Races: GBR (car #19); ITA (#46)

PIERO CARINI (ITA; AGE: 32) 0 PTS

Ferrari 553 S4
Scuderia Ferrari
Races: ITA (car #12)

LOUIS CHIRON (MON; AGE: 54) 0 PTS

OSCA 20 S6
Driver
Races: FRA; ITA (both car #32)

JOHNNY CLAES (BEL; AGE: 36) 0 PTS

Connaught A-Lea-Francis S4
Écurie Belge
Races: NED (car #30); FRA (#48); GER (#12); ITA (#26)

JOHNNY CLAES (CONTD)

Maserati A6GCM S6
Officine Alfieri Maserati
Races: BEL (car #6)

PETER COLLINS (GBR; AGE: 21) 0 PTS

HWM 53-Alta S4
Hersham & Walton Motors
Races: NED (car #36); BEL (#26); FRA (#28); GBR (#2)

1953

CHAMPIONSHIP CAR-BY-CAR

TONY CROOK (GBR; AGE: 33) 0 PTS

Cooper T24-Alta S4
Driver
Races: GBR (car #22)

PICTURED AT NON-CHAMPIONSHIP RACE

JACK FAIRMAN (GBR; AGE: 40) 0 PTS

HWM 52/53-Alta S4
Hersham & Walton Motors
Races: GBR (car #4)

JACK FAIRMAN (CONTD)

Connaught A-Lea-Francis S4
Connaught Engineering
Races: ITA (car #20)

JOHN FITCH (USA; AGE: 36) 0 PTS

HWM 52/53-Alta S4
Hersham & Walton Motors
Races: ITA (car #18)

THEO FITZAU (GER; AGE: 30) 0 PTS

AFM 7-BMW S6
Helmut Niedermayr
Races: GER (car #28)

PAUL FRÈRE (BEL; AGE: 36) 0 pts

HWM 53-Alta S4
Hersham & Walton Motors
Races: BEL (car #24); SUI (#14)

BOB GERARD (GBR; AGE: 39) 0 PTS

Cooper T23-Bristol S6
Driver
Races: FRA (car #38); GBR (#17)

YVES GIRAUD-CABANTOUS (FRA; AGE: 48) 0 PTS

HWM 53-Alta S4
Hersham & Walton Motors
Races: FRA (car #30); ITA (#16)

DUNCAN HAMILTON (GBR; AGE: 33) 0 PTS

HWM 53-Alta S4
Hersham & Walton Motors
Races: GBR (car #3)

WILLI HEEKS (GER; AGE: 31) 0 PTS

Veritas Meteor S6
Driver
Races: GER (car #23)

THEO HELFRICH (GER; AGE: 40) 0 PTS

Veritas RS S6
Driver
Races: GER (car #24)

HANS HERRMANN (GER; AGE: 25) 0 PTS

Veritas Meteor S6
Hans Klenk
Races: GER (car #31)

PETER HIRT (SUI; AGE: 43) 0 PTS

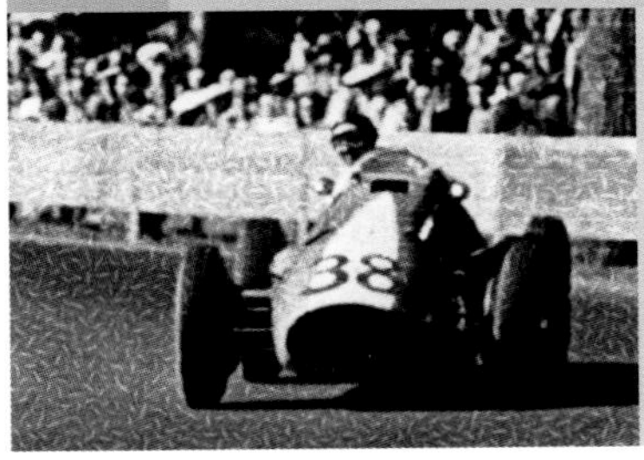

Ferrari 500 S4
Écurie Espadon
Races: SUI (car #38)

OSWALD KARCH (GER; AGE: 36) 0 PTS

Veritas RS S6
Driver
Races: GER (car #26)

ERNST KLODWIG (DDR; AGE: 50) 0 PTS

Heck-BMW S6
Driver
Races: GER (car #37)

1953

CHAMPIONSHIP CAR-BY-CAR

RUDOLF KRAUSE (DDR; AGE: 46) 0 PTS

BMW Special S6
Dora Greifzu
Races: GER (car #36)

CHICO LANDI (BRA; AGE: 46) 0 PTS

Maserati A6GCM S6
Driver/Scuderia Milano
Races: SUI (car #4); ITA (#42)

ARTHUR LEGAT (BEL; AGE: 54) 0 PTS

Veritas Meteor S6
Driver
Races: BEL (car #36)

ERNST LOOF (GER; AGE: 46) 0 PTS

Veritas Meteor S6
Driver
Races: GER (car #30)

LANCE MACKLIN (GBR; AGE: 33) 0 PTS

HWM 53-Alta S4
Hersham & Walton Motors
Races: NED (car #38); BEL (#22); FRA (#26); GBR (#1); SUI (#16); ITA (#14)

UMBERTO MAGLIOLI (ITA; AGE: 25) 0 PTS

Ferrari 553 S4
Scuderia Ferrari
Races: ITA (car #10)

SERGIO MANTOVANI (ITA; AGE: 24) 0 PTS
LUIGI MUSSO (ITA; AGE: 29)

(shared car)
Maserati A6GCM S6
Officine Alfieri Maserati
Races: ITA (car #56)

ROBERT MANZON (FRA; AGE: 35) 0 PTS

Gordini 16 S6
Équipe Gordini
Races: ARG (car #26)

KENNETH McALPINE (GBR; AGE: 32) 0 PTS

Connaught A-Lea-Francis S4
Connaught Engineering
Races: NED (car #28); GBR (#11); GER (#16); ITA (#24)

CARLOS MENDITÉGUY (ARG; AGE: 37) 0 PTS

Gordini 16 S6
Équipe Gordini
Races: ARG (car #32)

ROBERTO MIÈRES (ARG; AGE: 28) 0 PTS

Gordini 16 S6
Équipe Gordini
Races: NED (car #22); FRA (#8); ITA (#40)

STIRLING MOSS (GBR; AGE: 23) 0 PTS

Connaught A-Lea-Francis S4
Connaught Engineering
Races: NED (car #34)

STIRLING MOSS (CONTD)

Cooper T24-Alta S4
Cooper Car Co
Races: FRA (car #36); GER (#19); ITA (#28)

RODNEY NUCKEY (GBR; AGE: 24) 0 PTS

Cooper T23-Bristol S6
Driver
Races: GER (car #40)

ANDRÉ PILETTE (BEL; AGE: 34) 0 PTS

Connaught A-Lea-Francis S4
Écurie Belge
Races: BEL (car #40)

1953

CHAMPIONSHIP CAR-BY-CAR

TONY ROLT (GBR; AGE: 34) 0 PTS

Connaught A-Lea-Francis S4
Rob Walker Racing
Races: GBR (car #14)

LOUIS ROSIER (FRA; AGE: 47) 0 PTS

Ferrari 500 S4
Écurie Rosier
Races: NED (car #10); BEL (#32); FRA (#44); GBR (#9); GER (#20); SUI (#10); ITA (#64)

ROY SALVADORI (GBR; AGE: 31) 0 PTS

Connaught A-Lea-Francis S4
Connaught Engineering
Races: NED (car #26); FRA (#50); GBR (#12); GER (#15); ITA (#22)

HARRY SCHELL (USA; AGE: 32) 0 PTS

Gordini 16 S6
Équipe Gordini
Races: ARG (car #28); NED; BEL (both #20); FRA (#6); GBR (#28); GER (#11); ITA (#38)

ALBERT SCHERRER (SUI; AGE: 45) 0 PTS

HWM 53-Alta S4
Hersham & Walton Motors
Races: SUI (car #18)

ADOLFO SCHWELM CRUZ (ARG; AGE: 29) 0 PTS

Cooper T20-Bristol S6
Cooper Car Co
Races: ARG (car #24)

WOLFGANG SEIDEL (GER; AGE: 27) 0 PTS

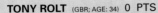

Veritas RS S6
Driver
Races: GER (car #22)

IAN STEWART (GBR; AGE: 24) 0 PTS

Connaught A-Lea-Francis S4
Écurie Ecosse
Races: GBR (car #15)

JIMMY STEWART (GBR; AGE: 22) 0 PTS

Cooper T20-Bristol S6
Écurie Ecosse
Races: GBR (car #18)

HANS STUCK (GER; AGE: 52) 0 pts

AFM 4-Kuchen V8
Driver
Races: GER (car #21); ITA (#48)

JACQUES SWATERS (BEL; AGE: 26) 0 PTS

Ferrari 500 S4
Écurie Francorchamps
Races: GER (car #18); SUI (#2)

MAX DE TERRA (SUI; AGE: 34) 0 PTS

Ferrari 166C V12
Écurie Espadon
Races: SUI (car #40)

FRED WACKER (USA; AGE: 34) 0 PTS

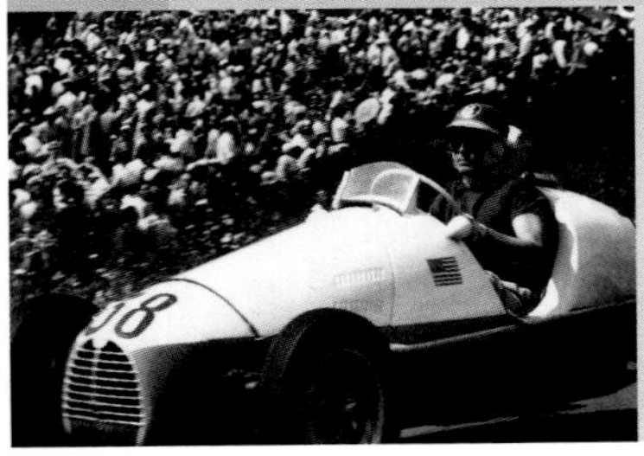

Gordini 16 S6
Équipe Gordini
Races: BEL (car #38)

KEN WHARTON (GBR; AGE: 37) 0 PTS

Cooper T23-Bristol S6
Driver/Cooper Car Co
Races: NED (car #32); FRA (#40); GBR (#16); SUI (#20); ITA (#30)

PETER WHITEHEAD (GBR; AGE: 38) 0 PTS

Cooper T24-Alta S4
Atlantic Stable
Races: GBR (car #20)

1953

CHAMPIONSHIP CAR-BY-CAR

GRAND PRIX WINNERS 1953

	RACE (CIRCUIT)	WINNER (CAR)
ARG	ARGENTINE GRAND PRIX (BUENOS AIRES)	ALBERTO ASCARI (FERRARI 500 S4)
NED	DUTCH GRAND PRIX (ZANDVOORT)	ALBERTO ASCARI (FERRARI 500 S4)
BEL	BELGIAN GRAND PRIX (SPA-FRANCORCHAMPS)	ALBERTO ASCARI (FERRARI 500 S4)
FRA	FRENCH GRAND PRIX (REIMS)	MIKE HAWTHORN (FERRARI 500 S4)
GBR	BRITISH GRAND PRIX (SILVERSTONE)	ALBERTO ASCARI (FERRARI 500 S4)
GER	GERMAN GRAND PRIX (NÜRBURGRING)	GIUSEPPE FARINA (FERRARI 500 S4)
SUI	SWISS GRAND PRIX (BREMGARTEN)	ALBERTO ASCARI (FERRARI 500 S4)
ITA	ITALIAN GRAND PRIX (PEDRALBES)	JUAN MANUEL FANGIO (ALFA ROMEO 159 S8 SC)

LUIGI VILLORESI

1954

SILVER ARROWS STRIKE GOLD

Far left
Leaders united: Fangio (18) and team-mate Kling qualified their Mercedes W196 streamliners first and second when the team made its world championship debut in France. They finished more than a lap clear of their closest rival

Above
Eifel power: Froilan Gonzalez leads Fangio et al at the Nürburgring. The leading W196 featured conventional single-seater bodywork here, but it had the same genius at the wheel. The Argentine duly scored his fourth win of the season

Left
Stirling work: a young Englishman by the name of Moss started his campaign in a privately-entered Maserati but was swiftly drafted into the works team

Ever since grand prix racing resumed after World War Two, it had been very much the preserve of specialist teams rather than the major motor manufacturers that had previously dominated. Alfa Romeo was an exception to this rule but its programme was based on pre-war hardware that already existed and was therefore inexpensive.

In 1954, however, both Mercedes-Benz and Lancia announced that they were going to compete in the new, 2.5-litre Formula One: the factories were returning. Mercedes appeared first and promptly recorded a one-two in the French Grand Prix, courtesy of Juan Manuel Fangio and Karl Kling. Fangio won twice at the start of the season in a Maserati 250F and picked up four wins with Mercedes to become world champion for the second time.

The Lancia didn't appear until the Spanish GP, the final race of the season, where Alberto Ascari qualified on pole position by more than a second. Clutch failure put him out of the race but the car's potential was very clear.

The Mercedes W196 and Lancia D50 were considerably more advanced than the designs used by specialists such as Ferrari and Maserati and the competitive benefits of the factories' greater resources were very obvious.

Stirling Moss drove his first F1 complete season, initially as a privateer in a Maserati. He created such a stir that he was soon a member of the factory team. The Englishman was on course to win the Italian GP until his engine failed.

Top left
Spa turn: Farina's Ferrari leads Fangio's Maserati in Belgium. It would be 1957 before the Argentine started another world championship race in the charismatic, enduring 250F

Top right
Better late than never: Lancia pledged its support for the new F1 regs. Not being German, however, the team wasn't ready to compete until the final race of the season. It was worth the wait: Ascari qualified the V8-powered D50 on pole

Above right
Speedy Gonzalez: the British GP winner zaps past a wooden timekeeping hut – an architectural classic that was strangely unique to the UK. Forty years later, some had still to be bulldozed

Right
Grey elegy: Mercedes ran a single W196 streamliner in its home race. Hans Herrmann qualified fourth and had the decency to pose for an evocative shot before a broken fuel line forced him out

1954

CHAMPIONSHIP CAR-BY-CAR

1ST JUAN MANUEL FANGIO (ARG; AGE: 43)
42(+15.14) PTS

Maserati 250F S6
Officine Alfieri Maserati
Races: ARG (car #2); BEL (#26)

JUAN MANUEL FANGIO (CONTD)

Mercedes-Benz W196 S8
Daimler-Benz
Races: FRA (car #18); GBR (#1); GER (#18); SUI (#4); ITA (#16); ESP (#2)

2ND JOSÉ FROILÁN GONZÁLEZ (ARG; AGE: 31)
25.14(+1.5) PTS

Ferrari 625 S4
Scuderia Ferrari
Races: ARG (car #12); BEL (#10); GBR (#9); GER (#1); SUI (#20); ITA (#38)

JOSÉ FROILÁN GONZÁLEZ (CONTD)

Ferrari 553 Squalo S4
Scuderia Ferrari
Races: BEL (car #6); FRA (#2); ITA (#32)

3RD MIKE HAWTHORN (GBR; AGE: 25) 24.64 PTS

Ferrari 625 S4
Scuderia Ferrari
Races: ARG (car #14); BEL (#10); GBR (#11); GER (#3 and #1); SUI (#22); ITA (#40)

MIKE HAWTHORN (CONTD)

Ferrari 553 Squalo S4
Scuderia Ferrari
Races: FRA (car #6); ESP (#38)

4TH MAURICE TRINTIGNANT (FRA; AGE: 36) 17 PTS

Ferrari 625 S4
Écurie Rosier/Scuderia Ferrari
Races: ARG (car #26); BEL (#8); FRA (#4); GBR (#10); GER (#2); SUI (#26); ITA (#30)

MAURICE TRINTIGNANT (CONTD)

Ferrari 553 Squalo S4
Scuderia Ferrari
Races: ESP (car #40)

5TH KARL KLING (GER; AGE: 43) 12 pts

Mercedes-Benz W196 S8
Daimler-Benz
Races: FRA (#20); GBR (#2); GER (#19); SUI (#8); ITA (#14); ESP (#4)

6TH HANS HERRMANN (GER; AGE: 26) 8 PTS

Mercedes-Benz W196 S8
Daimler-Benz
Races: FRA (car #22); GER (#20); SUI (#6); ITA (#12); ESP (#6)

7TH= GIUSEPPE FARINA (ITA; AGE: 47) 6 PTS

Ferrari 625 S4
Scuderia Ferrari
Races: ARG (car #10)

GIUSEPPE FARINA (CONTD)

Ferrari 553 Squalo S4
Scuderia Ferrari
Races: BEL (car #4)

7TH= ROBERTO MIÈRES (ARG; AGE: 29) 6 PTS

Maserati 250F S6
Driver/Officine Alfieri Maserati
Races: ARG (car #32); BEL (#24); FRA (#16); GBR (#4); GER (#8); SUI (#30); ITA (#24); ESP (#10)

7TH= LUIGI MUSSO (ITA; AGE: 30) 6 PTS

Maserati 250F S6
Officine Alfieri Maserati
Races: ITA (car #20); ESP (#14)

10TH= ONOFRÉ MARIMON (ARG; AGE: 30) 4.14 PTS

Maserati 250F S6
Officine Alfieri Maserati
Races: ARG (car #4); BEL (#28); FRA (#12); GBR (#33)

1954

CHAMPIONSHIP CAR-BY-CAR

10TH= STIRLING MOSS (GBR; AGE: 24) 4.14 PTS

Maserati 250F S6
Équipe Moss/Officine Alfieri Maserati
Races: BEL (car #22); GBR (#7); GER (#16); SUI (#32); ITA (#28); ESP (#8)

12TH= SERGIO MANTOVANI (ITA; AGE: 25) 4 PTS

Maserati 250F S6
Officine Alfieri Maserati
Races: BEL (car #30); GER (#7); SUI (#28); ITA (#18); ESP (#12)

12TH= ROBERT MANZON (FRA; AGE: 37) 4 PTS

Ferrari 625 S4
Écurie Rosier
Races: FRA (car #34); GBR (#14); GER (#24); ITA (#6); ESP (#20)

14TH "B BIRA" (THA; AGE: 40) 3 PTS

Maserati 250F S6
Officine Alfieri Maserati/Driver
Races: ARG (car #8); BEL (#20); FRA (#46); GBR (#6); GER (#14); ESP (#18)

15TH= ÉLIE BAYOL (FRA; AGE: 39) 2 PTS

Gordini 16 S6
Équipe Gordini
Races: ARG (car #20)

15TH= UMBERTO MAGLIOLI (ITA; AGE: 26) 2 PTS

Ferrari 625 S4
Scuderia Ferrari
Races: ARG (car #16); ITA (#38)

UMBERTO MAGLIOLI (CONTD)

Ferrari 553 Squalo S4
Scuderia Ferrari
Races: SUI (car #24)

15TH= ANDRÉ PILETTE (BEL; AGE: 35) 2 PTS

Gordini 16 S6
Équipe Gordini
Races: BEL (car #18); GBR (#19); GER (#12)

PICTURED AT NON-CHAMPIONSHIP RACE

15TH= LUIGI VILLORESI (ITA; AGE: 45) 2 PTS

Maserati 250F S6
Officine Alfieri Maserati
Races: FRA (car #14); GBR (#32); ITA (#22)

LUIGI VILLORESI (CONTD)

Lancia D50 V8
Scuderia Lancia
Races: ESP (car #36)

19TH ALBERTO ASCARI (ITA; AGE: 36) 1.14 PTS

Maserati 250F S6
Officine Alfieri Maserati
Races: FRA (car #10); GBR (#31 and #32)

ALBERTO ASCARI (CONTD)

Ferrari 625 S4
Scuderia Ferrari
Races: ITA (car #34)

ALBERTO ASCARI (CONTD)

Lancia D50 V8
Scuderia Lancia
Races: ESP (car #34)

20TH JEAN BEHRA (FRA; AGE: 33) 0.14 PTS

Gordini 16 S6
Équipe Gordini
Races: ARG (car #18); BEL (#12); FRA (#24); GBR (#17); GER (#9); SUI (#10); ITA (#44); ESP (#46)

DON BEAUMAN (GBR; AGE: 26) 0 PTS

Connaught A-Lea-Francis S4
Sir Jeremy Boles
Races: GBR (car #25)

PICTURED AT NON-CHAMPIONSHIP RACE

1954

CHAMPIONSHIP CAR-BY-CAR

GEORGES BERGER (BEL; AGE: 35) 0 PTS

Gordini 16 S6
Équipe Gordini
Races: FRA (car #30)

ERIC BRANDON (GBR; AGE: 34) 0 PTS

Cooper T23-Bristol S6
Écurie Richmond
Races: GBR (car #30)

CLEMAR BUCCI (ARG; AGE: 33) 0 PTS

Gordini 16 S6
Équipe Gordini
Races: GBR (car #18); GER (#11); SUI (#12); ITA (#46)

PETER COLLINS (GBR; AGE: 22) 0 PTS

Vanwall Special S4
Vandervell Products
Races: GBR (car #20); ITA (#10)

JORGE DAPONTE (ARG; AGE: 30) 0 PTS

Maserati 250F S6
Driver
Races: ARG (car #34); ITA (#8)

RON FLOCKHART (GBR; AGE: 31) 0 PTS

Maserati 250F S6
"B Bira"
Races: GBR (car #6)

PAUL FRÈRE (BEL; AGE: 37) 0 PTS

Gordini 16 S6
Équipe Gordini
Races: BEL (car #16); FRA (#28); GER (#10)

BOB GERARD (GBR; AGE: 40) 0 PTS

Cooper T23-Bristol S6
Driver
Races: GBR (car #29)

PICTURED AT NON-CHAMPIONSHIP RACE

CHICO GODIA-SALES (ESP; AGE: 33) 0 PTS

Maserati 250F S6
Officine Alfieri Maserati
Races: ESP (car #16)

HORACE GOULD (GBR; AGE: 32) 0 PTS

Cooper T23-Bristol S6
Goulds' Garage (Bristol)
Races: GBR (car #28)

PICTURED AT NON-CHAMPIONSHIP RACE

EMMANUEL DE GRAFFENRIED (SUI; AGE: 40) 0 PTS

Maserati 250F S6
Driver
Races: ARG (car #30); BEL (#50); ESP (#22)

THEO HELFRICH (GER; AGE: 41) 0 PTS

Klenk Meteor-BMW S6
Hans Klenk
Races: GER (car #22)

HERMANN LANG (GER; AGE: 45) 0 PTS

Mercedes-Benz W196 S8
Daimler-Benz
Races: GER (car #21)

ROGER LOYER (FRA; AGE: 46) 0 PTS

Gordini 16 S6
Équipe Gordini
Races: ARG (car #22)

LANCE MACKLIN (GBR; AGE: 34) 0 PTS

HWM 54-Alta S4
Hersham & Walton Motors
Races: FRA (car #32)

PICTURED AT NON-CHAMPIONSHIP RACE

1954

CHAMPIONSHIP CAR-BY-CAR

LESLIE MARR (GBR; AGE: 31) 0 PTS

Connaught A-Lea-Francis S4
Driver
Races: GBR (car #23)

PICTURED AT NON-CHAMPIONSHIP RACE

REG PARNELL (GBR; AGE: 43) 0 PTS

Ferrari 625 S4
Scuderia Ambrosiana
Races: GBR (car #12)

PICTURED AT NON-CHAMPIONSHIP RACE

JACQUES POLLET (FRA; AGE: 32) 0 PTS

Gordini 16 S6
Équipe Gordini
Races: FRA (car #26); ESP (#48)

JOHN RISELEY-PRICHARD (GBR; AGE: 30) 0 PTS

Connaught A-Lea-Francis S4
Rob Walker Racing
Races: GBR (car #24)

PICTURED AT NON-CHAMPIONSHIP RACE

LOUIS ROSIER (FRA; AGE: 48) 0 PTS

Ferrari 625 S4
Écurie Rosier
Races: ARG (car #24); FRA (#36); GBR (#15); GER (#25)

LOUIS ROSIER (CONTD)

Maserati 250F S6
Officine Alfieri Maserati/Écurie Rosier
Races: ITA; ESP (both car #26)

ROY SALVADORI (GBR; AGE: 32) 0 PTS

Maserati 250F S6
Gilby Engineering
Races: FRA (car #44); GBR (#5)

HARRY SCHELL (USA; AGE: 33) 0 PTS

Maserati 250F S6
Driver/Officine Alfieri Maserati
Races: ARG (car #28); FRA (#48); GBR (#3); GER (#15); SUI (#34); ESP (#24)

JACQUES SWATERS (BEL; AGE: 27) 0 PTS

Ferrari 625 S4
Écurie Francorchamps
Races: BEL; SUI (both car #2); ESP (#30)

PIERO TARUFFI (ITA; AGE: 47) 0 PTS

Ferrari 625 S4
Scuderia Ferrari
Races: GER (car #4)

LESLIE THORNE (GBR; AGE: 38) 0 PTS

Connaught A-Lea-Francis S4
Écurie Ecosse
Races: GBR (car #26)

OTTORINO VOLONTERIO (SUI; AGE: 36) 0 PTS

Maserati 250F S6
Baron Emmanuel de Graffenried
Races: ESP (car #22)

FRED WACKER (USA; AGE: 36) 0 PTS

Gordini 16 S6
Équipe Gordini
Races: SUI (car #14); ITA (#42)

KEN WHARTON (GBR; AGE: 38) 0 PTS

Maserati 250F S6
Owen Racing Organisation
Races: FRA (car #42); GBR (#8); SUI (#18); ESP (#28)

PETER WHITEHEAD (GBR; AGE: 39) 0 PTS

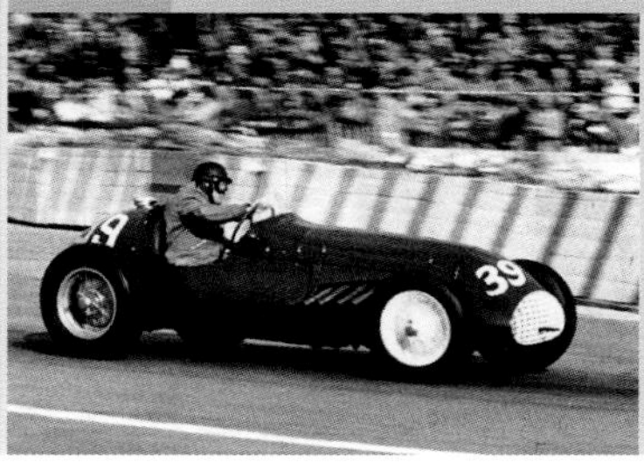

Cooper T24-Alta S4
Driver
Races: GBR (car #21)

PICTURED AT NON-CHAMPIONSHIP RACE

1954

CHAMPIONSHIP CAR-BY-CAR

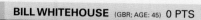

BILL WHITEHOUSE (GBR; AGE: 45) 0 PTS

Connaught A-Lea-Francis S4
Driver
Races: GBR (car #22)

GRAND PRIX WINNERS 1954

	RACE (CIRCUIT)	WINNER (CAR)
ARG	ARGENTINE GRAND PRIX (BUENOS AIRES)	JUAN MANUEL FANGIO (MASERATI 250F S6)
BEL	BELGIAN GRAND PRIX (SPA-FRANCORCHAMPS)	JUAN MANUEL FANGIO (MASERATI 250F S6)
FRA	FRENCH GRAND PRIX (REIMS)	JUAN MANUEL FANGIO (MERCEDES-BENZ W196 S8)
GBR	BRITISH GRAND PRIX (SILVERSTONE)	JOSÉ FROILÁN GONZÁLEZ (FERRARI 625 S4)
GER	GERMAN GRAND PRIX (NÜRBURGRING)	JUAN MANUEL FANGIO (MERCEDES-BENZ W196 S8)
SUI	SWISS GRAND PRIX (BREMGARTEN)	JUAN MANUEL FANGIO (MERCEDES-BENZ W196 S8)
ITA	ITALIAN GRAND PRIX (MONZA)	JUAN MANUEL FANGIO (MERCEDES-BENZ W196 S8)
ESP	SPANISH GRAND PRIX (PEDRALBES)	MIKE HAWTHORN (FERRARI 553 SQUALO S4)

JOSÉ FROILÁN GONÁLEZ

1955

THE SPORT'S FUTURE HANGS IN THE BALANCE

Left
Monte Carlo – and bust: Fangio qualified on pole in Monaco but transmission problems caused his retirement just before half-distance. The race covered 100 laps back then and lasted almost three hours

Above
Heady Mercs: Fangio edges ahead of Moss at Aintree. The positions were reversed by the end and the Englishman finally secured the first of his 16 GP victories

Right
Mersey beaucoup: Moss celebrates after winning the first of five British GPs to take place in the Liverpool suburbs. Did Fangio let him win? We've no idea – and neither, to this day, has Moss

This was a catastrophic season. Frenchman Pierre Levegh's Mercedes-Benz somersaulted into the crowd during the Le Mans 24 Hours: the driver and more than 80 spectators were killed and the ramifications were felt throughout the sport. Motor racing's very right to exist came under severe scrutiny and several Formula One grands prix were immediately cancelled. Switzerland imposed a blanket ban on circuit racing and it remains in force to this day.

Juan Manuel Fangio and Mercedes-Benz secured a second consecutive title, but at the end of the season the company understandably withdrew from the sport. It wouldn't be back for a very long time.

Stirling Moss drove alongside Fangio and won his first grand prix. Fittingly, his maiden success came on home soil at Aintree. To this day, though, Moss is unsure whether or not the Argentine let him win.

The Mercedes W196 was defeated only once all season – Maurice Trintignant's Ferrari won in Monaco, where both Fangio and Moss were forced to retire with mechanical problems. It was during this race that Alberto Ascari crashed his Lancia into the harbour when poised to

inherit the lead from Moss. Rescued by frogmen, he was only slightly hurt. A few days later, however, the double world champion was killed while testing a Ferrari sports car at Monza. This spelt the end of the Lancia F1 project, which the company had been struggling to afford.

The withdrawals of Mercedes-Benz and Lancia left the sport exclusively in the hands of the specialists once again.

STIRLING MOSS DROVE ALONGSIDE FANGIO AND WON HIS FIRST GRAND PRIX. FITTINGLY, HIS MAIDEN SUCCESS CAME ON HOME SOIL AT AINTREE

Above
Pop into your local Spa: fans dunk their chips in mayonnaise while waiting for a car to come past in Belgium

Left
Home straits: Mike Hawthorn poses before the start of the British GP. He felt ill during the race and so handed his car over to Luigi Castellotti, who brought it home sixth

Above right
Farewell to a king: Ascari leads Lancia team-mate Chiron in Monaco. The Italian escaped almost unhurt after plunging into the sea on lap 81. A few days later, however, he perished when he crashed a Ferrari sports car during a test at Monza

Right:
Double Dutch: the Mercedes W196s ruled the roost again at Zandvoort, where Fangio beat Moss by 0.2s

1955

CHAMPIONSHIP CAR-BY-CAR

1ST JUAN MANUEL FANGIO (ARG; AGE: 43) 40(+1) PTS

Mercedes-Benz W196 S8
Daimler-Benz
Races: ARG; MON (both car #2); BEL (#10); NED (#8); GBR (#10); ITA (#18)

2ND STIRLING MOSS (GBR; AGE: 25) 23 PTS

Mercedes-Benz W196 S8
Daimler-Benz
Races: ARG (car #6 and #8); MON (#6); BEL (#14); NED (#10); GBR (#12); ITA (#16)

3RD EUGENIO CASTELLOTTI (ITA; AGE: 24) 12 PTS

Lancia D50 V8
Scuderia Lancia
Races: ARG (car #36); MON; BEL (both #30)

EUGENIO CASTELLOTTI (CONTD)

Ferrari 555 Supersqualo S4
Scuderia Ferrari
Races: NED (car #6); ITA (#4)

EUGENIO CASTELLOTTI (CONTD)

Ferrari 625 S4
Scuderia Ferrari
Races: GBR (car #20 and #16)

4TH MAURICE TRINTIGNANT (FRA; AGE: 37) 11.33 PTS

Ferrari 625 S4
Scuderia Ferrari
Races: ARG (car #14, #12 and #10); MON (#44); GBR (#18)

MAURICE TRINTIGNANT (CONTD)

Ferrari 555 Supersqualo S4
Scuderia Ferrari
Races: BEL; NED (both car #4); ITA (#8)

5TH GIUSEPPE FARINA (ITA; AGE: 48) 10.33 PTS

Ferrari 625 S4
Scuderia Ferrari
Races: ARG (car #12 and #10); MON (#42)

GIUSEPPE FARINA (CONTD)

Ferrari 555 Supersqualo S4
Scuderia Ferrari
Races: BEL (car #2)

6TH PIERO TARUFFI (ITA; AGE: 48) 9 PTS

Ferrari 555 Supersqualo S4
Scuderia Ferrari
Races: MON (car #48)

PIERO TARUFFI (CONTD)

Mercedes-Benz W196 S8
Daimler-Benz
Races: GBR (car #50); ITA (#14)

7TH ROBERTO MIÈRES (ARG; AGE: 30) 7 PTS

Maserati 250F S6
Officine Alfieri Maserati
Races: ARG (car #18); MON (#36); BEL (#24); NED (#16); GBR (#6); ITA (#28)

8TH= JEAN BEHRA (FRA; AGE: 34) 6 PTS

Maserati 250F S6
Officine Alfieri Maserati
Races: ARG (car #16, #20 and #28); MON (#40 and #34); BEL (#20 and #24); NED (#14); GBR (#2); ITA (#36)

8TH= LUIGI MUSSO (ITA; AGE: 30) 6 PTS

Maserati 250F S6
Officine Alfieri Maserati
Races: ARG (car #20 and #22); MON (#38); BEL (#22); NED (#18); GBR (#4); ITA (#30)

10TH KARL KLING (GER; AGE: 44) 5 PTS

Mercedes-Benz W196 S8
Daimler-Benz
Races: ARG (car #4 and #8); BEL; NED (both #12); GBR (#14); ITA (#20)

1955

CHAMPIONSHIP CAR-BY-CAR

11TH PAUL FRÈRE (BEL; AGE: 38) 3 PTS

Ferrari 555 Supersqualo S4
Scuderia Ferrari
Races: MON (car #48); BEL (#6)

12TH= JOSÉ FROILÁN GONZÁLEZ (ARG; AGE: 32) 2 PTS

Ferrari 625 S4
Scuderia Ferrari
Races: ARG (car #12)

12TH= CARLOS MENDITÉGUY (ARG; AGE: 39) 2 PTS

Maserati 250F S6
Officine Alfieri Maserati
Races: ARG (car #24 and #26); ITA (#34)

12TH= CESARE PERDISA (ITA; AGE: 22) 2 PTS

Maserati 250F S6
Officine Alfieri Maserati
Races: MON (car #40 and #34); BEL (#26)

12TH= LUIGI VILLORESI (ITA; AGE: 45) 2 PTS

Lancia D50 V8
Scuderia Lancia
Races: ARG (car #34 and #36); MON (#28)

16TH UMBERTO MAGLIOLI (ITA; AGE: 26) 1.33 PTS

Ferrari 625 S4
Scuderia Ferrari
Races: ARG (car #10)

UMBERTO MAGLIOLI (CONTD)

Ferrari 555 Supersqualo S4
Scuderia Ferrari
Races: ITA (car #12)

17TH HANS HERRMANN (GER; AGE: 26) 1 pt

Mercedes-Benz W196 S8
Daimler-Benz
Races: ARG (car #8)

ALBERTO ASCARI (ITA; AGE: 36) 0 PTS

Lancia D50 V8
Scuderia Lancia
Races: ARG (car #32); MON (#26)

ÉLIE BAYOL (FRA; AGE: 41) 0 PTS

Gordini 16 S6
Équipe Gordini
Races: ARG (car #38); MON (#12)

PABLO BIRGER (ARG; AGE: 31) 0 PTS

Gordini 16 S6
Équipe Gordini
Races: ARG (car #40)

JACK BRABHAM (AUS; AGE: 29) 0 PTS

Cooper T40-Bristol S6
Cooper Car Co
Races: GBR (car #40)

CLEMAR BUCCI (ARG; AGE: 34) 0 PTS

Maserati 250F S6
Officine Alfieri Maserati
Races: ARG (car #26)

LOUIS CHIRON (MON; AGE: 55) 0 PTS

Lancia D50 V8
Scuderia Lancia
Races: MON (car #32)

JOHNNY CLAES (BEL; AGE: 38) 0 PTS

Ferrari 625 S4
Écurie Nationale Belge
Races: NED (car #30)

1955

CHAMPIONSHIP CAR-BY-CAR

PETER COLLINS (GBR; AGE: 23) 0 PTS

Maserati 250F S6
Owen Racing Organisation/Officine Alfieri Maserati
Races: GBR (car #42); ITA (#32)

JOHN FITCH (USA; AGE: 38) 0 PTS

Maserati 250F S6
Stirling Moss
Races: ITA (car #40)

HORACE GOULD (GBR; AGE: 33) 0 PTS

Maserati 250F S6
Goulds' Garage (Bristol)/Officine Alfieri Maserati
Races: NED (car #32); GBR (#48); ITA (#38)

MIKE HAWTHORN (GBR; AGE: 26) 0 PTS

Vanwall S4
Vandervell Products
Races: MON (car #18); BEL (#40)

MIKE HAWTHORN (CONTD)

Ferrari 555 Supersqualo S4
Scuderia Ferrari
Races: NED (car #2); ITA (#6)

MIKE HAWTHORN (CONTD)

Ferrari 625 S4
Scuderia Ferrari
Races: GBR (car #16)

JÉSUS IGLESIAS (ARG; AGE: 32) 0 PTS

Gordini 16 S6
Équipe Gordini
Races: ARG (car #42)

JEAN LUCAS (FRA; AGE: 38) 0 PTS

Gordini 32 S8
Équipe Gordini
Races: ITA (car #24)

LANCE MACKLIN (GBR; AGE: 35) 0 PTS

Maserati 250F S6
Stirling Moss
Races: GBR (car #46)

PICTURED DURING MON PRACTICE

SERGIO MANTOVANI (ITA; AGE: 25) 0 PTS

Maserati 250F S6
Officine Alfieri Maserati
Races: ARG (car #20 and #22)

ROBERT MANZON (FRA; AGE: 38) 0 PTS

Gordini 16 S6
Équipe Gordini
Races: MON (car #8); NED (#20); GBR (#22)

LESLIE MARR (GBR; AGE: 32) 0 PTS

Connaught B-Alta S4
Driver
Races: GBR (car #38)

KENNETH McALPINE (GBR; AGE: 34) 0 PTS

Connaught B-Alta S4
Connaught Engineering
Races: GBR (car #32)

JACQUES POLLET (FRA; AGE: 32) 0 PTS

Gordini 16 S6
Équipe Gordini
Races: MON (car #10); NED (#24); ITA (#26)

TONY ROLT (GBR; AGE: 36) 0 PTS
PETER WALKER (GBR; AGE: 42)

(shared car)
Connaught B-Alta S4
Rob Walker Racing
Races: GBR (car #36)

ALSO SEE PETER WALKER

1955

CHAMPIONSHIP CAR-BY-CAR

LOUIS ROSIER (FRA; AGE: 49) 0 PTS

Maserati 250F S6
Écurie Rosier
Races: MON (car #14); BEL; NED (both #28)

ROY SALVADORI (GBR; AGE: 33) 0 PTS

Maserati 250F S6
Gilby Engineering
Races: GBR (car #44)

HARRY SCHELL (USA; AGE: 33) 0 PTS

Maserati 250F S6
Officine Alfieri Maserati
Races: ARG (car #26, #28 and #22)

PICTURE SHOWS JEAN BEHRA WHO TOOK OVER SCHELL'S CAR

HARRY SCHELL (CONTD)

Ferrari 555 Supersqualo S4
Scuderia Ferrari
Races: MON (car #46)

HARRY SCHELL (CONTD)

Vanwall S4
Vandervell Products
Races: GBR (car #30 and #28); ITA (#42)

HERMANO DA SILVA RAMOS (FRA/BRA; AGE: 29) 0 PTS

Gordini 16 S6
Équipe Gordini
Races: NED (car #22); GBR (#24); ITA (#22)

ANDRÉ SIMON (FRA; AGE: 35) 0 PTS

Mercedes-Benz W196 S8
Daimler-Benz
Races: MON (car #4)

ANDRÉ SIMON (CONTD)

Maserati 250F S6
Officine Alfieri Maserati
Races: GBR (car #8)

MIKE SPARKEN (FRA; AGE: 25) 0 PTS

Gordini 16 S6
Équipe Gordini
Races: GBR (car #26)

ALBERTO URIA (URU; AGE: 30) 0 PTS

Maserati 250F S6
Driver
Races: ARG (car #30)

PETER WALKER (GBR; AGE: 42) 0 PTS

Maserati 250F S6
Stirling Moss
Races: NED (car #26)

ALSO SEE TONY ROLT

KEN WHARTON (GBR; AGE: 39) 0 PTS

Vanwall S4
Vandervell Products
Races: GBR (car #28); ITA (#44)

GRAND PRIX WINNERS 1955

	RACE (CIRCUIT)	WINNER (CAR)
ARG	ARGENTINE GRAND PRIX (BUENOS AIRES)	JUAN MANUEL FANGIO (MERCEDES-BENZ W196 S8)
MON	MONACO GRAND PRIX (MONTE CARLO)	MAURICE TRINTIGNANT (FERRARI 625 S4)
BEL	BELGIAN GRAND PRIX (SPA-FRANCORCHAMPS)	JUAN MANUEL FANGIO (MERCEDES-BENZ W196 S8)
NED	DUTCH GRAND PRIX (ZANDVOORT)	JUAN MANUEL FANGIO (MERCEDES-BENZ W196 S8)
GBR	BRITISH GRAND PRIX (AINTREE)	STIRLING MOSS (MERCEDES-BENZ W196 S8)
ITA	ITALIAN GRAND PRIX (MONZA)	JUAN MANUEL FANGIO (MERCEDES-BENZ W196 S8)

1956

FERRARI – DRIVEN BY SUCCESS BUT RIVEN BY POLITICS

Above
Every picture tells a story: irrespective of his continued success, Fangio never felt entirely comfortable at Ferrari

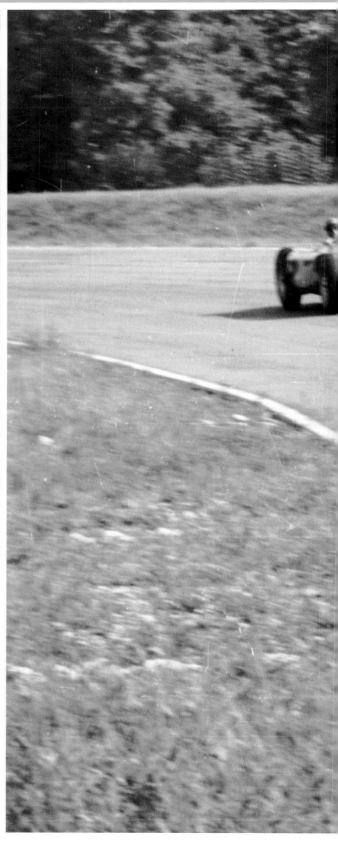

Far right
A question of sportsmanship: the champion heads Moss and Collins at Monza, where the latter sacrificed his own title chances on Fangio's behalf

Right
Brief encounter: Bugatti made its world championship debut at Reims with a transversely-mounted straight eight in its T251. It hasn't been back since

Above
Prancing horseplay: Castellotti leads team-mate Collins around the fast, open sweep Reims. They were just 0.3s apart at the chequered flag, albeit in reverse order

Below right
Reims beau rising: Peter Collins and assorted well-wishers in the wake of his French GP success

Right
The way we were: the Reims pit straight in 1956. The track closed in the early 1970s but the buildings remain in place today. Nature has taken its course – but that's much better than allowing property developers to get involved

Enzo Ferrari's shrewdness was very apparent when he contrived to be paid to take over the assets of the Lancia Formula One programme. This included the D50 chassis that were considerably more advanced than the cars his team had been fielding.

When he recruited Juan Manuel Fangio, who was on the market following Mercedes-Benz's withdrawal from the sport, it seemed Ferrari was a shoo-in for the championship. Fangio duly delivered title number four, but his partnership with Ferrari was uneasy from beginning to end and there was a great deal of mutual distrust.

By the time the series reached Monza for the Italian Grand Prix, eighth and final race of the season, Ferrari's favoured driver Peter Collins was vying with Fangio for the title. The Argentine was forced to retire with steering arm failure after 17 laps. In those days drivers were allowed to share cars and any points scored would be split between them. When third Ferrari driver Luigi Musso made a routine pit stop the team asked him to get out and hand his car to Fangio, but he refused.

Collins later made his stop from a position that virtually ensured he was going to win the title. When he saw Fangio standing there Collins immediately got out of his car and offered it to his team-mate. Fangio accepted and went on to finish second, which secured him the title. Asked why he had done this for Fangio, Collins replied: "Because he deserved it." It was sportsmanship of the very highest order.

Stirling Moss (Maserati 250F) was the only driver to win a grand prix in anything other than a Ferrari. He triumphed at Monte Carlo and Monza.

1956

CHAMPIONSHIP CAR-BY-CAR

1ST JUAN MANUEL FANGIO (ARG; AGE: 44) 30(+4.5) PTS

Lancia-Ferrari D50 V8
Scuderia Ferrari
Races: ARG (car #30 and #34); MON (#26 and #20); BEL (#2); FRA (#10); GBR; GER (both #1); ITA (#26 and #22)

2ND STIRLING MOSS (GBR; AGE: 26) 27(+1) PTS

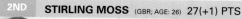

Maserati 250F S6
Officine Alfieri Maserati
Races: ARG (car #2); MON (#28); BEL (#30 and #34); FRA (#2 and #6); GBR; GER (both #7); ITA (#36)

3RD PETER COLLINS (GBR; AGE: 24) 25 PTS

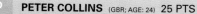

Ferrari 555 Supersqualo S4
Scuderia Ferrari
Races: ARG (car #36)

PETER COLLINS (CONTD)

Lancia-Ferrari D50 V8
Scuderia Ferrari
Races: MON (car #26); BEL (#8); FRA (#14); GBR (#2 and 4); GER (#2 and #5); ITA (#26)

4TH JEAN BEHRA (FRA; AGE: 35) 22 PTS

Maserati 250F S6
Officine Alfieri Maserati
Races: ARG (car #4); MON (#30); BEL (#32); FRA (#4); GBR (#8); GER (#6); ITA (#32 and #46)

5TH EUGENIO CASTELLOTTI (ITA; AGE: 25) 7.5 PTS

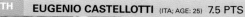

Lancia-Ferrari D50 V8
Scuderia Ferrari
Races: ARG (car #32); MON (#22 and #20); BEL (#4); FRA (#12); GBR (#3); GER (#3 and #4); ITA (#24 and #22)

6TH= PAUL FRÈRE (BEL; AGE: 39) 6 PTS

Lancia-Ferrari D50 V8
Scuderia Ferrari
Races: BEL (car #6)

6TH= CHICO GODIA-SALES (ESP; AGE: 35) 6 PTS

Maserati 250F S6
Officine Alfieri Maserati
Races: BEL (car #36); FRA (#40); GBR (#10); GER (#20); ITA (#38)

8TH JACK FAIRMAN (GBR; AGE: 43) 5 PTS

Connaught B-Alta S4
Connaught Engineering
Races: GBR (car #21); ITA (#6)

9TH= RON FLOCKHART (GBR; AGE: 33) 4 PTS

BRM P25 S4
Owen Racing Organisation
Races: GBR (car #25)

RON FLOCKHART (CONTD)

Connaught B-Alta S4
Connaught Engineering
Races: ITA (car #4)

9TH= MIKE HAWTHORN (GBR; AGE: 27) 4 PTS

Maserati 250F S6
Owen Racing Organisation
Races: ARG (car #14)

PICTURED AT BEL PRACTICE

MIKE HAWTHORN (CONTD)

Vanwall S4
Vandervell Products
Races: FRA (car #24)

MIKE HAWTHORN (CONTD)

BRM P25 S4
Owen Racing Organisation
Races: GBR (car #23)

9TH= LUIGI MUSSO (ITA; AGE: 31) 4 PTS

Lancia-Ferrari D50 V8
Scuderia Ferrari
Races: ARG (car #30 and #34); MON (#24); GER (#4); ITA (#28)

1956

CHAMPIONSHIP CAR-BY-CAR

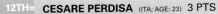

12TH= CESARE PERDISA (ITA; AGE: 23) 3 PTS

Maserati 250F S6
Officine Alfieri Maserati
Races: MON (car #32); BEL (#34); FRA (#6); GBR (#9)

12TH= ALFONSO DE PORTAGO (ESP; AGE: 27) 3 PTS

Lancia-Ferrari D50 V8
Scuderia Ferrari
Races: FRA (car #16); GBR (#4 and #3); GER (#5); ITA (#30)

12TH= HARRY SCHELL (USA; AGE: 35) 3 PTS

Vanwall S4
Vandervell Products
Races: MON (car #16); BEL (#10); FRA (#22 and #24); GBR (#16); ITA (#18)

HARRY SCHELL (CONTD)

Maserati 250F S6
Scuderia Centro Sud
Races: GER (car #12)

15TH= OLIVIER GENDEBIEN (BEL; AGE: 32) 2 PTS

Lancia-Ferrari D50 V8
Scuderia Ferrari
Races: ARG (car #38); FRA (#44)

15TH= HORACE GOULD (GBR; AGE: 34) 2 PTS

Maserati 250F S6
Goulds' Garage (Bristol)
Races: MON (car #18); BEL (#26); GBR (#31); GER (#19)

15TH= LOUIS ROSIER (FRA; AGE: 50) 2 PTS

Maserati 250F S6
Écurie Rosier
Races: MON (car #8); BEL (#24); FRA (#36); GBR (#27); GER (#15)

15TH= HERMANO DA SILVA RAMOS (FRA/BRA; AGE: 30) 2 PTS

Gordini 16 S6
Équipe Gordini
Races: MON (car #6)

HERMANO DA SILVA RAMOS (CONTD)

Gordini 32 S8
Équipe Gordini
Races: FRA (car #32); GBR (#14); ITA (#8)

15TH= LUIGI VILLORESI (ITA; AGE: 47) 2 PTS

Maserati 250F S6
Scuderia Centro Sud/ Luigi Piotti/Officine Alfieri Maserati
Races: BEL (car #22); FRA (#38); GBR (#11); GER (#17); ITA (#34)

20TH= GERINO GERINI (ITA; AGE: 27) 1.5 PTS

Maserati 250F S6
Officine Alfieri Maserati/Scuderia Guastalla
Races: ARG (car #10); ITA (#42)

20TH= CHICO LANDI (BRA; AGE: 48) 1.5 PTS

Maserati 250F S6
Officine Alfieri Maserati
Races: ARG (car #10)

ÉLIE BAYOL (FRA; AGE: 42) 0 PTS
ANDRÉ PILETTE (BEL; AGE: 37)

(shared car)
Gordini 32 S8
Équipe Gordini
Races: MON (car #4)

JO BONNIER (SWE; AGE: 26) 0 PTS
LUIGI VILLORESI (ITA; AGE: 47)

(shared car)
Maserati 250F S6
Officine Alfieri Maserati
Races: ITA (car #34)

JACK BRABHAM (AUS; AGE: 30) 0 PTS

Maserati 250F S6
Driver
Races: GBR (car #30)

PICTURED AT NON-CHAMPIONSHIP RACE

1956

CHAMPIONSHIP CAR-BY-CAR

TONY BROOKS (GBR; AGE: 24) 0 PTS

BRM P25 S4
Owen Racing Organisation
Races: GBR (car #24)

PICTURED AT NON-CHAMPIONSHIP RACE

PAUL EMERY (GBR; AGE: 39) 0 PTS

Emeryson Mk1-Alta S4
Emeryson Cars
Races: GBR (car #32)

PICTURED AT NON-CHAMPIONSHIP RACE

BOB GERARD (GBR; AGE: 42) 0 PTS

Cooper T23-Bristol S6
Driver
Races: GBR (car #26)

PICTURED AT NON-CHAMPIONSHIP RACE

JOSÉ FROILÁN GONZÁLEZ (ARG; AGE: 33) 0 PTS

Maserati 250F S6
Officine Alfieri Maserati
Races: ARG (car #12)

JOSÉ FROILÁN GONZÁLEZ (CONTD)

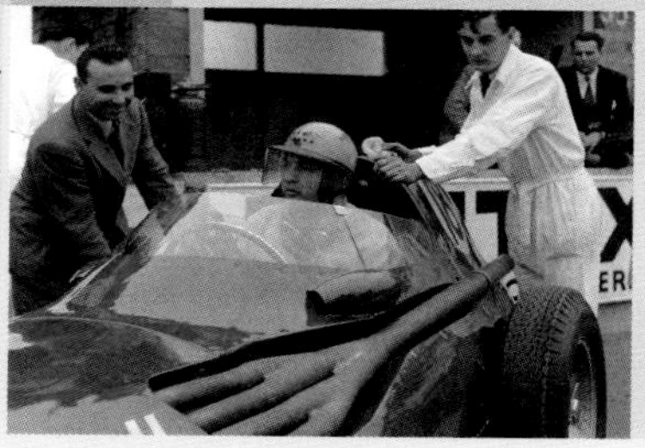

Vanwall S4
Vandervell Products
Races: GBR (car #18)

OSCAR GONZÁLEZ (URU; AGE: 32) 0 PTS
ALBERTO URIA (URU; AGE: 31)

(shared car)
Maserati 250F S6
Alberto Uria
Races: ARG (car #16)

EMMANUEL DE GRAFFENRIED (SUI; AGE: 42) 0 PTS

Maserati 250F S6
Scuderia Centro Sud
Races: ITA (car #14)

BRUCE HALFORD (GBR; AGE: 25) 0 PTS

Maserati 250F S6
Driver
Races: GBR (car #29); GER (#21); ITA (#48)

LES LESTON (GBR; AGE: 35) 0 PTS

Connaught B-Alta S4
Connaught Engineering
Races: ITA (car #2)

UMBERTO MAGLIOLI (ITA; AGE: 28) 0 PTS

Maserati 250F S6
Scuderia Guastalla/ Officine Alfieri Maserati
Races: GBR (car #12); GER (#8); ITA (#46)

ROBERT MANZON (FRA; AGE: 39) 0 PTS

Gordini 16 S6
Équipe Gordini
Races: MON (car #2)

PICTURED IN PRACTICE IN GORDINI 32

ROBERT MANZON (CONTD)

Gordini 32 S8
Équipe Gordini
Races: FRA (car #30); GBR (#15); GER; ITA (both #10)

CARLOS MENDITÉGUY (ARG; AGE: 40) 0 PTS

Maserati 250F S6
Officine Alfieri Maserati
Races: ARG (car #6)

ANDRÉ MILHOUX (BEL; AGE: 27) 0 PTS

Gordini 32 S8
Équipe Gordini
Races: GER (car #11)

ANDRÉ PILETTE (BEL; AGE: 37) 0 PTS

Lancia-Ferrari D50 V8
Scuderia Ferrari
Races: BEL (car #20)

ALSO SEE ÉLIE BAYOL

1956

CHAMPIONSHIP CAR-BY-CAR

ANDRÉ PILETTE (CONTD)

Gordini 16 S6
Equipe Gordini
Races: FRA (car #34)

LUIGI PIOTTI (ITA; AGE: 42) 0 PTS

Maserati 250F S6
Officine Alfieri Maserati/Driver
Races: ARG (car #8); GER (#18); ITA (#40)

ROY SALVADORI (GBR; AGE: 34) 0 PTS

Maserati 250F S6
Gilby Engineering
Races: GBR (car #28); GER (#16); ITA (#44)

GIORGIO SCARLATTI (ITA; AGE: 34) 0 PTS

Ferrari 500 S4
Scuderia Centro Sud
Races: GER (car #14)

ARCHIE SCOTT-BROWN (GBR; AGE: 29) 0 PTS

Connaught B-Alta S4
Connaught Engineering
Races: GBR (car #19)

PIERO SCOTTI (ITA; AGE: 46) 0 PTS

Connaught B-Alta S4
Driver
Races: BEL (car #28)

PICTURED AT NON-CHAMPIONSHIP RACE

ANDRÉ SIMON (FRA; AGE: 36) 0 PTS

Maserati 250F S6
Driver
Races: FRA (car #42)

ANDRÉ SIMON (CONTD)

Gordini 16 S6
Équipe Gordini
Races: ITA (car #12)

PIERO TARUFFI (ITA; AGE: 49) 0 PTS

Maserati 250F S6
Officine Alfieri Maserati
Races: FRA (car #8)

PIERO TARUFFI (CONTD)

Vanwall S4
Vandervell Products
Races: ITA (car #16)

DESMOND TITTERINGTON (GBR; AGE: 28) 0 PTS

Connaught B-Alta S4
Connaught Engineering
Races: GBR (car #20)

MAURICE TRINTIGNANT (FRA; AGE: 38) 0 PTS

Vanwall S4
Vandervell Products
Races: MON (car #14); BEL (#12); GBR (#17); ITA (#20)

MAURICE TRINTIGNANT (CONTD)

Bugatti T251 S8
Automobiles Bugatti
Races: FRA (car #28)

OTTORINO VOLONTERIO (SUI; AGE: 38) 0 PTS

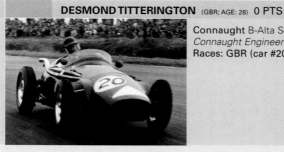

Maserati 250F S6
Driver
Races: GER (car #22)

1956

CHAMPIONSHIP CAR-BY-CAR

GRAND PRIX WINNERS 1956

	RACE (CIRCUIT)	WINNER (CAR)
ARG	ARGENTINE GRAND PRIX (BUENOS AIRES)	MUSSO/FANGIO (LANCIA-FERRARI D50 V8)
MON	MONACO GRAND PRIX (MONTE CARLO)	STIRLING MOSS (MASERATI 250F S6)
BEL	BELGIAN GRAND PRIX (SPA-FRANCORCHAMPS)	PETER COLLINS (LANCIA-FERRARI D50 V8)
FRA	FRENCH GRAND PRIX (REIMS)	PETER COLLINS (LANCIA-FERRARI D50 V8)
GBR	BRITISH GRAND PRIX (SILVERSTONE)	JUAN MANUEL FANGIO (LANCIA-FERRARI D50 V8)
GER	GERMAN GRAND PRIX (NÜRBURGRING)	JUAN MANUEL FANGIO (LANCIA-FERRARI D50 V8)
ITA	ITALIAN GRAND PRIX (MONZA)	STIRLING MOSS (MASERATI 250F S6)

PETER COLLINS

1957

FANGIO'S FIFTH – AND ALSO HIS BEST

Above
Come on you red: Fangio crosses the line after cementing the 24th and final win of his career. This was one of his greatest drives and it earned him a fifth title, a feat that would remain unequalled for 45 years

Right
History in the making: Tony Brooks took the start at Aintree but was still suffering from the after-effects of an accident at Le Mans. He handed his Vanwall over to Stirling Moss – and the latter went on to secure the maiden world championship win for a British car

Left
I'd like to teach the world to sing: first, though, Moss takes a well-earned post-race swig after completing his victorious stint at Aintree

FANGIO SAID THAT HE'D DRIVEN AT A LEVEL HE'D NEVER PREVIOUSLY REACHED – AND HE DIDN'T WANT TO GO THERE AGAIN. IT VERGED ON THE MYSTICAL

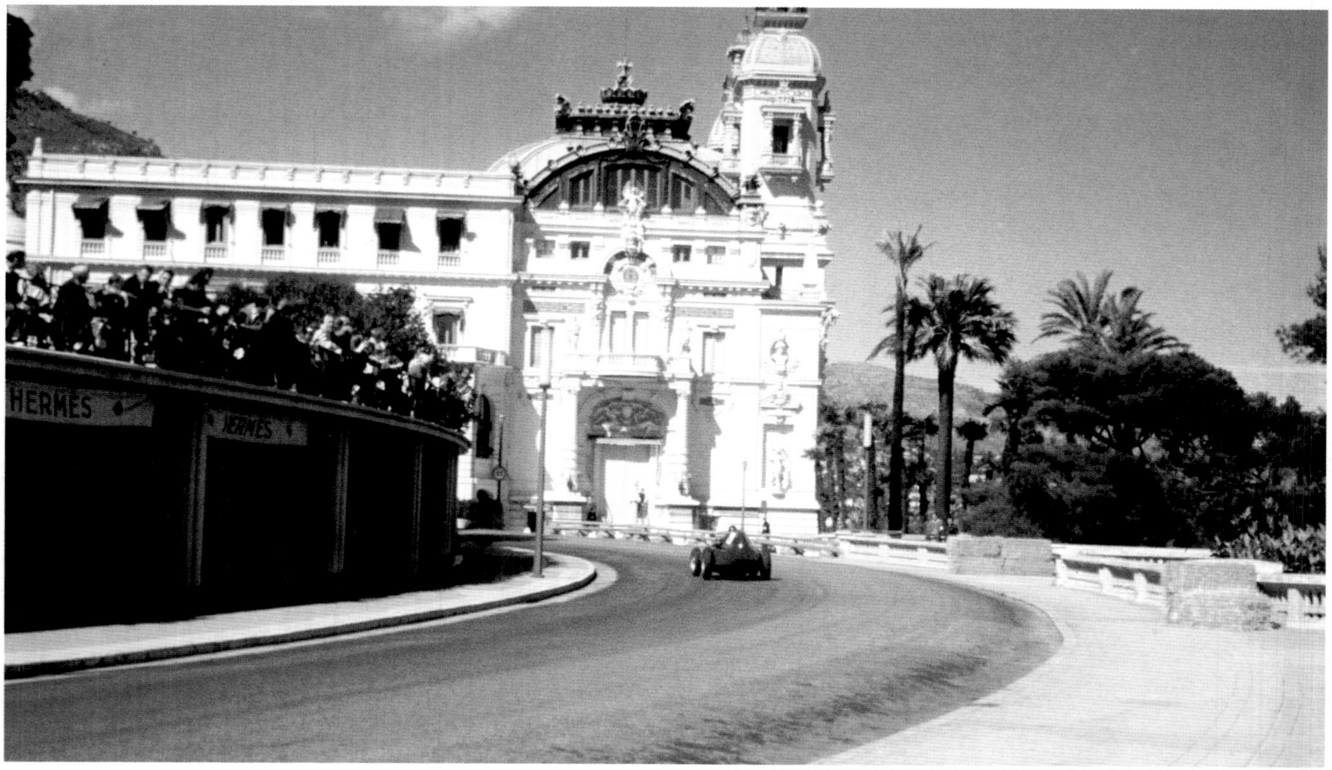

Above
Groundhog Day: Fangio triumphed in the opening two grands prix of 1954 at the wheel of a Maserati 250F – and repeated the trick three years later. He won from pole position in Monaco, where Peter Collins and Stirling Moss joined him on the front row

Left
Seconds out: Brooks trailed Fangio across the line in Monaco – although he was more than 25s adrift by the end

Far right, top
Hurry up Harry: Schell guides his Maserati towards third place in Pescara. The Italian track measured 16.055 miles (25.838 km) and is the longest to have staged a world championship grand prix

Right
Storm in a port: wreckage begins to tarnish the Monaco seafront after Hawthorn and Collins come to grief

Juan Manuel Fangio, still the world's greatest driver at 46 years of age, drove the finest season of his staggering career to win his fifth and final Formula One championship.

Having switched from Ferrari to Maserati for the new season, the Argentine was soon on his winning way. The Maserati 250F had been honed during the previous three years: it was a responsive chassis with beautifully delicate handling – exactly the sort of car in which Fangio could really demonstrate his genius.

Nowhere was this more apparent than at the Nürburgring, where he overcame a badly fluffed mid-race pit stop to defeat the Ferraris and clinch the title. During his fightback he repeatedly broke the lap record by an astonishing margin. He later said that he'd driven at a level he'd never previously reached – and he didn't want to go there again. It verged on the mystical.

While the Maserati represented an artisan's approach to creating an F1 car, the new Vanwall reflected a more scientific philosophy. With low-drag bodywork designed by an aircraft aerodynamicist, it was the fastest car in F1 by the end of the season. The team scored its breakthrough victory in the British Grand Prix at Aintree, where Stirling Moss and Tony Brooks shared the winning car. More impressive, however, was Moss's virtuoso performance in Pescara: despite stopping for a drink and a precautionary oil top-up, he finished more than three minutes clear of second-placed Fangio.

1957

CHAMPIONSHIP CAR-BY-CAR

1ST JUAN MANUEL FANGIO (ARG; AGE: 46) 40(+6) PTS

Maserati 250F S6
Officine Alfieri Maserati
Races: ARG (car #2); MON (#32); FRA; GBR (both #2); GER (#1); PES; ITA (both #2)

PICTURE IN MON PRACTICE

2ND STIRLING MOSS (GBR; AGE: 27) 25 PTS

Maserati 250F S6
Officine Alfieri Maserati
Races: ARG (car #4)

STIRLING MOSS (CONTD)

Vanwall S4
Vandervell Products
Races: MON (car #18); GBR (#18 and #20); GER (#10); PES (#26); ITA (#18)

3RD LUIGI MUSSO (ITA; AGE: 32) 16 PTS

Lancia-Ferrari D50 V8
Scuderia Ferrari
Races: ARG (car #12); FRA (#10); GBR (#14); GER (#6); PES (#34); ITA (#32)

4TH MIKE HAWTHORN (GBR; AGE: 28) 13 PTS

Lancia-Ferrari D50 V8
Scuderia Ferrari
Races: ARG (car #16); MON (#28 and #24); FRA (#14); GBR (#10); GER (#8); ITA (#34)

5TH TONY BROOKS (GBR; AGE: 25) 11 PTS

Vanwall S4
Vandervell Products
Races: MON (car #20); GBR (#18 and #20); GER (#11); PES (#28); ITA (#22)

6TH= MASTEN GREGORY (USA; AGE: 25) 10 PTS

Maserati 250F S6
Scuderia Centro Sud
Races: MON (car #2); GER (#16); PES (#14); ITA (#26)

6TH= HARRY SCHELL (USA; AGE: 36) 10 PTS

Maserati 250F S6
Scuderia Centro Sud/ Officine Alfieri Maserati
Races: ARG (car #22); MON (#38 and #34); FRA; GBR (both #6); GER (#3); PES (#6); ITA (#4 and #8)

8TH PETER COLLINS (GBR; AGE: 25) 8 PTS

Lancia-Ferrari D50 V8
Scuderia Ferrari
Races: ARG (car #10 and #18); MON (#26); FRA (#12); GBR (#12 and #16); GER (#7); ITA (#30)

See also Cesare Perdisa

9TH JEAN BEHRA (FRA; AGE: 36) 6 PTS

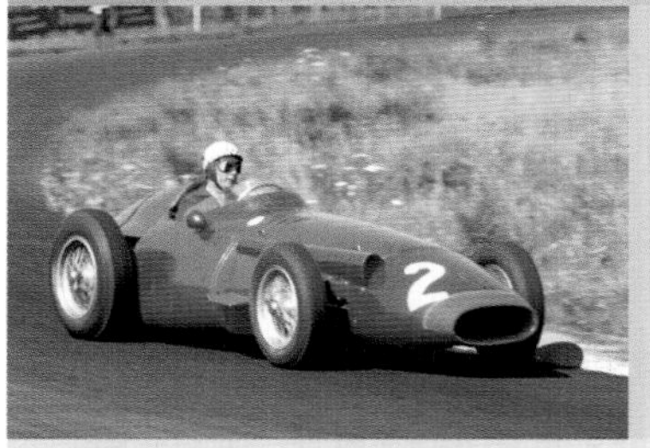

Maserati 250F S6 (V12 at ITA)
Officine Alfieri Maserati
Races: ARG (car #6); FRA (#4); GBR (#4); GER (#2); PES (#4); ITA (#6)

10TH= STUART LEWIS-EVANS (GBR; AGE: 27) 5 PTS

Connaught B-Alta S4
Connaught Engineering
Races: MON (car #10)

STUART LEWIS-EVANS (CONTD)

Vanwall S4
Vandervell Products
Races: FRA (car #18); GBR (#22); GER (#12); PES (#30); ITA (#20)

10TH= MAURICE TRINTIGNANT (FRA; AGE: 39) 5 PTS

Lancia-Ferrari D50 V8
Scuderia Ferrari
Races: MON (car #30); FRA (#16); GBR (#16)

12TH= CARLOS MENDITÉGUY (ARG; AGE: 41) 4 PTS

Maserati 250F S6
Officine Alfieri Maserati
Races: ARG (car #8); MON (#36); FRA; GBR (both #8)

12TH= WOLFGANG VON TRIPS (GER; AGE: 29) 4 PTS

Lancia-Ferrari D50 V8
Scuderia Ferrari
Races: ARG (car #18); MON (#24); ITA (#36)

See also Cesare Perdisa

1957

CHAMPIONSHIP CAR-BY-CAR

14TH ROY SALVADORI (GBR; AGE: 35) 2 PTS

Vanwall S4
Vandervell Products
Races: FRA (car #20)

ROY SALVADORI (CONTD)

Cooper T43-Climax S4
Cooper Car Co
Races: GBR (car #36); GER (#23); PES (#22)

15TH= JOSÉ FROILÁN GONZÁLEZ (ARG; AGE: 34) 1 PT

Lancia-Ferrari D50 V8
Scuderia Ferrari
Races: ARG (car #20)

15TH= ALFONSO DE PORTAGO (ESP; AGE: 28) 1 PT

Lancia-Ferrari D50 V8
Scuderia Ferrari
Races: ARG (car #20)

15TH= GIORGIO SCARLATTI (ITA; AGE: 35) 1 PT

Maserati 250F S6
Officine Alfieri Maserati
Races: MON (car #34); GER (#4); PES; ITA (both #8)

EDGAR BARTH (DDR; AGE: 40) 0 PTS

Porsche 550RS F4
Porsche
Races: GER (car #21)

CAREL GODIN DE BEAUFORT (NED; AGE: 23) 0 PTS

Porsche 550RS F4
Écurie Maarsbergen
Races: GER (car #27)

JO BONNIER (SWE; AGE: 27) 0 PTS

Maserati 250F S6
Scuderia Centro Sud/ Driver
Races: ARG (car #24); GBR (#28); PES (#16); ITA (#24)

JACK BRABHAM (AUS; AGE: 31) 0 PTS

Cooper T43-Climax S4
Cooper Car Co/ Rob Walker Racing
Races: MON (car #14); FRA (#22 and #24); GBR (#34); GER; PES (both #24)

IVOR BUEB (GBR; AGE: 34) 0 PTS

Connaught B-Alta S4
Connaught Engineering
Races: MON (car #12)

IVOR BUEB (CONTD)

Maserati 250F S6
Gilby Engineering
Races: GBR (car #32)

EUGENIO CASTELLOTTI (ITA; AGE: 26) 0 PTS

Lancia-Ferrari D50 V8
Scuderia Ferrari
Races: ARG (car #14)

PAUL ENGLAND (AUS; AGE: 28) 0 PTS

Cooper T41-Climax S4
Ridgeway Managements
Races: GER (car #26)

JACK FAIRMAN (GBR; AGE: 44) 0 PTS

BRM P25 S4
Owen Racing Organisation
Races: GBR (car #24)

RON FLOCKHART (GBR; AGE: 34) 0 PTS

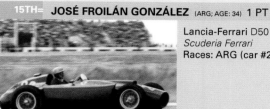

BRM P25 S4
Owen Racing Organisation
Races: MON (car #6); FRA (#26)

1957

CHAMPIONSHIP CAR-BY-CAR

BOB GERARD (GBR; AGE: 43) 0 PTS

Cooper T43-Bristol S6
Driver
Races: GBR (car #38)

DICK GIBSON (GBR; AGE: 39) 0 PTS

Cooper T43-Climax S4
Driver
Races: GER (car #29)

CHICO GODIA-SALES (ESP; AGE: 36) 0 PTS

Maserati 250F S6
Driver
Races: GER (car #18); PES; ITA (both #10)

HORACE GOULD (GBR; AGE: 35) 0 PTS

Maserati 250F S6
Driver
Races: MON (car #22); FRA (#30); GER (#19); PES (#18); ITA (#14)

BRUCE HALFORD (GBR; AGE: 26) 0 PTS

Maserati 250F S6
Driver
Races: GER (car #15); PES (#20); ITA (#16)

HANS HERRMANN (GER; AGE: 29) 0 PTS

Maserati 250F S6
Scuderia Centro Sud
Races: GER (car #17)

LES LESTON (GBR; AGE: 36) 0 PTS

BRM P25 S4
Owen Racing Organisation
Races: GBR (car #26)

MIKE MacDOWEL (GBR; AGE: 24) 0 PTS

Cooper T43-Climax S4
Cooper Car Co
Races: FRA (car #24)

HERBERT MacKAY-FRASER (USA; AGE: 30) 0 PTS

BRM P25 S4
Owen Racing Organisation
Races: FRA (car #28)

UMBERTO MAGLIOLI (ITA; AGE: 29) 0 PTS

Porsche 550RS F4
Porsche
Races: GER (car #20)

TONY MARSH (GBR; AGE: 26) 0 PTS

Cooper T43-Climax S4
Ridgeway Managements
Races: GER (car #25)

BRIAN NAYLOR (GBR; AGE: 34) 0 PTS

Cooper T43-Climax S4
Driver
Races: GER (car #28)

CESARE PERDISA (ITA; AGE: 24) 0 PTS
PETER COLLINS (GBR; AGE: 25)
WOLFGANG VON TRIPS (GER; AGE: 29)

(shared car)
Lancia-Ferrari D50 V8
Scuderia Ferrari
Races: ARG (car #18)

Also see Peter Collins and Wolfgang Von Trips

LUIGI PIOTTI (ITA; AGE: 43) 0 PTS

Maserati 250F S6
Driver
Races: ARG (car #28); PES; ITA (both #12)

PICTURED DURING MON PRACTICE

ANDRÉ SIMON (FRA; AGE: 37) 0 PTS
OTTORINO VOLONTERIO (SUI; AGE: 39)

(shared car)
Maserati 250F S6
Ottorino Volonterio
Races: ITA (car #28)

1957

CHAMPIONSHIP CAR-BY-CAR

ALEJANDRO DE TOMASO (ARG; AGE: 28) 0 PTS

Ferrari 625 S4
Scuderia Centro Sud
Races: ARG (car #26)

GRAND PRIX WINNERS 1957

	RACE (CIRCUIT)	**WINNER** (CAR)
ARG	ARGENTINE GRAND PRIX (BUENOS AIRES)	JUAN MANUEL FANGIO (MASERATI 250F S6)
MON	MONACO GRAND PRIX (MONTE CARLO)	JUAN MANUEL FANGIO (MASERATI 250F S6)
FRA	FRENCH GRAND PRIX (ROUEN-LES-ESSARTS)	JUAN MANUEL FANGIO (MASERATI 250F S6)
GBR	BRITISH GRAND PRIX (AINTREE)	BROOKS/MOSS (VANWALL S4)
GER	GERMAN GRAND PRIX (NÜRBURGRING)	JUAN MANUEL FANGIO (MASERATI 250F S6)
PES	PESCARA GRAND PRIX (PESCARA)	STIRLING MOSS (VANWALL S4)
ITA	ITALIAN GRAND PRIX (MONZA)	STIRLING MOSS (VANWALL S4)

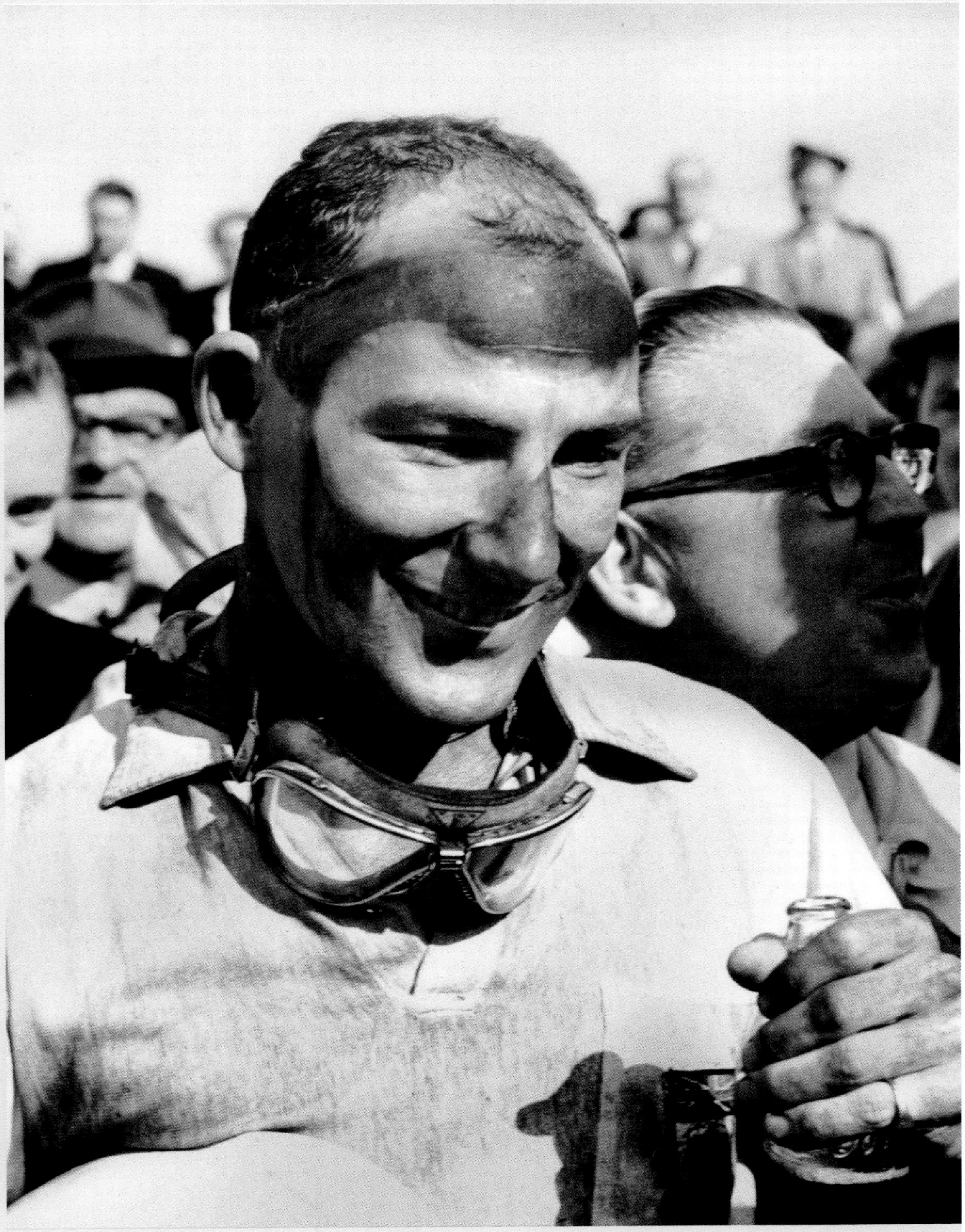

STIRLING MOSS

1958

HAWTHORN TAKES TITLE BY STEALTH AS BRITS DOMINATE

Left
Drier straights: Stirling Moss leads Phil Hill's Ferrari in the arid setting of Ain-Diab, during the season-closing – and only, to date – Moroccan GP. The Englishman recorded his fourth win of the campaign, but still the world title remained elusive

Above
Hawthorn amid the bushes: the champion finished second on five occasions in 1958 and started his collection here at Spa. The Englishman was the last driver to win the world title at the wheel of a front-engined car

Right:
Queen of the stone age: Maria Teresa de Filippis (Maserati 250F) made history in 1958 as the first woman to attempt qualification for a world championship grand prix. She failed to make the cut here in Monaco but later finished 10th in Belgium

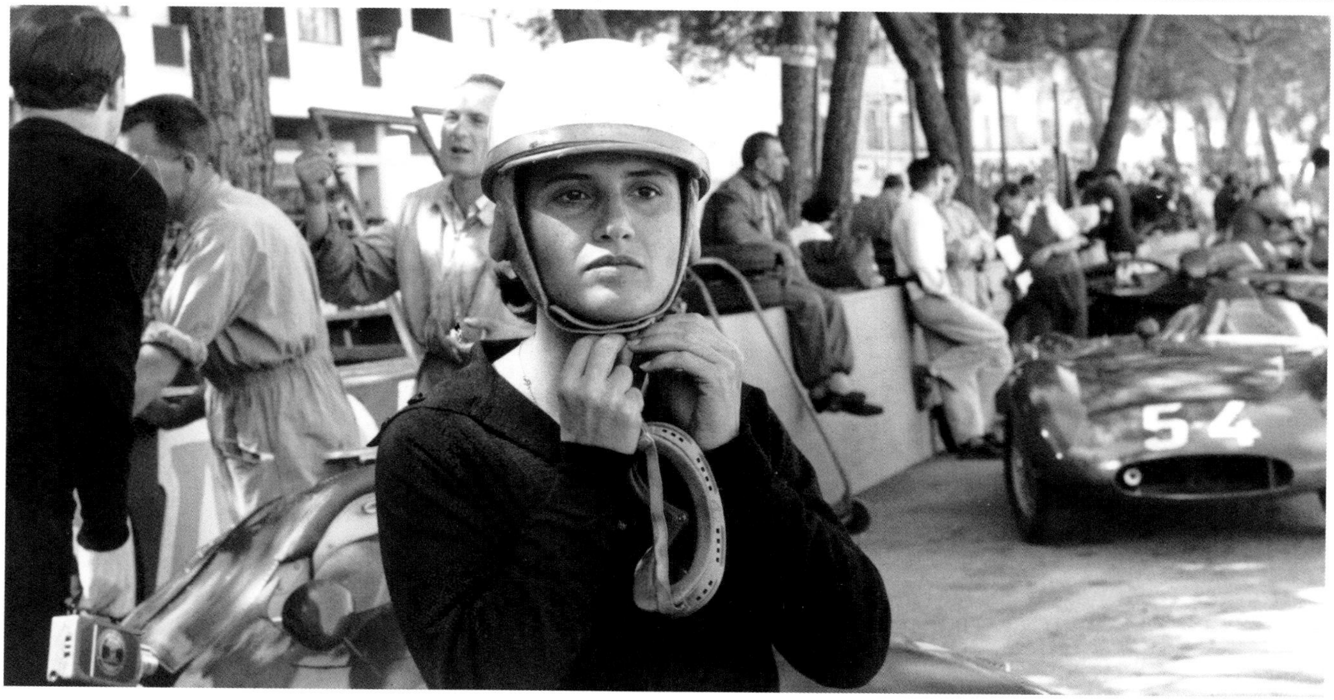

Left
Fields of dreams: Gerino Gerini (Maserati) leads Jean Behra (BRM), Stirling Moss (Vanwall) and Francesco Godia-Sales (Maserati) between the lush fields in the heart of France's Champagne region.

Below
You say want a revolution: The mid-engined Coopers pointed the way ahead for F1. Here Brabham leads winner Trintignant in Monaco

Bottom left
On your marques: Lotus made its Formula One world championship debut in 1958 and Cliff Allison scored the team's first points at Spa, where he finished fourth

Bottom right
Duke of hurl: at pavement level, the chap in the centre appears to ordering a drink from the Monaco station bar and thus misses a glorious opportunity to appreciate the art of opposite lock, as demonstrated by Peter Collins in his Ferrari 246 Dino

Three English drivers fought out the destiny of the world title. Two drove for a British team, Vanwall, the other for Ferrari. It was the season that provided final confirmation of the British movement's arrival as a force in grand prix racing.

Mike Hawthorn (Ferrari) finally edged out Vanwall rivals Stirling Moss and Tony Brooks to take the crown, but his tally of one victory – Moss took four and Brooks three – made many question the scoring system's worth.

There was some consolation in that Vanwall won the newly-instigated world championship for constructors. It was to be its first and last, though, because team boss Tony Vandervell – suffering ill-health and deeply upset at the death of his third driver Stuart Lewis-Evans, who succumbed to injuries sustained in the Moroccan Grand Prix – would never again run a serious Formula One programme.

Lewis-Evans was not the season's only casualty. Hawthorn's close friend and Ferrari team-mate Peter Collins was killed during the German GP while trying to stay in touch with Brooks's winning Vanwall. Luigi Musso, another Ferrari driver, was killed in a high-speed accident at Reims. It was against this oppressive backdrop that Hawthorn decided to retire after clinching the title. Cruelly, he was killed in a road accident early the following year.

The great Juan Manuel Fangio retired midway through the year, which signalled the end of an era. The first grand prix of the season, in Argentina, hinted at a new one to come. Stirling Moss won at the wheel of a tiny, bizarre-looking car with its engine behind the driver – the Cooper. Although it was nothing more than a bored-out F2 chassis, the benefits of its layout gave it a decisive advantage over the classic, front-engined thoroughbreds. It won in Monaco, too, and Cooper began to realise it had really stumbled onto something.

1958

CHAMPIONSHIP CAR-BY-CAR

1ST MIKE HAWTHORN (GBR; AGE: 29) 42 PTS

Ferrari Dino 246 V6
Scuderia Ferrari
Races: ARG (car #20); MON (#38); NED (#5); BEL (#16); FRA (#4); GBR (#2); GER (#3); POR (#22); ITA (#14); MAR (#6)

2ND STIRLING MOSS (GBR; AGE: 28) 41 PTS

Cooper T43-Climax S4
Rob Walker Racing
Races: ARG (car #14)

STIRLING MOSS (CONTD)

Vanwall S4
Vandervell Products
Races: MON (car #28); NED (#1); BEL (#2); FRA (#8); GBR; GER (both #7); POR (#2); ITA (#26); MAR (#8)

3RD TONY BROOKS (GBR; AGE: 26) 24 PTS

Vanwall S4
Vandervell Products
Races: MON (car #30); NED (#2); BEL (#4); FRA (#10 and #12); GBR; GER (both #8); POR (#4); ITA (#28); MAR (#10)

4TH ROY SALVADORI (GBR; AGE: 36) 15 PTS

Cooper T45-Climax S4
Cooper Car Co
Races: MON (car #18); NED (#7); BEL (#24); FRA (#20); GBR; GER (both #10); POR (#16); ITA (#6); MAR (#28)

5TH= PETER COLLINS (GBR; AGE: 26) 14 PTS

Ferrari Dino 246 V6
Scuderia Ferrari
Races: ARG (car #18); MON (#36); NED (#4); BEL (#14); FRA (#42); GBR (#1); GER (#2)

5TH= HARRY SCHELL (USA; AGE: 37) 14 PTS

Maserati 250F S6
Joakim Bonnier
Races: ARG (car #8)

HARRY SCHELL (CONTD)

BRM P25 S4
Owen Racing Organisation
Races: MON (car #8); NED (#15); BEL (#10); FRA (#16); GBR (#20); GER (#6); POR; ITA (both #10); MAR (#16)

7TH= LUIGI MUSSO (ITA; AGE: 33) 12 PTS

Ferrari Dino 246 V6
Scuderia Ferrari
Races: ARG (car #16); MON (#34); NED (#6); BEL (#18); FRA (#2)

7TH= MAURICE TRINTIGNANT (FRA; AGE: 40) 12 PTS

Cooper T45-Climax S4
Rob Walker Racing
Races: MON (car #20); NED (#9); GER (#11); POR (#12); ITA (#2); MAR (#32)

MAURICE TRINTIGNANT (CONTD)

Maserati 250F S6
Scuderia Centro Sud
Races: BEL (car #28)

MAURICE TRINTIGNANT (CONTD)

BRM P25 S4
Owen Racing Organisation
Races: FRA (car #18)

MAURICE TRINTIGNANT (CONTD)

Cooper T43-Climax S4
Rob Walker Racing
Races: GBR (car #4)

9TH STUART LEWIS-EVANS (GBR; AGE: 28) 11 PTS

Vanwall S4
Vandervell Products
Races: MON (car #32); NED (#3); BEL (#6); FRA (#12); GBR (#9); POR (#6); ITA (#30); MAR (#12)

10TH= JEAN BEHRA (FRA; AGE: 37) 9 PTS

Maserati 250F S6
Ken Kavanagh
Races: ARG (car #4)

1958

CHAMPIONSHIP CAR-BY-CAR

JEAN BEHRA (CONTD)

BRM P25 S4
Owen Racing Organisation
Races: MON (car #6); NED (#14); BEL (#8); FRA (#14); GBR (#19); GER (#5); POR (#8); ITA (#8); MAR (#14)

10TH= PHIL HILL (USA; AGE: 31) 9 PTS

Maserati 250F S6
Joakim Bonnier
Races: FRA (car #36)

PHIL HILL (CONTD)

Ferrari Dino 156 V6
Scuderia Ferrari
Races: GER (car #23)

PHIL HILL (CONTD)

Ferrari Dino 246 V6
Scuderia Ferrari
Races: ITA (car #18); MAR (#4)

10TH= WOLFGANG VON TRIPS (GER; AGE: 30) 9 PTS

Ferrari Dino 246 V6
Scuderia Ferrari
Races: MON (car #40); FRA (#6); GBR (#3); GER (#4); POR (#24); ITA (#16)

13TH JUAN MANUEL FANGIO (ARG; AGE: 46) 7 PTS

Maserati 250F S6
Scuderia Sud Americana/Driver
Races: ARG (car #2); FRA (#34)

14TH= CLIFF ALLISON (GBR; AGE: 26) 3 PTS

Lotus 12-Climax S4
Team Lotus
Races: MON (car #24); NED (#17); BEL (#40); FRA (#26); GBR (#17); ITA (#36); MAR (#34)

CLIFF ALLISON (CONTD)

Lotus 16-Climax S4
Team Lotus
Races: GER (car #12)

CLIFF ALLISON (CONTD)

Maserati 250F S6
Team Lotus
Races: POR (car #18)

14TH= JO BONNIER (SWE; AGE: 28) 3 PTS

Maserati 250F S6
Driver/Giorgio Scarlatti/Scuderia Centro Sud
Races: MON (car #58); NED (#11); BEL (#36); FRA (#38); GBR (#22); GER (#16); POR (#32)

JO BONNIER (CONTD)

BRM P25 S4
Owen Racing Organisation
Races: ITA (car #12); MAR (#18)

14TH= JACK BRABHAM (AUS; AGE: 32) 3 PTS

Cooper T45-Climax S4
Cooper Car Co
Races: MON (car #16); NED (#8); BEL; FRA (both #22); GBR (#11); GER (#24); POR (#14); ITA (#4); MAR (#50)

EDGAR BARTH (DDR; AGE: 41) 0 PTS

Porsche RSK F4
Porsche
Races: GER (car #21)

CAREL GODIN DE BEAUFORT (NED; AGE: 24) 0 PTS

Porsche RSK F4
Écurie Maarsbergen
Races: NED; GER (both car #18)

TOMMY BRIDGER (GBR; AGE: 24) 0 PTS

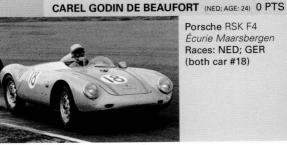

Cooper T45-Climax S4
British Racing Partnership
Races: MAR (car #56)

1958

CHAMPIONSHIP CAR-BY-CAR

IVOR BUEB (GBR; AGE: 35) 0 PTS

Connaught B-Alta S4
BC Ecclestone
Races: GBR (car #15)

IVOR BUEB (CONTD)

Lotus 12-Climax S4
Écurie Demi Litre
Races: GER (car #28)

IAN BURGESS (GBR; AGE: 28) 0 PTS

Cooper T45-Climax S4
Cooper Car Co
Races: GBR (car #12)

IAN BURGESS (CONTD)

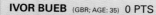

Cooper T43-Climax S4
High Efficiency Motors
Races: GER (car #26)

GIULIO CABIANCA (ITA; AGE: 35) 0 PTS

Maserati 250F S6
Joakim Bonnier
Races: ITA (car #22)

ROBERT LA CAZE (MAR; AGE: 41) 0 PTS

Cooper T45-Climax S4
Driver
Races: MAR (car #58)

JACK FAIRMAN (GBR; AGE: 45) 0 PTS

Connaught B-Alta S4
BC Ecclestone
Races: GBR (car #14)

JACK FAIRMAN (CONTD)

Cooper T45-Climax S4
Cooper Car Co
Races: MAR (car #32)

MARIA TERESA DE FILIPPIS (ITA; AGE: 31) 0 PTS

Maserati 250F S6
Driver/Scuderia Centro Sud
Races: BEL (car #26); POR (#30); ITA (#42)

RON FLOCKHART (GBR; AGE: 35) 0 PTS

BRM P25 S4
Owen Racing Organisation
Races: MAR (car #20)

OLIVIER GENDEBIEN (BEL; AGE: 34) 0 PTS

Ferrari Dino 246 V6
Scuderia Ferrari
Races: BEL; ITA (both car #20); MAR (#2)

GERINO GERINI (ITA; AGE: 30) 0 PTS

Maserati 250F S6
Scuderia Centro Sud
Races: FRA (car #32); GBR (#6); ITA (#40); MAR (#26)

PICTURED DURING MON PRACTICE

DICK GIBSON (GBR; AGE: 40) 0 PTS

Cooper T43-Climax S4
Driver
Races: GER (car #19)

CHICO GODIA-SALES (ESP; AGE: 37) 0 PTS

Maserati 250F S6
Driver
Races: ARG (car #10); BEL (#38); FRA (#40)

CHRISTIAN GOETHALS (BEL; AGE: 30) 0 PTS

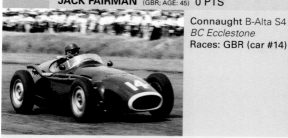

Cooper T43-Climax S4
Écurie Eperon d'Or
Races: GER (car #27)

1958

CHAMPIONSHIP CAR-BY-CAR

HORACE GOULD (GBR; AGE: 36) 0 PTS

Maserati 250F S6
Driver
Races: ARG (car #12)

MASTEN GREGORY (USA; AGE: 26) 0 PTS

Maserati 250F S6
Horace Gould/Scuderia Centro Sud/Temple Buell
Races: NED (car #12); BEL (#30); ITA (#32); MAR (#22)

ANDRÉ GUELFI (FRA; AGE: 39) 0 PTS

Cooper T45-Climax S4
Driver
Races: MAR (car #48)

PICTURED IN PRACTICE

HANS HERRMANN (GER; AGE: 30) 0 PTS

Maserati 250F S6
Scuderia Centro Sud/ Joakim Bonnier
Races: GER (car #17); ITA (#24); MAR (#38)

GRAHAM HILL (GBR; AGE: 29) 0 PTS

Lotus 12-Climax S4
Team Lotus
Races: MON (car #26); NED (#16); BEL (#42)

GRAHAM HILL (CONTD)

Lotus 16-Climax S4
Team Lotus
Races: FRA (car #24); GBR (#16); GER (#25); POR (#20); ITA (#38); MAR (#36)

TONY MARSH (GBR; AGE: 27) 0 PTS

Cooper T45-Climax S4
Driver
Races: GER (car #30)

BRUCE McLAREN (NZL; AGE: 21) 0 PTS

Cooper T45-Climax S4
Cooper Car Co
Races: GER (car #20); MAR (#52)

CARLOS MENDITÉGUY (ARG; AGE: 42) 0 PTS

Maserati 250F S6
Scuderia Sud Americana
Races: ARG (car #6)

BRIAN NAYLOR (GBR; AGE: 35) 0 PTS

Cooper T45-Climax S4
Driver
Races: GER (car #29)

FRANÇOIS PICARD (FRA; AGE: 37) 0 PTS

Cooper T43-Climax S4
Rob Walker Racing
Races: MAR (car #54)

TROY RUTTMAN (USA; AGE: 28) 0 PTS

Maserati 250F S6
Scuderia Centro Sud
Races: FRA (car #30)

GIORGIO SCARLATTI (ITA; AGE: 36) 0 PTS

Maserati 250F S6
Driver
Races: MON (car #46); NED (#10)

WOLFGANG SEIDEL (GER; AGE: 32) 0 PTS

Maserati 250F S6
Scuderia Centro Sud
Races: BEL (car #32); MAR (#24)

WOLFGANG SEIDEL (CONTD)

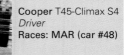

Cooper T43-Climax S4
Rob Walker Racing
Races: GER (car #22)

1958

CHAMPIONSHIP CAR-BY-CAR

CARROLL SHELBY (USA; AGE: 35) 0 PTS

Maserati 250F S6
Scuderia Centro Sud/ Temple Buell
Races: FRA (car #28); GBR (#5); POR (#28); ITA (#34 and #32)

ALAN STACEY (GBR; AGE: 24) 0 PTS

Lotus 16-Climax S4
Team Lotus
Races: GBR (car #18)

GRAND PRIX WINNERS 1958

	RACE (CIRCUIT)	WINNER (CAR)
ARG	ARGENTINE GRAND PRIX (BUENOS AIRES)	STIRLING MOSS (COOPER T43-CLIMAX S4)
MON	MONACO GRAND PRIX (MONTE CARLO)	MAURICE TRINTIGNANT (COOPER T45-CLIMAX S4)
NED	DUTCH GRAND PRIX (ZANDVOORT)	STIRLING MOSS (VANWALL S4)
BEL	BELGIAN GRAND PRIX (SPA-FRANCORCHAMPS)	TONY BROOKS (VANWALL S4)
FRA	FRENCH GRAND PRIX (REIMS)	MIKE HAWTHORN (FERRARI DINO 246 V6)
GBR	BRITISH GRAND PRIX (SILVERSTONE)	PETER COLLINS (FERRARI DINO 246 V6)
GER	GERMAN GRAND PRIX (NÜRBURGRING)	TONY BROOKS (VANWALL S4)
POR	PORTUGUESE GRAND PRIX (OPORTO)	STIRLING MOSS (VANWALL S4)
ITA	ITALIAN GRAND PRIX (MONZA)	TONY BROOKS (VANWALL S4)
MAR	MOROCCAN GRAND PRIX (AIN DIAB, CASABLANCA)	STIRLING MOSS (VANWALL S4)

MIKE HAWTHORN – WORLD CHAMPION 1958

1959

BRABHAM AND COOPER CATALYSE F1 REVOLUTION

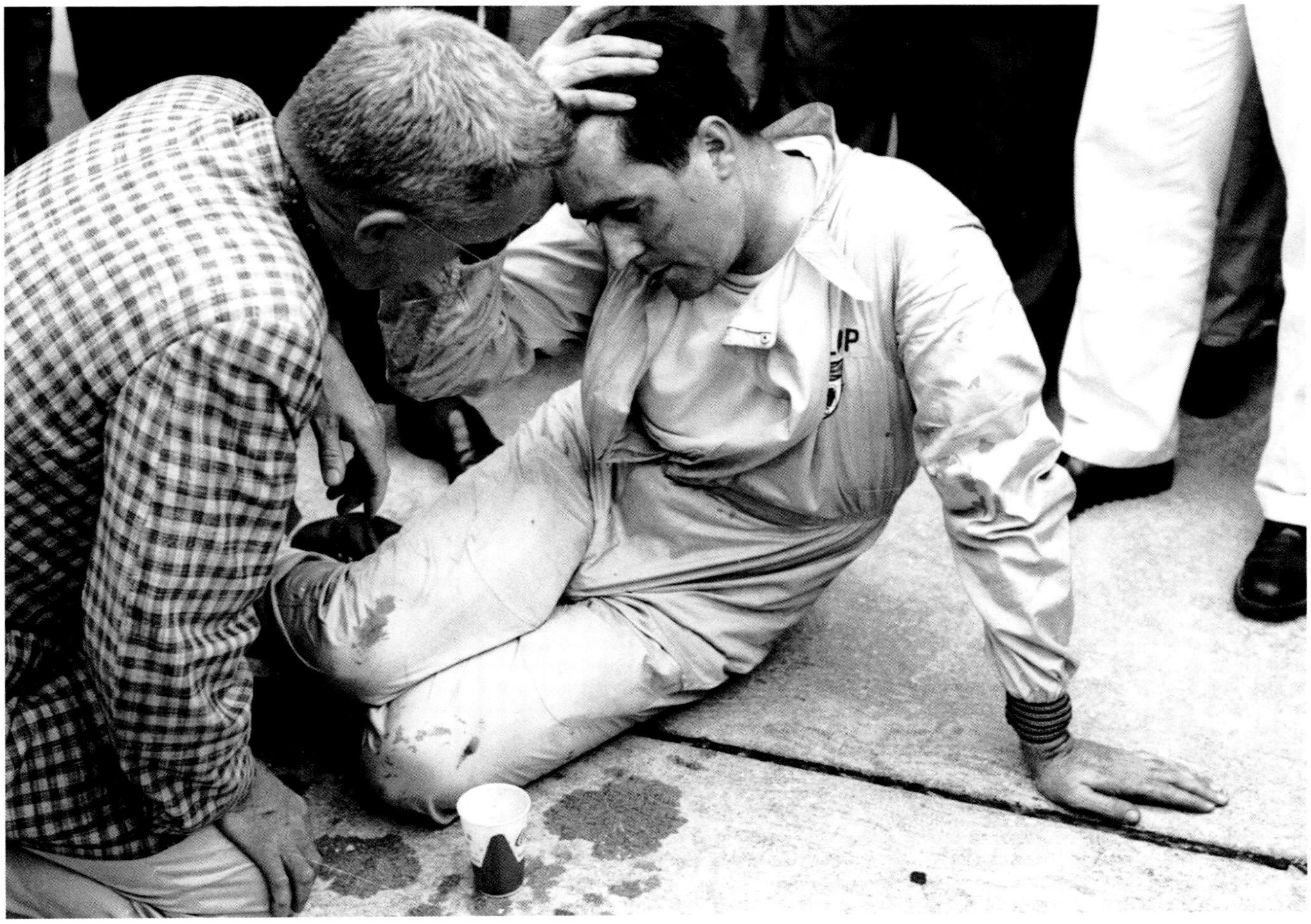

Left
Back to the future: it might look stubby and spindly – a bit like a cigar tube with a wheel at each corner – but Jack Brabham's Cooper, here heading for third at Reims, represents the principle on which all modern grand prix cars are based: engine tucked snugly behind the driver, weight over the driven wheels

Above
Tired and unemotional: Brabham pushed his car across the line to claim fourth place in the seasonal finale at Sebring. That was enough to make him champion – but he was far too knackered to celebrate

Right
Big bother: Moss coaxes his BRP-run BRM towards the finish in France. He was initially classified eighth, but officials turfed him out because marshals had given him an illegal push-start after an earlier spin

Left
Days of yaw: Brooks, Moss, Gregory, Brabham, Bonnier and Gurney try to stick between the white lines at Avus, Germany – the only world championship race to have taken place on what was effectively two sides of an autobahn linked by banked hairpins

Above
Fastest lip: part of the prize for winning the first United States GP involved being snogged senseless. Formula One's youngest winner Bruce McLaren accepted gracefully

Below:
Dying breed: Ferrari's Dino 246 was the ultimate realisation of the classic front-engined grand prix car, for which extinction beckoned. Dan Gurney heads for third in Portugal

During the previous season Cooper had scored sensational, unexpected successes in Argentina and Monaco with what was little more than a beefed-up Formula Two car. This time the company went the whole hog and developed a pukka, mid-engined F1 machine.

Ranged against this new-generation racer was the ultimate development of the classic, front-engined grand prix car – the Ferrari Dino 246. Its V6 engine might have been in what was gradually transpiring to be the wrong place, but it had 60bhp more than the 2.5-litre, four-cylinder Coventry Climax in the back of the Cooper. It was a great rearguard action against the inevitable and it allowed the Italian team to fight with great dignity.

Having left Vanwall at the end of the previous season, when the British team announced it was quitting the sport, Tony Brooks emerged as the leading Ferrari driver. He won at Reims and Avus and went to the championship showdown in America with a real chance of pipping Cooper star Jack Brabham to the title. Unfortunately Brooks was hit at the start – by team-mate Wolfgang von Trips – and decided to pit for a damage inspection rather than take an unnecessary risk. He recovered to finish third, but Brabham took the title and the mid-engined revolution was complete.

Stirling Moss drove a Cooper, too, but it was owned by private entrant Rob Walker and proved to be less reliable than Brabham's factory car. When it held together, though, Moss could usually be relied upon to win.

JACK BRABHAM – WORLD CHAMPION 1959, 1960 & 1966

1959

CHAMPIONSHIP CAR-BY-CAR

1ST JACK BRABHAM (AUS; AGE: 33) 31(+3) PTS

Cooper T51-Climax S4
Cooper Car Co
Races: MON (car #24); NED; FRA (both #8); GBR (#12); GER; POR (both #1); USA (#8)

JACK BRABHAM (CONTD)

Cooper T45-Climax S4
Cooper Car Co
Races: ITA (car #12)

2ND TONY BROOKS (GBR; AGE: 27) 27 PTS

Ferrari Dino 246 V6
Scuderia Ferrari
Races: MON (car #50); NED (#2); FRA (#24); GER (#4); POR (#14); ITA (#30); USA (#2)

TONY BROOKS (CONTD)

Vanwall S4
Vandervell Products
Races: GBR (car #20)

3RD STIRLING MOSS (GBR; AGE: 29) 25.5 PTS

Cooper T51-Climax S4
Rob Walker Racing
Races: MON (car #30); NED (#11); GER (#7); POR (#4); ITA (#14); USA (#7)

STIRLING MOSS (CONTD)

BRM P25 S4
British Racing Partnership
Races: FRA (car #2); GBR (#6)

4TH PHIL HILL (USA; AGE: 32) 20 PTS

Ferrari Dino 246 V6
Scuderia Ferrari
Races: MON (car #48); NED (#3); FRA (#26); GER (#5); POR (#15); ITA (#32); USA (#5)

5TH MAURICE TRINTIGNANT (FRA; AGE: 41) 19 PTS

Cooper T51-Climax S4
Rob Walker Racing
Races: MON (car #32); NED (#10); FRA (#14); GBR (#18); GER (#8); POR (#5); ITA (#16); USA (#6)

6TH BRUCE McLAREN (NZL; AGE: 21) 16.5 PTS

Cooper T51-Climax S4
Cooper Car Co
Races: MON (car #22); ITA (#8)

BRUCE McLAREN (CONTD)

Cooper T45-Climax S4
Cooper Car Co
Races: FRA (car #12); GBR (#16); GER (#2); POR (#3); USA (#9)

7TH DAN GURNEY (USA; AGE: 28) 13 PTS

Ferrari Dino 246 V6
Scuderia Ferrari
Races: FRA (car #28); GER (#6); POR (#16); ITA (#36)

8TH= JO BONNIER (SWE; AGE: 29) 10 PTS

BRM P25 S4
Owen Racing Organisation
Races: MON (car #18); NED (#7); FRA (#4); GBR (#10); GER (#9); POR (#7); ITA (#6)

8TH= MASTEN GREGORY (USA; AGE: 27) 10 PTS

Cooper T45-Climax S4
Cooper Car Co
Races: MON (car #26)

MASTEN GREGORY (CONTD)

Cooper T51-Climax S4
Cooper Car Co
Races: NED (car #9); FRA (#10); GBR (#14); GER (#3); POR (#2)

10TH= INNES IRELAND (GBR; AGE: 29) 5 PTS

Lotus 16-Climax S4
Team Lotus
Races: NED (car #12); FRA (#34); GER (#15); POR (#12); ITA (#20); USA (#10)

1959

CHAMPIONSHIP CAR-BY-CAR

10TH= HARRY SCHELL (USA; AGE: 38) 5 PTS

BRM P25 S4
Owen Racing Organisation
Races: MON (car #16); NED; FRA (both #6); GBR (#8); GER (#10); POR (#6); ITA (#2)

HARRY SCHELL (CONTD)

Cooper T51-Climax S4
Écurie Bleue
Races: USA (car #19)

12TH OLIVIER GENDEBIEN (BEL; AGE: 35) 3 PTS

Ferrari Dino 246 V6
Scuderia Ferrari
Races: FRA (car #22); ITA (#38)

13TH= CLIFF ALLISON (GBR; AGE: 27) 2 PTS

Ferrari Dino 156 V6
Scuderia Ferrari
Races: MON (car #52)

CLIFF ALLISON (CONTD)

Ferrari Dino 246 V6
Scuderia Ferrari
Races: NED (car #16); GER (#17); ITA (#34); USA (#3)

13TH= JEAN BEHRA (FRA; AGE: 38) 2 PTS

Ferrari Dino 246 V6
Scuderia Ferrari
Races: MON (car #46); NED (#1); FRA (#30)

PETER ASHDOWN (GBR; AGE: 24) 0 PTS

Cooper T45-Climax S4
Alan Brown Équipe
Races: GBR (car #52)

CAREL GODIN DE BEAUFORT (NED; AGE: 25) 0 PTS

Porsche RSK F4
Écurie Maarsbergen
Races: NED (car #15)

CAREL GODIN DE BEAUFORT (CONTD)

Maserati 250F S6
Scuderia Ugolini
Races: FRA (car #42)

HARRY BLANCHARD (USA; AGE: 28) 0 PTS

Porsche RSK F4
Blanchard Automobile Co
Races: USA (car #17)

CHRIS BRISTOW (GBR; AGE: 21) 0 PTS

Cooper T51-Borgward
British Racing Partnership
Races: GBR (car #48)

IVOR BUEB (GBR; AGE: 36) 0 PTS

Cooper T51-Borgward
British Racing Partnership
Races: GBR (car #46)

IAN BURGESS (GBR; AGE: 29) 0 PTS

Cooper T51-Maserati S4
Scuderia Centro Sud
Races: FRA (car #18); GBR (#22); GER (#18); ITA (#42)

GIULIO CABIANCA (ITA; AGE: 36) 0 PTS

Maserati 250F S6
Ottorino Volonterio
Races: ITA (car #28)

MARIO ARAUJO DE CABRAL (POR; AGE: 25) 0 PTS

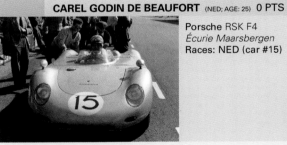

Cooper T51-Maserati S4
Scuderia Centro Sud
Races: POR (car #18)

1959

CHAMPIONSHIP CAR-BY-CAR

GEORGE CONSTANTINE (USA; AGE: 41) 0 PTS

Cooper T45-Climax S4
Mike Taylor
Races: USA (car #16)

COLIN DAVIS (GBR; AGE: 26) 0 PTS

Cooper T51-Maserati S4
Scuderia Centro Sud
Races: FRA (car #20); ITA (#40)

JACK FAIRMAN (GBR; AGE: 46) 0 PTS

Cooper T43-Climax S4
High Efficiency Motors
Races: GBR (car #38)

JACK FAIRMAN (CONTD)

Cooper T45-Maserati S4
High Efficiency Motors
Races: ITA (car #22)

RON FLOCKHART (GBR; AGE: 36) 0 PTS

BRM P25 S4
Owen Racing Organisation
Races: MON (car #20); FRA (#44); GBR (#42); POR (#8); ITA (#4)

BRUCE HALFORD (GBR; AGE: 28) 0 PTS

Lotus 16-Climax S4
John Fisher
Races: MON (car #44)

HANS HERRMANN (GER; AGE: 31) 0 PTS

Cooper T51-Maserati S4
Scuderia Centro Sud
Races: GBR (car #24)

HANS HERRMANN (CONTD)

BRM P25 S4
British Racing Partnership
Races: GER (car #11)

GRAHAM HILL (GBR; AGE: 30) 0 PTS

Lotus 16-Climax S4
Team Lotus
Races: MON (car #40); NED (#14); FRA (#32); GBR (#28); GER (#16); POR (#11); ITA (#18)

BRIAN NAYLOR (GBR; AGE: 36) 0 PTS

JBW-Maserati S4
Driver
Races: GBR (car #36)

FRITZ D'OREY (BRA; AGE: 21) 0 PTS

Maserati 250F S6
Scuderia Centro Sud
Races: FRA (car #38); GBR (#40)

FRITZ D'OREY (CONTD)

Tec-Mec F415-Maserati S6
Camoradi USA
Races: USA (car #15)

DAVID PIPER (GBR; AGE: 28) 0 PTS

Lotus 16-Climax S4
Dorchester Service Station
Races: GBR (car #64)

BOB SAID (USA; AGE: 27) 0 PTS

Connaught C-Alta S4
Connaught Engineering
Races: USA (car #18)

ROY SALVADORI (GBR; AGE: 37) 0 PTS

Cooper T45-Maserati S4
High Efficiency Motors
Races: MON (car #38); FRA (#16); USA (#12)

1959

CHAMPIONSHIP CAR-BY-CAR

ROY SALVADORI (CONTD)

Aston Martin DBR4/250 S6
David Brown Corporation
Races: NED (car #4); GBR (#2); POR (#10); ITA (#24)

GIORGIO SCARLATTI (ITA; AGE: 37) 0 PTS

Maserati 250F S6
Scuderia Ugolini
Races: FRA (car #40)

GIORGIO SCARLATTI (CONTD)

Cooper T51-Climax S4
Cooper Car Co
Races: ITA (car #10)

CARROLL SHELBY (USA; AGE: 36) 0 PTS

Aston Martin DBR4/250 S6
David Brown Corporation
Races: NED (car #5); GBR (#4); POR (#9); ITA (#26)

ALAN STACEY (GBR; AGE: 26) 0 PTS

Lotus 16-Climax S4
Team Lotus
Races: GBR (car #30); USA (#11)

HENRY TAYLOR (GBR; AGE: 26) 0 PTS

Cooper T51-Climax S4
Reg Parnell Racing
Races: GBR (car #58)

GRAND PRIX WINNERS 1959

	RACE (CIRCUIT)	WINNER (CAR)
MON	MONACO GRAND PRIX (MONTE CARLO)	JACK BRABHAM (COOPER T51-CLIMAX S4)
NED	DUTCH GRAND PRIX (ZANDVOORT)	JO BONNIER (BRM P25 S4)
FRA	FRENCH GRAND PRIX (REIMS)	TONY BROOKS (FERRARI DINO 246 V6)
GBR	BRITISH GRAND PRIX (AINTREE)	JACK BRABHAM (COOPER T51-CLIMAX S4)
GER	GERMAN GRAND PRIX (AVUS)	TONY BROOKS (FERRARI DINO 246 V6)
POR	PORTUGUESE GRAND PRIX (MONSANTO)	STIRLING MOSS (COOPER T51-CLIMAX S4)
ITA	ITALIAN GRAND PRIX (MONZA)	STIRLING MOSS (COOPER T51-CLIMAX S4)
USA	UNITED STATES GRAND PRIX (SEBRING)	BRUCE McLAREN (COOPER T45-CLIMAX S4)

MIKE TAYLOR (GBR; AGE: 25) 0 PTS

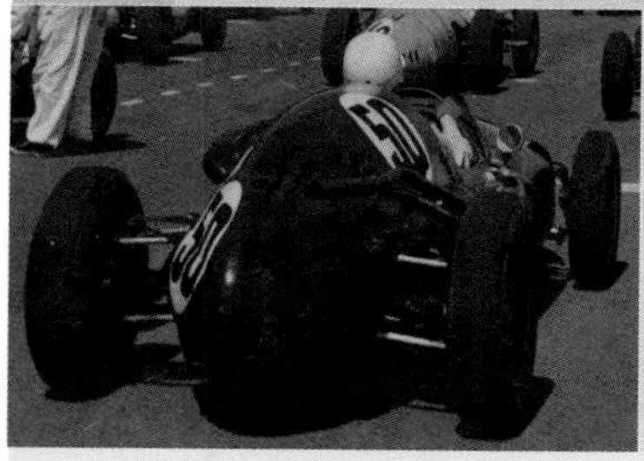

Cooper T45-Climax S4
Alan Brown Équipe
Races: GBR (car #50)

ALEJANDRO DE TOMASO (ARG; AGE: 31) 0 PTS

Cooper T43-OSCA
Officine Specializate Costruzione Automobili
Races: USA (car #14)

WOLFGANG VON TRIPS (GER; AGE: 31) 0 PTS

Porsche 718 F4
Porsche
Races: MON (car #6)

WOLFGANG VON TRIPS (CONTD)

Ferrari Dino 246 V6
Scuderia Ferrari
Races: USA (car #4)

RODGER WARD (USA; AGE: 38) 0 PTS

Kurtis-Offenhauser S4
Leader Card Racers
Races: USA (car #1)

BP
BP ENERGOL
28

1960s

1960

LOTUS BLOSSOMS – BUT BRABHAM TAKES TWO ON THE TROT

Left
Distraction derby: double world champion Jack Brabham fails to concentrate on the cameras at Riverside, during a US GP photo-shoot. Hollywood actress Jayne Mansfield and team boss Charles Cooper don't appear to be having the same trouble

Right
Smooth operator: Moss scored Lotus's first world championship success when he guided his privately-entered 18 to victory in Monaco. Lotus built the season's quickest chassis, but it often proved frail

Below:
Streetwise: Brabham won a string of races in mid-season to underline the strength of his title challenge. Here he negotiates Oporto's straw bales and tramlines – no longer a feature of F1 circuits, oddly – en route to a fifth straight victory

Jack Brabham reeled off a second consecutive world title for Cooper – but Stirling Moss might have pushed him harder had he not been seriously injured during practice for the Belgian Grand Prix. The Englishman crashed heavily after his Lotus shed a wheel and he was sidelined for much of the year, although he returned in time to win the seasonal finale in America.

The Lotus 18, Colin Chapman's first mid-engined single-seater, was probably quicker than Brabham's title-winning Cooper – but it was also more frail. The Australian took full advantage of his "low-line" Cooper's speed and reliability to score five wins and become the first driver since Juan Manuel Fangio to win back-to-back titles. He would be the last to do so until Alain Prost in the mid-1980s.

BRM joined the mid-engined crusade and Graham Hill came close to winning the British GP, but after a terrific comeback drive he spun away his chances in the closing stages.

Ferrari effectively wrote off the season and campaigned its old-fashioned D246 chassis while making plans for the future. It scored one victory – the last-ever world championship success for front-engined car – but it was somewhat hollow. When the Italian GP organisers decided to use the old banked track at Monza, to help the powerful Ferraris overcome their chassis handicap, the British teams withdrew in protest because they felt the circuit was too dangerous. The race went ahead anyway and Phil Hill won against makeweight opposition.

Above
Absinthe makes the heart grow fonder: the bloke who was drinking at the Monaco station bar two years earlier appears still to be there as Maurice Trintignant's Cooper T51 heads a queue into the hairpin

Far left
Take your pick: Willy Mairesse ponders tyre options during a pit stop at Monza, where he finished third

Centre left
Time to go home: Hill retired in Portugal after clipping the straw bales

Left
American's cup: Phil Hill celebrates after beating makeshift opposition at Monza – he had just scored the final victory for a front-engined GP car

1960

CHAMPIONSHIP CAR-BY-CAR

1ST JACK BRABHAM (AUS; AGE: 34) 43 PTS

Cooper T51-Climax S4
Cooper Car Co
Races: ARG (car #18)

JACK BRABHAM (CONDT)

Cooper T53-Climax S4
Cooper Car Co
Races: MON (car #8); NED (#11); BEL (#2); FRA (#16); GBR (#1); POR; USA (both #2)

2ND BRUCE McLAREN (NZL; AGE: 22) 34(+3) PTS

Cooper T45-Climax S4
Cooper Car Co
Races: ARG (car #16)

BRUCE McLAREN (CONDT)

Cooper T53-Climax S4
Cooper Car Co
Races: MON (car #10); NED (#12); BEL (#4); FRA (#18); GBR (#2); POR (#4); USA (#3)

3RD STIRLING MOSS (GBR; AGE: 30) 19 PTS

Cooper T51-Climax S4
Rob Walker Racing
Races: ARG (car #36 and #38)

STIRLING MOSS (CONDT)

Lotus 18-Climax S4
Rob Walker Racing
Races: MON (car #28); NED (#7); POR (#12); USA (#5)

4TH INNES IRELAND (GBR; AGE: 30) 18 PTS

Lotus 18-Climax S4
Team Lotus
Races: ARG (car #20); MON (#22); NED (#4); BEL (#14); FRA (#20); GBR (#7); POR (#16); USA (#10)

5TH PHIL HILL (USA; AGE: 33) 16 PTS

Ferrari Dino 246 V6
Scuderia Ferrari
Races: ARG (car #26); MON (#36); NED (#1); BEL (#24); FRA (#2); GBR (#10); POR (#26); ITA (#20)

PHIL HILL (CONDT)

Cooper T51-Climax S4
Yeoman Credit Racing Team
Races: USA (car #9)

6TH= OLIVIER GENDEBIEN (BEL; AGE: 36) 10 PTS

Cooper T51-Climax S4
Yeoman Credit Racing Team
Races: BEL (car #34); FRA (#44); GBR (#14); POR (#8); USA (#7)

6TH= WOLFGANG VON TRIPS (GER; AGE: 32) 10 PTS

Ferrari Dino 246 V6
Scuderia Ferrari
Races: ARG (car #30); MON (#38); NED (#2); BEL (#26); FRA (#4); GBR (#11); POR (#28)

WOLFGANG VON TRIPS (CONDT)

Ferrari Dino 156P V6
Scuderia Ferrari
Races: ITA (car #22)

WOLFGANG VON TRIPS (CONDT)

Cooper T51-Maserati S4
Scuderia Centro Sud
Races: USA (car #26)

8TH= JIM CLARK (GBR; AGE: 24) 8 PTS

Lotus 18-Climax S4
Team Lotus
Races: NED (car #6); BEL (#18); FRA (#24); GBR (#8); POR (#14); USA (#12)

8TH= RICHIE GINTHER (USA; AGE: 29) 8 PTS

Ferrari Dino 246P V6
Scuderia Ferrari
Races: MON (car #34)

1960

CHAMPIONSHIP CAR-BY-CAR

RICHIE GINTHER (CONDT)

Ferrari Dino 246 V6
Scuderia Ferrari
Races: NED (car #3); ITA (#18)

10TH TONY BROOKS (GBR; AGE: 28) 7 PTS

Cooper T51-Climax S4
Yeoman Credit Racing Team
Races: MON (car #18); NED (#9); BEL (#38); GBR (#12); POR; USA (both #6)

TONY BROOKS (GBR; AGE: 28)

Vanwall S4
Vandervell Products
Races: FRA (car #14)

11TH= CLIFF ALLISON (GBR; AGE: 28) 6 PTS

Ferrari Dino 246 V6
Scuderia Ferrari
Races: ARG (car #24)

11TH= JOHN SURTEES (GBR; AGE: 26) 6 PTS

Lotus 18-Climax S4
Team Lotus
Races: MON (car #26); GBR (#9); POR (#18); USA (#11)

13TH= JO BONNIER (SWE; AGE: 30) 4 PTS

BRM P25 S4
Owen Racing Organisation
Races: ARG (car #40)

PICTURED AT NON-CHAMPIONSHIP RACE

JO BONNIER (CONDT)

BRM P48 S4
Owen Racing Organisation
Races: MON (car #2); NED (#14); BEL (#6); FRA (#8); GBR (#6); POR (#20); USA (#15)

13TH= GRAHAM HILL (GBR; AGE: 31) 4 PTS

BRM P25 S4
Owen Racing Organisation
Races: ARG (car #42)

GRAHAM HILL (CONDT)

BRM P48 S4
Owen Racing Organisation
Races: MON (car #6); NED (#16); BEL (#10); FRA (#12); GBR (#4); POR (#22); USA (#17)

13TH= WILLY MAIRESSE (BEL; AGE: 31) 4 PTS

Ferrari Dino 246 V6
Scuderia Ferrari
Races: BEL (car #22); FRA (#6); ITA (#16)

16TH= GIULIO CABIANCA (ITA; AGE: 37) 3 PTS

Cooper T51-Ferrari S4
Scuderia Castellotti
Races: ITA (car #2)

16TH= CARLOS MENDITÉGUY (ARG; AGE: 44) 3 PTS

Cooper T51-Maserati S4
Scuderia Centro Sud
Races: ARG (car #6)

16TH= HENRY TAYLOR (GBR; AGE: 27) 3 PTS

Cooper T51-Climax S4
Yeoman Credit Racing Team
Races: NED (car #10); FRA (#46); GBR (#15); USA (#8)

19TH= LUCIEN BIANCHI (BEL; AGE: 25) 1 PT

Cooper T45-Climax S4
Fred Tuck Cars
Races: BEL (car #32); FRA (#36); GBR (#24)

19TH= RON FLOCKHART (GBR; AGE: 37) 1 PT

Lotus 18-Climax S4
Team Lotus
Races: FRA (car #22)

1960

CHAMPIONSHIP CAR-BY-CAR

RON FLOCKHART (CONTD)

Cooper T51-Climax S4
Cooper Car Co
Races: USA (car #4)

19TH= HANS HERRMANN (GER; AGE: 32) 1 PT

Porsche 718 F4
Porsche
Races: ITA (car #26)

EDGAR BARTH (DDR; AGE: 43) 0 PTS

Porsche 718 F4
Porsche
Races: ITA (car #24)

CAREL GODIN DE BEAUFORT (NED; AGE: 26) 0 PTS

Cooper T51-Climax S4
Écurie Maarsbergen
Races: NED (car #20)

ROBERTO BONOMI (ARG; AGE: 40) 0 PTS

Cooper T51-Maserati S4
Scuderia Centro Sud
Races: ARG (car #4)

CHRIS BRISTOW (GBR; AGE: 22) 0 PTS

Cooper T51-Climax S4
Yeoman Credit Racing Team
Races: MON (car #16); NED (#8); BEL (#36)

IAN BURGESS (GBR; AGE: 30) 0 PTS

Cooper T51-Maserati S4
Scuderia Centro Sud
Races: FRA (car #42); GBR (#17); USA (#19)

PICTURED AT NON-CHAMPIONSHIP RACE

MARIO ARAUJO DE CABRAL (POR; AGE: 26) 0 PTS

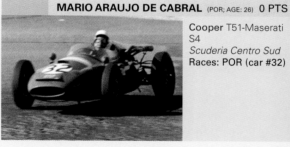

Cooper T51-Maserati S4
Scuderia Centro Sud
Races: POR (car #32)

ETTORE CHIMERI (VEN; AGE: 38) 0 PTS

Maserati 250F S6
Escuderia Sorocaima
Races: ARG (car #44)

ANTONIO CREUS (ESP; AGE: 40) 0 PTS

Maserati 250F S6
Driver
Races: ARG (car #12)

CHUCK DAIGH (USA; AGE: 36) 0 PTS

Scarab S4
Reventlow Automobiles
Races: BEL (car #30); USA (#23)

PICTURED DURING MON PRACTICE

CHUCK DAIGH (CONTD)

Cooper T51-Climax S4
Cooper Car Co
Races: GBR (car #3)

BOB DRAKE (USA; AGE: 40) 0 PTS

Maserati 250F S6
Joe Lubin
Races: USA (car #20)

PIERO DROGO (VEN; AGE: 34) 0 PTS

Cooper T43-Climax S4
Scuderia Colonia
Races: ITA (car #12)

NASIF ESTEFANO (ARG; AGE: 27) 0 PTS

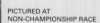

Maserati 250F S6
Camoradi International
Races: ARG (car #10)

1960

CHAMPIONSHIP CAR-BY-CAR

JACK FAIRMAN (GBR; AGE: 47) 0 PTS

Cooper T51-Climax S4
High Efficiency Motors
Races: GBR (car #23)

FRED GAMBLE (USA; AGE: 28) 0 PTS

Behra-Porsche F4
Camoradi International
Races: ITA (car #28)

JOSÉ FROILÁN GONZÁLEZ (ARG; AGE: 37) 0 PTS

Ferrari Dino 246 V6
Scuderia Ferrari
Races: ARG (car #32)

KEITH GREENE (GBR; AGE: 22) 0 PTS

Cooper T45-Maserati S4
Gilby Engineering
Races: GBR (car #22)

PICTURED AT NON-CHAMPIONSHIP RACE

MASTEN GREGORY (USA; AGE: 28) 0 PTS

Behra-Porsche F4
Camoradi International
Races: ARG (car #2)

MASTEN GREGORY (CONTD)

Cooper T51-Maserati S4
Scuderia Centro Sud
Races: FRA (car #40); GBR (#16); POR (#30)

DAN GURNEY (USA; AGE: 29) 0 PTS

BRM P48 S4
Owen Racing Organisation
Races: MON (car #4); NED (#15); BEL (#8); FRA (#10); GBR (#5); POR (#24); USA (#16)

BRUCE HALFORD (GBR; AGE: 29) 0 PTS

Cooper T51-Climax S4
Yeoman Credit Racing Team
Races: FRA (car #48)

JIM HALL (USA; AGE: 25) 0 PTS

Lotus 18-Climax S4
Driver
Races: USA (car #24)

ALBERTO RODRIGUEZ LARRETA (ARG; AGE: 26) 0 pts

Lotus 16-Climax S4
Team Lotus
Races: ARG (car #46)

PETE LOVELY (USA; AGE: 34) 0 PTS

Cooper T51-Ferrari S4
Fred Armbruster
Races: USA (car #25)

GINO MUNARON (ITA; AGE: 32) 0 PTS

Maserati 250F S6
Driver
Races: ARG (car #14)

GINO MUNARON (CONTD)

Cooper T51-Ferrari S4
Scuderia Castellotti
Races: FRA (car #30); GBR (#21); ITA (#4)

BRIAN NAYLOR (GBR; AGE: 37) 0 PTS

JBW-Maserati S4
Driver
Races: GBR (car #25); ITA (#6); USA (#21)

ARTHUR OWEN (GBR; AGE: 45) 0 PTS

Cooper T45-Climax S4
Driver
Races: ITA (car #8)

1960

CHAMPIONSHIP CAR-BY-CAR

DAVID PIPER (GBR; AGE: 29) 0 PTS

Lotus 16-Climax S4
Robert Bodle
Races: GBR (car #26)

LANCE REVENTLOW (USA; AGE: 24) 0 PTS

Scarab S4
Reventlow Automobiles
Races: BEL (car #28)

PICTURED DURING MON PRACTICE

ROY SALVADORI (GBR; AGE: 38) 0 PTS

Cooper T51-Climax S4
High Efficiency Motors
Races: MON; USA (both car #14)

ROY SALVADORI (CONTD)

Aston Martin DBR5/250 S6
David Brown Corporation
Races: GBR (car #18)

GIORGIO SCARLATTI (ITA; AGE: 38) 0 PTS

Maserati 250F S6
Scuderia Centro Sud
Races: ARG (car #8)

GIORGIO SCARLATTI (CONTD)

Cooper T51-Maserati S4
Scuderia Centro Sud
Races: ITA (car #36)

PICTURED AT NON-CHAMPIONSHIP RACE

HARRY SCHELL (USA; AGE: 38) 0 PTS

Cooper T51-Climax S4
Écurie Bleue
Races: ARG (car #34)

PICTURED AT NON-CHAMPIONSHIP RACE

WOLFGANG SEIDEL (GER; AGE: 34) 0 PTS

Cooper T45-Climax S4
Scuderia Colonia
Races: ITA (car #10)

ALAN STACEY (GBR; AGE: 26) 0 PTS

Lotus 16-Climax S4
Team Lotus
Races: ARG (car #22)

ALAN STACEY (CONTD)

Lotus 18-Climax S4
Team Lotus
Races: MON (car #24); NED (#5); BEL (#16)

ALFONSO THIELE (USA; AGE: 38) 0 PTS

Cooper T51-Maserati S4
Scuderia Centro Sud
Races: ITA (car #34)

MAURICE TRINTIGNANT (FRA; AGE: 42) 0 PTS

Cooper T51-Climax S4
Rob Walker Racing
Races: ARG (car #38)

MAURICE TRINTIGNANT (CONTD)

Cooper T51-Maserati S4
Scuderia Centro Sud
Races: MON (car #44); NED (#18); FRA (#38); USA (#18)

MAURICE TRINTIGNANT (CONTD)

Aston Martin DBR5/250 S6
David Brown Corporation
Races: GBR (car #19)

VIC WILSON (GBR; AGE: 29) 0 PTS

Cooper T43-Climax S4
Équipe Prideaux
Races: ITA (car #30)

1960

CHAMPIONSHIP CAR-BY-CAR

GRAND PRIX WINNERS 1960

	RACE (CIRCUIT)	**WINNER** (CAR)
ARG	ARGENTINE GRAND PRIX (BUENOS AIRES)	BRUCE McLAREN (COOPER T45-CLIMAX S4)
MON	MONACO GRAND PRIX (MONTE CARLO)	STIRLING MOSS (LOTUS 18-CLIMAX S4)
NED	DUTCH GRAND PRIX (ZANDVOORT)	JACK BRABHAM (COOPER T53-CLIMAX S4)
BEL	BELGIAN GRAND PRIX (SPA-FRANCORCHAMPS)	JACK BRABHAM (COOPER T53-CLIMAX S4)
FRA	FRENCH GRAND PRIX (REIMS)	JACK BRABHAM (COOPER T53-CLIMAX S4)
GBR	BRITISH GRAND PRIX (SILVERSTONE)	JACK BRABHAM (COOPER T53-CLIMAX S4)
POR	PORTUGUESE GRAND PRIX (OPORTO)	JACK BRABHAM (COOPER T53-CLIMAX S4)
ITA	ITALIAN GRAND PRIX (MONZA)	PHIL HILL (FERRARI DINO 246 V6)
USA	UNITED STATES GRAND PRIX (RIVERSIDE)	STIRLING MOSS (LOTUS 18-CLIMAX S4)

BRUCE McLAREN

1961

TRAGEDY TAINTS FERRARI'S RETURN TO FORM

Far left
Shark-nose attack: Phil Hill, von Trips and Ginther strike a customarily dominant pose at the start of the French GP. The works Ferraris won all but three of the races for which they were entered – but this wasn't one of them…

Left
French resistance: with the factory Ferraris having run into bother, the semi-official 156 of Giancarlo Baghetti was on hand to pick up the pieces and outrun Dan Gurney's Porsche to the line. The Italian became the first – and so far only – F1 driver to triumph on his world championship debut. Peculiarly, he never won again

Above
Let us prey: Phil Hill tracks down Clark's Lotus at Zandvoort. They finished second and third

THE BRITISH FELT THE REGULATIONS WOULD FAVOUR FERRARI – AND THEIR FEARS WERE DULY REALISED. THE ITALIAN TEAM HAD BEEN MAKING 1.5-LITRE ENGINES FOR A NUMBER OF YEARS AND WAS SEVERAL STEPS AHEAD BEFORE THE SEASON BEGAN

Ferrari was the only team properly prepared for the first season of the new 1.5-litre engine regulations, which were introduced because the previous 2.5-litre racers were thought to be outgrowing the circuits. The change met stiff opposition, mainly from British teams who struggled to find suitable, commercially available power units in the short term.

They felt the regulations would favour Ferrari – and their fears were duly realised. The Italian team produced a beautiful new mid-engined car that was nicknamed the "shark-nose", on account of its distinctive front end.

Ferrari had been making 1.5-litre F2 engines for a number of seasons before the new formula was introduced and so was several steps ahead before the season began. By the end of the campaign, however, Coventry Climax had introduced a new 1.5-litre V8 for customer teams and promised power parity for 1962.

It was no surprise that the championship turned out to be a contest between Ferrari team-mates Phil Hill and Wolfgang von Trips, although they didn't have things all their own way. The sheer driving genius of Stirling Moss twice overcame them – in Monaco and Germany – even though he was driving an underpowered Lotus belonging to privateer entrant Rob Walker.

Hill clinched the title in tragic circumstances at Monza. He won the race but team-mate von Trips tangled with Jim Clark's Lotus on the second lap. The German's Ferrari speared off the track, slammed into an earth bank packed with fans and reared into the air, throwing its driver out. By the time the car came to rest von Trips and 14 spectators had perished.

Far left
Strength through finesse: Moss gives Ginther a hard time at Zandvoort. The Englishman's dextrous touch occasionally allowed him to overcome Ferrari's power advantage and he steered his private Lotus 18 to epic victories in Monaco and Germany

Above
Jack of all tirades: defending champ Brabham had a miserable season and didn't muster a single podium finish. At the Nürburgring he qualified on the front row in his first race with the V8-powered Cooper, but a jammed throttle caused him to crash on the opening lap

Left
Victory V: Innes Ireland and Colin Chapman revel in their success at Watkins Glen – the first world championship win for a factory-entered Lotus

PHIL HILL – WORLD CHAMPION 1961

1961

CHAMPIONSHIP CAR-BY-CAR

1ST PHIL HILL (USA; AGE: 34) 34(+4) PTS

Ferrari Dino 156 V6
Scuderia Ferrari
Races: MON (car #38); NED (#1); BEL (#4); FRA (#16); GBR (#2); GER (#4); ITA (#2)

2ND WOLFGANG VON TRIPS (GER; AGE: 33) 33 PTS

Ferrari Dino 156 V6
Scuderia Ferrari
Races: MON (car #40); NED (#3); BEL (#2); FRA (#20); GBR (#4); GER (#3); ITA (#4)

3RD= DAN GURNEY (USA; AGE: 30) 21 PTS

Porsche 718 F4
Porsche System Engineering
Races: MON (car #4); BEL (#20); FRA (#12); GBR (#10); GER (#9); ITA (#46); USA (#12)

DAN GURNEY (CONTD)

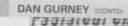

Porsche 787 F4
Porsche System Engineering
Races: NED (car #7)

3RD= STIRLING MOSS (GBR; AGE: 31) 21 PTS

Lotus 18-Climax S4
Rob Walker Racing
Races: MON (car #20); NED (#14)

Also see Jack Fairman below

STIRLING MOSS (CONTD)

Lotus 18/21-Climax S4
Rob Walker Racing
Races: BEL (car #14); FRA (#26); GBR (#28); GER; USA (both #7)

STIRLING MOSS (CONTD)

Lotus 21-Climax S4
Rob Walker Racing
Races: ITA (car #28)

5TH RICHIE GINTHER (USA; AGE: 30) 16 PTS

Ferrari Dino 156 V6
Scuderia Ferrari
Races: MON (car #36); NED (#2); BEL (#6); FRA (#18); GBR (#6); GER (#5); ITA (#6)

6TH INNES IRELAND (GBR; AGE: 31) 12 PTS

Lotus 21-Climax S4
Team Lotus
Races: BEL (car #32); FRA (#6); GBR (#16); GER; USA (both #15)

INNES IRELAND (CONTD)

Lotus 18/21-Climax S4
Team Lotus
Races: ITA (car #38)

7TH= JIM CLARK (GBR; AGE: 25) 11 PTS

Lotus 21-Climax S4
Team Lotus
Races: MON (car #28); NED (#15); BEL (#34); FRA (#8); GBR (#18); GER (#14); ITA (#36); USA (#14)

7TH= BRUCE McLAREN (NZL; AGE: 23) 11 PTS

Cooper T55-Climax S4
Cooper Car Co
Races: MON (car #26); NED (#11); BEL (#30); FRA (#4); GBR (#14); GER (#2); ITA (#12); USA (#2)

9TH GIANCARLO BAGHETTI (ITA; AGE: 26) 9 PTS

Ferrari Dino 156 V6
FISA/Scuderia Sant Ambroeus
Races: FRA (car #50); GBR (#58); ITA (#32)

10TH TONY BROOKS (GBR; AGE: 29) 6 PTS

BRM P48/57-Climax S4
Owen Racing Organisation
Races: MON (car #16); NED (#5); BEL (#38); FRA (#24); GBR (#22); GER (#16); ITA (#26); USA (#5)

11TH= JACK BRABHAM (AUS; AGE: 35) 4 PTS

Cooper T55-Climax S4
Cooper Car Co
Races: MON (car #24); NED (#10); BEL (#28); FRA (#2); GBR (#12)

1961

CHAMPIONSHIP CAR-BY-CAR

JACK BRABHAM (CONTD)

Cooper T58-Climax V8
Cooper Car Co
Races: GER (car #1); ITA (#10); USA (#1)

11TH= JOHN SURTEES (GBR; AGE: 27) 4 PTS

Cooper T53-Climax S4
Reg Parnell Racing
Races: MON (car #22); NED (#12); BEL (#24); FRA (#40); GBR (#34); GER (#18); ITA (#42); USA (#18)

13TH= JO BONNIER (SWE; AGE: 31) 3 PTS

Porsche 787 F4
Porsche System Engineering
Races: MON (car #2); NED (#6)

JO BONNIER (CONTD)

Porsche 718 F4
Porsche System Engineering
Races: BEL (car #18); FRA (#10); GBR; GER (both #8); ITA (#44); USA (#11)

13TH= OLIVIER GENDEBIEN (BEL; AGE: 37) 3 PTS

Ferrari Dino 156 V6
Scuderia Ferrari
Races: BEL (car #8)

OLIVIER GENDEBIEN (CONTD)

Lotus 18/21-Climax S4
UDT-Laystall Racing Team
Races: USA (car #21)

13TH= GRAHAM HILL (GBR; AGE: 32) 3 PTS

BRM P48/57-Climax S4
Owen Racing Organisation
Races: MON (car #18); NED (#4); BEL (#36); FRA (#22); GBR (#20); GER (#17); ITA (#24); USA (#4)

13TH= JACKIE LEWIS (GBR; AGE: 24) 3 PTS

Cooper T53-Climax S4
H&L Motors
Races: BEL (car #40); FRA (#44); GBR (#46); GER (#28); ITA (#60)

17TH ROY SALVADORI (GBR; AGE: 39) 2 PTS

Cooper T53-Climax S4
Reg Parnell Racing
Races: FRA (car #42); GBR (#36); GER (#19); ITA (#40); USA (#19)

CLIFF ALLISON (GBR; AGE: 29) 0 PTS

Lotus 18-Climax S4
UDT-Laystall Racing Team
Races: MON (car #32)

GERRY ASHMORE (GBR; AGE: 25) 0 PTS

Lotus 18-Climax S4
Driver
Races: GBR (car #40); GER (#27); ITA (#18)

LORENZO BANDINI (ITA; AGE: 25) 0 PTS

Cooper T53-Maserati S4
Scuderia Centro Sud
Races: BEL (car #46); GBR (#60); GER (#32); ITA (#62)

CAREL GODIN DE BEAUFORT (NED; AGE: 27) 0 PTS

Porsche 718 F4
Écurie Maarsbergen
Races: NED (car #8); BEL (#22); FRA (#14); GBR (#56); GER (#31); ITA (#74)

LUCIEN BIANCHI (BEL; AGE: 26) 0 PTS

Lotus 18-Climax S4
Écurie Nationale Belge
Races: BEL (car #12)

LUCIEN BIANCHI (CONTD)

Lotus 18/21-Climax S4
UDT-Laystall Racing Team
Races: FRA (car #28); GBR (#32)

1961

CHAMPIONSHIP CAR-BY-CAR

IAN BURGESS (GBR; AGE: 31) 0 PTS

Lotus 18-Climax S4
Camoradi International
Races: FRA (car #38); GBR (#44)

IAN BURGESS (CONTD)

Cooper T53-Climax S4
Camoradi International
Races: GER (car #30)

ROBERTO BUSSINELLO (ITA; AGE: 33) 0 PTS

De Tomaso F1/004-Alfa Romeo 4
Scuderia de Tomaso
Races: ITA (car #54)

BERNARD COLLOMB (FRA; AGE: 30) 0 PTS

Cooper T53-Climax S4
Driver
Races: FRA (car #52); GER (#38)

JACK FAIRMAN (GBR; AGE: 48) 0 PTS
STIRLING MOSS (GBR; AGE: 31)

(shared car)
Ferguson P99-Climax S4
Rob Walker Racing
Races: GBR (car #26)

ALSO SEE STIRLING MOSS

JACK FAIRMAN (GBR; AGE: 48) 0 PTS

Cooper T45-Climax S4
Fred Tuck Cars
Races: ITA (car #30)

KEITH GREENE (GBR; AGE: 23) 0 PTS

Gilby-Climax S4
Gilby Engineering
Races: GBR (car #54)

PICTURED AT NON-CHAMPIONSHIP RACE

MASTEN GREGORY (USA; AGE: 29) 0 PTS

Cooper T53-Climax S4
Camoradi International
Races: BEL (car #44); FRA (#36); GBR (#42)

MASTEN GREGORY (CONTD)

Lotus 18/21-Climax S4
UDT-Laystall Racing Team
Races: ITA (car #22); USA (#22 and #21)

JIM HALL (USA; AGE: 26) 0 PTS

Lotus 18/21-Climax S4
Driver
Races: USA (car #17)

WALT HANSGEN (USA; AGE: 41) 0 PTS

Cooper T53-Climax S4
Momo Corporation
Races: USA (car #60)

HANS HERRMANN (GER; AGE: 33) 0 PTS

Porsche 718 F4
Porsche System Engineering/Écurie Maarsbergen
Races: MON (car #6); NED (#9); GER (#11)

ROBERTO LIPPI (ITA; AGE: 34) 0 PTS

De Tomaso F1/002-OSCA 4
Scuderia Settecolli
Races: ITA (car #52)

TONY MAGGS (RSA; AGE: 24) 0 PTS

Lotus 18-Climax S4
Louise Bryden-Brown
Races: GBR (car #50); GER (#33)

WILLY MAIRESSE (BEL; AGE: 32) 0 PTS

Lotus 18-Climax S4
Écurie Nationale Belge
Races: BEL (car #10)

1961

CHAMPIONSHIP CAR-BY-CAR

WILLY MAIRESSE (CONTD)

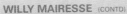

Lotus 21-Climax S4
Team Lotus
Races: FRA (car #48)

WILLY MAIRESSE (CONTD)

Ferrari Dino 156 V6
Scuderia Ferrari
Races: GER (car #6)

TONY MARSH (GBR; AGE: 30) 0 PTS

Lotus 18-Climax S4
Driver
Races: GBR (car #48); GER (#37)

PICTURED AT NON-CHAMPIONSHIP RACE

MICHEL MAY (SUI; AGE: 26) 0 PTS

Lotus 18-Climax S4
Scuderia Colonia
Races: MON (car #8); FRA (#46)

MASSIMO NATILI (ITA; AGE: 26) 0 PTS

Cooper T51-Maserati S4
Scuderia Centro Sud
Races: GBR (car #62)

PICTURED AT NON-CHAMPIONSHIP RACE

BRIAN NAYLOR (GBR; AGE: 38) 0 PTS

JBW-Climax S4
Driver
Races: ITA (car #14)

TIM PARNELL (GBR; AGE: 29) 0 PTS

Lotus 18-Climax S4
Driver
Races: GBR (car #38); ITA (#16)

PICTURED AT NON-CHAMPIONSHIP RACE

ROGER PENSKE (USA; AGE: 24) 0 PTS

Cooper T53-Climax S4
John M Wyatt III
Races: USA (car #6)

RENATO PIROCCHI (ITA; AGE: 28) 0 PTS

Cooper T51-Maserati S4
Pescara Racing Club
Races: ITA (car #58)

RICARDO RODRIGUEZ (MEX; AGE: 19) 0 PTS

Ferrari Dino 156 V6
Scuderia Ferrari
Races: ITA (car #8)

LLOYD RUBY (USA; AGE: 33) 0 PTS

Lotus 18-Climax S4
J Frank Harrison
Races: USA (car #26)

PETER RYAN (CAN; AGE: 21) 0 PTS

Lotus 18/21-Climax S4
J Wheeler Autosport
Races: USA (car #16)

GIORGIO SCARLATTI (ITA; AGE: 39) 0 PTS

De Tomaso F1/001-OSCA 4
Scuderia Serenissima
Races: FRA (car #34)

WOLFGANG SEIDEL (GER; AGE: 35) 0 PTS

Lotus 18-Climax S4
Scuderia Colonia
Races: GBR (car #52); GER (#26); ITA (#56)

PICTURED AT NON-CHAMPIONSHIP RACE

HAP SHARP (USA; AGE: 33) 0 PTS

Cooper T53-Climax S4
Driver
Races: USA (car #3)

1961

CHAMPIONSHIP CAR-BY-CAR

GAETANO STARRABBA (ITA; AGE: 28) 0 PTS

Lotus 18-Maserati S4
Driver
Races: ITA (car #72)

HENRY TAYLOR (GBR; AGE: 28) 0 PTS

Lotus 18/21-Climax S4
UDT-Laystall Racing Team
Races: FRA; GBR (both car #30); ITA (#20)

TREVOR TAYLOR (GBR; AGE: 24) 0 PTS

Lotus 18-Climax S4
Team Lotus
Races: NED (car #16)

MAURICE TRINTIGNANT (FRA; AGE: 43) 0 PTS

Cooper T51-Maserati S4
Scuderia Serenissima
Races: MON (car #42); BEL (#26); FRA (#32); GER (#20); ITA (#48)

NINO VACCARELLA (ITA; AGE: 28) 0 PTS

DeTomaso F1/003-Alfa Romeo S4
Scuderia Serenissima
Races: ITA (car #50)

GRAND PRIX WINNERS 1961

	RACE (CIRCUIT)	**WINNER** (CAR)
MON	MONACO GRAND PRIX (MONTE CARLO)	STIRLING MOSS (LOTUS 18-CLIMAX S4)
NED	DUTCH GRAND PRIX (ZANDVOORT)	WOLFGANG VON TRIPS (FERRARI DINO 156 V6)
BEL	BELGIAN GRAND PRIX (SPA-FRANCORCHAMPS)	PHIL HILL (FERRARI DINO 156 V6)
FRA	FRENCH GRAND PRIX (REIMS)	GIANCARLO BAGHETTI (FERRARI DINO 156 V6)
GBR	BRITISH GRAND PRIX (AINTREE)	WOLFGANG VON TRIPS (FERRARI DINO 156 V6)
GER	GERMAN GRAND PRIX (NÜRBURGRING)	STIRLING MOSS (LOTUS 18/21-CLIMAX S4)
ITA	ITALIAN GRAND PRIX (MONZA)	PHIL HILL (FERRARI DINO 156 V6)
USA	UNITED STATES GRAND PRIX (WATKINS GLEN)	INNES IRELAND (LOTUS 21-CLIMAX S4)

1962

HILL GETS THE VERDICT AS CLARK'S HOPES GO UP IN SMOKE

Opposite page
You wait several seasons for a grand prix win – and then four come along at once: Graham Hill was classified only sixth here in Monaco but was usually on hand to pick up the pieces whenever Clark retired

Above
Pleased as punch: delighted that his Lotus has lasted 100 laps without anything falling off, Clark savours the sensation of crossing the line at Watkins Glen

Far left
Perishable goods: Clark leads away from pole at Rouen, where suspension failure put him out. Hill and McLaren follow

Left
Things you don't see any more, number one in a series: Clark tries rival Ferrari's 156 for size while Lotus boss Colin Chapman makes technical observations

Right
New breed: British manufacturer Lola made its world championship debut in 1962. Roy Salvadori's Climax-powered Mk4 is pictured leading Trevor Taylor's Lotus in Monaco

Below
Unequal struggle: reigning champion Phil Hill began the year with three podium finishes – but Ferrari was swiftly eclipsed and he didn't score again

Below right
No smoke without ire: Clark had the world title in the bag until an oil leak forced him to retire from the lead in South Africa. He had been 21 laps away from his first world title

Colin Chapman rewrote the Formula One design rules when he introduced the Lotus 25. With a monocoque chassis instead of the traditional spaceframe, it was lighter, stiffer, faster and safer. Jim Clark led on the car's debut in the season-opening Dutch Grand Prix, but a clutch problem forced him to retire and gifted victory to Graham Hill's BRM. The future, though, was clear.

Clark's form made it evident that he was the world's new number one – a mantle he inherited from Stirling Moss, who was sidelined by serious injuries sustained in an accident during a non-championship race early in the season at Goodwood. Although the Englishman subsequently made a full recovery he felt his skills had been impaired and chose not to return to the sport.

The general pattern of the season was that Clark would win if his Lotus didn't break, which it tended to do rather too often. Suspension failure forced him to retire in France while engine problems accounted for him in Monaco and Italy (when he was running behind Hill, for once). Even so, he remained on course for the world title until another engine failure caused him to retire from the lead of the final race in East London, South Africa, where Hill swept through to take the title. The BRM's powerful engine helped offset some of the Lotus's chassis superiority and Hill was a tough, tenacious competitor.

Between them Clark and Hill won all but two races. Bruce McLaren (Cooper) triumphed in Monaco while Dan Gurney gave Porsche its only championship-status grand prix success in France. On both occasions Clark and Hill had been running ahead of the eventual winners when forced to retire. Former Cooper driver Jack Brabham set up his own team and his BT3 chassis made its world championship debut in Germany.

GRAHAM HILL – WORLD CHAMPION 1962 & 1968

1962

CHAMPIONSHIP CAR-BY-CAR

1ST GRAHAM HILL (GBR; AGE: 33) 42(+10) PTS

BRM P57 V8
Owen Racing Organisation
Races: NED (car #17); MON (#10); BEL (#1); FRA (#8); GBR (#12); GER (#11); ITA (#14); USA (#4); RSA (#3)

2ND JIM CLARK (GBR; AGE: 26) 30 PTS

Lotus 25-Climax V8
Team Lotus
Races: NED (car #4); MON (#18); BEL (#16); FRA (#12); GBR (#20); GER (#5); ITA (#20); USA (#8); RSA (#1)

3RD BRUCE McLAREN (NZL; AGE: 24) 27(+5) PTS

Cooper T60-Climax V8
Cooper Car Co
Races: NED (car #6); MON (#14); BEL (#25); FRA (#22); GBR (#16); GER (#9); ITA (#28); USA (#21); RSA (#8)

4TH JOHN SURTEES (GBR; AGE: 28) 19 PTS

Lola Mk4-Climax V8
Reg Parnell Racing
Races: NED (car #19); MON (#28); BEL (#5); FRA (#18); GBR (#24); GER (#14); ITA (#46); USA (#18); RSA (#6)

5TH DAN GURNEY (USA; AGE: 31) 15 PTS

Porsche 804 F8
Porsche System Engineering
Races: NED (car #12); MON (#4); FRA (#30); GBR (#8); GER (#7); ITA (#16); USA (#10)

6TH PHIL HILL (USA; AGE: 35) 14 PTS

Ferrari Dino 156 V6
Scuderia Ferrari
Races: NED (car #1); MON (#36); BEL (#9); GBR (#2); GER (#1); ITA (#10)

7TH TONY MAGGS (RSA; AGE: 25) 13 PTS

Cooper T55-Climax S4
Cooper Car Co
Races: NED (car #7); MON (#16); GER (#10)

TONY MAGGS (CONTD)

Cooper T60-Climax V8
Cooper Car Co
Races: BEL (car #26); FRA (#24); GBR (#18); ITA (#30); USA (#22); RSA (#9)

8TH RICHIE GINTHER (USA; AGE: 32) 10 PTS

BRM P48/57 V8
Owen Racing Organisation
Races: NED (car #18); MON (#8)

RICHIE GINTHER (CONTD)

BRM P57 V8
Owen Racing Organisation
Races: BEL (car #2); FRA (#10); GBR (#14); GER; ITA (both #12); USA (#5); RSA (#4)

9TH JACK BRABHAM (AUS; AGE: 36) 9 PTS

Lotus 24-Climax V8
Brabham Racing Organisation
Races: NED (car #8); MON (#22); BEL (#15); FRA (#26); GBR (#30)

JACK BRABHAM (CONTD)

Brabham BT3-Climax V8
Brabham Racing Organisation
Races: GER (car #16); USA (#17); RSA (#10)

10TH TREVOR TAYLOR (GBR; AGE: 25) 6 PTS

Lotus 24-Climax V8
Team Lotus
Races: NED (car #5); MON (#20); BEL (#17); GBR (#22); GER (#6)

TREVOR TAYLOR (CONTD)

Lotus 25-Climax V8
Team Lotus
Races: FRA (car #14); ITA (#22); USA (#9); RSA (#2)

11TH GIANCARLO BAGHETTI (ITA; AGE: 27) 5 PTS

Ferrari Dino 156 V6
Scuderia Ferrari
Races: NED (car #2); BEL (#11); GER; ITA (both #2)

1962

CHAMPIONSHIP CAR-BY-CAR

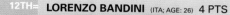

12TH= LORENZO BANDINI (ITA; AGE: 26) 4 PTS

Ferrari Dino 156 V6
Scuderia Ferrari
Races: MON (car #38); GER (#4); ITA (#6)

12TH= RICARDO RODRIGUEZ (MEX; AGE: 20) 4 PTS

Ferrari Dino 156 V6
Scuderia Ferrari
Races: NED (car #3); BEL (#12); GER (#3); ITA (#4)

14TH= JO BONNIER (SWE; AGE: 32) 3 PTS

Porsche 804 F8
Porsche System Engineering
Races: NED (car #11); FRA (#32); GBR (#10); GER (#8); ITA (#18); USA (#11)

JO BONNIER (CONTD)

Porsche 718 F4
Porsche System Engineering
Races: MON (car #2)

14TH= WILLY MAIRESSE (BEL; AGE: 33) 3 PTS

Ferrari Dino 156 V6
Scuderia Ferrari
Races: MON (car #40); BEL (#10); ITA (#8)

16TH= CAREL GODIN DE BEAUFORT (NED; AGE: 28) 2 PTS

Porsche 718 F4
Écurie Maarsbergen
Races: NED (car #14); BEL (#7); FRA (#38); GBR (#54); GER (#18); ITA (#32); USA (#12); RSA (#15)

16TH= INNES IRELAND (GBR; AGE: 32) 2 PTS

Lotus 24-Climax V8
UDT-Laystall Racing Team
Races: NED (car #9); MON (#34); BEL (#20); FRA (#36); GBR (#32); ITA (#40); USA (#15); RSA (#11)

18TH= MASTEN GREGORY (USA; AGE: 30) 1 PT

Lotus 18/21-Climax S4
UDT-Laystall Racing Team
Races: NED (car #10)

MASTEN GREGORY (CONTD)

Lotus 24-BRM V8
UDT-Laystall Racing Team
Races: BEL (car #21); FRA (#34); ITA (#38); USA (#16)

MASTEN GREGORY (CONTD)

Lotus 24-Climax V8
UDT-Laystall Racing Team
Races: GBR (car #34)

18TH= NEVILLE LEDERLE (RSA; AGE: 24) 1 PT

Lotus 21-Climax S4
Driver
Races: RSA (car #20)

LUCIEN BIANCHI (BEL; AGE: 27) 0 PTS

Lotus 18/21-Climax S4
Écurie Nationale Belge
Races: BEL (car #19)

LUCIEN BIANCHI (CONTD)

ENB-Maserati S4
Écurie Nationale Belge
Races: GER (car #21)

IAN BURGESS (GBR; AGE: 32) 0 PTS

Cooper T59-Climax S4
Anglo-American Equipe
Races: GBR (car #36); GER (#25)

JOHN CAMPBELL-JONES (GBR; AGE: 32) 0 PTS

Lotus 18-Climax S4
Emeryson Cars
Races: BEL (car #4)

1962

CHAMPIONSHIP CAR-BY-CAR

JAY CHAMBERLAIN (USA; AGE: 36) 0 PTS

Lotus 18-Climax S4
Écurie Excelsior
Races: GBR (car #46)

BERNARD COLLOMB (FRA; AGE: 31) 0 PTS

Cooper T53-Climax S4
Bernard Collomb
Races: GER (car #31)

PICTURED AT A NON-CHAMPIONSHIP RACE

KEITH GREENE (GBR; AGE: 24) 0 PTS

Gilby-BRM V8
Gilby Engineering
Races: GER (car #27)

MIKE HARRIS (RSR; AGE: 23) 0 PTS

Cooper T53-Alfa Romeo S4
Driver
Races: RSA (car #22)

BRUCE JOHNSTONE (RSA; AGE: 25) 0 PTS

BRM P48/57 V8
Driver
Races: RSA (car #5)

JACKIE LEWIS (GBR; AGE: 25) 0 PTS

Cooper T53-Climax S4
Écurie Galloise
Races: NED (car #21); FRA; GBR (both #42); GER (#20)

JOHN LOVE (RSR; AGE: 38) 0 PTS

Cooper T55-Climax S4
John Love
Races: RSA (car #18)

TIMMY MAYER (USA; AGE: 24) 0 PTS

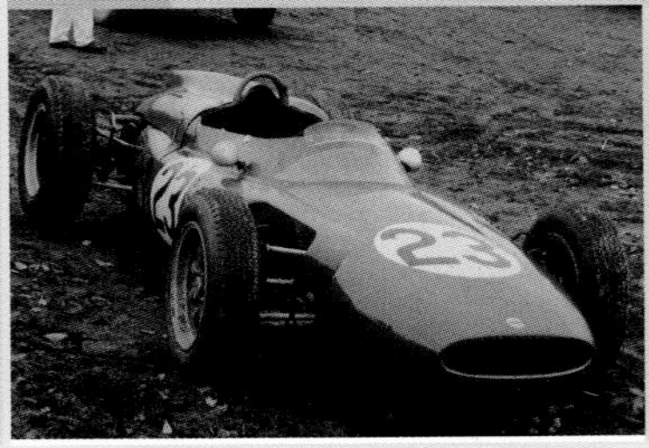

Cooper T53-Climax S4
Cooper Car Co
Races: USA (car #23)

ROGER PENSKE (USA; AGE: 25) 0 PTS

Lotus 24-Climax V8
Dupont Team Zerex
Races: USA (car #14)

ERNEST PIETERSE (RSA; AGE: 24) 0 PTS

Lotus 21-Climax S4
Driver
Races: RSA (car #14)

BEN PON (NED; AGE: 25) 0 PTS

Porsche 787 F4
Écurie Maarsbergen
Races: NED (car #15)

ROY SALVADORI (GBR; AGE: 40) 0 PTS

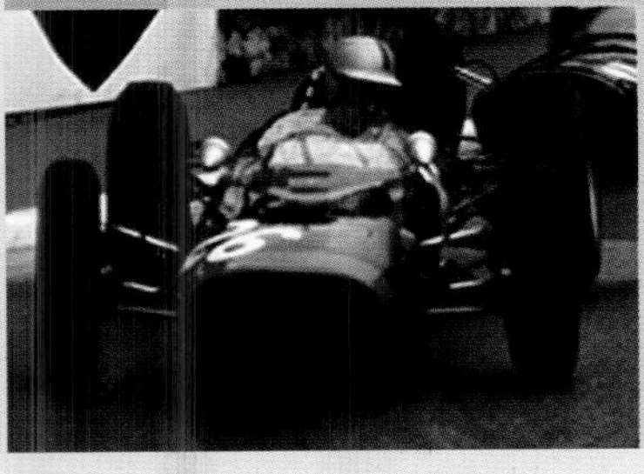

Lola Mk4-Climax V8
Reg Parnell Racing
Races: NED (car #20); MON (#26); FRA (#20); GBR (#26); GER (#15); ITA (#44); RSA (#7)

HEINZ SCHILLER (SUI; AGE: 32) 0 PTS

Lotus 24-BRM V8
Écurie Filipinetti
Races: GER (car #28)

ROB SCHROEDER (USA; AGE: 36) 0 PTS

Lotus 24-Climax V8
John Mecom
Races: USA (car #26)

WOLFGANG SEIDEL (GER; AGE: 36) 0 PTS

Emeryson Mk2-Climax S4
Écurie Maarsbergen
Races: NED (car #16)

1962

CHAMPIONSHIP CAR-BY-CAR

WOLFGANG SEIDEL (CONTD)

Lotus 24-BRM V8
Autosport Team Wolfgang Seidel
Races: GBR (car #44)

DOUG SERRURIER (RSA; AGE: 42) 0 PTS

LDS Mk1-Alfa Romeo S4
Otelle Nucci
Races: RSA (car #21)

TONY SETTEMBER (USA; AGE: 36) 0 PTS

Emeryson Mk2-Climax S4
Emeryson Cars
Races: GBR (car #40); ITA (#48)

PICTURED AT NON-CHAMPIONSHIP RACE

HAP SHARP (USA; AGE: 34) 0 PTS

Cooper T53-Climax S4
Driver
Races: USA (car #24)

TONY SHELLY (NZL; AGE: 25) 0 PTS

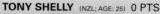

Lotus 18/21-Climax S4
John Dalton
Races: GBR (car #48)

PICTURED AT NON-CHAMPIONSHIP RACE

JO SIFFERT (SUI; AGE: 26) 0 PTS

Lotus 21-Climax S4
Écurie Filipinetti
Races: BEL (car #22); GER (#19)

GRAND PRIX WINNERS 1962

	RACE (CIRCUIT)	WINNER (CAR)
NED	DUTCH GRAND PRIX (ZANDVOORT)	GRAHAM HILL (BRM P57 V8)
MON	MONACO GRAND PRIX (MONTE CARLO)	BRUCE McLAREN (COOPER T60-CLIMAX V8)
BEL	BELGIAN GRAND PRIX (SPA-FRANCORCHAMPS)	JIM CLARK (LOTUS 25-CLIMAX V8)
FRA	FRENCH GRAND PRIX (ROUEN-LES-ESSARTS)	DAN GURNEY (PORSCHE 804 F8)
GBR	BRITISH GRAND PRIX (AINTREE)	JIM CLARK (LOTUS 25-CLIMAX V8)
GER	GERMAN GRAND PRIX (NÜRBURGRING)	GRAHAM HILL (BRM P57 V8)
ITA	ITALIAN GRAND PRIX (MONZA)	GRAHAM HILL (BRM P57 V8)
USA	UNITED STATES GRAND PRIX (WATKINS GLEN)	JIM CLARK (LOTUS 25-CLIMAX V8)
RSA	SOUTH AFRICAN GRAND PRIX (EAST LONDON)	GRAHAM HILL (BRM P57 V8)

JO SIFFERT (CONTD)

Lotus 24-BRM V8
Écurie Filipinetti
Races: FRA (car #40)

MAURICE TRINTIGNANT (FRA; AGE: 44) 0 PTS

Lotus 24-Climax V8
Rob Walker Racing
Races: MON (car #30); BEL (#18); FRA (#28); GER (#17); ITA (#36); USA (#6)

NINO VACCARELLA (ITA; AGE: 29) 0 PTS

Porsche 718 F4
Scuderia SSS Republica di Venezia
Races: GER (car #26)

NINO VACCARELLA (CONTD)

Lotus 24-Climax V8
Scuderia SSS Republica di Venezia
Races: ITA (car #24)

HEINI WALTER (SUI; AGE: 35) 0 PTS

Porsche 718 F4
Écurie Filipinetti
Races: GER (car #32)

1963

CLARK AND LOTUS REALISE THEIR POTENTIAL – AT LAST

Left
Action station: Hill leads the field past the local SNCF HQ on the opening lap of the Monaco GP. The railway line no longer runs through this bit of the principality. The same site nowadays houses the Grand Hotel and its casino, where you might find modern-day Ferrari star Rubens Barrichello playing the fruit machines if you stumble in at the right time

Above
Ticket to ride: team boss Colin Chapman sits astride Jim Clark's Lotus 25 to complete an FA Cup Final-style lap of honour in the wake of their title triumph at Monza

Right
Into South Africa: to most people East London conjures images of West Ham football club being given a good drubbing, the Docklands Light Railway breaking down or traffic jams in Leytonstone. In1963, however, it was one of the world championship's host circuits. Here, Trevor Blokdyk leads fellow local Paddy Driver

Jim Clark and Lotus won seven of the championship's 10 rounds – but that bald statistic doesn't properly reflect Scot's dominance. He lapped the entire field in the Dutch Grand Prix, for instance, and overcame a broken valve to triumph in France. As the fastest man in the fastest car, he was properly rewarded – in sharp contrast to the previous season.

John Surtees, the former motorcycle champion who had shown immense promise ever since setting pole position for only his second grand prix, switched to Ferrari. The Italian team's new technical regime came up with a car that was a big improvement on the previous season's old-fashioned "shark-nose" chassis. Surtees scored his maiden grand prix victory at the Nürburgring but wasn't able to repeat that success elsewhere. He led briefly at Monza, though, and the partnership looked destined for great things.

BRM struggled to match its 1962 form but Graham Hill managed to win twice. He capitalised in Monaco, when Clark retired from the lead with a broken gearbox, and was helped immensely at Watkins Glen when a faulty battery caused his Lotus rival to be left behind at the start. Clark's only genuine defeat of the season came courtesy of Surtees at the Nürburgring – although even there the Scot was troubled by a misfire.

The Brabhams became increasingly competitive as the season wore on, so much so that Dan Gurney and Jack Brabham came closest to matching Clark's pace in the South African finale.

Left
Two into four will go: former motorcycle world champion John Surtees continued to show terrific promise. He won for Ferrari in Germany and finished second here at Silverstone. Graham Hill follows

Top
Fading star: 1961 world champ Phil Hill had a miserable season in the uncompetitive ATS. Jo Bonnier (Cooper), Trevor Taylor (Lotus), Chris Amon (Lola) and Innes Ireland (BRP) give chase at Zandvoort

Above
Art of poise: nowadays this would be called a mistake; back then it was known as car control. Graham Hill heads for third in South Africa

1963

CHAMPIONSHIP CAR-BY-CAR

1ST JIM CLARK (GBR; AGE: 27) 54(+19) PTS

Lotus 25-Climax V8
Team Lotus
Races: MON (car #9); BEL (#1); NED (#6); FRA (#18); GBR (#4); GER (#3); ITA; USA; MEX (all #8); RSA (#1)

2ND= RICHIE GINTHER (USA; AGE: 33) 29(+5) PTS

BRM P57 V8
Owen Racing Organisation
Races: MON (car #5); BEL (#8); NED (#14); FRA (#4); GBR; GER (both #2); ITA (#10); USA; MEX (both #2); RSA (#6)

2ND= GRAHAM HILL (GBR; AGE: 34) 29 PTS

BRM P57 V8
Owen Racing Organisation
Races: MON (car #6); BEL (#7); NED (#12); GBR; GER; USA; MEX (all #1); RSA (#5)

GRAHAM HILL (CONTD)

BRM P61 V8
Owen Racing Organisation
Races: FRA (car #2); ITA (#12)

4TH JOHN SURTEES (GBR; AGE: 29) 22 PTS

Ferrari Dino 156 V6
Scuderia Ferrari
Races: MON (car #21); BEL (#9); NED (#2); FRA (#16); GBR (#10); GER (#7); ITA (#4); USA; MEX (both #23); RSA (#3)

5TH DAN GURNEY (USA; AGE: 32) 19 PTS

Brabham BT7-Climax V8
Brabham Racing Organisation
Races: MON (car #4); BEL; NED (both #18); FRA (#8); GBR (#9); GER (#10); ITA (#24); USA; MEX (both #6); RSA (#9)

6TH= BRUCE McLAREN (NZL; AGE: 26) 17 PTS

Cooper T66-Climax V8
Cooper Car Co
Races: MON (car #7); BEL (#14); NED (#20); FRA (#10); GBR (#6); GER (#5); ITA (#18); USA; MEX (both #3); RSA (#10)

7TH JACK BRABHAM (AUS; AGE: 37) 14 PTS

Lotus 25-climax V8
Brabham Racing Organisation
Races: MON (car #3)

JACK BRABHAM (CONTD)

Brabham BT3-Climax V8
Brabham Racing Organisation
Races: BEL (car #17); ITA (#22)

PICTURED AT NON-CHAMPIONSHIP RACE

JACK BRABHAM (CONTD)

Brabham BT7-Climax V8
Brabham Racing Organisation
Races: NED (car #16); FRA (#6); GBR (#8); GER (#9); USA; MEX (both #5); RSA (#8)

9TH TONY MAGGS (RSA; AGE: 26) 9 PTS

Cooper T66-Climax V8
Cooper Car Co
Races: MON (car #8); BEL (#15); NED (#22); FRA (#12); GBR (#7); GER (#6); ITA (#20); USA; MEX (both #4); RSA (#11)

9TH= LORENZO BANDINI (ITA; AGE: 27) 6 PTS

BRM P57 V8
Scuderia Centro Sud
Races: FRA (car #46); GBR (#3); GER (#15)

LORENZO BANDINI (CONTD)

Ferrari Dino 156 V6
Scuderia Ferrari
Races: ITA (car #2); USA; MEX (both #24); RSA (#4)

9TH= JO BONNIER (SWE; AGE: 33) 6 PTS

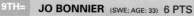

Cooper T60-Climax V8
Rob Walker Racing
Races: MON (car #11); BEL (#12); NED (#28); FRA (#44)

JO BONNIER (CONTD)

Cooper T66-Climax V8
Rob Walker Racing
Races: GBR (car #14); GER (#16); ITA (#58); USA; MEX (both #11); RSA (#12)

1963

CHAMPIONSHIP CAR-BY-CAR

9TH= INNES IRELAND (GBR; AGE: 33) 6 PTS

Lotus 24-BRM V8
British Racing Partnership
Races: MON; GER (both car #14)

INNES IRELAND (CONTD)

BRP 1-BRM V8
British Racing Partnership
Races: BEL (car #4); NED (#30); FRA (#32); GBR (#11); ITA (#32)

12TH= JIM HALL (USA; AGE: 28) 3 PTS

Lotus 24-BRM V8
British Racing Partnership
Races: MON (car #12); BEL (#5); NED (#42); FRA (#34); GBR (#12); GER (#20); ITA (#30); USA; MEX (both #16)

12TH= GERHARD MITTER (GER; AGE: 27) 3 PTS

Porsche 718 F4
Écurie Maarsbergen
Races: NED (car #34); GER (#26)

14TH CAREL GODIN DE BEAUFORT (NED; AGE: 29) 2 PTS

Porsche 718 F4
Écurie Maarsbergen
Races: BEL (car #29); NED (#32); GBR (#23); GER (#17); USA; MEX (both #12); RSA (#14)

15TH= LUDOVICO SCARFIOTTI (ITA; AGE: 29) 1 PT

Ferrari Dino 156 V6
Scuderia Ferrari
Races: NED (car #4)

15TH= JO SIFFERT (SUI; AGE: 27) 1 PT

Lotus 24-BRM V8
Siffert Racing Team
Races: MON (car #25); BEL (#28); NED; FRA (both #36); GBR (#25); GER (#18); ITA (#54); USA; MEX (both #14)

15TH= TREVOR TAYLOR (GBR; AGE: 26) 1 PT

Lotus 25-Climax V8
Team Lotus
Races: MON (car #10); BEL (#2); NED (#8); FRA (#20); GBR (#5); GER (#4); USA; MEX (both #9); RSA (#2)

CHRIS AMON (NZL; AGE: 20) 0 PTS

Lola Mk4-Climax V8
Reg Parnell Racing
Races: BEL (car #21); NED (#10); FRA (#30); GBR (#19); GER (#21)

CHRIS AMON (CONTD)

Lotus 24-BRM V8
Reg Parnell Racing
Races: MEX (car #18)

NOTE: OBSCURED BEHIND CAR #25

BOB ANDERSON (RSR; AGE: 32) 0 PTS

Lola Mk4-Climax V8
DW Racing Enterprises
Races: GBR (car #22); ITA (#48)

GIANCARLO BAGHETTI (ITA; AGE: 28) 0 PTS

ATS 100 V8
Automobili Turismo e Sport
Races: BEL (car #27); NED (#26); ITA (#14); USA; MEX (both #26)

LUCIEN BIANCHI (BEL; AGE: 28) 0 PTS

Lola Mk4-Climax V8
Reg Parnell Racing
Races: BEL (car #22)

TREVOR BLOKDYK (RSA; AGE: 28) 0 PTS

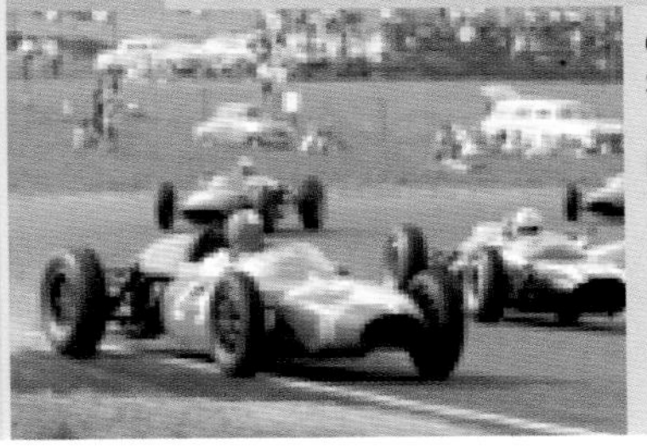

Cooper T51-Maserati S4
Scuderia Lupini
Races: RSA (car #23)

PETER BROEKER (CAN; AGE: 34) 0 PTS

Stebro 4-Ford S4
Canadian Stebro Racing
Races: USA (car #21)

1963

CHAMPIONSHIP CAR-BY-CAR

IAN BURGESS (GBR; AGE: 33) 0 PTS

Scirocco 02-BRM V8
Scirocco-Powell Racing Cars
Races: GBR (car #16); GER (#24)

MARIO ARAUJO DE CABRAL (POR; AGE: 29) 0 PTS

Cooper T60-Climax V8
Scuderia Centro Sud
Races: GER (car #22)

JOHN CAMPBELL-JONES (GBR; AGE: 33) 0 PTS

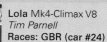

Lola Mk4-Climax V8
Tim Parnell
Races: GBR (car #24)

BERNARD COLLOMB (FRA; AGE: 32) 0 PTS

Lotus 24-Climax V8
Driver
Races: GER (car #28)

MASTEN GREGORY (USA; AGE: 31) 0 PTS

Lotus 24-BRM V8
Reg Parnell Racing
Races: FRA (car #48); GBR (#21); ITA (#42)

MASTEN GREGORY (CONTD)

Lola Mk4-Climax V8
Reg Parnell Racing
Races: USA; MEX (both car #17)

MIKE HAILWOOD (GBR; AGE: 23) 0 PTS

Lotus 24-Climax V8
Reg Parnell Racing
Races: GBR (car #20)

MIKE HAILWOOD (CONTD)

Lola Mk4-Climax V8
Reg Parnell Racing
Races: ITA (car #40)

PHIL HILL (USA; AGE: 36) 0 PTS

ATS 100 V8
Automobili Turismo e Sport
Races: BEL (car #26); NED (#24); ITA (#16); USA; MEX (both #25)

PHIL HILL (CONTD)

Lotus 24-BRM V8
Écurie Filipinetti
Races: FRA (car #42)

PIET DE KLERK (RSA; AGE: 27) 0 PTS

Alfa Special S4
Otelle Nucci
Races: RSA (car #18)

JOHN LOVE (RSR; AGE: 39) 0 PTS

Cooper T55-Climax S4
Driver
Races: RSA (car #19)

WILLY MAIRESSE (BEL; AGE: 34) 0 PTS

Ferrari Dino 156 V6
Scuderia Ferrari
Races: MON (car #20); BEL (#10); GER (#8)

BRAUSCH NIEMANN (RSA; AGE: 25) 0 PTS

Lotus 22-Ford S4
Ted Lanfear
Races: RSA (car #21)

ERNEST PIETERSE (RSA; AGE: 25) 0 PTS

Lotus 21-Climax S4
Team Lawson
Races: RSA (car #7)

1963

CHAMPIONSHIP CAR-BY-CAR

DAVID PROPHET (GBR; AGE: 26) 0 PTS

Brabham BT6-Ford S4
David Prophet Racing
Races: RSA (car #22)

IAN RABY (GBR; AGE: 41) 0 PTS

Gilby-BRM V8
Ian Raby Racing
Races: GBR (car #26)

PICTURED DURING ITA PRACTICE

PEDRO RODRIGUEZ (MEX; AGE: 23) 0 PTS

Lotus 25-Climax V8
Team Lotus
Races: USA; MEX (both car #10)

DOUG SERRURIER (RSA; AGE: 43) 0 PTS

LDS Mk1-Alfa Romeo S4
Otelle Nucci
Races: RSA (car #16)

TONY SETTEMBER (USA; AGE: 37) 0 PTS

Scirocco 01-BRM V8
Scirocco-Powell Racing Cars
Races: BEL (car #24); FRA (#38); GBR (#15); GER (#23)

HAP SHARP (USA; AGE: 35) 0 PTS

Lotus 24-BRM V8
Reg Parnell Racing
Races: USA; MEX (both car #22)

MOISES SOLANA (MEX; AGE: 27) 0 PTS

BRM P57 V8
Scuderia Centro Sud
Races: MEX (car #13)

MIKE SPENCE (GBR; AGE: 26) 0 PTS

Lotus 25-Climax V8
Team Lotus
Races: ITA (car #6)

SAM TINGLE (RSR; AGE: 42) 0 PTS

LDS Mk1-Alfa Romeo S4
Driver
Races: RSA (car #20)

PICTURED AT NON-CHAMPIONSHIP RACE

MAURICE TRINTIGNANT (FRA; AGE: 45) 0 PTS

Lola Mk4-Climax V8
Reg Parnell Racing
Races: MON (car #17)

MAURICE TRINTIGNANT (CONTD)

Lotus 24-Climax V8
Reg Parnell Racing
Races: FRA (car #28)

PICTURED AT NON-CHAMPIONSHIP RACE

MAURICE TRINTIGNANT (CONTD)

BRM P57 V8
Scuderia Centro Sud
Races: ITA (car #66)

RODGER WARD (USA; AGE: 42) 0 PTS

Lotus 24-BRM V8
Reg Parnell Racing
Races: USA (car #18)

1963

CHAMPIONSHIP CAR-BY-CAR

GRAND PRIX WINNERS 1963

	RACE (CIRCUIT)	**WINNER** (CAR)
MON	MONACO GRAND PRIX (MONTE CARLO)	GRAHAM HILL (BRM P57 V8)
BEL	BELGIAN GRAND PRIX (SPA-FRANCORCHAMPS)	JIM CLARK (LOTUS 25-CLIMAX V8)
NED	DUTCH GRAND PRIX (ZANDVOORT)	JIM CLARK (LOTUS 25-CLIMAX V8)
FRA	FRENCH GRAND PRIX (REIMS)	JIM CLARK (LOTUS 25-CLIMAX V8)
GBR	BRITISH GRAND PRIX (SILVERSTONE)	JIM CLARK (LOTUS 25-CLIMAX V8)
GER	GERMAN GRAND PRIX (NÜRBURGRING)	JOHN SURTEES (FERRARI DINO 156 V6)
ITA	ITALIAN GRAND PRIX (MONZA)	JIM CLARK (LOTUS 25-CLIMAX V8)
USA	UNITED STATES GRAND PRIX (WATKINS GLEN)	GRAHAM HILL (BRM P57 V8)
MEX	MEXICAN GRAND PRIX (MEXICO CITY)	JIM CLARK (LOTUS 25-CLIMAX V8)
RSA	SOUTH AFRICAN GRAND PRIX (EAST LONDON)	JIM CLARK (LOTUS 25-CLIMAX V8)

DAN GURNEY

1964

SURTEES CREATES A SLICE OF SPORTING HISTORY

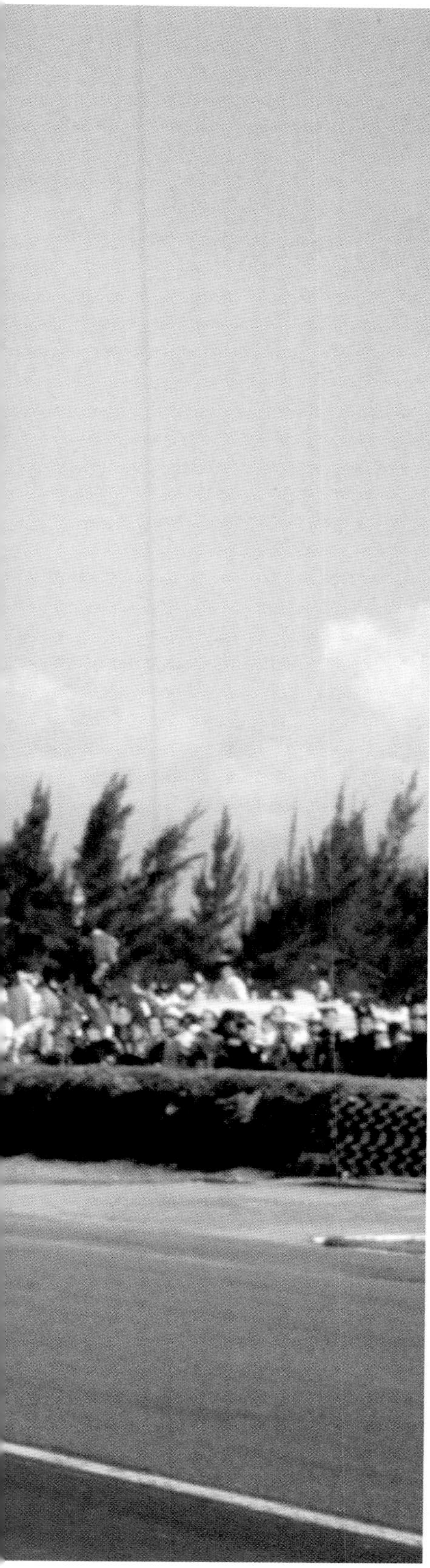

Far left
White knights: the works Ferraris ran in North American Racing Team colours for the season's final two races. Surtees leads Bandini in Mexico, where the Italian had moved over to allow his team-mate to claim the second place he needed to become world champion

Above
That petrol emotion: Dan Gurney (left) led in Belgium before running out of fuel. The same thing happened to Graham Hill and Bruce McLaren – and that allowed Jim Clark to snatch victory within sight of the chequered flag. The Scot then ran dry on his slowing-down lap, which gave him the chance to stop and discuss economical throttle techniques with Gurney

Left
Emerging threat: Hill and Surtees at the Nürburgring, where the Ferrari driver won to kick-start his title challenge

Three British drivers headed for the final event of the year in Mexico with a chance of taking the world title – and all of them had at least one hand on the trophy during the dramatic closing stages. Canny teamwork, however, ensured that John Surtees got the verdict.

Defending champion Jim Clark had dominated the race and seemed certain to secure victory – and the title – until a fractured oil pipe brought his Lotus to a halt with little more than a lap to run. That handed the advantage to pre-race points leader Graham Hill, even though his BRM was two laps adrift after a collision with Surtees's Ferrari team-mate Lorenzo Bandini.

There was a further twist to come, though. With Clark out and Hill a long way back, Surtees needed to finish second to take the title. Going into the final lap he lay third, behind Dan Gurney's Brabham and Bandini… who duly pulled aside to allow his team-mate to become the first man to win world titles on two wheels and four – a feat that remains unique.

Surtees's challenge didn't begin in earnest until mid-season, when he scored his second consecutive victory at the Nürburgring. It was the pattern of the time for Ferrari's Formula One effort to be compromised until June, because of the effort it put into winning the Le Mans 24 Hours, the world's most prestigious sports car race. Once that was out of the way, the Ferrari V8's potential started to become apparent. After Germany the world championship paid its first visit to Austria, where a makeshift circuit – on the Zeltweg military airfield – played havoc with cars' suspension systems and most front-runners retired with breakages. Bandini came through to give Ferrari another victory. Championship pace-setters Clark and Hill failed to score both here and at Monza, where Surtees notched up the win he needed to reinforce his title challenge. He then finished second to Hill in America, after Clark retired, to set up a three-way title shoot-out in Mexico.

Gurney scored Brabham's maiden victory, in France, and Honda became the first Japanese manufacturer to race an F1 car. Its complex, V12-engined chassis made its debut in Germany and, in the hands of American rookie Ronnie Bucknum, showed increasing promise as the campaign went on.

Above
A spanner in the works: frantic preparations on the grid at Brands Hatch, which hosted its first Formula One grand prix in 1964

Right
Up with the Clark: Hill, Gurney, Arundell and Surtees head the pursuit of the pace-setting Scot during the Dutch GP's opening stages. The Lotus driver was still ahead 80 laps later, however

Above right
Breaking point: the first Austrian GP took place at the Zeltweg military aerodrome, where the rough concrete played havoc with suspension systems. Lorenzo Bandini (Ferrari) passes Trevor Taylor's abandoned BRP en route to his only world championship success. Bandini and Richie Ginther (BRM) finished three laps clear of their few surviving rivals

JOHN SURTEES – WORLD CHAMPION 1964

1964

CHAMPIONSHIP CAR-BY-CAR

1ST JOHN SURTEES (GBR; AGE: 30) 40 PTS

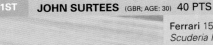

Ferrari 158 V8
Scuderia Ferrari/North American Racing Team
Races: MON (car #21); NED (#2); BEL (#10); FRA (#24); GBR; GER; AUT (all #7); ITA (#2); USA; MEX (both #7)

2ND GRAHAM HILL (GBR; AGE: 35) 39(+2) PTS

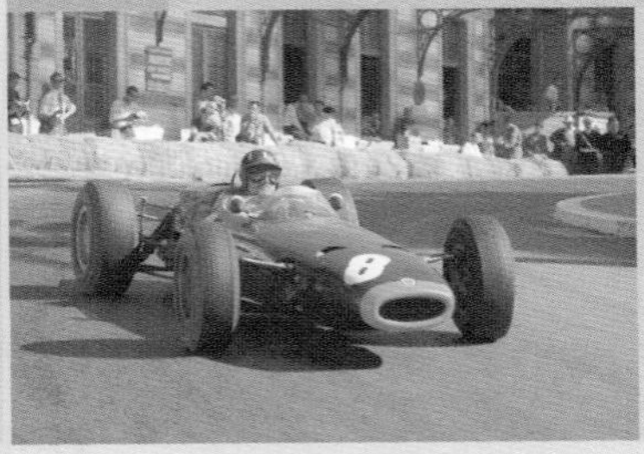

BRM P261 V8
Owen Racing Organisation
Races: MON (car #8); NED (#6); BEL (#1); FRA (#8); GBR; GER; AUT (all #3); ITA (#18); USA; MEX (both #3)

3RD JIM CLARK (GBR; AGE: 28) 32 PTS

Lotus 25-Climax V8
Team Lotus
Races: MON (car #12); NED (#18); BEL (#23); FRA (#2); GBR (#1); ITA (#8); USA (#1)

JIM CLARK (CONTD)

Lotus 33-Climax V8
Team Lotus
Races: GER; AUT (both car #1); USA (#2); MEX (#1)

4TH= LORENZO BANDINI (ITA; AGE: 28) 23 PTS

Ferrari Dino 156 V6
Scuderia Ferrari
Races: MON (car #20); GBR; GER; AUT (all #8)

LORENZO BANDINI (CONTD)

Ferrari 158 V8
Scuderia Ferrari
Races: NED (car #4); BEL (#11); FRA (#26); ITA (#4)

LORENZO BANDINI (CONTD)

Ferrari 1512 F12
North American Racing Team
Races: USA; MEX (both car #8)

4TH= RICHIE GINTHER (USA; AGE: 34) 23 PTS

BRM P261 V8
Owen Racing Organisation
Races: MON (car #7); NED (#8); BEL (#2); FRA (#10); GBR; GER; AUT (all #4); ITA (#20); USA; MEX (both #4)

6TH DAN GURNEY (USA; AGE: 33) 19 PTS

Brabham BT7-Climax V8
Brabham Racing Organisation
Races: MON (car #6); NED (#16); BEL (#15); FRA (#22); GBR (#6); GER; AUT (both #5); ITA (#16); USA; MEX (both #6)

7TH BRUCE McLAREN (NZL; AGE: 26) 13 PTS

Cooper T66-Climax V8
Cooper Car Co
Races: MON (car #10)

BRUCE McLAREN (CONTD)

Cooper T73-Climax V8
Cooper Car Co
Races: NED (car #24); BEL (#20); FRA (#12); GBR; GER; AUT (all #9); ITA (#26); USA; MEX (both #9)

8TH= PETER ARUNDELL (GBR; AGE: 30) 11 PTS

Lotus 25-Climax V8
Team Lotus
Races: MON (car #11); NED (#20); BEL (#24); FRA (#4)

8TH= JACK BRABHAM (AUS; AGE: 38) 11 PTS

Brabham BT7-Climax V8
Brabham Racing Organisation
Races: MON (car #5); NED; BEL (both #14); FRA (#20); GBR (#5); GER (#6)

JACK BRABHAM (CONTD)

Brabham BT11-Climax V8
Brabham Racing Organisation
Races: AUT (car #6); ITA (#14); USA; MEX (both #5)

10TH JO SIFFERT (SUI; AGE: 28) 7 PTS

Lotus 24-BRM V8
Siffert Racing Team
Races: MON (car #24)

1964

CHAMPIONSHIP CAR-BY-CAR

JO SIFFERT (CONTD)

Brabham BT11-BRM V8
Siffert Racing Team/ Rob Walker Racing
Races: NED (car #36); BEL (#17); FRA (#30); GBR (#20); GER (#19); AUT (#20); ITA (#12); USA; MEX (both #22)

11TH BOB ANDERSON (RSR; AGE: 33) 5 PTS

Brabham BT11-Climax V8
DW Racing Enterprises
Races: MON (car #16); NED (#34); FRA (#32); GBR (#19); GER (#16); AUT; ITA (both #22)

12TH= INNES IRELAND (GBR; AGE: 34) 4 PTS

BRP 1-BRM V8
British Racing Partnership
Races: BEL (car #3); FRA (#16)

INNES IRELAND (CONTD)

BRP 2-BRM V8
British Racing Partnership
Races: GBR (car #11); AUT (#14); ITA (#46); USA; MEX (both #11)

12TH= TONY MAGGS (RSA; AGE: 27) 4 PTS

BRM P57 V8
Scuderia Centro Sud
Races: GBR (car #17); GER (#26); AUT (#19)

12TH= MIKE SPENCE (GBR; AGE: 27) 4 PTS

Lotus 25-Climax V8
Team Lotus
Races: GBR (car #2); USA (#1); MEX (#2)

MIKE SPENCE (CONTD)

Lotus 33-Climax V8
Team Lotus
Races: GER; AUT (both car #2); ITA (#10); USA (#2)

15TH JO BONNIER (SWE; AGE: 34) 3 PTS

Cooper T66-Climax V8
Rob Walker Racing
Races: MON (car #19)

JO BONNIER (CONTD)

Brabham BT11-BRM V8
Rob Walker Racing
Races: NED (car #26); BEL; GBR (both #16); GER (#11)

JO BONNIER (CONTD)

Brabham BT7-Climax V8
Rob Walker Racing
Races: AUT (car #11); ITA (#34); USA; MEX (both #16)

16TH= CHRIS AMON (NZL; AGE: 21) 2 PTS

Lotus 25-BRM V8
Reg Parnell Racing
Races: NED (car #10); BEL (#27); FRA (#34); GBR (#15); GER (#14); USA; MEX (both #15)

CHRIS AMON (CONTD)

Lotus 25-Climax V8
Reg Parnell Racing
Races: AUT (car #16)

16TH= WALT HANSGEN (USA; AGE: 44) 2 PTS

Lotus 33-Climax V8
Team Lotus
Races: USA (car #17)

16TH= MAURICE TRINTIGNANT (FRA; AGE: 46) 2 PTS

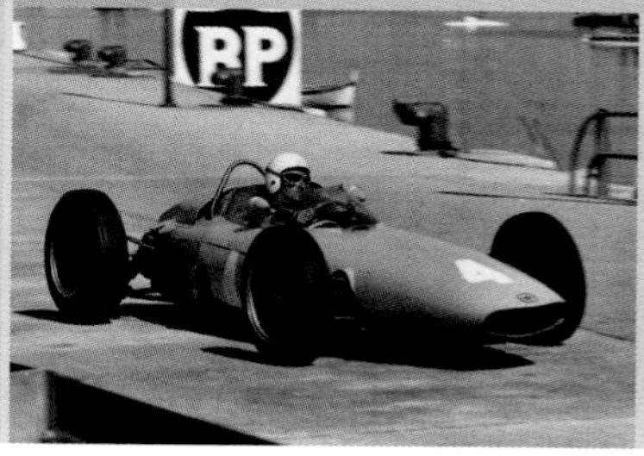

BRM P57 V8
Driver
Races: MON (car #4); FRA (#28); GER (#22); ITA (#48)

19TH= MIKE HAILWOOD (GBR; AGE: 24) 1 PT

Lotus 25-BRM V8
Reg Parnell Racing
Races: MON (car #18); NED (#12); FRA (#36); GBR (#14); GER (#15); AUT (#17); ITA (#40); USA; MEX (both #14)

1964

CHAMPIONSHIP CAR-BY-CAR

19TH= PHIL HILL (USA; AGE: 37) 1 PT

Cooper T73-Climax V8
Cooper Car Co
Races: MON (car #9); NED (#22); BEL (#21); FRA (#14); GBR; GER; USA; MEX (all #10)

PHIL HILL (CONTD)

Cooper T66-Climax V8
Cooper Car Co
Races: AUT (car #10)

19TH= PEDRO RODRIGUEZ (MEX; AGE: 24) 1 PT

Ferrari Dino 156 V6
North American Racing Team
Races: MEX (car #18)

19TH= TREVOR TAYLOR (GBR; AGE: 27) 1 PT

BRP 1-BRM V8
British Racing Partnership
Races: MON; AUT (both car #15)

TREVOR TAYLOR (CONTD)

BRP 2-BRM V8
British Racing Partnership
Races: BEL (car #4); FRA (#18); USA; MEX (both #12)

TREVOR TAYLOR (CONTD)

Lotus 24-BRM V8
British Racing Partnership
Races: GBR (car #12)

GIANCARLO BAGHETTI (ITA; AGE: 29) 0 PTS

BRM P57 V8
Scuderia Centro Sud
Races: NED (car #32); BEL (#6); GBR; GER; AUT (all #18); ITA (#30)

EDGAR BARTH (DDR; AGE: 47) 0 PTS

Cooper T66-Climax V8
Rob Walker Racing
Races: GER (car #12)

CAREL GODIN DE BEAUFORT (NED; AGE: 30) 0 PTS

Porsche 718 F4
Écurie Maarsbergen
Races: NED (car #28)

PICTURED IN GER PRACTICE

RONNIE BUCKNUM (USA; AGE: 28) 0 PTS

Honda RA271 V12
Honda Research & Development
Races: GER (car #20); ITA (#28); USA (#25)

MARIO ARAUJO DE CABRAL (POR; AGE: 30) 0 PTS

ATS 100 V8
Derrington-Francis Racing Team
Races: ITA (car #50)

FRANK GARDNER (AUS; AGE: 33) 0 PTS

Brabham BT10-Ford S4
John Willment Automobiles
Races: GBR (car #26)

GERHARD MITTER (GER; AGE: 28) 0 PTS

Lotus 25-Climax V8
Team Lotus
Races: GER (car #23)

ANDRÉ PILETTE (BEL; AGE: 45) 0 PTS

Scirocco 02-Climax V8
Équipe Scirocco Belge
Races: BEL (car #28)

IAN RABY (GBR; AGE: 42) 0 PTS

Brabham BT3-BRM V8
Ian Raby Racing
Races: GBR (car #23)

1964

CHAMPIONSHIP CAR-BY-CAR

PETER REVSON (USA; AGE: 25) 0 PTS

Lotus 24-BRM V8
Revson Racing
Races: BEL (car #29); GBR (#24); GER (#27); ITA (#38)

JOCHEN RINDT (AUT; AGE: 22) 0 PTS

Brabham BT11-BRM V8
Rob Walker Racing
Races: AUT (car #12)

LUDOVICO SCARFIOTTI (ITA; AGE: 30) 0 PTS

Ferrari Dino 156 V6
Scuderia Ferrari
Races: ITA (car #6)

HAP SHARP (USA; AGE: 36) 0 PTS

Brabham BT11-BRM V8
Rob Walker Racing
Races: USA; MEX (both car #23)

MOISES SOLANA (MEX; AGE: 28) 0 PTS

Lotus 33-Climax V8
Team Lotus
Races: MEX (car #17)

JOHN TAYLOR (GBR; AGE: 31) 0 PTS

Cooper T71/73-Ford S4
FR Gerard
Races: GBR (car #22)

GRAND PRIX WINNERS 1964

	RACE (CIRCUIT)	**WINNER** (CAR)
MON	MONACO GRAND PRIX (MONTE CARLO)	GRAHAM HILL (BRM P261 V8)
NED	DUTCH GRAND PRIX (ZANDVOORT)	JIM CLARK (LOTUS 25-CLIMAX V8)
BEL	BELGIAN GRAND PRIX (SPA-FRANCORCHAMPS)	JIM CLARK (LOTUS 25-CLIMAX V8)
FRA	FRENCH GRAND PRIX (ROUEN-LES-ESSARTS)	DAN GURNEY (BRABHAM BT7-CLIMAX V8)
GBR	BRITISH GRAND PRIX (BRANDS HATCH)	JIM CLARK (LOTUS 25-CLIMAX V8)
GER	GERMAN GRAND PRIX (NÜRBURGRING)	JOHN SURTEES (FERRARI 158 V8)
AUT	AUSTRIAN GRAND PRIX (ZELTWEG)	LORENZO BANDINI (FERRARI DINO 156 V6)
ITA	ITALIAN GRAND PRIX (MONZA)	JOHN SURTEES (FERRARI 158 V8)
USA	UNITED STATES GRAND PRIX (WATKINS GLEN)	GRAHAM HILL (BRM P261 V8)
MEX	MEXICAN GRAND PRIX (MEXICO CITY)	DAN GURNEY (BRABHAM BT7-CLIMAX V8)

1965

NO STOPPING CLARK – AND HE EVEN TAKES TIME OUT TO WIN INDY

Left
Discomfort zone: Jim Clark didn't like Spa-Francorchamps at the best of times, but his uncanny sense of feel and touch always served him well – no matter how dismal the conditions. This was his fourth straight Belgian GP win

Above
Spray rise: Hill leads Stewart, Ginther, Siffert, Surtees, Gurney and the rest on the climb through Eau Rouge shortly after the start in Belgium

Right
Richie pickings: Ginther's Mexican GP success established a number of benchmarks. It was a first world championship win for Honda, Goodyear and for him. Of the three parties, the American was the only one not to enjoy further F1 success

Left
Privateers on parade: the Brabhams of Bob Anderson (DW Racing), Frank Gardner (Willment) and Jo Siffert (Rob Walker) vie for position in Monaco

Below
Weapons of mass eruption: Hill passes Rindt's abandoned Cooper at Clermont-Ferrand, a new venue for the French GP. The track was built amid a range of extinct volcanoes

Bottom
Balancing act: Clark, first-time winner Stewart, Hill and Gurney demonstrate the art of the four-wheel drift at Monza's Parabolica. Gorgeous, basically

Jim Clark and Lotus were back to peak form and won six of the nine grands prix they contested. The Scot missed Monaco in order to take part in the Indianapolis 500 – and won that, too.

The Lotus 25 was updated and relabelled as the 33, but in essence it was the same Coventry Climax-powered monocoque chassis that Clark had been using to great effect since 1962. When things ran reliably he was generally unbeatable.

BRM recruited new boy Jackie Stewart to race alongside Graham Hill and the pair were Clark's most consistent challengers. Hill was runner-up in the title race and Stewart took a remarkable third. The promising rookie won his first grand prix at Monza after depriving his team-mate of the lead on the final lap.

The Ferrari challenge faded and John Surtees had a difficult year. Late in the season the 1964 world champion suffered serious back injuries when he crashed while practising for a sports car race at Mosport Park, Canada. He would be sidelined until the following spring.

Honda continued with its Formula One effort and was rewarded when Richie Ginther won the seasonal finale in Mexico. It was a first grand prix success for both the Japanese company and its tyre supplier Goodyear. It was also the last world championship race governed by the 1.5-litre engine regulations that had been in place for the past five seasons. With the possible exception of Clark and Lotus boss Colin Chapman, nobody was sad to see them phased out.

JIM CLARK – WORLD CHAMPION 1963 & 1965

1965

CHAMPIONSHIP CAR-BY-CAR

1ST JIM CLARK (GBR; AGE: 29) 54 PTS

Lotus 33-Climax V8
Team Lotus
Races: RSA (car #5); BEL (#17); GBR (#5); NED (#6); GER (#1); ITA (#24); USA; MEX (both #5)

JIM CLARK (CONTD)

Lotus 25-Climax V8
Team Lotus
Races: FRA (car #6)

2ND GRAHAM HILL (GBR; AGE: 36) 40 PTS

BRM P261 V8
Owen Racing Organisation
Races: RSA; MON (both car #3); BEL (#7); FRA (#10); GBR (#3); NED (#10); GER (#9); ITA (#30); USA; MEX (both #3)

3RD JACKIE STEWART (GBR; AGE: 26) 33 PTS

BRM P261 V8
Owen Racing Organisation
Races: RSA; MON (both car #4); BEL (#8); FRA (#12); GBR (#4); NED (#12); GER (#10); ITA (#32); USA; MEX (both #4)

4TH DAN GURNEY (USA; AGE: 34) 25 PTS

Brabham BT11-Climax V8
Brabham Racing Organisation
Races: RSA (car #8); BEL (#15); FRA (#14); GBR (#7); NED (#16); GER (#5); ITA (#12); USA; MEX (both #8)

5TH JOHN SURTEES (GBR; AGE: 31) 17 PTS

Ferrari 158 V8
Eugenio Dragoni/ Scuderia Ferrari
Races: RSA (car #1); MON (#18); BEL (#1); FRA (#2)

JOHN SURTEES (CONTD)

Ferrari 1512 F12
Scuderia Ferrari
Races: GBR (car #1); NED (#2); GER (#7); ITA (#8)

6TH LORENZO BANDINI (ITA; AGE: 29) 13 PTS

Ferrari 1512 F12
Eugenio Dragoni/ Scuderia Ferrari
Races: RSA (car #2); MON (#17); BEL (#2); FRA; ITA (both #4); USA; MEX (both #2)

LORENZO BANDINI (CONTD)

Ferrari 158 V8
Scuderia Ferrari
Races: GBR (car #2); NED (#4); GER (#8)

7TH RICHIE GINTHER (USA; AGE: 35) 11 PTS

Honda RA272 V12
Honda Research & Development
Races: MON (car #20); BEL (#10); FRA (#26); GBR (#11); NED (#22); ITA (#20); USA; MEX (both #11)

8TH= BRUCE McLAREN (NZL; AGE: 27) 10 PTS

Cooper T73-Climax V8
Cooper Car Co
Races: RSA (car #9)

BRUCE McLAREN (CONTD)

Cooper T77-Climax V8
Cooper Car Co
Races: MON (car #7); BEL (#4); FRA (#18); GBR (#9); NED (#18); GER (#11); ITA (#16); USA; MEX (both #9)

8TH= MIKE SPENCE (GBR; AGE: 28) 10 PTS

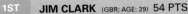

Lotus 33-Climax V8
Team Lotus
Races: RSA (car #6); BEL (#18); FRA (#8); GBR (#6); GER (#2); ITA (#26); USA; MEX (both #6)

MIKE SPENCE (CONTD)

Lotus 25-Climax V8
Team Lotus
Races: NED (car #8)

10TH JACK BRABHAM (AUS; AGE: 39) 9 PTS

Brabham BT11-Climax V8
Brabham Racing Organisation
Races: RSA (car #7); MON (#1); BEL (#14); GER (#4); USA; MEX (both #7)

1965

CHAMPIONSHIP CAR-BY-CAR

11TH= DENNY HULME (NZL; AGE: 29) 5PT

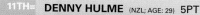

Brabham BT7-Climax V8
Brabham Racing Organisation
Races: MON (car #2); GBR (#14); GER (#6)

DENNY HULME (CONTD)

Brabham BT11-Climax V8
Brabham Racing Organisation
Races: FRA (car #16); NED; ITA (both #14)

11TH= JO SIFFERT (SUI; AGE: 29) 5 PTS

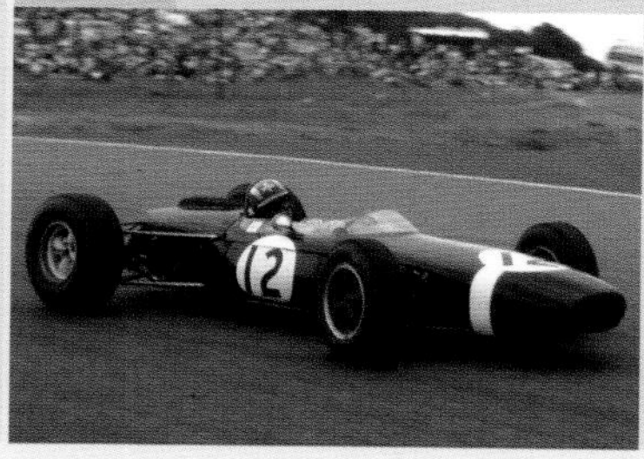

Brabham BT11-BRM V8
Rob Walker Racing
Races: RSA (car #12); MON (#14); BEL (#21); FRA (#36); GBR (#16); NED (#28); GER (#17); ITA (#44); USA; MEX (both #16)

13TH JOCHEN RINDT (AUT; AGE: 23) 4 PTS

Cooper T73-Climax V8
Cooper Car Co
Races: RSA (car #10); ITA (#18)

JOCHEN RINDT (CONTD)

Cooper T77-Climax V8
Cooper Car Co
Races: BEL (car #5); FRA (#20); GBR (#10); NED (#20); GER (#12); USA; MEX (both #10)

14TH= RICHARD ATTWOOD (GBR; AGE: 25) 2 PTS

Lotus 25-BRM V8
Reg Parnell Racing
Races: MON (car #15); BEL (#23); GBR (#22); NED (#34); GER (#20); ITA (#40); USA; MEX (both #21)

14TH= RONNIE BUCKNUM (USA; AGE: 29) 2 PTS

Honda RA272 V12
Honda Research & Development
Races: MON (car #19); BEL (#11); FRA (#28); ITA (#22); USA; MEX (both #12)

14TH= PEDRO RODRIGUEZ (MEX; AGE: 25) 2 PTS

Ferrari 1512 F12
North American Racing Team
Races: USA; MEX (both car #14)

CHRIS AMON (NZL; AGE: 22) 0 PTS

Lotus 25-BRM V8
Reg Parnell Racing
Races: FRA (car #24); GER (#19)

BOB ANDERSON (RSR; AGE: 34) 0 PTS

Brabham BT11-Climax V8
DW Racing Enterprises
Races: RSA (car #14); MON (#9); FRA (#30); GBR (#18); NED (#36)

GIANCARLO BAGHETTI (ITA; AGE: 30) 0 PTS

Brabham BT7-Climax V8
Brabham Racing Organisation
Races: ITA (car #10)

GIORGIO BASSI (ITA; AGE: 31) 0 PTS

BRM P57 V8
Scuderia Centro Sud
Races: ITA (car #52)

LUCIEN BIANCHI (BEL; AGE: 30) 0 PTS

BRM P57 V8
Scuderia Centro Sud
Races: BEL (car #27)

BOB BONDURANT (USA; AGE: 32) 0 PTS

Ferrari 158 V8
North American Racing Team
Races: USA (car #24)

BOB BONDURANT (CONTD)

Lotus 33-BRM V8
Reg Parnell Racing
Races: MEX (car #22)

1965

CHAMPIONSHIP CAR-BY-CAR

JO BONNIER (SWE; AGE: 35) 0 PTS

Brabham BT7-Climax V8
Rob Walker Racing
Races: RSA (car #11); MON (#12); BEL (#20); FRA (#34); GBR (#15); NED (#26); GER (#16); ITA (#42); USA (#15)

JO BONNIER (CONTD)

Brabham BT11-Climax V8
Rob Walker Racing
Races: MEX (car #15)

ROBERTO BUSSINELLO (ITA; AGE: 37) 0 PTS

BRM P57 V8
Scuderia Centro Sud
Races: ITA (car #50)

FRANK GARDNER (AUS; AGE: 34) 0 PTS

Brabham BT11-BRM V8
John Willment Automobiles
Races: RSA (car #16); MON (#11); BEL (#26); GBR (#17); NED (#30); GER (#21); ITA (#46)

MASTEN GREGORY (USA; AGE: 33) 0 PTS

BRM P57 V8
Scuderia Centro Sud
Races: BEL (car #29); GBR (#12); GER (#24); ITA (#48)

MIKE HAILWOOD (GBR; AGE: 25) 0 PTS

Lotus 25-BRM V8
Reg Parnell Racing
Races: MON (car #16)

PAUL HAWKINS (AUS; AGE: 27) 0 PTS

Brabham BT10-Ford S4
John Willment Automobiles
Races: RSA (car #18)

PAUL HAWKINS (CONTD)

Lotus 33-Climax V8
DW Racing Enterprises
Races: MON (car #10); GER (#22)

INNES IRELAND (GBR; AGE: 35) 0 PTS

Lotus 25-BRM V8
Reg Parnell Racing
Races: BEL (car #22); FRA (#22); GBR (#23); NED (#38)

INNES IRELAND (CONTD)

Lotus 33-BRM V8
Reg Parnell Racing
Races: ITA (car #38); USA (#22)

PIET DE KLERK (RSA; AGE: 28) 0 PTS

Alfa Special S4
Otelle Nucci
Races: RSA (car #20)

JOHN LOVE (RSR; AGE: 40) 0 PTS

Cooper T55-Climax S4
Driver
Races: RSA (car #17)

TONY MAGGS (RSA; AGE: 27) 0 PTS

Lotus 25-BRM V8
Reg Parnell Racing
Races: RSA (car #15)

GERHARD MITTER (GER; AGE: 29) 0 PTS

Lotus 25-Climax V8
Team Lotus
Races: GER (car #3)

DAVID PROPHET (GBR; AGE: 27) 0 PTS

Brabham BT10-Ford S4
David Prophet Racing
Races: RSA (car #19)

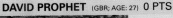

1965

CHAMPIONSHIP CAR-BY-CAR

IAN RABY (GBR; AGE: 43) 0 PTS

Brabham BT3-BRM V8
Ian Raby Racing
Races: GBR (car #24)

JOHN RHODES (GBR; AGE: 37) 0 PTS

Cooper T60-Climax V8
FR Gerard
Races: GBR (car #20)

GEKI RUSSO (ITA; AGE: 27) 0 PTS

Lotus 25-Climax V8
Team Lotus
Races: ITA (car #28)

MOISES SOLANA (MEX; AGE: 29) 0 PTS

Lotus 25-Climax V8
Team Lotus
Races: USA; MEX (both car #18)

SAM TINGLE (RSR; AGE: 43) 0 PTS

LDS Mk1-Alfa Romeo S4
Driver
Races: RSA (car #25)

NINO VACCARELLA (ITA; AGE: 32) 0 PTS

Ferrari 158 V8
Scuderia Ferrari
Races: ITA (car #6)

GRAND PRIX WINNERS 1965

	RACE (CIRCUIT)	WINNER (CAR)
RSA	SOUTH AFRICAN GRAND PRIX (EAST LONDON)	JIM CLARK (LOTUS 33-CLIMAX V8)
MON	MONACO GRAND PRIX (MONTE CARLO)	GRAHAM HILL (BRM P261 V8)
BEL	BELGIAN GRAND PRIX (SPA-FRANCORCHAMPS)	JIM CLARK (LOTUS 33-CLIMAX V8)
FRA	FRENCH GRAND PRIX (CLERMONT-FERRAND)	JIM CLARK (LOTUS 25-CLIMAX V8)
GBR	BRITISH GRAND PRIX (SILVERSTONE)	JIM CLARK (LOTUS 33-CLIMAX V8)
NED	DUTCH GRAND PRIX (ZANDVOORT)	JIM CLARK (LOTUS 33-CLIMAX V8)
GER	GERMAN GRAND PRIX (NÜRBURGRING)	JIM CLARK (LOTUS 33-CLIMAX V8)
ITA	ITALIAN GRAND PRIX (MONZA)	JACKIE STEWART (BRM P261 V8)
USA	UNITED STATES GRAND PRIX (WATKINS GLEN)	GRAHAM HILL (BRM P261 V8)
MEX	MEXICAN GRAND PRIX (MEXICO CITY)	RICHIE GINTHER (HONDA RA272 V12)

1966

BRABHAM POSTPONES RETIREMENT – AND TAKES TITLE NUMBER THREE

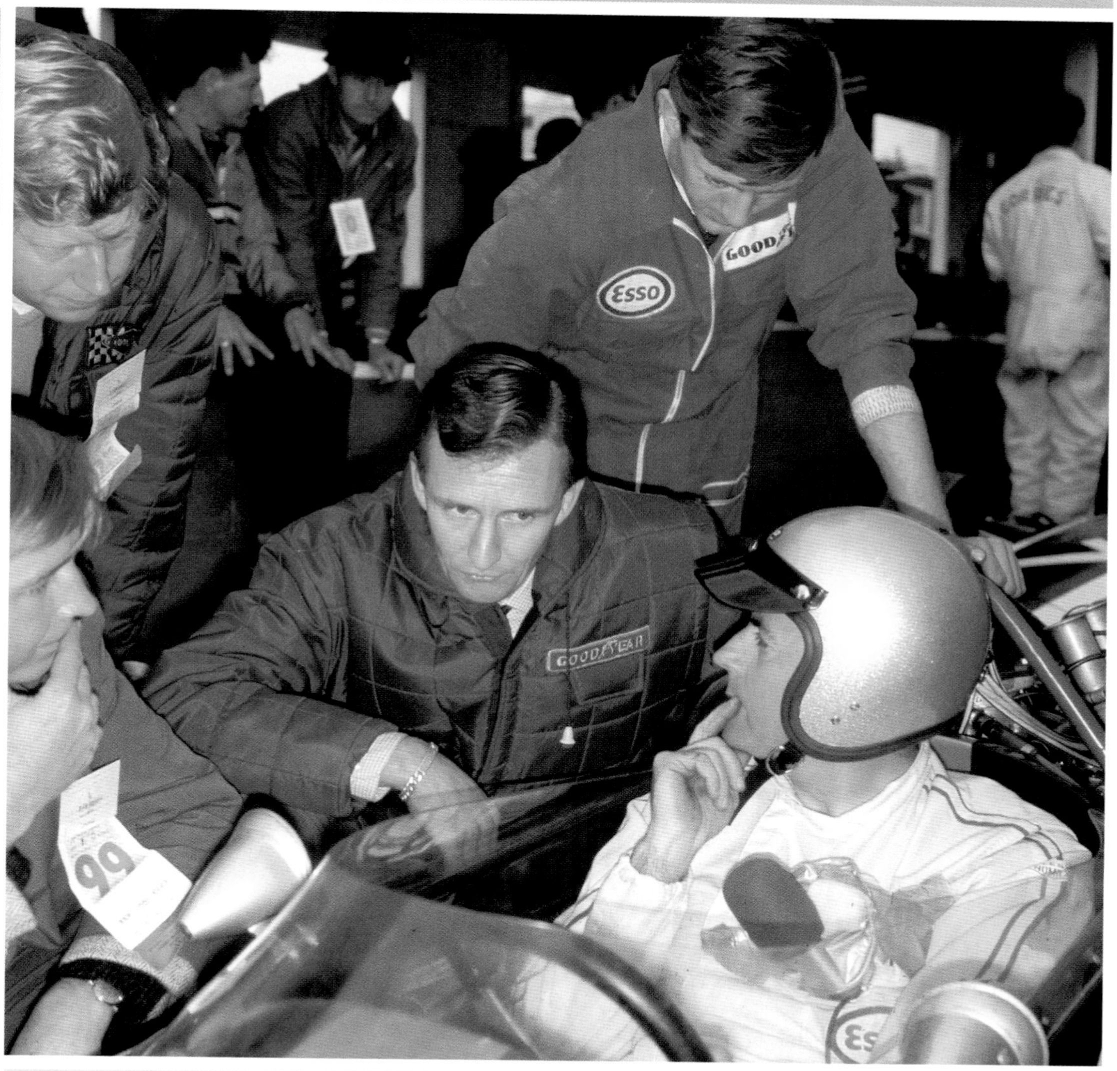

Left
Dunes in July: Brabham leads team-mate Hulme, Clark and Hill at Zandvoort, where the Australian scored the third of his four consecutive mid-summer wins

Above
Scene of tranquillity: conference in the Brabham pit during the American GP weekend. The title was already in the bag before the team crossed the Atlantic at the end of the year

Right
Changing vrooms: Bandini duels with former team-mate Surtees at Watkins Glen. The Englishman quit Ferrari after a mid-season row, transferred to Cooper and went on to finish a distant second in the championship

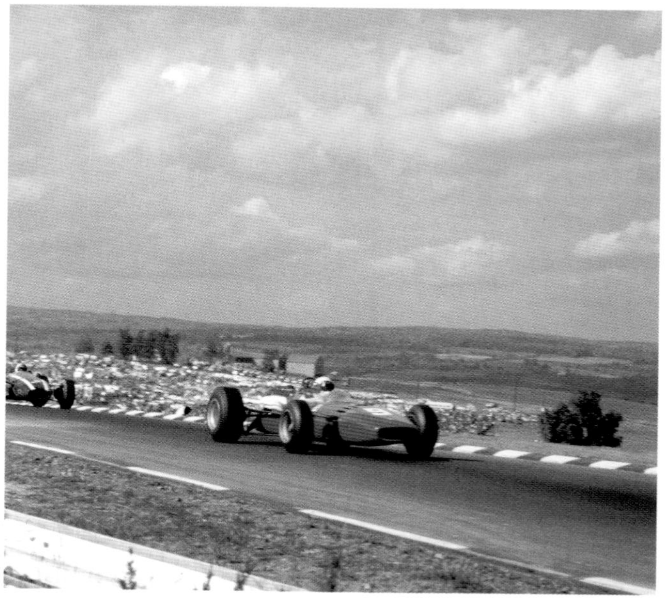

With his 40th birthday approaching, Jack Brabham originally envisaged stepping down from the cockpit in order to concentrate on running his team. He had hoped Dan Gurney would spearhead Brabham's attack in 1966, but then the American announced he was leaving to set up on his own. Brabham consequently postponed his retirement plans for the time being. Remarkably, he ended the year as world champion – the first man to achieve the feat in a car bearing his own name.

This was the opening season of a new three-litre engine formula, but doubling the cubic capacity didn't immediately lead to the dramatic performance surge that had been anticipated. It took time for engines designed specifically for the new rules to appear and most teams opted for short-term compromises.

Engine choice was largely responsible for Brabham's terrific year. Opting for simplicity and reliability he commissioned Australian firm Repco to modify a roadgoing General Motors V8 to racing spec. Despite having only single overhead camshafts, when every serious F1 engine had for a long time employed twin cams for each head, it proved perfect for its time. Light and economical, it enabled the Brabhams to line up on the grid weighing substantially less than rivals. This, in turn, allowed them to run softer-compound tyres that gave them a grip advantage.

Brabham won for the first time in France and rarely stopped doing so thereafter as he enjoyed a fairly comfortable jaunt to his third title. Ferrari was expected to benefit from the new rules but relied on a reworked version of an old sports car engine that was too heavy and thirsty. John Surtees left following a row with the team shortly after winning in Belgium. He joined Cooper and won the season-closing Mexican Grand Prix using an adapted Maserati engine that had its origins in the 1950s. Unsurprisingly, this was overweight.

The same was true of BRM's complex H16, which had been purpose-built for the new regulations. It scored its only victory in the United States GP, when installed in the back of Jim Clark's Lotus 43.

Top
Stars on film: work proceeds on John Frankenheimer's cinematic epic *Grand Prix* in Monaco. Note to Sylvester Stallone: this is how to make a motor racing movie

Above centre
Cruise control: Stewart breezes to a comfortable victory in Monaco, where five laps covered the four finishers

Right
Talking point: from the left, Surtees, camera-car driver Phil Hill, Ginther, Graham Hill, Stewart, journalist Peter Garnier, Spence, Bonnier and Siffert in discussion at Spa, where half the field would be eliminated in a series of opening lap accidents

Far right
All dressed up, no place to slow: Bandini prepares for the last French GP to take place at Reims

1966

CHAMPIONSHIP CAR-BY-CAR

1ST JACK BRABHAM (AUS; AGE: 40) 42(+3) PTS

Brabham BT19-Repco V8
Brabham Racing Organisation
Races: MON (car #7); BEL (#3); FRA (#12); GBR (#5); NED (#16); GER (#3); ITA (#10)

JACK BRABHAM (CONTD)

Brabham BT20-Repco V8
Brabham Racing Organisation
Races: USA; MEX (both car #5)

2ND JOHN SURTEES (GBR; AGE: 32) 28 PTS

Ferrari 312 V12
Scuderia Ferrari
Races: MON (car #17); BEL (#6)

JOHN SURTEES (CONTD)

Cooper T81-Maserati V12
Cooper Car Co
Races: FRA (car #10); GBR (#12); NED (#24); GER (#7); ITA (#14); USA; MEX (both #7)

3RD JOCHEN RINDT (AUT; AGE: 24) 22(+2) PTS

Cooper T81-Maserati V12
Cooper Car Co
Races: MON (car #10); BEL (#19); FRA (#6); GBR (#11); NED (#26); GER (#8); ITA (#16); USA; MEX (both #8)

4TH DENNY HULME (NZL; AGE: 30) 18 PTS

Brabham BT11-Climax V8
Brabham Racing Organisation
Races: MON (car #8); BEL (#4)

DENNY HULME (CONTD)

Brabham BT20-Repco V8
Brabham Racing Organisation
Races: FRA (car #14); GBR (#6); NED (#18); GER (#4); ITA (#12); USA; MEX (both #6)

5TH GRAHAM HILL (GBR; AGE: 37) 17 PTS

BRM P261 V8
Owen Racing Organisation
Races: MON (car #11); BEL (#14); FRA (#16); GBR (#3); NED (#12); GER (#5)

GRAHAM HILL (CONTD)

BRM P83 H16
Owen Racing Organisation
Races: ITA (car #26); USA; MEX (both #3)

6TH JIM CLARK (GBR; AGE: 30) 16 PTS

Lotus 33-Climax V8
Team Lotus
Races: MON (car #4); BEL (#10); GBR (#1); NED (#6); GER (#1)

JIM CLARK (CONTD)

Lotus 43-BRM H16
Team Lotus
Races: ITA (car #22); USA; MEX (both #1)

7TH JACKIE STEWART (GBR; AGE: 27) 14 PTS

BRM P261 V8
Owen Racing Organisation
Races: MON (car #12); BEL (#15); GBR (#4); NED (#14); GER (#6)

JACKIE STEWART (CONTD)

BRM P83 H16
Owen Racing Organisation
Races: ITA (car #28); USA; MEX (both #4)

8TH= LORENZO BANDINI (ITA; AGE: 30) 12 PTS

Ferrari 158/246 V6
Scuderia Ferrari
Races: MON (car #16); BEL (#7)

LORENZO BANDINI (CONTD)

Ferrari 312 V12
Scuderia Ferrari
Races: FRA (car #20); NED (#2); GER (#9); ITA (#2); USA (#9)

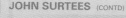

1966

CHAMPIONSHIP CAR-BY-CAR

8TH= MICHAEL PARKES (GBR; AGE: 34) 12 PTS

Ferrari 312 V12
Scuderia Ferrari
Races: FRA (car #22); NED (#4); GER (#10); ITA (#4)

10TH LUDOVICO SCARFIOTTI (ITA; AGE: 32) 9 PTS

Ferrari 158/246 V6
Scuderia Ferrari
Races: GER (car #11)

LUDOVICO SCARFIOTTI (CONTD)

Ferrari 312 V12
Scuderia Ferrari
Races: ITA (car #6)

11TH RICHIE GINTHER (USA; AGE: 36) 5 PTS

Cooper T81-Maserati V12
Cooper Car Co
Races: MON (car #9); BEL (#18)

RICHIE GINTHER (CONTD)

Honda RA273 V12
Honda Racing
Races: ITA (car #18); USA; MEX (both #12)

12TH= DAN GURNEY (USA; AGE: 35) 4 PTS

Eagle AAR101-Climax S4
Anglo-American Racers
Races: BEL (car #27); FRA (#26); GBR (#16); NED (#10); GER (#12); MEX (#15)

DAN GURNEY (CONTD)

Eagle AAR102-Weslake V12
Anglo-American Racers
Races: ITA (car #30); USA (#15)

12TH= MIKE SPENCE (GBR; AGE: 29) 4 PTS

Lotus 33-BRM V8
Reg Parnell Racing
Races: MON (car #6); BEL (#16); FRA (#32); GBR (#17); NED (#32); GER (#15); ITA (#32)

MIKE SPENCE (CONTD)

Lotus 25-BRM V8
Reg Parnell Racing
Races: USA (car #18)

14TH= BOB BONDURANT (USA; AGE: 33) 3 PTS

BRM P261 V8
Team Chamaco Collect/ Bernard White Racing
Races: MON (car #19); BEL (#24); GBR (#25); GER (#14); ITA (#48)

BOB BONDURANT (CONTD)

Eagle AAR101-Climax S4
Anglo-American Racers
Races: USA (car #16)

BOB BONDURANT (CONTD)

Eagle AAR102-Weslake V12
Anglo-American Racers
Races: MEX (car #16)

14TH= BRUCE McLAREN (NZL; AGE: 29) 3 PTS

McLaren M2B-Ford V8
Bruce McLaren Motor Racing
Races: MON (car #2); USA; MEX (both #17)

BRUCE McLAREN (CONTD)

McLaren M2B-Serenissima V8
Bruce McLaren Motor Racing
Races: GBR (car #14)

14TH= JO SIFFERT (SUI; AGE: 30) 3 PTS

Brabham BT11-BRM V8
Rob Walker Racing
Races: MON (car #14)

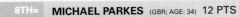

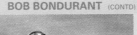

1966

CHAMPIONSHIP CAR-BY-CAR

JO SIFFERT (CONTD)

Cooper T81-Maserati V12
Rob Walker Racing
Races: BEL (car #21); FRA (#38); GBR (#20); NED (#28); ITA (#36); USA; MEX (both #19)

17TH= BOB ANDERSON (RSR; AGE: 35) 1 PT

Brabham BT11-Climax V8
DW Racing Enterprises
Races: MON (car #15); FRA (#36); GBR (#21); NED (#34); GER (#19); ITA (#40)

17TH= PETER ARUNDELL (GBR; AGE: 32) 1 PT

Lotus 43-BRM H16
Team Lotus
Races: FRA (car #4)

PETER ARUNDELL (CONTD)

Lotus 33-BRM V8
Team Lotus
Races: GBR (car #2); NED (#8); GER (#2); ITA (#24); MEX (#2)

PETER ARUNDELL (CONTD)

Lotus 33-Climax V8
Team Lotus
Races: USA (car #2)

17TH= JO BONNIER (SWE; AGE: 36) 1 PT

Cooper T81-Maserati V12
Anglo-Suisse Racing Team
Races: MON (car #18); BEL (#20); NED (#30); GER (#17); ITA (#38); USA; MEX (both #22)

JO BONNIER (CONTD)

Brabham BT11-Climax V8
Anglo-Suisse Racing Team
Races: FRA (car #30)

JO BONNIER (CONTD)

Brabham BT7-Climax V8
Anglo-Suisse Racing Team
Races: GBR (car #18)

17TH= JOHN TAYLOR (GBR; AGE: 33) 1 PT

Brabham BT11-BRM V8
David Bridges
Races: FRA (car #44); GBR (#22); NED (#38); GER (#16)

KURT AHRENS JR (GER; AGE: 26) 0 PTS

Brabham BT18-Ford S4
Caltex Racing Team
Races: GER (car #25)

CHRIS AMON (NZL; AGE: 23) 0 PTS

Cooper T81-Maserati V12
Cooper Car Co
Races: FRA (car #8)

GIANCARLO BAGHETTI (ITA; AGE: 31) 0 PTS

Ferrari 158/246 V6
Reg Parnell Racing
Races: ITA (car #44)

JEAN-PIERRE BELTOISE (FRA; AGE: 29) 0 PTS

Matra MS5-Ford S4
Matra Sports
Races: GER (car #34)

RONNIE BUCKNUM (USA; AGE: 30) 0 PTS

Honda RA273 V12
Honda Racing
Races: USA; MEX (both car #14)

PIERS COURAGE (GBR; AGE: 24) 0 PTS

Lotus 44-Ford S4
Ron Harris Team Lotus
Races: GER (car #32)

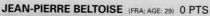

1966

CHAMPIONSHIP CAR-BY-CAR

HUBERT HAHNE (GER; AGE: 31) 0 PTS

Matra MS5-BRM S4
Tyrrell Racing Organisation
Races: GER (car #26)

HANS HERRMANN (GER; AGE: 38) 0 PTS

Brabham BT18-Ford S4
Roy Winkelmann Racing
Races: GER (car #28)

JACKY ICKX (BEL; AGE: 21) 0 PTS

Matra MS5-Ford S4
Tyrrell Racing Organisation
Races: GER (car #27)

INNES IRELAND (GBR; AGE: 36) 0 PTS

BRM P261 V8
Bernard White Racing
Races: USA; MEX (both car #10)

CHRIS IRWIN (GBR; AGE: 24) 0 PTS

Brabham BT11-Climax V8
Brabham Racing Organisation
Races: GBR (car #7)

CHRIS LAWRENCE (GBR; AGE: 33) 0 PTS

Cooper T73-Ferrari V12
JA Pearce Engineering
Races: GBR (car #24); GER (#20)

GUY LIGIER (FRA; AGE: 36) 0 PTS

Cooper T81-Maserati V12
Driver
Races: MON (car #21); BEL (#22); FRA (#42); GBR (#19); NED (#36)

ALAN REES (GBR; AGE: 28) 0 PTS

Brabham BT18-Ford S4
Roy Winkelmann Racing
Races: GER (car #29)

PEDRO RODRIGUEZ (MEX; AGE: 26) 0 PTS

Lotus 33-Climax V8
Team Lotus
Races: FRA (car #2); MEX (#11)

PEDRO RODRIGUEZ (CONTD)

Lotus 44-Ford S4
Ron Harris Team Lotus
Races: GER (car #31)

PEDRO RODRIGUEZ (CONTD)

Lotus 33-BRM V8
Team Lotus
Races: USA (car #11)

GEKI RUSSO (ITA; AGE: 28) 0 PTS

Lotus 33-Climax V8
Team Lotus
Races: ITA (car #20)

JO SCHLESSER (FRA; AGE: 38) 0 PTS

Matra MS5-Ford S4
Matra Sports
Races: GER (car #33)

MOISES SOLANA (MEX; AGE: 30) 0 PTS

Cooper T81-Maserati V12
Cooper Car Co
Races: MEX (car #9)

TREVOR TAYLOR (GBR; AGE: 29) 0 PTS

Shannon SH1-Climax V8
Aiden Jones/Paul Emery
Races: GBR (car #23)

1966

CHAMPIONSHIP CAR-BY-CAR

GRAND PRIX WINNERS 1966

	RACE (CIRCUIT)	WINNER (CAR)
MON	MONACO GRAND PRIX (MONTE CARLO)	JACKIE STEWART (BRM P261 V8)
BEL	BELGIAN GRAND PRIX (SPA-FRANCORCHAMPS)	JOHN SURTEES (FERRARI 312 V12)
FRA	FRENCH GRAND PRIX (REIMS)	JACK BRABHAM (BRABHAM BT19-REPCO V8)
GBR	BRITISH GRAND PRIX (BRANDS HATCH)	JACK BRABHAM (BRABHAM BT19-REPCO V8)
NED	DUTCH GRAND PRIX (ZANDVOORT)	JACK BRABHAM (BRABHAM BT19-REPCO V8)
GER	GERMAN GRAND PRIX (NÜRBURGRING)	JACK BRABHAM (BRABHAM BT19-REPCO V8)
ITA	ITALIAN GRAND PRIX (MONZA)	LUDOVICO SCARFIOTTI (FERRARI 312 V12)
USA	UNITED STATES GRAND PRIX (WATKINS GLEN)	JIM CLARK (LOTUS 43-BRM H16)
MEX	MEXICAN GRAND PRIX (MEXICO CITY)	JOHN SURTEES (COOPER T81-MASERATI V12)

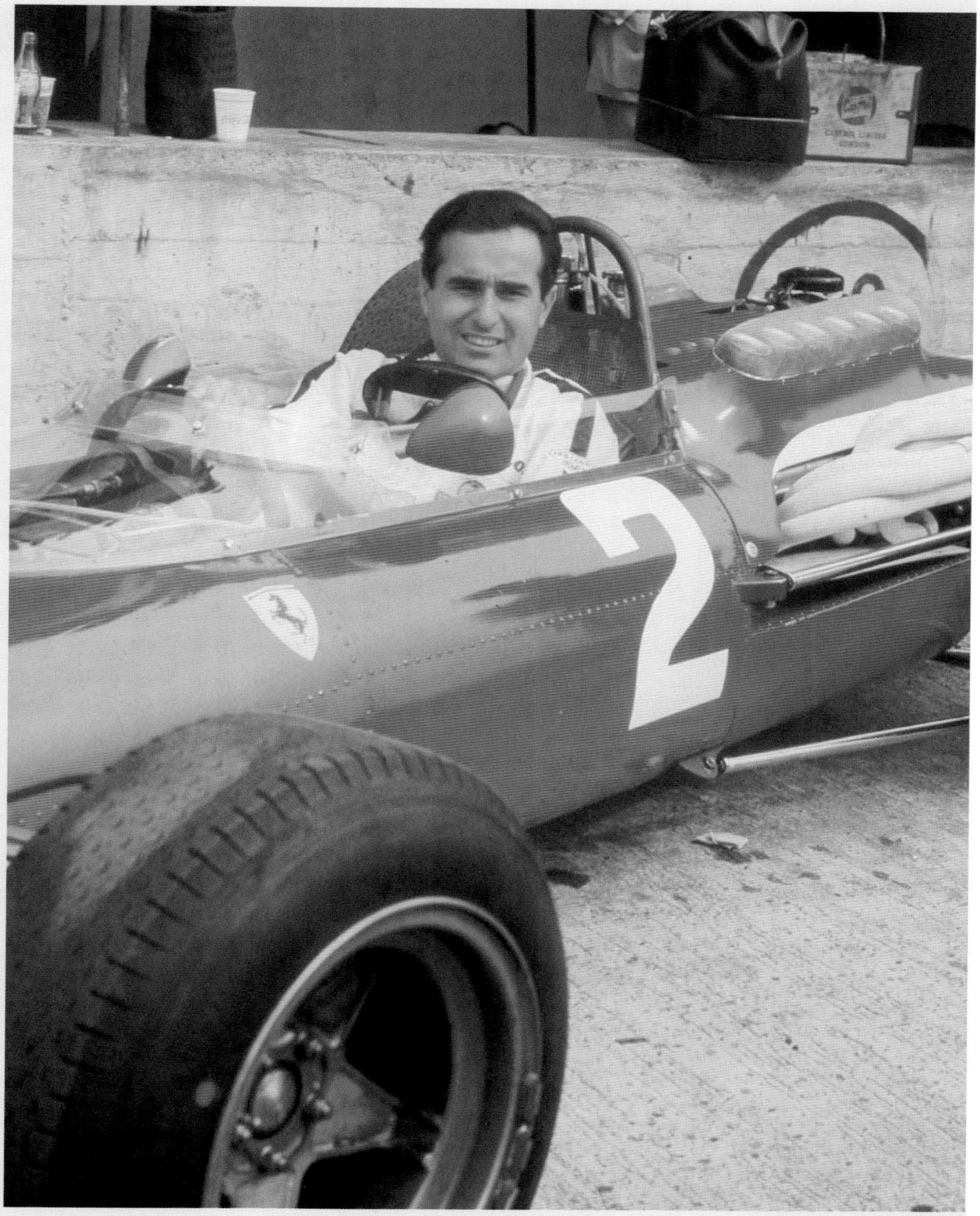

LORENZO BANDINI

1967

RELIABILITY THE KEY FOR HULME AND BRABHAM

Opposite page
Kiwi polish: Hulme heads for second place behind team-mate Brabham in the French GP, which was staged for the first and only time at the Le Mans Bugatti circuit

Above
And they're off: from left, Clark, Hulme, Stewart and Gurney spearhead the 25-car field in Germany

Far left
Power and glory: the Ford-backed Cosworth DFV made its debut in Holland and swiftly proved to be the best engine in the field

Left
One day, son, all this will be yours: Graham Hill and bored-looking world champion-to-be Damon at Monza

A FORD-SPONSORED COSWORTH V8 ENGINE, THE DFV, WAS THE KEY TO LOTUS'S SUCCESS. IT RENDERED OTHER CONTEMPORARY POWER UNITS OBSOLETE. ONLY TEETHING PROBLEMS PREVENTED CLARK AND HILL FROM DOMINATING WHAT WAS LEFT OF THE SEASON

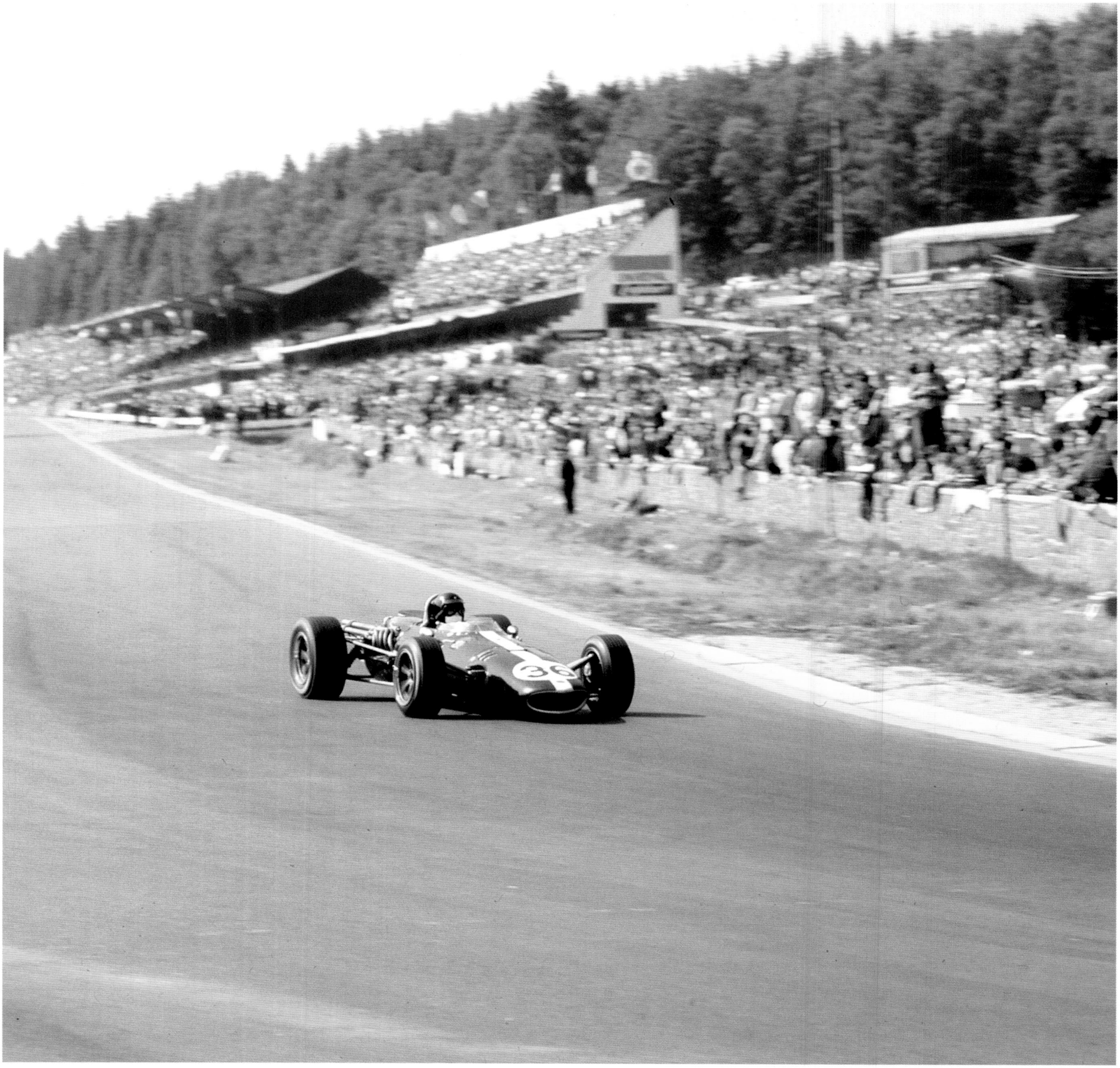

This was the last season before someone thought to apply wings to the cars, so their shapes still had an unadorned purity of line. The Eagle was probably most elegant of them all – and Dan Gurney used it to score a memorable Belgian Grand Prix victory. Like Jack Brabham, this gave him the distinction of having won a race driving his own car for his own team.

The fastest machine was the new Lotus 49, which Jim Clark steered to victory on its debut in Holland – the third of the season's 11 races. A new Ford-sponsored Cosworth V8 engine, the DFV, was the key to Lotus's success. It rendered other contemporary power units obsolete thanks to its compactness, rigidity – it was used as a structural part of the 49's chassis – and power. Only teething problems prevented Clark and Graham Hill from dominating what was left of the season.

As it was, Clark's poor finishing record meant the title fight was between the slower, but steadier, Brabhams of Jack Brabham and Denny Hulme. This was Hulme's first full season with the team – although he'd made occasional appearances during the previous two years – and defending champion Brabham was expected to be the main challenger. Engine supplier Repco kept trying to squeeze more power from its simple V8, however, and the latest developments were fitted to Jack's car. These proved to be less reliable than Hulme's standard parts: Denny won at Monaco and the Nürburgring and scored very consistently in-between to give New Zealand its first – and only, to date – world champion. Hulme's fellow Kiwi Chris Amon joined F1's major league by signing for Ferrari and he put in some brilliant performances, although none yielded victory. He was thrust into a team leadership role early in the year after Lorenzo Bandini succumbed to burns sustained in a horrific, fiery accident during the Monaco GP. Mexican Pedro Rodriguez won the year's opening event in South Africa – and this turned out to be the final world championship success for pioneering British manufacturer Cooper.

Opposite page
Purity in motion: Gurney qualified the handsome Eagle second to Clark at Spa but went on to win after the Scot made an unscheduled stop. This was the fourth and last of the gifted American's world championship successes – and the only one he scored in his own car

Left
I could be a celebrity, get me out of here: Jochen Rindt had to make do with indifferent equipment during his third year with Cooper. Here at Silverstone his Maserati engine packed up. He only finished twice all season

Above, far right
"Sorry – somebody appears to have dropped a packet of custard creams in one of the inlet trumpets": Jackie Stewart suffered appalling unreliability in his third year at BRM. Highlight was a second place at Spa – where he had to hold the car in gear for much of the race

Above
Flake speed: Michael Schumacher eats carefully measured portions of rice and pasta; Jim Clark was happy to partake in a round of ice creams between practice sessions

DENNY HULME – WORLD CHAMPION 1967

1967

CHAMPIONSHIP CAR-BY-CAR

1ST DENNY HULME (NZL; AGE: 31) 51 PTS

Brabham BT20-Repco V8
Brabham Racing Organisation
Races: RSA (car #2); MON (#9); NED (#2)

DENNY HULME (CONTD)

Brabham BT19-Repco V8
Brabham Racing Organisation
Races: BEL (car #26)

DENNY HULME (CONTD)

Brabham BT24-Repco V8
Brabham Racing Organisation
Races: FRA (car #4); GBR; GER; CAN (all #2); ITA (#18); USA; MEX (both #2)

2ND JACK BRABHAM (AUS; AGE: 41) 46 PTS

Brabham BT20-Repco V8
Brabham Racing Organisation
Races: RSA (car #1)

JACK BRABHAM (CONTD)

Brabham BT19-Repco V8
Brabham Racing Organisation
Races: MON (car #8); NED (#1)

JACK BRABHAM (CONTD)

Brabham BT24-Repco V8
Brabham Racing Organisation
Races: BEL (car #25); FRA (#3); GBR; GER; CAN (all #1); ITA (#16); USA; MEX (both #1)

3RD JIM CLARK (GBR; AGE: 31) 41 PTS

Lotus 43-BRM H16
Team Lotus
Races: RSA (car #7)

JIM CLARK (CONTD)

Lotus 33-Climax V8
Team Lotus
Races: MON (car #12)

JIM CLARK (CONTD)

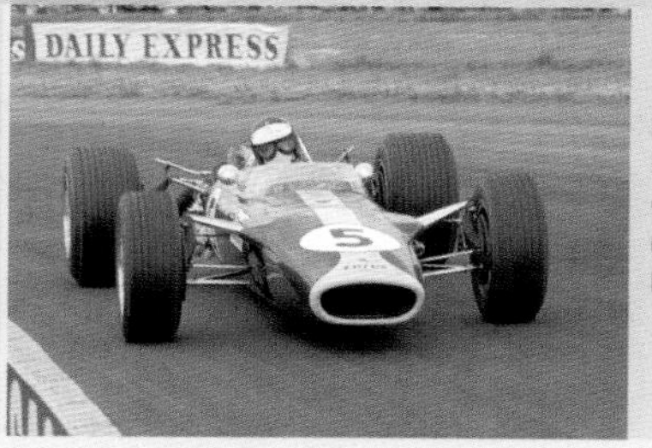

Lotus 49-Ford V8
Team Lotus
Races: NED (car #5); BEL (#21); FRA (#6); GBR (#5); GER; CAN (both #3); ITA (#20); USA; MEX (both #5)

4TH= CHRIS AMON (NZL; AGE: 24) 20 PTS

Ferrari 312 V12
Scuderia Ferrari
Races: MON (car #20); NED (#3); BEL (#1); FRA (#2); GBR; GER (both #8); CAN (#20); ITA (#2); USA; MEX (both #9)

4TH= JOHN SURTEES (GBR; AGE: 33) 20 PTS

Honda RA273 V12
Honda Racing
Races: RSA (car #11); MON; NED; BEL; GBR; GER (all #7)

JOHN SURTEES (CONTD)

Honda RA300 V12
Honda Racing
Races: ITA (car #14); USA; MEX (both #3)

6TH= GRAHAM HILL (GBR; AGE: 38) 15 PTS

Lotus 43-BRM H16
Team Lotus
Races: RSA (car #8)

GRAHAM HILL (CONTD)

Lotus 33-BRM V8
Team Lotus
Races: MON (car #14)

GRAHAM HILL (CONTD)

Lotus 49-Ford V8
Team Lotus
Races: NED (car #6); BEL (#22); FRA (#7); GBR (#6); GER; CAN (both #4); ITA (#22); USA; MEX (both #6)

PICTURED AT GER PRACTICE

1967

CHAMPIONSHIP CAR-BY-CAR

6TH= PEDRO RODRIGUEZ (MEX; AGE: 27) 15 PTS

Cooper T81-Maserati V12
Cooper Car Co
Races: RSA (car #4); MON (#11); NED (#14); BEL (#30); FRA (#14); GBR (#12); GER (#6); MEX (#21)

8TH DAN GURNEY (USA; AGE: 36) 13 PTS

Eagle AAR101-Climax S4
Anglo-American Racers
Races: RSA (car #9)

DAN GURNEY (CONTD)

Eagle AAR103-Weslake V12
Anglo-American Racers
Races: MON (car #23); CAN (#10)

DAN GURNEY (CONTD)

Eagle AAR104-Weslake V12
Anglo-American Racers
Races: NED (car #15); BEL (#36); FRA; GBR; GER (all #9); ITA (#8); USA; MEX (both #11)

9TH JACKIE STEWART (GBR; AGE: 28) 10 PTS

BRM P83 H16
Owen Racing Organisation
Races: RSA (car #5); NED (#9); BEL (#14); GBR (#3); GER (#11); CAN (#15); ITA (#34); USA; MEX (both #7)

JACKIE STEWART (CONTD)

BRM P261 V8
Owen Racing Organisation
Races: MON (car #4); FRA (#10)

10TH MIKE SPENCE (GBR; AGE: 30) 9 PTS

BRM P83 H16
Owen Racing Organisation
Races: RSA (car #6); MON (#5); NED (#10); BEL (#12); FRA (#11); GBR (#4); GER (#12); CAN (#16); ITA (#36); USA; MEX (both #8)

11TH= JOHN LOVE (RSR; AGE: 42) 6 PTS

Cooper T79-Climax S4
Driver
Races: RSA (car #17)

11TH= JOCHEN RINDT (AUT; AGE: 25) 6 PTS

Cooper T81-Maserati V12
Cooper Car Co
Races: RSA (car #3); MON (#10); NED (#12); BEL (#29); FRA (#12); CAN (#71); ITA (#30); USA (#4)

JOCHEN RINDT (CONTD)

Cooper T86-Maserati V12
Cooper Car Co
Races: GBR (car #11); GER (#5)

11TH= JO SIFFERT (SUI; AGE: 31) 6 PTS

Cooper T81-Maserati V12
Rob Walker Racing
Races: RSA (car #12); MON (#17); NED (#20); BEL (#34); FRA (#18); GBR (#17); GER (#14); ITA (#6); USA; MEX (both #15)

14TH= JO BONNIER (SWE; AGE: 37) 3 PTS

Cooper T81-Maserati V12
Joakim Bonnier Racing Team
Races: RSA (car #15); BEL (#39); GBR (#23); GER (#16); CAN (#9); ITA (#26); USA; MEX (both #16)

14TH= BRUCE McLAREN (NZL; AGE: 29) 3 PTS

McLaren M4B-BRM V8
Bruce McLaren Motor Racing
Races: MON (car #16); NED (#17)

BRUCE McLAREN (CONTD)

Eagle AAR102-Weslake V12
Anglo-American Racers
Races: FRA (car #8); GBR; GER (both #10)

BRUCE McLAREN (CONTD)

McLaren M5A-BRM V12
Bruce McLaren Motor Racing
Races: CAN (car #19); ITA (#4); USA; MEX (both #14)

1967

CHAMPIONSHIP CAR-BY-CAR

16TH= BOB ANDERSON (RSR; AGE: 36) 2 PTS

Brabham BT11-Climax V8
Driver
Races: RSA (car #14); NED (#21); BEL (#19); FRA (#17); GBR (#19)

16TH CHRIS IRWIN (GBR; AGE: 25) 2 PTS

Lotus 33-BRM V8
Reg Parnell Racing
Races: NED (car #18)

CHRIS IRWIN (CONTD)

BRM P261 V8
Reg Parnell Racing
Races: BEL (car #17); GBR (#15)

CHRIS IRWIN (CONTD)

BRM P83 H16
Reg Parnell Racing
Races: FRA (car #15); GER (#18); CAN (#17); ITA (#38); USA; MEX (both #17)

16TH= MICHAEL PARKES (GBR; AGE: 35) 2 PTS

Ferrari 312 V12
Scuderia Ferrari
Races: NED (car #4); BEL (#3)

PICTURED AT NON-CHAMPIONSHIP RACE

18TH= JACKY ICKX (BEL; AGE: 22) 1PT

Matra MS5-Cosworth S4
Tyrrell Racing Organisation
Races: GER (car #29)

JACKY ICKX (CONTD)

Cooper T81-Maserati V12
Cooper Car Co
Races: ITA (car #32)

JACKY ICKX (CONTD)

Cooper T86-Maserati V12
Cooper Car Co
Races: USA (car #21)

18TH= GUY LIGIER (FRA; AGE: 37) 1PT

Cooper T81-Maserati V12
Driver
Races: BEL (car #32); FRA (#16)

GUY LIGIER (CONTD)

Brabham BT20-Repco V8
Driver/Brabham Racing Organisation
Races: GBR (car #18); GER (#15); ITA (#12); USA; MEX (both #19)

19TH= LUDOVICO SCARFIOTTI (ITA; AGE: 33) 1PT

Ferrari 312 V12
Scuderia Ferrari
Races: NED (car #22); BEL (#2)

LUDOVICO SCARFIOTTI (CONTD)

Eagle AAR103-Weslake V12
Anglo-American Racers
Races: ITA (car #10)

KURT AHRENS JR (GER; AGE: 27) 0 PTS

Protos-Cosworth S4
Ron Harris
Races: GER (car #26)

RICHARD ATTWOOD (GBR; AGE: 27) 0 PTS

Cooper T81-Maserati V12
Cooper Car Co
Races: CAN (car #8)

GIANCARLO BAGHETTI (ITA; AGE: 32) 0 PTS

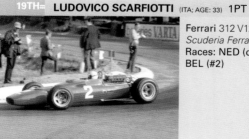

Lotus 49-Ford V8
Team Lotus
Races: ITA (car #24)

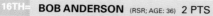

1967

CHAMPIONSHIP CAR-BY-CAR

LORENZO BANDINI (ITA; AGE: 31) 0 PTS

Ferrari 312 V12
Scuderia Ferrari
Races: MON (car #18)

JEAN-PIERRE BELTOISE (FRA; AGE: 30) 0 PTS

Matra MS7-Cosworth S4
Matra Sports
Races: USA; MEX (both car #22)

LUKI BOTHA (RSA; AGE: 37) 0 PTS

Brabham BT11-Climax V8
Driver
Races: RSA (car #20)

DAVE CHARLTON (RSA; AGE: 30) 0 PTS

Brabham BT11-Climax V8
Scuderia Scribante
Races: RSA (car #19)

PIERS COURAGE (GBR; AGE: 24) 0 PTS

Lotus 25-BRM V8
Reg Parnell Racing
Races: RSA (car #16)

PIERS COURAGE (CONTD)

BRM P261 V8
Reg Parnell Racing
Races: MON (car #6)

MIKE FISHER (USA; AGE: 24) 0 PTS

Lotus 33-BRM V8
Driver
Races: CAN (car #6); MEX (#10)

HUBERT HAHNE (GER; AGE: 32) 0 PTS

Lola T100-BMW S4
BMW
Races: GER (car #17)

BRIAN HART (GBR; AGE: 30) 0 PTS

Protos-Cosworth S4
Ron Harris
Races: GER (car #25)

DAVID HOBBS (GBR; AGE: 28) 0 PTS

BRM P261 V8
Bernard White Racing
Races: GBR (car #20); CAN (#12)

DAVID HOBBS (CONTD)

Lola T100-BMW S4
Lola Cars
Races: GER (car #27)

GERHARD MITTER (GER; AGE: 31) 0 PTS

Brabham BT23-Cosworth S4
Driver
Races: GER (car #20)

SILVIO MOSER (SUI; AGE: 26) 0 PTS

Cooper T77-ATS V8
Charles Vogele
Races: GBR (car #22)

JACKIE OLIVER (GBR; AGE: 25) 0 PTS

Lotus 48-Cosworth S4
Lotus Components
Races: GER (car #24)

AL PEASE (CAN; AGE: 45) 0 PTS

Eagle AAR101-Climax S4
Castrol Oils
Races: CAN (car #11)

1967

CHAMPIONSHIP CAR-BY-CAR

ALAN REES (GBR; AGE: 29) 0 PTS

Cooper T81-Maserati V12
Cooper Car Co
Races: GBR (car #14)

ALAN REES (CONTD)

Brabham BT23-Cosworth S4
Roy Winkelmann Racing
Races: GER (car #22)

JO SCHLESSER (FRA; AGE: 39) 0 PTS

Matra MS5-Cosworth S4
Écurie Ford France
Races: GER (car #23)

JOHNNY SERVOZ-GAVIN (FRA; AGE: 25) 0 PTS

Matra MS5-Ford S4
Matra Sports
Races: MON (car #2)

MOISES SOLANA (MEX; AGE: 31) 0 PTS

Lotus 49-Ford V8
Team Lotus
Races: USA; MEX (both car #18)

SAM TINGLE (RSR; AGE: 45) 0 PTS

LDS Mk3-Climax S4
Driver
Races: RSA (car #18)

EPPIE WIETZES (CAN; AGE: 29) 0 PTS

Lotus 49-Ford V8
Team Lotus
Races: CAN (car #5)

JONATHAN WILLIAMS (GBR; AGE: 25) 0 PTS

Ferrari 312 V12
Scuderia Ferrari
Races: MEX (car #12)

GRAND PRIX WINNERS 1967

	RACE (CIRCUIT)	WINNER (CAR)
RSA	SOUTH AFRICAN GRAND PRIX (KYALAMI)	PEDRO RODRIGUEZ (COOPER T81-MASERATI V12)
MON	MONACO GRAND PRIX (MONTE CARLO)	DENNY HULME (BRABHAM BT20-REPCO V8)
NED	DUTCH GRAND PRIX (ZANDVOORT)	JIM CLARK (LOTUS 49-FORD V8)
BEL	BELGIAN GRAND PRIX (SPA-FRANCORCHAMPS)	DAN GURNEY (EAGLE AAR104-WESLAKE V12)
FRA	FRENCH GRAND PRIX (LE MANS BUGATTI CIRCUIT)	JACK BRABHAM (BRABHAM BT24-REPCO V8)
GBR	BRITISH GRAND PRIX (SILVERSTONE)	JIM CLARK (LOTUS 49-FORD V8)
GER	GERMAN GRAND PRIX (NÜRBURGRING)	DENNY HULME (BRABHAM BT24-REPCO V8)
CAN	CANADIAN GRAND PRIX (MOSPORT PARK)	JACK BRABHAM (BRABHAM BT24-REPCO V8)
ITA	ITALIAN GRAND PRIX (MONZA)	JOHN SURTEES (HONDA RA300 V12)
USA	UNITED STATES GRAND PRIX (WATKINS GLEN)	JIM CLARK (LOTUS 49-FORD V8)
MEX	MEXICAN GRAND PRIX (MEXICO CITY)	JIM CLARK (LOTUS 49-FORD V8)

1968

MOTOR SPORT MOURNS ITS TALISMAN

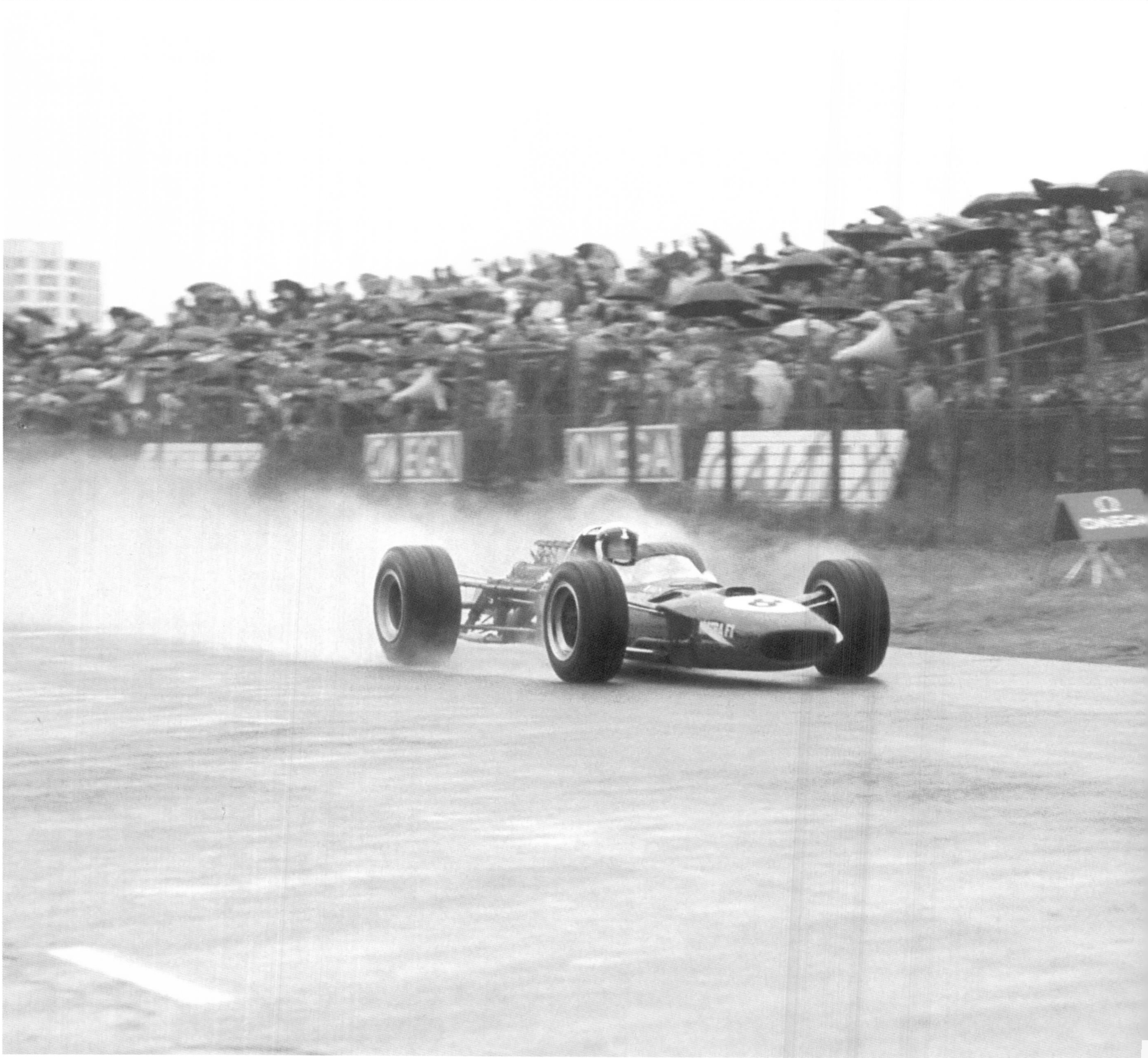

Far left
'Ring of bright water: Jackie Stewart put in one the greatest drives of his career in the rain-swept German GP. Irresistible in the mist, he finished more than four minutes ahead of Hill's Lotus

Above
Coronation streets: Hill mastered Monaco once again. It was his fourth win – and sixth consecutive podium finish – in the principality

Left
Jim Clark: March 4 1936-April 7 1968

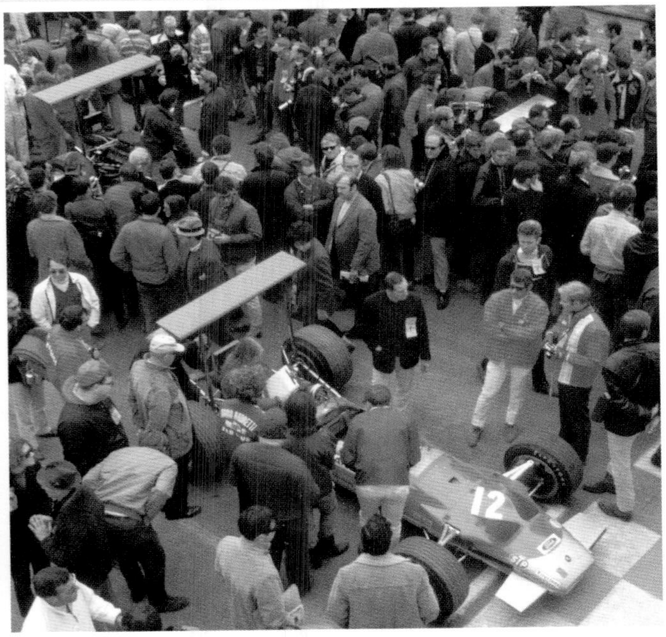

For many, April 7 1968 was the day the music died. The incomparable Jim Clark was killed while competing in a Formula Two event at Hockenheim, Germany. Earlier in the year he had won the season-opening South African Grand Prix to take his world championship victory tally to 25 – one more than previous record-holder Juan Manuel Fangio. Few doubted that Clark was on his way to a third F1 title with Lotus, but fate decreed otherwise. Devastated Lotus boss Colin Chapman seriously contemplated pulling out of the sport, but the gritty determination of Graham Hill, his other driver, helped to pull the team through. Hill won in Spain, the first grand prix after Clark's death, and immediately followed up with victory in Monaco.

When Hill arrived in Mexico City for the finale, he had two men to beat if he was to take the crown: Jackie Stewart and Denny Hulme. Stewart was newly reunited with Ken Tyrrell, the man who set the Scot's career on its way by guiding him to victory in the 1964 British F3 Championship. Tyrrell had persuaded French company Matra, which was entering F1 for the first time with its own car and engine, to allow him to run a Matra chassis with Ford Cosworth DFV power. With arguably the best chassis, unquestionably the best engine and a great driver in Stewart, the partnership was an instant success. Were it not for a wrist injury that obliged him to miss a couple of races, Stewart might have sealed the title well before Mexico. He scythed through the Nürburgring's rain and fog to win the German GP by more than four minutes.

Defending champion Hulme had switched to McLaren and took up where he'd left off at Brabham, winning regularly and without fuss. In Mexico he suffered a suspension failure and posted an early retirement, so the race became a thrilling battle between Hill and Stewart. They were out front and fighting for the title, but Stewart's car eventually suffered fuel starvation because of a metering unit problem and Hill was free to win the race and the crown.

Top left
Monarch of Watkins Glen: Stewart scored his third win of the year in the United States. Had a wrist injury not forced him to miss Spain and Monaco, the world title might have been his

Top right
Super Mario: Andretti caused a sensation by qualifying on pole position at Watkins Glen. It was only his second grand prix appearance. He practised at Monza but was not allowed to participate because he had competed in America within the previous 24 hours

Right
The gain in Spain: Rodriguez (BRM) and Hulme (McLaren) outgun fast-but-unlucky pole-winner Amon off the line at Jarama

1968

CHAMPIONSHIP CAR-BY-CAR

1ST GRAHAM HILL (GBR; AGE: 39) 48 PTS

Lotus 49-Ford V8
Team Lotus
Races: RSA (car #5); ESP (#10); MON (#9); BEL (#1); NED (#3); FRA (#12); GBR (#8); GER (#3); ITA (#16); CAN (#3); USA; MEX (both #10)

2ND JACKIE STEWART (GBR; AGE: 29) 36 PTS

Matra MS9-Ford V8
Matra International
Races: RSA (car #16)

JACKIE STEWART (CONTD)

Matra MS10-Ford V8
Matra International
Races: BEL (car #7); NED (#8); FRA (#28); GBR (#14); GER (#6); ITA (#4); CAN (#14); USA; MEX (both #15)

3RD DENNY HULME (NZL; AGE: 32) 33 PTS

McLaren M5A-BRM V12
Bruce McLaren Motor Racing
Races: RSA (car #1)

DENNY HULME (CONTD)

McLaren M7A-Ford V8
Bruce McLaren Motor Racing
Races: ESP (car #1); MON (#12); BEL (#6); NED (#1); FRA (#8); GBR; GER; ITA; CAN; USA; MEX (all #1)

4TH JACKY ICKX (BEL; AGE: 23) 27 PTS

Ferrari 312 V12
Scuderia Ferrari
Races: RSA (car #9); ESP (#21); BEL (#23); NED (#10); FRA (#26); GBR (#6); GER (#9); ITA (#8); MEX (#7)

5TH BRUCE McLAREN (NZL; AGE: 30) 22 PTS

McLaren M7A-Ford V8
Bruce McLaren Motor Racing
Races: ESP (car #2); MON (#14); BEL (#5); NED (#2); FRA (#10); GBR; GER; ITA; CAN; USA; MEX (all #2)

6TH PEDRO RODRIGUEZ (MEX; AGE: 28) 18 PTS

BRM P126 V12
Owen Racing Organisation
Races: RSA (car #11)

PEDRO RODRIGUEZ (CONTD)

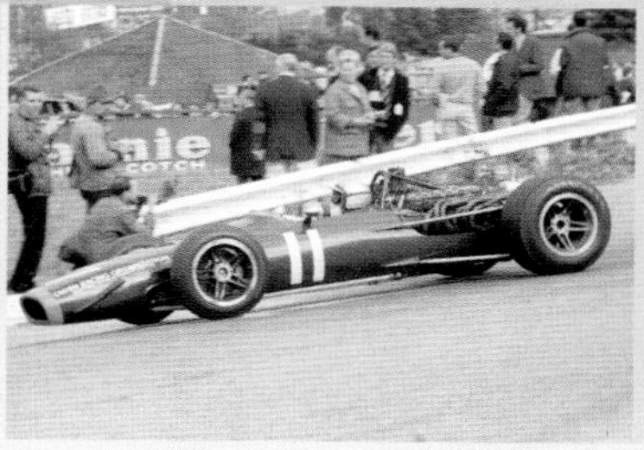

BRM P133 V12
Owen Racing Organisation
Races: ESP (car #9); MON (#4); BEL (#11); NED (#15); FRA (#20); GBR; GER (both #10); CAN (#16); USA; MEX (both #8)

PEDRO RODRIGUEZ (CONTD)

BRM P138 V12
Owen Racing Organisation
Races: ITA (car #26)

7TH= JO SIFFERT (SUI; AGE: 32) 12 PTS

Cooper T81-Maserati V12
Rob Walker/Jack Durlacher Racing
Races: RSA (car #19)

JO SIFFERT (CONTD)

Lotus 49-Ford V8
Rob Walker/Jack Durlacher Racing
Races: ESP (car #16); MON (#17); BEL (#3); NED (#21); FRA (#34); GBR (#22); GER (#16); ITA (#20); CAN (#12); USA; MEX (both #16)

7TH= JOHN SURTEES (GBR; AGE: 34) 12 PTS

Honda RA300 V12
Honda Racing
Races: RSA (car #7)

JOHN SURTEES (CONTD)

Honda RA301 V12
Honda Racing
Races: ESP (car #7); MON (#8); BEL (#20); NED (#7); FRA (#16); GBR; GER (both #7); ITA (#14); CAN (#8); USA; MEX (both #5)

9TH JEAN-PIERRE BELTOISE (FRA; AGE: 31) 11 PTS

Matra MS7-Cosworth S4
Matra Sports
Races: RSA (car #21)

1968

CHAMPIONSHIP CAR-BY-CAR

JEAN-PIERRE BELTOISE (CONTD)

Matra MS10-Ford V8
Matra International
Races: ESP (car #6)

JEAN-PIERRE BELTOISE (CONTD)

Matra MS11 V12
Matra Sports
Races: MON (car #1); BEL (#10); NED (#17); FRA (#6); GBR (#18); GER (#12); ITA (#6); CAN (#18); USA; MEX (both #21)

10TH CHRIS AMON (NZL; AGE: 25) 10 PTS

Ferrari 312 V12
Scuderia Ferrari
Races: RSA (car #8); ESP (#19); BEL (#22); NED (#9); FRA (#24); GBR (#5); GER (#8); ITA; CAN (both #9); USA (#6); MEX (#6)

11TH JIM CLARK (GBR; AGE: 31) 9 PTS

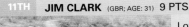

Lotus 49-Ford V8
Team Lotus
Races: RSA (car #4)

12TH JOCHEN RINDT (AUT; AGE: 26) 8 PTS

Brabham BT24-Repco V8
Brabham Racing Organisation
Races: RSA (car #3); ESP (#4); MON (#3)

JOCHEN RINDT (CONTD)

Brabham BT26-Repco V8
Brabham Racing Organisation
Races: BEL (car #19); NED (#6); FRA (#2); GBR (#4); GER (#5); ITA (#11); CAN (#6); USA; MEX (both #4)

13TH= RICHARD ATTWOOD (GBR; AGE: 28) 6 PTS

BRM P126 V12
Owen Racing Organisation
Races: MON (car #15); BEL (#12); NED (#16); FRA (#22); GBR; GER (both #11)

13TH= JACKIE OLIVER (GBR; AGE: 26) 6 PTS

Lotus 49-Ford V8
Team Lotus
Races: MON (car #10); BEL (#2); NED (#4); GBR (#9); GER (#21); ITA (#19); CAN (#4); MEX (#11)

13TH= LUDOVICO SCARFIOTTI (ITA; AGE: 34) 6 PTS

Cooper T86-Maserati V12
Cooper Car Co
Races: RSA (car #15)

LUDOVICO SCARFIOTTI (CONTD)

Cooper T86B-BRM V12
Cooper Car Co
Races: ESP (car #15); MON (#6)

13TH= JOHNNY SERVOZ-GAVIN (FRA; AGE: 26) 6 PTS

Matra MS10-Ford V8
Matra International
Races: MON (car #11); ITA (#5); CAN (#15); MEX (#23)

JOHNNY SERVOZ-GAVIN (CONTD)

Cooper T86B-BRM V12
Cooper Car Co
Races: FRA (car #32)

16TH= LUCIEN BIANCHI (BEL; AGE: 33) 5 PTS

Cooper T86B-BRM V12
Cooper Car Co
Races: MON (car #7); BEL (#15); NED (#14); GER (#19); CAN (#20); USA; MEX (both #19)

16TH= VIC ELFORD (GBR; AGE: 33) 5 PTS

Cooper T86B-BRM V12
Cooper Car Co
Races: FRA (car #30); GBR (#15); GER (#20); ITA (#23); CAN (#21); USA; MEX (both #18)

18TH= PIERS COURAGE (GBR; AGE: 26) 4 PTS

BRM P126 V12
Reg Parnell Racing
Races: ESP (car #5); MON (#16); BEL (#14); NED (#20); FRA (#36); GBR (#20); GER (#22); ITA (#27); CAN (#24); USA; MEX (both #22)

1968

CHAMPIONSHIP CAR-BY-CAR

18TH= BRIAN REDMAN (GBR; AGE: 31) 4 PTS

Cooper T81-Maserati V12
Cooper Car Co
Races: RSA (car #14)

BRIAN REDMAN (CONTD)

Cooper T86B-BRM V12
Cooper Car Co
Races: ESP (car #14); BEL (#16)

20TH= JO BONNIER (SWE; AGE: 38) 3 PTS

Cooper T81-Maserati V12
Joakim Bonnier Racing Team
Races: RSA (car #20)

JO BONNIER (CONTD)

McLaren M5A-BRM V12
Joakim Bonnier Racing Team
Races: BEL (car #17); NED (#19); GBR (#23); ITA (#3); CAN (#22); USA (#17)

JO BONNIER (CONTD)

Honda RA301 V12
Joakim Bonnier Racing Team
Races: MEX (car #17)

20TH= DAN GURNEY (USA; AGE: 37) 3 PTS

Eagle AAR104-Weslake V12
Anglo-American Racers
Races: RSA (car #6); MON (#19); GBR (#24); GER (#14); ITA (#21)

DAN GURNEY (CONTD)

Brabham BT24-Repco V8
Brabham Racing Organisation
Races: NED (car #18)

DAN GURNEY (CONTD)

McLaren M7A-Ford V8
Anglo-American Racers
Races: CAN (car #11); USA; MEX (both #14)

22ND JACK BRABHAM (AUS; AGE: 42) 2 PTS

Brabham BT24-Repco V8
Brabham Racing Organisation
Races: RSA (car #2)

JACK BRABHAM (CONTD)

Brabham BT26-Repco V8
Brabham Racing Organisation
Races: MON (car #2); BEL (#18); NED (#5); FRA (#4); GBR (#3); GER (#4); ITA (#10); CAN (#5); USA; MEX (both #3)

22ND SILVIO MOSER (SUI; AGE: 27) 2 PTS

Brabham BT20-Repco V8
Écurie Charles Vogele
Races: NED (car #22); GBR (#19)

ANDREA DE ADAMICH (ITA; AGE: 26) 0 PTS

Ferrari 312 V12
Scuderia Ferrari
Races: RSA (car #10)

KURT AHRENS JR (GER; AGE: 28) 0 PTS

Brabham BT24-Repco V8
Brabham Racing Organisation
Races: GER (car #17)

MARIO ANDRETTI (USA; AGE: 28) 0 PTS

Lotus 49B-Ford V8
Team Lotus
Races: USA (car #12)

DEREK BELL (GBR; AGE: 26) 0 PTS

Ferrari 312 V12
Scuderia Ferrari
Races: ITA; USA (both car #7)

1968

CHAMPIONSHIP CAR-BY-CAR

BILL BRACK (CAN; AGE: 32) 0 PTS

Lotus 49B-Ford V8
Team Lotus
Races: CAN (car #27)

DAVE CHARLTON (RSA; AGE: 31) 0 PTS

Brabham BT11-Repco V8
Scuderia Scribante
Races: RSA (car #22)

HUBERT HAHNE (GER; AGE: 33) 0 PTS

Lola T100-BMW S4
BMW
Races: GER (car #18)

DAVID HOBBS (GBR; AGE: 29) 0 PTS

Honda RA301 V12
Honda Racing
Races: ITA (car #15)

JOHN LOVE (RSR; AGE: 43) 0 PTS

Brabham BT20-Repco V8
Team Gunston
Races: RSA (car #17)

HENRI PESCAROLO (FRA; AGE: 26) 0 PTS

Matra MS11 V12
Matra Sports
Races: CAN (car #19); MEX (#9)

JACKIE PRETORIUS (RSA; AGE: 33) 0 PTS

Brabham BT7-Climax V8
Team Pretoria
Races: RSA (car #23)

BASIL VAN ROOYEN (RSA; AGE: 28) 0 pts

Cooper T75-Climax S4
John Love
Races: RSA (car #25)

JO SCHLESSER (FRA; AGE: 40) 0 PTS

Honda RA302 V8
Honda Racing
Races: FRA (car #18)

MOISES SOLANA (MEX; AGE: 32) 0 PTS

Lotus 49B-Ford V8
Team Lotus
Races: MEX (car #12)

MIKE SPENCE (GBR; AGE: 31) 0 PTS

BRM P83 H16
Owen Racing Organisation
Races: RSA (car #12)

SAM TINGLE (RSR; AGE: 46) 0 PTS

LDS Mk5-Repco V8
Team Gunston
Races: RSA (car #18)

BOBBY UNSER (USA; AGE: 34) 0 PTS

BRM P138 V12
Owen Racing Organisation
Races: USA (car #9)

ROBIN WIDDOWS (GBR; AGE: 26) 0 PTS

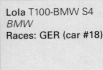

Cooper T86B-BRM V12
Cooper Car Co
Races: GBR (car #16)

1968

CHAMPIONSHIP CAR-BY-CAR

GRAND PRIX WINNERS 1968

	RACE (CIRCUIT)	WINNER (CAR)
RSA	SOUTH AFRICAN GRAND PRIX (KYALAMI)	JIM CLARK (LOTUS 49-FORD V8)
ESP	SPANISH GRAND PRIX (JARAMA)	GRAHAM HILL (LOTUS 49-FORD V8)
MON	MONACO GRAND PRIX (MONTE CARLO)	GRAHAM HILL (LOTUS 49-FORD V8)
BEL	BELGIAN GRAND PRIX (SPA-FRANCORCHAMPS)	BRUCE McLAREN (McLAREN M7A-FORD V8)
NED	DUTCH GRAND PRIX (ZANDVOORT)	JACKIE STEWART (MATRA MS10-FORD V8)
FRA	FRENCH GRAND PRIX (ROUEN-LES-ESSARTS)	JACKY ICKX (FERRARI 312 V12)
GBR	BRITISH GRAND PRIX (BRANDS HATCH)	JO SIFFERT (LOTUS 49-FORD V8)
GER	GERMAN GRAND PRIX (NÜRBURGRING)	JACKIE STEWART (MATRA MS10-FORD V8)
ITA	ITALIAN GRAND PRIX (MONZA)	DENNY HULME (McLAREN M7A-FORD V8)
CAN	CANADIAN GRAND PRIX (ST JOVITE)	DENNY HULME (McLAREN M7A-FORD V8)
USA	UNITED STATES GRAND PRIX (WATKINS GLEN)	JACKIE STEWART (MATRA MS10-FORD V8)
MEX	MEXICAN GRAND PRIX (MEXICO CITY)	GRAHAM HILL (LOTUS 49-FORD V8)

JACKY ICKX

1969

PLAIN SAILING FOR STEWART

Above
Walking tall: Stewart kicked his season off in style with victory at Kyalami. F1's tall, spindly wings lasted for just one more grand prix: dramatic structural failures at the next race in Spain led to their banishment

Left
Forest jump: Hill gets airborne at the Nürburgring, where he picked up one of only four points finishes during a low-key campaign

Right
Chequered past: Rindt had been threatening to win a GP for sometime – and everything finally held together for Rindt at Watkins Glen, the penultimate race of the season

TWEED

Jackie Stewart, Ken Tyrrell and Matra had a clean run through the season and the previous year's niggling problems were forgotten as the Scot swept to the world title – a first for all three members of the partnership.

In terms of pace, Jochen Rindt (Lotus) was Stewart's only rival. The Austrian's car proved repeatedly frail, however, and it was only in the penultimate race of the season that it held together to give Rindt his first grand prix win. His success was marred by an unfortunate accident that befell team-mate Graham Hill, who suffered serious leg injuries after being thrown from his car when it somersaulted. Hill had scored an unprecedented fifth Monaco victory earlier in the year but had an otherwise barren campaign and at no stage looked likely to retain his championship crown.

Hill and Rindt suffered enormous, near-identical accidents during the Spanish GP when the stalks supporting their high-downforce wings snapped as they crested a rise on the Montjuich Park track. In both instances their cars became airborne before smashing hard into the barriers. Hill climbed out unhurt while Rindt was fortunate to get away with a broken nose. It had been a lucky escape and the sport's governing body decided it was time to act. At the next race it decreed that wings were banned.

A subsequent compromise was reached: teams were allowed to continue using wings, but no longer could they be mounted directly to the suspension and their size and height were drastically restricted.

Jacky Ickx (Brabham) was a distant runner-up in the title race, although he defeated Stewart fair and square at the challenging Nürburgring. Ferrari, the team that Ickx left at the end of the previous season, fell into disarray and lead driver Chris Amon had a dispiriting year. The obvious promise of the previous two seasons was conspicuous by its absence.

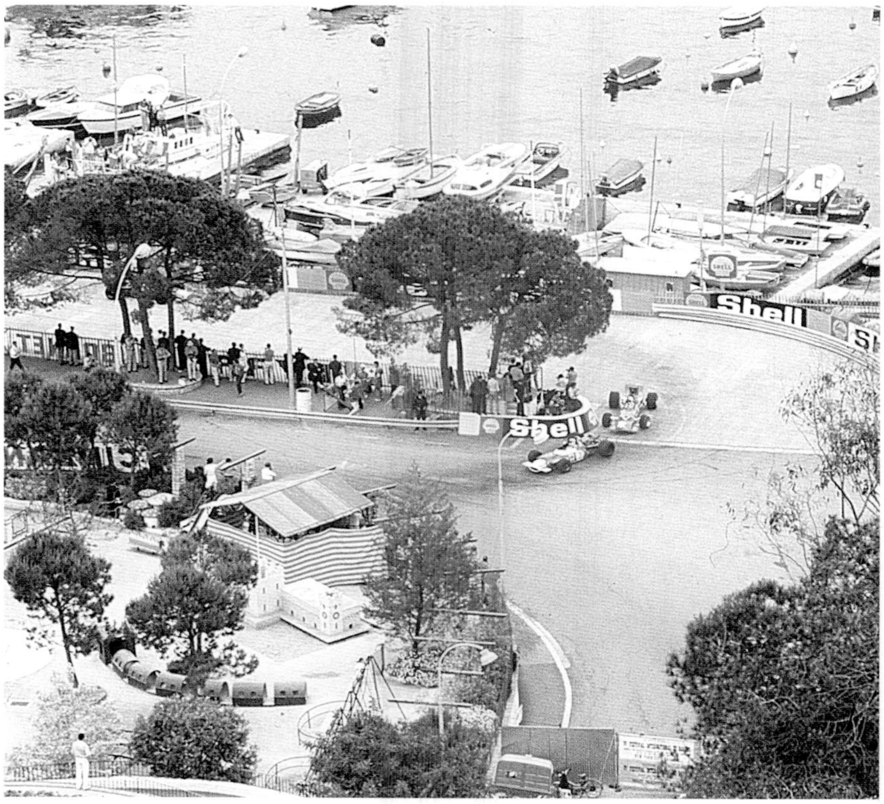

Top left
Wing driven things: McLaren holds off Amon and Siffert during the early stages of the South African GP

Top right
Ickx of the best: Brabham's new signing was second in the title race, albeit miles behind Stewart. Here he confers with designer Ron Tauranac in Canada, where he scored his second win of the campaign

Above
Monte's flying circus: Stewart and Amon streaked away in the early stages of the Monaco GP, but both dropped out and handed the wily Graham Hill his fifth win around the Mediterranean-fringed streets

JACKIE STEWART – WORLD CHAMPION 1969, 1971 & 1973

1969

CHAMPIONSHIP CAR-BY-CAR

1ST JACKIE STEWART (GBR; AGE: 30) 63 pts

Matra MS10-Ford V8
Matra International
Races: RSA (car #7)

JACKIE STEWART (CONTD)

Matra MS80-Ford V8
Matra International
Races: ESP; MON (both car #7); NED (#4); FRA (#2); GBR (#3); GER (#7); ITA (#20); CAN (#17); USA; MEX (both #3)

2ND JACKY ICKX (BEL; AGE: 24) 37 PTS

Brabham BT26-Ford V8
Motor Racing Developments
Races: RSA (car #15); ESP (#4); MON (#6); NED (#12); FRA (#11); GBR (#7); GER (#6); ITA (#26); CAN (#11); USA; MEX (both #7)

3RD BRUCE McLAREN (NZL; AGE: 31) 26 PTS

McLaren M7A-Ford V8
Bruce McLaren Motor Racing
Races: RSA (car #6)

BRUCE McLAREN (CONTD)

McLaren M7C-Ford V8
Bruce McLaren Motor Racing
Races: ESP (car #6); MON (#4); NED (#6); FRA (#5); GBR (#6); GER (#10); ITA (#18); CAN (#4)

4TH JOCHEN RINDT (AUT; AGE: 27) 22 PTS

Lotus 49B-Ford V8
Gold Leaf Team Lotus
Races: RSA; ESP; NED (all car #2); FRA (#15); GBR; GER (both #2); ITA (#4); CAN; USA; MEX (all #2)

5TH JEAN-PIERRE BELTOISE (FRA; AGE: 32) 21 PTS

Matra MS10-Ford V8
Matra International
Races: RSA (car #8)

JEAN-PIERRE BELTOISE (CONTD)

Matra MS80-Ford V8
Matra International
Races: ESP; MON (both car #8); NED (#5); FRA (#7); GER (#8); ITA (#18); CAN (#18); USA; MEX (both #4)

JEAN-PIERRE BELTOISE (CONTD)

Matra MS84-Ford V8
Matra International
Races: GBR (car #4)

6TH DENNY HULME (NZL; AGE: 33) 20 PTS

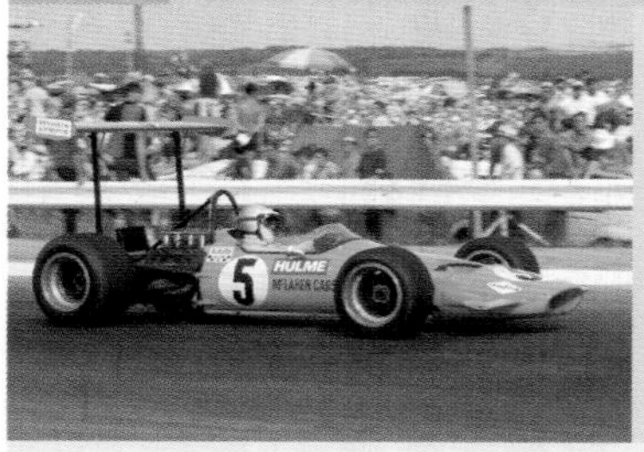

McLaren M7A-Ford V8
Bruce McLaren Motor Racing
Races: RSA; ESP (both car #5); MON (#3); NED (#7); FRA (#4); GBR (#5); GER (#9); ITA (#16); CAN; USA; MEX (all #5)

7TH GRAHAM HILL (GBR; AGE: 40) 19 PTS

Lotus 49B-Ford V8
Gold Leaf Team Lotus
Races: RSA; ESP; MON; NED; FRA; GBR; GER (all car #1); ITA (#2); CAN; USA (both #1)

8TH PIERS COURAGE (GBR; AGE: 27) 16 PTS

Brabham BT26-Ford V8
Frank Williams Racing Cars
Races: ESP (car #11); MON; NED (both #16); FRA (#9); GBR (#16); GER (#17); ITA (#32); CAN (#21); USA; MEX (both #18)

9TH JO SIFFERT (SUI; AGE: 33) 15 PTS

Lotus 49B-Ford V8
Rob Walker/Jack Durlacher Racing
Races: RSA (car #4); ESP (#10); MON (#9); NED (#10); FRA (#3); GBR (#10); GER (#11); ITA (#30); CAN (#9); USA; MEX (both #10)

10TH JACK BRABHAM (AUS; AGE: 43) 14 PTS

Brabham BT26-Ford V8
Motor Racing Developments
Races: RSA (car #14); ESP (#3); MON (#5); NED (#11); ITA (#28); CAN (#12); USA; MEX (both #8)

11TH JOHN SURTEES (GBR; AGE: 35) 6 PTS

BRM P138 V12
Owen Racing Organisation
Races: RSA (car #10); ESP; MON; NED (all #14)

1969

CHAMPIONSHIP CAR-BY-CAR

JOHN SURTEES (CONTD)

BRM P139 V12
Owen Racing Organisation
Races: GBR; ITA; CAN; USA; MEX (all car #14)

12TH CHRIS AMON (NZL; AGE: 25) 4 PTS

Ferrari 312 V12
Scuderia Ferrari
Races: RSA (car #9); ESP (#15); MON (#11); NED (#8); FRA (#6); GBR (#11)

13TH= RICHARD ATTWOOD (GBR; AGE: 29) 3 PTS

Lotus 49-Ford V8
Gold Leaf Team Lotus
Races: MON (car #2)

RICHARD ATTWOOD (CONTD)

Brabham BT30-Cosworth S4
Frank Williams Racing Cars
Races: GER (car #29)

13TH= VIC ELFORD (GBR; AGE: 34) 3 PTS

Cooper T86B-Maserati V12
Colin Crabbe-Antique Automobiles
Races: MON (car #12)

VIC ELFORD (CONTD)

McLaren M7A/M7B-Ford V8
Colin Crabbe-Antique Automobiles
Races: NED (car #18); FRA (#10); GBR (#19); GER (#12)

13TH= PEDRO RODRIGUEZ (MEX; AGE: 29) 3 PTS

BRM P126 V12
Reg Parnell Racing
Races: RSA (car #12); ESP (#9); MON (#10)

PEDRO RODRIGUEZ (CONTD)

Ferrari 312 V12
Scuderia Ferrari/North American Racing Team
Races: GBR (car #12); ITA (#10); CAN (#6); USA; MEX (both #12)

16TH= SILVIO MOSER (SUI; AGE: 28) 1 PT

Brabham BT24-Ford V8
Silvio Moser Racing Team
Races: MON; NED (both car #17); FRA (#12); ITA (#36); CAN (#20); USA; MEX (both #19)

16TH= JACKIE OLIVER (GBR; AGE: 26) 1 PT

BRM P133 V12
Owen Racing Organisation
Races: RSA (car #11); ESP (#12); MON; NED; GBR (all #15)

JACKIE OLIVER (CONTD)

BRM P138 V12
Owen Racing Organisation
Races: GER (car #15)

JACKIE OLIVER (CONTD)

BRM P139 V12
Owen Racing Organisation
Races: ITA (car #12); CAN; USA; MEX (all #15)

16TH= JOHNNY SERVOZ-GAVIN (FRA; AGE: 27) 1 PT

Matra MS7-Cosworth S4
Matra International
Races: GER (car #27)

JOHNNY SERVOZ-GAVIN (CONTD)

Matra MS84-Ford V8
Matra International
Races: CAN (car #19); USA; MEX (both #16)

KURT AHRENS JR (GER; AGE: 29) 0 PTS

Brabham BT30-Cosworth S4
Ahrens Racing Team
Races: GER (car #20)

1969

CHAMPIONSHIP CAR-BY-CAR

MARIO ANDRETTI (USA; AGE: 29) 0 PTS

Lotus 49B-Ford V8
Gold Leaf Team Lotus
Races: RSA (car #3)

MARIO ANDRETTI (CONTD)

Lotus 63-Ford V8
Gold Leaf Team Lotus
Races: GER (car #3); USA (#9)

DEREK BELL (GBR; AGE: 27) 0 PTS

McLaren M9A-Ford V8
Bruce McLaren Motor Racing
Races: GBR (car #20)

JO BONNIER (SWE; AGE: 39) 0 PTS

Lotus 63-Ford V8
Écurie Bonnier
Races: GBR (car #18)

JO BONNIER (CONTD)

Lotus 49B-Ford V8
Écurie Bonnier
Races: GER (car #16)

BILL BRACK (CAN; AGE: 33) 0 PTS

BRM P138 V12
Owen Racing Organisation
Races: CAN (car #16)

FRANÇOIS CEVERT (FRA; AGE: 25) 0 PTS

Tecno 306-Cosworth S4
Tecno Racing
Races: GER (car #28)

JOHN CORDTS (CAN; AGE: 34) 0 PTS

Brabham BT23B-Ford S4
Paul Seitz
Races: CAN (car #26)

GEORGE EATON (CAN; AGE: 23) 0 PTS

BRM P138 V12
Owen Racing Organisation
Races: USA (car #22)

GEORGE EATON (CONTD)

BRM P139 V12
Owen Racing Organisation
Races: MEX (car #22)

PIET DE KLERK (RSA; AGE: 33) 0 PTS

Brabham BT20-Repco V8
Jack Holme
Races: RSA (car #19)

JOHN LOVE (RSR; AGE: 44) 0 PTS

Lotus 49-Ford V8
Team Gunston
Races: RSA (car #16)

PETE LOVELY (USA; AGE: 43) 0 PTS

Lotus 49B-Ford V8
Pete Lovely Volkswagen
Races: CAN (car #25); USA; MEX (both #21)

JOHN MILES (GBR; AGE: 26) 0 PTS

Lotus 63-Ford V8
Gold Leaf Team Lotus
Races: FRA (car #14); GBR (#9); ITA (#6); CAN (#3); MEX (#9)

AL PEASE (CAN; AGE: 47) 0 PTS

Eagle AAR101-Climax S4
John Maryon
Races: CAN (car #69)

1969

CHAMPIONSHIP CAR-BY-CAR

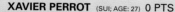

XAVIER PERROT (SUI; AGE: 27) 0 PTS

Brabham BT23C-Cosworth S4
Squadra Tartaruga
Races: GER (car #30)

HENRI PESCAROLO (FRA; AGE: 26) 0 PTS

Matra MS7-Cosworth S4
Matra Sports
Races: GER (car #26)

BASIL VAN ROOYEN (RSA; AGE: 29) 0 PTS

McLaren M7A-Ford V8
Team Lawson
Races: RSA (car #18)

ROLF STOMMELEN (GER; AGE: 26) 0 PTS

Lotus 59B-Cosworth S4
Roy Winkelmann Racing
Races: GER (car #22)

SAM TINGLE (RSR; AGE: 47) 0 PTS

Brabham BT24-Repco V8
Team Gunston
Races: RSA (car #17)

PETER WESTBURY (GBR; AGE: 31) 0 PTS

Brabham BT30-Cosworth S4
Felday Engineering
Races: GER (car #31)

GRAND PRIX WINNERS 1969

	RACE (CIRCUIT)	WINNER (CAR)
RSA	SOUTH AFRICAN GRAND PRIX (KYALAMI)	JACKIE STEWART (MATRA MS10-FORD V8)
ESP	SPANISH GRAND PRIX (MONTJUICH PARK)	JACKIE STEWART (MATRA MS80-FORD V8)
MON	MONACO GRAND PRIX (MONTE CARLO)	GRAHAM HILL (LOTUS 49B-FORD V8)
NED	DUTCH GRAND PRIX (ZANDVOORT)	JACKIE STEWART (MATRA MS80-FORD V8)
FRA	FRENCH GRAND PRIX (CLERMONT-FERRAND)	JACKIE STEWART (MATRA MS80-FORD V8)
GBR	BRITISH GRAND PRIX (SILVERSTONE)	JACKIE STEWART (MATRA MS80-FORD V8)
GER	GERMAN GRAND PRIX (NÜRBURGRING)	JACKY ICKX (BRABHAM BT26-FORD V8)
ITA	ITALIAN GRAND PRIX (MONZA)	JACKIE STEWART (MATRA MS80-FORD V8)
CAN	CANADIAN GRAND PRIX (MOSPORT PARK)	JACKY ICKX (BRABHAM BT26-FORD V8)
USA	UNITED STATES GRAND PRIX (WATKINS GLEN)	JOCHEN RINDT (LOTUS 49B-FORD V8)
MEX	MEXICAN GRAND PRIX (MEXICO CITY)	DENNY HULME (McLAREN M7A-FORD V8)

Ronnie
Peterson

1970s

1970

RINDT'S POSTHUMOUS TITLE – THE LEGACY OF A CRUEL SEASON

Left
Final flourish: Rindt finished five of the nine races he started – and won every time. At Hockenheim he fought an epic battle with Ickx's Ferrari and crossed the line just 0.7s to the good

Above
Quick off the blocks: originally drafted into the Lotus team to drive a third car on an occasional basis, Emerson Fittipaldi responded superbly when he was given a more prominent role in the wake of Rindt's death. He won at Watkins Glen and made sure the title went to his late team-mate. It was only his fifth GP start

Right
A worthy champion: Rindt prepares to practise at Monza, where he would have started his 61st grand prix. He scored just six victories at this level – a tally that didn't reflect his gift

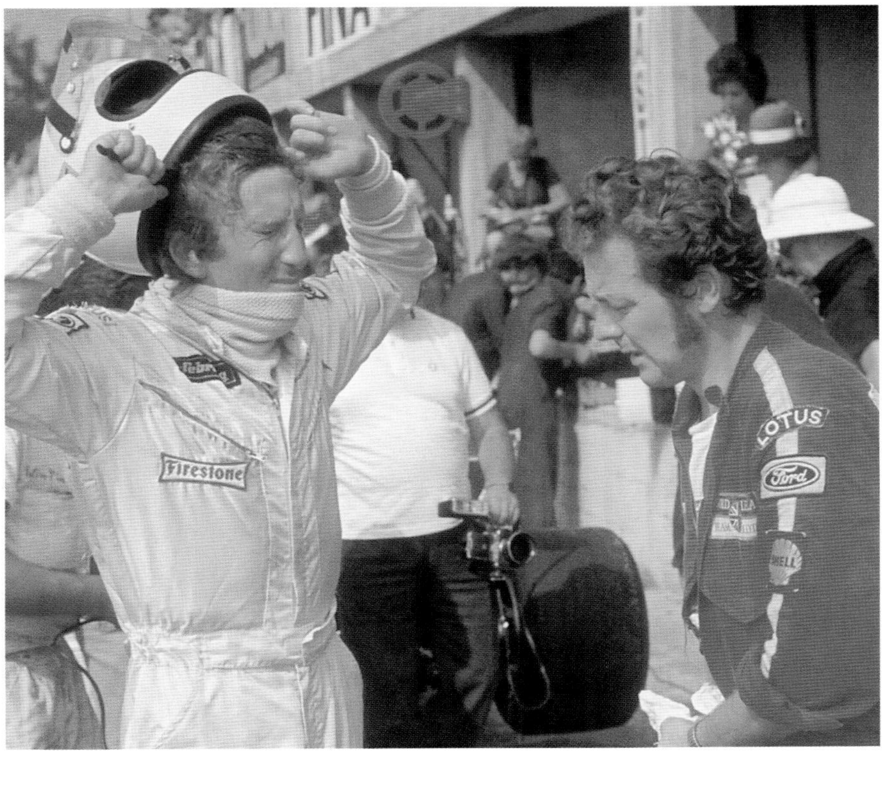

In one of the sport's most tragic seasons, Lotus driver Jochen Rindt's story was perhaps the most poignant. The Austrian all but secured the world title after winning the German Grand Prix at Hockenheim, his fifth victory of the season, but he never got to celebrate his accomplishment. He was killed during practice for the Italian GP and, in the four remaining races, no one managed to overhaul his points tally. He became the sport's first posthumous world champion. Piers Courage and Bruce McLaren were also killed during the season, adding yet greater urgency to a Jackie Stewart-led safety crusade.

Stewart's competitive circumstances had taken a dive before the season started, because chassis builder Matra ended its association with the Tyrrell team – despite their successful world title conquest the previous year. Matra was now owned by Chrysler and the prospect of using a Ford engine, which Stewart and Tyrrell insisted was vital for success, was politically unacceptable. Instead, Tyrrell opted to run with March – a new Formula One manufacturer – but although Stewart won the Spanish GP the car was not up to the task of sustaining a championship challenge.

At the end of the year Tyrrell unveiled his secret weapon – an eponymous new car. Stewart used it to dominate in both America and Mexico before breaking down, but its potential was clear. His retirement in America allowed Lotus rookie Emerson Fittipaldi to win what was only his fifth grand prix. Fittingly, this sealed his late team-mate Rindt's world title.

Jack Brabham won the year's opening race in South Africa and, at 44, had a very competitive final season before retiring from the cockpit and moving back to Australia. Jacky Ickx (Ferrari) won in Canada, Austria and Mexico while Clay Regazzoni triumphed in Italy. The Scuderia's cars were often the fastest around and Ickx finished second in the championship. He and Stewart were co-favourites for 1971.

Below
Spa trek: McLaren and Andretti pass the aftermath of a fiery collision between Ickx and Oliver during the Spanish GP. Neither driver was badly hurt in the first-lap incident, but their cars burned for much of the race because some of the marshals had apparently never seen an extinguisher before

Above
End of an era: from right to left, Stewart, Rindt and Amon lead away at the start of the final grand prix to take place on the full, 8.76-mile Ardennes circuit. The track was increasingly regarded as too fast to be made safe. Stewart averaged 151.638mph to annexe pole – and yes he was driving a March 701

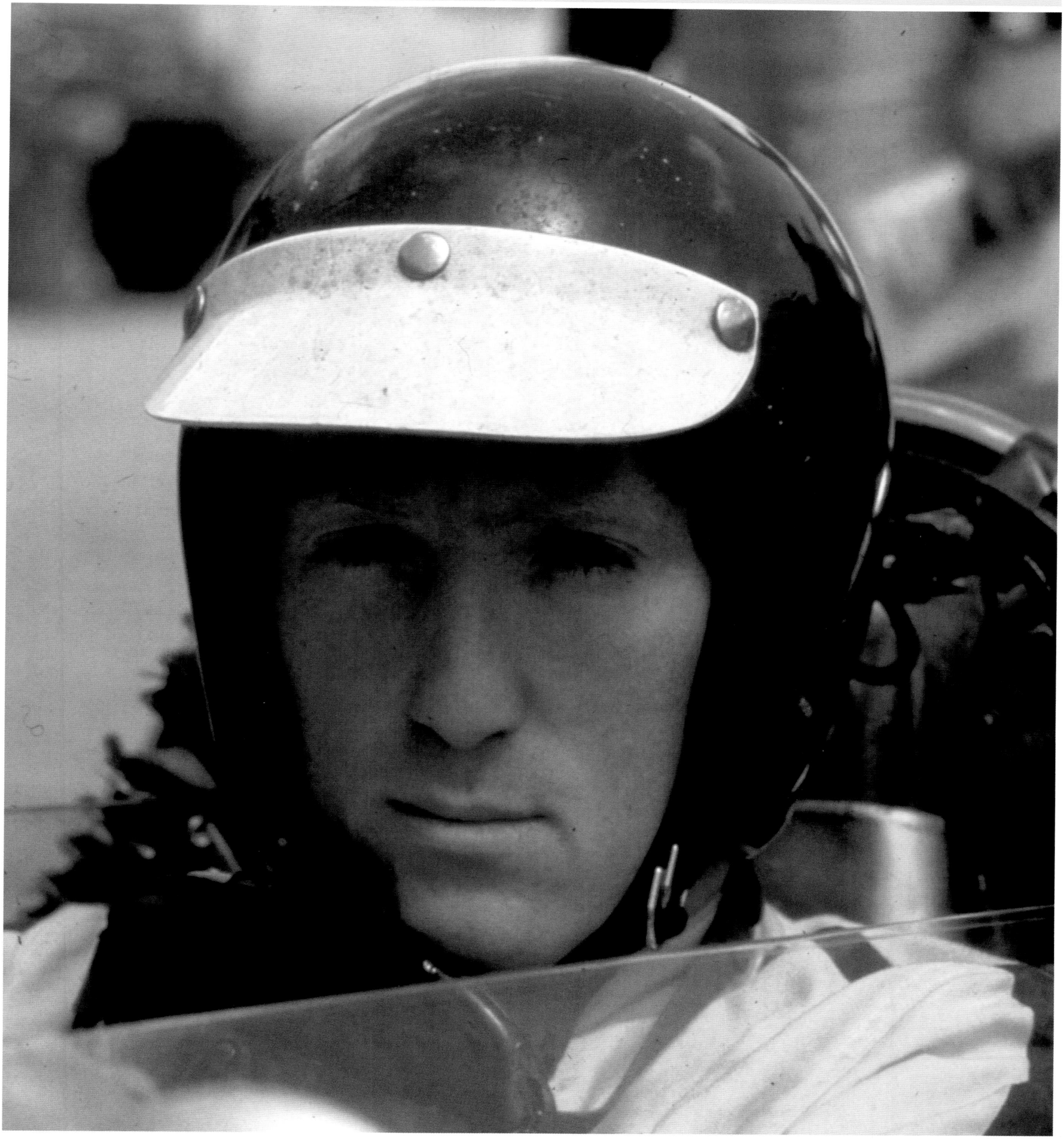

JOCHEN RINDT – WORLD CHAMPION 1970

1970

CHAMPIONSHIP CAR-BY-CAR

1ST JOCHEN RINDT (AUT; AGE: 28) 45 PTS

Lotus 49C-Ford V8
Gold Leaf Team Lotus
Races: RSA (car #9); MON (#3); BEL (#20)

JOCHEN RINDT (CONTD)

Lotus 72-Ford V8
Gold Leaf Team Lotus
Races: ESP (car #3); NED (#10); FRA (#6); GBR (#5); GER (#2); AUT (#6)

2ND JACKY ICKX (BEL; AGE: 25) 40 PTS

Ferrari 312B F12
Scuderia Ferrari
Races: RSA (car #17); ESP (#2); MON (#26); BEL (#27); NED (#25); FRA (#10); GBR (#3); GER (#10); AUT (#12); ITA (#2); CAN (#18); USA; MEX (both #3)

3RD CLAY REGAZZONI (SUI; AGE: 31) 33 PTS

Ferrari 312B F12
Scuderia Ferrari
Races: NED (car #26); GBR (#4); GER (#15); AUT (#27); ITA (#4); CAN (#19); USA; MEX (both #4)

4TH DENNY HULME (NZL; AGE: 34) 27 PTS

McLaren M14A-Ford V8
Bruce McLaren Motor Racing
Races: RSA (car #6); ESP (#5); MON (#11); GER (#4); AUT (#21); ITA (#30); CAN (#5); USA; MEX (both #8)

DENNY HULME (CONTD)

McLaren M14D-Ford V8
Bruce McLaren Motor Racing
Races: FRA (car #19); GBR (#9)

5TH= JACK BRABHAM (AUS; AGE: 44) 25 PTS

Brabham BT33-Ford V8
Motor Racing Developments
Races: RSA (car #12); ESP (#7); MON (#5); BEL; NED (both #18); FRA (#23); GBR (#17); GER (#3); AUT (#10); ITA (#44); CAN (#11); USA; MEX (both #15)

5TH= JACKIE STEWART (GBR; AGE: 31) 25 PTS

March 701-Ford V8
Tyrrell Racing Organisation
Races: RSA; ESP (both car #1); MON (#21); BEL (#11); NED (#5); FRA; GBR; GER; AUT (all #1); ITA (#18)

JACKIE STEWART (CONTD)

Tyrrell 001-Ford V8
Tyrrell Racing Organisation
Races: CAN (car #3); USA; MEX (both #1)

7TH= CHRIS AMON (NZL; AGE: 27) 23 PTS

March 701-Ford V8
March Engineering
Races: RSA (car #15); ESP (#9); MON (#28); BEL (#10); NED (#8); FRA (#14); GBR (#16); GER (#5); AUT (#4); ITA (#48); CAN (#20); USA; MEX (both #12)

7TH= PEDRO RODRIGUEZ (MEX; AGE: 30) 23 PTS

BRM P153 V12
Yardley Team BRM
Races: RSA (car #20); ESP (#10); MON (#17); BEL; NED (both #1); FRA (#3); GBR (#22); GER (#6); AUT (#17); ITA (#10); CAN (#14); USA; MEX (both #19)

9TH JEAN-PIERRE BELTOISE (FRA; AGE: 33) 16 PTS

Matra-Simca MS120 V12
Équipe Matra Elf
Races: RSA (car #3); ESP (#4); MON (#8); BEL (#25); NED (#23); FRA (#21); GBR (#7); GER (#8); AUT (#19); ITA (#40); CAN (#23); USA; MEX (both #6)

10TH EMERSON FITTIPALDI (BRA; AGE: 23) 12 PTS

Lotus 49C-Ford V8
Gold Leaf Team Lotus
Races: GBR (car #28); GER (#17); AUT (#8)

EMERSON FITTIPALDI (CONTD)

Lotus 72-Ford V8
Gold Leaf Team Lotus
Races: USA; MEX (both car #24)

11TH ROLF STOMMELEN (GER; AGE: 27) 10 PTS

Brabham BT33-Ford V8
Motor Racing Developments
Races: RSA (car #14); ESP (#24); BEL (#19); FRA (#22); GER (#21); AUT (#11); ITA (#46); CAN (#12); USA; MEX (both #16)

1970

CHAMPIONSHIP CAR-BY-CAR

12TH HENRI PESCAROLO (FRA; AGE: 27) 8 PTS

Matra-Simca MS120 V12
Équipe Matra Elf
Races: RSA (car #4); ESP (#22); MON (#9); BEL (#26); NED (#24); FRA (#20); GBR (#8); GER (#14); AUT (#20); ITA (#42); CAN (#24); USA; MEX (both #7)

13TH GRAHAM HILL (GBR; AGE: 41) 7 PTS

Lotus 49C-Ford V8
Brooke Bond Oxo Racing Team/Rob Walker
Races: RSA (car #11); ESP (#6); MON (#1); BEL (#23); NED (#15); FRA (#8); GBR (#14); GER (#9)

GRAHAM HILL (CONTD)

Lotus 72-Ford V8
Brooke Bond Oxo Racing Team/Rob Walker
Races: CAN (car #9); USA; MEX (both #14)

14TH BRUCE McLAREN (NZL; AGE: 32) 6 PTS

McLaren M14A-Ford V8
Bruce McLaren Motor Racing
Races: RSA (car #5); ESP (#11); MON (#12)

15TH= MARIO ANDRETTI (USA; AGE: 30) 4 PTS

March 701-Ford V8
STP Corporation
Races: RSA (car #8); ESP (#18); GBR (#26); GER (#11); AUT (#5)

15TH= REINE WISELL (SWE; AGE: 29) 4 PTS

Lotus 72-Ford V8
Gold Leaf Team Lotus
Races: USA; MEX (both car #23)

17TH= IGNAZIO GIUNTI (ITA; AGE: 28) 3 PTS

Ferrari 312B F12
Scuderia Ferrari
Races: BEL (car #28); FRA (#11); AUT (#14); ITA (#6)

17TH= JOHN SURTEES (GBR; AGE: 36) 3 PTS

McLaren M7C-Ford V8
Team Surtees
Races: RSA (car #7); ESP (#8); MON (#14); NED (#16)

JOHN SURTEES (CONTD)

Surtees TS7-Ford V8
Team Surtees
Races: GBR (car #20); GER (#7); AUT (#15); ITA (#14); CAN (#4); USA; MEX (both #17)

19TH= JOHN MILES (GBR; AGE: 27) 2 PTS

Lotus 49C-Ford V8
Gold Leaf Team Lotus
Races: RSA (car #10)

JOHN MILES (CONTD)

Lotus 72-Ford V8
Gold Leaf Team Lotus
Races: BEL (car #21); NED (#12); FRA (#7); GBR (#6); GER (#16); AUT (#7)

19TH= JACKIE OLIVER (GBR; AGE: 27) 2 PTS

BRM P153 V12
Yardley Team BRM
Races: RSA (car #19); ESP (#15); MON (#16); BEL; NED (both #2); FRA (#5); GBR (#23); GER (#18); AUT (#16); ITA (#8); CAN (#15); USA; MEX (both #20)

19TH= JOHNNY SERVOZ-GAVIN (FRA; AGE: 28) 2 PTS

March 701-Ford V8
Tyrrell Racing Organisation
Races: RSA (car #2); ESP (#16)

22ND DEREK BELL (GBR; AGE: 28) 1 PT

Brabham BT26-Ford V8
Team Wheatcroft Racing
Races: BEL (car #8)

DEREK BELL (CONTD)

Surtees TS7-Ford V8
Team Surtees
Races: USA (car #18)

1970

CHAMPIONSHIP CAR-BY-CAR

22ND FRANÇOIS CEVERT (FRA; AGE: 26) 1 PT

March 701-Ford V8
Tyrrell Racing Organisation
Races: NED (car #6); FRA; GBR (both #2); GER (#23); AUT (#2); ITA (#20); CAN; USA; MEX (all #2)

22ND PETER GETHIN (GBR; AGE: 30) 1 PT

McLaren M14A-Ford V8
Bruce McLaren Motor Racing
Races: NED (car #20); GER (#24); AUT (#23); ITA (#32); CAN (#6); USA; MEX (both #9)

22ND DAN GURNEY (USA; AGE: 39) 1 PT

McLaren M14A-Ford V8
Bruce McLaren Motor Racing
Races: NED (car #32); FRA (#17); GBR (#10)

ANDREA DE ADAMICH (ITA; AGE: 28) 0 PTS

McLaren M7D-Alfa Romeo V8
Bruce McLaren Motor Racing
Races: FRA (car #16)

ANDREA DE ADAMICH (CONTD)

McLaren M14D-Alfa Romeo V8
Bruce McLaren Motor Racing
Races: AUT (car #22); ITA (#34); CAN (#8)

JO BONNIER (SWE; AGE: 40) 0 PTS

McLaren M7C-Ford V8
Écurie Bonnier
Races: USA (car #27)

DAVE CHARLTON (RSA; AGE: 33) 0 PTS

Lotus 49C-Ford V8
Scuderia Scribante
Races: RSA (car #25)

PIERS COURAGE (GBR; AGE: 28) 0 PTS

De Tomaso 505/38-Ford V8
Frank Williams Racing Cars
Races: RSA (car #22); MON (#24); BEL (#7); NED (#4)

GEORGE EATON (CAN; AGE: 24) 0 PTS

BRM P139 V12
Yardley Team BRM
Races: RSA (car #21)

GEORGE EATON (CONTD)

BRM P153 V12
Yardley Team BRM
Races: NED (car #3); FRA (#4); GBR (#24); AUT (#18); ITA (#12); CAN (#16); USA (#21)

GUS HUTCHISON (USA; AGE: 33) 0 PTS

Brabham BT26-Ford V8
Driver
Races: USA (car #31)

PIET DE KLERK (RSA; AGE: 34) 0 PTS

Brabham BT26-Ford V8
Team Gunston
Races: RSA (car #24)

JOHN LOVE (RSR; AGE: 45) 0 PTS

Lotus 49-Ford V8
Team Gunston
Races: RSA (car #23)

PETE LOVELY (USA; AGE: 44) 0 PTS

Lotus 49B-Ford V8
Pete Lovely Volkswagen
Races: GBR (car #29)

PICTURED DURING FRA PRACTICE

SILVIO MOSER (SUI; AGE: 29) 0 PTS

Bellasi F170-Ford V8
Silvio Moser Racing Team
Races: AUT (car #24)

PICTURED DURING FRA PRACTICE

1970

CHAMPIONSHIP CAR-BY-CAR

RONNIE PETERSON (SWE; AGE: 26) 0 PTS

March 701-Ford V8
Antique Automobiles Racing Team
Races: MON (car #23); BEL (#14); NED (#22); FRA (#18); GBR (#27); GER (#22); ITA (#52); CAN (#26); USA (#29)

TIM SCHENKEN (AUS; AGE: 27) 0 PTS

De Tomaso 505/38-Ford V8
Frank Williams Racing Cars
Races: AUT (car #26); ITA (#54); CAN (#10); USA (#30)

JO SIFFERT (SUI; AGE: 34) 0 PTS

March 701-Ford V8
March Engineering
Races: RSA (car #16); MON (#19); BEL; NED (both #9); FRA (#12); GBR (#15); GER (#12); AUT (#3); ITA (#50); CAN (#21); USA; MEX (both #11)

GRAND PRIX WINNERS 1970

	RACE (CIRCUIT)	**WINNER** (CAR)
RSA	SOUTH AFRICAN GRAND PRIX (KYALAMI)	JACK BRABHAM (BRABHAM BT33-FORD V8)
ESP	SPANISH GRAND PRIX (JARAMA)	JACKIE STEWART (MARCH 701-FORD V8)
MON	MONACO GRAND PRIX (MONTE CARLO)	JOCHEN RINDT (LOTUS 49C-FORD V8)
BEL	BELGIAN GRAND PRIX (SPA-FRANCORCHAMPS)	PEDRO RODRIGUEZ (BRM P153 V12)
NED	DUTCH GRAND PRIX (ZANDVOORT)	JOCHEN RINDT (LOTUS 72-FORD V8)
FRA	FRENCH GRAND PRIX (CLERMONT-FERRAND)	JOCHEN RINDT (LOTUS 72-FORD V8)
GBR	BRITISH GRAND PRIX (BRANDS HATCH)	JOCHEN RINDT (LOTUS 72-FORD V8)
GER	GERMAN GRAND PRIX (HOCKENHEIM)	JOCHEN RINDT (LOTUS 72-FORD V8)
AUT	AUSTRIAN GRAND PRIX (ÖSTERREICHRING)	JACKY ICKX (FERRARI 312B F12)
ITA	ITALIAN GRAND PRIX (MONZA)	CLAY REGAZZONI (FERRARI 312B F12)
CAN	CANADIAN GRAND PRIX (ST JOVITE)	JACKY ICKX (FERRARI 312B F12)
USA	UNITED STATES GRAND PRIX (WATKINS GLEN)	EMERSON FITTIPALDI (LOTUS 72-FORD V8)
MEX	MEXICAN GRAND PRIX (MEXICO CITY)	JACKY ICKX (FERRARI 312B F12)

1971

STEWART IN A LEAGUE OF HIS OWN

Far right
No stopping him – literally: Stewart, by now well able to afford a yacht like the one in the background, stroked to victory in Monaco. None of his rivals had a clue that his rear brakes had been disconnected through necessity

Above
Nice trophy, rubbish garland: Regazzoni (left) and Cevert join Stewart on the podium in Germany, after the fifth of the Scot's six wins

Right
British flag and name, Swedish passport: Ronnie Peterson underlined his credentials as a star of the future

The new Tyrrell marque had hinted at its potential during the final two races of 1970 – and this was well and truly fulfilled in '71, when Jackie Stewart enjoyed one of the most dominant seasons in the sport's history.

The Scot won six of the 11 championship races, gliding from one immaculate performance to another in his blue, Ford-powered chassis. At Monaco he even managed to win with substantially reduced stopping power. It was discovered on the warm-up lap that there was a problem with the brake balance bar and the only short-term solution in the time available was to disconnect the system at the rear. He led from start to finish and none of his rivals knew there was even a hint of a problem.

Of the five races not won by Stewart, one was taken by his junior team-mate François Cevert, two by the Ferraris of Mario Andretti and Jacky Ickx and two by the BRMs of Jo Siffert and Peter Gethin. The latter triumphed at Monza in the final year before chicanes were installed to make the track slower. His winning average was 150.755mph – and at the time of writing this remained the fastest grand prix of all time.

The Ferraris didn't show their expected form because the new 312B2 proved very difficult to balance. BRM had its most competitive season for a while, but this was a campaign blighted by tragedy: Siffert was killed in an end-of-season non-championship race at Brands Hatch while team-mate Pedro Rodriguez had perished in a sports car event earlier in the year.

Although missing from the list of winners, March driver Ronnie Peterson finished as distant championship runner-up in his first full F1 season. The quiet Swede often proved to be best of the rest behind Stewart and was clearly a driver of enormous potential.

Below
Statistical nirvana: Peter Gethin wins the fastest – and closest – grand prix in history. The BRM driver averaged 150.755mph at Monza and 0.18s covered the top four cars

Above
Breakthrough: in his first F1 race for Ferrari, Andretti leads Rodriguez and Siffert at Kyalami. The American scored his maiden grand prix win at only the 10th attempt

1971

CHAMPIONSHIP CAR-BY-CAR

1ST JACKIE STEWART (GBR; AGE: 32) 62 PTS

Tyrrell 001-Ford V8
Elf Team Tyrrell
Races: RSA (car #9)

JACKIE STEWART (CONTD)

Tyrrell 003-Ford V8
Elf Team Tyrrell
Races: ESP (car #11); MON (#11); NED (#5); FRA (#11); GBR (#12); GER (#2); AUT (#11); ITA (#30); CAN (#11); USA (#8)

2ND RONNIE PETERSON (SWE; AGE: 27) 33 PTS

March 711-Ford V8
STP March Racing Team
Races: RSA (car #7); ESP (#18); MON (#17); NED (#16); GBR (#18); GER (#15); AUT (#17); ITA (#25); CAN (#17); USA (#25)

RONNIE PETERSON (CONTD)

March 711-Alfa Romeo V8
STP March Racing Team
Races: FRA (car #17)

3RD FRANÇOIS CEVERT (FRA; AGE: 27) 26 PTS

Tyrrell 002-Ford V8
Elf Team Tyrrell
Races: RSA (car #10); ESP; MON (both #12); NED (#6); FRA (#12); GBR (#14); GER (#3); AUT (#12); ITA (#2); CAN (#12); USA (#9)

4TH= JACKY ICKX (BEL; AGE: 26) 19 PTS

Ferrari 312B F12
Scuderia Ferrari
Races: RSA (car #4); ESP (#4); ITA (#3); USA (#32)

JACKY ICKX (CONTD)

Ferrari 312B2 F12
Scuderia Ferrari
Races: MON (car #4); NED (#2); FRA; GBR; GER; AUT; CAN (all #4)

4TH= JO SIFFERT (SUI; AGE: 35) 19 PTS

BRM P153 V12
Yardley Team BRM
Races: RSA (car #17)

JO SIFFERT (CONTD)

BRM P160 V12
Yardley Team BRM
Races: ESP (car #15); MON (#14); NED (#9); FRA (#14); GBR (#16); GER (#21); AUT (#14); ITA (#20); CAN; USA (both #14)

6TH EMERSON FITTIPALDI (BRA; AGE: 24) 16 PTS

Lotus 72-Ford V8
Gold Leaf Team Lotus
Races: RSA; ESP (both car #2); MON; FRA; GBR (all #1); GER (#8); AUT; CAN; USA (all #2)

EMERSON FITTIPALDI (CONTD)

Lotus 56B-Pratt & Whitney turbine
World Wide Racing
Races: ITA (car #5)

7TH CLAY REGAZZONI (SUI; AGE: 31) 13 PTS

Ferrari 312B F12
Scuderia Ferrari
Races: RSA; ESP (both car #5)

CLAY REGAZZONI (CONTD)

Ferrari 312B2 F12
Scuderia Ferrari
Races: MON (car #5); NED (#3); FRA; GBR (both #5); GER (#6); AUT (#5); ITA (#4); CAN; USA (both #5)

8TH MARIO ANDRETTI (USA; AGE: 31) 12 PTS

Ferrari 312B F12
Scuderia Ferrari
Races: RSA; ESP (both car #6); NED (#4)

MARIO ANDRETTI (CONTD)

Ferrari 312B2 F12
Scuderia Ferrari
Races: GER (car #5); CAN (#6)

1971

CHAMPIONSHIP CAR-BY-CAR

9TH= CHRIS AMON (NZL; AGE: 28) 9 PTS

Matra-Simca MS120B V12
Équipe Matra Sports
Races: RSA (car #19); ESP; MON; NED; FRA (all #20); GBR (#21); GER (#10); ITA (#12); CAN (#20); USA (#11)

9TH= PETER GETHIN (GBR; AGE: 31) 9 PTS

McLaren M14A-Ford V8
Bruce McLaren Motor Racing
Races: RSA (car #12); ESP; MON (both #10)

PETER GETHIN (CONTD)

McLaren M19A-Ford V8
Bruce McLaren Motor Racing
Races: NED (car #28); FRA; GBR (both #10); GER (#20)

PETER GETHIN (CONTD)

BRM P160 V12
Yardley Team BRM
Races: AUT (car #23); ITA (#18); CAN; USA (both #15)

9TH= DENNY HULME (NZL; AGE: 35) 9 PTS

McLaren M19A-Ford V8
Bruce McLaren Motor Racing
Races: RSA (car #11); ESP; MON (both #9); NED (#26); FRA; GBR (both #9); GER (#18); AUT; CAN (both #9); USA (#7)

9TH= PEDRO RODRIGUEZ (MEX; AGE: 31) 9 PTS

BRM P160 V12
Yardley Team BRM
Races: RSA (car #16); ESP (#14); MON (#15); NED (#8); FRA (#15)

9TH= REINE WISELL (SWE; AGE: 29) 9 PTS

Lotus 72-Ford V8
Gold Leaf Team Lotus
Races: RSA; ESP (both car #3); MON (#2); NED (#14); FRA (#2); GER (#9); AUT; CAN; USA (all #3)

REINE WISELL (CONTD)

Lotus 56B-Pratt & Whitney turbine
Gold Leaf Team Lotus
Races: GBR (car #3)

14TH= HOWDEN GANLEY (NZL; AGE: 29) 5 PTS

BRM P153 V12
Yardley Team BRM
Races: RSA (car #27); ESP (#16); NED (#10); FRA (#16); GBR (#17); GER (#23)

HOWDEN GANLEY (CONTD)

BRM P160 V12
Yardley Team BRM
Races: AUT (car #15); ITA (#19); USA (#16)

14TH= TIM SCHENKEN (AUS; AGE: 27) 5 PTS

Brabham BT33-Ford V8
Motor Racing Developments
Races: ESP; MON (both car #8); NED (#25); FRA; GBR (both #8); GER (#25); AUT (#8); ITA (#11); CAN (#8); USA (#23)

16TH= MARK DONOHUE (USA; AGE: 34) 4 PTS

McLaren M19A-Ford V8
Penske-White Racing
Races: CAN (car #10)

16TH= HENRI PESCAROLO (FRA; AGE: 28) 4 PTS

March 701-Ford V8
Frank Williams Racing Cars
Races: RSA (car #22)

HENRI PESCAROLO (CONTD)

March 711-Ford V8
Frank Williams Racing Cars
Races: ESP; MON (both car #27); NED (#31); FRA (#27); GBR (#26); GER (#14); AUT (#25); ITA (#16); USA (#21)

18TH= MIKE HAILWOOD (GBR; AGE: 31) 3 PTS

Surtees TS9-Ford V8
Team Surtees
Races: ITA (car #9); USA (#20)

1971

CHAMPIONSHIP CAR-BY-CAR

18TH= ROLF STOMMELEN (GER; AGE: 28) 3 PTS

Surtees TS7-Ford V8
Team Surtees
Races: RSA (car #21)

ROLF STOMMELEN (CONTD)

Surtees TS9-Ford V8
Team Surtees
Races: ESP (car #25); MON (#24); NED (#29); FRA; GBR (both #24); GER (#12); AUT; CAN (both #24)

18TH= JOHN SURTEES (GBR; AGE: 37) 3 PTS

Surtees TS9-Ford V8
Team Surtees
Races: RSA (car #20); ESP (#24); MON (#22); NED (#23); FRA (#22); GBR (#23); GER (#7); AUT (#22); ITA (#7); CAN (#22); USA (#18)

21ST GRAHAM HILL (GBR; AGE: 42) 2 PTS

Brabham BT33-Ford V8
Motor Racing Developments
Races: RSA (car #14)

GRAHAM HILL (CONTD)

Brabham BT34-Ford V8
Motor Racing Developments
Races: ESP; MON (both car #7); NED (#24); FRA; GBR (both #7); GER (#24); AUT (#7); ITA (#10); CAN (#37); USA (#22)

22ND JEAN-PIERRE BELTOISE (FRA; AGE: 34) 1 PT

Matra-Simca MS120B V12
Équipe Matra Sports
Races: ESP; MON; NED; FRA (all car #21); GBR (#22); CAN (#21); USA (#12)

ANDREA DE ADAMICH (ITA; AGE: 29) 0 PTS

March 711-Alfa Romeo V8
STP March Racing Team
Races: RSA (car #8); ESP (#17); FRA; GBR (both #19); GER (#16); ITA (#23); USA (#27)

SKIP BARBER (USA; AGE: 34) 0 PTS

March 711-Ford V8
Gene Mason Racing
Races: NED (car #22); CAN; USA (both #33)

DEREK BELL (GBR; AGE: 29) 0 PTS

Surtees TS9-Ford V8
Team Surtees
Races: GBR (car #25)

MIKE BEUTTLER (GBR; AGE: 31) 0 PTS

March 711-Ford V8
Clarke-Mordaunt-Guthrie Racing/STP March Racing Team
Races: GBR (car #6); GER (#28); AUT (#27); ITA (#24); CAN (#19)

JO BONNIER (SWE; AGE: 41) 0 PTS

McLaren M7C-Ford V8
Écurie Bonnier
Races: RSA (car #23); ITA (#28); USA (#29)

PICTURED DURING GER PRACTICE

JOHN CANNON (CAN; AGE: 34) 0 PTS

BRM P153 V12
Yardley Team BRM
Races: USA (car #28)

DAVE CHARLTON (RSA; AGE: 34) 0 PTS

Brabham BT33-Ford V8
Motor Racing Developments
Races: RSA (car #15)

DAVE CHARLTON (CONTD)

Lotus 72-Ford V8
Gold Leaf Team Lotus
Races: GBR (car #2)

CHRIS CRAFT (GBR; AGE: 31) 0 PTS

Brabham BT33-Ford V8
Motor Racing Developments
Races: USA (car #24)

PICTURED DURING CAN PRACTICE

1971

CHAMPIONSHIP CAR-BY-CAR

GEORGE EATON (CAN; AGE: 25) 0 PTS

BRM P160 V12
Yardley Team BRM
Races: CAN (car #28)

VIC ELFORD (GBR; AGE: 36) 0 PTS

BRM P160 V12
Yardley Team BRM
Races: GER (car #22)

NANNI GALLI (ITA; AGE: 30) 0 PTS

March 711-Alfa Romeo V8
STP March Racing Team
Races: NED (car #18); GER (#17); AUT (#19)

NANNI GALLI (CONTD)

March 711-Ford V8
STP March Racing Team
Races: GBR (car #20); ITA (#22); CAN (#18); USA (#26)

DAVID HOBBS (GBR; AGE: 32) 0 PTS

McLaren M19A-Ford V8
Penske-White Racing
Races: USA (car #31)

JEAN-PIERRE JARIER (FRA; AGE: 25) 0 PTS

March 701-Ford V8
Shell-Arnold Team
Races: ITA (car #26)

NIKI LAUDA (AUT; AGE: 22) 0 PTS

March 711-Ford V8
STP March Racing Team
Races: AUT (car #26)

GIJS VAN LENNEP (NED; AGE: 29) 0 PTS

Surtees TS7-Ford V8
Stichting Autoraces Nederland
Races: NED (car #30)

JOHN LOVE (RSR; AGE: 46) 0 PTS

March 701-Ford V8
Team Gunston
Races: RSA (car #24)

PETE LOVELY (USA; AGE: 45) 0 PTS

Lotus 69-Ford S4
Pete Lovely Volkswagen
Races: CAN (car #35); USA (#30)

HELMUT MARKO (AUT; AGE: 28) 0 PTS

BRM P153 V12
Yardley Team BRM
Races: AUT (car #16); ITA (#21); CAN (#31)

HELMUT MARKO (CONTD)

BRM P160 V12
Yardley Team BRM
Races: USA (car #17)

JEAN MAX (FRA; AGE: 27) 0 PTS

March 701-Ford V8
Frank Williams Racing Cars
Races: FRA (car #28)

FRANÇOIS MAZET (FRA; AGE: 28) 0 PTS

March 701-Ford V8
Jo Siffert Automobiles
Races: FRA (car #34)

SILVIO MOSER (SUI; AGE: 30) 0 PTS

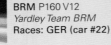

Bellasi F170-Ford V8
Jolly Club of Switzerland
Races: ITA (car #27)

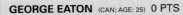

1971

CHAMPIONSHIP CAR-BY-CAR

JACKIE OLIVER (GBR; AGE: 29) 0 PTS

McLaren M14A-Ford V8
Bruce McLaren Motor Racing
Races: GBR (car #11); ITA (#14)

JACKIE OLIVER (CONTD)

McLaren M19A-Ford V8
Bruce McLaren Motor Racing
Races: AUT (car #10)

SAM POSEY (USA; AGE: 27) 0 PTS

Surtees TS9-Ford V8
Team Surtees
Races: USA (car #19)

JACKIE PRETORIUS (RSA; AGE: 36) 0 PTS

Brabham BT26-Ford V8
Team Gunston
Races: RSA (car #25)

BRIAN REDMAN (GBR; AGE: 34) 0 PTS

Surtees TS7-Ford V8
Team Surtees
Races: RSA (car #28)

PETER REVSON (USA; AGE: 32) 0 PTS

Tyrrell 001-Ford V8
Elf Team Tyrrell
Races: USA (car #10)

ALEX SOLER-ROIG (ESP; AGE: 38) 0 PTS

March 711-Ford V8
STP March Racing Team
Races: RSA (car #26); ESP; NED (both #19); FRA (#18)

DAVE WALKER (AUS; AGE: 30) 0 PTS

Lotus 56B-Pratt & Whitney turbine
Gold Leaf Team Lotus
Races: NED (car #15)

GRAND PRIX WINNERS 1971

	RACE (CIRCUIT)	**WINNER** (CAR)
RSA	SOUTH AFRICAN GRAND PRIX (KYALAMI)	MARIO ANDRETTI (FERRARI 312B F12)
ESP	SPANISH GRAND PRIX (MONTJUICH PARK)	JACKIE STEWART (TYRRELL 003-FORD V8)
MON	MONACO GRAND PRIX (MONTE CARLO)	JACKIE STEWART (TYRRELL 003-FORD V8)
NED	DUTCH GRAND PRIX (ZANDVOORT)	JACKY ICKX (FERRARI 312B2 F12)
FRA	FRENCH GRAND PRIX (PAUL RICARD)	JACKIE STEWART (TYRRELL 003-FORD V8)
GBR	BRITISH GRAND PRIX (SILVERSTONE)	JACKIE STEWART (TYRRELL 003-FORD V8)
GER	GERMAN GRAND PRIX (NÜRBURGRING)	JACKIE STEWART (TYRRELL 003-FORD V8)
AUT	AUSTRIAN GRAND PRIX (ÖSTERREICHRING)	JO SIFFERT (BRM P160 V12)
ITA	ITALIAN GRAND PRIX (MONZA)	PETER GETHIN (BRM P160 V12)
CAN	CANADIAN GRAND PRIX (MOSPORT PARK)	JACKIE STEWART (TYRRELL 003-FORD V8)
USA	UNITED STATES GRAND PRIX (WATKINS GLEN)	FRANÇOIS CEVERT (TYRRELL 002-FORD V8)

1972

FITTIPALDI STRIKES A BLOW FOR YOUTH

Above
Brazilian blend: Fittipaldi sets the pace in Spain, where he scored the first of five victories en route to becoming the sport's youngest world champion

Far left
Neat, stylish, elegant: one of the best crash helmet designs ever. The driver (Fittipaldi) wasn't bad either

Left
Champagne reception: after missing the Belgian GP to have an ulcer treated, Stewart scored a mildly fortuitous victory on his return in France – then managed to drench some of the spectators in row 27 of the main grandstand

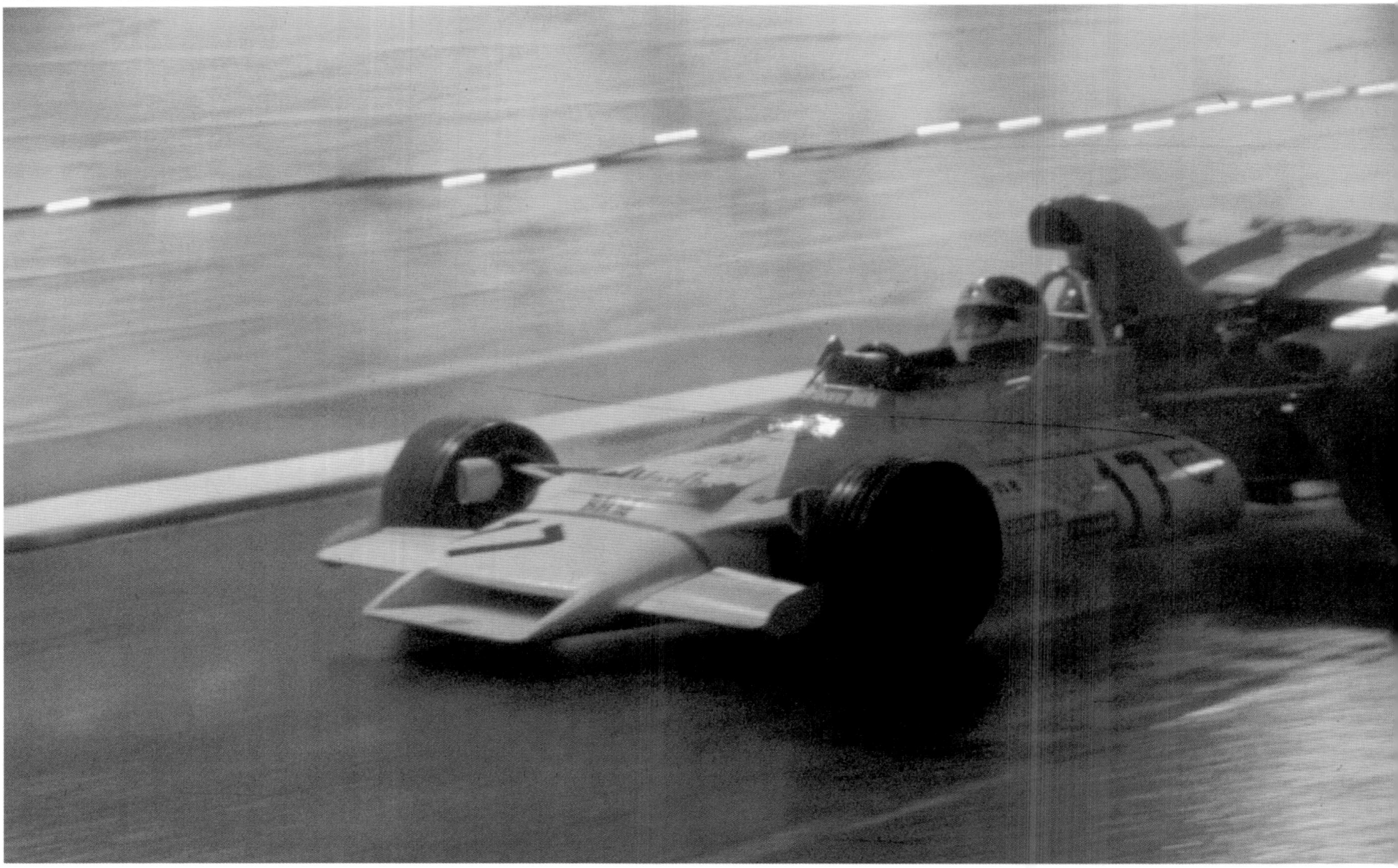

BRM ATTEMPTED TO RUN AS MANY AS FIVE CARS WITH ITS NEW BACKING BUT, APART FROM JEAN-PIERRE BELTOISE'S INSPIRED WIN AT A WET MONACO, IT SUFFERED A POOR SEASON

Above
Saturation point: 21 years after BRM made its world championship debut, Jean-Pierre Beltoise gave the company its 17th – and final – grand prix win at a rain-hit Monaco

Far left
Wilson, brother of the wizard: Fittipaldi Snr (left) and Brabham team-mate Carlos Reutemann take a breather in Austria

Left
It takes tools to tango: BRM mechanics wonder if they have enough wheel nuts to go round. The team only brought three cars to Germany but occasionally ran five.

Right
Denny lane: Hulme won in South Africa and was hugely consistent all season. Seven podium finishes put him third in the championship

This was the year in which Emerson Fittipaldi became Formula One's youngest world champion. When he clinched the crown for Lotus at the Italian Grand Prix he was just 25, yet he had shown great maturity with a series of fast and immaculate drives.

Fittipaldi's path to the crown was made easier because Tyrrell talisman Jackie Stewart spent much of the year bugged by what turned out to be a stomach ulcer. He performed below his own exceptional standards in a few races before the problem was nailed and he then had to miss a grand prix. Only at the start of the year and the end – he won in Argentina and dominated the final two races in Canada and the USA – did he look at full strength, though he scored a somewhat lucky mid-season win in France.

Chris Amon (Matra) delivered a sensational performance in that Clermont-Ferrand race and was without doubt the moral victor. He led until suffering a puncture, then made a stunning comeback drive to third, shattering the lap record many times in the process. Had the race continued a few more laps he could almost certainly have caught Stewart and Fittipaldi. After six years at the top, ill luck continued to dog the New Zealander and it was unbelievable that he had yet to win a championship-status grand prix.

Ferrari spent most of the year making its 312B2 reliable and team leader Jacky Ickx won only once, at his beloved Nürburgring. For a spell during the middle of the season this was clearly the fastest car, which showed that a lot of potential remained untapped within the Italian team. McLaren was beginning to emerge as a serious force after a few quiet seasons. BRM attempted to run as many as five cars with its new Marlboro backing but, apart from Jean-Pierre Beltoise's inspired win at a wet Monaco, it suffered a poor season.

EMERSON FITTIPALDI – WORLD CHAMPION 1972 & 1974

1972

CHAMPIONSHIP CAR-BY-CAR

1ST EMERSON FITTIPALDI (BRA; AGE: 25) 61 PTS

Lotus 72-Ford V8
John Player Team Lotus
Races: ARG (car #11); RSA (#8); ESP (#5); MON (#8); BEL (#32); FRA (#1); GBR (#8); GER (#2); AUT (#31); ITA (#6); CAN (#5); USA (#10)

2ND JACKIE STEWART (GBR; AGE: 33) 45 PTS

Tyrrell 003/004-Ford V8
Elf Team Tyrrell
Races: ARG (car #21); RSA; ESP; MON (all #1); FRA (#4); GBR; GER (both #1)

JACKIE STEWART (CONTD)

Tyrrell 005-Ford V8
Elf Team Tyrrell
Races: AUT; ITA; CAN; USA (all car #1)

3RD DENNY HULME (NZL; AGE: 36) 39 PTS

McLaren M19A-Ford V8
Yardley Team McLaren
Races: ARG (car #17); RSA (#12); ESP (#11)

DENNY HULME (CONTD)

McLaren M19C-Ford V8
Yardley Team McLaren
Races: MON (car #14); BEL (#9); FRA (#2); GBR (#18); GER (#3); AUT (#12); ITA (#14); CAN (#18); USA (#19)

4TH JACKY ICKX (BEL; AGE: 27) 27 PTS

Ferrari 312B2 F12
Scuderia Ferrari
Races: ARG (car #8); RSA (#5); ESP (#4); MON (#6); BEL (#29); FRA (#3); GBR (#5); GER (#4); AUT (#18); ITA (#4); CAN (#10); USA (#7)

5TH PETER REVSON (USA; AGE: 33) 23 PTS

McLaren M19A-Ford V8
Yardley Team McLaren
Races: ARG (car #18); RSA (#14); ESP (#20); BEL (#10); GBR (#19)

PETER REVSON (CONTD)

McLaren M19C-Ford V8
Yardley Team McLaren
Races: AUT (car #14); ITA (#15); CAN (#19); USA (#20)

6TH= FRANÇOIS CEVERT (FRA; AGE: 28) 15 PTS

Tyrrell 002-Ford V8
Elf Team Tyrrell
Races: ARG (car #22); RSA (#2); ESP (#3); MON (#2); BEL (#8); FRA (#7); GBR (#2); GER (#7); AUT; ITA (both #2)

FRANÇOIS CEVERT (CONTD)

Tyrrell 006-Ford V8
Elf Team Tyrrell
Races: CAN; USA (both car #2)

6TH= CLAY REGAZZONI (SUI; AGE: 32) 15 PTS

Ferrari 312B2 F12
Scuderia Ferrari
Races: ARG (car #9); RSA; ESP (both #6); MON (#7); BEL (#30); GER (#9); AUT (#19); ITA (#5); CAN (#11); USA (#8)

8TH MIKE HAILWOOD (GBR; AGE: 32) 13 PTS

Surtees TS9B-Ford V8
Team Surtees
Races: RSA (car #17); ESP (#15); MON (#11); BEL (#34); FRA (#26); GBR (#21); GER (#14); AUT (#25); ITA (#10); USA (#23)

9TH= CHRIS AMON (NZL; AGE: 29) 12 pts

Matra-Simca MS120C V12
Équipe Matra
Races: RSA (car #15); ESP (#9); MON (#16); BEL (#5); GBR (#17)

PICTURED DURING ARG PRACTICE

CHRIS AMON (CONTD)

Matra-Simca MS120D V12
Équipe Matra
Races: FRA (car #9); GER (#8); AUT (#10); ITA (#20); CAN (#4); USA (#18)

9TH= RONNIE PETERSON (SWE; AGE: 28) 12 PTS

March 721-Ford V8
STP March Racing Team
Races: ARG (car #14); RSA (#3)

1972

CHAMPIONSHIP CAR-BY-CAR

RONNIE PETERSON (CONTD)

March 721X-Ford V8
STP March Racing Team
Races: ESP (car #2); MON (#3); BEL (#11)

RONNIE PETERSON (CONTD)

March 721G-Ford V8
STP March Racing Team
Races: FRA (car #12); GBR (#3); GER (#10); AUT (#5); ITA (#19); CAN (#25); USA (#4)

11TH JEAN-PIERRE BELTOISE (FRA; AGE: 35) 9 PTS

BRM P160 V12
Marlboro Team BRM
Races: RSA (car #10); ESP (#19); MON (#17); BEL (#23); FRA (#5); GBR (#11); GER (#6); AUT (#7)

JEAN-PIERRE BELTOISE (CONTD)

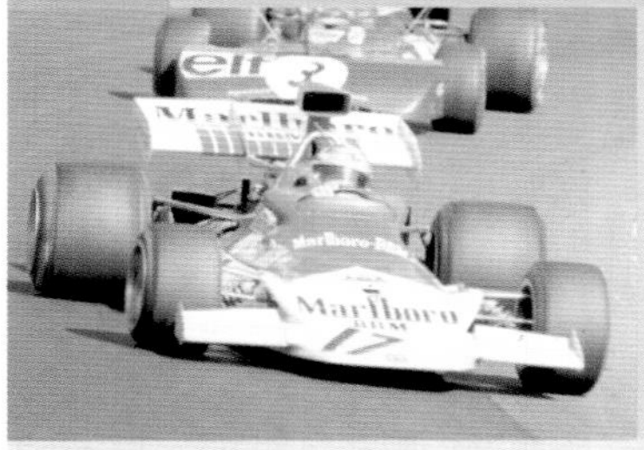

BRM P180 V12
Marlboro Team BRM
Races: ITA (car #21); CAN (#14); USA (#17)

12TH= MARIO ANDRETTI (USA; AGE: 32) 4 PTS

Ferrari 312B2 F12
Scuderia Ferrari
Races: ARG (car #10); RSA; ESP (both #7); ITA (#3); USA (#9)

12TH= HOWDEN GANLEY (NZL; AGE: 30) 4 PTS

BRM P160 V12
Marlboro Team BRM
Races: ARG (car #3); RSA (#23); ESP; BEL (both #25); GER (#17); AUT (#9); ITA (#22); CAN (#15); USA (#16)

HOWDEN GANLEY (CONTD)

BRM P180 V12
Marlboro Team BRM
Races: MON (car #19)

12TH= GRAHAM HILL (GBR; AGE: 43) 4 PTS

Brabham BT33-Ford V8
Motor Racing Developments
Races: ARG (car #1); RSA (#19)

GRAHAM HILL (CONTD)

Brabham BT37-Ford V8
Motor Racing Developments
Races: ESP (car #18); MON (#20); BEL (#17); FRA (#18); GBR (#26); GER (#11); AUT (#16); ITA (#28); CAN (#7); USA (#28)

12TH= BRIAN REDMAN (GBR; AGE: 35) 4 PTS

McLaren M19A-Ford V8
Yardley Team McLaren
Races: MON (car #15); FRA (#11); GER (#5)

BRIAN REDMAN (CONTD)

BRM P180 V12
Marlboro Team BRM
Races: USA (car #15)

16TH= ANDREA DE ADAMICH (ITA; AGE: 30) 3 PTS

Surtees TS9B-Ford V8
Team Surtees
Races: ARG (car #20); RSA (#18); ESP (#26); MON (#12); BEL (#36); FRA (#28); GBR (#23); GER (#16); AUT (#11); ITA (#9); CAN (#23); USA (#25)

16TH= CARLOS PACE (BRA; AGE: 27) 3 PTS

March 711-Ford V8
Team Williams Motul
Races: RSA (car #22); ESP (#29); MON (#23); BEL (#16); FRA (#17); GBR (#25); GER (#21); AUT (#23); ITA (#26); CAN (#29); USA (#27)

16TH= CARLOS REUTEMANN (ARG; AGE: 30) 3 PTS

Brabham BT34-Ford V8
Motor Racing Developments
Races: ARG (car #2); RSA (#20)

CARLOS REUTEMANN (CONTD)

Brabham BT37-Ford V8
Motor Racing Developments
Races: BEL (car #19); FRA (#20); GBR (#27); GER (#12); AUT (#17); ITA (#30); CAN (#8); USA (#29)

1972

CHAMPIONSHIP CAR-BY-CAR

19TH TIM SCHENKEN (AUS; AGE: 28) 2 PTS

Surtees TS9B-Ford V8
Team Surtees
Races: ARG (car #19); RSA (#16); ESP (#12); MON (#10); BEL (#35); FRA (#27); GBR (#22); GER (#15); AUT (#24); ITA (#8); CAN (#22)

TIM SCHENKEN (CONTD)

Surtees TS14-Ford V8
Team Surtees
Races: USA (car #24)

20TH= PETER GETHIN (GBR; AGE: 32) 1 PT

BRM P160 V12
Marlboro Team BRM
Races: ARG (car #5); RSA (#11); MON (#18); BEL (#24); GBR (#12); AUT (#6); ITA (#23); CAN (#16); USA (#14)

PETER GETHIN (CONTD)

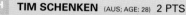

BRM P180 V12
Marlboro Team BRM
Races: ESP (car #8)

20TH= ARTURO MERZARIO (ITA; AGE: 29) 1 PT

Ferrari 312B2 F12
Scuderia Ferrari
Races: GBR (car #6); GER (#19)

SKIP BARBER (USA; AGE: 35) 0 PTS

March 711-Ford V8
Gene Mason Racing
Races: CAN; USA (both car #33)

DEREK BELL (GBR; AGE: 30) 0 PTS

Tecno PA123 F12
Martini Racing Team
Races: GER (car #27); USA (#31)

MIKE BEUTTLER (GBR; AGE: 32) 0 PTS

March 721G-Ford V8
Clarke-Mordaunt-Guthrie-Durlacher Racing
Races: MON (car #5); BEL (#14); FRA (#15); GBR (#31); GER (#28); AUT (#3); ITA (#16); CAN (#27); USA (#6)

PICTURED DURING ESP PRACTICE

BILL BRACK (CAN; AGE: 36) 0 PTS

BRM P180 V12
Marlboro Team BRM
Races: CAN (car #17)

DAVE CHARLTON (RSA; AGE: 35) 0 PTS

Lotus 72-Ford V8
Lucky Strike Scuderia Scribante
Races: RSA (car #26); GBR; GER (both #29)

PATRICK DEPAILLER (FRA; AGE: 28) 0 PTS

Tyrrell 004-Ford V8
Elf Team Tyrrell
Races: FRA (car #8); USA (#3)

WILSON FITTIPALDI (BRA; AGE: 28) 0 PTS

Brabham BT33-Ford V8
Motor Racing Developments
Races: ESP (car #22); MON (#21)

WILSON FITTIPALDI (CONTD)

Brabham BT34-Ford V8
Motor Racing Developments
Races: BEL (car #18); FRA (#19); GBR (#28); GER (#26); AUT (#28); ITA (#29); CAN (#9); USA (#30)

NANNI GALLI (ITA; AGE: 31) 0 PTS

Tecno PA123 F12
Martini Racing Team
Races: BEL (car #22); GBR (#30); AUT (#15); ITA (#11)

NANNI GALLI (CONTD)

Ferrari 312B2 F12
Scuderia Ferrari
Races: FRA (car #30)

1972

CHAMPIONSHIP CAR-BY-CAR

NIKI LAUDA (AUT; AGE: 23) 0 PTS

March 721-Ford V8
STP March Racing Team
Races: ARG (car #15); RSA (#4)

NIKI LAUDA (CONTD)

March 721X-Ford V8
STP March Racing Team
Races: ESP (car #24); MON (#4); BEL (#12)

NIKI LAUDA (CONTD)

March 721G-Ford V8
STP March Racing Team
Races: FRA (car #14); GBR (#4); GER (#23); AUT (#4); ITA (#18); CAN (#26); USA (#5)

JOHN LOVE (RSR; AGE: 47) 0 PTS

Surtees TS9-Ford V8
Team Gunston
Races: RSA (car #27)

HELMUT MARKO (AUT; AGE: 29) 0 PTS

BRM P153 V12
Marlboro Team BRM
Races: ARG (car #7); RSA (#24); MON (#26); BEL (#27)

HELMUT MARKO (CONTD)

BRM P160 V12
Marlboro Team BRM
Races: FRA (car #25)

FRANÇOIS MIGAULT (FRA; AGE: 27) 0 PTS

Connew PC1-Ford V8
Darnval Connew Racing Team
Races: AUT (car #29)

JACKIE OLIVER (GBR; AGE: 29) 0 PTS

BRM P160 V12
Marlboro Team BRM
Races: GBR (car #14)

HENRI PESCAROLO (FRA; AGE: 29) 0 PTS

March 721-Ford V8
Team Williams Motul
Races: ARG (car #23); RSA (#21); ESP (#14); MON (#22); BEL (#15); GER (#20); CAN (#28); USA (#26)

HENRI PESCAROLO (CONTD)

Politoys FX3-Ford V8
Team Williams Motul
Races: GBR (car #24)

SAM POSEY (USA; AGE: 28) 0 PTS

Surtees TS9B-Ford V8
ChampCarr Inc.
Races: USA (car #34)

JODY SCHECKTER (RSA; AGE: 22.7) 0 PTS

McLaren M19A-Ford V8
Yardley Team McLaren
Races: USA (car #21)

ALEX SOLER-ROIG (ESP; AGE: 39) 0 PTS

BRM P160 V12
Marlboro Team BRM
Races: ARG (car #6); ESP (#28)

ROLF STOMMELEN (GER; AGE: 28) 0 PTS

Eifelland 21-Ford V8
Team Eifelland Caravans
Races: RSA (car #25); ESP (#16); MON (#27); BEL (#6); FRA (#10); GBR (#33); GER (#22); AUT (#27)

JOHN SURTEES (GBR; AGE: 38) 0 PTS

Surtees TS14-Ford V8
Team Surtees
Races: ITA (car #7)

1972

CHAMPIONSHIP CAR-BY-CAR

DAVE WALKER (AUS; AGE: 31) 0 PTS

Lotus 72-Ford V8
John Player
Team Lotus
Races: ARG (car #12); RSA (#9); ESP (#21); MON (#9); BEL (#33); FRA (#6); GBR (#9); GER (#25); AUT (#21); USA (#11)

REINE WISELL (SWE; AGE: 30) 0 PTS

BRM P153 V12
Marlboro Team BRM
Races: ARG (car #4)

REINE WISELL (CONTD)

BRM P160 V12
Marlboro Team BRM
Races: ESP (car #10); MON (#28); FRA (#24); GER (#18); ITA (#24)

REINE WISELL (CONTD)

Lotus 72-Ford V8
John Player
Team Lotus
Races: CAN (car #6); USA (#12)

GRAND PRIX WINNERS 1972

	RACE (CIRCUIT)	WINNER (CAR)
ARG	ARGENTINE GRAND PRIX (BUENOS AIRES)	JACKIE STEWART (TYRRELL 003-FORD V8)
RSA	SOUTH AFRICAN GRAND PRIX (KYALAMI)	DENNY HULME (McLAREN M19A-FORD V8)
ESP	SPANISH GRAND PRIX (JARAMA)	EMERSON FITTIPALDI (LOTUS 72-FORD V8)
MON	MONACO GRAND PRIX (MONTE CARLO)	JEAN-PIERRE BELTOISE (BRM P160B V12)
BEL	BELGIAN GRAND PRIX (NIVELLES)	EMERSON FITTIPALDI (LOTUS 72-FORD V8)
FRA	FRENCH GRAND PRIX (CLERMONT-FERRAND)	JACKIE STEWART (TYRRELL 003-FORD V8)
GBR	BRITISH GRAND PRIX (BRANDS HATCH)	EMERSON FITTIPALDI (LOTUS 72-FORD V8)
GER	GERMAN GRAND PRIX (NÜRBURGRING)	JACKY ICKX (FERRARI 312B2 F12)
AUT	AUSTRIAN GRAND PRIX (ÖSTERREICHRING)	EMERSON FITTIPALDI (LOTUS 72-FORD V8)
ITA	ITALIAN GRAND PRIX (MONZA)	EMERSON FITTIPALDI (LOTUS 72-FORD V8)
CAN	CANADIAN GRAND PRIX (MOSPORT PARK)	JACKIE STEWART (TYRRELL 005-FORD V8)
USA	UNITED STATES GRAND PRIX (WATKINS GLEN)	JACKIE STEWART (TYRRELL 005-FORD V8)

1973

STEWART BOWS OUT AT THE TOP

Above
A portrait of respect: François Cevert (left) was a perfect foil for team-mate Jackie Stewart – and the two combined friendship with rivalry as successfully as any partnership in F1 history. His death during practice for the final race of the year at Watkins Glen cast a shadow over the Scot's farewell season

Right
Kind of French blue: Stewart and Tyrrell 006 in classic pose at the Nürburgring, scene of his 27th and final grand prix victory

Left
Hedging the best: yes, it's another gratuitous shot of the original Nürburgring – but would you rather look at this or the contemporary version? Thought so. Carlos Reutemann (Brabham BT42) qualified sixth in Germany but engine failure forced him out

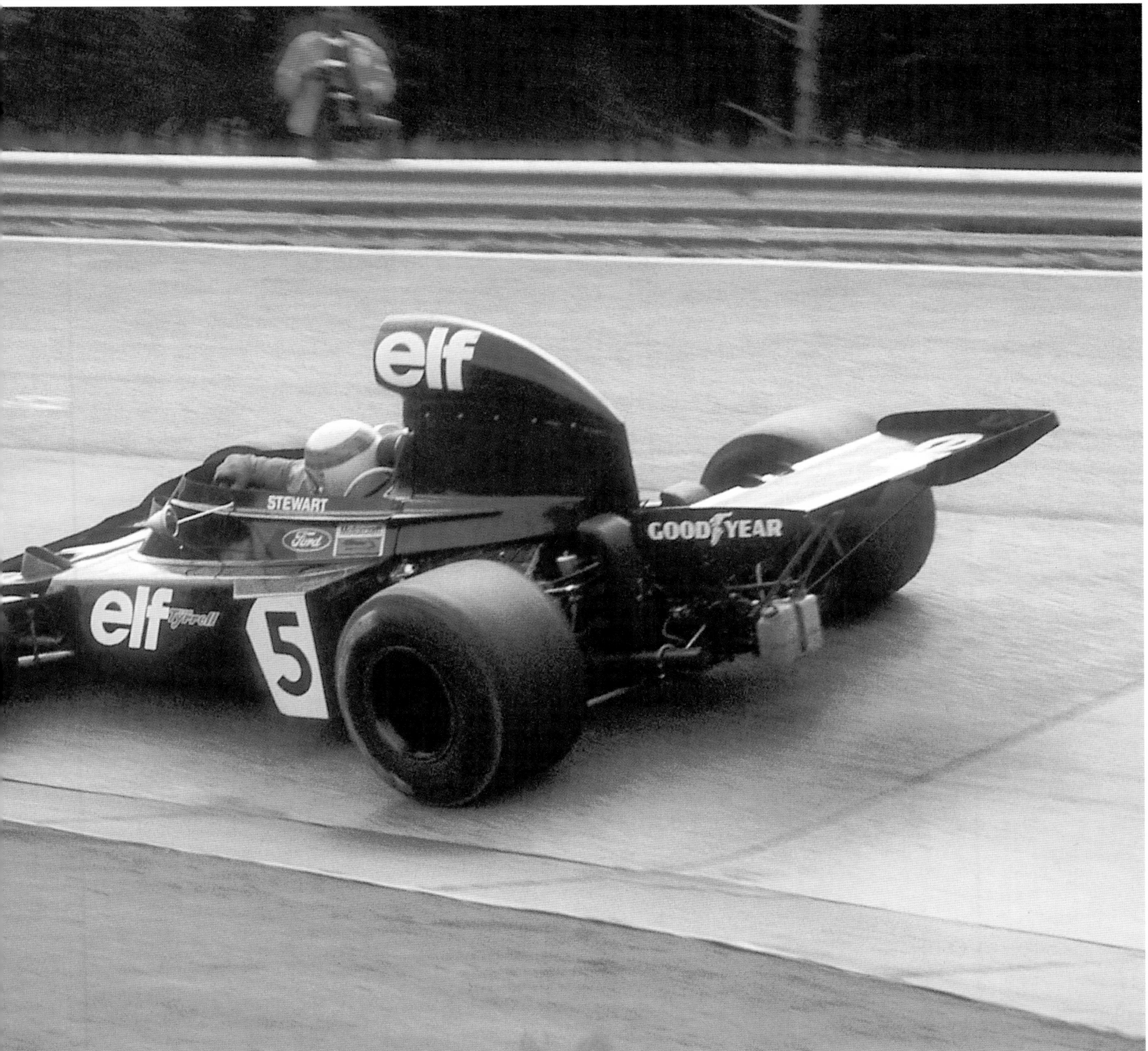
elf
STEWART
GOODYEAR
elf
Tyrrell
5

Jackie Stewart gave his great career a final flourish by establishing a new all-time record for Formula One grand prix wins en route to a third world title. His victory in Holland raised his career tally to a record-breaking 26, one more than his late friend Jim Clark. Seven days later he added a 27th success at the German Grand Prix and few in F1 suspected that this might be his last, because only a very tight circle of friends knew that he planned to retire at the end of the year.

He clinched the title with a fantastic recovery drive to fourth during the Italian GP and was looking forward to bowing out after the season's American finale, which was due to be his 100th world championship grand prix. Sadly, it wasn't to be. His Tyrrell team-mate François Cevert was killed in a violent qualifying accident. Stewart withdrew from the event and later made his decision to retire known to the world.

Cevert had three times followed his Scottish mentor across the line to give the Tyrrell team one-two finishes during the year. The gifted Frenchman had been due to assume the role of team leader once Jackie stepped down.

Stewart's closest title rival, once again, was Lotus star Emerson Fittipaldi – even though the Brazilian was frequently outpaced by his new team-mate Ronnie Peterson. The Swede set a record nine pole positions during the year in the John Player Special-liveried Lotus 72. When team boss Colin Chapman refused to ask Peterson to cede the lead in the Italian GP, to keep Fittipaldi's title challenge alive, it was the final straw for Emerson. He decided to leave at the end of the year.

McLaren was the other front-runner. Its M23 chassis won three times in the hands of Peter Revson and Denny Hulme. A third car was run occasionally for the wild, but fast, Jody Scheckter, who had impressed on his debut with the team late in 1972. He caused what was then the biggest pile-up in F1 history when he crashed at the end of the opening lap during the British GP – but no one doubted his potential. Rookie James Hunt impressed, too, at the wheel of a Hesketh Racing March, while Niki Lauda occasionally looked remarkable in the outclassed BRM. The search for Stewart's successor was on.

Above
Wrecks harassin': "I know. I'll just keep my boot in. That should sort things out. Oh." Jody Scheckter takes an unconventional line through Silverstone's Woodcote Corner (top) and prompts a gargantuan pile-up that stopped the race

Below
Swede and sour: Ronnie Peterson qualified his Lotus 72 on pole position nine times during the season, but here in Spain gearbox failure forced him to retire. He finally broke his grand prix duck in France, one of four victories during the season

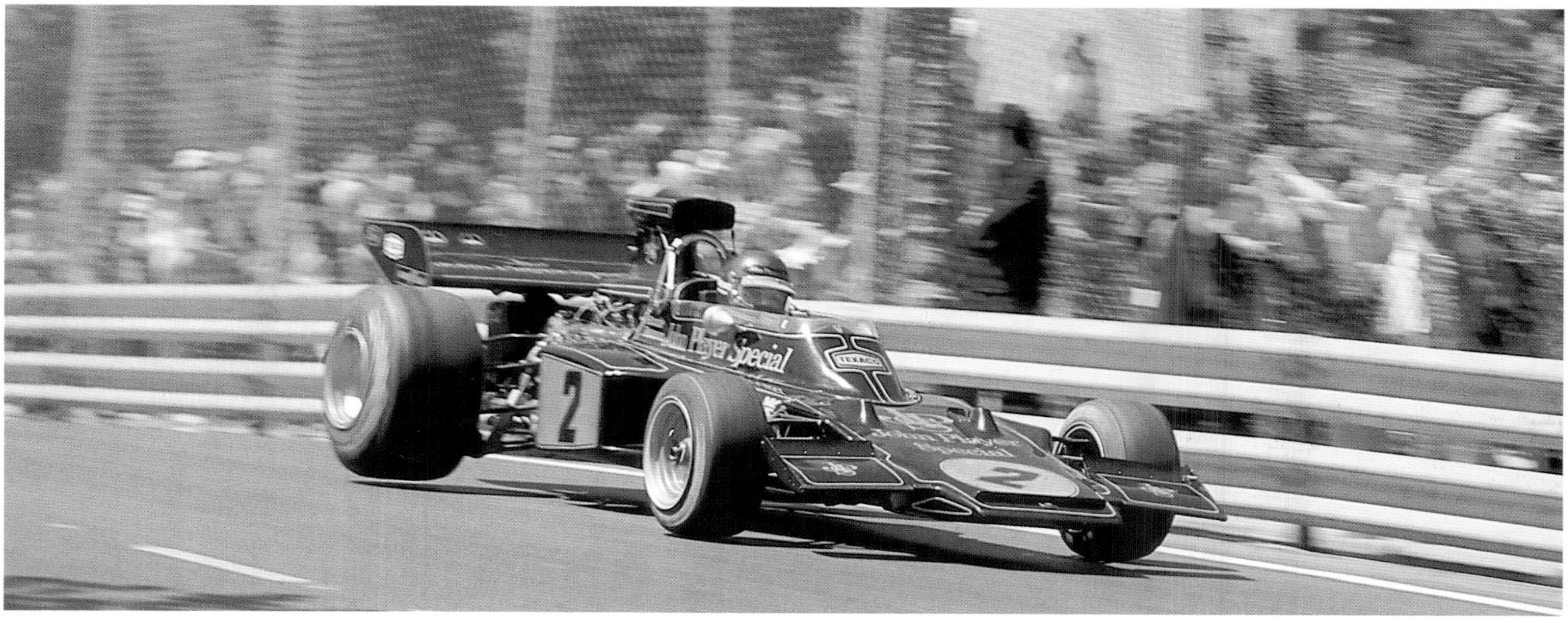

1973

CHAMPIONSHIP CAR-BY-CAR

1ST JACKIE STEWART (GBR; AGE: 34) 71 PTS

Tyrrell 005/006-Ford V8
Elf Team Tyrrell
Races: ARG (car #6); BRA; RSA; ESP (all #3); BEL; MON; SWE; FRA; GBR; NED; GER; AUT; ITA; CAN (all #5)

2ND EMERSON FITTIPALDI (BRA; AGE: 26) 55 PTS

Lotus 72-Ford V8
John Player Team Lotus
Races: ARG (car #2); BRA; RSA; ESP; BEL; MON; SWE; FRA; GBR; NED; GER; AUT; ITA; CAN; USA (all #1)

3RD RONNIE PETERSON (SWE; AGE: 29) 52 PTS

Lotus 72-Ford V8
John Player Team Lotus
Races: ARG (car #4); BRA; RSA; ESP; BEL; MON; SWE; FRA; GBR; NED; GER; AUT; ITA; CAN; USA (all #2)

4TH FRANÇOIS CEVERT (FRA; AGE: 29) 47 PTS

Tyrrell 005/006-Ford V8
Elf Team Tyrrell
Races: ARG (car #8); BRA; RSA; ESP (all #4); BEL; MON; SWE; FRA; GBR; NED; GER; AUT; ITA; CAN (all #6)

5TH PETER REVSON (USA; AGE: 34) 38 PTS

McLaren M19C-Ford V8
Yardley Team McLaren
Races: ARG (car #16); BRA (#8); RSA (#6)

PETER REVSON (CONTD)

McLaren M23-Ford V8
Yardley Team McLaren
Races: ESP (car #6); BEL; MON; SWE; GBR; NED; GER; AUT; ITA; CAN; USA (all #8)

6TH DENNY HULME (NZL; AGE: 37) 26 PTS

McLaren M19C-Ford V8
Yardley Team McLaren
Races: ARG (car #14); BRA (#7)

DENNY HULME (CONTD)

McLaren M23-Ford V8
Yardley Team McLaren
Races: RSA; ESP (both car #5); BEL; MON; SWE; FRA; GBR; NED; GER; AUT; ITA; CAN; USA (all #7)

7TH CARLOS REUTEMANN (ARG; AGE: 31) 16 PTS

Brabham BT37-Ford V8
Motor Racing Developments
Races: ARG (car #10); BRA (#17); RSA (#18)

CARLOS REUTEMANN (CONTD)

Brabham BT42-Ford V8
Motor Racing Developments
Races: ESP (car #18); BEL; MON; SWE; FRA; GBR; NED; GER; AUT; ITA; CAN; USA (all #10)

8TH JAMES HUNT (GBR; AGE: 25) 14 PTS

March 731-Ford V8
Hesketh Racing
Races: MON ; FRA; GBR; NED; AUT; CAN; USA (all car #27)

9TH JACKY ICKX (BEL; AGE: 28) 12 PTS

Ferrari 312B2 F12
Scuderia Ferrari
Races: ARG (car #18); BRA (#9); RSA (#8)

PICTURED DURING ARG PRACTICE

JACKY ICKX (CONTD)

Ferrari 312B3 F12
Scuderia Ferrari
Races: ESP (car #7); BEL; MON; SWE; FRA; GBR (all #3)

JACKY ICKX (CONTD)

McLaren M23-Ford V8
Yardley Team McLaren
Races: GER (car #30)

JACKY ICKX (CONTD)

Ferrari 312B3S F12
Scuderia Ferrari
Races: ITA (car #3)

1973

CHAMPIONSHIP CAR-BY-CAR

JACKY ICKX (CONTD)

Williams IR01-Ford V8
Frank Williams Racing Cars
Races: USA (car #26)

10TH JEAN-PIERRE BELTOISE (FRA; AGE: 36) 9 PTS

BRM P160 V12
Marlboro Team BRM
Races: ARG (car #30); BRA (#15); RSA (#16); ESP (#15); BEL; MON; SWE; FRA; GBR; NED; GER; AUT; ITA; CAN; USA (all #20)

11TH CARLOS PACE (BRA; AGE: 28) 7 PTS

Surtees TS14A-Ford V8
Team Surtees
Races: ARG (car #28); BRA (#6); RSA (#11); ESP (#10); BEL; MON; SWE; FRA; GBR; NED; GER; AUT; ITA; CAN; USA (all #24)

12TH ARTURO MERZARIO (ITA; AGE: 30) 6 PTS

Ferrari 312B2 F12
Scuderia Ferrari
Races: ARG (car #20); BRA (#10); RSA (#9)

ARTURO MERZARIO (CONTD)

Ferrari 312B3 F12
Scuderia Ferrari
Races: MON; FRA (both car #4)

ARTURO MERZARIO (CONTD)

Ferrari 312B3S F12
Scuderia Ferrari
Races: AUT; ITA; CAN; USA (all car #4)

13TH GEORGE FOLLMER (USA; AGE: 39) 5 PTS

Shadow DN1A-Ford V8
UOP Shadow Racing Team
Races: RSA (car #23); ESP (#20); BEL; SWE; FRA; GBR; NED; GER; AUT; ITA; CAN; USA (all #16)

14TH JACKIE OLIVER (GBR; AGE: 30) 4 PTS

Shadow DN1A-Ford V8
UOP Shadow Racing Team
Races: RSA (car #22); ESP (#19); BEL; MON; SWE; FRA; GBR; NED; GER; AUT; ITA; CAN; USA (all #17)

15TH= ANDREA DE ADAMICH (ITA; AGE: 31) 3 PTS

Surtees TS9B-Ford V8
Team Surtees
Races: RSA (car #12)

ANDREA DE ADAMICH (CONTD)

Brabham BT37-Ford V8
Motor Racing Developments
Races: ESP (car #21); BEL; MON; FRA (all #9)

ANDREA DE ADAMICH (CONTD)

Brabham BT42-Ford V8
Motor Racing Developments
Races: GBR (car #9)

15TH= WILSON FITTIPALDI (BRA; AGE: 29) 3 PTS

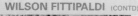

Brabham BT37-Ford V8
Motor Racing Developments
Races: ARG (car #12); BRA (#18); RSA (#19)

WILSON FITTIPALDI (CONTD)

Brabham BT42-Ford V8
Motor Racing Developments
Races: ESP (car #17); BEL; MON; SWE; FRA; GBR; NED; GER; AUT; ITA; CAN; USA (all #11)

17TH= NIKI LAUDA (AUT; AGE: 24) 2 PTS

BRM P160 V12
Marlboro Team BRM
Races: ARG (car #34); BRA (#16); RSA (#17); ESP (#16); BEL; MON; SWE; FRA; GBR; NED; GER; ITA; CAN; USA (all #21)

17TH= CLAY REGAZZONI (SUI; AGE: 33) 2 PTS

BRM P160 V12
Marlboro Team BRM
Races: ARG (car #32); BRA (#14); RSA (#15); ESP (#14); BEL; MON; SWE; FRA; GBR; NED; GER; AUT; ITA; USA (all #19)

1973

CHAMPIONSHIP CAR-BY-CAR

19TH= CHRIS AMON (NZL; AGE: 30) 1 PT

Tecno PA123 F12
Martini Racing Team
Races: BEL; MON; GBR; NED (all car #22)

CHRIS AMON (CONTD)

Tyrrell 005-Ford V8
Elf Team Tyrrell
Races: CAN (car #29)

19TH= HOWDEN GANLEY (NZL; AGE: 31) 1 PT

Williams FX3B-Ford V8
Frank Williams Racing Cars
Races: ARG (car #38); BRA (#19); RSA (#21)

HOWDEN GANLEY (CONTD)

Williams IR02/IR03-Ford V8
Frank Williams Racing Cars
Races: ESP (car #23); BEL; MON; SWE; FRA; GBR; NED; AUT; ITA; CAN; USA (all #25)

19TH= GIJS VAN LENNEP (NED; AGE: 31) 1 PT

Williams IR01-Ford V8
Frank Williams Racing Cars
Races: NED; AUT; ITA (all car #26)

MIKE BEUTTLER (GBR; AGE: 32) 0 PTS

March 721G-Ford V8
Clarke-Mordaunt-Guthrie-Durlacher Racing
Races: ARG (car #22); BRA (#12); RSA (#24)

MIKE BEUTTLER (CONTD)

March 731-Ford V8
Clarke-Mordaunt-Guthrie-Durlacher Racing
Races: ESP (car #12); BEL; MON; SWE; GBR; NED; GER; AUT; ITA; CAN; USA (all #15)

LUIZ-PEREIRA BUENO (BRA; AGE: 36) 0 PTS

Surtees TS9B-Ford V8
Team Surtees
Races: BRA (car #23)

DAVE CHARLTON (RSA; AGE: 36) 0 PTS

Lotus 72-Ford V8
Lucky Strike Scuderia Scribante
Races: RSA (car #25)

NANNI GALLI (ITA; AGE: 32) 0 PTS

Williams FX3B-Ford V8
Frank Williams Racing Cars
Races: ARG (car #36); BRA (#20)

NANNI GALLI (CONTD)

Williams IR01-Ford V8
Frank Williams Racing Cars
Races: ESP (car #24); BEL; MON (both #26)

PETER GETHIN (GBR; AGE: 33) 0 PTS

BRM P160 V12
Marlboro Team BRM
Races: CAN (car #19)

MIKE HAILWOOD (GBR; AGE: 33) 0 PTS

Surtees TS14A-Ford V8
Team Surtees
Races: ARG (car #26); BRA (#5); RSA (#10); ESP (#9); BEL; MON; SWE; FRA; GBR; NED; GER; AUT; ITA; CAN; USA (all #23)

GRAHAM HILL (GBR; AGE: 44) 0 PTS

Shadow DN1A-Ford V8
Embassy Racing with Graham Hill
Races: ESP (car #25); BEL; MON; SWE; FRA; GBR; NED; GER; AUT; ITA; CAN; USA (all #12)

JEAN-PIERRE JARIER (FRA; AGE: 26) 0 PTS

March 721G-Ford V8
March Engineering
Races: ARG (car #24); BRA (#11); RSA (#14)

1973

CHAMPIONSHIP CAR-BY-CAR

JEAN-PIERRE JARIER (CONTD)

March 731-Ford V8
March Engineering
Races: BEL; MON; SWE; FRA (all car #14); AUT; CAN; USA (all #18)

EDDIE KEIZAN (RSA; AGE: 28) 0 PTS

Tyrrell 004-Ford V8
Blignaut Lucky Strike Racing
Races: RSA (car #26)

JOCHEN MASS (GER; AGE: 26) 0 PTS

Surtees TS14A-Ford V8
Team Surtees
Races: GBR; GER (both car #31); USA (#30)

GRAHAM McRAE (NZL; AGE: 33) 0 PTS

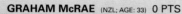

Williams IR01-Ford V8
Frank Williams Racing Cars
Races: GBR (car #26)

RIKKY VON OPEL (LIE; AGE: 25) 0 PTS

Ensign N173-Ford V8
Team Ensign
Races: FRA (car #29); GBR; AUT; ITA; CAN; USA (all #28)

HENRI PESCAROLO (FRA; AGE: 30) 0 PTS

March 731-Ford V8
March Engineering
Races: ESP (car #11)

HENRI PESCAROLO (CONTD)

Williams IR01-Ford V8
Frank Williams Racing Cars
Races: FRA; GER (both car #26)

JACKIE PRETORIUS (RSA; AGE: 38) 0 PTS

Williams FX3B-Ford V8
Frank Williams Racing Cars
Races: RSA (car #20)

DAVID PURLEY (GBR; AGE: 28) 0 PTS

March 731-Ford V8
Lec Refrigeration
Races: MON; NED; GER (all car #18); ITA (#29)

BRIAN REDMAN (GBR; AGE: 36) 0 PTS

Shadow DN1A-Ford V8
UOP Shadow Racing Team
Races: USA (car #31)

JODY SCHECKTER (RSA; AGE: 23) 0 PTS

McLaren M19C-Ford V8
Yardley Team McLaren
Races: RSA (car #7)

JODY SCHECKTER (CONTD)

McLaren M23-Ford V8
Yardley Team McLaren
Races: FRA (car #8); GBR (#30); CAN; USA (both#0)

TIM SCHENKEN (AUS; AGE: 30) 0 PTS

Williams IR01-Ford V8
Frank Williams Racing Cars
Races: CAN (car #26)

ROLF STOMMELEN (GER; AGE: 30) 0 PTS

Brabham BT42-Ford V8
Motor Racing Developments
Races: GER; AUT; ITA; CAN (all car #9)

JOHN WATSON (GBR; AGE: 27) 0 PTS

Brabham BT37-Ford V8
Motor Racing Developments
Races: GBR (car #29)

1973

CHAMPIONSHIP CAR-BY-CAR

JOHN WATSON (CONTD)

Brabham BT42-Ford V8
Motor Racing Developments
Races: USA (car #9)

REINE WISELL (SWE; AGE: 31) 0 PTS

March 731-Ford V8
Clarke-Mordaunt-Guthrie-Durlacher Racing
Races: FRA (car #15)

ROGER WILLIAMSON (GBR; AGE: 25) 0 PTS

March 731-Ford V8
March Engineering
Races: GBR; NED (both car #14)

GRAND PRIX WINNERS 1973

	RACE (CIRCUIT)	WINNER (CAR)
ARG	ARGENTINE GRAND PRIX (BUENOS AIRES)	EMERSON FITTIPALDI (LOTUS 72-FORD V8)
BRA	BRAZILIAN GRAND PRIX (INTERLAGOS)	EMERSON FITTIPALDI (LOTUS 72-FORD V8)
RSA	SOUTH AFRICAN GRAND PRIX (KYALAMI)	JACKIE STEWART (TYRRELL 006-FORD V8)
ESP	SPANISH GRAND PRIX (MONTJUICH PARK)	EMERSON FITTIPALDI (LOTUS 72-FORD V8)
BEL	BELGIAN GRAND PRIX (ZOLDER)	JACKIE STEWART (TYRRELL 006-FORD V8)
MON	MONACO GRAND PRIX (MONTE CARLO)	JACKIE STEWART (TYRRELL 006-FORD V8)
SWE	SWEDISH GRAND PRIX (ANDERSTORP)	DENNY HULME (McLAREN M23-FORD V8)
FRA	FRENCH GRAND PRIX (PAUL RICARD)	RONNIE PETERSON (LOTUS 72-FORD V8)
GBR	BRITISH GRAND PRIX (SILVERSTONE)	PETER REVSON (McLAREN M23-FORD V8)
NED	DUTCH GRAND PRIX (ZANDVOORT)	JACKIE STEWART (TYRRELL 006-FORD V8)
GER	GERMAN GRAND PRIX (NÜRBURGRING)	JACKIE STEWART (TYRRELL 006-FORD V8)
AUT	AUSTRIAN GRAND PRIX (ÖSTERREICHRING)	RONNIE PETERSON (LOTUS 72-FORD V8)
ITA	ITALIAN GRAND PRIX (MONZA)	RONNIE PETERSON (LOTUS 72-FORD V8)
CAN	CANADIAN GRAND PRIX (MOSPORT PARK)	PETER REVSON (McLAREN M23-FORD V8)
USA	UNITED STATES GRAND PRIX (WATKINS GLEN)	RONNIE PETERSON (LOTUS 72-FORD V8)

1974

FITTIPALDI'S SECOND TITLE – AND McLAREN'S FIRST

Above
"Yes! It's almost time to get out of Belgium": Fittipaldi is exultant after holding off Lauda at Nivelles, one of the least distinguished tracks to have hosted a world championship grand prix

Left
Get my drift: Depailler holds off hard-trying Tyrrell team-mate Scheckter in Buenos Aires, where the Frenchman finished sixth

Right
Merry of the fourth form: three points at Watkins Glen were enough to give Fittipaldi the crown. Trademark corduroy cap still in place, former champion Jackie Stewart steps in as poacher-turned-question master

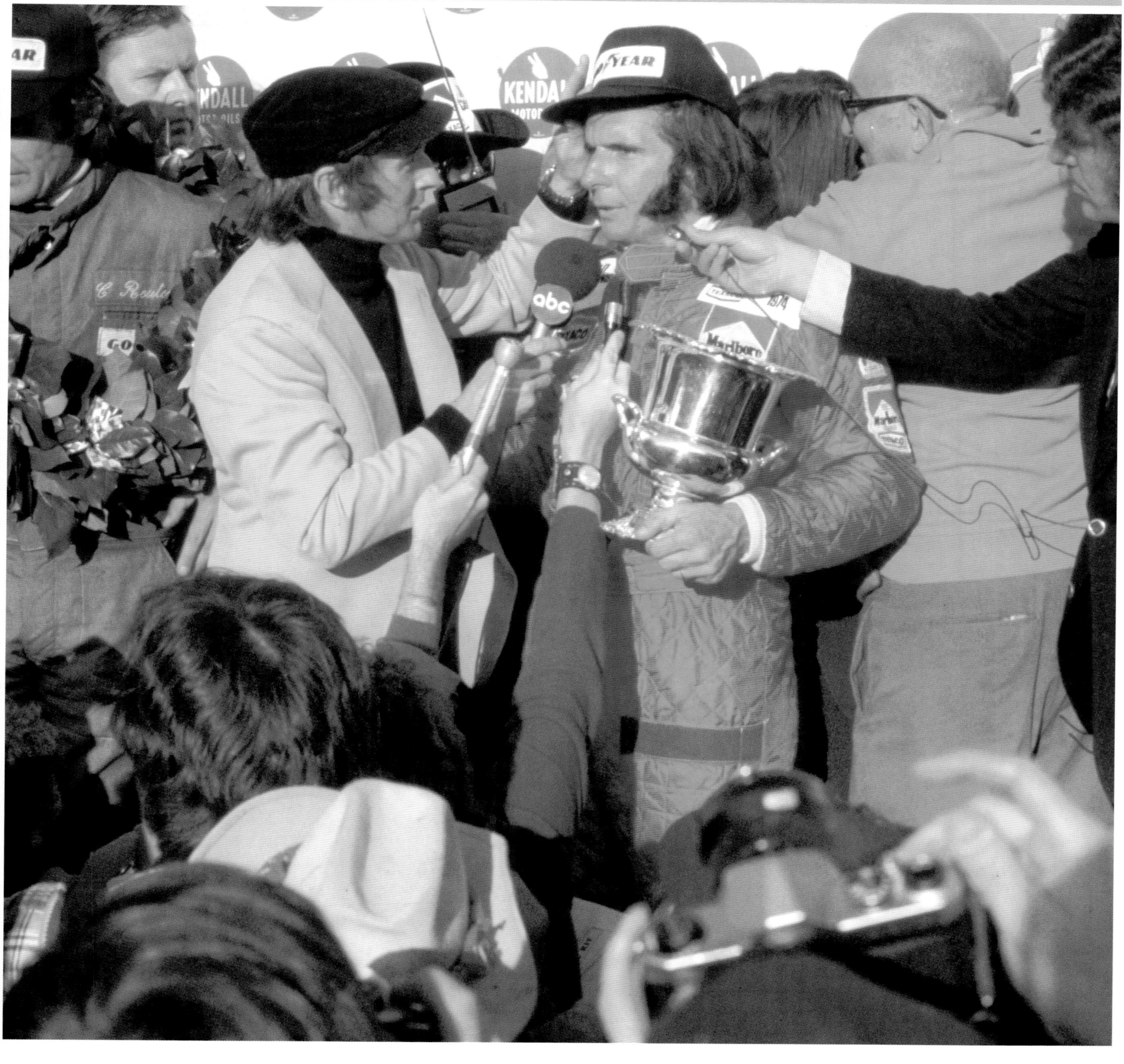
KENDALL
abc
Marlboro
1974

At the end of a very open season three drivers went to the final race with a chance of lifting the world crown: McLaren's Emerson Fittipaldi, Ferrari's Clay Regazzoni and Tyrrell's Jody Scheckter. Fittipaldi emerged victorious to take his second world title and McLaren's first.

It was a typically professional performance from the Brazilian, but it was far from clear if anybody had established themselves as an obvious natural heir to the retired Jackie Stewart.

Ronnie Peterson won three races for Lotus, each of them a brilliant performance in an outdated car. The team reverted to its 72 model – introduced in 1970 – because its intended replacement, the innovative 76, proved slower. Scheckter took over Stewart's old seat at Tyrrell – and it said everything about his potential that he should emerge as a title contender in his first full year of F1.

Then there was Niki Lauda, the young Austrian who set a record-equalling nine pole positions in his first season for Ferrari. He scored his maiden grand prix win in Spain and followed it with another in Holland, but his title chances were compromised by a touch of impetuosity in Germany – where he tangled with Scheckter – and an accident in Canada, when he hit a patch of oil after marshals failed to warn him of its presence. His team-mate, the more experienced Regazzoni, carried the Ferrari torch to the finale at Watkins but Lauda had proved clearly quicker and would go on to lead the team.

Ferrari's form was probably the story of the season. The team bounced back from a disastrous, winless 1973 to prove it had the fastest car in the field. Founder Enzo Ferrari had reorganised his troops, bringing Mauro Forghieri back from a year in the wilderness to head up the technical department and recruiting a young lawyer called Luca di Montezemelo as team manager. This and Lauda's appetite for development work at the team's new Fiorano test track had turned things around – but it was still hungry to do even better.

Above
Traction speaks Lauda: Ferrari's pole-winner gets away ahead of Peterson, Reutemann and winner Scheckter at Brands Hatch

Far left
Chequered fag: a promotional escapade on behalf of something anti-social and deeply unpleasant

Left
Patriotic missile: designer Harvey Postlethwaite watches over the unsponsored Hesketh 308. James Hunt gave the independent team's new chassis its world championship debut in South Africa

1974

CHAMPIONSHIP CAR-BY-CAR

1ST EMERSON FITTIPALDI (BRA; AGE: 27) 55 PTS

McLaren M23-Ford V8
Marlboro Team Texaco
Races: ARG; BRA; RSA; ESP; BEL; MON; SWE; NED; FRA; GBR; GER; AUT; ITA; CAN; USA (all car #5)

2ND CLAY REGAZZONI (SUI; AGE: 34) 52 PTS

Ferrari 312B3 F12
Scuderia Ferrari
Races: ARG; BRA; RSA; ESP; BEL; MON; SWE; NED; FRA; GBR; GER; AUT; ITA; CAN; USA (all car #11)

3RD JODY SCHECKTER (RSA; AGE: 24) 45 PTS

Tyrrell 006-Ford V8
Elf Team Tyrrell
Races: ARG; BRA; RSA (all car #3)

JODY SCHECKTER (CONTD)

Tyrrell 007-Ford V8
Elf Team Tyrrell
Races: ESP; BEL; MON; SWE; NED; FRA; GBR; GER; AUT; ITA; CAN; USA (all car #3)

4TH NIKI LAUDA (AUT; AGE: 25) 38 PTS

Ferrari 312B3 F12
Scuderia Ferrari
Races: ARG; BRA; RSA; ESP; BEL; MON; SWE; NED; FRA; GBR; GER; AUT; ITA; CAN; USA (all car #12)

5TH RONNIE PETERSON (SWE; AGE: 30) 35 PTS

Lotus 72-Ford V8
John Player Team Lotus
Races: ARG; BRA; MON; SWE; NED; FRA; GBR; AUT; ITA; CAN; USA (all car #1)

RONNIE PETERSON (CONTD)

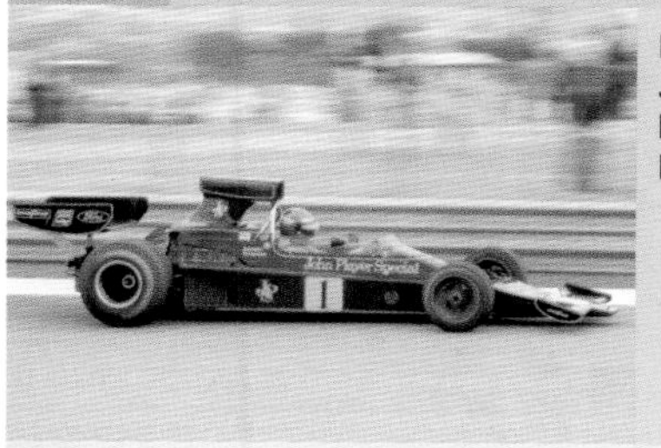

Lotus 76-Ford V8
John Player Team Lotus
Races: RSA; ESP; BEL; GER (all car #1)

6TH CARLOS REUTEMANN (ARG; AGE: 32) 32 PTS

Brabham BT44-Ford V8
Motor Racing Developments
Races: ARG; BRA; RSA; ESP; BEL; MON; SWE; NED; FRA; GBR; GER; AUT; ITA; CAN; USA (all car #7)

7TH DENNY HULME (NZL; AGE: 38) 20 PTS

McLaren M23-Ford V8
Marlboro Team Texaco
Races: ARG; BRA; RSA (all car #6); ESP (#56); BEL; MON; SWE; NED; FRA; GBR; GER; AUT; ITA; CAN; USA (all #6)

8TH JAMES HUNT (GBR; AGE: 26) 15 PTS

March 731-Ford V8
Hesketh Racing
Races: ARG; BRA (both car #24)

JAMES HUNT (CONTD)

Hesketh 308-Ford V8
Hesketh Racing
Races: RSA; ESP; BEL; MON; SWE; NED; FRA; GBR; GER; AUT; ITA; CAN; USA (all car #24)

9TH PATRICK DEPAILLER (FRA; AGE: 29) 14 PTS

Tyrrell 005/006-Ford V8
Elf Team Tyrrell
Races: ARG; BRA; RSA; ESP; MON; FRA (all car #4)

PATRICK DEPAILLER (CONTD)

Tyrrell 007-Ford V8
Elf Team Tyrrell
Races: BEL; SWE; NED; GBR; GER; AUT; ITA; CAN; USA (all car #4)

10TH= MIKE HAILWOOD (GBR; AGE: 34) 12 PTS

McLaren M23-Ford V8
Yardley Team McLaren
Races: ARG; BRA; RSA; ESP; BEL; MON; SWE; NED; FRA; GBR; GER (all car #33)

10TH= JACKY ICKX (BEL; AGE: 29) 12 PTS

Lotus 72-Ford V8
John Player Team Lotus
Races: ARG; BRA; MON; SWE; NED; FRA; GBR; GER; CAN; USA (all car #2)

1974

CHAMPIONSHIP CAR-BY-CAR

JACKY ICKX (CONTD)

Lotus 76-Ford V8
John Player Team Lotus
Races: RSA; ESP; BEL; AUT; ITA (all car #2)

12TH CARLOS PACE (BRA; AGE: 29) 11 PTS

Surtees TS16-Ford V8
Bang & Olufsen Team Surtees
Races: ARG; BRA; RSA; ESP; BEL; MON; SWE (all car #18)

CARLOS PACE (CONTD)

Brabham BT44-Ford V8
Motor Racing Developments
Races: GBR; GER; AUT; ITA; CAN; USA (all car #8)

13TH JEAN-PIERRE BELTOISE (FRA; AGE: 37) 10 PTS

BRM P160 V12
Team Motul BRM
Races: ARG; BRA (both car #14)

JEAN-PIERRE BELTOISE (CONTD)

BRM P201 V12
Team Motul BRM
Races: RSA; ESP; BEL; MON; SWE; NED; FRA; GBR; GER; AUT; ITA; CAN (all car #14)

14TH= JEAN-PIERRE JARIER (FRA; AGE: 27) 6 PTS

Shadow DN1A-Ford V8
UOP Shadow Racing Team
Races: ARG; BRA (both car #17)

JEAN-PIERRE JARIER (CONTD)

Shadow DN3A-Ford V8
UOP Shadow Racing Team
Races: ESP; BEL; MON; SWE; NED; FRA; GBR; GER; AUT; ITA; CAN; USA (all car #17)

14TH= JOHN WATSON (GBR; AGE: 28) 6 PTS

Brabham BT42-Ford V8
John Goldie Racing
Races: ARG; BRA; RSA; ESP; BEL; MON; SWE; NED; FRA; GBR (all car #28)

JOHN WATSON (CONTD)

Brabham BT44-Ford V8
John Goldie Racing
Races: GER; AUT; ITA; CAN; USA (all car #28)

16TH HANS-JOACHIM STUCK (GER; AGE: 23) 5 PTS

March 741-Ford V8
March Engineering
Races: ARG; BRA; RSA; ESP; BEL; MON; NED; GBR; GER; AUT; ITA; CAN (all car #9)

17TH ARTURO MERZARIO (ITA; AGE: 31) 4 PTS

Williams FW01/FW03-Ford V8
Frank Williams Racing Cars
Races: ARG; BRA; RSA; ESP; BEL; MON; NED; FRA; GBR; GER; AUT; ITA; CAN; USA (all car #20)

18TH= VITTORIO BRAMBILLA (ITA; AGE: 36) 1 PT

March 741-Ford V8
March Engineering
Races: RSA; BEL; MON; SWE; NED; FRA; GBR; GER; AUT; ITA; USA (all car #10)

19TH= GRAHAM HILL (GBR; AGE: 45) 1 PT

Lola T370-Ford V8
Embassy Racing with Graham Hill
Races: ARG; BRA; RSA; ESP; BEL; MON; SWE; NED; FRA; GBR; GER; AUT; ITA; CAN; USA (all car #26)

18TH= TOM PRYCE (GBR; AGE: 25) 1 PT

Token RJ02-Ford V8
Token Racing
Races: BEL (car #42)

TOM PRYCE (CONTD)

Shadow DN3A-Ford V8
UOP Shadow Racing Team
Races: NED; FRA; GBR; GER; AUT; ITA; CAN; USA (all car #16)

1974

CHAMPIONSHIP CAR-BY-CAR

CHRIS AMON (NZL; AGE: 31) 0 PTS

Amon AF101-Ford V8
Chris Amon Racing
Races: ESP (car #30)

CHRIS AMON (CONTD)

BRM P201 V12
Team Motul BRM
Races: CAN; USA (both car #15)

MARIO ANDRETTI (USA; AGE: 34) 0 PTS

Parnelli VPJ4-Ford V8
Vel's Parnelli Jones Racing
Races: CAN; USA (both car #55)

IAN ASHLEY (GBR; AGE: 26) 0 PTS

Token RJ02-Ford V8
Token Racing
Races: GER (car #32); AUT (#35)

DEREK BELL (GBR; AGE: 32) 0 PTS

Surtees TS16-Ford V8
Bang & Olufsen Team Surtees
Races: GER (car #18)

PICTURED DURING GBR PRACTICE

TOM BELSO (DEN; AGE: 31) 0 PTS

Williams FW01/FW02-Ford V8
Frank Williams Racing Cars
Races: RSA; SWE (both car #21)

PICTURED DURING GBR PRACTICE

DAVE CHARLTON (RSA; AGE: 37) 0 PTS

McLaren M23-Ford V8
Lucky Strike Scuderia Scribante
Races: RSA (car #23)

JOSÉ DOLHEM (FRA; AGE: 30) 0 PTS

Surtees TS16-Ford V8
Team Surtees
Races: USA (car #18)

PICTURED DURING FRA PRACTICE

MARK DONOHUE (USA; AGE: 37) 0 PTS

Penske PC1-Ford V8
Penske Cars
Races: CAN; USA (both car #66)

PADDY DRIVER (RSA; AGE: 39) 0 PTS

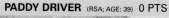

Lotus 72-Ford V8
Team Gunston
Races: RSA (car #30)

GUY EDWARDS (GBR; AGE: 31) 0 PTS

Lola T370-Ford V8
Embassy Racing with Graham Hill
Races: ARG; BRA; BEL; MON; SWE; NED; FRA (all car #27)

HOWDEN GANLEY (NZL; AGE: 32) 0 PTS

March 741-Ford V8
March Engineering
Races: ARG; BRA (both car #10)

PETER GETHIN (GBR; AGE: 34) 0 PTS

Lola T370-Ford V8
Embassy Racing with Graham Hill
Races: GBR (car #27)

DAVID HOBBS (GBR; AGE: 35) 0 PTS

McLaren M23-Ford V8
Yardley Team McLaren
Races: AUT; ITA (both car #33)

EDDIE KEIZAN (RSA; AGE: 29) 0 PTS

Tyrrell 004-Ford V8
Blignaut Embassy Racing
Races: RSA (car #32)

1974

CHAMPIONSHIP CAR-BY-CAR

LEO KINNUNEN (FIN; AGE: 30) 0 PTS

Surtees TS16-Ford V8
AAW Racing Team
Races: SWE (car #23)

HELMUTH KOINIGG (AUT; AGE: 25) 0 PTS

Surtees TS16-Ford V8
Team Surtees
Races: CAN; USA (both car #19)

JACQUES LAFFITE (FRA; AGE: 30) 0 PTS

Williams FW02-Ford V8
Frank Williams Racing Cars
Races: GER; AUT; ITA; CAN; USA (all car #21)

GÉRARD LARROUSSE (FRA; AGE: 34) 0 PTS

Brabham BT42-Ford V8
Scuderia Finotto
Races: BEL (car #43)

GIJS VAN LENNEP (NED; AGE: 32) 0 PTS

Williams FW02-Ford V8
Frank Williams Racing Cars
Races: BEL (car #21)

JOCHEN MASS (GER; AGE: 27) 0 PTS

Surtees TS16-Ford V8
Bang & Olufsen Team Surtees
Races: ARG; BRA; RSA; ESP; BEL; SWE; NED; FRA; GBR; GER (all car #19)

JOCHEN MASS (CONTD)

McLaren M23-Ford V8
Yardley Team McLaren
Races: CAN; USA (both car #33)

FRANÇOIS MIGAULT (FRA; AGE: 29) 0 PTS

BRM P160 V12
Team Motul BRM
Races: ARG; BRA; RSA; ESP; BEL; MON; FRA; GBR (all car #37)

FRANÇOIS MIGAULT (CONTD)

BRM P201 V12
Team Motul BRM
Races: NED; ITA (both car #37)

RIKKY VON OPEL (LIE; AGE: 26) 0 PTS

Brabham BT44-Ford V8
Motor Racing Developments
Races: ESP; BEL; SWE; NED (all car #8)

HENRI PESCAROLO (FRA; AGE: 31) 0 PTS

BRM P160 V12
Team Motul BRM
Races: ARG; BRA; RSA; ESP; BEL; MON; NED (all car #15)

HENRI PESCAROLO (CONTD)

BRM P201 V12
Team Motul BRM
Races: SWE; FRA; GBR; GER; ITA (all car #15)

TEDDY PILETTE (BEL; AGE: 31) 0 PTS

Brabham BT42-Ford V8
Motor Racing Developments
Races: BEL car #34)

DIETER QUESTER (AUT; AGE: 35) 0 PTS

Surtees TS16-Ford V8
Team Surtees
Races: AUT (car #30)

BRIAN REDMAN (GBR; AGE: 37) 0 PTS

Shadow DN3A-Ford V8
UOP Shadow Racing Team
Races: ESP; BEL; MON (all car #16)

1974

CHAMPIONSHIP CAR-BY-CAR

PETER REVSON (USA; AGE: 34) 0 PTS

Shadow DN3A-Ford V8
UOP Shadow Racing Team
Races: ARG; BRA (both car #16)

RICHARD ROBARTS (GBR; AGE: 29) 0 PTS

Brabham BT44-Ford V8
Motor Racing Developments
Races: ARG; BRA; RSA (all car #8)

BERTIL ROOS (SWE; AGE: 30) 0 PTS

Shadow DN3A-Ford V8
UOP Shadow Racing Team
Races: SWE (car #16)

IAN SCHECKTER (RSA; AGE: 26) 0 PTS

Lotus 72-Ford V8
Team Gunston
Races: RSA (car #29)

TIM SCHENKEN (AUS; AGE: 30) 0 PTS

Trojan T103-Ford V8
Trojan-Tauranac Racing
Races: ESP (car #23); BEL (#41); MON; GBR; AUT (all #23); ITA (#29)

TIM SCHENKEN (CONTD)

Lotus 76-Ford V8
John Player Team Lotus
Races: USA (car #31)

VERN SCHUPPAN (AUS; AGE: 31) 0 PTS

Ensign N174-Ford V8
Team Ensign
Races: BEL; MON; SWE; NED; GER (all car #22)

ROLF STOMMELEN (GER; AGE: 31) 0 PTS

Lola T370-Ford V8
Embassy Racing with Graham Hill
Races: AUT; ITA; CAN; USA (all car #27)

GRAND PRIX WINNERS 1974

	RACE (CIRCUIT)	WINNER (CAR)
ARG	ARGENTINIAN GRAND PRIX (BUENOS AIRES)	DENNY HULME (McLAREN M23-FORD V8)
BRA	BRAZILIAN GRAND PRIX (INTERLAGOS)	EMERSON FITTIPALDI (McLAREN M23-FORD V8)
RSA	SOUTH AFRICAN GRAND PRIX (KYALAMI)	CARLOS REUTEMANN (BRABHAM BT44-FORD V8)
ESP	SPANISH GRAND PRIX (JARAMA)	NIKI LAUDA (FERRARI 312B3 F12)
BEL	BELGIAN GRAND PRIX (NIVELLES)	EMERSON FITTIPALDI (McLAREN M23-FORD V8)
MON	MONACO GRAND PRIX (MONTE CARLO)	RONNIE PETERSON (LOTUS 72-FORD V8)
SWE	SWEDISH GRAND PRIX (ANDERSTORP)	JODY SCHECKTER (TYRRELL 007-FORD V8)
NED	DUTCH GRAND PRIX (ZANDVOORT)	NIKI LAUDA (FERRARI 312B3 F12)
FRA	FRENCH GRAND PRIX (DIJON-PRENOIS)	RONNIE PETERSON (LOTUS 72-FORD V8)
GBR	BRITISH GRAND PRIX (BRANDS HATCH)	JODY SCHECKTER (TYRRELL 007-FORD V8)
GER	GERMAN GRAND PRIX (NÜRBURGRING)	CLAY REGAZZONI (FERRARI 312B3 F12)
AUT	AUSTRIAN GRAND PRIX (ÖSTERREICHRING)	CARLOS REUTEMANN (BRABHAM BT44-FORD V8)
ITA	ITALIAN GRAND PRIX (MONZA)	RONNIE PETERSON (LOTUS 72-FORD V8)
CAN	CANADIAN GRAND PRIX (MOSPORT PARK)	EMERSON FITTIPALDI (McLAREN M23-FORD V8)
USA	UNITED STATES GRAND PRIX (WATKINS GLEN)	CARLOS REUTEMANN (BRABHAM BT44-FORD V8)

EPPIE WIETZES (CAN; AGE: 36) 0 PTS

Brabham BT42-Ford V8
Team Canada Formula 1 Racing
Races: CAN (car #50)

MIKE WILDS (GBR; AGE: 28) 0 PTS

Ensign N174-Ford V8
Team Ensign
Races: USA (car #22)

REINE WISELL (SWE; AGE: 32) 0 PTS

March 741-Ford V8
March Engineering
Races: SWE (car #9)

1975

LAUDA ENDS FERRARI DROUGHT

Far left
Carlos whispers: Brabham team-mates Pace and Reutemann lead away in South Africa – but it was Jody Scheckter, third here, who went on to score a popular home win

Above
Blurred on the wing: Lauda inspires a spot of photographic creativity at Watkins Glen, where he notched up his fifth victory of the season

Left
Sing if you're glad to be Clay: Regazzoni savours success at Monza, where the tifosi also had the satisfaction of celebrating Ferrari's first title for 11 years

This was the year that Ferrari cemented its long-awaited return to form. The key to its world title success was designer Mauro Forghieri's ultra-effective 312T chassis, complete with transverse gearbox and powerful flat-12 engine. A series of polished, dominant drives put Niki Lauda on course for his first world title. Team-mate Clay Regazzoni backed him up all the way and won the Italian Grand Prix, where Lauda's third place sealed the crown.

This was also the first time that the Cosworth DFV engine had been beaten to the title since it was first used for a full world championship campaign in 1968. No DFV-powered team was able to challenge the Ferraris consistently. Emerson Fittipaldi won twice for McLaren and finished as distant runner-up to Lauda. Carlos Reutemann and Carlos Pace took one win each for Bernie Ecclestone's Brabham, which put the team second in the championship for constructors, and Jody Scheckter scored a home win in South Africa for Tyrrell. The most remarkable non-Ferrari win, however, was James Hunt's defeat of Lauda during the Dutch GP at Zandvoort.

Driving for the small, privately-funded Hesketh team, Hunt took a brave decision to pit early for dry tyres in what had started out as a wet race. Lauda made his stop later, by which time Hunt had established himself at the front. Lauda tried everything he knew to pass the Hesketh but, for lap after lap, Hunt calmly soaked up the pressure and went on to score his, and the team's, first grand prix success. For Hunt there would be many more in future. For Hesketh, sadly, there would not. At the end of the season the team announced it was scaling down its operation for financial reasons.

THE KEY TO FERRARI'S SUCCESS WAS DESIGNER MAURO FORGHIERI'S ULTRA-EFFECTIVE 312T CHASSIS, COMPLETE WITH POWERFUL FLAT-12. IT WAS THE FIRST TIME COSWORTH'S DFV ENGINE HAD BEEN BEATEN TO THE TITLE SINCE 1968

Left
Monza gorilla in the mist: Brambilla celebrates his maiden F1 win in Austria, where he spun, clipped the barrier and rumpled his works March moments after taking the chequered flag

Top
Redwing takes flight: Mass heads for first place in the accident-shortened Spanish GP

Above
Fittipaldi: possibly hasn't yet realised quite how good the Ferrari is – or that his watch is full of water

Right
Me and my Shadow: out of the car Tom Pryce was quiet and reserved type – in it he was anything but

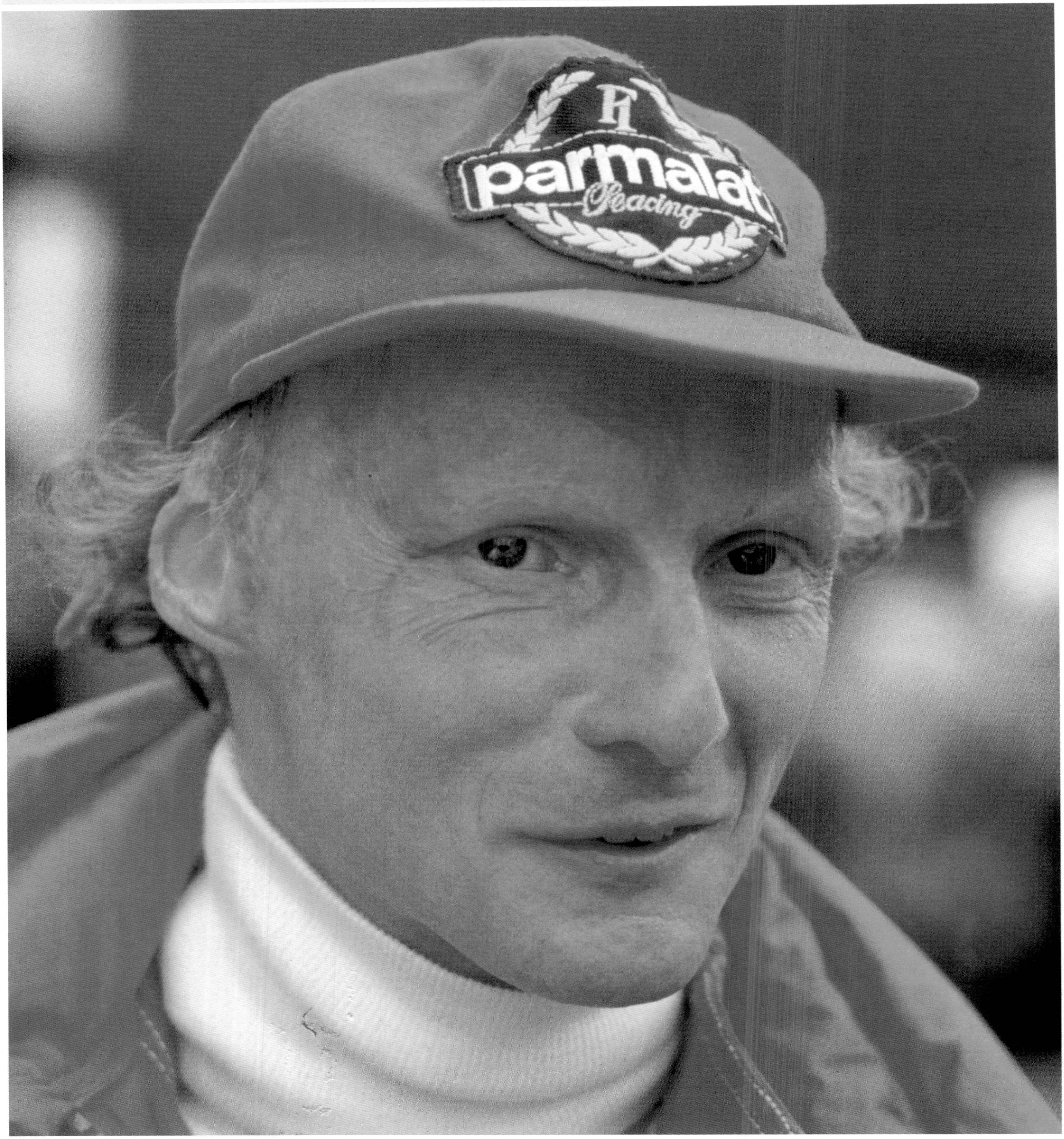

NIKI LAUDA – WORLD CHAMPION 1975, 1977 & 1984

1975

CHAMPIONSHIP CAR-BY-CAR

1ST NIKI LAUDA (AUT; AGE: 26) 64.5 PTS

Ferrari 312B3 F12
Scuderia Ferrari
Races: ARG; BRA (both car #12)

NIKI LAUDA (CONTD)

Ferrari 312T F12
Scuderia Ferrari
Races: RSA; ESP; MON; BEL; SWE; NED; FRA; GBR; GER; AUT; ITA; USA (all car #12)

2ND EMERSON FITTIPALDI (BRA; AGE: 28) 45 PTS

McLaren M23-Ford V8
Marlboro Team Texaco
Races: ARG; BRA; RSA; MON; BEL; SWE; NED; FRA; GBR; GER; AUT; ITA; USA (all car #1)

3RD CARLOS REUTEMANN (ARG; AGE: 33) 37 PTS

Brabham BT44B-Ford V8
Martini Racing
Races: ARG; BRA; RSA; ESP; MON; BEL; SWE; NED; FRA; GBR; GER; AUT; ITA; USA (all car #7)

4TH JAMES HUNT (GBR; AGE: 27) 33 PTS

Hesketh 308-Ford V8
Hesketh Racing
Races: ARG; BRA; RSA; ESP; MON; BEL; SWE; NED; FRA; GBR; GER; AUT (all car #24)

JAMES HUNT (CONTD)

Hesketh 308C-Ford V8
Hesketh Racing
Races: ITA; USA (both car #24)

5TH CLAY REGAZZONI (SUI; AGE: 35) 25 PTS

Ferrari 312B3 F12
Scuderia Ferrari
Races: ARG; BRA (both car #11)

CLAY REGAZZONI (CONTD)

Ferrari 312T F12
Scuderia Ferrari
Races: RSA; ESP; MON; BEL; SWE; NED; FRA; GBR; GER; AUT; ITA; USA (all car #11)

6TH CARLOS PACE (BRA; AGE: 30) 24 PTS

Brabham BT44B-Ford V8
Martini Racing
Races: ARG; BRA; RSA; ESP; MON; BEL; SWE; NED; FRA; GBR; GER; AUT; ITA; USA (all car #8)

7TH= JOCHEN MASS (GER; AGE: 28) 20 PTS

McLaren M23-Ford V8
Marlboro Team Texaco
Races: ARG; BRA; RSA; ESP; MON; BEL; SWE; NED; FRA; GBR; GER; AUT; ITA; USA (all car #2)

7TH= JODY SCHECKTER (RSA; AGE: 25) 20 PTS

Tyrrell 007-Ford V8
Elf Team Tyrrell
Races: ARG; BRA; RSA; ESP; MON; BEL; SWE; NED; FRA; GBR; GER; AUT; ITA; USA (all car #3)

9TH PATRICK DEPAILLER (FRA; AGE: 30) 12 PTS

Tyrrell 007-Ford V8
Elf Team Tyrrell
Races: ARG; BRA; RSA; ESP; MON; BEL; SWE; NED; FRA; GBR; GER; AUT; ITA; USA (all car #4)

10TH TOM PRYCE (GBR; AGE: 26) 8 PTS

Shadow DN3B-Ford V8
UOP Shadow Racing Team
Races: ARG; BRA (both car #16)

TOM PRYCE (CONTD)

Shadow DN5A-Ford V8
UOP Shadow Racing Team
Races: RSA; ESP; MON; BEL; SWE; NED; FRA; GBR; GER; AUT; ITA; USA (all car #16)

11TH VITTORIO BRAMBILLA (ITA; AGE: 37) 6.5 PTS

March 741-Ford V8
March Engineering
Races: ARG; BRA (both car #9)

1975

CHAMPIONSHIP CAR-BY-CAR

VITTORIO BRAMBILLA (CONTD)

March 751-Ford V8
March Engineering
Races: RSA; ESP; MON; BEL; SWE; NED; FRA; GBR; GER; AUT; ITA; USA (all car #9)

12TH= JACQUES LAFFITE (FRA; AGE: 31) 6 PTS

Williams FW02-Ford V8
Frank Williams Racing Cars
Races: ARG; BRA; RSA (all car #21)

JACQUES LAFFITE (CONTD)

Williams FW04-Ford V8
Frank Williams Racing Cars
Races: BEL; NED; FRA; GBR; GER; AUT; ITA (all car #21)

12TH= RONNIE PETERSON (SWE; AGE: 31) 6 PTS

Lotus 72-Ford V8
John Player Team Lotus
Races: ARG; BRA; RSA; ESP; MON; BEL; SWE; NED; FRA; GBR; GER; AUT; ITA; USA (all car #5)

14TH MARIO ANDRETTI (USA; AGE: 35) 5 PTS

Parnelli VPJ4-Ford V8
Vel's Parnelli Jones Racing
Races: ARG; BRA; RSA; ESP; MON; SWE; FRA; GBR; GER; AUT; ITA; USA (all car #27)

15TH MARK DONOHUE (USA; AGE: 38) 4 PTS

Penske PC1-Ford V8
Penske Cars
Races: ARG; BRA; RSA; ESP; MON; BEL; SWE; NED; FRA (all car #28)

MARK DONOHUE (CONTD)

March 751-Ford V8
Penske Cars
Races: GBR; GER (both car #28)

16TH JACKY ICKX (BEL; AGE: 30) 3 PTS

Lotus 72-Ford V8
John Player Team Lotus
Races: ARG; BRA; RSA; ESP; MON; BEL; SWE; NED; FRA (all car #6)

17TH ALAN JONES (AUS; AGE: 28) 2 PTS

Hesketh 308-Ford V8
Custom Made Harry Stiller Racing
Races: ESP (car #25); MON; BEL; SWE (all #26)

ALAN JONES (CONTD)

Hill GH1-Ford V8
Embassy Racing with Graham Hill
Races: NED; FRA; GBR; GER (all car #22)

18TH JEAN-PIERRE JARIER (FRA; AGE: 28) 1.5 PTS

Shadow DN5A-Ford V8
UOP Shadow Racing Team
Races: BRA; RSA; ESP; MON; BEL; SWE; NED; FRA; GBR; GER; USA (all car #17)

JEAN-PIERRE JARIER (CONTD)

Shadow DN7A-Matra V12
UOP Shadow Racing Team
Races: AUT; ITA (both car #17)

19TH= TONY BRISE (GBR; AGE: 23) 1 PT

Williams FW03-Ford V8
Frank Williams Racing Cars
Races: ESP (car #21)

TONY BRISE (CONTD)

Hill GH1-Ford V8
Embassy Racing with Graham Hill
Races: BEL; SWE; NED; FRA; GBR; GER; AUT; ITA; USA (all car #23)

19TH= GIJS VAN LENNEP (NED; AGE: 33) 1 PT

Ensign N174-Ford V8
HB Bewaking Team Ensign
Races: NED (car #31)

1975

CHAMPIONSHIP CAR-BY-CAR

GIJS VAN LENNEP (CONTD)

Ensign N175-Ford V8
HB Bewaking Team Ensign
Races: FRA (car #31); GER (#19)

21ST LELLA LOMBARDI (ITA; AGE: 34) 0.5 PTS

March 741-Ford V8
March Engineering
Races: RSA (car #10)

LELLA LOMBARDI (CONTD)

March 751-Ford V8
March Engineering
Races: ESP; BEL; SWE; NED; FRA (all car #10); GBR; GER; AUT; ITA (all #29)

CHRIS AMON (NZL; AGE: 32) 0 PTS

Ensign N175-Ford V8
HB Bewaking Team Ensign
Races: AUT (car #31); ITA (#32)

DAVE CHARLTON (RSA; AGE: 38) 0 PTS

McLaren M23-Ford V8
Lucky Strike Scuderia Scribante
Races: RSA (car #31)

JIM CRAWFORD (GBR; AGE: 27) 0 PTS

Lotus 72-Ford V8
John Player Team Lotus
Races: GBR; ITA (both car #6)

HARALD ERTL (AUT; AGE: 27) 0 PTS

Hesketh 308-Ford V8
Warsteiner Brewery
Races: GER (car #25); AUT (#32); ITA (#34)

BOB EVANS (GBR; AGE: 28) 0 PTS

Stanley BRM P201 V12
Stanley BRM
Races: RSA; ESP; BEL; SWE; NED; FRA; AUT; ITA (all car #14)

WILSON FITTIPALDI (BRA; AGE: 31) 0 PTS

Fittipaldi FD01/FD03-Ford V8
Copersucar-Fittipaldi Automotive
Races: ARG; BRA; ESP; BEL; SWE; NED; FRA; GBR; GER; USA (all car #30)

BRIAN HENTON (GBR; AGE: 28) 0 PTS

Lotus 72-Ford V8
John Player Team Lotus
Races: GBR (car #15); USA (#6)

GRAHAM HILL (GBR; AGE: 45) 0 PTS

Lola T370-Ford V8
Embassy Racing with Graham Hill
Races: ARG; BRA (both car #22)

JEAN-PIERRE JABOUILLE (FRA; AGE: 32) 0 PTS

Tyrrell 007-Ford V8
Elf Team Tyrrell
Races: FRA (car #15)

EDDIE KEIZAN (RSA; AGE: 30) 0 PTS

Lotus 72-Ford V8
Team Gunston
Races: RSA (car #33)

MICHEL LECLÈRE (FRA; AGE: 29) 0 PTS

Tyrrell 007-Ford V8
Elf Team Tyrrell
Races: USA (car #15)

BRETT LUNGER (USA; AGE: 29) 0 PTS

Hesketh 308-Ford V8
Hesketh Racing
Races: AUT; ITA; USA (all car #25)

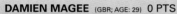

1975

CHAMPIONSHIP CAR-BY-CAR

DAMIEN MAGEE (GBR; AGE: 29) 0 PTS

Williams FW03-Ford V8
Frank Williams Racing Cars
Races: SWE (car #20)

ARTURO MERZARIO (ITA; AGE: 32) 0 PTS

Williams FW03-Ford V8
Frank Williams Racing Cars
Races: ARG; BRA; RSA; BEL (all car #20)

ARTURO MERZARIO (CONTD)

Williams FW04-Ford V8
Frank Williams Racing Cars
Races: ESP (car #20)

ARTURO MERZARIO (CONTD)

Fittipaldi FD03-Ford V8
Copersucar-Fittipaldi Automotive
Races: ITA (car #30)

FRANÇOIS MIGAULT (FRA; AGE: 30) 0 PTS

Hill GH1-Ford V8
Embassy Racing with Graham Hill
Races: ESP (car #23); BEL (#22)

DAVE MORGAN (GBR; AGE: 30) 0 PTS

Surtees TS16-Ford V8
Team Surtees
Races: GBR (car #19)

JOHN NICHOLSON (NZL; AGE: 33) 0 PTS

Lyncar 009-Ford V8
Lyncar Engineering
Races: GBR (car #32)

TORSTEN PALM (SWE; AGE: 27) 0 PTS

Hesketh 308-Ford V8
Hesketh Racing
Races: SWE (car #32)

IAN SCHECKTER (RSA; AGE: 27) 0 PTS

Tyrrell 007-Ford V8
Lexington Racing
Races: RSA (car #32)

IAN SCHECKTER (CONTD)

Williams FW04-Ford V8
Frank Williams Racing Cars
Races: SWE (car #21)

IAN SCHECKTER (CONTD)

Williams FW03-Ford V8
Frank Williams Racing Cars
Races: NED (car #20)

VERN SCHUPPAN (AUS; AGE: 32) 0 PTS

Hill GH1-Ford V8
Embassy Racing with Graham Hill
Races: SWE (car #22)

ROLF STOMMELEN (GER; AGE: 31) 0 PTS

Lola T370-Ford V8
Embassy Racing with Graham Hill
Races: ARG; BRA (both car #23)

ROLF STOMMELEN (CONTD)

Lola T371-Ford V8
Embassy Racing with Graham Hill
Races: RSA (car #23)

ROLF STOMMELEN (CONTD)

Hill GH1-Ford V8
Embassy Racing with Graham Hill
Races: ESP; AUT; ITA (all car #22)

1975

CHAMPIONSHIP CAR-BY-CAR

HANS-JOACHIM STUCK (GER; AGE: 24) 0 PTS

March 751-Ford V8
March Engineering
Races: GBR; GER; AUT; ITA; USA (all car #10)

GUY TUNMER (RSA; AGE: 26) 0 PTS

Lotus 72-Ford V8
Team Gunston
Races: RSA (car #34)

JOSEPH VONLANTHEN (SUI; AGE: 33) 0 PTS

Williams FW03-Ford V8
Frank Williams Racing Cars
Races: AUT (car #20)

JOHN WATSON (GBR; AGE: 29) 0 PTS

Surtees TS16-Ford V8
Team Surtees
Races: ARG; BRA; RSA; ESP; MON; BEL; SWE; NED; FRA; GBR; AUT (all car #18)

JOHN WATSON (CONTD)

Lotus 72-Ford V8
John Player Team Lotus
Races: GER (car #6)

JOHN WATSON (CONTD)

Penske PC1-Ford V8
Penske Cars
Races: USA (car #28)

MIKE WILDS (GBR; AGE: 29) 0 PTS

Stanley BRM P201 V12
Stanley BRM
Races: ARG; BRA (both car #14)

ROELOF WUNDERINK (NED; AGE: 26) 0 PTS

Ensign N174-Ford V8
HB Bewaking Team Ensign
Races: ESP (car #31); AUT (#33)

ROELOF WUNDERINK (CONTD)

Ensign N175-Ford V8
HB Bewaking Team Ensign
Races: USA (car #31)

RENZO ZORZI (ITA; AGE: 28) 0 PTS

Williams FW03-Ford V8
Frank Williams Racing Cars
Races: ITA (car #20)

GRAND PRIX WINNERS 1975

	RACE (CIRCUIT)	WINNER (CAR)
ARG	ARGENTINE GRAND PRIX (BUENOS AIRES)	EMERSON FITTIPALDI (McLAREN M23-FORD V8)
BRA	BRAZILIAN GRAND PRIX (INTERLAGOS)	CARLOS PACE (BRABHAM BT44B-FORD V8)
RSA	SOUTH AFRICAN GRAND PRIX (KYALAMI)	JODY SCHECKTER (TYRRELL 007-FORD V8)
ESP	SPANISH GRAND PRIX (MONTJUICH PARK)	JOCHEN MASS (McLAREN M23-FORD V8)
MON	MONACO GRAND PRIX (MONTE CARLO)	NIKI LAUDA (FERRARI 312T F12)
BEL	BELGIAN GRAND PRIX (ZOLDER)	NIKI LAUDA (FERRARI 312T F12)
SWE	SWEDISH GRAND PRIX (ANDERSTORP)	NIKI LAUDA (FERRARI 312T F12)
NED	DUTCH GRAND PRIX (ZANDVOORT)	JAMES HUNT (HESKETH 308-FORD V8)
FRA	FRENCH GRAND PRIX (PAUL RICARD)	NIKI LAUDA (FERRARI 312T F12)
GBR	BRITISH GRAND PRIX (SILVERSTONE)	EMERSON FITTIPALDI (McLAREN M23-FORD V8)
GER	GERMAN GRAND PRIX (NÜRBURGRING)	CARLOS REUTEMANN (BRABHAM BT44B-FORD V8)
AUT	AUSTRIAN GRAND PRIX (ÖSTERREICHRING)	VITTORIO BRAMBILLA (MARCH 751-FORD V8)
ITA	ITALIAN GRAND PRIX (MONZA)	CLAY REGAZZONI (FERRARI 312T F12)
USA	UNITED STATES GRAND PRIX (WATKINS GLEN)	NIKI LAUDA (FERRARI 312T F12)

1976

DRAMA, DEBATE – AND LAST-GASP TITLE FOR HUNT

Far left
Sodden movement: Hunt and Andretti dribble off the line in the rain-delayed seasonal finale at Fuji, where the American gave Lotus its first GP win since Monza 1974

Above
I'm a celebrity getting out of here: Lauda's accident in Germany heightened his appreciation of life. He baled out after completing a couple of gentle laps in Japan and the destiny of the title rested in Hunt's hands alone

Left
Holland perk: Hunt hit a rich seam of form in the second half of the season and scored win number four at Zandvoort, one of two races Lauda had to miss

This remarkable Formula One season helped popularise the sport's appeal enormously as James Hunt and Niki Lauda fought out a dramatic world championship duel. Lauda suffered serious burns when he crashed during the German Grand Prix and was subsequently read the last rites in his hospital bed. Just six weeks later, however, he returned to the cockpit and finished fourth in the Italian GP. It stands as one of the most remarkable sporting achievements in history.

Lauda began the season much as he finished 1975, with a series of searing performances for Ferrari. There were, however, some brilliant showings from Hunt, who joined McLaren as a late-notice replacement when Emerson Fittipaldi opted to switch to his brother's fledgling team. In a season of relentless controversy, Hunt was disqualified from victory in the Spanish GP because his car was too wide, although he would later be reinstated. Lauda, meanwhile, won four of the first six races and was second in the other two. In Sweden, round seven, Jody Scheckter led home team-mate Patrick Depailler in a historic one-two for Tyrrell's six-wheeled P34. Lauda, of course, was on the third step of the podium.

Hunt defeated Lauda on the track at Brands Hatch – but later had his win taken away because he had supposedly breached the sporting regulations when returning to the grid for a restart, which was necessary in the wake of a first-corner pile-up. Germany came next – and with it Lauda's life-threatening injury. Hunt won here and in Holland – one of two subsequent races Lauda missed – but the Austrian still held the points lead when he returned at Monza, with four races to go. Hunt's form was almost unstoppable, though, and he won in Canada and America to be within three points of Lauda as they headed for a title showdown in Japan.

In teeming rain that produced near-zero visibility, Lauda was understandably unwilling to expose himself to unseemly risk and he retired after two laps. Hunt needed to finish third to take the title. He led most of the way but a deflated tyre forced him to make a late pit stop and he rejoined fifth. In a suitably spectacular finish to this most dramatic of seasons, he passed two of the four cars ahead before the flag fell – and the title was his. Almost overlooked amid all the drama was the fact that Mario Andretti had won for Lotus, the beginning of the team's comeback after a couple of years in the doldrums.

LAUDA SUFFERED SERIOUS BURNS AND WAS SUBSEQUENTLY READ THE LAST RITES. JUST SIX WEEKS LATER, HOWEVER, HE FINISHED FOURTH IN THE ITALIAN GP. IT STANDS AS ONE OF THE MOST REMARKABLE SPORTING ACHIEVEMENTS IN HISTORY

Far left
Frame academy: fans at Monza scramble for the best view. Is this safe? No. Do they do it every year? Er, yes

Left
Patter of tiny feat: the innovative Tyrrell P34's quartet of small front wheels created a) reduced drag and b) production headaches for tyre supplier Goodyear

Above
Chapter and reverse: Regazzoni tries to tackle Brands Hatch's Paddock Hill Bend gearbox-first and race-stopping chaos is but seconds away

Right
Alternative Ulsterman: Steely Dan and Genesis aficionado John Watson scored his first – and Penske's only – world championship win in Austria

JAMES HUNT – WORLD CHAMPION 1976

1976

CHAMPIONSHIP CAR-BY-CAR

1ST JAMES HUNT (GBR; AGE: 28) 69 PTS

McLaren M23-Ford V8
Marlboro Team McLaren
Races: BRA; RSA; LB; ESP; BEL; MON; SWE; FRA; GBR; GER; AUT; NED; ITA; CAN; USA; JPN (all car #11)

2ND NIKI LAUDA (AUT; AGE: 27) 68 PTS

Ferrari 312T F12
Scuderia Ferrari
Races: BRA; RSA; LB (all car #1)

NIKI LAUDA (CONTD)

Ferrari 312T2 F12
Scuderia Ferrari
Races: ESP; BEL; MON; SWE; FRA; GBR; GER; ITA; CAN; USA; JPN (all car #1)

3RD JODY SCHECKTER (RSA; AGE: 26) 49 PTS

Tyrrell 007-Ford V8
Elf Team Tyrrell
Races: BRA; RSA; LB; ESP (all car #3)

JODY SCHECKTER (CONTD)

Tyrrell P34-Ford V8
Elf Team Tyrrell
Races: BEL; MON; SWE; FRA; GBR; GER; AUT; NED; ITA; CAN; USA; JPN (all car #3)

4TH PATRICK DEPAILLER (FRA; AGE: 31) 39 PTS

Tyrrell 007-Ford V8
Elf Team Tyrrell
Races: BRA; RSA; LB (all car #4)

PATRICK DEPAILLER (CONTD)

Tyrrell P34-Ford V8
Elf Team Tyrrell
Races: ESP; BEL; MON; SWE; FRA; GBR; GER; AUT; NED; ITA; CAN; USA; JPN (all car #4)

5TH CLAY REGAZZONI (SUI; AGE: 36) 31 PTS

Ferrari 312T F12
Scuderia Ferrari
Races: BRA; RSA; LB (all car #2)

CLAY REGAZZONI (CONTD)

Ferrari 312T2 F12
Scuderia Ferrari
Races: ESP; BEL; MON; SWE; FRA; GBR; GER; NED; ITA; CAN; USA; JPN (all car #2)

6TH MARIO ANDRETTI (USA; AGE: 36) 22 PTS

Lotus 77-Ford V8
John Player Team Lotus
Races: BRA (car #6); ESP; BEL; SWE; FRA; GBR; GER; AUT; NED; ITA; CAN; USA; JPN (all #5)

MARIO ANDRETTI (CONTD)

Parnelli VPJ4B-Ford V8
Vel's Parnelli Jones Racing
Races: RSA; LB (both car #27)

7TH= JACQUES LAFFITE (FRA; AGE: 32) 20 PTS

Ligier JS5-Matra V12
Équipe Ligier Gitanes
Races: BRA; RSA; LB; ESP; BEL; MON; SWE; FRA; GBR; GER; AUT; NED; ITA; CAN; USA; JPN (all car #26)

7TH= JOHN WATSON (GBR; AGE: 30) 20 PTS

Penske PC3-Ford V8
Citibank Team Penske
Races: BRA; RSA; LB; ESP; BEL; MON (all car #28)

JOHN WATSON (CONTD)

Penske PC4-Ford V8
Citibank Team Penske
Races: SWE; FRA; GBR; GER; AUT; NED; ITA; CAN; USA; JPN (all car #28)

9TH JOCHEN MASS (GER; AGE: 29) 19 PTS

McLaren M23-Ford V8
Marlboro Team McLaren
Races: BRA; RSA; LB; ESP; BEL; MON; SWE; FRA; GBR; GER; AUT; CAN; USA; JPN (all car #12)

1976

CHAMPIONSHIP CAR-BY-CAR

JOCHEN MASS (CONTD)

McLaren M26-Ford V8
Marlboro Team McLaren
Races: NED; ITA (both car #12)

10TH GUNNAR NILSSON (SWE; AGE: 27) 11 PTS

Lotus 77-Ford V8
John Player Team Lotus
Races: RSA; LB; ESP; BEL; MON; SWE; FRA; GBR; GER; AUT; NED; ITA; CAN; USA; JPN (all car #6)

11TH= RONNIE PETERSON (SWE; AGE: 32) 10 PTS

Lotus 77-Ford V8
John Player Team Lotus
Races: BRA (car #5)

RONNIE PETERSON (CONTD)

March 761-Ford V8
March Engineering
Races: RSA; LB; ESP; BEL; MON; SWE; FRA; GBR; GER; AUT; NED; ITA; CAN; USA; JPN (all car #10)

11TH= TOM PRYCE (GBR; AGE: 27) 10 PTS

Shadow DN5B-Ford V8
Shadow Racing Team
Races: BRA; RSA; LB; ESP; BEL; MON; SWE; FRA; GBR; GER; AUT (all car #16)

TOM PRYCE (CONTD)

Shadow DN8A-Ford V8
Shadow Racing Team
Races: NED; ITA; CAN; USA; JPN (all car #16)

13TH HANS-JOACHIM STUCK (GER; AGE: 25) 8 PTS

March 761-Ford V8
March Engineering
Races: BRA; RSA; LB; ESP; BEL; MON; SWE; FRA; GBR; GER; AUT; NED; ITA; CAN; USA; JPN (all car #34)

14TH= ALAN JONES (AUS; AGE: 29) 7 PTS

Surtees TS19-Ford V8
Team Surtees
Races: LB; ESP; BEL; MON; SWE; FRA; GBR; GER; AUT; NED; ITA; CAN; USA; JPN (all car #19)

14TH= CARLOS PACE (BRA; AGE: 31) 7 PTS

Brabham BT45-Alfa Romeo F12
Martini Racing
Races: BRA; RSA; LB; ESP; BEL; MON; SWE; FRA; GBR; GER; AUT; NED; ITA; CAN; USA; JPN (all car #8)

16TH= EMERSON FITTIPALDI (BRA; AGE: 29) 3 PTS

Fittipaldi FD04-Ford V8
Copersucar-Fittipaldi Automotive
Races: BRA; RSA; LB; ESP; MON; SWE; FRA; GBR; GER; AUT; NED; ITA; CAN; USA; JPN (all car #30)

16TH= CARLOS REUTEMANN (ARG; AGE: 34) 3 PTS

Brabham BT45-Alfa Romeo F12
Martini Racing
Races: BRA; RSA; LB; ESP; BEL; MON; SWE; FRA; GBR; GER; AUT; NED (all car #7)

CARLOS REUTEMANN (CONTD)

Ferrari 312T2 F12
Scuderia Ferrari
Races: ITA (car #35)

18TH CHRIS AMON (NZL; AGE: 32) 2 PTS

Ensign N174-Ford V8
Team Ensign
Races: RSA; LB (both car #22)

CHRIS AMON (CONTD)

Ensign N176-Ford V8
Team Ensign
Races: ESP; BEL; MON; SWE; GBR; GER (all car #22)

19TH= VITTORIO BRAMBILLA (ITA; AGE: 38) 1 PT

March 761-Ford V8
March Engineering
Races: BRA; RSA; LB; ESP; BEL; MON; SWE; FRA; GBR; GER; AUT; NED; ITA; CAN; USA; JPN (all car #9)

1976

CHAMPIONSHIP CAR-BY-CAR

19TH= **ROLF STOMMELEN** (GER; AGE: 33) 1 PT

Brabham BT45-Alfa Romeo F12
Martini Racing
Races: GER (car #77); ITA (#7)

ROLF STOMMELEN (CONTD)

Hesketh 308D-Ford V8
Hesketh Racing
Races: NED (car #25)

CONNY ANDERSSON (SWE; AGE: 36) 0 PTS

Surtees TS19-Ford V8
Team Surtees
Races: NED (car #18)

IAN ASHLEY (GBR; AGE: 28) 0 PTS

Stanley BRM P201B V12
Stanley BRM
Races: BRA (car #14)

HANS BINDER (AUT; AGE: 28) 0 PTS

Ensign N176-Ford V8
Team Ensign
Races: AUT (car #22)

HANS BINDER (CONTD)

Williams FW05-Ford V8
Frank Williams Racing Cars
Races: JPN (car #21)

WARWICK BROWN (AUS; AGE: 26) 0 PTS

Williams FW05-Ford V8
Frank Williams Racing Cars
Races: USA (car #21)

GUY EDWARDS (GBR; AGE: 33) 0 PTS

Hesketh 308D-Ford V8
Hesketh Racing
Races: FRA; GBR; GER; CAN (all car #25)

HARALD ERTL (AUT; AGE: 27) 0 PTS

Hesketh 308D-Ford V8
Hesketh Racing
Races: RSA; BEL; SWE; FRA; GBR; GER; AUT; NED; ITA; USA; JPN (all car #24)

BOB EVANS (GBR; AGE: 28) 0 PTS

Lotus 77-Ford V8
John Player Team Lotus
Races: RSA (car #5)

BOB EVANS (GBR; AGE: 28)

Brabham BT44B-Ford V8
RAM Racing
Races: GBR (car #32)

MASAHIRO HASEMI (JPN; AGE: 30) 0 PTS

Kojima KE007-Ford V8
Kojima Engineering
Races: JPN (car #51)

BOY HAYJE (NED; AGE: 27) 0 PTS

Penske PC3-Ford V8
F&S Properties
Races: NED (car #39)

INGO HOFFMANN (BRA; AGE: 22) 0 PTS

Fittipaldi FD03-Ford V8
Copersucar-Fittipaldi Automotive
Races: BRA (car #31)

KAZUYOSHI HOSHINO (JPN; AGE: 29) 0 PTS

Tyrrell 007-Ford V8
Heros Racing Corporation
Races: JPN (car #52)

1976

CHAMPIONSHIP CAR-BY-CAR

JACKY ICKX (BEL; AGE: 31) 0 PTS

Williams FW05-Ford V8
Frank Williams Racing Cars
Races: BRA; RSA; ESP; FRA (all car #20)

JACKY ICKX (CONTD)

Ensign N176-Ford V8
Team Ensign
Races: NED; ITA; CAN; USA (all car #22)

JEAN-PIERRE JARIER (FRA; AGE: 30) 0 PTS

Shadow DN5B-Ford V8
Shadow Racing Team
Races: BRA; RSA; LB; ESP; BEL; MON; SWE; FRA; GBR; GER; AUT; NED; ITA; CAN; USA; JPN (all car #17)

LORIS KESSEL (SUI; AGE: 26) 0 PTS

Brabham BT44B-Ford V8
RAM Racing
Races: BEL; SWE; AUT (all car #32)

MICHEL LECLÈRE (FRA; AGE: 30) 0 PTS

Williams FW05-Ford V8
Frank Williams Racing Cars
Races: RSA; ESP; BEL; MON; SWE; FRA (all car #21)

LELLA LOMBARDI (ITA; AGE: 35) 0 PTS

March 761-Ford V8
March Engineering
Races: BRA (car #10)

LELLA LOMBARDI (CONTD)

Brabham BT44B-Ford V8
RAM Racing
Races: AUT (car #33)

PICTURED DURING GER PRACTICE

BRETT LUNGER (USA; AGE: 30) 0 PTS

Surtees TS19-Ford V8
Team Surtees
Races: RSA; BEL; SWE; FRA; GBR; GER; AUT; ITA; CAN; USA (all car #18)

ARTURO MERZARIO (ITA; AGE: 33) 0 PTS

March 761-Ford V8
March Engineering
Races: ESP; BEL; SWE; FRA; GBR (all car #35)

ARTURO MERZARIO (CONTD)

Williams FW05-Ford V8
Frank Williams Racing Cars
Races: GER; AUT; NED; CAN; USA; JPN (all car #20)

PATRICK NEVE (BEL; AGE: 26) 0 PTS

Brabham BT44B-Ford V8
RAM Racing
Races: BEL (car #33)

PATRICK NEVE (CONTD)

Ensign N176-Ford V8
Team Ensign
Races: FRA (car #22)

LARRY PERKINS (AUS; AGE: 26) 0 PTS

Boro-Ensign N175-Ford V8
HB Bewaking Alarm Systems
Races: ESP; BEL; SWE (all car #37); NED (#27); ITA (#40)

LARRY PERKINS (CONTD)

Brabham BT45-Alfa Romeo F12
Martini Racing
Races: CAN; USA; JPN (all car #7)

HENRI PESCAROLO (FRA; AGE: 33) 0 PTS

Surtees TS19-Ford V8
Team Norev Racing with BS Fabrications
Races: FRA; GBR; AUT; NED; ITA; CAN; USA (all car #38)

1976

CHAMPIONSHIP CAR-BY-CAR

ALESSANDRO PESENTI-ROSSI (ITA; AGE: 34) 0 PTS

Tyrrell 007-Ford V8
Scuderia Gulf Rondini
Races: GER (car #40); AUT (#39); ITA (#37)

ALEX RIBEIRO (BRA; AGE: 27) 0 PTS

Hesketh 308D-Ford V8
Hesketh Racing
Races: USA (car #25)

IAN SCHECKTER (RSA; AGE: 28) 0 PTS

Tyrrell 007-Ford V8
Lexington Racing
Races: RSA (car #15)

NORITAKE TAKAHARA (JPN; AGE: 25) 0 PTS

Surtees TS19-Ford V8
Team Surtees
Races: JPN (car #18)

RENZO ZORZI (ITA; AGE: 29) 0 PTS

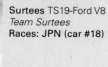

Williams FW04-Ford V8
Frank Williams Racing Cars
Races: BRA (car #21)

GRAND PRIX WINNERS 1976

	RACE (CIRCUIT)	**WINNER** (CAR)
BRA	BRAZILIAN GRAND PRIX (INTERLAGOS)	NIKI LAUDA (FERRARI 312T F12)
RSA	SOUTH AFRICAN GRAND PRIX (KYALAMI)	NIKI LAUDA (FERRARI 312T F12)
LB	LONG BEACH GRAND PRIX (LONG BEACH)	CLAY REGAZZONI (FERRARI 312T F12)
ESP	SPANISH GRAND PRIX (JARAMA)	JAMES HUNT (McLAREN M23-FORD V8)
BEL	BELGIAN GRAND PRIX (ZOLDER)	NIKI LAUDA (FERRARI 312T2 F12)
MON	MONACO GRAND PRIX (MONTE CARLO)	NIKI LAUDA (FERRARI 312T2 F12)
SWE	SWEDISH GRAND PRIX (ANDERSTORP)	JODY SCHECKTER (TYRRELL P34-FORD V8)
FRA	FRENCH GRAND PRIX (PAUL RICARD)	JAMES HUNT (McLAREN M23-FORD V8)
GBR	BRITISH GRAND PRIX (BRANDS HATCH)	NIKI LAUDA (FERRARI 312T2 F12)
GER	GERMAN GRAND PRIX (NÜRBURGRING)	JAMES HUNT (McLAREN M23-FORD V8)
AUT	AUSTRIAN GRAND PRIX (ÖSTERREICHRING)	JOHN WATSON (PENSKE PC4-FORD V8)
NED	DUTCH GRAND PRIX (ZANDVOORT)	JAMES HUNT (McLAREN M23-FORD V8)
ITA	ITALIAN GRAND PRIX (MONZA)	RONNIE PETERSON (MARCH 761-FORD V8)
CAN	CANADIAN GRAND PRIX (MOSPORT PARK)	JAMES HUNT (McLAREN M23-FORD V8)
USA	UNITED STATES GRAND PRIX (WATKINS GLEN)	JAMES HUNT (McLAREN M23-FORD V8)
JPN	JAPANESE GRAND PRIX (FUJI)	MARIO ANDRETTI (LOTUS 77-FORD V8)

1977

CANNY LAUDA DELIVERS PERFECT RIPOSTE

Above
Niki knack: the traumas of the previous season had done nothing to dilute Lauda's dexterity at the wheel

Right
Flash cordon: the Buenos Aires police force turned out in force to escort Jody Scheckter in the wake of his unexpected triumph for F1 newcomer Wolf in the season's opening race

Far right
Potting the black-and-gold: Lauda fends off Mario Andretti's pole-winning Lotus at Zandvoort, where he scored his third victory of the season.

MICHELIN
John Player Special
Valvoline
GOOD-YEAR
Agip
arexons
11
5

The dramatic events of 1976 had a fitting postscript the following year when Niki Lauda regained the world championship. It was a story given an extra little twist when Lauda walked out on Ferrari as soon as he had clinched the crown, despite there still being three races to go. This was in retribution for the lack of support he felt the team had given him during his fightback from injury the year before.

Lauda's title was the product of reliability more than speed. The new, ground-effect Lotus 78 of Mario Andretti was usually the fastest car and the Italo-American won more races – four – than anyone else, but engine failures cost him dearly and he was restricted to third in the championship. Jody Scheckter was runner-up after a remarkable season with Wolf. He gave the new team an unexpected debut victory when the season opened in Argentina, added two further wins during the year and was a consistent challenger throughout.

Lauda's 1976 title foe James Hunt had an indifferent first half-season while McLaren tried to develop its new M26 chassis. This finally came good in the summer and Hunt made his seasonal breakthrough at Silverstone, the first of three wins. This, though, was an inherited success. John Watson retired his Brabham-Alfa Romeo from the lead – and that was typical of the Ulsterman's form and luck during the year. Only two weeks earlier he had lost what appeared to be a certain French GP victory when he ran short of fuel on the final lap.

Top
Campaign for real frail: Andretti streaks away from Hunt and the rest in Canada. The American often had the fastest car and won more races than champion Lauda, but unreliability plagued him. On this occasion his engine blew when he was just a couple of laps from home

Above
Fuel if you think it's over: Andretti wasn't the only driver who could justly complain about ill fortune. Here he trails John Watson's Brabham in France – and he stayed behind until the final lap, when his rival's car began to run dry. The Ulsterman coasted home second

1977

CHAMPIONSHIP CAR-BY-CAR

1ST NIKI LAUDA (AUT; AGE: 28) 72 PTS

Ferrari 312T2 F12
Scuderia Ferrari
Races: ARG; BRA; RSA; LB; MON; BEL; SWE; FRA; GBR; GER; AUT; NED; ITA; USA (all car #11)

2ND JODY SCHECKTER (RSA; AGE: 27) 55 PTS

Wolf WR1/WR3-Ford V8
Walter Wolf Racing
Races: ARG; BRA; RSA; LB; ESP; MON; BEL; SWE; FRA; GBR; GER; AUT; NED; ITA; CAN; USA; JPN (all car #20)

3RD MARIO ANDRETTI (USA; AGE: 37) 47 PTS

Lotus 78-Ford V8
John Player Team Lotus
Races: ARG; BRA; RSA; LB; ESP; MON; BEL; SWE; FRA; GBR; GER; AUT; NED; ITA; USA; CAN; JPN (all car #5)

4TH CARLOS REUTEMANN (ARG; AGE: 35) 42 PTS

Ferrari 312T2 F12
Scuderia Ferrari
Races: ARG; BRA; RSA; LB; ESP; MON; BEL; SWE; FRA; GBR; GER; AUT; NED; ITA; USA; CAN; JPN (all car #12)

5TH JAMES HUNT (GBR; AGE: 29) 40 PTS

McLaren M23-Ford V8
Marlboro Team McLaren
Races: ARG; BRA; RSA; LB; MON (all car #1)

JAMES HUNT (CONTD)

McLaren M26-Ford V8
Marlboro Team McLaren
Races: ESP; BEL; SWE; FRA; GBR; GER; AUT; NED; ITA; USA; CAN; JPN (all car #1)

6TH JOCHEN MASS (GER; AGE: 30) 25 PTS

McLaren M23-Ford V8
Marlboro Team McLaren
Races: ARG; BRA; RSA; LB; ESP; MON; BEL; SWE; FRA (all car #2)

JOCHEN MASS (CONTD)

McLaren M26-Ford V8
Marlboro Team McLaren
Races: GBR; GER; AUT; NED; ITA; USA; CAN; JPN (all car #2)

7TH ALAN JONES (AUS; AGE: 30) 22 PTS

Shadow DN8A-Ford V8
Shadow Racing Team
Races: RSA; LB; ESP; MON; BEL; SWE; FRA; GBR; GER; AUT; NED; ITA; USA; CAN; JPN (all car #17)

8TH= PATRICK DEPAILLER (FRA; AGE: 32) 20 PTS

Tyrrell P34-Ford V8
Elf Team Tyrrell
Races: ARG; BRA; RSA; LB; ESP; MON; BEL; SWE; FRA; GBR; GER; AUT; NED; ITA; USA; CAN; JPN (all car #4)

8TH= GUNNAR NILSSON (SWE; AGE: 28) 20 PTS

Lotus 78-Ford V8
John Player Team Lotus
Races: BRA; RSA; LB; ESP; MON; BEL; SWE; FRA; GBR; GER; AUT; NED; ITA; USA; CAN; JPN (all car #6)

10TH JACQUES LAFFITE (FRA; AGE: 33) 18 PTS

Ligier JS7-Matra V12
Équipe Ligier Gitanes
Races: ARG; BRA; RSA; LB; ESP; MON; BEL; SWE; FRA; GBR; GER; AUT; NED; ITA; USA; CAN; JPN (all car #26)

11TH HANS-JOACHIM STUCK (GER; AGE: 26) 12 PTS

March 761B-Ford V8
March Engineering
Races: RSA (car #10)

HANS-JOACHIM STUCK (GER; AGE: 26)

Brabham BT45B-Alfa Romeo F12
Martini Racing
Races: LB; ESP; MON; BEL; SWE; FRA; GBR; GER; AUT; NED; ITA; USA; CAN; JPN (all car #8)

12TH EMERSON FITTIPALDI (BRA; AGE: 30) 11 PTS

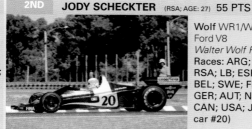

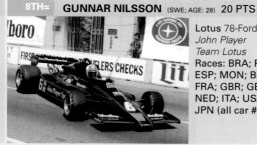

Fittipaldi FD04-Ford V8
Copersucar-Fittipaldi Automotive
Races: ARG; BRA; RSA; LB; ESP; MON; SWE (all car #28)

1977

CHAMPIONSHIP CAR-BY-CAR

EMERSON FITTIPALDI (CONTD)

Fittipaldi F5-Ford V8
Copersucar-Fittipaldi Automotive
Races: BEL; FRA; GBR; AUT; NED; USA; CAN (all car #28)

13TH JOHN WATSON (GBR; AGE: 31) 9 PTS

Brabham BT45-Alfa Romeo F12
Martini Racing
Races: ARG; BRA; RSA; LB; ESP; MON; BEL; SWE; FRA; GBR; GER; AUT; NED; ITA; USA; CAN; JPN (all car #7)

14TH RONNIE PETERSON (SWE; AGE: 33) 7 PTS

Tyrrell P34-Ford V8
Elf Team Tyrrell
Races: ARG; BRA; RSA; LB; ESP; MON; BEL; SWE; FRA; GBR; GER; AUT; NED; ITA; USA; CAN; JPN (all car #3)

15TH= VITTORIO BRAMBILLA (ITA; AGE: 39) 6 PTS

Surtees TS19-Ford V8
Team Surtees
Races: ARG; BRA; RSA; LB; ESP; MON; BEL; SWE; FRA; GBR; GER; AUT; NED; ITA; USA; CAN; JPN (all car #19)

15TH= CARLOS PACE (BRA; AGE: 32) 6 PTS

Brabham BT45-Alfa Romeo F12
Martini Racing
Races: ARG; BRA; RSA (all car #8)

17TH= CLAY REGAZZONI (SUI; AGE: 37) 5 PTS

Ensign N177-Ford V8
Team Tissot Ensign with Castrol
Races: ARG; BRA; RSA; LB; ESP; BEL; SWE; FRA; GER; AUT; NED; ITA; USA; CAN; JPN (all car #22)

17TH= PATRICK TAMBAY (FRA; AGE: 28) 5 PTS

Ensign N177-Ford V8
Theodore Racing Hong Kong
Races: GBR; GER; AUT; NED; ITA; CAN; JPN (all car #23)

19TH= JEAN-PIERRE JARIER (FRA; AGE: 31) 1 PT

Penske PC4-Ford V8
ATS Racing Team
Races: LB; MON; BEL; SWE; FRA; GBR; GER; AUT; NED; ITA (all car #34)

JEAN-PIERRE JARIER (CONTD)

Shadow DN8A-Ford V8
Shadow Racing Team
Races: USA (car #16)

JEAN-PIERRE JARIER (CONTD)

Ligier JS7-Matra V12
Équipe Ligier Gitanes
Races: JPN (car #27)

19TH= RICCARDO PATRESE (ITA; AGE: 23) 1 PT

Shadow DN8A-Ford V8
Shadow Racing Team
Races: MON; BEL; FRA; GBR; GER; NED; ITA; CAN; JPN (all car #16)

19TH= RENZO ZORZI (ITA; AGE: 30) 1 PT

Shadow DN5B-Ford V8
Shadow Racing Team
Races: ARG; BRA (both car #17)

RENZO ZORZI (CONTD)

Shadow DN8A-Ford V8
Shadow Racing Team
Races: RSA (car #17); LB; ESP (both #16)

IAN ASHLEY (GBR; AGE: 29) 0 PTS

Hesketh 308E-Ford V8
Hesketh Racing
Races: USA (car #25)

HANS BINDER (AUT; AGE: 29) 0 PTS

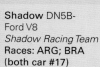

Surtees TS19-Ford V8
Team Surtees
Races: ARG; BRA; RSA; LB; ESP; MON; USA; CAN; JPN (all car #18)

1977

CHAMPIONSHIP CAR-BY-CAR

HANS BINDER (CONTD)

Penske PC4-Ford V8
ATS Racing Team
Races: AUT (car #33); NED (#35)

HARALD ERTL (AUT; AGE: 28) 0 PTS

Hesketh 308E-Ford V8
Hesketh Racing
Races: ESP; BEL; SWE (all car #25)

BRUNO GIACOMELLI (ITA; AGE: 25) 0 PTS

McLaren M23-Ford V8
Marlboro Team McLaren
Races: ITA (car #14)

BOY HAYJE (NED; AGE: 28) 0 PTS

March 761-Ford V8
RAM Racing
Races: RSA; BEL (both car #33)

PICTURED DURING ESP PRACTICE

BRIAN HENTON (GBR; AGE: 30) 0 PTS

March 761B-Ford V8
March Engineering
Races: LB (car #10)

PICTURED DURING ESP PRACTICE

BRIAN HENTON (CONTD)

Boro-Ensign N175-Ford V8
HB Bewaking Alarm Systems
Races: NED (car #38)

HANS HEYER (GER; AGE: 34) 0 PTS

Penske PC4-Ford V8
ATS Racing Team
Races: GER (car #35)

INGO HOFFMANN (BRA; AGE: 23) 0 PTS

Fittipaldi FD04-Ford V8
Copersucar-Fittipaldi Automotive
Races: ARG; BRA (both car #29)

KAZUYOSHI HOSHINO (JPN; AGE: 30) 0 PTS

Kojima KE009-Ford V8
Heros Racing Corporation
Races: JPN (car #52)

JACKY ICKX (BEL; AGE: 32) 0 PTS

Ensign N177-Ford V8
Team Tissot Ensign with Castrol
Races: MON (car #22)

JEAN-PIERRE JABOUILLE (FRA; AGE: 34) 0 PTS

Renault RS01 V6 tc
Équipe Renault Elf
Races: GBR; NED; ITA; USA (all car #15)

RUPERT KEEGAN (GBR; AGE: 22) 0 PTS

Hesketh 308E-Ford V8
Hesketh Racing
Races: ESP; MON; BEL; SWE; FRA; GBR; GER; AUT; NED; ITA; USA; CAN (all car #24)

BRETT LUNGER (USA; AGE: 31) 0 PTS

March 761-Ford V8
Chesterfield Racing
Races: RSA; LB; ESP (all car #30)

BRETT LUNGER (CONTD)

McLaren M23-Ford V8
Chesterfield Racing
Races: SWE; GBR; GER; AUT; NED; ITA; USA; CAN (all car #30)

ARTURO MERZARIO (ITA; AGE: 34) 0 PTS

March 761B-Ford V8
Team Merzario
Races: ESP; BEL; FRA; GBR (all car #37)

1977

CHAMPIONSHIP CAR-BY-CAR

ARTURO MERZARIO (CONTD)

Shadow DN8A-Ford V8
Shadow Racing Team
Races: AUT (car #16)

PATRICK NEVE (BEL; AGE: 27) 0 PTS

March 761-Ford V8
Williams Grand Prix Engineering
Races: ESP; BEL; SWE; GBR; AUT; ITA; USA; CAN (all car #27)

JACKIE OLIVER (GBR; AGE: 34) 0 PTS

Shadow DN8A-Ford V8
Shadow Racing Team
Races: SWE (car #16)

PICTURED AT NON-CHAMPIONSHIP RACE

DANNY ONGAIS (USA; AGE: 35) 0 PTS

Penske PC4-Ford V8
Interscope Racing
Races: USA; CAN (both car #14)

LARRY PERKINS (AUS; AGE: 27) 0 PTS

Stanley BRM P207 V12
Rotary Watches Stanley BRM
Races: BRA (car #14)

LARRY PERKINS (CONTD)

Stanley BRM P201B/204 V12
Rotary Watches Stanley BRM
Races: RSA (car #14)

LARRY PERKINS (CONTD)

Surtees TS19-Ford V8
Team Surtees
Races: BEL (car #18)

TOM PRYCE (GBR; AGE: 27) 0 PTS

Shadow DN8A-Ford V8
Shadow Racing Team
Races: ARG; BRA; RSA (all car #16)

DAVID PURLEY (GBR; AGE: 32) 0 PTS

Lec CRP1-Ford V8
Lec Refrigeration Racing
Races: BEL; SWE; FRA (all car #31)

HECTOR REBAQUE (MEX; AGE: 21) 0 PTS

Hesketh 308E-Ford V8
Hesketh Racing
Races: GER (car #25)

PICTURED DURING NED PRACTICE

ALEX RIBEIRO (BRA; AGE: 28) 0 PTS

March 761B-Ford V8
March Engineering
Races: ARG; BRA; RSA; LB; GER; NED; USA; CAN; JPN (all car #9)

IAN SCHECKTER (RSA; AGE: 29) 0 PTS

March 761B-Ford V8
March Engineering
Races: ARG; BRA; ESP; BEL; SWE; FRA; GBR; GER; AUT (all car #10)

IAN SCHECKTER (CONTD)

March 771-Ford V8
March Engineering
Races: NED; ITA; USA; CAN (all car #10)

VERN SCHUPPAN (AUS; AGE: 34) 0 PTS

Surtees TS19-Ford V8
Team Surtees
Races: GBR; GER; AUT (all car #18)

NORITAKE TAKAHARA (JPN; AGE: 26) 0 PTS

Kojima KE009-Ford V8
Kojima Engineering
Races: JPN (car #51)

1977

CHAMPIONSHIP CAR-BY-CAR

KUNIMITSU TAKAHASHI (JPN; AGE: 37) 0 PTS

Tyrrell 007-Ford V8
Meiritsu Racing Team
Races: JPN (car #50)

GILLES VILLENEUVE (CAN; AGE: 27) 0 PTS

McLaren M23-Ford V8
Marlboro Team McLaren
Races: GBR (car #40)

GILLES VILLENEUVE (CONTD)

Ferrari 312T2 F12
Scuderia Ferrari
Races: CAN (car #21); JPN (#11)

EMILIO DE VILLOTA (ESP; AGE: 30) 0 PTS

McLaren M23-Ford V8
Iberia Airlines
Races: ESP; AUT (both car #36)

GRAND PRIX WINNERS 1977

	RACE (CIRCUIT)	**WINNER** (CAR)
ARG	ARGENTINIAN GRAND PRIX (BUENOS AIRES)	JODY SCHECKTER (WOLF WR1-FORD V8)
BRA	BRAZILIAN GRAND PRIX (INTERLAGOS)	CARLOS REUTEMANN (FERRARI 312T2 F12)
RSA	SOUTH AFRICAN GRAND PRIX (KYALAMI)	NIKI LAUDA (FERRARI 312T2 F12)
LB	LONG BEACH GRAND PRIX (LONG BEACH)	MARIO ANDRETTI (LOTUS 78-FORD V8)
ESP	SPANISH GRAND PRIX (JARAMA)	MARIO ANDRETTI (LOTUS 78-FORD V8)
MON	MONACO GRAND PRIX (MONTE CARLO)	JODY SCHECKTER (WOLF WR1-FORD V8)
BEL	BELGIAN GRAND PRIX (ZOLDER)	GUNNAR NILSSON (LOTUS 78-FORD V8)
SWE	SWEDISH GRAND PRIX (ANDERSTORP)	JACQUES LAFFITE (LIGIER JS7-MATRA V12)
FRA	FRENCH GRAND PRIX (DIJON-PRENOIS)	MARIO ANDRETTI (LOTUS 78-FORD V8)
GBR	BRITISH GRAND PRIX (SILVERSTONE)	JAMES HUNT (McLAREN M26-FORD V8)
GER	GERMAN GRAND PRIX (HOCKENHEIM)	NIKI LAUDA (FERRARI 312T2 F12)
AUT	AUSTRIAN GRAND PRIX (ÖSTERREICHRING)	ALAN JONES (SHADOW DN8A-FORD V8)
NED	DUTCH GRAND PRIX (ZANDVOORT)	NIKI LAUDA (FERRARI 312T2 F12)
ITA	ITALIAN GRAND PRIX (MONZA)	MARIO ANDRETTI (LOTUS 78-FORD V8)
USA	UNITED STATES GRAND PRIX (WATKINS GLEN)	JAMES HUNT (McLAREN M26-FORD V8)
CAN	CANADIAN GRAND PRIX (MOSPORT PARK)	JODY SCHECKTER (WOLF WR1-FORD V8)
JPN	JAPANESE GRAND PRIX (FUJI)	JAMES HUNT (McLAREN M26-FORD V8)

1978

LOTUS HAS THE TECHNICAL EDGE IN BITTER-SWEET CAMPAIGN

Left
Sign of the lap times: Andretti got his hands on the new Lotus 79 in Belgium – and rivals didn't see him again until the podium ceremony

Above
Don't throw away your old 78s: Peterson leads Jones in South Africa, where he gave the outgoing Lotus its final victory

Right:
Game, sept and match: France had F1 strength in depth during the 1970s. Top row, from left: Jarier, Tambay, Pironi and Depailler. Front: Laffite, Jabouille and Arnoux

Far right
Poignant encounter: former racer Gunnar Nilsson in the Brands Hatch pits with compatriot Ronnie Peterson and Lotus engineer Nigel Bennett. Both Swedes would be dead by October: Nilsson succumbed to cancer; Peterson died as a result of injuries sustained at Monza

John Player Spe
n Player Special
GOODYEAR
saudia
6

TOTAL
Marlboro
TEXACO
elf
parmalat

GOODYEAR
POLAR

Lotus finally reaped full benefit of the aerodynamic breakthrough it had made the previous season. The black-and-gold, ground-effect Lotus 79s of Mario Andretti and contracted number two Ronnie Peterson dominated the campaign and were usually able to reduce the rest of the field to bit players.

Andretti took the title in tragic circumstances at the Italian Grand Prix. Peterson was involved in a serious, multi-car accident shortly after the start and succumbed to his injuries the following morning.

Lotus began the year with the previous season's 78 model – and even that was good enough to win two of the first five races. The 79 addressed the old car's singular weakness – lack of straightline speed – and Andretti gave it a victorious debut in the Belgian GP, leading home Peterson's 78. By the next race in Spain both drivers were equipped with the new car and duly left their rivals far behind. The venturi channels in the car's sidepods created a suction effect when the pods were sealed to the track surface via sliding lateral skirts. This was the key to their massive superiority.

Brabham designer Gordon Murray attempted to combat them midway through the year with his own interpretation of ground-effect aerodynamics. This involved fitting the rear of the car with skirts and a massive fan to create suction. Niki Lauda and John Watson used the infamous BT46B to finish first and second in the Swedish GP, but thereafter it was banned on the grounds that the fan constituted a movable aerodynamic device.

Ferrari won five times – four with Carlos Reutemann and once with exciting rookie Gilles Villeneuve – thanks to a combination of occasional Michelin tyre superiority and great reliability.

Above left
Heir Canada: Gilles Villeneuve scored his maiden F1 win on home soil. It was also the first grand prix to be staged in Montreal

Above
Dark side of the mood: Carlos Reutemann on one of his more sombre days. He did score four wins during the season, mind

Left
Plane sailing: James Hunt tried this unusual front wing set-up during practice in Spain, but his McLaren was more conventionally appended in the race

Right
Dive, dive, dive: Watson lunges inside Reutemann on the opening lap of the Long Beach GP as Villeneuve, Lauda and Andretti tuck in behind. A leaky oil tank soon forced Watson out and Reutemann went on to win

THE VENTURI CHANNELS IN THE LOTUS 79's SIDEPODS CREATED A SUCTION EFFECT WHEN THE PODS WERE SEALED TO THE TRACK SURFACE VIA SLIDING LATERAL SKIRTS. THIS WAS THE KEY TO ITS MASSIVE SUPERIORITY

MARIO ANDRETTI – WORLD CHAMPION 1978

1978

CHAMPIONSHIP CAR-BY-CAR

1ST MARIO ANDRETTI (USA; Age: 38) 64 pts

Lotus 78-Ford V8
John Player Team Lotus
Races: ARG; BRA; RSA; LB; MON (all car #5)

MARIO ANDRETTI (CONTD)

Lotus 79-Ford V8
John Player Team Lotus
Races: BEL; ESP; SWE; FRA; GBR; GER; AUT; NED; ITA; USA; CAN (all car #5)

2ND RONNIE PETERSON (SWE; AGE: 34) 51 PTS

Lotus 78-Ford V8
John Player Team Lotus
Races: ARG; BRA; RSA; LB; MON; BEL; ITA (all car #6)

RONNIE PETERSON (CONTD)

Lotus 79-Ford V8
John Player Team Lotus
Races: ESP; SWE; FRA; GBR; GER; AUT; NED (all car #6)

3RD CARLOS REUTEMANN (ARG; AGE: 36) 48 PTS

Ferrari 312T2 F12
Scuderia Ferrari
Races: ARG; BRA (both car #11)

CARLOS REUTEMANN (CONTD)

Ferrari 312T3 F12
Scuderia Ferrari
Races: RSA; LB; MON; BEL; ESP; SWE; FRA; GBR; GER; AUT; NED; ITA; USA; CAN (all car #11)

4TH NIKI LAUDA (AUT; AGE: 29) 44 PTS

Brabham BT45C-Alfa Romeo F12
Parmalat Racing Team
Races: ARG; BRA (both car #1)

NIKI LAUDA (CONTD)

Brabham BT46-Alfa Romeo F12
Parmalat Racing Team
Races: RSA; LB; MON; BEL; ESP; FRA; GBR; GER; AUT; NED; ITA; USA; CAN (all car #1)

NIKI LAUDA (CONTD)

Brabham BT46B-Alfa Romeo F12 "fan car"
Parmalat Racing Team
Races: SWE (car #1)

5TH PATRICK DEPAILLER (FRA; AGE: 33) 34 PTS

Tyrrell 008-Ford V8
Elf Team Tyrrell
Races: ARG; BRA; RSA; LB; MON; BEL; ESP; SWE; FRA; GBR; GER; AUT; NED; ITA; USA; CAN (all car #4)

6TH JOHN WATSON (GBR; AGE: 32) 25 PTS

Brabham BT45C-Alfa Romeo F12
Parmalat Racing Team
Races: ARG; BRA (both car #2)

JOHN WATSON (CONTD)

Brabham BT46-Alfa Romeo F12
Parmalat Racing Team
Races: RSA; LB; MON; BEL; ESP; FRA; GBR; GER; AUT; NED; ITA; USA; CAN (all car #2)

JOHN WATSON (CONTD)

Brabham BT46B-Alfa Romeo F12 "fan car"
Parmalat Racing Team
Races: SWE (car #2)

7TH JODY SCHECKTER (RSA; AGE: 28) 24 PTS

Wolf WR1/WR4-Ford V8
Walter Wolf Racing
Races: ARG; BRA; RSA; LB; MON (all car #20)

JODY SCHECKTER (CONTD)

Wolf WR5/WR6-Ford V8
Walter Wolf Racing
Races: BEL; ESP; SWE; FRA; GBR; GER; AUT; NED; ITA; USA; CAN (all car #20)

1978

CHAMPIONSHIP CAR-BY-CAR

8TH JACQUES LAFFITE (FRA; AGE: 34) 19 PTS

Ligier JS7-Matra V12
Équipe Ligier Gitanes
Races: ARG; BRA; LB (all car #26)

JACQUES LAFFITE (CONTD)

Ligier JS7/9-Matra V12
Équipe Ligier Gitanes
Races: RSA; BEL; FRA; GBR (all car #26)

JACQUES LAFFITE (CONTD)

Ligier JS9-Matra V12
Équipe Ligier Gitanes
Races: MON; ESP; SWE; GER; AUT; NED; ITA; USA; CAN (all car #26)

9TH= EMERSON FITTIPALDI (BRA; AGE: 31) 17 PTS

Fittipaldi F5A-Ford V8
Fittipaldi Automotive
Races: ARG; BRA; RSA; LB; MON; BEL; ESP; SWE; FRA; GBR; GER; AUT; NED; ITA; USA; CAN (all car #14)

9TH= GILLES VILLENEUVE (CAN; AGE: 28) 17 PTS

Ferrari 312T2 F12
Scuderia Ferrari
Races: ARG; BRA (both car #12)

GILLES VILLENEUVE (CONTD)

Ferrari 312T3 F12
Scuderia Ferrari
Races: RSA; LB; MON; BEL; ESP; SWE; FRA; GBR; GER; AUT; NED; ITA; USA; CAN (all car #12)

11TH= ALAN JONES (AUS; AGE: 31) 11 PTS

Williams FW06-Ford V8
Williams Grand Prix Engineering
Races: ARG; BRA; RSA; LB; MON; BEL; ESP; SWE; FRA; GBR; GER; AUT; NED; ITA; USA; CAN (all car #27

11TH= RICCARDO PATRESE (ITA; AGE: 24) 11 PTS

Arrows FA1-Ford V8
Arrows Racing Team
Races: BRA; RSA; LB; MON; BEL; ESP; SWE; FRA; GBR; GER (all car #35)

RICCARDO PATRESE (CONTD)

Arrows A1-Ford V8
Arrows Racing Team
Races: AUT; NED; ITA; CAN (all car #35)

13TH= JAMES HUNT (GBR; AGE: 30) 8 PTS

McLaren M26-Ford V8
Marlboro Team McLaren
Races: ARG; BRA; RSA; LB; MON; BEL; ESP; SWE; FRA; GBR; GER; AUT; NED; ITA; USA; CAN (all car #7)

13TH= PATRICK TAMBAY (FRA; AGE: 29) 8 PTS

McLaren M26-Ford V8
Marlboro Team McLaren
Races: ARG; BRA; RSA; LB; MON; ESP; SWE; FRA; GBR; GER; AUT; NED; ITA; USA; CAN (all car #8)

15TH DIDIER PIRONI (FRA; AGE: 26) 7 PTS

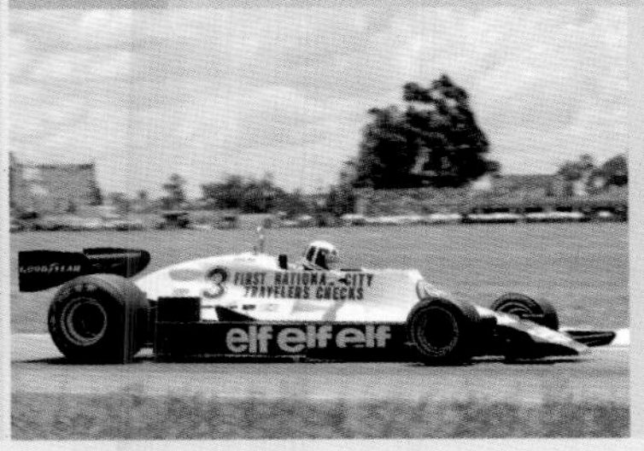

Tyrrell 008-Ford V8
Elf Team Tyrrell
Races: ARG; BRA; RSA; LB; MON; BEL; ESP; SWE; FRA; GBR; GER; AUT; NED; ITA; USA; CAN (all car #3)

16TH CLAY REGAZZONI (SUI; AGE: 38) 4 PTS

Shadow DN8A-Ford V8
Shadow Racing Team
Races: ARG; BRA; LB (all car #17)

PICTURED DURING RSA PRACTICE

CLAY REGAZZONI (CONTD)

Shadow DN9A-Ford V8
Shadow Racing Team
Races: BEL; ESP; SWE; FRA; GBR; AUT; ITA; USA (all car #17)

17TH JEAN-PIERRE JABOUILLE (FRA; AGE: 35) 3 PTS

Renault RS01 V6 tc
Équipe Renault Elf
Races: RSA; LB; MON; BEL; ESP; SWE; FRA; GBR; GER; AUT; NED; ITA; USA; CAN (all car #15)

1978

CHAMPIONSHIP CAR-BY-CAR

18TH HANS-JOACHIM STUCK (GER; AGE: 27) 2 PTS

Shadow DN8A-Ford V8
Shadow Racing Team
Races: ARG; BRA (both car #16)

HANS-JOACHIM STUCK (CONTD)

Shadow DN9A-Ford V8
Shadow Racing Team
Races: MON; BEL; ESP; SWE; FRA; GBR; GER; AUT; NED; ITA; USA; CAN (all car #16)

19TH= VITTORIO BRAMBILLA (ITA; AGE: 40) 1 PT

Surtees TS19-Ford V8
Team Surtees
Races: ARG; RSA; LB (all car #19)

VITTORIO BRAMBILLA (CONTD)

Surtees TS20-Ford V8
Team Surtees
Races: BEL; ESP; SWE; FRA; GBR; GER; AUT; NED; ITA (all car #19)

19TH= DEREK DALY (IRL; AGE: 25) 1 PT

Ensign N177-Ford V8
Team Tissot Ensign
Races: GBR; AUT; NED; ITA; USA; CAN (all car #22)

19TH= HECTOR REBAQUE (MEX; AGE: 22) 1 PT

Lotus 78-Ford V8
Team Rebaque
Races: BRA; RSA; ESP; SWE; GBR; GER; AUT; NED; USA (all car #25)

RENÉ ARNOUX (FRA; AGE: 30) 0 PTS

Martini MK23-Ford V8
Automobiles Martini
Races: BEL; FRA; AUT; NED (all car #31)

PICTURED DURING RSA PRACTICE

RENÉ ARNOUX (CONTD)

Surtees TS20-Ford V8
Team Surtees
Races: USA; CAN (both car #18)

MICHAEL BLEEKEMOLEN (NED; AGE: 29) 0 pts

ATS HS1-Ford V8
ATS Racing Team
Races: USA (car #9)

EDDIE CHEEVER (USA; AGE: 20) 0 PTS

Hesketh 308E-Ford V8
Olympus Cameras with Hesketh
Races: RSA (car #24)

HARALD ERTL (AUT; AGE: 29) 0 PTS

Ensign N177-Ford V8
Sachs Racing
Races: GER; AUT (both car #23)

BRUNO GIACOMELLI (ITA; AGE: 25) 0 PTS

McLaren M26-Ford V8
Marlboro Team McLaren
Races: BEL; FRA; GBR; NED; ITA (all car #33)

JACKY ICKX (BEL; AGE: 33) 0 PTS

Ensign N177-Ford V8
Team Tissot Ensign
Races: MON; BEL; ESP (all car #22)

JEAN-PIERRE JARIER (FRA; AGE: 31) 0 PTS

ATS HS1-Ford V8
ATS Racing Team
Races: ARG; RSA; LB (all car #10)

JEAN-PIERRE JARIER (CONTD)

Lotus 79-Ford V8
John Player Team Lotus
Races: USA; CAN (both car #55)

1978

CHAMPIONSHIP CAR-BY-CAR

RUPERT KEEGAN (GBR; AGE: 23) 0 PTS

Surtees TS19-Ford V8
Team Surtees
Races: ARG; BRA; RSA; MON (all car #18)

RUPERT KEEGAN (CONTD)

Surtees TS20-Ford V8
Team Surtees
Races: ESP; FRA (both car #18)

PICTURED DURING SWE PRACTICE

LAMBERTO LEONI (ITA; AGE: 24) 0 PTS

Ensign N177-Ford V8
Team Tissot Ensign
Races: ARG (car #23)

BRETT LUNGER (USA; AGE: 32) 0 PTS

McLaren M23-Ford V8
Liggett Group with BS Fabrications
Races: ARG; BRA; RSA (all car #30)

PICTURED DURING LB PRACTICE

BRETT LUNGER (CONTD)

McLaren M26-Ford V8
Liggett Group with BS Fabrications
Races: BEL; FRA; GBR; AUT; NED; ITA (all car #30)

BRETT LUNGER (CONTD)

Ensign N177-Ford V8
Team Tissot Ensign
Races: USA (car #23)

JOCHEN MASS (GER; AGE: 31) 0 PTS

ATS HS1-Ford V8
ATS Racing Team
Races: ARG; BRA; RSA; LB; BEL; ESP; SWE; FRA; GBR; GER (all car #9)

PICTURED DURING MON PRACTICE

ARTURO MERZARIO (ITA; AGE: 35) 0 PTS

Merzario A1-Ford V8
Team Merzario
Races: ARG; RSA; LB; SWE; GBR; NED; ITA; USA (all car #37)

DANNY ONGAIS (USA; AGE: 35) 0 PTS

Ensign N177-Ford V8
Team Tissot Ensign
Races: ARG; BRA (both car #22)

NELSON PIQUET (BRA; AGE: 26) 0 PTS

Ensign N177-Ford V8
Team Tissot Ensign
Races: GER (car #22)

NELSON PIQUET (CONTD)

McLaren M23-Ford V8
Liggett Group with BS Fabrications
Races: AUT; NED; ITA (all car #29)

NELSON PIQUET (CONTD)

Brabham BT46-Alfa Romeo F12
Parmalat Racing Team
Races: CAN (car #66)

BOBBY RAHAL (USA; AGE: 25) 0 PTS

Wolf WR5-Ford V8
Walter Wolf Racing
Races: USA (car #21)

BOBBY RAHAL (CONTD)

Wolf WR1-Ford V8
Walter Wolf Racing
Races: CAN (car #21)

KEKE ROSBERG (FIN; AGE: 29) 0 PTS

Theodore TR1-Ford V8
Theodore Racing Hong Kong
Races: RSA (car #32)

PICTURED DURING MON PRACTICE

1978

CHAMPIONSHIP CAR-BY-CAR

KEKE ROSBERG (CONTD)

ATS HS1-Ford V8
ATS Racing Team
Races: SWE; FRA; GBR (all car #10)

KEKE ROSBERG (CONTD)

Wolf WR3/WR4-Ford V8
Theodore Racing Hong Kong
Races: GER; AUT; NED (all car #32)

KEKE ROSBERG (CONTD)

ATS D1-Ford V8
ATS Racing Team
Races: USA; CAN (both car #10)

ROLF STOMMELEN (GER; AGE: 34) 0 PTS

Arrows FA1-Ford V8
Arrows Racing Team
Races: RSA; LB; MON; BEL; ESP; SWE; FRA; GER (all car #36)

ROLF STOMMELEN (CONTD)

Arrows A1-Ford V8
Arrows Racing Team
Races: USA (car #36)

GRAND PRIX WINNERS 1978

	RACE (CIRCUIT)	WINNER (CAR)
ARG	ARGENTINE GRAND PRIX (BUENOS AIRES)	MARIO ANDRETTI (LOTUS 78-FORD V8)
BRA	BRAZILIAN GRAND PRIX (RIO DE JANEIRO)	CARLOS REUTEMANN (FERRARI 312T2 F12)
RSA	SOUTH AFRICAN GRAND PRIX (KYALAMI)	RONNIE PETERSON (LOTUS 78-FORD V8)
LB	LONG BEACH GRAND PRIX (LONG BEACH)	CARLOS REUTEMANN (FERRARI 312T3 F12)
MON	MONACO GRAND PRIX (MONTE CARLO)	PATRICK DEPAILLER (TYRRELL 008-FORD V8)
BEL	BELGIAN GRAND PRIX (ZOLDER)	MARIO ANDRETTI (LOTUS 79-FORD V8)
ESP	SPANISH GRAND PRIX (JARAMA)	MARIO ANDRETTI (LOTUS 79-FORD V8)
SWE	SWEDISH GRAND PRIX (ANDERSTORP)	NIKI LAUDA (BRABHAM BT46B-ALFA ROMEO F12)
FRA	FRENCH GRAND PRIX (PAUL RICARD)	MARIO ANDRETTI (LOTUS 79-FORD V8)
GBR	BRITISH GRAND PRIX (BRANDS HATCH)	CARLOS REUTEMANN (FERRARI 312T3 F12)
GER	GERMAN GRAND PRIX (HOCKENHEIM)	MARIO ANDRETTI (LOTUS 79-FORD V8)
AUT	AUSTRIAN GRAND PRIX (ÖSTERREICHRING)	RONNIE PETERSON (LOTUS 79-FORD V8)
NED	DUTCH GRAND PRIX (ZANDVOORT)	MARIO ANDRETTI (LOTUS 79-FORD V8)
ITA	ITALIAN GRAND PRIX (MONZA)	NIKI LAUDA (BRABHAM BT46-ALFA ROMEO F12)
USA	UNITED STATES GRAND PRIX (WATKINS GLEN)	CARLOS REUTEMANN (FERRARI 312T3 F12)
CAN	CANADIAN GRAND PRIX (MONTRÉAL)	GILLES VILLENEUVE (FERRARI 312T3 F12)

1979

CONSISTENCY THE KEY FOR SCHECKTER AND FERRARI

Far left
Keeping up with the Jones: Villeneuve tracks the pace-setting Australian at Zandvoort. The Williams team scored its maiden GP win in 1979 – and had racked up five by the season's end

Above
Red, steady, go: Scheckter finished in the top six 12 times in 15 starts and wrapped up the title at Monza

Left
Things you don't see any more, sadly: Gilles Villeneuve as the sport will forever remember him – giving his all irrespective of circumstance

Ligier was the dominant force at the start of the season and Williams was the team to beat by the end – but Ferrari maintained a rock solid beat throughout the campaign and swept to a one-two in the world championship for drivers as Jody Scheckter edged out friend and team-mate Gilles Villeneuve.

In the wake of Lotus's devastating 1978 form, ground-effect technology arrived in a big way. Ligier's JS11 and Williams's FW07 adopted the Lotus principle but took fuller advantage by coupling it with stronger, stiffer chassis. The Ligier was ready right from the start of the season and Jacques Laffite dominated the opening two races. Team-mate Patrick Depailler was his closest challenger.

Ferrari then introduced its own ground-effect car and monopolised the next two events. Villeneuve beat Scheckter on both occasions, although the latter made his winning breakthrough at Zolder and immediately followed it up with another victory in Monaco. Ligier lost impetus in the summer, shortly after Depailler injured his legs in a hang-gliding accident. That coincided with Renault's emergence as a serious contender and the French manufacturer earned a permanent place in the history books on home soil, at Dijon, when Jean-Pierre Jabouille recorded the first F1 world championship victory for a turbocharged car. Jabouille's achievement was almost overlooked, however, because of a stunning fight for second place between his team-mate René Arnoux and Villeneuve. In the closing stages, the pair rubbed wheels countless times before Villeneuve finally gained the upper hand.

Williams took its first F1 victory at Silverstone two weeks later, courtesy of Clay Regazzoni. His team-mate Alan Jones had retired from a big lead but went on to a score a flurry of victories during what was left of the season. It was too late for the Australian to overhaul the Ferrari drivers' big points advantage, however, and Scheckter went on to seal the title – appropriately at Monza. It would be a long time before the tifosi would be able to celebrate so wildly again.

Above
Wrong Beach: Patrick Tambay had gained several places by the time he reached the Queens Hairpin on the opening lap of the US GP West. Unfortunately he couldn't then stop. Well, not until he hit Niki Lauda

Below
Jacques be nimble: Laffite was 17 points clear of eventual champion Scheckter after winning the opening two races in Argentina and Brazil, but the Ligier team was unable to sustain its stunning early-season pace

JODY SCHECKTER – WORLD CHAMPION 1979

1979

CHAMPIONSHIP CAR-BY-CAR

1ST JODY SCHECKTER (RSA; AGE: 29) 51(+9) PTS

Ferrari 312T3 F12
Scuderia Ferrari
Races: ARG; BRA (both car #11)

JODY SCHECKTER (CONTD)

Ferrari 312T4 F12
Scuderia Ferrari
Races: RSA; LB; ESP; BEL; MON; FRA; GBR; GER; AUT; NED; ITA; CAN; USA (all car #11)

2ND GILLES VILLENEUVE (CAN; AGE: 29) 47(+6) PTS

Ferrari 312T3 F12
Scuderia Ferrari
Races: ARG; BRA (both car #12)

GILLES VILLENEUVE (CONTD)

Ferrari 312T4 F12
Scuderia Ferrari
Races: RSA; LB; ESP; BEL; MON; FRA; GBR; GER; AUT; NED; ITA; CAN; USA (all car #12)

3RD ALAN JONES (AUS; AGE: 32) 40(+3) PTS

Williams FW06-Ford V8
Albilad-Saudia Racing Team
Races: ARG; BRA; RSA; LB (all car #27)

ALAN JONES (CONTD)

Williams FW07-Ford V8
Albilad-Saudia Racing Team
Races: ESP; BEL; MON; FRA; GBR; GER; AUT; NED; ITA; CAN; USA (all car #27)

4TH JACQUES LAFFITE (FRA; AGE: 35) 36 PTS

Ligier JS11-Ford V8
Équipe Ligier Gitanes
Races: ARG; BRA; RSA; LB; ESP; BEL; MON; FRA; GBR; GER; AUT; NED; ITA; CAN; USA (all car #26)

5TH CLAY REGAZZONI (SUI; AGE: 39) 29(+3) PTS

Williams FW06-Ford V8
Albilad-Saudia Racing Team
Races: ARG; BRA; RSA; LB (all car #28)

CLAY REGAZZONI (CONTD)

Williams FW07-Ford V8
Albilad-Saudia Racing Team
Races: ESP; BEL; MON; FRA; GBR; GER; AUT; NED; ITA; CAN; USA (all car #28)

6TH= PATRICK DEPAILLER (FRA; AGE: 34) 20(+2) PTS

Ligier JS11-Ford V8
Équipe Ligier Gitanes
Races: ARG; BRA; RSA; LB; ESP; BEL; MON (all car #25)

6TH= CARLOS REUTEMANN (ARG; AGE: 37) 20(+5) PTS

Lotus 79-Ford V8
Martini Racing Team Lotus
Races: ARG; BRA; RSA; LB; ESP; BEL; MON; FRA; GBR; GER; AUT; NED; ITA; CAN; USA (all car #2)

8TH RENÉ ARNOUX (FRA; AGE: 31) 17 PTS

Renault RS01 V6 tc
Équipe Renault Elf
Races: ARG; BRA; RSA; ESP; BEL (all car #16)

RENÉ ARNOUX (CONTD)

Renault RE10 V6 tc
Équipe Renault Elf
Races: MON; FRA; GBR; GER; AUT; NED; ITA; CAN; USA (all car #16)

9TH JOHN WATSON (GBR; AGE: 33) 15 PTS

McLaren M28-Ford V8
Marlboro Team McLaren
Races: ARG; BRA; RSA; LB; ESP; BEL; MON; FRA (all car #7)

JOHN WATSON (CONTD)

McLaren M29-Ford V8
Marlboro Team McLaren
Races: GBR; GER; AUT; NED; ITA; CAN; USA (all car #7)

1979

CHAMPIONSHIP CAR-BY-CAR

10TH= MARIO ANDRETTI (USA; AGE: 39) 14 PTS

Lotus 79-Ford V8
Martini Racing Team Lotus
Races: ARG; BRA; RSA; LB; BEL; GBR; GER; AUT; NED; ITA; CAN; USA (all car #1)

MARIO ANDRETTI (CONTD)

Lotus 80-Ford V8
Martini Racing Team Lotus
Races: ESP; MON; FRA (all car #1)

10TH= JEAN-PIERRE JARIER (FRA; AGE: 32) 14 PTS

Tyrrell 009-Ford V8
Candy Team Tyrrell
Races: ARG; RSA; LB; ESP; BEL; MON; FRA; GBR; NED; ITA; CAN; USA (all car #4)

10TH= DIDIER PIRONI (FRA; AGE: 27) 14 PTS

Tyrrell 009-Ford V8
Candy Team Tyrrell
Races: ARG; BRA; RSA; LB; ESP; BEL; MON; FRA; GBR; GER; AUT; NED; ITA; CAN; USA (all car #3)

13TH JEAN-PIERRE JABOUILLE (FRA; AGE: 36) 9 PTS

Renault RS01 V6 tc
Équipe Renault Elf
Races: ARG; BRA; RSA (all car #15)

JEAN-PIERRE JABOUILLE (CONTD)

Renault RE10 V6 tc
Équipe Renault Elf
Races: ESP; BEL; MON; FRA; GBR; GER; AUT; NED; ITA; CAN; USA (all car #15)

14TH NIKI LAUDA (AUT; AGE: 30) 4 PTS

Brabham BT48-Alfa Romeo V12
Parmalat Racing Team
Races: ARG; BRA; RSA; LB; ESP; BEL; MON; FRA; GBR; GER; AUT; NED; ITA (all car #5)

15TH= ELIO DE ANGELIS (ITA; AGE: 21) 3 PTS

Shadow DN9B-Ford V8
Shadow Racing Team
Races: ARG; BRA; RSA; LB; ESP; BEL; FRA; GBR; GER; AUT; NED; ITA; CAN; USA (all car #18)

15TH= JACKY ICKX (BEL; AGE: 34) 3 PTS

Ligier JS11-Ford V8
Équipe Ligier Gitanes
Races: FRA; GBR; GER; AUT; NED; ITA; CAN; USA (all car #25)

15TH= JOCHEN MASS (GER; AGE: 32) 3 PTS

Arrows A1-Ford V8
Warsteiner Arrows Racing Team
Races: ARG; BRA; RSA; LB; ESP; BEL; MON (all car #30)

JOCHEN MASS (CONTD)

Arrows A2-Ford V8
Warsteiner Arrows Racing Team
Races: FRA; GBR; GER; AUT; NED; ITA (all car #30)

15TH= NELSON PIQUET (BRA; AGE: 26) 3 PTS

Brabham BT46-Alfa Romeo F12
Parmalat Racing Team
Races: ARG (car #6)

NELSON PIQUET (CONTD)

Brabham BT48-Alfa Romeo V12
Parmalat Racing Team
Races: BRA; RSA; LB; ESP; BEL; MON; FRA; GBR; GER; AUT; NED; ITA (all car #6)

NELSON PIQUET (CONTD)

Brabham BT49-Ford V8
Parmalat Racing Team
Races: CAN; USA (both car #6)

19TH= RICCARDO PATRESE (ITA; AGE: 25) 2 PTS

Arrows A1-Ford V8
Warsteiner Arrows Racing Team
Races: BRA; RSA; LB; ESP; BEL; MON; CAN (all car #29)

1979

CHAMPIONSHIP CAR-BY-CAR

RICCARDO PATRESE (CONTD)

Arrows A2-Ford V8
Warsteiner Arrows Racing Team
Races: FRA; GBR; GER; AUT; NED; ITA; USA (all car #29)

19TH= HANS-JOACHIM STUCK (GER; AGE: 28) 2 PTS

ATS D2-Ford V8
ATS Wheels
Races: BRA; RSA; LB; ESP; BEL; MON; GER (all car #9)

PICTURED DURING FRA PRACTICE

HANS-JOACHIM STUCK (CONTD)

ATS D3-Ford V8
ATS Wheels
Races: AUT; NED; ITA; CAN; USA (all car #9)

20TH EMERSON FITTIPALDI (BRA; AGE: 32) 1 PT

Fittipaldi F5A-Ford V8
Fittipaldi Automotive
Races: ARG; BRA; LB; ESP; BEL; MON; FRA; GBR (all car #14)

EMERSON FITTIPALDI (CONTD)

Fittipaldi F6-Ford V8
Fittipaldi Automotive
Races: RSA; GER; AUT; NED; ITA; CAN; USA (all car #14)

VITTORIO BRAMBILLA (ITA; AGE: 41) 0 PTS

Alfa Romeo 177 F12
Autodelta
Races: ITA (car #36)

VITTORIO BRAMBILLA (CONTD)

Alfa Romeo 179 V12
Autodelta
Races: CAN (car #36)

DEREK DALY (IRL; AGE: 26) 0 PTS

Ensign N177-Ford V8
Team Ensign
Races: ARG; BRA (both car #22)

PICTURED DURING ESP PRACTICE

DEREK DALY (CONTD)

Ensign N179-Ford V8
Team Ensign
Races: LB (car #22)

PICTURED DURING RSA PRACTICE

DEREK DALY (CONTD)

Tyrrell 009-Ford V8
Candy Team Tyrrell
Races: AUT (car #4); CAN; USA (both #33)

PATRICK GAILLARD (FRA; AGE: 27) 0 PTS

Ensign N179-Ford V8
Team Ensign
Races: GBR; AUT (both car #22)

BRUNO GIACOMELLI (ITA; AGE: 26) 0 PTS

Alfa Romeo 177 F12
Autodelta
Races: BEL; FRA (both car #35)

BRUNO GIACOMELLI (CONTD)

Alfa Romeo 179 V12
Autodelta
Races: ITA; USA (both car #35)

JAMES HUNT (GBR; AGE: 31) 0 PTS

Wolf WR7/WR8-Ford V8
Olympus Cameras Wolf Racing
Races: ARG; BRA; RSA; LB; ESP; BEL; MON (all car #20)

JAN LAMMERS (NED; AGE: 23) 0 PTS

Shadow DN9B-Ford V8
Shadow Racing Team
Races: ARG; BRA; RSA; LB; ESP; BEL; FRA; GBR; GER; AUT; NED; CAN (all car #17)

1979

CHAMPIONSHIP CAR-BY-CAR

GEOFF LEES (GBR; AGE: 28) 0 PTS

Tyrrell 009-Ford V8
Candy Team Tyrrell
Races: GER (car #4)

ARTURO MERZARIO (ITA; AGE: 36) 0 PTS

Merzario A1B-Ford V8
Team Merzario
Races: ARG; LB (both car #24)

PICTURED DURING CAN PRACTICE

HECTOR REBAQUE (MEX; AGE: 23) 0 PTS

Lotus 79-Ford V8
Team Rebaque
Races: ARG; RSA; LB; ESP; BEL; FRA; GBR; GER; NED (all car #31)

HECTOR REBAQUE (CONTD)

Rebaque HR100-Ford V8
Team Rebaque
Races: CAN (car #31)

KEKE ROSBERG (FIN; AGE: 30) 0 PTS

Wolf WR7/WR9-Ford V8
Olympus Cameras Wolf Racing
Races: FRA; GBR; GER; AUT; NED; ITA; USA (all car #20)

MARC SURER (SUI; AGE: 28) 0 PTS

Ensign N179-Ford V8
Team Ensign
Races: USA (car #22)

PICTURED DURING CAN PRACTICE

PATRICK TAMBAY (FRA; AGE: 30) 0 PTS

McLaren M28-Ford V8
Marlboro Team McLaren
Races: ARG; RSA; LB; ESP; FRA; GBR (all car #8)

PATRICK TAMBAY (CONTD)

McLaren M26-Ford V8
Marlboro Team McLaren
Races: BRA (car #8)

PICTURED DURING BEL PRACTICE

PATRICK TAMBAY (CONTD)

McLaren M29-Ford V8
Marlboro Team McLaren
Races: GER; AUT; NED; ITA; CAN; USA (all car #8)

RICARDO ZUNINO (ARG; AGE: 30) 0 PTS

Brabham BT49-Ford V8
Parmalat Racing Team
Races: CAN; USA (both car #5)

GRAND PRIX WINNERS 1979

	RACE (CIRCUIT)	**WINNER** (CAR)
ARG	ARGENTINE GRAND PRIX (BUENOS AIRES)	JACQUES LAFFITE (LIGIER JS11-FORD V8)
BRA	BRAZILIAN GRAND PRIX (INTERLAGOS)	JACQUES LAFFITE (LIGIER JS11-FORD V8)
RSA	SOUTH AFRICAN GRAND PRIX (KYALAMI)	GILLES VILLENEUVE (FERRARI 312T4 F12)
LB	LONG BEACH GRAND PRIX (LONG BEACH)	GILLES VILLENEUVE (FERRARI 312T4 F12)
ESP	SPANISH GRAND PRIX (JARAMA)	PATRICK DEPAILLER (LIGIER JS11-FORD V8)
BEL	BELGIAN GRAND PRIX (ZOLDER)	JODY SCHECKTER (FERRARI 312T4 F12)
MON	MONACO GRAND PRIX (MONTE CARLO)	JODY SCHECKTER (FERRARI 312T4 F12)
FRA	FRENCH GRAND PRIX (DIJON-PRENOIS)	JEAN-PIERRE JABOUILLE (RENAULT RE10 V6 TC)
GBR	BRITISH GRAND PRIX (SILVERSTONE)	CLAY REGAZZONI (WILLIAMS FW07-FORD V8)
GER	GERMAN GRAND PRIX (HOCKENHEIM)	ALAN JONES (WILLIAMS FW07-FORD V8)
AUT	AUSTRIAN GRAND PRIX (ÖSTERREICHRING)	ALAN JONES (WILLIAMS FW07-FORD V8)
NED	DUTCH GRAND PRIX (ZANDVOORT)	ALAN JONES (WILLIAMS FW07-FORD V8)
ITA	ITALIAN GRAND PRIX (MONZA)	JODY SCHECKTER (FERRARI 312T4 F12)
CAN	CANADIAN GRAND PRIX (MONTRÉAL)	ALAN JONES (WILLIAMS FW07-FORD V8)
USA	UNITED STATES GRAND PRIX (WATKINS GLEN)	GILLES VILLENEUVE (FERRARI 312T4 F12)

Marlboro
SAIMA
SAIMA
SAIMA
Marlboro
7
HERCULES
HERCULES
UNIPART

RENAULT elf
elf
RENAULT
GOODYEAR

1980s

1980

JONES COMPLETES WILLIAMS'S RISE TO THE TOP

Above
Grimace and bear it: Alan Jones tries to explain why he qualified only third fastest in Austria; team boss Frank Williams doesn't have the relaxed demeanour of a man on the way to his first world title but looks as though he wants to punch somebody – probably the photographer rather than Jones

Right
Buoyed from Brazil: Piquet celebrates the first of three wins during the year, at Long Beach. Fittipaldi (left, on the podium for the last time in his F1 career) and Patrese join him

Far right
Glen raider: Jones ended his season on a winning note in America. Villeneuve gives chase in the inadequate Ferrari 312T5. Science is powerless to explain how the French-Canadian managed to qualify it in the top 10 on seven occasions

saudia
saudia
27

Alan Jones gave Williams its first world championship title thanks to a string of aggressive performances in Patrick Head's superb FW07 chassis. The Australian swatted off an early-season challenge from Renault and Ligier and proved to be equally effective against the emerging threat of Nelson Piquet's Brabham.

René Arnoux (Renault) became something of a pole position specialist and racked up early back-to-back wins in Brazil and South Africa. His highly-stressed turbo engine was faster than it was reliable, however, which left French title hopes resting on Ligier, whose effective JS11/15 chassis often gave Didier Pironi and Jacques Laffite the fastest car in the field. The team couldn't capitalise on its speed as regularly as Williams or Brabham, however.

Piquet recorded his maiden F1 win at Long Beach, went on to score two more and his title chances only ended when his engine blew during the penultimate race.

The Ferraris suffered a dramatic fall from grace after their triumphant 1979 season and only Gilles Villeneuve's genius gave the team any respectability at all. His team-mate Jody Scheckter retired from the sport at the end of the year, as did double world champion Emerson Fittipaldi.

As two greats stepped down, so another appeared on the horizon: Alain Prost put together a deeply-impressive rookie season for the outpaced McLaren team – a bright spot in a year that took its toll. Patrick Depailler was killed while testing his Alfa Romeo at Hockenheim; Clay Regazzoni was left paralysed from the waist down after crashing at Long Beach when his Ensign's brake pedal snapped. This was still a lethally dangerous sport.

Top
Let us spray: René Arnoux fails to heed the hoarding that's urging him to make Coca-Cola his drink of choice. The Frenchman scored back-to-back wins in Brazil and South Africa but a string of niggling problems stifled his title bid

Above
Flair's fair: the McLaren M29 was not a competitive proposition – but it still allowed rookie Alain Prost to underline his immense promise

Left
Striking Frenchmen: the Ligiers of Didier Pironi and Jacques Laffite lead away at Brands Hatch, where they set the pace before retiring. The elegant JS11/15 chassis was occasionally devastating and consistently finished strongly, but its drivers only scored one win apiece

ALAN JONES – WORLD CHAMPION 1980

1980

CHAMPIONSHIP CAR-BY-CAR

1ST ALAN JONES (AUS; AGE: 33) 67(+4) PTS

Williams FW07B-Ford V8
Albilad-Williams Racing Team
Races: ARG; BRA; RSA; LB; BEL; MON; FRA; GBR; GER; AUT; NED; ITA; CAN; USA (all car #27)

2ND NELSON PIQUET (BRA; AGE: 27) 54 PTS

Brabham BT49-Ford V8
Parmalat Racing Team
Races: ARG; BRA; RSA; LB; BEL; MON; FRA; GBR; GER; AUT; NED; ITA; CAN; USA (all car #5)

3RD CARLOS REUTEMANN (ARG; AGE: 38) 42(+7) PTS

Williams FW07B-Ford V8
Albilad-Williams Racing Team
Races: ARG; BRA; RSA; LB; BEL; MON; FRA; GBR; GER; AUT; NED; ITA; CAN; USA (all car #28)

4TH JACQUES LAFFITE (FRA; AGE: 36) 34 PTS

Ligier JS11/15-Ford V8
Équipe Ligier Gitanes
Races: ARG; BRA; RSA; LB; BEL; MON; FRA; GBR; GER; AUT; NED; ITA; CAN; USA (all car #26)

5TH DIDIER PIRONI (FRA; AGE: 28) 32 PTS

Ligier JS11/15-Ford V8
Équipe Ligier Gitanes
Races: ARG; BRA; RSA; LB; BEL; MON; FRA; GBR; GER; AUT; NED; ITA; CAN; USA (all car #25)

6TH RENÉ ARNOUX (FRA; AGE: 31) 29 PTS

Renault RE20 V6 tc
Équipe Renault Elf
Races: ARG; BRA; RSA; LB; BEL; MON; FRA; GBR; GER; AUT; NED; ITA; CAN; USA (all car #16)

7TH ELIO DE ANGELIS (ITA; AGE: 22) 13 PTS

Lotus 81-Ford V8
Team Essex Lotus
Races: ARG; BRA; RSA; LB; BEL; MON; FRA; GBR; GER; AUT; NED; ITA; CAN; USA (all car #12)

8TH JEAN-PIERRE JABOUILLE (FRA; AGE: 37) 9 PTS

Renault RE20 V6 tc
Équipe Renault Elf
Races: ARG; BRA; RSA; LB; BEL; MON; FRA; GBR; GER; AUT; NED; ITA; CAN (all car #15)

9TH RICCARDO PATRESE (ITA; AGE: 26) 7 PTS

Arrows A3-Ford V8
Warsteiner Arrows Racing Team
Races: ARG; BRA; RSA; LB; BEL; MON; FRA; GBR; GER; AUT; NED; ITA; CAN; USA (all car #29)

10TH= DEREK DALY (IRL; AGE: 27) 6 PTS

Tyrrell 009-Ford V8
Candy Tyrrell Team
Races: ARG; BRA (both car #4)

DEREK DALY (CONTD)

Tyrrell 010-Ford V8
Candy Tyrrell Team
Races: RSA; LB; BEL; MON; FRA; GBR; GER; AUT; NED; ITA; CAN; USA (all car #4)

10TH= JEAN-PIERRE JARIER (FRA; AGE: 33) 6 PTS

Tyrrell 009-Ford V8
Candy Tyrrell Team
Races: ARG; BRA (both car #3)

JEAN-PIERRE JARIER (CONTD)

Tyrrell 010-Ford V8
Candy Tyrrell Team
Races: RSA; LB; BEL; MON; FRA; GBR; GER; AUT; NED; ITA; CAN; USA (all car #3)

10TH= KEKE ROSBERG (FIN; AGE: 31) 6 PTS

Fittipaldi F7-Ford V8
Skol Fittipaldi Team
Races: ARG; BRA; RSA; LB; BEL; FRA (all car #21)

KEKE ROSBERG (CONTD)

Fittipaldi F8-Ford V8
Skol Fittipaldi Team
Races: GER; AUT; ITA; CAN; USA (all car #21)

1980

CHAMPIONSHIP CAR-BY-CAR

10TH= GILLES VILLENEUVE (CAN; AGE: 30) 6 PTS

Ferrari 312T5 F12
Scuderia Ferrari
Races: ARG; BRA; RSA; LB; BEL; MON; FRA; GBR; GER; AUT; NED; ITA; CAN; USA (all car #2)

10TH= JOHN WATSON (GBR; AGE: 34) 6 PTS

McLaren M29-Ford V8
Marlboro Team McLaren
Races: ARG; BRA; RSA; LB; BEL; FRA; GBR; GER; AUT; NED; ITA; CAN; USA (all car #7)

15TH= EMERSON FITTIPALDI (BRA; AGE: 33) 5 PTS

Fittipaldi F7-Ford V8
Skol Fittipaldi Team
Races: ARG; BRA; RSA; LB; BEL; MON; FRA (all car #20)

EMERSON FITTIPALDI (CONTD)

Fittipaldi F8-Ford V8
Skol Fittipaldi Team
Races: GBR; GER; AUT; NED; ITA; CAN; USA (all car #20)

15TH= ALAIN PROST (FRA; AGE: 25) 5 PTS

McLaren M29-Ford V8
Marlboro Team McLaren
Races: ARG; BRA; BEL; MON; FRA; GBR; GER; AUT all car (#8)

ALAIN PROST (CONTD)

McLaren M30-Ford V8
Marlboro Team McLaren
Races: NED; ITA; CAN (all car #8)

17TH= BRUNO GIACOMELLI (ITA; AGE: 27) 4 PTS

Alfa Romeo 179B V12
Marlboro Team Alfa Romeo
Races: ARG; BRA; RSA; LB; BEL; MON; FRA; GBR; GER; AUT; NED; ITA; CAN; USA (all car #23)

17TH= JOCHEN MASS (GER; AGE: 33) 4 PTS

Arrows A3-Ford V8
Warsteiner Arrows Racing Team
Races: ARG; BRA; RSA; LB; BEL; MON; FRA; GBR; GER; CAN; USA (all car #30)

19TH JODY SCHECKTER (RSA; AGE: 30) 2 PTS

Ferrari 312T5 F12
Scuderia Ferrari
Races: ARG; BRA; RSA; LB; BEL; MON; FRA; GBR; GER; AUT; NED; ITA; USA (all car #1)

20TH MARIO ANDRETTI (USA; AGE: 40) 1 PT

Lotus 81-Ford V8
Team Essex Lotus
Races: ARG; BRA; RSA; LB; BEL; MON; FRA; GBR; GER; AUT; NED; ITA; CAN; USA (all car #11)

20TH= HECTOR REBAQUE (MEX; AGE: 24) 1 PT

Brabham BT49-Ford V8
Parmalat Racing Team
Races: GBR; GER; AUT; NED; ITA; CAN; USA (all car #6)

VITTORIO BRAMBILLA (ITA; AGE: 42) 0 PTS

Alfa Romeo 179B V12
Marlboro Team Alfa Romeo
Races: NED; ITA (both car #22)

ANDREA DE CESARIS (ITA; AGE: 21) 0 PTS

Alfa Romeo 179B V12
Marlboro Team Alfa Romeo
Races: CAN; USA (both car #22)

EDDIE CHEEVER (USA; AGE: 22) 0 PTS

Osella FA1-Ford V8
Osella Squadra Corse
Races: RSA; LB; FRA; GBR; GER; AUT; NED (all car #31)

PICTURED DURING ARG PRACTICE

EDDIE CHEEVER (CONTD)

Osella FA1B-Ford V8
Osella Squadra Corse
Races: ITA; CAN; USA (all car #31)

1980

CHAMPIONSHIP CAR-BY-CAR

PATRICK DEPAILLER (FRA; AGE: 35) 0 PTS

Alfa Romeo 179B V12
Marlboro Team Alfa Romeo
Races: ARG; BRA; RSA; LB; BEL; MON; FRA; GBR (all car #22)

RUPERT KEEGAN (GBR; AGE: 25) 0 PTS

Williams FW07-Ford V8
RAM Racing Team
Races: GBR; AUT; ITA; USA (all car #50)

JAN LAMMERS (NED; AGE: 24) 0 PTS

ATS D4-Ford V8
Team ATS
Races: LB; BEL; MON (all car #9)

JAN LAMMERS (CONTD)

Ensign N180-Ford V8
Unipart Racing Team
Races: GER; CAN; USA (all car #14)

GEOFF LEES (GBR; AGE: 29) 0 PTS

Shadow DN11A-Ford V8
Shadow Cars
Races: RSA (car #17)

PICTURED DURING LB PRACTICE

GEOFF LEES (CONTD)

Ensign N180-Ford V8
Unipart Racing Team
Races: NED (car #41)

NIGEL MANSELL (GBR; AGE: 27) 0 PTS

Lotus 81-Ford V8
Team Essex Lotus
Races: AUT; NED (both car #43)

TIFF NEEDELL (GBR; AGE: 28) 0 PTS

Ensign N180-Ford V8
Unipart Racing Team
Races: BEL (car #14)

PICTURED DURING MON PRACTICE

CLAY REGAZZONI (SUI; AGE: 40) 0 PTS

Ensign N180-Ford V8
Unipart Racing Team
Races: ARG; BRA; RSA; LB (all car #14)

MARC SURER (SUI; AGE: 28) 0 PTS

ATS D3-Ford V8
Team ATS
Races: ARG; BRA (both car #9)

MARC SURER (CONTD)

ATS D4-Ford V8
Team ATS
Races: FRA; GBR; GER; AUT; NED; ITA; USA (all car #9)

MIKE THACKWELL (NZL; AGE: 19) 0 PTS

Tyrrell 010-Ford V8
Candy Tyrrell Team
Races: CAN (car #43)

RICARDO ZUNINO (ARG; AGE: 30) 0 PTS

Brabham BT49-Ford V8
Parmalat Racing Team
Races: ARG; BRA; RSA; LB; BEL; FRA (all car #6)

1980

CHAMPIONSHIP CAR-BY-CAR

GRAND PRIX WINNERS 1980

	RACE (CIRCUIT)	WINNER (CAR)
ARG	ARGENTINE GRAND PRIX (BUENOS AIRES)	ALAN JONES (WILLIAMS FW07B-FORD V8)
BRA	BRAZILIAN GRAND PRIX (INTERLAGOS)	RENÉ ARNOUX (RENAULT RE20 V6 TC)
RSA	SOUTH AFRICAN GRAND PRIX (KYALAMI)	RENÉ ARNOUX (RENAULT RE20 V6 TC)
LB	LONG BEACH GRAND PRIX (LONG BEACH)	NELSON PIQUET (BRABHAM BT49-FORD V8)
BEL	BELGIAN GRAND PRIX (ZOLDER)	DIDIER PIRONI (LIGIER JS11/15-FORD V8)
MON	MONACO GRAND PRIX (MONTE CARLO)	CARLOS REUTEMANN (WILLIAMS FW07B-FORD V8)
FRA	FRENCH GRAND PRIX (PAUL RICARD)	ALAN JONES (WILLIAMS FW07B-FORD V8)
GBR	BRITISH GRAND PRIX (BRANDS HATCH)	ALAN JONES (WILLIAMS FW07B-FORD V8)
GER	GERMAN GRAND PRIX (HOCKENHEIM)	JACQUES LAFFITE (LIGIER JS11/15-FORD V8)
AUT	AUSTRIAN GRAND PRIX (ÖSTERREICHRING)	JEAN-PIERRE JABOUILLE (RENAULT RE20 V6 TC)
NED	DUTCH GRAND PRIX (ZANDVOORT)	NELSON PIQUET (BRABHAM BT49-FORD V8)
ITA	ITALIAN GRAND PRIX (IMOLA)	NELSON PIQUET (BRABHAM BT49-FORD V8)
CAN	CANADIAN GRAND PRIX (MONTRÉAL)	ALAN JONES (WILLIAMS FW07B-FORD V8)
USA	UNITED STATES GRAND PRIX (WATKINS GLEN)	ALAN JONES (WILLIAMS FW07B-FORD V8)

GILLES VILLENEUVE

1981

PIQUET SNATCHES TITLE IN A LAS VEGAS CAR PARK

Far left
Argentine beef: Piquet won from pole position in Buenos Aires early in a closely-fought season. Seven drivers shared 15 victories between them

Above
Bare necessities: today they use high-tech pit counters with a barrage of monitors, back then they had a sunshade, a pencil and a notebook. The Williams team keeps an eye on rivals' progress in Spain. Note that Reutemann (right) is practising his moody look

Left
"Sorry, sir, you can't bring that in here": Lotus persisted with its twin-chassis concept, the 88, but scrutineers usually refused it permission to run. The team gave up the unequal struggle after Silverstone, where the car was used on the opening day before being barred – again

The season began badly as leading teams fought a vicious battle with the governing body in a bid to gain control of Formula One. It ended well, though, with the disagreements patched up and a down-to-the-wire title fight between Nelson Piquet (Brabham) and Carlos Reutemann (Williams).

The authorities had attempted to outlaw ground-effect aerodynamics by introducing regulations that stipulated a minimum ride height. The teams got around this by using hydraulically-adjustable suspension: cars met legal requirements when measured at standstill but ran lower when out on the track. This kept the specialist teams – almost all of whom relied on the underpowered, normally-aspirated Cosworth DFV for motive power – in the hunt against the increasingly powerful Renault and Ferrari turbos.

Alain Prost won three grands prix for Renault in just his second season of F1, while Gilles Villeneuve scored two extraordinary wins in a powerful but gripless Ferrari. Neither team was consistently successful, however, and this handed the initiative to Williams and Brabham. Reutemann had earned a big championship lead by mid-season, but Piquet was form man in the second half of the year.

Tyre manufacturer Goodyear pulled out of the sport before the first event, leaving Michelin to fill the breach. The American company was not away for long: it returned in France, round eight, and hooked up with pace-setters Williams and Brabham. Ligier opted to stay with Michelin and Jacques Laffite remained an outside title contender to the end. Piquet was crowned, however, after Reutemann faded dramatically during the Las Vegas finale. The Argentine's team-mate Alan Jones won the closing race – and it was due to be his last. The Australian former champ intended to retire from the sport and return to his homeland at the end of the year.

Other highlights included John Watson winning his home grand prix at Silverstone to give McLaren its first victory for four years. The car he used, the MP4/1, was the first F1 machine to be constructed from carbon-fibre. Soon all cars would be made this way. But they wouldn't be made the same way as the revolutionary Lotus 88, a car the governing body banned because its twin-chassis set-up was controversially deemed to be illegal.

Above left
No drought about it: Watson scores a popular success at Silverstone – the first for a British driver (and McLaren, come to that) since James Hunt won the 1977 seasonal finale at Fuji

Above
Renault brio: Alain Prost notched up his maiden F1 victory in France and added two more towards the end of the season. Here he leads team-mate Arnoux at Monza

Left
Fever Las Vegas: the world title reaches a gripping climax – and they choose to stage it in a Caesars Palace parking lot. Jones grabs the lead at the start from Villeneuve, Prost and Reutemann, who had a nightmare afternoon, finished a lapped eighth and gifted the title to Piquet

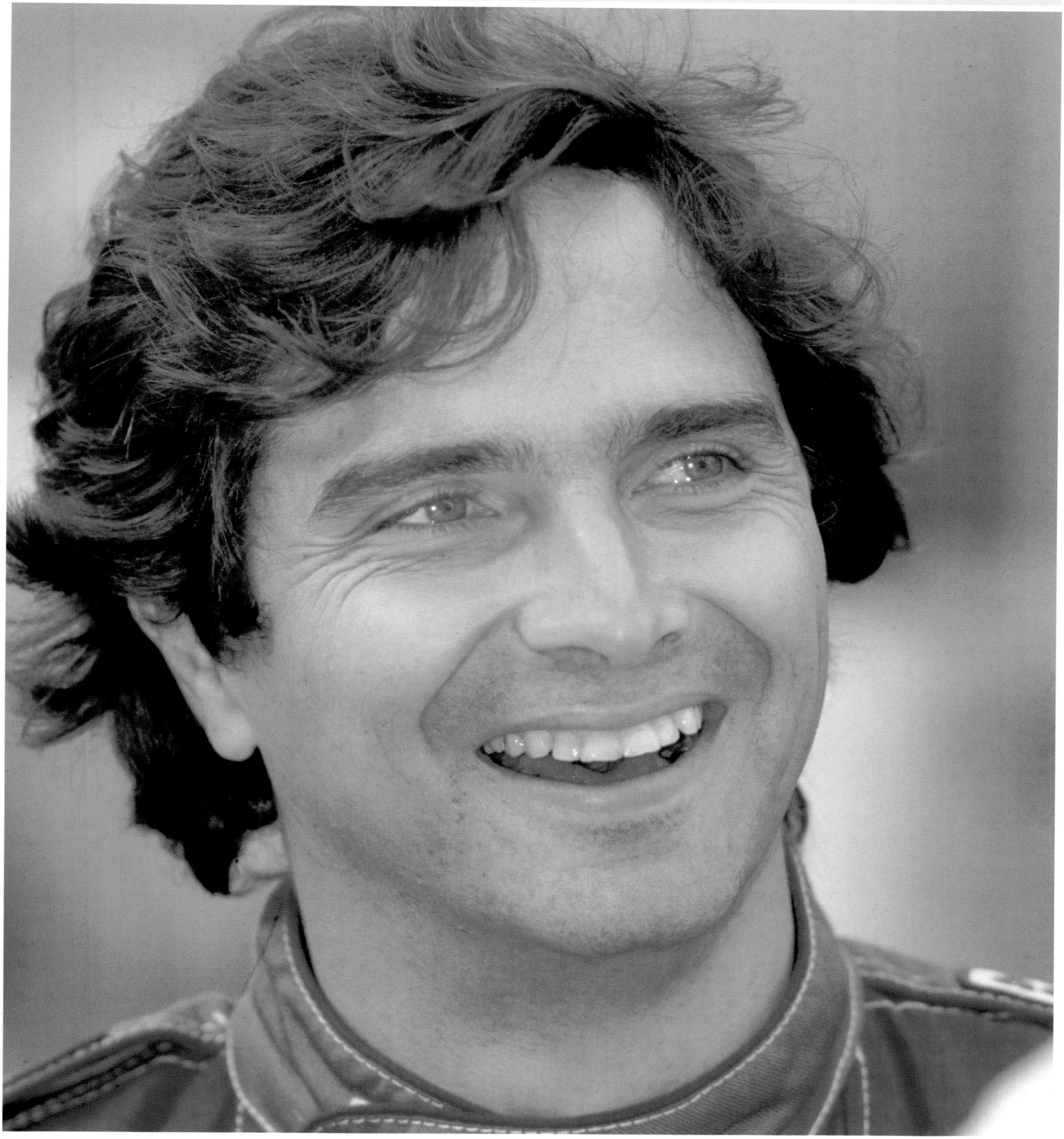

NELSON PIQUET – WORLD CHAMPION 1981, 1983 & 1987

1981

CHAMPIONSHIP CAR-BY-CAR

1ST NELSON PIQUET (BRA; AGE: 28) 50 PTS

Brabham BT49C-Ford V8
Parmalat Racing Team
Races: LB; BRA; ARG; SMR; BEL; MON; ESP; FRA; GBR; GER; AUT; NED; ITA; CAN; LV (all car #5)

2ND CARLOS REUTEMANN (ARG; AGE: 39) 49 PTS

Williams FW07C-Ford V8
Albilad-Williams Racing Team
Races: LB; BRA; ARG; SMR; BEL; MON; ESP; FRA; GBR; GER; AUT; NED; ITA; CAN; LV (all car #2)

3RD ALAN JONES (AUS; AGE: 34) 46 PTS

Williams FW07C-Ford V8
Albilad-Williams Racing Team
Races: LB; BRA; ARG; SMR; BEL; MON; ESP; FRA; GBR; GER; AUT; NED; ITA; CAN; LV (all car #1)

4TH JACQUES LAFFITE (FRA; AGE: 37) 44 PTS

Ligier JS17-Matra V12
Équipe Talbot Gitanes
Races: LB; BRA; ARG; SMR; BEL; MON; ESP; FRA; GBR; GER; AUT; NED; ITA; CAN; LV (all car #26)

5TH ALAIN PROST (FRA; AGE: 26) 43 PTS

Renault RE20B V6 tc
Équipe Renault Elf
Races: LB; BRA; ARG; SMR (all car #15)

ALAIN PROST (CONTD)

Renault RE30 V6 tc
Équipe Renault Elf
Races: BEL; MON; ESP; FRA; GBR; GER; AUT; NED; ITA; CAN; LV (all car #15)

6TH JOHN WATSON (GBR; AGE: 35) 27 PTS

McLaren M29F-Ford V8
Marlboro McLaren International
Races: LB; BRA (both car #7)

JOHN WATSON (GBR; AGE: 35)

McLaren MP4/1-Ford V8
Marlboro McLaren International
Races: ARG; SMR; BEL; MON; ESP; FRA; GBR; GER; AUT; NED; ITA; CAN; LV (all car #7)

7TH GILLES VILLENEUVE (CAN; AGE: 31) 25 PTS

Ferrari 126CK V6 tc
Scuderia Ferrari
Races: LB; BRA; ARG; SMR; BEL; MON; ESP; FRA; GBR; GER; AUT; NED; ITA; CAN; LV (all car #27)

8TH ELIO DE ANGELIS (ITA; AGE: 23) 14 PTS

Lotus 81-Ford V8
Team Essex Lotus
Races: LB; BRA; ARG; BEL (all car #11)

ELIO DE ANGELIS (CONTD)

Lotus 87-Ford V8
Team Essex Lotus/ John Player Team Lotus
Races: MON; ESP; FRA; GBR; GER; AUT; NED; ITA; CAN; LV (all car #11)

9TH= RENÉ ARNOUX (FRA; AGE: 33) 11 PTS

Renault RE20B V6 tc
Équipe Renault Elf
Races: LB; BRA; ARG; SMR; MON (all car #16)

RENÉ ARNOUX (CONTD)

Renault RE30 V6 tc
Équipe Renault Elf
Races: ESP; FRA; GBR; GER; AUT; NED; ITA; CAN; LV (all car #16)

9TH= HECTOR REBAQUE (MEX; AGE: 25) 11 PTS

Brabham BT49C-Ford V8
Parmalat Racing Team
Races: LB; BRA; ARG; SMR; BEL; ESP; FRA; GBR; GER; AUT; NED; ITA; CAN; LV (all car #6)

11TH= EDDIE CHEEVER (USA; AGE: 23) 10 PTS

Tyrrell 010-Ford V8
Tyrrell Racing Organisation
Races: LB; BRA; ARG; SMR; BEL; MON; ESP; FRA; GBR (all car #3)

1981

CHAMPIONSHIP CAR-BY-CAR

EDDIE CHEEVER (CONTD)

Tyrrell 011-Ford V8
Tyrrell Racing Organisation
Races: GER; NED; ITA; CAN; LV (all car #3)

11TH= RICCARDO PATRESE (ITA; AGE: 27) 10 PTS

Arrows A3-Ford V8
Arrows Racing Team
Races: LB; BRA; ARG; SMR; BEL; MON; ESP; FRA; GBR; GER; AUT; NED; ITA; CAN; LV (all car #29)

13TH DIDIER PIRONI (FRA; AGE: 29) 9 PTS

Ferrari 126CK V6 tc
Scuderia Ferrari
Races: LB; BRA; ARG; SMR; BEL; MON; ESP; FRA; GBR; GER; AUT; NED; ITA; CAN; LV (all car #28)

14TH NIGEL MANSELL (GBR; AGE: 27) 8 PTS

Lotus 81-Ford V8
Team Essex Lotus
Races: LB; BRA; ARG; BEL (all car #12)

NIGEL MANSELL (CONTD)

Lotus 87-Ford V8
Team Essex Lotus
John Player Team Lotus
Races: MON; ESP; FRA; GER; AUT; NED; ITA; CAN; LV (all car #12)

15TH BRUNO GIACOMELLI (ITA; AGE: 28) 7 PTS

Alfa Romeo 179 V12
Marlboro Team Alfa Romeo
Races: LB; BRA; ARG; SMR; BEL; MON; ESP; FRA; GBR; GER; AUT; NED; ITA; CAN; LV (all car #23)

16TH MARC SURER (SUI; AGE: 29) 4 PTS

Ensign N180B-Ford V8
Ensign Racing
Races: LB; BRA; ARG; SMR; BEL; MON (all car #14)

MARC SURER (CONTD)

Theodore TY01-Ford V8
Theodore Racing Team
Races: FRA; GBR; GER; NED; CAN; LV (all car #33)

17TH MARIO ANDRETTI (USA; AGE: 41) 3 PTS

Alfa Romeo 179 V12
Marlboro Team Alfa Romeo
Races: LB; BRA; ARG; SMR; BEL; MON; ESP; FRA; GBR; GER; AUT; NED; ITA; CAN; LV (all car #22)

SLIM BORGUDD (SWE; AGE: 34) 1 PT

ATS D4-Ford V8
Team ATS
Races: SMR (car #10)

SLIM BORGUDD (CONTD)

ATS HGS1-Ford V8
Team ATS
Races: GBR; GER; AUT; NED; ITA; CAN (all car #9)

18TH= ANDREA DE CESARIS (ITA; AGE: 22) 1 PT

McLaren M29F-Ford V8
Marlboro McLaren International
Races: LB; BRA; ARG; SMR; BEL (all car #8)

ANDREA DE CESARIS (CONTD)

McLaren MP4/1-Ford V8
Marlboro McLaren International
Races: MON; ESP; FRA; GBR; GER; AUT; ITA; CAN; LV (all car #8)

18TH= ELISEO SALAZAR (CHI; AGE: 26) 1 PT

March 811-Ford V8
March Grand Prix
Races: SMR (car #17)

PICTURED DURING LB PRACTICE

ELISEO SALAZAR (CONTD)

Ensign N180B-Ford V8
Ensign Racing
Races: ESP; FRA; GER; AUT; NED; ITA; CAN; LV (all car #14)

1981

CHAMPIONSHIP CAR-BY-CAR

18TH= PATRICK TAMBAY (FRA; AGE: 32) 1 PT

Theodore TY01-Ford V8
Theodore Racing Team
Races: LB; BRA; ARG; SMR; MON; ESP (all car #33)

PATRICK TAMBAY (CONTD)

Ligier JS17-Matra V12
Équipe Talbot Gitanes
Races: FRA; GBR; GER; AUT; NED; ITA; CAN; LV (all car #25)

MICHELE ALBORETO (ITA; AGE: 24) 0 PTS

Tyrrell 010-Ford V8
Tyrrell Racing Organisation
Races: SMR; BEL; MON; FRA; GBR; AUT (all car #4)

MICHELE ALBORETO (CONTD)

Tyrrell 011-Ford V8
Tyrrell Racing Organisation
Races: NED; ITA; CAN; LV (all car #4)

DEREK DALY (IRL; AGE: 28) 0 PTS

March 811-Ford V8
March Grand Prix
Races: ESP; FRA; GBR; GER; AUT; NED; ITA; CAN (all car #17)

BEPPE GABBIANI (ITA; AGE: 24) 0 PTS

Osella FA1B-Ford V8
Osella Squadra Corse
Races: LB; SMR; BEL (all car #32)

PICTURED DURING BRA PRACTICE

PIERCARLO GHINZANI (ITA; AGE: 29) 0 PTS

Osella FA1B-Ford V8
Osella Squadra Corse
Races: BEL (car #31)

PICTURED DURING MON PRACTICE

MIGUEL ANGEL GUERRA (ARG; AGE: 27) 0 PTS

Osella FA1B-Ford V8
Osella Squadra Corse
Races: SMR (car #31)

PICTURED DURING LB PRACTICE

BRIAN HENTON (GBR; AGE: 35) 0 PTS

Toleman TG181-Hart S4 tc
Candy Toleman Motorsport
Races: ITA (car #35)

PICTURED DURING CAN PRACTICE

JEAN-PIERRE JABOUILLE (FRA; AGE: 38) 0 PTS

Ligier JS17-Matra V12
Équipe Talbot Gitanes
Races: SMR; BEL; ESP (all car #25)

JEAN-PIERRE JARIER (FRA; AGE: 35) 0 PTS

Ligier JS17-Matra V12
Équipe Talbot Gitanes
Races: LB; BRA (both car #25)

JEAN-PIERRE JARIER (CONTD)

Osella FA1B-Ford V8
Osella Squadra Corse
Races: GBR; GER; AUT; NED (all car #32)

JEAN-PIERRE JARIER (CONTD)

Osella FA1C-Ford V8
Osella Squadra Corse
Races: ITA; CAN; LV (all car #32)

JAN LAMMERS (NED; AGE: 24) 0 PTS

ATS D4-Ford V8
Team ATS
Races: LB; ARG (both car #9)

KEKE ROSBERG (FIN; AGE: 32) 0 PTS

Fittipaldi F8C-Ford V8
Fittipaldi Automotive
Races: LB; BRA; ARG; SMR; BEL; ESP; FRA; GBR; LV (all car #20)

1981

CHAMPIONSHIP CAR-BY-CAR

CHICO SERRA (BRA; AGE: 24) 0 PTS

Fittipaldi F8C-Ford V8
Fittipaldi Automotive
Races: LB; BRA; ARG; BEL; ESP (all car #21)

SIEGFRIED STOHR (ITA; AGE: 28) 0 PTS

Arrows A3-Ford V8
Arrows Racing Team
Races: BRA; ARG; BEL; MON; ESP; GBR; GER; AUT; NED (all car #30)

DEREK WARWICK (GBR; AGE: 27) 0 PTS

Toleman TG181-Hart S4 tc
Candy Toleman Motorsport
Races: LV (car #36)

RICARDO ZUNINO (ARG; AGE: 32) 0 pts

Tyrrell 010-Ford V8
Tyrrell Racing Organisation
Races: BRA; ARG (both car #4)

GRAND PRIX WINNERS 1981

	RACE (CIRCUIT)	**WINNER** (CAR)
LB	LONG BEACH GRAND PRIX (LONG BEACH)	ALAN JONES (WILLIAMS FW07C-FORD V8)
BRA	BRAZILIAN GRAND PRIX (RIO DE JANEIRO)	CARLOS REUTEMANN (WILLIAMS FW07C-FORD V8)
ARG	ARGENTINE GRAND PRIX (BUENOS AIRES)	NELSON PIQUET (BRABHAM BT49C-FORD V8)
SMR	SAN MARINO GRAND PRIX (IMOLA)	NELSON PIQUET (BRABHAM BT49C-FORD V8)
BEL	BELGIAN GRAND PRIX (ZOLDER)	CARLOS REUTEMANN (WILLIAMS FW07C-FORD V8)
MON	MONACO GRAND PRIX (MONTE CARLO)	GILLES VILLENEUVE (FERRARI 126CK V6 TC)
ESP	SPANISH GRAND PRIX (JARAMA)	GILLES VILLENEUVE (FERRARI 126CK V6 TC)
FRA	FRENCH GRAND PRIX (DIJON-PRENOIS)	ALAIN PROST (RENAULT RE30 V6 TC)
GBR	BRITISH GRAND PRIX (SILVERSTONE)	JOHN WATSON (McLAREN MP4/1-FORD V8)
GER	GERMAN GRAND PRIX (HOCKENHEIM)	NELSON PIQUET (BRABHAM BT49C-FORD V8)
AUT	AUSTRIAN GRAND PRIX (ÖSTERREICHRING)	JACQUES LAFFITE (LIGIER JS17-MATRA V12)
NED	DUTCH GRAND PRIX (ZANDVOORT)	ALAIN PROST (RENAULT RE30 V6 TC)
ITA	ITALIAN GRAND PRIX (MONZA)	ALAIN PROST (RENAULT RE30 V6 TC)
CAN	CANADIAN GRAND PRIX (MONTRÉAL)	JACQUES LAFFITE (LIGIER JS17-MATRA V12)
LV	LAS VEGAS GRAND PRIX (CAESARS PALACE)	ALAN JONES (WILLIAMS FW07C-FORD V8)

1982

ONE WIN ENOUGH FOR ROSBERG IN F1'S MOST TURBULENT SEASON

Left
Chuckle, merry Finn: fifth place in Las Vegas clinched the title for Keke Rosberg, even though he averaged only 2.75 points per race. John Watson, one of 11 drivers to win during the 16-event season, looks on

Above
Last battle: Pironi leads Villeneuve at Imola, where he dified team orders to win – much to the Canadian's displeasure. Villeneuve was killed at Zolder two weeks later; the two men never spoke to each other again

Right
Dignified silence: the furious Villeneuve struggles to find words for Jackie Stewart on the Imola podium

Right:
Stop me and try one: Brabham reintroduced tactical mid-race refuelling, although it didn't yield any victories. Patrese comes in for a service in Austria

RITMO
GOMMA
28

GIACOBAZZI
brut N.H. gran premio

parmalat
parmalat

No driver scored more than two wins in the most open championship for seasons – and Williams team leader Keke Rosberg picked up only one en route to becoming the first Finn to lift Formula One's main prize.

For all that it was close and exciting, however, this was a turbulent season. There was a drivers' strike on the eve of the opening race in South Africa. Gilles Villeneuve was killed during qualifying for the Belgian Grand Prix and rookie Riccardo Paletti perished in a startline accident in Canada, two races later. At Hockenheim, Didier Pironi suffered career-ending leg injuries just as he appeared to be on his way to the world title. There was also a fierce, enduring dispute between the teams and the authorities – and this led many entrants to boycott the San Marino GP.

Ferrari had coupled big turbo horsepower with a modern chassis, courtesy of new chief designer Harvey Postlethwaite, and the combination looked set to be a winning one. The Ferrari 126C2 was almost certainly the fastest car of the year but tragedy overtook the team as Villeneuve and, later, Pironi suffered their appalling accidents. At the age of 42, Mario Andretti provided some late-season solace when he stood in at Monza and qualified on pole, to the locals' great delight.

Halfway through the season Brabham designer Gordon Murray re-introduced the tactical pit stop to F1 after a gap of more than 25 years. He realised that the greater speed of a car with a low fuel load and grippy, soft-compound tyres would more than compensate for any time lost in the pits. The tactic showed potential, but reliability issues prevented it paying off. The team managed two wins before this innovation, however: Riccardo Patrese triumphed in Monaco and Nelson Piquet in Montreal.

Niki Lauda made an F1 comeback with McLaren after two years in retirement – and won third time out, at Long Beach. His team-mate John Watson was a title contender up to the final race. Renault dominated the early events but couldn't sustain its reliability. In addition, drivers Alain Prost and René Arnoux fell out after the latter went against team orders to win in France – another element of discord in a very troubled season.

ALAIN PROST AND RENÉ ARNOUX FELL OUT AFTER THE LATTER WENT AGAINST TEAM ORDERS TO WIN IN FRANCE – ANOTHER ELEMENT OF DISCORD IN A VERY TROUBLED SEASON

Above
Quit stop: the season almost didn't start in South Africa because drivers staged a strike in protest at the latest licensing system. Here they leave the track prior to locking themselves away in hotel

Above right
Nelson ready: Piquet's victory in Canada was BMW's first in Formula One. It was only the fifth time the engine had been used at a world championship grand prix

Above far right
Mixed feelings: hired to replace the late Gilles Villeneuve, Patrick Tambay scored his maiden grand prix victory at Hockenheim. It was a bitter-sweet success, however. His Ferrari team-mate Didier Pironi suffered terrible leg injuries in a practice accident and never raced in F1 again

Right
Fraction stations: just five-hundredths of a second separated first-time winner Elio de Angelis from Keke Rosberg in Austria. They finished more than a lap clear of anybody else. Title contender Rosberg was still looking for his maiden world championship success. The Finn broke his duck a fortnight later when he won the Swiss GP, which wasn't particularly Swiss at all because it took place in Dijon, France

parmalat
santal

Jules
MOULIN ROUGE
PARIS
Agip

John Player
Special
GOODYEAR
11

KEKE ROSBERG – WORLD CHAMPION 1982

1982

CHAMPIONSHIP CAR-BY-CAR

1ST KEKE ROSBERG (FIN; AGE: 33) 44 PTS

Williams FW07C-Ford V8
TAG Williams Team
Races: RSA; BRA; LB (all car #6)

KEKE ROSBERG (CONTD)

Williams FW08-Ford V8
TAG Williams Team
Races: BEL; MON; DET; CAN; NED; GBR; FRA; GER; AUT; SUI; ITA; LV (all car #6)

2ND= DIDIER PIRONI (FRA; AGE: 30) 39 PTS

Ferrari 126C2 V6 tc
Scuderia Ferrari
Races: RSA; BRA; LB; SMR; MON; DET; CAN; NED; GBR; FRA (all car #28)

2ND= JOHN WATSON (GBR; AGE: 36) 39 PTS

McLaren MP4/1B-Ford V8
Marlboro McLaren International
Races: RSA; BRA; LB; BEL; MON; DET; CAN; NED; GBR; FRA; GER; AUT; SUI; ITA; LV (all car #7)

4TH ALAIN PROST (FRA; AGE: 27) 34 PTS

Renault RE30B V6 tc
Équipe Renault Elf
Races: RSA; BRA; LB; SMR; BEL; MON; DET; CAN; NED; GBR; FRA; GER; AUT; SUI; ITA; LV (all car #15)

5TH NIKI LAUDA (AUT; AGE: 33) 30 PTS

McLaren MP4/1B-Ford V8
Marlboro McLaren International
Races: RSA; BRA; LB; BEL; MON; DET; CAN; NED; GBR; FRA; AUT; SUI; ITA; LV (all car #8)

6TH RENÉ ARNOUX (FRA; AGE: 34) 28 PTS

Renault RE30B V6 tc
Équipe Renault Elf
Races: RSA; BRA; LB; SMR; BEL; MON; DET; CAN; NED; GBR; FRA; GER; AUT; SUI; ITA; LV (all car #16)

7TH= MICHELE ALBORETO (ITA; AGE: 25) 25 PTS

Tyrrell 011-Ford V8
Team Tyrrell
Races: RSA; BRA; LB; SMR; BEL; MON; DET; CAN; NED; GBR; FRA; GER; AUT; SUI; ITA; LV (all car #3)

7TH= PATRICK TAMBAY (FRA; AGE: 33) 25 PTS

Ferrari 126C2 V6 tc
Scuderia Ferrari
Races: NED; GBR; FRA; GER; AUT; ITA (all car #27)

9TH ELIO DE ANGELIS (ITA; AGE: 24) 23 PTS

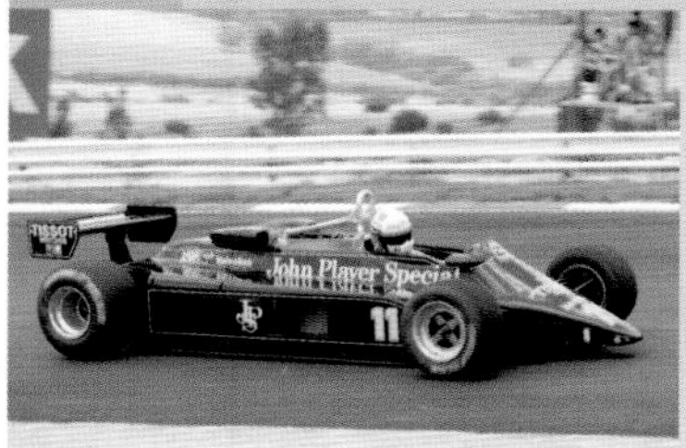

Lotus 87B-Ford V8
John Player Team Lotus
Races: RSA (car #11)

ELIO DE ANGELIS (CONTD)

Lotus 91-Ford V8
John Player Team Lotus
Races: BRA; LB; BEL; MON; DET; CAN; NED; GBR; FRA; GER; AUT; SUI; ITA; LV (all car #11)

10TH RICCARDO PATRESE (ITA; AGE: 28) 21 PTS

Brabham BT50-BMW S4 tc
Parmalat Racing Team
Races: RSA; BEL; NED; GBR; FRA; GER; AUT; SUI; ITA; LV (all car #2)

RICCARDO PATRESE (CONTD)

Brabham BT49D-Ford V8
Parmalat Racing Team
Races: BRA; LB; MON; DET; CAN (all car #2)

11TH NELSON PIQUET (BRA; AGE: 29) 20 PTS

Brabham BT50-BMW S4 tc
Parmalat Racing Team
Races: RSA; BEL; MON; CAN; NED; GBR; FRA; GER; AUT; SUI; ITA; LV (all car #1)

NELSON PIQUET (CONTD)

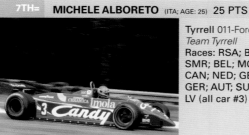

Brabham BT49D-Ford V8
Parmalat Racing Team
Races: BRA; LB (both car #1)

1982

CHAMPIONSHIP CAR-BY-CAR

12TH EDDIE CHEEVER (USA; AGE: 24) 15 PTS

Ligier JS17-Matra V12
Équipe Talbot Gitanes
Races: RSA; BRA; LB; BEL; DET; CAN; GBR (all car #25)

EDDIE CHEEVER (CONTD)

Ligier JS19-Matra V12
Équipe Talbot Gitanes
Races: MON; FRA; GER; AUT; SUI; ITA; LV (all car #25)

13TH DEREK DALY (IRL; AGE: 29) 8 PTS

Theodore TY01-Ford V8
Theodore Racing Team
Races: RSA (car #33)

DEREK DALY (CONTD)

Theodore TY02-Ford V8
Theodore Racing Team
Races: BRA; LB (both car #33)

DEREK DALY (CONTD)

Williams FW08-Ford V8
TAG Williams Team
Races: BEL; MON; DET; CAN; NED; GBR; FRA; GER; AUT; SUI; ITA; LV (all car #5)

14TH NIGEL MANSELL (GBR; AGE: 28) 7 PTS

Lotus 87B-Ford V8
John Player Team Lotus
Races: RSA (car #12)

NIGEL MANSELL (CONTD)

Lotus 91-Ford V8
John Player Team Lotus
Races: BRA; LB; BEL; MON; DET; CAN; GBR; GER; AUT; SUI; ITA; LV (all car #12)

15TH= CARLOS REUTEMANN (ARG; AGE: 39) 6 PTS

Williams FW07C-Ford V8
TAG Williams Team
Races: RSA; BRA (both car #5)

15TH= GILLES VILLENEUVE (CAN; AGE: 32) 6 PTS

Ferrari 126C2 V6 tc
Scuderia Ferrari
Races: RSA; BRA; LB; SMR (all car #27)

17TH= ANDREA DE CESARIS (ITA; AGE: 23) 5 PTS

Alfa Romeo 179D V12
Marlboro Team Alfa Romeo
Races: RSA (car #22)

ANDREA DE CESARIS (CONTD)

Alfa Romeo 182 V12
Marlboro Team Alfa Romeo
Races: BRA; LB; SMR; BEL; MON; DET; CAN; NED; GBR; FRA; GER; AUT; SUI; ITA; LV (all car #22)

17TH= JACQUES LAFFITE (FRA; AGE: 38) 5 PTS

Ligier JS17-Matra V12
Équipe Talbot Gitanes
Races: RSA; BRA; LB; BEL; DET; CAN; NED (all car #26)

JACQUES LAFFITE (CONTD)

Ligier JS19-Matra V12
Équipe Talbot Gitanes
Races: MON; GBR; FRA; GER; AUT; SUI; ITA; LV (all car #26)

19TH MARIO ANDRETTI (USA; AGE: 42) 4 PTS

Williams FW07C-Ford V8
TAG Williams Team
Races: LB (car #5)

MARIO ANDRETTI (CONTD)

Ferrari 126C2 V6 tc
Scuderia Ferrari
Races: ITA; LV (both car #28)

1982

CHAMPIONSHIP CAR-BY-CAR

20TH= JEAN-PIERRE JARIER (FRA; AGE: 35) 3 PTS

Osella FA1C-Ford V8
Osella Squadra Corse
Races: RSA; BRA; LB; SMR; BEL; DET; CAN; NED; GBR; FRA; GER; SUI; ITA (all car #31)

20TH= MARC SURER (SUI; AGE: 30) 3 PTS

Arrows A4-Ford V8
Arrows Racing Team
Races: BEL; MON; DET; CAN; NED; GBR; FRA; GER; AUT; ITA (all car #29)

MARC SURER (CONTD)

Arrows A5-Ford V8
Arrows Racing Team
Races: SUI; LV (both car #29)

22ND MAURO BALDI (ITA; AGE: 28) 2 PTS

Arrows A4-Ford V8
Arrows Racing Team
Races: BRA; BEL; DET; CAN; NED; GBR; FRA; GER; AUT; LV (all car #30)

MAURO BALDI (CONTD)

Arrows A5-Ford V8
Arrows Racing Team
Races: ITA (car #30)

22ND BRUNO GIACOMELLI (ITA; AGE: 29) 2 PTS

Alfa Romeo 179D V12
Marlboro Team Alfa Romeo
Races: RSA (car #23)

BRUNO GIACOMELLI (CONTD)

Alfa Romeo 182 V12
Marlboro Team Alfa Romeo
Races: BRA; LB; SMR; BEL; MON; DET; CAN; NED; GBR; FRA; GER; AUT; SUI; ITA; LV (all car #23)

22ND ELISEO SALAZAR (CHI; AGE: 27) 2 PTS

ATS D5-Ford V8
Team ATS
Races: RSA; BRA; LB; SMR; BEL; MON; DET; CAN; NED; FRA; GER; SUI; ITA (all car #10)

22ND MANFRED WINKELHOCK (GER; AGE: 30) 2 PTS

ATS D5-Ford V8
Team ATS
Races: RSA; BRA; LB; SMR; BEL; MON; DET; NED; FRA; GER; AUT; SUI; LV (all car #9)

CHICO SERRA (BRA; AGE: 25) 1 PT

Fittipaldi F8D-Ford V8
Fittipaldi Automotive
Races: RSA; BRA; BEL; DET; NED; GBR (all car #20)

CHICO SERRA (CONTD)

Fittipaldi F9-Ford V8
Fittipaldi Automotive
Races: GER; AUT; ITA (all car #20)

RAUL BOESEL (BRA; AGE: 24) 0 PTS

March 821-Ford V8
Rothmans March Grand Prix
Races: RSA; BRA; LB; BEL; DET; CAN; NED; GER; SUI; LV (all car #18)

SLIM BORGUDD (SWE; AGE: 35) 0 PTS

Tyrrell 011-Ford V8
Team Tyrrell
Races: RSA; BRA; LB (all car #4)

TOMMY BYRNE (IRL; AGE: 24) 0 PTS

Theodore TY02-Ford V8
Theodore Racing Team
Races: AUT; LV (both car #33)

TEO FABI (ITA; AGE: 27) 0 PTS

Toleman TG181C-Hart S4 tc
Toleman Group Motorsport
Races: SMR; BEL; GBR; FRA; AUT; SUI; ITA (all car #36)

1982

CHAMPIONSHIP CAR-BY-CAR

ROBERTO GUERRERO (COL; AGE: 23) 0 PTS

Ensign N181-Ford V8
Ensign Racing
Races: LB; DET; CAN; GBR; GER; AUT; SUI; ITA (all car #14)

PICTURED DURING MON PRACTICE

BRIAN HENTON (GBR; AGE: 35) 0 PTS

Arrows A4-Ford V8
Arrows Racing Team
Races: LB (car #29)

BRIAN HENTON (CONTD)

Tyrrell 011-Ford V8
Team Tyrrell
Races: SMR; BEL; MON; DET; CAN; NED; GBR; FRA; GER; AUT; SUI; ITA; LV (all car #4)

RUPERT KEEGAN (GBR; AGE: 27) 0 PTS

March 821-Ford V8
Rothmans March Grand Prix
Races: AUT; SUI; LV (all car #17)

JAN LAMMERS (NED; AGE: 26) 0 PTS

Theodore TY02-Ford V8
Theodore Racing Team
Races: NED (car #33)

PICTURED DURING GBR PRACTICE

GEOFF LEES (GBR; AGE: 31) 0 PTS

Theodore TY02-Ford V8
Theodore Racing Team
Races: CAN (car #33)

GEOFF LEES (CONTD)

Lotus 91-Ford V8
John Player Team Lotus
Races: FRA (car #12)

JOCHEN MASS (GER; AGE: 35) 0 PTS

March 821-Ford V8
Rothmans March Grand Prix
Races: RSA; BRA; LB; BEL; DET; CAN; NED; GBR; FRA (all car #17)

PICTURED DURING MON PRACTICE

RICCARDO PALETTI (ITA; AGE: 23) 0 PTS

Osella FA1C-Ford V8
Osella Squadra Corse
Races: SMR; CAN (both car #32)

PICTURED DURING LB PRACTICE

DEREK WARWICK (GBR; AGE: 27) 0 PTS

Toleman TG181C-Hart S4 tc
Toleman Group Motorsport
Races: RSA; BEL; NED; GBR; FRA; GER; AUT; SUI (all car #35)

DEREK WARWICK (CONTD)

Toleman TG183-Hart S4 tc
Toleman Group Motorsport
Races: ITA; LV (both car #35)

1982

CHAMPIONSHIP CAR-BY-CAR

GRAND PRIX WINNERS 1982

	RACE (CIRCUIT)	WINNER (CAR)
RSA	SOUTH AFRICAN GRAND PRIX (KYALAMI)	ALAIN PROST (RENAULT RE30B V6 TC)
BRA	BRAZILIAN GRAND PRIX (RIO DE JANEIRO)	ALAIN PROST (RENAULT RE30B V6 TC)
LB	LONG BEACH GRAND PRIX (LONG BEACH)	NIKI LAUDA (McLAREN MP4/1B-FORD V8)
SMR	SAN MARINO GRAND PRIX (IMOLA)	DIDIER PIRONI (FERRARI 126C2 V6 TC)
BEL	BELGIAN GRAND PRIX (ZOLDER)	JOHN WATSON (McLAREN MP4/1B-FORD V8)
MON	MONACO GRAND PRIX (MONTE CARLO)	RICCARDO PATRESE (BRABHAM BT49D-FORD V8)
DET	DETROIT GRAND PRIX (DETROIT)	JOHN WATSON (McLAREN MP4/1B-FORD V8)
CAN	CANADIAN GRAND PRIX (MONTRÉAL)	NELSON PIQUET (BRABHAM BT50-BMW S4 TC)
NED	DUTCH GRAND PRIX (ZANDVOORT)	DIDIER PIRONI (FERRARI 126C2 V6 TC)
GBR	BRITISH GRAND PRIX (BRANDS HATCH)	NIKI LAUDA (McLAREN MP4/1B-FORD V8)
FRA	FRENCH GRAND PRIX (PAUL RICARD)	RENÉ ARNOUX (RENAULT RE30B V6 TC)
GER	GERMAN GRAND PRIX (HOCKENHEIM)	PATRICK TAMBAY (FERRARI 126C2 V6 TC)
AUT	AUSTRIAN GRAND PRIX (ÖSTERREICHRING)	ELIO DE ANGELIS (LOTUS 91-FORD V8)
SUI	SWISS GRAND PRIX (DIJON-PRENOIS)	KEKE ROSBERG (WILLIAMS FW08-FORD V8)
ITA	ITALIAN GRAND PRIX (MONZA)	RENÉ ARNOUX (RENAULT RE30B V6 TC)
LV	LAS VEGAS GRAND PRIX (CAESARS PALACE)	MICHELE ALBORETO (TYRRELL 011-FORD V8)

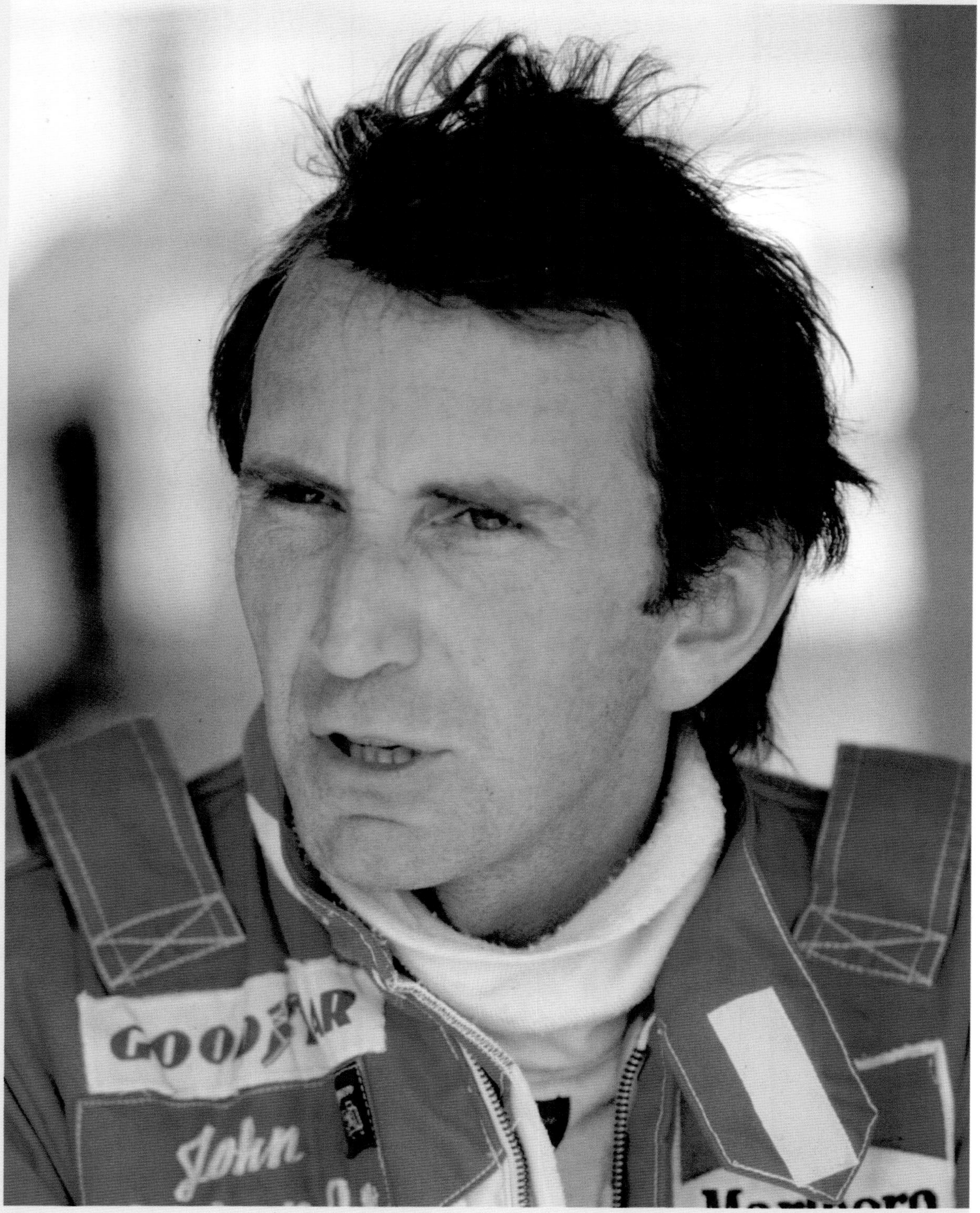

JOHN WATSON

1983

PIQUET BECOMES THE SPORT'S FIRST TURBOCHARGED CHAMPION

Right
Fizzy veldt: Piquet (left) backed off after arch-rival Prost retired from the Kyalami finale. He cruised to third place – and the title. His team-mate Patrese won – but somebody appears to have forgotten to hand runner-up Andrea de Cesaris a bottle of podium bubbly. Perhaps they thought he might drop it

Above
Forlorn hero: Prost's buckled Renault lies abandoned after his clash with Piquet in Holland

Left
Kind of blew: a McLaren expires during practice at Imola

SOUTHERN SUN HOTELS
MICHELIN
parmalat
MOET
CHANDON

By three-quarters of the way through the season Alain Prost and Renault appeared to be locked into their first world titles – but specialist-team ingenuity and flexibility would beat factory might at the 11th hour.

Renault had changed the face of Formula One when it introduced the turbocharged engine in 1977. It threatened to end small, specialist teams' domination of the sport and its pioneering approach was poised to reap dividends... until Brabham came up with an interesting interpretation of the fuel-composition regulations. Suddenly, Nelson Piquet's Brabham-BMW was transformed and his late-season run of form enabled him to overhaul Prost in the championship finale at Kyalami, South Africa. Ferrari was a title threat, too, though it ultimately lost out because drivers René Arnoux and Patrick Tambay took too many points off each other. The team had the consolation of retaining the championship for constructors, however.

There was big news just before the start of the season: new regulations stipulated that cars must feature flat undersides. In other words, ground-effect aerodynamics would be a thing of the past. This and further advances in the latest engine technology increased the performance gap between the turbos and the more conventional, normally-aspirated cars. In addition, the turbos had become reasonably reliable and were able to convert superior power into hard results. The old Cosworth DFV was left gasping and won just two races, courtesy of Keke Rosberg (Williams, Monaco) and Michele Alboreto (Tyrrell, Detroit). They were to the final moments of contemporary F1 glory for an engine that had made its grand prix debut back in 1967.

It was increasingly clear that specialist teams needed to find more horsepower if they were to combat the major manufacturers. Brabham's association with BMW had shown the way forward.

THE TEAM CAME UP WITH AN INTERESTING INTERPRETATION OF THE FUEL REGULATIONS. SUDDENLY, NELSON PIQUET'S BRABHAM-BMW WAS TRANSFORMED AND HIS LATE-SEASON RUN OF FORM ENABLED HIM TO OVERHAUL PROST IN THE CHAMPIONSHIP FINALE

Above
Second helping: Britain hosted two world championship races for the first time after Brands Hatch managed to wangle an autumn fixture – the GP of Europe. Patrese beats pole-winner de Angelis, Piquet and Mansell into Paddock Hill Bend on the opening lap

Far left
Still crazy after all these years: Monza fans stage their customary post-race invasion in recognition of René Arnoux's second place for Ferrari. Former motorcycle star Johnny Cecotto (Theodore) is also trying to dodge the sea of humanity after finishing 12th

Centre left
A wish called Honda: the Japanese giant returned to F1 in the second half of the season in partnership with fledgling British team Spirit. Its V6 turbo failed after just four laps at Monza

Left
End of an era: Michele Alboreto scored the naturally-aspirated Ford-Cosworth V8's 155th – and final – world championship success in Detroit, 16 years after it made its debut

1983

CHAMPIONSHIP CAR-BY-CAR

1ST NELSON PIQUET (BRA; AGE: 30) 59 PTS

Brabham BT52-BMW S4 tc
Fila Sport
Races: BRA; LB; FRA; SMR; MON; BEL; DET; CAN (all car #5)

NELSON PIQUET (CONTD)

Brabham BT52B-BMW S4 tc
Fila Sport
Races: GBR; GER; AUT; NED; ITA; EUR; RSA (all car #5)

2ND ALAIN PROST (FRA; AGE: 28) 57 PTS

Renault RE30C V6 tc
Équipe Renault Elf
Races: BRA (car #15)

ALAIN PROST (CONTD)

Renault RE40 V6 tc
Équipe Renault Elf
Races: LB; FRA; SMR; MON; BEL; DET; CAN; GBR; GER; AUT; NED; ITA; EUR; RSA (all car #15)

3RD RENÉ ARNOUX (FRA; AGE: 35) 49 PTS

Ferrari 126C2B V6 tc
Scuderia Ferrari
Races: BRA; LB; FRA; SMR; MON; BEL; DET; CAN (all car #28)

RENÉ ARNOUX (CONTD)

Ferrari 126C3 V6 tc
Scuderia Ferrari
Races: GBR; GER; AUT; NED; ITA; EUR; RSA (all car #28)

4TH PATRICK TAMBAY (FRA; AGE: 34) 40 PTS

Ferrari 126C2B V6 tc
Scuderia Ferrari
Races: BRA; LB; FRA; SMR; MON; BEL; DET; CAN (all car #27)

PATRICK TAMBAY (CONTD)

Ferrari 126C3 V6 tc
Scuderia Ferrari
Races: GBR; GER; AUT; NED; ITA; EUR; RSA (all car #27)

5TH KEKE ROSBERG (FIN; AGE: 34) 27 PTS

Williams FW08C-Ford V8
TAG Williams Team
Races: BRA; LB; FRA; SMR; MON; BEL; DET; CAN; GBR; GER; AUT; NED; ITA; EUR (all car #1)

KEKE ROSBERG (CONTD)

Williams FW09-Honda V6 tc
TAG Williams Team
Races: RSA (car #1)

6TH= EDDIE CHEEVER (USA; AGE: 25) 22 PTS

Renault RE30C V6 tc
Équipe Renault Elf
Races: BRA; LB (both car #16)

EDDIE CHEEVER (CONTD)

Renault RE40 V6 tc
Équipe Renault Elf
Races: FRA; SMR; MON; BEL; DET; CAN; GBR; GER; AUT; NED; ITA; EUR; RSA (all car #16)

6TH= JOHN WATSON (GBR; AGE: 37) 22 PTS

McLaren MP4/1C-Ford V8
Marlboro McLaren International
Races: BRA; LB; FRA; SMR; BEL; DET; CAN; GBR; GER; AUT; NED (all car #7)

JOHN WATSON (CONTD)

McLaren MP4/1E-TAG V6 tc
Marlboro McLaren International
Races: ITA; EUR; RSA (all car #7)

8TH ANDREA DE CESARIS (ITA; AGE: 24) 15 PTS

Alfa Romeo 183T V8 tc
Marlboro Team Alfa Romeo
Races: LB; FRA; SMR; MON; BEL; DET; CAN; GBR; GER; AUT; NED; ITA; EUR; RSA (all car #22)

PICTURED DURING BRA PRACTICE

1983

CHAMPIONSHIP CAR-BY-CAR

9TH RICCARDO PATRESE (ITA; AGE: 29) 13 PTS

Brabham BT52-BMW S4 tc
Fila Sport
Races: BRA; LB; FRA; SMR; MON; BEL; DET; CAN (all car #6)

RICCARDO PATRESE (CONTD)

Brabham BT52B-BMW S4 tc
Fila Sport
Races: GBR; GER; AUT; NED; ITA; EUR; RSA (all car #6)

10TH NIKI LAUDA (AUT; AGE: 34) 12 PTS

McLaren MP4/1C-Ford V8
Marlboro McLaren International
Races: BRA; LB; FRA; SMR; BEL; DET; CAN; GBR; GER; AUT (all car #8)

NIKI LAUDA (CONTD)

McLaren MP4/1E-TAG V6 tc
Marlboro McLaren International
Races: NED; ITA; EUR; RSA (all car #8)

11TH JACQUES LAFFITE (FRA; AGE: 39) 11 PTS

Williams FW08C-Ford V8
TAG Williams Team
Races: BRA; LB; FRA; SMR; MON; BEL; DET; CAN; GBR; GER; AUT; NED (all car #2)

JACQUES LAFFITE (CONTD)

Williams FW09-Honda V6 tc
TAG Williams Team
Races: RSA (car #2)

12TH= MICHELE ALBORETO (ITA; AGE: 26) 10 PTS

Tyrrell 011-Ford V8
Benetton Tyrrell Team
Races: BRA; LB; FRA; SMR; MON; BEL; DET; CAN; GBR; GER; AUT (all car #3)

MICHELE ALBORETO (CONTD)

Tyrrell 012-Ford V8
Benetton Tyrrell Team
Races: NED; ITA; EUR; RSA (all car #3)

12TH= NIGEL MANSELL (GBR; AGE: 29) 10 PTS

Lotus 92-Ford V8
John Player Team Lotus
Races: BRA; LB; FRA; SMR; MON; BEL; DET; CAN (all car #12)

NIGEL MANSELL (CONTD)

Lotus 94T-Renault V6 tc
John Player Team Lotus
Races: GBR; AUT; NED; ITA; EUR; RSA (all car #12)

NIGEL MANSELL (CONTD)

Lotus 93T-Renault V6 tc
John Player Team Lotus
Races: GER (car #12)

14TH= DEREK WARWICK (GBR; AGE: 28) 9 PTS

Toleman TG183B-Hart S4 tc
Candy Toleman Motorsport
Races: BRA; LB; FRA; SMR; MON; BEL; DET; CAN; GBR; GER; AUT; NED; ITA; EUR; RSA (all car #35)

15TH MARC SURER (SUI; AGE: 31) 4 PTS

Arrows A6-Ford V8
Arrows Racing Team
Races: BRA; LB; FRA; SMR; MON; BEL; DET; CAN; GBR; GER; AUT; NED; ITA; EUR; RSA (all car #29)

16TH MAURO BALDI (ITA; AGE: 29) 3 PTS

Alfa Romeo 183T V8 tc
Marlboro Team Alfa Romeo
Races: BRA; LB; FRA; SMR; MON; BEL; DET; CAN; GBR; GER; AUT; NED; ITA; EUR; RSA (all car #23)

17TH= ELIO DE ANGELIS (ITA; AGE: 25) 2 PTS

Lotus 92-Ford V8
John Player Team Lotus
Races: BRA (car #11)

1983

CHAMPIONSHIP CAR-BY-CAR

ELIO DE ANGELIS (CONTD)

Lotus 93T-Renault V6 tc
John Player Team Lotus
Races: LB; FRA; SMR; MON; BEL; DET; CAN (all car #11)

ELIO DE ANGELIS (CONTD)

Lotus 94T-Renault V6 tc
John Player Team Lotus
Races: GBR; GER; AUT; NED; ITA; EUR; RSA (all car #11)

17TH= DANNY SULLIVAN (USA; AGE: 33) 2 PTS

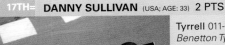

Tyrrell 011-Ford V8
Benetton Tyrrell Team
Races: BRA; LB; FRA; SMR; MON; BEL; DET; CAN; GBR; GER; AUT; NED; ITA (all car #4)

DANNY SULLIVAN (CONTD)

Tyrrell 012-Ford V8
Benetton Tyrrell Team
Races: EUR; RSA (both car #4)

18TH= JOHNNY CECOTTO (VEN; AGE: 27) 1 PT

Theodore N183-Ford V8
Theodore Racing Team
Races: BRA; LB; FRA; SMR; BEL; DET; CAN; GER; ITA (all car #34)

PICTURED DURING NED PRACTICE

18TH= BRUNO GIACOMELLI (ITA; AGE: 30) 1 PT

Toleman TG183B-Hart S4 tc
Candy Toleman Motorsport
Races: BRA; LB; FRA; SMR; BEL; DET; CAN; GBR; GER; AUT; NED; ITA; EUR; RSA (all car #36)

KENNETH ACHESON (GBR; AGE: 25) 0 PTS

RAM-March 01-Ford V8
RAM Automotive Team March
Races: RSA (car #17)

PICTURED DURING NED PRACTICE

RAUL BOESEL (BRA; AGE: 25) 0 PTS

Ligier JS21-Ford V8
Équipe Ligier Gitanes
Races: BRA; LB; FRA; SMR; MON; BEL; DET; CAN; GBR; GER; NED; EUR; RSA (all car #26)

THIERRY BOUTSEN (BEL; AGE: 26) 0 PTS

Arrows A6-Ford V8
Arrows Racing Team
Races: BEL; DET; CAN; GBR; GER; AUT; NED; ITA; EUR; RSA (all car #30)

CORRADO FABI (ITA; AGE: 22) 0 PTS

Osella FA1D-Ford V8
Osella Squadra Corse
Races: BRA; FRA; SMR; BEL; CAN (all car #31)

PICTURED DURING MON PRACTICE

CORRADO FABI (CONTD)

Osella FA1E-Alfa Romeo V12
Osella Squadra Corse
Races: AUT; NED; ITA; RSA (all car #31)

PICTURED DURING EUR PRACTICE

PIERCARLO GHINZANI (ITA; AGE: 31) 0 PTS

Osella FA1E-Alfa Romeo V12
Osella Squadra Corse
Races: DET; GBR; GER; AUT; ITA; EUR; RSA (all car #32)

PICTURED DURING NED PRACTICE

ROBERTO GUERRERO (COL; AGE: 24) 0 PTS

Theodore N183-Ford V8
Theodore Racing Team
Races: BRA; LB; FRA; SMR; BEL; DET; CAN; GBR; GER; AUT; NED; ITA; EUR (all car #33)

JEAN-PIERRE JARIER (FRA; AGE: 36) 0 PTS

Ligier JS21-Ford V8
Équipe Ligier Gitanes
Races: BRA; LB; FRA; SMR; MON; BEL; DET; CAN; GBR; GER; AUT; NED; ITA; RSA (all car #25)

STEFAN JOHANSSON (SWE; AGE: 27) 0 PTS

Spirit 201-Honda V6 tc
Spirit Racing
Races: GBR; GER; AUT; NED; ITA; EUR (all car #40)

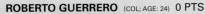

1983

CHAMPIONSHIP CAR-BY-CAR

ALAN JONES (AUS; AGE: 36) 0 PTS

Arrows A6-Ford V8
Arrows Racing Team
Races: LB (car #30)

JONATHAN PALMER (GBR; AGE: 26) 0 PTS

Williams FW08C-Ford V8
TAG Williams Team
Races: EUR (car #42)

ELISEO SALAZAR (CHI; AGE: 28) 0 PTS

RAM-March 01-Ford V8
RAM Automotive Team March
Races: BRA; LB (both car #17)

PICTURED DURING BEL PRACTICE

CHICO SERRA (BRA; AGE: 26) 0 PTS

Arrows A6-Ford V8
Arrows Racing Team
Races: BRA; FRA; SMR; MON (all car #30)

MANFRED WINKELHOCK (GER; AGE: 31) 0 PTS

ATS D6-BMW S4 tc
Team ATS
Races: BRA; LB; FRA; SMR; MON; BEL; DET; CAN; GBR; AUT; NED; ITA; EUR; RSA (all car #9)

GRAND PRIX WINNERS 1983

	RACE (CIRCUIT)	WINNER (CAR)
BRA	BRAZILIAN GRAND PRIX (RIO DE JANEIRO)	NELSON PIQUET (BRABHAM BT52-BMW S4 TC)
LB	LONG BEACH GRAND PRIX (LONG BEACH)	JOHN WATSON (McLAREN MP4/1C-FORD V8)
FRA	FRENCH GRAND PRIX (PAUL RICARD)	ALAIN PROST (RENAULT RE40 V6 TC)
SMR	SAN MARINO GRAND PRIX (IMOLA)	PATRICK TAMBAY (FERRARI 126C2B V6 TC)
MON	MONACO GRAND PRIX (MONTE CARLO)	KEKE ROSBERG (WILLIAMS FW08C-FORD V8)
BEL	BELGIAN GRAND PRIX (SPA-FRANCORCHAMPS)	ALAIN PROST (RENAULT RE40 V6 TC)
DET	DETROIT GRAND PRIX (DETROIT)	MICHELE ALBORETO (TYRRELL 011-FORD V8)
CAN	CANADIAN GRAND PRIX (MONTRÉAL)	RENÉ ARNOUX (FERRARI 126C2B V6 TC)
GBR	BRITISH GRAND PRIX (SILVERSTONE)	ALAIN PROST (RENAULT RE40 V6 TC)
GER	GERMAN GRAND PRIX (HOCKENHEIM)	RENÉ ARNOUX (FERRARI 126C3 V6 TC)
AUT	AUSTRIAN GRAND PRIX (ÖSTERREICHRING)	ALAIN PROST (RENAULT RE40 V6 TC)
NED	DUTCH GRAND PRIX (ZANDVOORT)	RENÉ ARNOUX (FERRARI 126C3 V6 TC)
ITA	ITALIAN GRAND PRIX (MONZA)	NELSON PIQUET (BRABHAM BT52B-BMW S4 TC)
EUR	EUROPEAN GRAND PRIX (BRANDS HATCH)	NELSON PIQUET (BRABHAM BT52B-BMW S4 TC)
RSA	SOUTH AFRICAN GRAND PRIX (KYALAMI)	RICCARDO PATRESE (BRABHAM BT52B-BMW S4 TC)

1984

PROST HAS THE EDGE – BUT LAUDA TAKES THE TITLE

Far left
Paint it black: the yachts weren't the only things bobbing up and down in water during the Monaco GP. Prost leads in the early stages from Mansell, who soon assumed control and was heading for victory until he ran over slippery road markings, slid wide and creamed the barrier

Above
Champagne in Burgundy: Lauda scored the second of his five victories at Dijon, where Prost was delayed by a loose wheel. Tambay (left) and Mansell (looking at somebody else's camera) trailed him across the line

Left
Hot property: you could always rely on Ayrton Senna to be on fire – and sometimes the same was true of his Toleman, too. This happened during practice at Brands Hatch, where the Brazilian finished third

This was the year when economy came to the fore. Mid-race fuel stops were banned and a maximum capacity of 220 litres was imposed (30 litres fewer than before). Concurrently, Bosch was making great strides with electronic control of fuel and ignition settings on the TAG-Porsche engine in the back of the new McLaren MP4/2. John Barnard's design proved extremely efficient aerodynamically and the sum of McLaren's parts led the team to enjoy an utterly dominant season. The battle for the championship was an all-McLaren affair and team-mates Niki Lauda and Alain Prost slugged it out until the final round.

Lauda or Prost scooped all but four of the season's 16 races. Nelson Piquet won a couple for Brabham-BMW while Michele Alboreto (Ferrari) and Keke Rosberg (Williams-Honda) scored one victory apiece. Ayrton Senna came close to giving Toleman a maiden victory with a sensational performance at a drenched Monaco. It was only the Brazilian's fifth grand prix, but although he was catching leader Prost he was denied a chance to challenge because conditions led to the race being stopped after 31 of the 77 scheduled laps.

Lauda led Prost by a scant 3.5 points prior to the final showdown at Estoril, Portugal – and there were nine up for grabs. After qualifying the odds favoured Prost, who lined up on the front row, while Lauda was only 11th. Prost led the early going with Lauda stuck in the lower order, but gradually the Austrian veteran began to pick cars off until there was only Nigel Mansell's Lotus between him and Prost. Second place was all Lauda needed to clinch the title and he was handed this on a plate when Mansell's brakes wore out. Rarely has a race winner looked so downcast as Prost. He'd won the battle, but Lauda had won the war.

Far right
Solitary consignment: Ferrari was often best of the rest behind McLaren – but Alboreto won only once, in Belgium

Below
Making pains for Nigel: Mansell pushed his damaged Lotus across the line in Dallas and collapsed with exhaustion, although he was fine once they had poured water over (and into) him

Right
Bard of prey: they were still using the instrumental break from Fleetwood Mac's *The Chain* as F1's theme music in 1984. In Monaco the 'danger – approaching shark' score from *Jaws* would have been more appropriate. Senna (pictured) and Tyrrell driver Stefan Bellof were reeling Prost in when the race had to be stopped

RARELY HAS A RACE WINNER LOOKED SO DOWNCAST AS PROST. HE'D WON THE BATTLE, BUT LAUDA HAD WON THE WAR

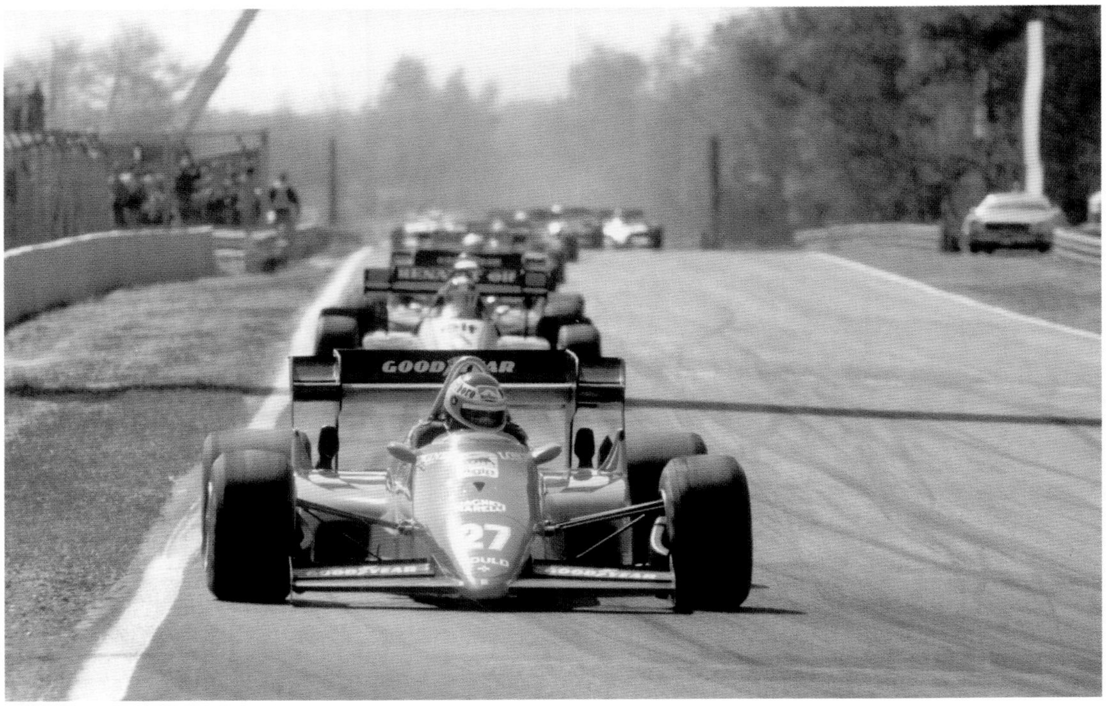

1984

CHAMPIONSHIP CAR-BY-CAR

1ST NIKI LAUDA (AUT; AGE: 35) 72 PTS

McLaren MP4/2-TAG V6 tc
Marlboro McLaren International
Races: BRA; RSA; BEL; SMR; FRA; MON; CAN; DET; DAL; GBR; GER; AUT; NED; ITA; EUR; POR (all car #8)

2ND ALAIN PROST (FRA; AGE: 29) 71.5 PTS

McLaren MP4/2-TAG V6 tc
Marlboro McLaren International
Races: BRA; RSA; BEL; SMR; FRA; MON; CAN; DET; DAL; GBR; GER; AUT; NED; ITA; EUR; POR (all car #7)

3RD ELIO DE ANGELIS (ITA; AGE: 26) 34 PTS

Lotus 95T-Renault V6 tc
John Player Team Lotus
Races: BRA; RSA; BEL; SMR; FRA; MON; CAN; DET; DAL; GBR; GER; AUT; NED; ITA; EUR; POR (all car #11)

4TH MICHELE ALBORETO (ITA; AGE: 27) 30.5 PTS

Ferrari 126C4 V6 tc
Scuderia Ferrari
Races: BRA; RSA; BEL; SMR; FRA; MON; CAN; DET; DAL; GBR; GER; AUT; NED; ITA; EUR; POR (all car #27)

5TH NELSON PIQUET (BRA; AGE: 31) 29 PTS

Brabham BT53-BMW S4 tc
Motor Racing Developments
Races: BRA; RSA; BEL; SMR; FRA; MON; CAN; DET; DAL; GBR; GER; AUT; NED; ITA; EUR; POR (all car #1)

6TH RENÉ ARNOUX (FRA; AGE: 36) 27 PTS

Ferrari 126C4 V6 tc
Scuderia Ferrari
Races: BRA; RSA; BEL; SMR; FRA; MON; CAN; DET; DAL; GBR; GER; AUT; NED; ITA; EUR; POR (all car #28)

7TH EREK WARWICK (GBR; AGE: 29) 23 PTS

Renault RE50 V6 tc
Équipe Renault Elf
Races: BRA; RSA; BEL; SMR; FRA; MON; CAN; DET; DAL; GBR; GER; AUT; NED; ITA; EUR; POR (all car #16)

8TH KEKE ROSBERG (FIN; AGE: 35) 20.5 PTS

Williams FW09-Honda V6 tc
Williams Grand Prix Engineering
Races: BRA; RSA; BEL; SMR; FRA; MON; CAN; DET; DAL; GBR; GER; AUT; NED; ITA; EUR; POR (all car #6)

9TH= NIGEL MANSELL (GBR; AGE: 30) 13 PTS

Lotus 95T-Renault V6 tc
John Player Team Lotus
Races: BRA; RSA; BEL; SMR; FRA; MON; CAN; DET; DAL; GBR; GER; AUT; NED; ITA; EUR; POR (all car #12)

9TH= AYRTON SENNA (BRA; AGE: 24) 13 PTS

Toleman TG183B-Hart S4 tc
Toleman Group Motorsport
Races: BRA; RSA; BEL (all car #19)

AYRTON SENNA (CONTD)

Toleman TG184-Hart S4 tc
Toleman Group Motorsport
Races: FRA; MON; CAN; DET; DAL; GBR; GER; AUT; NED; EUR; POR (all car #19)

11TH PATRICK TAMBAY (FRA; AGE: 35) 11 PTS

Renault RE50 V6 tc
Équipe Renault Elf
Races: BRA; RSA; BEL; SMR; FRA; MON; DET; DAL; GBR; GER; AUT; NED; ITA; EUR; POR (all car #15)

12TH TEO FABI (ITA; AGE: 29) 9 PTS

Brabham BT53-BMW S4 tc
Motor Racing Developments
Races: BRA; RSA; BEL; SMR; FRA; DET; GBR; GER; AUT; NED; ITA; EUR (all car #2)

13TH RICCARDO PATRESE (ITA; AGE: 30) 8 PTS

Alfa Romeo 184T V8 tc
Benetton Team Alfa Romeo
Races: BRA; RSA; BEL; SMR; FRA; MON; CAN; DET; DAL; GBR; GER; AUT; NED; ITA; EUR; POR (all car #22)

14TH= THIERRY BOUTSEN (BEL; AGE: 27) 5 PTS

Arrows A6-Ford V8
Barclay Nordica Arrows
Races: BRA; RSA; SMR (all car #18)

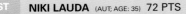

1984

CHAMPIONSHIP CAR-BY-CAR

THIERRY BOUTSEN (CONTD)

Arrows A7-BMW S4 tc
Barclay Nordica Arrows BMW
Races: BEL; FRA; CAN; DET; DAL; GBR; GER; AUT; NED; ITA; EUR; POR (all car #18)

14TH= JACQUES LAFFITE (FRA; AGE: 40) 5 PTS

Williams FW09-Honda V6 tc
Williams Grand Prix Engineering
Races: BRA; RSA; BEL; SMR; FRA; MON; CAN; DET; DAL; GBR; GER; AUT; NED; ITA; EUR; POR (all car #5)

16TH= ANDREA DE CESARIS (ITA; AGE: 25) 3 PTS

Ligier JS23-Renault V6 tc
Ligier LOTO
Races: BRA; RSA; BEL; SMR; FRA; MON; CAN; DET; DAL; GBR; GER; AUT; NED; ITA; EUR; POR (all car #26)

16TH= EDDIE CHEEVER (USA; AGE: 26) 3 PTS

Alfa Romeo 184T V8 tc
Benetton Team Alfa Romeo
Races: BRA; RSA; BEL; SMR; FRA; CAN; DET; DAL; GBR; GER; AUT; NED; ITA; EUR; POR (all car #23)

16TH= STEFAN JOHANSSON (SWE; AGE: 28) 3 PTS

Tyrrell 012-Ford V8
Tyrrell Racing Organisation
Races: GBR; GER; NED (all car #3)

STEFAN JOHANSSON (CONTD)

Toleman TG184-Hart S4 tc
Toleman Group Motorsport
Races: ITA (car #19); EUR; POR (both #20)

19TH PIERCARLO GHINZANI (ITA; AGE: 32) 2 PTS

Osella FA1F-Alfa Romeo V8 tc
Osella Squadra Corse
Races: BRA; BEL; FRA; MON; CAN; DET; DAL; GBR; GER; AUT; NED; ITA; EUR; POR (all car #24)

20TH MARC SURER (SUI; AGE: 32) 1 PT

Arrows A6-Ford V8
Barclay Nordica Arrows
Races: BRA; RSA; BEL; FRA; CAN; DET (all car #17)

MARC SURER (CONTD)

Arrows A7-BMW S4 tc
Barclay Nordica Arrows BMW
Races: SMR; DAL; GBR; GER; AUT; NED; ITA; EUR; POR (all car #17)

PHILIPPE ALLIOT (FRA; AGE: 30) 0 PTS

RAM 02-Hart S4 tc
Skoal Bandit Formula 1 Team
Races: BRA; RSA; SMR; FRA; CAN; DET; GBR; GER; AUT; NED; ITA; EUR; POR (all car #9)

MAURO BALDI (ITA; AGE: 30) 0 PTS

Spirit 101B-Hart S4 tc
Spirit Racing
Races: BRA; RSA; BEL; SMR; FRA; EUR; POR (all car #21)

STEFAN BELLOF (GER; AGE: 26) 0 PTS

Tyrrell 012-Ford V8
Tyrrell Racing Organisation
Races: BRA; RSA; BEL; SMR; FRA; MON; CAN; DET; DAL; GBR; NED (all car #4)

GERHARD BERGER (AUT; AGE: 25) 0 PTS

ATS D7-BMW S4 tc
Team ATS
Races: AUT; ITA; EUR (all car #31); POR(#14)

MARTIN BRUNDLE (GBR; AGE: 24) 0 PTS

Tyrrell 012-Ford V8
Tyrrell Racing Organisation
Races: BRA; RSA; BEL; SMR; FRA; CAN; DET (all car #3)

JOHNNY CECOTTO (VEN; AGE: 28) 0 PTS

Toleman TG183B-Hart S4 tc
Toleman Group Motorsport
Races: BRA; RSA; BEL; SMR (all car #20)

1984

CHAMPIONSHIP CAR-BY-CAR

JOHNNY CECOTTO (CONTD)

Toleman TG184-Hart S4 tc
Toleman Group Motorsport
Races: FRA; MON; CAN; DET; DAL (all car #20)

CORRADO FABI (ITA; AGE: 23) 0 PTS

Brabham BT53-BMW S4 tc
Motor Racing Developments
Races: MON; CAN; DAL (all car #2)

JO GARTNER (AUT; AGE: 30) 0 PTS

Osella FA1E-Alfa Romeo V12
Osella Squadra Corse
Races: SMR (car #30)

JO GARTNER (CONTD)

Osella FA1F-Alfa Romeo V8 tc
Osella Squadra Corse
Races: GBR; GER; AUT; NED; ITA; EUR; POR (all car #30)

FRANÇOIS HESNAULT (FRA; AGE: 27) 0 PTS

Ligier JS23-Renault V6 tc
Ligier LOTO
Races: BRA; RSA; BEL; SMR; MON; CAN; DET; DAL; GBR; GER; AUT; NED; ITA; EUR; POR (all car #25)

JONATHAN PALMER (GBR; AGE: 27) 0 PTS

RAM 01-Hart S4 tc
Skoal Bandit Formula 1 Team
Races: BRA; RSA (both car #10)

JONATHAN PALMER (CONTD)

RAM 02-Hart S4 tc
Skoal Bandit Formula 1 Team
Races: BEL; SMR; FRA; DET; DAL; GBR; GER; AUT; NED; ITA; EUR; POR (all car #10)

HUUB ROTHENGATTER (NED; AGE: 29) 0 PTS

Spirit 101B-Hart S4 tc
Spirit Racing
Races: CAN; DAL; GBR; GER; AUT; NED; ITA (all car #21)

PHILIPPE STREIFF (FRA; AGE: 29) 0 PTS

Renault RE50 V6 tc
Équipe Renault Elf
Races: POR (car #33)

MIKE THACKWELL (NZL; AGE: 23) 0 PTS

RAM 02-Hart S4 tc
Skoal Bandit Formula 1 Team
Races: CAN (car #10)

MANFRED WINKELHOCK (GER; AGE: 32) 0 PTS

ATS D7-BMW S4 tc
Team ATS
Races: RSA; BEL; SMR; FRA; MON; CAN; DET; DAL; GBR; GER; NED (all car #14)

MANFRED WINKELHOCK (CONTD)

Brabham BT53-BMW S4 tc
Motor Racing Developments
Races: POR (car #2)

1984

CHAMPIONSHIP CAR-BY-CAR

GRAND PRIX WINNERS 1984

	RACE (CIRCUIT)	WINNER (CAR)
BRA	BRAZILIAN GRAND PRIX (RIO DE JANEIRO)	ALAIN PROST (McLAREN MP4/2-TAG V6 TC)
RSA	SOUTH AFRICAN GRAND PRIX (KYALAMI)	NIKI LAUDA (McLAREN MP4/2-TAG V6 TC)
BEL	BELGIAN GRAND PRIX (ZOLDER)	MICHELE ALBORETO (FERRARI 126C4 V6 TC)
SMR	SAN MARINO GRAND PRIX (IMOLA)	ALAIN PROST (McLAREN MP4/2-TAG V6 TC)
FRA	FRENCH GRAND PRIX (DIJON-PRENOIS)	NIKI LAUDA (McLAREN MP4/2-TAG V6 TC)
MON	MONACO GRAND PRIX (MONTE CARLO)	ALAIN PROST (McLAREN MP4/2-TAG V6 TC)
CAN	CANADIAN GRAND PRIX (MONTRÉAL)	NELSON PIQUET (BRABHAM BT53-BMW S4 TC)
DET	DETROIT GRAND PRIX (DETROIT)	NELSON PIQUET (BRABHAM BT53-BMW S4 TC)
DAL	DALLAS GP (FAIR PARK)	KEKE ROSBERG (WILLIAMS FW09-HONDA V6 TC)
GBR	BRITISH GRAND PRIX (BRANDS HATCH)	NIKI LAUDA (McLAREN MP4/2-TAG V6 TC)
GER	GERMAN GRAND PRIX (HOCKENHEIM)	ALAIN PROST (McLAREN MP4/2-TAG V6 TC)
AUT	AUSTRIAN GRAND PRIX (ÖSTERREICHRING)	NIKI LAUDA (McLAREN MP4/2-TAG V6 TC)
NED	DUTCH GRAND PRIX (ZANDVOORT)	ALAIN PROST (McLAREN MP4/2-TAG V6 TC)
ITA	ITALIAN GRAND PRIX (MONZA)	NIKI LAUDA (McLAREN MP4/2-TAG V6 TC)
EUR	EUROPEAN GRAND PRIX (NÜRBURGRING)	ALAIN PROST (McLAREN MP4/2-TAG V6 TC)
POR	PORTUGUESE GRAND PRIX (ESTORIL)	ALAIN PROST (McLAREN MP4/2-TAG V6 TC)

RENÉ ARNOUX

1985

PROST GETS HIS JUST DESERTS – AT LAST

Above
Kent buy me love: Mansell (left) scored his maiden F1 victory in the GP of Europe at Brands Hatch. Prost (centre) finished fourth and finally won the world title, something he'd been threatening to do since 1982. Senna looks a trifle sour, possibly because some idiot has just sprayed champagne in his eyes

Left
Tyre brigade: Rosberg and Mansell push on at Kyalami. The Englishman eventually moved ahead after his team-mate ran wide. Having waited 72 races for his first grand prix success, he picked up his second within a fortnight

Right
Genius, in a word: while rivals were busy crashing on the main straight, Senna's touch and balance came into their own during the sodden Portuguese GP. He beat Alboreto's Ferrari by more than a minute and lapped everyone else. Some first win

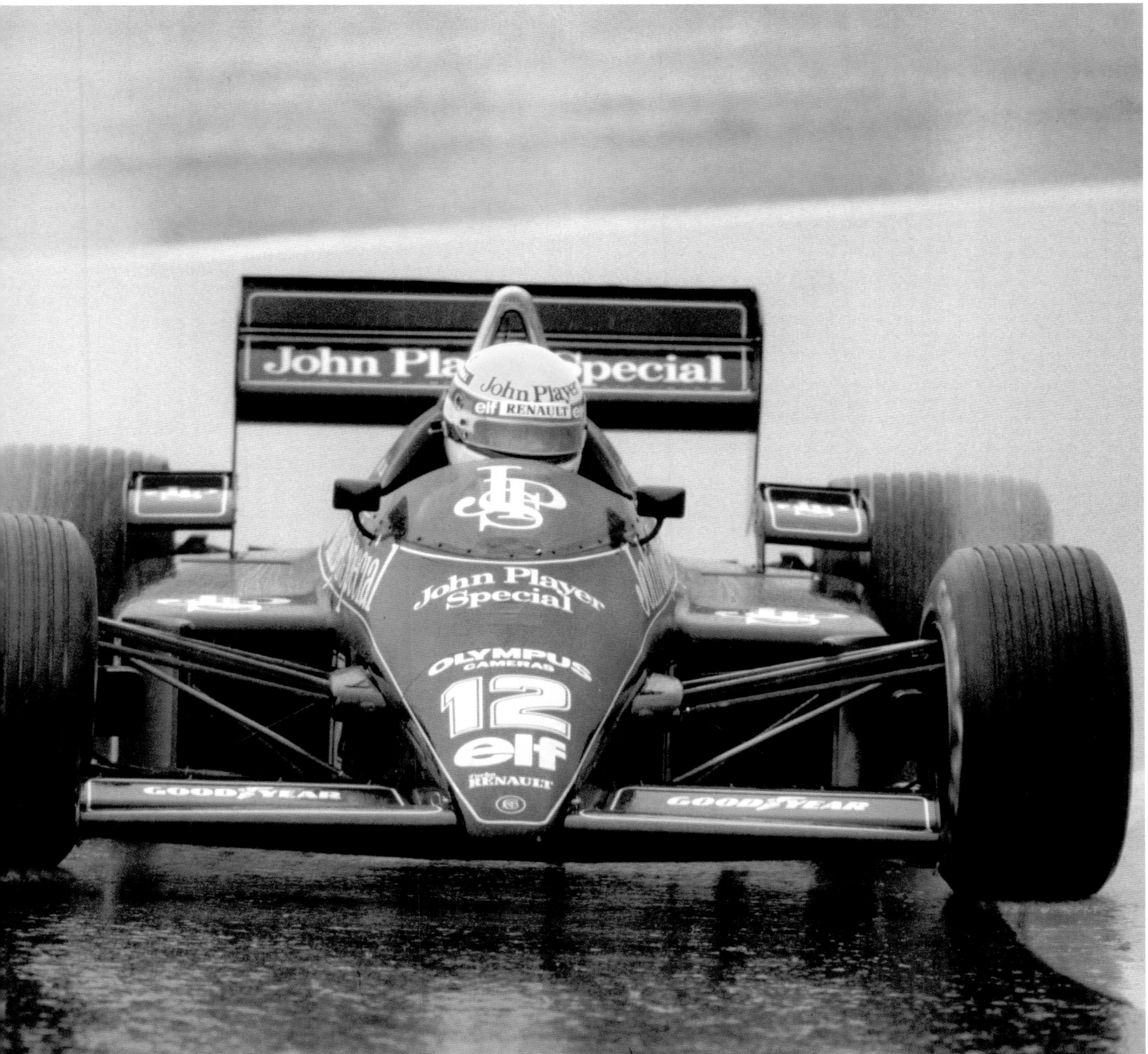
John Player Special
John Player
elf RENAULT
John Player Special
OLYMPUS CAMERAS
12
elf
RENAULT
GOODYEAR
GOODYEAR

McLaren continued its winning form of the year before, but this time its successes were due almost entirely to Alain Prost, who duly took his – and France's – first world title. Team-mate Niki Lauda suffered from appalling unreliability and won only once, at the Dutch Grand Prix. At the end of the year he retired from racing – this time for good.

In the first half of the season Ferrari looked a credible title threat to McLaren. The Italian team's new car, the 156/85, appeared quite McLaren-like in its aerodynamic layout. Michele Alboreto used it to good effect to win in Canada and Germany and kept Prost within striking distance until mid-season. Then electronics specialist Bosch made a big step forward with the management system of McLaren's TAG-Porsche engine. Drastically improved fuel efficiency allowed Prost and Lauda to run more turbo boost, which left the Ferraris a long way behind. As the Italian team tried to coax more power from its engines, reliability suffered.

In the second half of the year the Williams-Hondas came on so strongly that they were the fastest cars of all by the season's end. Honda horsepower gains allowed Williams to untap the potential of the FW10 – its first carbon-fibre chassis – and it won the last three races. Two of these victories came courtesy of Nigel Mansell, who finally made his winning breakthrough. Fittingly it came in front of his home crowd, in the GP of Europe at Brands Hatch. Prost finished fourth here to seal the crown.

In his final year with Brabham, Nelson Piquet gave tyre manufacturer Pirelli its first F1 victory since 1957 by winning in France, while Ayrton Senna and Elio de Angelis won three races between them in the Renault-powered Lotus 97T.

IMPROVED FUEL EFFICIENCY ALLOWED PROST AND LAUDA TO RUN MORE TURBO BOOST, WHICH LEFT THE FERRARIS A LONG WAY BEHIND. AS THE ITALIAN TEAM TRIED TO COAX MORE POWER FROM ITS ENGINES, RELIABILITY SUFFERED

Far left
Blazing saddle: Alboreto peels into the Brands Hatch pit lane and the Prancing Horse's title challenge grids to a halt for another year

Left
Whose line is it anyway? Unfortunately this didn't happen in the United States, thereby ruling out the possibility of a caption about Detroit spinners. Marc Surer (Brabham) passes Derek Warwick's clumsily-parked Renault at Spa

Above
Tight fit: Monaco is an anachronism, discuss. A passing Williams gets in the way of all the pit lane hangers-on during the season's most cramped grand prix

Above left
Calm before the storm: having broken down during the dry morning warm-up in Portugal, Senna watches team-mate de Angelis in action. It started to rain about 90 minutes later – and didn't stop thereafter

1985

CHAMPIONSHIP CAR-BY-CAR

1ST ALAIN PROST (FRA; AGE: 30) 73(+3) PTS

McLaren MP4/2B-TAG V6 tc
Marlboro McLaren International
Races: BRA; POR; SMR; MON; CAN; DET; FRA; GBR; GER; AUT; NED; ITA; BEL; EUR; RSA; AUS (all car #2)

2ND MICHELE ALBORETO (ITA; AGE: 28) 53 PTS

Ferrari 156/85 V6 tc
Scuderia Ferrari
Races: BRA; POR; SMR; MON; CAN; DET; FRA; GBR; GER; AUT; NED; ITA; BEL; EUR; RSA; AUS (all car #27)

3RD KEKE ROSBERG (FIN; AGE: 36) 40 PTS

Williams FW10-Honda V6 tc
Canon Williams Honda Team
Races: BRA; POR; SMR; MON; CAN; DET; FRA; GBR; GER; AUT; NED; ITA; BEL; EUR; RSA; AUS (all car #6)

4TH AYRTON SENNA (BRA; AGE: 25) 38 PTS

Lotus 97T-Renault V6 tc
John Player Special Team Lotus
Races: BRA; POR; SMR; MON; CAN; DET; FRA; GBR; GER; AUT; NED; ITA; BEL; EUR; RSA; AUS (all car #12)

5TH ELIO DE ANGELIS (ITA; AGE: 27) 33 PTS

Lotus 97T-Renault V6 tc
John Player Special Team Lotus
Races: BRA; POR; SMR; MON; CAN; DET; FRA; GBR; GER; AUT; NED; ITA; BEL; EUR; RSA; AUS (all car #11)

6TH NIGEL MANSELL (GBR; AGE: 32) 31 PTS

Williams FW10-Honda V6 tc
Canon Williams Honda Team
Races: BRA; POR; SMR; MON; CAN; DET; GBR; GER; AUT; NED; ITA; BEL; EUR; RSA; AUS (all car #5)

7TH STEFAN JOHANSSON (SWE; AGE: 28) 26 PTS

Tyrrell 012-Ford V8
Tyrrell Racing Organisation
Races: BRA (car #4)

STEFAN JOHANSSON (CONTD)

Ferrari 156/85 V6 tc
Scuderia Ferrari
Races: POR; SMR; MON; CAN; DET; FRA; GBR; GER; AUT; NED; ITA; BEL; EUR; RSA; AUS (all car #28)

8TH NELSON PIQUET (BRA; AGE: 32) 21 PTS

Brabham BT54-BMW S4 tc
Motor Racing Developments
Races: BRA; POR; SMR; MON; CAN; DET; FRA; GBR; GER; AUT; NED; ITA; BEL; EUR; RSA; AUS (all car #7)

9TH JACQUES LAFFITE (FRA; AGE: 41) 16 PTS

Ligier JS25-Renault V6 tc
Équipe Ligier Gitanes
Races: BRA; POR; SMR; MON; CAN; DET; FRA; GBR; GER; AUT; NED; ITA; BEL; EUR; AUS (all car #26)

10TH NIKI LAUDA (AUT; AGE: 36) 14 PTS

McLaren MP4/2B-TAG V6 tc
Marlboro McLaren International
Races: BRA; POR; SMR; MON; CAN; DET; FRA; GBR; GER; AUT; NED; ITA; RSA; AUS (all car #1)

11TH= THIERRY BOUTSEN (BEL; AGE: 28) 11 PTS

Arrows A8-BMW S4 tc
Barclay Arrows BMW
Races: BRA; POR; SMR; MON; CAN; DET; FRA; GBR; GER; AUT; NED; ITA; BEL; EUR; RSA; AUS (all car #18)

11TH= PATRICK TAMBAY (FRA; AGE: 36) 11 PTS

Renault RE60 V6 tc
Équipe Renault Elf
Races: BRA; POR; SMR; MON; CAN; DET; FRA; GBR; GER; AUT; NED; ITA; BEL; EUR; AUS (all car #15)

13TH= MARC SURER (SUI; AGE: 33) 5 PTS

Brabham BT54-BMW S4 tc
Motor Racing Developments
Races: CAN; DET; FRA; GBR; GER; AUT; NED; ITA; BEL; EUR; RSA; AUS (all car #8)

13TH= DEREK WARWICK (GBR; AGE: 30) 5 PTS

Renault RE60 V6 tc
Équipe Renault Elf
Races: BRA; POR; SMR; MON; CAN; DET; FRA; GBR; GER; AUT; NED; ITA; BEL; EUR; AUS (all car #16)

1985

CHAMPIONSHIP CAR-BY-CAR

13TH= STEFAN BELLOF (GER; AGE: 27) 4 PTS

Tyrrell 012-Ford V8
Tyrrell Racing Organisation
Races: POR; SMR; CAN; DET; FRA; GBR (all car #4)

STEFAN BELLOF (CONTD)

Tyrrell 014-Renault V6 tc
Tyrrell Racing Organisation
Races: GER; AUT (both car #3); NED (#4)

15TH= PHILIPPE STREIFF (FRA; AGE: 30) 4 PTS

Ligier JS25-Renault V6 tc
Équipe Ligier Gitanes
Races: ITA; BEL; EUR; AUS (all car #25)

PHILIPPE STREIFF (CONTD)

Tyrrell 014-Renault V6 tc
Tyrrell Racing Organisation
Races: RSA (car #4)

17TH= RENÉ ARNOUX (FRA; AGE: 36) 3 PTS

Ferrari 156/85 V6 tc
Scuderia Ferrari
Races: BRA (car #28)

17TH= GERHARD BERGER (AUT; AGE: 25) 3 PTS

Arrows A8-BMW S4 tc
Barclay Arrows BMW
Races: BRA; POR; SMR; MON; CAN; DET; FRA; GBR; GER; AUT; NED; ITA; BEL; EUR; RSA; AUS (all car #17)

17TH= IVAN CAPELLI (ITA; AGE: 22) 3 PTS

Tyrrell 014-Renault V6 tc
Tyrrell Racing Organisation
Races: EUR; AUS (both car #4

17TH= ANDREA DE CESARIS (ITA; AGE: 26) 3 PTS

Ligier JS25-Renault V6 tc
Équipe Ligier Gitanes
Races: BRA; POR; SMR; MON; CAN; DET; FRA; GBR; GER; AUT; NED (all car #25)

KENNETH ACHESON (GBR; AGE: 27) 0 PTS

RAM 03-Hart S4 tc
Skoal Bandit Formula 1 Team
Races: AUT; ITA (both car #10)

PHILIPPE ALLIOT (FRA; AGE: 31) 0 PTS

RAM 03-Hart S4 tc
Skoal Bandit Formula 1 Team
Races: BRA; POR; SMR; CAN; DET; FRA; GBR; GER (all car #10); AUT; NED; ITA; BEL; EUR (all #9)

MAURO BALDI (ITA; AGE: 31) 0 PTS

Spirit 101D-Hart S4 tc
Spirit Enterprises
Races: BRA; POR; SMR (all car #21)

MARTIN BRUNDLE (GBR; AGE: 26) 0 PTS

Tyrrell 012-Ford V8
Tyrrell Racing Organisation
Races: BRA; POR; SMR; MON; CAN; DET (all car #3); GER (#4)

MARTIN BRUNDLE (CONTD)

Tyrrell 014-Renault V6 tc
Tyrrell Racing Organisation
Races: FRA; GBR; NED; ITA; BEL; EUR; RSA; AUS (all car #3)

EDDIE CHEEVER (USA; AGE: 27) 0 PTS

Alfa Romeo 185T V8 tc
Benetton Team Alfa Romeo
Races: BRA; POR; SMR; MON; CAN; DET; FRA (all car #23)

EDDIE CHEEVER (CONTD)

Alfa Romeo 184TB V8 tc
Benetton Team Alfa Romeo
Races: GBR; GER; AUT; NED; ITA; BEL; EUR; RSA; AUS (all car #23)

1985

CHAMPIONSHIP CAR-BY-CAR

CHRISTIAN DANNER (GER; AGE: 27) 0 PTS

Zakspeed 841 S4 tc
West Zakspeed Racing
Races: BEL; EUR (both car #30)

TEO FABI (ITA; AGE: 30) 0 PTS

Toleman TG185-Hart S4 tc
Toleman Group Motorsport
Races: MON; CAN; DET; FRA; GBR; GER; AUT; NED; ITA; BEL; EUR; RSA; AUS (all car #19)

PIERCARLO GHINZANI (ITA; AGE: 33) 0 PTS

Osella FA1G-Alfa Romeo V8 tc
Osella Squadra Corse
Races: BRA; SMR; CAN; DET; FRA; GBR (all car #24)

PICTURED DURING MON PRACTICE

PIERCARLO GHINZANI (CONTD)

Osella FA1F-Alfa Romeo V8 tc
Osella Squadra Corse
Races: POR (car #24)

PIERCARLO GHINZANI (CONTD)

Toleman TG185-Hart S4 tc
Toleman Group Motorsport
Races: AUT; NED; ITA; BEL; EUR; RSA; AUS (all car #20)

FRANÇOIS HESNAULT (FRA; AGE: 28) 0 PTS

Brabham BT54-BMW S4 tc
Motor Racing Developments
Races: BRA; POR; SMR (all car #8)

FRANÇOIS HESNAULT (CONTD)

Renault RE60 V6 tc
Équipe Renault Elf
Races: GER (car #14)

ALAN JONES (AUS; AGE: 38) 0 PTS

Lola THL1-Hart S4 tc
Team Haas USA
Races: ITA; EUR; AUS (all car #33)

PIERLUIGI MARTINI (ITA; AGE: 24) 0 PTS

Minardi M185-Ford V8
Minardi Team
Races: BRA; POR (both car #29)

PIERLUIGI MARTINI (CONTD)

Minardi M185-Motori Moderni V6 tc
Minardi Team
Races: SMR; CAN; DET; FRA; GBR; GER; AUT; NED; ITA; BEL; EUR; RSA; AUS (all car #29)

JONATHAN PALMER (GBR; AGE: 28) 0 PTS

Zakspeed 841 S4 tc
West Zakspeed Racing
Races: POR; MON; FRA; GBR; GER; AUT; NED (all car #30)

RICCARDO PATRESE (ITA; AGE: 31) 0 PTS

Alfa Romeo 185T V8 tc
Benetton Team Alfa Romeo
Races: BRA; POR; SMR; MON; CAN; DET; FRA; GBR (all car #22)

RICCARDO PATRESE (CONTD)

Alfa Romeo 184TB V8 tc
Benetton Team Alfa Romeo
Races: GER; AUT; NED; ITA; BEL; EUR; RSA; AUS (all car #22)

HUUB ROTHENGATTER (NED; AGE: 30) 0 PTS

Osella FA1G-Alfa Romeo V8 tc
Osella Squadra Corse
Races: GER; AUT; NED; ITA; BEL; RSA; AUS (all car #24)

PICTURED DURING EUR PRACTICE

JOHN WATSON (GBR; AGE: 39) 0 PTS

McLaren MP4/2B-TAG V6 tc
Marlboro McLaren International
Races: EUR (car #1)

1985

CHAMPIONSHIP CAR-BY-CAR

MANFRED WINKELHOCK (GER; AGE: 33) 0 PTS

RAM 03-Hart S4 tc
Skoal Bandit Formula 1 Team
Races: BRA; POR; SMR; CAN; DET; FRA; GBR; GER (all car #9)

GRAND PRIX WINNERS 1985

	RACE (CIRCUIT)	WINNER (CAR)
BRA	BRAZILIAN GRAND PRIX (RIO DE JANEIRO)	ALAIN PROST (McLAREN MP4/2B-TAG V6 TC)
POR	PORTUGUESE GRAND PRIX (ESTORIL)	AYRTON SENNA (LOTUS 97T-RENAULT V6 TC)
SMR	SAN MARINO GRAND PRIX (IMOLA)	ELIO DE ANGELIS (LOTUS 97T-RENAULT V6 TC)
MON	MONACO GRAND PRIX (MONTE CARLO)	ALAIN PROST (McLAREN MP4/2B-TAG V6 TC)
CAN	CANADIAN GRAND PRIX (MONTRÉAL)	MICHELE ALBORETO (FERRARI 156/85 V6 TC)
DET	DETROIT GRAND PRIX (DETROIT)	KEKE ROSBERG (WILLIAMS FW10-HONDA V6 TC)
FRA	FRENCH GRAND PRIX (PAUL RICARD)	NELSON PIQUET (BRABHAM BT54-BMW S4 TC)
GBR	BRITISH GRAND PRIX (SILVERSTONE)	ALAIN PROST (McLAREN MP4/2B-TAG V6 TC)
GER	GERMAN GRAND PRIX (NÜRBURGRING)	MICHELE ALBORETO (FERRARI 156/85 V6 TC)
AUT	AUSTRIAN GRAND PRIX (ÖSTERREICHRING)	ALAIN PROST (McLAREN MP4/2B-TAG V6 TC)
NED	DUTCH GRAND PRIX (ZANDVOORT)	NIKI LAUDA (McLAREN MP4/2B-TAG V6 TC)
ITA	ITALIAN GRAND PRIX (MONZA)	ALAIN PROST (McLAREN MP4/2B-TAG V6 TC)
BEL	BELGIAN GRAND PRIX (SPA-FRANCORCHAMPS)	AYRTON SENNA (LOTUS 97T-RENAULT V6 TC)
EUR	EUROPEAN GRAND PRIX (BRANDS HATCH)	NIGEL MANSELL (WILLIAMS FW10-HONDA V6 TC)
RSA	SOUTH AFRICAN GRAND PRIX (KYALAMI)	NIGEL MANSELL (WILLIAMS FW10-HONDA V6 TC)
AUS	AUSTRALIAN GRAND PRIX (ADELAIDE)	KEKE ROSBERG (WILLIAMS FW10-HONDA V6 TC)

MICHELE ALBORETO

1986

PROST HAS THE BRAIN TO BEAT WILLIAMS'S BRAWN

Above
Feeling wizard in Oz: having sealed the world title, Prost indulges in a spot of imaginary weightlifting. Piquet (left) summons up a grin in defeat. Johansson looks suitably embarrassed about the picture on the opposite page

Left
Advance Australia flair: Prost takes liberties with his McLaren during his early pursuit of Piquet in Adelaide

Far left
Twisted fiery starter: winner Piquet heads Prost, Mansell, Patrese, Alboreto, Arnoux and Fabi towards the first right-hander at Hockenheim. Just behind, Johansson is turning in a fraction too early

This season was the story of how one driver's individual brilliance led him to triumph over a technical shortfall. Armed with an underpowered McLaren-TAG Porsche, Alain Prost should not have been able to beat the faster Williams-Hondas of Nigel Mansell and Nelson Piquet. But, aided a little by luck and the duelling Williams drivers' habit of taking points off each other, he did just that and became the first back-to-back title winner for 26 years. Williams won the championship for constructors by way of consolation.

With up to 1200 horsepower in qualifying and more than 900 in races, the Honda was fantastically powerful, superbly reliable and very efficient – important with regulations that limited fuel capacity to 195 litres. The Renault turbo, as used by Lotus, was even more powerful in qualifying trim (up to 1400 horsepower), but less economical. The Lotus 98T wasn't as good aerodynamically as the Williams, either, and Ayrton Senna was able to conjure only two victories. The TAG Porsche engine in Prost's McLaren MP4/2C was fuel-efficient, however, and the Frenchman made highly intelligent use of it. He won in San Marino Imola, Monaco and Austria to keep himself in title contention prior to the final round in Australia.

With 19 laps to go in Adelaide, everything was looking good for Mansell. He lay third, with Piquet leading from Prost. If they finished in that order the title was the Englishman's. But at close to 200mph on the pit straight, his left-rear tyre exploded. Only incredible car control prevented him hitting anything, but his dream was over. Williams took the agonising, but understandable, decision to bring Piquet into the pits for a tyre check. Victory and the title were Prost's.

ALAIN PROST SHOULD NOT HAVE BEEN ABLE TO BEAT THE FASTER WILLIAMS-HONDAS OF NIGEL MANSELL AND NELSON PIQUET. BUT, AIDED A LITTLE BY LUCK AND THE DUELLING WILLIAMS DRIVERS' HABIT OF TAKING POINTS OFF EACH OTHER, HE DID

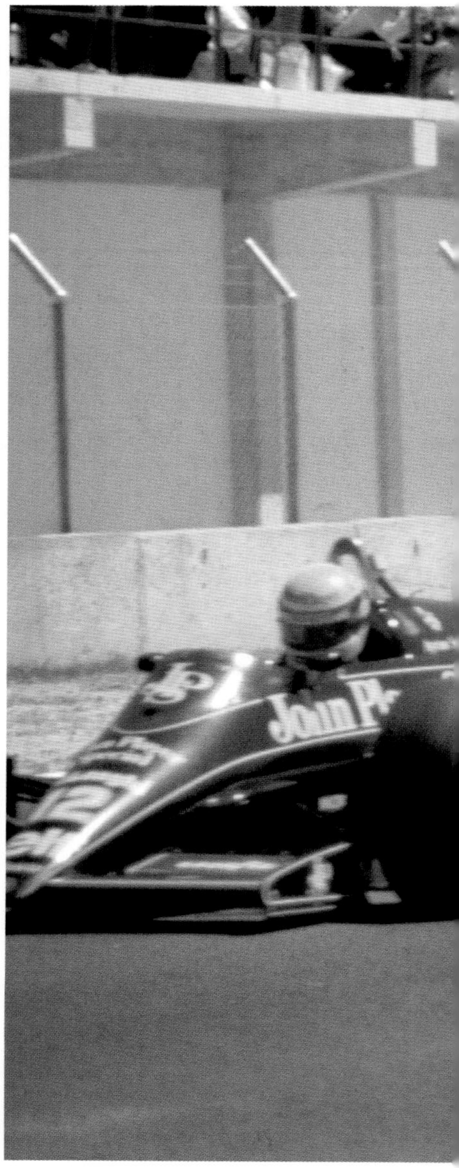

Right
Modestly ablaze: two seasons with Ferrari earned Johansson half a dozen podium finishes and a clutch of appearances in this book. This time he's included because of an engine failure during practice at Imola

Below
Hundredths and thousandths: Senna beat Mansell to the line by just 0.014s in a frantic sprint at Jerez, a recently-built facility in the heart of Spain's sherry-growing region. Anyone planning to visit the track is advised to fly in via Gibraltar, purely because of the fantastic mountain roads that lie between the colony and the circuit

Below left
Berger king: a tall Austrian broke his – and Benetton's – F1 duck in Mexico City. It was also the solitary success of the season for tyre supplier Pirelli

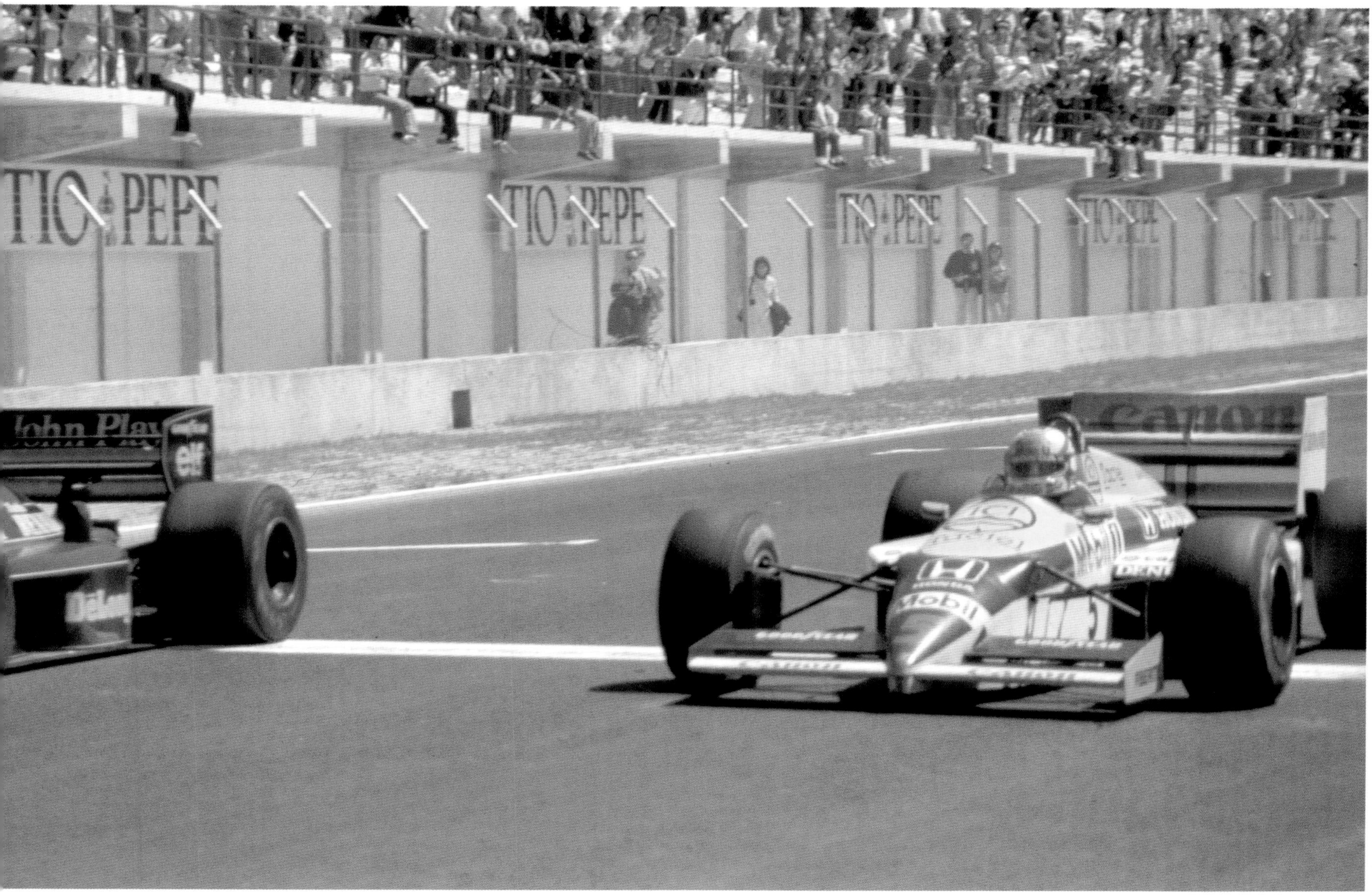

1986

CHAMPIONSHIP CAR-BY-CAR

1ST ALAIN PROST (FRA; AGE: 31) 72(+2) PTS

McLaren MP4/2C-TAG V6 tc
Marlboro McLaren International
Races: BRA; ESP; SMR; MON; BEL; CAN; DET; FRA; GBR; GER; HUN; AUT; ITA; POR; MEX; AUS (all car #1)

2ND NIGEL MANSELL (GBR; AGE: 32) 70(+2) PTS

Williams FW11-Honda V6 tc
Canon Williams Honda Team
Races: BRA; ESP; SMR; MON; BEL; CAN; DET; FRA; GBR; GER; HUN; AUT; ITA; POR; MEX; AUS (all car #5)

3RD NELSON PIQUET (BRA; AGE: 33) 69 PTS

Williams FW11-Honda V6 tc
Canon Williams Honda Team
Races: BRA; ESP; SMR; MON; BEL; CAN; DET; FRA; GBR; GER; HUN; AUT; ITA; POR; MEX; AUS (all car #6)

4TH AYRTON SENNA (BRA; AGE: 26) 55 PTS

Lotus 98T-Renault V6 tc
John Player Special Team Lotus
Races: BRA; ESP; SMR; MON; BEL; CAN; DET; FRA; GBR; GER; HUN; AUT; ITA; POR; MEX; AUS (all car #12)

5TH STEFAN JOHANSSON (SWE; AGE: 29) 23 PTS

Ferrari F186 V6 tc
Scuderia Ferrari
Races: BRA; ESP; SMR; MON; BEL; CAN; DET; FRA; GBR; GER; HUN; AUT; ITA; POR; MEX; AUS (all car #28)

6TH KEKE ROSBERG (FIN; AGE: 37) 22 PTS

McLaren MP4/2C-TAG V6 tc
Marlboro McLaren International
Races: BRA; ESP; SMR; MON; BEL; CAN; DET; FRA; GBR; GER; HUN; AUT; ITA; POR; MEX; AUS (all car #2)

7TH GERHARD BERGER (AUT; AGE: 26) 17 PTS

Benetton B186-BMW S4 tc
Benetton Formula
Races: BRA; ESP; SMR; MON; BEL; CAN; DET; FRA; GBR; GER; HUN; AUT; ITA; POR; MEX; AUS (all car #20)

8TH= MICHELE ALBORETO (ITA; AGE: 29) 14 PTS

Ferrari F186 V6 tc
Scuderia Ferrari
Races: BRA; ESP; SMR; MON; BEL; CAN; DET; FRA; GBR; GER; HUN; AUT; ITA; POR; MEX; AUS (all car #27)

8TH= RENÉ ARNOUX (FRA; AGE: 38) 14 PTS

Ligier JS27-Renault V6 tc
Équipe Ligier
Races: BRA; ESP; SMR; MON; BEL; CAN; DET; FRA; GBR; GER; HUN; AUT; ITA; POR; MEX; AUS (all car #25)

8TH= JACQUES LAFFITE (FRA; AGE: 42) 14 PTS

Ligier JS27-Renault V6 tc
Équipe Ligier
Races: BRA; ESP; SMR; MON; BEL; CAN; DET; FRA; GBR (all car #26)

11TH MARTIN BRUNDLE (GBR; AGE: 27) 8 PTS

Tyrrell 014-Renault V6 tc
Data General Team Tyrrell
Races: BRA; ESP; SMR (all car #3)

MARTIN BRUNDLE (CONTD)

Tyrrell 015-Renault V6 tc
Data General Team Tyrrell
Races: MON; BEL; CAN; DET; FRA; GBR; GER; HUN; AUT; ITA; POR; MEX; AUS (all car #3)

12TH= ALAN JONES (AUS; AGE: 39) 4 PTS

Lola THL1-Hart S4 tc
Team Haas USA
Races: BRA; ESP (both car #15)

ALAN JONES (CONTD)

Lola THL2-Ford V6 tc
Team Haas USA
Races: SMR; MON; BEL; CAN; DET; FRA; GBR; GER; HUN; AUT; ITA; POR; MEX; AUS (all car #15)

13TH= JOHNNY DUMFRIES (GBR; AGE: 28) 3 PTS

Lotus 98T-Renault V6 tc
John Player Special Team Lotus
Races: BRA; ESP; SMR; BEL; CAN; DET; FRA; GBR; GER; HUN; AUT; ITA; POR; MEX; AUS (all car #11)

PICTURED DURING MON PRACTICE

1986

CHAMPIONSHIP CAR-BY-CAR

13TH= PHILIPPE STREIFF (FRA; AGE: 31) 3 PTS

Tyrrell 014-Renault V6 tc
Data General Team Tyrrell
Races: BRA; ESP; SMR; CAN (all car #4)

PHILIPPE STREIFF (CONTD)

Tyrrell 015-Renault V6 tc
Data General Team Tyrrell
Races: MON; BEL; DET; FRA; GBR; GER; HUN; AUT; ITA; POR; MEX; AUS (all car #4)

15TH= TEO FABI (ITA; AGE: 31) 2 PTS

Benetton B186-BMW S4 tc
Benetton Formula
Races: BRA; ESP; SMR; MON; BEL; CAN; DET; FRA; GBR; GER; HUN; AUT; ITA; POR; MEX; AUS (all car #19)

15TH= RICCARDO PATRESE (ITA; AGE: 32) 2 PTS

Brabham BT55-BMW S4 tc
Motor Racing Developments
Races: BRA; ESP; SMR; MON; BEL; CAN; DET; FRA; GER; HUN; AUT; ITA; POR; MEX; AUS (all car #7)

RICCARDO PATRESE (CONTD)

Brabham BT54-BMW S4 tc
Motor Racing Developments
Races: GBR (car #7)

15TH= PATRICK TAMBAY (FRA; AGE: 37) 2 PTS

Lola THL1-Hart S4 tc
Team Haas USA
Races: BRA; ESP; SMR (all car #16)

PATRICK TAMBAY (CONTD)

Lola THL2-Ford V6 tc
Team Haas USA
Races: MON; BEL; FRA; GBR; GER; HUN; AUT; ITA; POR; MEX; AUS (all car #16)

17TH= PHILIPPE ALLIOT (FRA; AGE: 32) 1 PT

Ligier JS27-Renault V6 tc
Équipe Ligier
Races: GER; HUN; AUT; ITA; POR; MEX; AUS (all car #26)

17TH= CHRISTIAN DANNER (GER; AGE: 28) 1 PT

Osella FA1F-Alfa Romeo V8 tc
Osella Squadra Corse
Races: BRA; ESP; SMR; BEL; CAN (all car #22)

PICTURED DURING MON PRACTICE

CHRISTIAN DANNER (CONTD)

Arrows A8-BMW S4 tc
Barclay Arrows BMW
Races: DET; FRA; GBR; GER; AUT; ITA; POR; MEX; AUS (all car #17)

CHRISTIAN DANNER (CONTD)

Arrows A9-BMW S4 tc
Barclay Arrows BMW
Races: HUN (car #17)

ELIO DE ANGELIS (ITA; AGE: 28) 0 PTS

Brabham BT55-BMW S4 tc
Motor Racing Developments
Races: BRA; ESP; SMR; MON (all car #8)

ALLEN BERG (CAN; AGE: 25) 0 PTS

Osella FA1F-Alfa Romeo V8 tc
Osella Squadra Corse
Races: DET; GER; HUN; AUT; POR; MEX; AUS (all car #22)

ALLEN BERG (CONTD)

Osella FA1G-Alfa Romeo V8 tc
Osella Squadra Corse
Races: FRA (car #22)

ALLEN BERG (CONTD)

Osella FA1H-Alfa Romeo V8 tc
Osella Squadra Corse
Races: GBR (car #22)

1986

CHAMPIONSHIP CAR-BY-CAR

THIERRY BOUTSEN (BEL; AGE: 29) 0 PTS

Arrows A8-BMW S4 tc
Barclay Arrows BMW
Races: BRA; ESP; SMR; MON; BEL; CAN; DET; FRA; GBR; HUN; ITA; POR; MEX; AUS (all car #18)

THIERRY BOUTSEN (CONTD)

Arrows A9-BMW S4 tc
Barclay Arrows BMW
Races: GER; AUT (both car #18)

ALEX CAFFI (ITA; AGE: 22) 0 PTS

Osella FA1F-Alfa Romeo V8 tc
Osella Squadra Corse
Races: ITA (car #22)

IVAN CAPELLI (ITA; AGE: 23) 0 PTS

AGS JH21C-Motori Moderni V6 tc
Jolly Club
Races: ITA; POR (both car #31)

ANDREA DE CESARIS (ITA; AGE: 27) 0 PTS

Minardi M185B-Motori Moderni V6 tc
Minardi Team
Races: BRA; ESP; SMR; BEL; CAN; DET; FRA; GBR; GER; AUT (all car #23)

ANDREA DE CESARIS (CONTD)

Minardi M186-Motori Moderni V6 tc
Minardi Team
Races: HUN; ITA; POR; MEX; AUS (all car #23)

EDDIE CHEEVER (USA; AGE: 28) 0 PTS

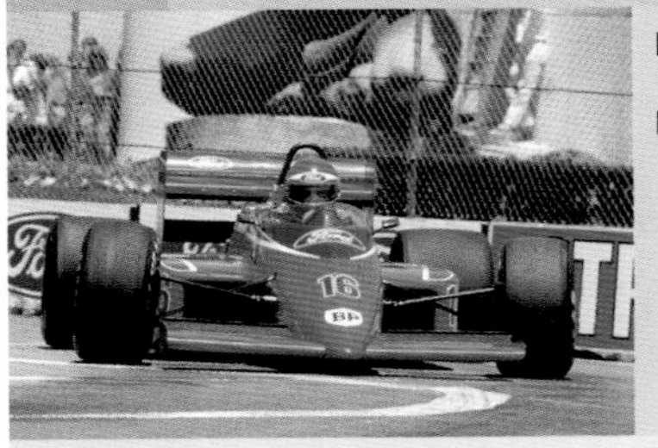

Lola THL2-Ford V6 tc
Team Haas USA
Races: DET (car #16)

PIERCARLO GHINZANI (ITA; AGE: 34) 0 PTS

Osella FA1G-Alfa Romeo V8 tc
Osella Squadra Corse
Races: BRA; ESP; SMR; BEL; CAN; DET; GBR; GER; HUN; AUT; ITA; POR; MEX; AUS (all car #21)

PIERCARLO GHINZANI (CONTD)

Osella FA1H-Alfa Romeo V8 tc
Osella Squadra Corse
Races: FRA (car #21)

ALESSANDRO NANNINI (ITA; AGE: 27) 0 PTS

Minardi M185B-Motori Moderni V6 tc
Minardi Team
Races: BRA; SMR; BEL; CAN; DET; FRA; GBR; GER; HUN; ITA; POR; MEX; AUS (all car #24)

ALESSANDRO NANNINI (CONTD)

Minardi M186-Motori Moderni V6 tc
Minardi Team
Races: AUT (car #24)

JONATHAN PALMER (GBR; AGE: 29) 0 PTS

Zakspeed 861 S4 tc
West Zakspeed Racing
Races: BRA; ESP; SMR; MON; BEL; CAN; DET; FRA; GBR; GER; HUN; AUT; ITA; POR; MEX; AUS (all car #14)

HUUB ROTHENGATTER (NED; AGE: 31) 0 PTS

Zakspeed 861 S4 tc
West Zakspeed Racing
Races: SMR; BEL; CAN; FRA; GBR; GER; HUN; AUT; ITA; POR; AUS (all car #29)

MARC SURER (SUI; AGE: 34) 0 PTS

Arrows A8-BMW S4 tc
Barclay Arrows BMW
Races: BRA; ESP; SMR; MON; BEL (all car #17)

DEREK WARWICK (GBR; AGE: 32) 0 PTS

Brabham BT55-BMW S4 tc
Motor Racing Developments
Races: CAN; DET; FRA; GBR; GER; HUN; ITA; POR; MEX; AUS (all car #8)

1986

CHAMPIONSHIP CAR-BY-CAR

GRAND PRIX WINNERS 1986

	RACE (CIRCUIT)	WINNER (CAR)
BRA	BRAZILIAN GRAND PRIX (RIO DE JANEIRO)	NELSON PIQUET (WILLIAMS FW11-HONDA V6 TC)
ESP	SPANISH GRAND PRIX (JEREZ)	AYRTON SENNA (LOTUS 98T-RENAULT V6 TC)
SMR	SAN MARINO GRAND PRIX (IMOLA)	ALAIN PROST (McLAREN MP4/2C-TAG V6 TC)
MON	MONACO GRAND PRIX (MONTE CARLO)	ALAIN PROST (McLAREN MP4/2C-TAG V6 TC)
BEL	BELGIAN GRAND PRIX (SPA-FRANCORCHAMPS)	NIGEL MANSELL (WILLIAMS FW11-HONDA V6 TC)
CAN	CANADIAN GRAND PRIX (MONTRÉAL)	NIGEL MANSELL (WILLIAMS FW11-HONDA V6 TC)
DET	DETROIT GRAND PRIX (DETROIT)	AYRTON SENNA (LOTUS 98T-RENAULT V6 TC)
FRA	FRENCH GRAND PRIX (PAUL RICARD)	NIGEL MANSELL (WILLIAMS FW11-HONDA V6 TC)
GBR	BRITISH GRAND PRIX (BRANDS HATCH)	NIGEL MANSELL (WILLIAMS FW11-HONDA V6 TC)
GER	GERMAN GRAND PRIX (HOCKENHEIM)	NELSON PIQUET (WILLIAMS FW11-HONDA V6 TC)
HUN	HUNGARIAN GRAND PRIX (HUNGARORING)	NELSON PIQUET (WILLIAMS FW11-HONDA V6 TC)
AUT	AUSTRIAN GRAND PRIX (ÖSTERREICHRING)	ALAIN PROST (McLAREN MP4/2C-TAG V6 TC)
ITA	ITALIAN GRAND PRIX (MONZA)	NELSON PIQUET (WILLIAMS FW11-HONDA V6 TC)
POR	PORTUGUESE GRAND PRIX (ESTORIL)	NIGEL MANSELL (WILLIAMS FW11-HONDA V6 TC)
MEX	MEXICAN GRAND PRIX (MEXICO CITY)	GERHARD BERGER (BENETTON B186-BMW S4 TC)
AUS	AUSTRALIAN GRAND PRIX (ADELAIDE)	ALAIN PROST (McLAREN MP4/2C-TAG V6 TC)

JACQUES LAFFITE

1987

PIQUET'S THREE WINS COUNT FOR MORE THAN MANSELL'S SIX

Far left
National stealth service: Piquet finished on the podium 11 times in the 15 races he started – and that was the key to his third world title

Above
Landmark: Prost celebrates his Jackie Stewart-beating 28th victory in Portugal

Centre left
Wages of spin: Derek Warwick fell off twice in Portugal and finished 13th, four laps adrift, as a consequence

Left
Pine Martin: Brundle's marmalised chassis awaits recovery in Austria, where it took three attempts to get the race started. Mind you, the Zakspeed wasn't a great deal faster with all its wheels attached

After a near miss the previous season, things finally worked out in Williams's favour. The team lifted both world titles – but its champion driver Nelson Piquet left at the end of the season and engine supplier Honda went with him.

The power of Honda's V6 turbo and the aerodynamic effectiveness of the Williams FW11B made for an unbeatable combination. Piquet and team-mate Nigel Mansell fought between themselves for the crown until the Englishman put himself out of contention by injuring his back in a practice accident prior to the Japanese Grand Prix, the penultimate race of the season. Before that, there had been some vintage battles between the two, none more so than during Mansell's home race at Silverstone. Here, after an unscheduled stop left him 30 seconds behind with 30 laps to go, Mansell closed dramatically on his rival and passed him at Stowe Corner on the penultimate lap. The crowd went delirious and mobbed the winner when he ran out of fuel shortly after taking the chequered flag. Mansellmania had reached new heights.

Gerhard Berger (Ferrari), Alain Prost (McLaren) and Ayrton Senna (Lotus) picked up the few crumbs the Williams drivers left behind. The Ferrari was the most aerodynamically advanced car on the grid and, by the end of the season, Berger was the man to beat. But Ferrari's slow development had given Williams too much of a head start. McLaren's TAG Porsche engine was now being outgunned while the Lotus was at a clear aerodynamic disadvantage against the similarly-powered Williams. Both Lotus and Williams ran their cars with active ride, but the system seemed to provide no definitive superiority over conventional springs. This would change in years to come.

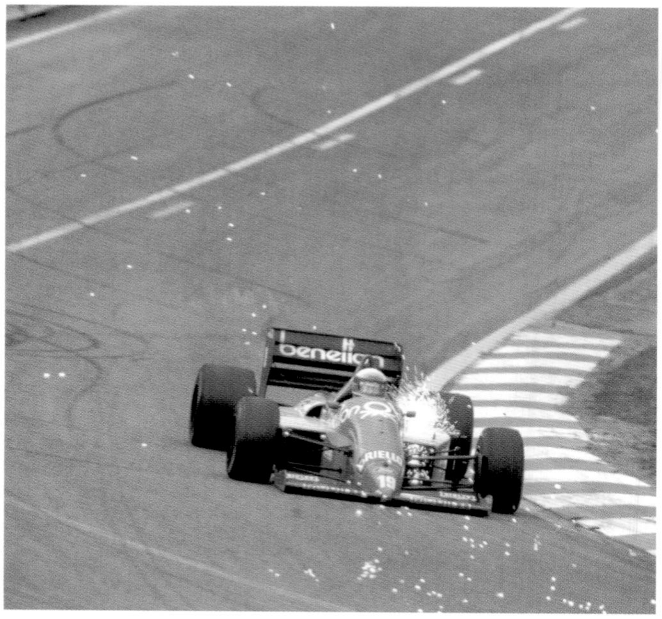

Top
Spark life: Mansell scored the finest of his six wins at Silverstone, where he had to make up 30 seconds in as many laps to track down Piquet

Far left
Turning Japanese: Berger leads Prost and the rest into the first corner at Suzuka, where the Austrian sealed the first of his back-to-back victories at the end of the season

Left
Benetton pullover: Fabi hammers through Spa's Eau Rouge kink before oil pump failure led to his retirement from the Belgian GP

1987

CHAMPIONSHIP CAR-BY-CAR

1ST NELSON PIQUET (BRA; AGE: 35) 73(+3) PTS

Williams FW11B-Honda V6 tc
Canon Williams Honda Team
Races: BRA; BEL; MON; DET; FRA; GBR; GER; HUN; AUT; ITA; POR; ESP; MEX; JPN; AUS (all car #6)

2ND NIGEL MANSELL (GBR; AGE: 33) 61 PTS

Williams FW11B-Honda V6 tc
Canon Williams Honda Team
Races; BRA; SMR; BEL; MON; DET; FRA; GBR; GER; HUN; AUT; ITA; POR; ESP; MEX; (all car #5)

3RD AYRTON SENNA (BRA; AGE: 27) 57 PTS

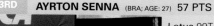

Lotus 99T-Honda V6 tc
Camel Team Lotus Honda
Races: BRA; SMR; BEL; MON; DET; FRA; GBR; GER; HUN; AUT; ITA; POR; ESP; MEX; JPN; AUS (all car #12)

4TH ALAIN PROST (FRA; AGE: 32) 46 PTS

McLaren MP4/3-TAG V6 tc
Marlboro McLaren International
Races: BRA; SMR; BEL; MON; DET; FRA; GBR; GER; HUN; AUT; ITA; POR; ESP; MEX; JPN; AUS (all car #1)

5TH GERHARD BERGER (AUT; AGE: 27) 36 PTS

Ferrari F187 V6 tc
Scuderia Ferrari
Races: BRA; SMR; BEL; MON; DET; FRA; GBR; GER; HUN; AUT; ITA; POR; ESP; MEX; JPN; AUS (all car #28)

6TH STEFAN JOHANSSON (SWE; AGE: 30) 30 PTS

McLaren MP4/3-TAG V6 tc
Marlboro McLaren International
Races: BRA; SMR; BEL; MON; DET; FRA; GBR; GER; HUN; AUT; ITA; POR; ESP; MEX; JPN; AUS (all car #2)

7TH MICHELE ALBORETO (ITA; AGE: 30) 17 PTS

Ferrari F187 V6 tc
Scuderia Ferrari
Races: BRA; SMR; BEL; MON; DET; FRA; GBR; GER; HUN; AUT; ITA; POR; ESP; MEX; JPN; AUS (all car #27)

8TH THIERRY BOUTSEN (BEL; AGE: 30) 16 PTS

Benetton B187-Ford V6 tc
Benetton Formula
Races: BRA; SMR; BEL; MON; DET; FRA; GBR; GER; HUN; AUT; ITA; POR; ESP; MEX; JPN; AUS (all car #20)

9TH TEO FABI (ITA; AGE: 32) 12 PTS

Benetton B187-Ford V6 tc
Benetton Formula
Races: BRA; SMR; BEL; MON; DET; FRA; GBR; GER; HUN; AUT; ITA; POR; ESP; MEX; JPN; AUS (all car #19)

10TH EDDIE CHEEVER (USA; AGE: 29) 8 PTS

Arrows A10-Megatron S4 tc
USF&G Arrows Megatron
Races: BRA; SMR; BEL; MON; DET; FRA; GBR; GER; HUN; AUT; ITA; POR; ESP; MEX; JPN; AUS (all car #18)

11TH= SATORU NAKAJIMA (JPN; AGE: 34) 7 PTS

Lotus 99T-Honda V6 tc
Camel Team Lotus Honda
Races: BRA; SMR; BEL; MON; DET; FRA; GBR; GER; HUN; AUT; ITA; POR; ESP; MEX; JPN; AUS (all car #11)

11TH= JONATHAN PALMER (GBR; AGE: 30) 7 PTS

Tyrrell 016-Ford V8
Data General Team Tyrrell
Races: BRA; SMR; BEL; MON; DET; FRA; GBR; GER; HUN; AUT; ITA; POR; ESP; MEX; JPN; AUS (all car #3)

13TH= RICCARDO PATRESE (ITA; AGE: 33) 6 PTS

Brabham BT56-BMW S4 tc
Motor Racing Developments
Races: BRA; SMR; BEL; MON; DET; FRA; GBR; GER; HUN; AUT; ITA; POR; ESP; MEX; JPN (all car #7)

RICCARDO PATRESE (CONTD)

Williams FW11B-Honda V6 tc
Canon Williams Honda Team
Races: AUS (car #5)

14TH= ANDREA DE CESARIS (ITA; AGE: 28) 4 PTS

Brabham BT56-BMW S4 tc
Motor Racing Developments
Races: BRA; SMR; BEL; MON; DET; FRA; GBR; GER; HUN; AUT; ITA; POR; ESP; MEX; JPN; AUS (all car #8)

1987

CHAMPIONSHIP CAR-BY-CAR

14TH= PHILIPPE STREIFF (FRA; AGE: 32) 4 PTS

Tyrrell 016-Ford V8
Data General Team Tyrrell
Races: BRA; SMR; BEL; MON; DET; FRA; GBR; GER; HUN; AUT; ITA; POR; ESP; MEX; JPN; AUS (all car #4)

16TH= PHILIPPE ALLIOT (FRA; AGE: 33) 3 PTS

Lola LC87-Ford V8
Larrousse Calmels
Races: SMR; BEL; MON; DET; FRA; GBR; GER; HUN; AUT; ITA; POR; ESP; MEX; JPN; AUS (all car #30)

16TH= DEREK WARWICK (GBR; AGE: 32) 3 PTS

Arrows A10-Megatron S4 tc
USF&G Arrows Megatron
Races: BRA; SMR; BEL; MON; DET; FRA; GBR; GER; HUN; AUT; ITA; POR; ESP; MEX; JPN; AUS (all car #17)

18TH MARTIN BRUNDLE (GBR; AGE: 28) 2 PTS

Zakspeed 861 S4 tc
West Zakspeed Racing
Races: BRA; DET (both car #9)

MARTIN BRUNDLE (CONTD)

Zakspeed 871 S4 tc
West Zakspeed Racing
Races: SMR; BEL; MON; FRA; GBR; GER; HUN; AUT; ITA; POR; ESP; MEX; JPN; AUS (all car #9)

19TH= RENÉ ARNOUX (FRA; AGE: 39) 1 PT

Ligier JS29-Megatron S4 tc
Ligier LOTO
Races: BEL; MON; DET; FRA; GBR; GER; HUN; AUT; ITA; POR; ESP; MEX; JPN; AUS (all car #25)

19TH= IVAN CAPELLI (ITA; AGE: 24) 1 PT

March 871-Ford V8
Leyton House March Racing Team
Races: SMR; BEL; MON; DET; FRA; GBR; GER; HUN; AUT; ITA; POR; ESP; MEX; JPN; AUS (all car #16)

19TH= ROBERTO MORENO (BRA; AGE: 28) 1 PT

AGS JH22-Ford V8
Team El Charro AGS
Races: JPN; AUS (both car #14)

ALEX CAFFI (ITA; AGE: 23) 0 PTS

Osella FA1I-Alfa Romeo V8 tc
Osella Squadra Corse
Races: BRA; SMR; BEL; MON; DET; FRA; GBR; GER; HUN; AUT; ITA; POR; MEX; JPN (all car #21)

ADRIAN CAMPOS (ESP; AGE: 27) 0 PTS

Minardi M187-Motori Moderni V6 tc
Minardi Team
Races: BRA; SMR; BEL; DET; FRA; GBR; GER; HUN; AUT; ITA; POR; ESP; MEX; JPN; AUS (all car #23)

PICTURED DURING MON PRACTICE

YANNICK DALMAS (FRA; AGE: 26) 0 PTS

Lola LC87-Ford V8
Larrousse Calmels
Races: MEX; JPN; AUS (all car #29)

CHRISTIAN DANNER (GER; AGE: 29) 0 PTS

Zakspeed 861 S4 tc
West Zakspeed Racing
Races: BRA; SMR (both car #10)

CHRISTIAN DANNER (CONTD)

Zakspeed 871 S4 tc
West Zakspeed Racing
Races: BEL; DET; FRA; GBR; GER; HUN; AUT; ITA; POR; ESP; MEX; JPN; AUS (all car #10)

PASCAL FABRE (FRA; AGE: 27) 0 PTS

AGS JH22-Ford V8
Team El Charro AGS
Races: BRA; SMR; BEL; MON; DET; FRA; GBR; GER; HUN; AUT; ESP (all car #14)

FRANCO FORINI (SUI; AGE: 29) 0 PTS

Osella FA1I-Alfa Romeo V8 tc
Osella Squadra Corse
Races: ITA; POR (both car #22)

1987

CHAMPIONSHIP CAR-BY-CAR

PIERCARLO GHINZANI (ITA; AGE: 35) 0 PTS

Ligier JS29-Megatron S4 tc
Ligier LOTO
Races: SMR; BEL; MON; DET; FRA; GER; HUN; AUT; ITA; POR; ESP; MEX; JPN; AUS (all car #26)

NICOLA LARINI (ITA; AGE: 23) 0 PTS

Coloni FC187-Ford V8
Enzo Coloni Racing Car System
Races: ESP (car #32)

PICTURED DURING ITA PRACTICE

STEFANO MODENA (ITA; AGE: 24) 0 PTS

Brabham BT56-BMW S4 tc
Motor Racing Developments
Races: AUS (car #7)

ALESSANDRO NANNINI (ITA; AGE: 28) 0 PTS

Minardi M187-Motori Moderni V6 tc
Minardi Team
Races: BRA; SMR; BEL; MON; DET; FRA; GBR; GER; HUN; AUT; ITA; POR; ESP; MEX; JPN; AUS (all car #24)

GABRIELE TARQUINI (ITA; AGE: 25) 0 PTS

Osella FA1H-Alfa Romeo V8 tc
Osella Squadra Corse
Races: SMR (car #22)

GRAND PRIX WINNERS 1987

	RACE (CIRCUIT)	**WINNER** (CAR)
BRA	BRAZILIAN GRAND PRIX (RIO DE JANEIRO)	ALAIN PROST (McLAREN MP4/3-TAG V6 TC)
SMR	SAN MARINO GRAND PRIX (IMOLA)	NIGEL MANSELL (WILLIAMS FW11B-HONDA V6 TC)
BEL	BELGIAN GRAND PRIX (SPA-FRANCORCHAMPS)	ALAIN PROST (McLAREN MP4/3-TAG V6 TC)
MON	MONACO GRAND PRIX (MONTE CARLO)	AYRTON SENNA (LOTUS 99T-HONDA V6 TC)
DET	DETROIT GRAND PRIX (DETROIT)	AYRTON SENNA (LOTUS 99T-HONDA V6 TC)
FRA	FRENCH GRAND PRIX (PAUL RICARD)	NIGEL MANSELL (WILLIAMS FW11B-HONDA V6 TC)
GBR	BRITISH GRAND PRIX (SILVERSTONE)	NIGEL MANSELL (WILLIAMS FW11B-HONDA V6 TC)
GER	GERMAN GRAND PRIX (HOCKENHEIM)	NELSON PIQUET (WILLIAMS FW11B-HONDA V6 TC)
HUN	HUNGARIAN GRAND PRIX (HUNGARORING)	NELSON PIQUET (WILLIAMS FW11B-HONDA V6 TC)
AUT	AUSTRIAN GRAND PRIX (ÖSTERREICHRING)	NIGEL MANSELL (WILLIAMS FW11B-HONDA V6 TC)
ITA	ITALIAN GRAND PRIX (MONZA)	NELSON PIQUET (WILLIAMS FW11B-HONDA V6 TC)
POR	PORTUGUESE GRAND PRIX (ESTORIL)	ALAIN PROST (McLAREN MP4/3-TAG V6 TC)
ESP	SPANISH GRAND PRIX (JEREZ)	NIGEL MANSELL (WILLIAMS FW11B-HONDA V6 TC)
MEX	MEXICAN GRAND PRIX (MEXICO CITY)	NIGEL MANSELL (WILLIAMS FW11B-HONDA V6 TC)
JPN	JAPANESE GRAND PRIX (SUZUKA)	GERHARD BERGER (FERRARI F187 V6 TC)
AUS	AUSTRALIAN GRAND PRIX (ADELAIDE)	GERHARD BERGER (FERRARI F187 V6 TC)

1988

McLAREN A CLEAN SWEEP

Above
Crowned prince: Senna stalled at the start in Japan, finally managed to get going and reeled in long-time leader Prost when it began to rain. Victory and the world title were his

Far left
Brace McLaren: Prost leads Senna, Berger, Alboreto, Nannini, Boutsen and Piquet at the start in Montreal, a great city where CDs are refreshingly inexpensive. Next up is Cheever, who appears to have been reading the Stefan Johansson race-driving manual

Left
Camel laird: Nelson Piquet left Williams and took engine supplier Honda with him to Lotus, but other than a trio of third places he had a rubbish season

McLaren did what wasn't supposed to be possible in the modern F1 era and dominated so completely that the biggest sensation of the season was its failure to win the Italian Grand Prix. Between them, Ayrton Senna and Alain Prost won every other race in their turbocharged, Honda-powered MP4/4s.

Having switched from Lotus to McLaren, Senna entered Prost's territory to form a superteam. The pair were widely recognised as F1's leading drivers, but Prost already had two world titles and a record number of race wins under his belt. Senna, on the other hand, felt he still had it all to do. As soon as he first tested the car and began to appreciate its superiority over the opposition, he made it his sole focus to defeat his new team-mate, who was widely recognised as the world's number one. With a bewitching blend of aggression, stunning speed and worrying commitment, Senna achieved his aim and took eight wins – one more than Prost.

The pair pushed each other to deliver supreme performances and their partnership was spiced from the start with an edge of animosity that would later develop into all-out warfare. In the middle of this most personal of battles, the team simply left them to get on with it and watched the silverware rack up.

It was a task made easier by rival teams' below-par performances. After being dropped by Honda, Williams was effectively out of the fray and had to fight on with a customer Judd engine. The team scored no wins but had the satisfaction of performing at a higher level than Honda-powered Lotus. Ferrari picked up the only race that McLaren failed to win just a few weeks after founder and boss Enzo Ferrari had died, aged 90, but at no stage were its cars a serious threat.

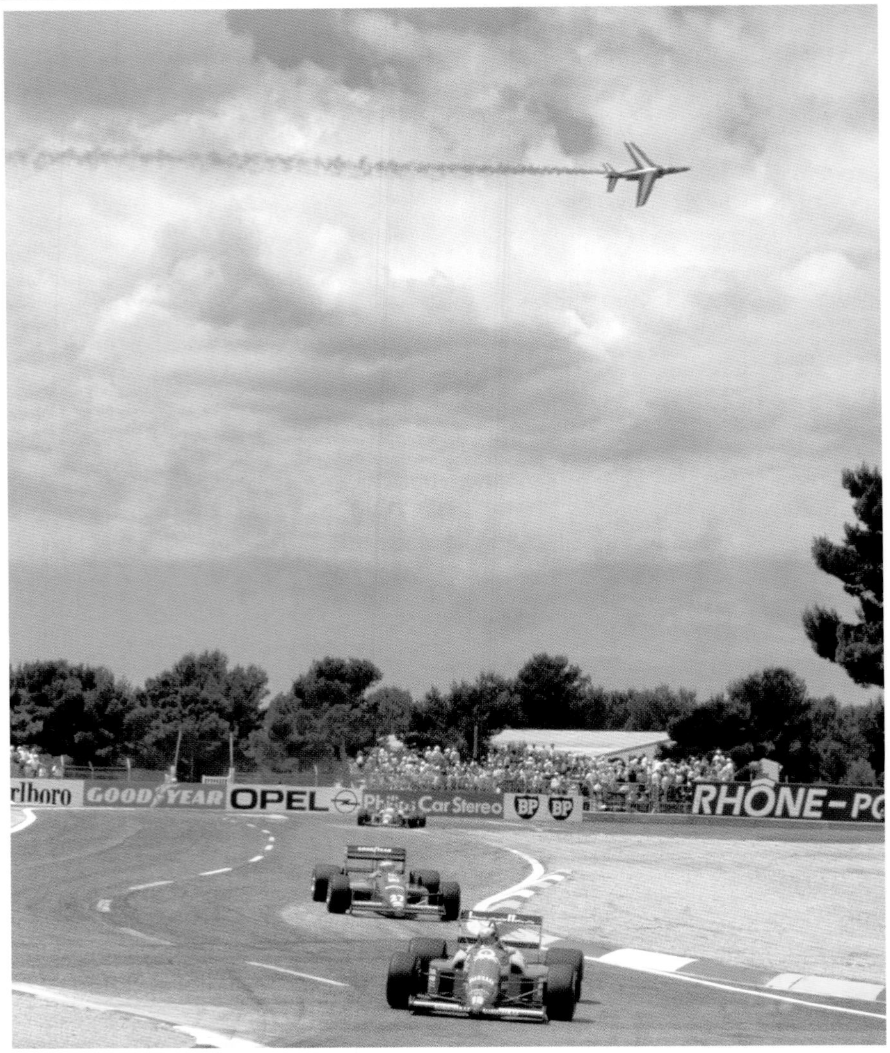

Above
Wings at the speed of sound: Nannini leads Alboreto and Boutsen in France, where the local air force is showing distinct Stefan Johansson tendencies

Left
Red cross code: after abandoning his broken Ferrari during practice at Hockenheim, Berger contemplates completing the lap on foot.

Below
Crowdburst: powered by a customer Judd V8, the Ferrari-bound Mansell had to settle for a couple of second places. His fans still loved him, though

1988

CHAMPIONSHIP CAR-BY-CAR

1ST AYRTON SENNA (BRA; AGE: 28) 90(+4) PTS

McLaren MP4/4-Honda V6 tc
Honda Marlboro McLaren
Races: BRA; SMR; MON; MEX; CAN; DET; FRA; GBR; GER; HUN; BEL; ITA; POR; ESP; JPN; AUS (all car #12)

2ND ALAIN PROST (FRA; AGE: 33) 87(+18) PTS

McLaren MP4/4-Honda V6 tc
Honda Marlboro McLaren
Races: BRA; SMR; MON; MEX; CAN; DET; FRA; GBR; GER; HUN; BEL; ITA; POR; ESP; JPN; AUS (all car #11)

3RD GERHARD BERGER (AUT; AGE: 28) 41 PTS

Ferrari F187/88C V6 tc
Scuderia Ferrari
Races: BRA; SMR; MON; MEX; CAN; DET; FRA; GBR; GER; HUN; BEL; ITA; POR; ESP; JPN; AUS (all car #28)

4TH THIERRY BOUTSEN (BEL; AGE: 31) 27 PTS

Benetton B188-Ford V8
Benetton Formula
Races: BRA; SMR; MON; MEX; CAN; DET; FRA; GBR; GER; HUN; BEL; ITA; POR; ESP; JPN; AUS (all car #20)

5TH MICHELE ALBORETO (ITA; AGE: 31) 24 pts

Ferrari F187/88C V6 tc
Scuderia Ferrari
Races: BRA; SMR; MON; MEX; CAN; DET; FRA; GBR; GER; HUN; BEL; ITA; POR; ESP; JPN; AUS (all car #27)

6TH NELSON PIQUET (BRA; AGE: 35) 22 PTS

Lotus 100T-Honda V6 tc
Camel Team Lotus Honda
Races: BRA; SMR; MON; MEX; CAN; DET; FRA; GBR; GER; HUN; BEL; ITA; POR; ESP; JPN; AUS (all car #1)

7TH= IVAN CAPELLI (ITA; AGE: 25) 17 PTS

March 881-Judd V8
Leyton House March Racing Team
Races: BRA; SMR; MON; MEX; CAN; FRA; GBR; GER; HUN; BEL; ITA; POR; ESP; JPN; AUS (all car #16)

7TH= DEREK WARWICK (GBR; AGE: 33) 17 PTS

Arrows A10B-Megatron S4 tc
USF&G Arrows Megatron
Races: BRA; SMR; MON; MEX; CAN; DET; FRA; GBR; GER; HUN; BEL; ITA; POR; ESP; JPN; AUS (all car #17)

9TH= NIGEL MANSELL (GBR; AGE: 34) 12 PTS

Williams FW12-Judd V8
Canon Williams Team
Races: BRA; SMR; MON; MEX; CAN; DET; FRA; GBR; GER; HUN; POR; ESP; JPN; AUS (all car #5)

9TH= ALESSANDRO NANNINI (ITA; AGE: 29) 12 PTS

Benetton B188-Ford V8
Benetton Formula
Races: BRA; SMR; MON; MEX; CAN; DET; FRA; GBR; GER; HUN; BEL; ITA; POR; ESP; JPN; AUS (all car #19)

11TH RICCARDO PATRESE (ITA; AGE: 34) 8 PTS

Williams FW12-Judd V8
Canon Williams Team
Races: BRA; SMR; MON; MEX; CAN; DET; FRA; GBR; GER; HUN; BEL; ITA; POR; ESP; JPN; AUS (all car #6)

12TH EDDIE CHEEVER (USA; AGE: 30) 6 PTS

Arrows A10B-Megatron S4 tc
USF&G Arrows Megatron
Races: BRA; SMR; MON; MEX; CAN; DET; FRA; GBR; GER; HUN; BEL; ITA; POR; ESP; JPN; AUS (all car #18)

13TH= MAURICIO GUGELMIN (BRA; AGE: 25) 5 PTS

March 881-Judd V8
Leyton House March Racing Team
Races: BRA; SMR; MON; MEX; CAN; DET; FRA; GBR; GER; HUN; BEL; ITA; POR; ESP; JPN; AUS (all car #15)

13TH= JONATHAN PALMER (GBR; AGE: 31) 5 PTS

Tyrrell 017-Ford V8
Tyrrell Racing Organisation
Races: BRA; SMR; MON; CAN; DET; FRA; GBR; GER; HUN; BEL; POR; ESP; JPN; AUS (all car #3)

15TH ANDREA DE CESARIS (ITA; AGE: 29) 3 PTS

Rial ARC1-Ford V8
Rial Racing
Races: BRA; SMR; MON; MEX; CAN; DET; FRA; GBR; GER; HUN; BEL; ITA; POR; ESP; JPN; AUS (all car #22)

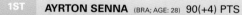

1988

CHAMPIONSHIP CAR-BY-CAR

16TH= PIERLUIGI MARTINI (ITA; AGE: 27) 1 PT

Minardi M188-Ford V8
Lois Minardi Team
Races: DET; FRA; GBR; HUN; ITA; POR; ESP; JPN; AUS (all car #23)

16TH= SATORU NAKAJIMA (JPN; AGE: 35) 1 PT

Lotus 100T-Honda V6 tc
Camel Team Lotus Honda
Races: BRA; SMR; MEX; CAN; FRA; GBR; GER; HUN; BEL; ITA; POR; ESP; JPN; AUS (all car #2)

PHILIPPE ALLIOT (FRA; AGE: 34) 0 PTS

Lola LC88-Ford V8
Larrousse Calmels
Races: BRA; SMR; MON; MEX; CAN; DET; FRA; GBR; GER; HUN; BEL; ITA; POR; ESP; JPN; AUS (all car #30)

RENÉ ARNOUX (FRA; AGE: 40) 0 PTS

Ligier JS31-Judd V8
Ligier LOTO
Races: BRA; MON; MEX; CAN; DET; GBR; GER; HUN; BEL; ITA; POR; ESP; JPN; AUS (all car #25)

JULIAN BAILEY (GBR; AGE: 26) 0 PTS

Tyrrell 017-Ford V8
Tyrrell Racing Organisation
Races: SMR; CAN; DET; GBR; ITA; JPN (all car #4)

MARTIN BRUNDLE (GBR; AGE: 29) 0 PTS

Williams FW12-Judd V8
Canon Williams Team
Races: BEL (car #5)

ALEX CAFFI (ITA; AGE: 24) 0 PTS

Dallara F188-Ford V8
Scuderia Italia
Races: SMR; MON; MEX; DET; FRA; GBR; GER; HUN; BEL; ITA; POR; ESP; JPN; AUS (all car #36)

ADRIAN CAMPOS (ESP; AGE: 27) 0 PTS

Minardi M188-Ford V8
Lois Minardi Team
Races: BRA; SMR (both car #23)

YANNICK DALMAS (FRA; AGE: 27) 0 PTS

Lola LC88-Ford V8
Larrousse Calmels
Races: BRA; SMR; MON; MEX; DET; FRA; GBR; GER; HUN; BEL; ITA; POR; ESP (all car #29)

PIERCARLO GHINZANI (ITA; AGE: 36) 0 PTS

Zakspeed 881 S4 tc
West Zakspeed Racing
Races: SMR; MON; MEX; CAN; GER; BEL; ITA; AUS (all car #9)

STEFAN JOHANSSON (SWE; AGE: 31) 0 PTS

Ligier JS31-Judd V8
Ligier LOTO
Races: BRA; MON; MEX; CAN; DET; HUN; BEL; POR; ESP; AUS (all car #26)

NICOLA LARINI (ITA; AGE: 24) 0 PTS

Osella FA1L-Alfa Romeo V8 tc
Osella Squadra Corse
Races: MON; DET; FRA; GBR; GER; BEL; ITA; POR; ESP; JPN (all car #21)

OSCAR LARRAURI (ARG; AGE: 33) 0 PTS

EuroBrun ER188-Ford V8
EuroBrun Racing
Races: MON; MEX; CAN; DET; FRA; GER; AUS (all car #32)

STEFANO MODENA (ITA; AGE: 25) 0 PTS

EuroBrun ER188-Ford V8
EuroBrun Racing
Races: BRA; SMR; CAN; DET; FRA; GBR; GER; HUN; ESP; AUS (all car #33)

LUIS PEREZ SALA (ESP; AGE: 29) 0 PTS

Minardi M188-Ford V8
Lois Minardi Team
Races: BRA; SMR; MON; MEX; CAN; DET; FRA; GBR; HUN; ITA; POR; ESP; JPN; AUS (all car #24)

1988

CHAMPIONSHIP CAR-BY-CAR

JEAN-LOUIS SCHLESSER (FRA; AGE: 40) 0 PTS

Williams FW12-Judd V8
Canon Williams Team
Races: ITA (car #5)

BERND SCHNEIDER (GER; AGE: 24) 0 PTS

Zakspeed 881 S4 tc
West Zakspeed Racing
Races: MEX; FRA; GER; BEL; ITA; JPN (all car #10)

PICTURED DURING GBR PRACTICE

PHILIPPE STREIFF (FRA; AGE: 33) 0 PTS

AGS JH23-Ford V8
Automobiles Gonfaronaise Sportive
Races: BRA; SMR; MEX; CAN; DET; FRA; GBR; GER; HUN; BEL; ITA; POR; ESP; JPN; AUS (all car #14)

AGURI SUZUKI (JPN; AGE: 28) 0 PTS

Lola LC88-Ford V8
Larrousse Calmels
Races: JPN (car #29)

GABRIELE TARQUINI (ITA; AGE: 26) 0 PTS

Coloni FC188-Ford V8
Coloni Racing
Races: BRA; SMR; MON; MEX; CAN; HUN; BEL; POR (all car #31)

PICTURED DURING ESP PRACTICE

GRAND PRIX WINNERS 1988

	RACE (CIRCUIT)	WINNER (CAR)
BRA	BRAZILIAN GRAND PRIX (RIO DE JANEIRO)	ALAIN PROST (McLAREN MP4/4-HONDA V6 TC)
SMR	SAN MARINO GRAND PRIX (IMOLA)	AYRTON SENNA (McLAREN MP4/4-HONDA V6 TC)
MON	MONACO GRAND PRIX (MONTE CARLO)	ALAIN PROST (McLAREN MP4/4-HONDA V6 TC)
MEX	MEXICAN GRAND PRIX (MEXICO CITY)	ALAIN PROST (McLAREN MP4/4-HONDA V6 TC)
CAN	CANADIAN GRAND PRIX (MONTRÉAL)	AYRTON SENNA (McLAREN MP4/4-HONDA V6 TC)
DET	DETROIT GRAND PRIX (DETROIT)	AYRTON SENNA (McLAREN MP4/4-HONDA V6 TC)
FRA	FRENCH GRAND PRIX (PAUL RICARD)	ALAIN PROST (McLAREN MP4/4-HONDA V6 TC)
GBR	BRITISH GRAND PRIX (SILVERSTONE)	AYRTON SENNA (McLAREN MP4/4-HONDA V6 TC)
GER	GERMAN GRAND PRIX (HOCKENHEIM)	AYRTON SENNA (McLAREN MP4/4-HONDA V6 TC)
HUN	HUNGARIAN GRAND PRIX (HUNGARORING)	AYRTON SENNA (McLAREN MP4/4-HONDA V6 TC)
BEL	BELGIAN GRAND PRIX (SPA-FRANCORCHAMPS)	AYRTON SENNA (McLAREN MP4/4-HONDA V6 TC)
ITA	ITALIAN GRAND PRIX (MONZA)	GERHARD BERGER (FERRARI F187/88C V6 TC)
POR	PORTUGUESE GRAND PRIX (ESTORIL)	ALAIN PROST (McLAREN MP4/4-HONDA V6 TC)
ESP	SPANISH GRAND PRIX (JEREZ)	ALAIN PROST (McLAREN MP4/4-HONDA V6 TC)
JPN	JAPANESE GRAND PRIX (SUZUKA)	AYRTON SENNA (McLAREN MP4/4-HONDA V6 TC)
AUS	AUSTRALIAN GRAND PRIX (ADELAIDE)	ALAIN PROST (McLAREN MP4/4-HONDA V6 TC)

1989

PROST AND SENNA – THE BEST OF ENEMIES

Far left
Escape road to victory: Senna (nearer camera) and Prost slither to an ignominious halt after trying to take Suzuka's chicane as one. Senna resumed to win, but was later excluded for rejoining the circuit in an inappropriate manner. The Frenchman had his third title

Above
Ricard lionheart: Prost celebrates the fourth of his six French GP wins. No, we don't know what Mansell is looking at, either

Left
Rio uncovered: the Ferrari 640 won on its debut in Brazil, despite barely being ready beforehand

McLaren team-mates Alain Prost and Ayrton Senna waged a fierce, uncompromising title battle that wasn't settled until the closing laps of the penultimate race, in Japan – and here the intensity of their rivalry was given its full perspective.

Prost had driven magnificently, setting the pace from the start. His attacking strategy reversed the season's usual pattern. It had become the norm for Senna to run at the front, leaving Prost to pick up wins through guile and default. But not today: the Frenchman was in no mood for compromise and had even issued a public warning that should Senna try to pass in his usual manner – by giving the defending driver the option to accede or crash – then he, Prost, was not going to comply.

With one more race remaining, in Australia, the points situation was such that Senna had to beat Prost to remain in the title hunt. Tension increased as Senna closed down the leader with just a few laps to go. With nothing to lose he took a dive down Prost's inside as they approached the tight chicane that leads on to the pit straight. Prost, as promised, refused to yield. The McLaren-Hondas tangled and the drivers gestured furiously to each other as they skated to a halt. Senna carried on, Prost didn't. The Brazilian went on to win but was later disqualified for rejoining the track in a dangerous manner. The title was Prost's.

Their rivalry stole the headlines at the dawn of the sport's post-turbo era: for the first time, the whole field ran with normally-aspirated 3.5-litre engines. It made little difference to McLaren's form. Benefiting from the most powerful engine – Honda's new V10 – and the best two drivers, the team dominated much as it had the previous season. Ferrari's Nigel Mansell and Gerhard Berger occasionally got close in the radical, John Barnard-designed 640, with semi-automatic transmission, but its reliability wasn't good enough. Williams entered a new partnership with Renault and Thierry Boutsen won two wet races, in Canada and Australia.

Above
Water margins: reunited with a major engine partner in the shape of Renault, Williams regained some of its old form. Thierry Boutsen was particularly strong whenever it tipped down: he won in Canada (pictured) and Australia

Below
Beware the slides of March: Mauricio Gugelmin was launched spectacularly on the opening lap of the French GP. The incident caused the race to be stopped and the Brazilian calmly restarted at the wheel of his team's badly-misfiring spare

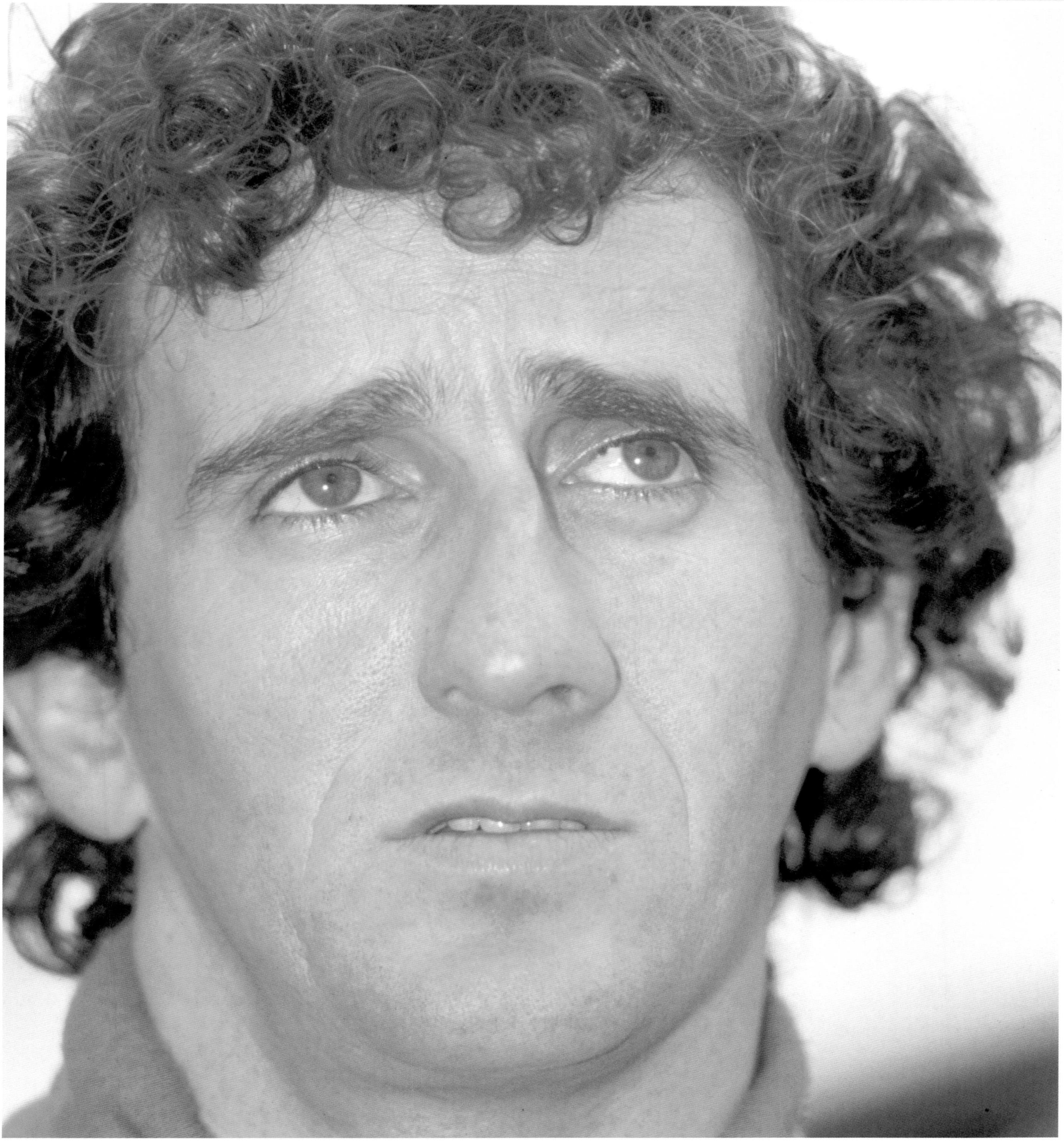

ALAIN PROST – WORLD CHAMPION 1985, 1986, 1989 & 1993

1989

CHAMPIONSHIP CAR-BY-CAR

1ST ALAIN PROST (FRA; AGE: 34) 76(+5) PTS

McLaren MP4/5-Honda V10
Honda Marlboro McLaren
Races: BRA; SMR; MON; MEX; USA; CAN; FRA; GBR; GER; HUN; BEL; ITA; POR; ESP; JPN; AUS (all car #2)

2ND AYRTON SENNA (BRA; AGE: 29) 60 PTS

McLaren MP4/5-Honda V10
Honda Marlboro McLaren
Races: BRA; SMR; MON; MEX; USA; CAN; FRA; GBR; GER; HUN; BEL; ITA; POR; ESP; JPN; AUS (all car #1)

3RD RICCARDO PATRESE (ITA; AGE: 35) 40 PTS

Williams FW12C-Renault V10
Canon Williams Team
Races: BRA; SMR; MON; MEX; USA; CAN; FRA; GBR; GER; HUN; BEL; ITA; ESP (all car #6)

RICCARDO PATRESE (CONTD)

Williams FW13-Renault V10
Canon Williams Team
Races: POR; JPN; AUS (all car #6)

4TH NIGEL MANSELL (GBR; AGE: 35) 38 PTS

Ferrari 640 V12
Scuderia Ferrari
Races: BRA; SMR; MON; MEX; USA; CAN; FRA; GBR; GER; HUN; BEL; ITA; POR; JPN; AUS (all car #27)

5TH THIERRY BOUTSEN (BEL; AGE: 32) 37 PTS

Williams FW12C-Renault V10
Canon Williams Team
Races: BRA; SMR; MON; MEX; USA; CAN; FRA; GBR; GER; HUN; BEL; ITA (all car #5)

THIERRY BOUTSEN (CONTD)

Williams FW13-Renault V10
Canon Williams Team
Races: POR; ESP; JPN; AUS (all car #5)

6TH ALESSANDRO NANNINI (ITA; AGE: 30) 32 PTS

Benetton B188-Ford V8
Benetton Formula
Races: BRA; SMR; MON; MEX; USA; CAN (all car #19)

ALESSANDRO NANNINI (CONTD)

Benetton B189-Ford V8
Benetton Formula
Races: FRA; GBR; GER; HUN; BEL; ITA; POR; ESP; JPN; AUS (all car #19)

7TH GERHARD BERGER (AUT; AGE: 29) PTS

Ferrari 640 V12
Scuderia Ferrari
Races: BRA; SMR; MEX; USA; CAN; FRA; GBR; GER; HUN; BEL; ITA; POR; ESP; JPN; AUS (all car #28)

8TH NELSON PIQUET (BRA; AGE: 36) 12 PTS

Lotus 101-Judd V8
Camel Team Lotus
Races: BRA; SMR; MON; MEX; USA; CAN; FRA; GBR; GER; HUN; ITA; POR; ESP; JPN; AUS (all car #11)

9TH JEAN ALESI (FRA; AGE: 25) 8 PTS

Tyrrell 018-Ford V8
Tyrrell Racing Organisation
Races: FRA; GBR; GER; HUN; ITA; ESP; JPN; AUS (all car #4)

10TH DEREK WARWICK (GBR; AGE: 34) 7 PTS

Arrows A11-Ford V8
Arrows Grand Prix International
Races: BRA; SMR; MON; MEX; USA; CAN; GBR; GER; HUN; BEL; ITA; POR; ESP; JPN; AUS (all car #9)

11TH MICHELE ALBORETO (ITA; AGE: 32) 6 PTS

Tyrrell 017B-Ford V8
Tyrrell Racing Organisation
Races: BRA (car #4)

MICHELE ALBORETO (CONTD)

Tyrrell 018-Ford V8
Tyrrell Racing Organisation
Races: MON; MEX; USA; CAN (all car #4)

1989

CHAMPIONSHIP CAR-BY-CAR

MICHELE ALBORETO (CONTD)

Lola LC89-Lamborghini V12
Équipe Larrousse
Races: GER; HUN; BEL; ITA; POR (all car #29)

11TH EDDIE CHEEVER (USA; AGE: 31) 6 PTS

Arrows A11-Ford V8
Arrows Grand Prix International
Races: BRA; SMR; MON; MEX; USA; CAN; FRA; GER; HUN; BEL; ESP; JPN; AUS (all car #10)

11TH STEFAN JOHANSSON (SWE; AGE: 32) 6 PTS

Onyx ORE1-Ford V8
Moneytron Onyx Formula One
Races: MEX; USA; CAN; FRA; GER; HUN; BEL; POR (all car #36)

14TH JOHNNY HERBERT (GBR; AGE: 24) 5 PTS

Benetton B188-Ford V8
Benetton Formula
Races: BRA; SMR; MON; MEX; USA (all car #20)

JOHNNY HERBERT (CONTD)

Tyrrell 018-Ford V8
Tyrrell Racing Organisation
Races: BEL (car #4)

PICTURED DURING POR PRACTICE

14TH PIERLUIGI MARTINI (ITA; AGE: 28) 5 PTS

Minardi M188B-Ford V8
Lois Minardi Team
Races: BRA; SMR; MON (all car #23)

PIERLUIGI MARTINI (CONTD)

Minardi M189-Ford V8
Lois Minardi Team
Races: MEX; USA; CAN; FRA; GBR; GER; HUN; BEL; ITA; POR; ESP; AUS (all car #23)

16TH= MARTIN BRUNDLE (GBR; AGE: 30) 4 PTS

Brabham BT58-Judd V8
Motor Racing Developments
Races: BRA; SMR; MON; MEX; USA; GBR; GER; HUN; BEL; ITA; POR; ESP; JPN; AUS (all car #7)

16TH= ALEX CAFFI (ITA; AGE: 25) 4 PTS

Dallara F189-Ford V8
Scuderia Italia
Races: SMR; MON; MEX; USA; CAN; FRA; GER; HUN; BEL; ITA; POR; ESP; JPN; AUS (all car #21)

16TH= ANDREA DE CESARIS (ITA; AGE: 30) 4 PTS

Dallara F189-Ford V8
Scuderia Italia
Races: BRA; SMR; MON; MEX; USA; CAN; GBR; GER; HUN; BEL; ITA; POR; ESP; JPN; AUS (all car #22)

16TH= MAURICIO GUGELMIN (BRA; AGE: 26) 4 PTS

March 881-Judd V8
Leyton House March Racing Team
Races: BRA; SMR (both car #15)

MAURICIO GUGELMIN (CONTD)

March CG891-Judd V8
Leyton House March Racing Team
Races: MON; USA; CAN; FRA; GBR; GER; HUN; BEL; ITA; POR; ESP; JPN; AUS (all car #15)

16TH= STEFANO MODENA (ITA; AGE: 26) 4 PTS

Brabham BT58-Judd V8
Motor Racing Developments
Races: BRA; SMR; MON; MEX; USA; CAN; FRA; GBR; GER; HUN; BEL; POR; ESP; JPN; AUS (all car #8)

21ST= CHRISTIAN DANNER (GER; AGE: 31) 3 PTS

Rial ARC2-Ford V8
Rial Racing
Races: BRA; MEX; USA; CAN (all car #38)

PICTURED DURING SMR PRACTICE

21ST= SATORU NAKAJIMA (JPN; AGE: 36) 3 PTS

Lotus 101-Judd V8
Camel Team Lotus
Races: BRA; SMR; MEX; USA; FRA; GBR; GER; HUN; ITA; POR; ESP; JPN; AUS (all car #12)

1989

CHAMPIONSHIP CAR-BY-CAR

23RD= RENÉ ARNOUX (FRA; AGE: 41) 2 PTS

Ligier JS33-Ford V8
Ligier LOTO
Races: MON; MEX; CAN; FRA; GER; BEL; ITA; POR; AUS (all car #25)

23RD= JONATHAN PALMER (GBR; AGE: 32) 2 PTS

Tyrrell 017B-Ford V8
Tyrrell Racing Organisation
Races: BRA (car #3)

JONATHAN PALMER (CONTD)

Tyrrell 018-Ford V8
Tyrrell Racing Organisation
Races: SMR; MON; MEX; USA; CAN; FRA; GBR; GER; HUN; BEL; ITA; POR; ESP; JPN (all car #3)

23RD= EMANUELE PIRRO (ITA; AGE: 27) 2 PTS

Benetton B188-Ford V8
Benetton Formula
Races: FRA; GBR (both car #20)

EMANUELE PIRRO (CONTD)

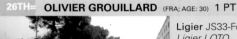

Benetton B189-Ford V8
Benetton Formula
Races: GER; HUN; BEL; ITA; POR; ESP; JPN; AUS (all car #20)

26TH= PHILIPPE ALLIOT (FRA; AGE: 35) 1 PT

Lola LC88C-Lamborghini V12
Larrousse Calmels
Races: BRA (car #30)

PHILIPPE ALLIOT (CONTD)

Lola LC89-Lamborghini V12
Équipe Larrousse
Races: SMR; MON; MEX; USA; CAN; FRA; GBR; GER; BEL; ITA; POR; ESP; JPN; AUS (all car #30)

26TH= OLIVIER GROUILLARD (FRA; AGE: 30) 1 PT

Ligier JS33-Ford V8
Ligier LOTO
Races: BRA; SMR; MON; MEX; FRA; GBR; GER; BEL; ITA; ESP; JPN; AUS (all car #26)

26TH= LUIS PEREZ SALA (ESP; AGE: 30) 1 PT

Minardi M188B-Ford V8
Lois Minardi Team
Races: BRA; SMR; MON (all car #24)

LUIS PEREZ SALA (CONTD)

Minardi M189-Ford V8
Lois Minardi Team
Races: USA; CAN; GBR; HUN; BEL; ITA; POR; ESP; JPN (all car #24)

26TH= GABRIELE TARQUINI (ITA; AGE: 27) 1 PT

AGS JH23B-Ford V8
Automobiles Gonfaronaise Sportive
Races: SMR; MON; MEX; USA; CAN; FRA (all car #40)

PAOLO BARILLA (ITA; AGE: 28) 0 PTS

Minardi M189-Ford V8
Lois Minardi Team
Races: JPN (car #23)

ÉRIC BERNARD (FRA; AGE: 24) 0 PTS

Lola LC89-Lamborghini V12
Équipe Larrousse
Races: FRA; GBR car #29)

IVAN CAPELLI (ITA; AGE: 26) 0 PTS

March 881-Judd V8
Leyton House March Racing Team
Races: BRA; SMR (both car #16)

IVAN CAPELLI (CONTD)

March CG891-Judd V8
Leyton House March Racing Team
Races: MON; MEX; USA; CAN; FRA; GBR; GER; HUN; BEL; ITA; POR; ESP; JPN; AUS (all car #16)

1989

CHAMPIONSHIP CAR-BY-CAR

MARTIN DONNELLY (GBR; AGE: 25) 0 PTS

Arrows A11-Ford V8
Arrows Grand Prix International
Races: FRA (car #9)

BERTRAND GACHOT (BEL/FRA; AGE: 26) 0 PTS

Onyx ORE1-Ford V8
Moneytron Onyx Formula One
Races: FRA; GBR; HUN; BEL; ITA (all car #37)

PIERCARLO GHINZANI (ITA; AGE: 37) 0 PTS

Osella FA1M-Ford V8
Osella Squadra Corse
Races: HUN; ESP; AUS (all car #18)

PICTURED DURING SMR PRACTICE

NICOLA LARINI (ITA; AGE: 25) 0 PTS

Osella FA1M-Ford V8
Osella Squadra Corse
Races: BRA; SMR; CAN; GBR; ITA; ESP; JPN; AUS (all car #17)

JJ LEHTO (FIN; AGE: 23) 0 PTS

Onyx ORE1-Ford V8
Moneytron Onyx Formula One
Races: ESP; AUS (both car #37)

ROBERTO MORENO (BRA; AGE: 30) 0 PTS

Coloni FC188C-Ford V8
Coloni Racing
Races: MON (car #31)

ROBERTO MORENO (CONTD)

Coloni C3-Ford V8
Coloni Racing
Races: CAN; GBR; POR (all car #31)

PIERRE-HENRI RAPHANEL (FRA; AGE: 27) 0 PTS

Coloni FC188C-Ford V8
Coloni Racing
Races: MON (car #32)

BERND SCHNEIDER (GER; AGE: 25) 0 PTS

Zakspeed 891-Yamaha V8
West Zakspeed Racing
Races: BRA; JPN (both car #34)

GRAND PRIX WINNERS 1989

	RACE (CIRCUIT)	WINNER (CAR)
BRA	BRAZILIAN GRAND PRIX (RIO DE JANEIRO)	NIGEL MANSELL (FERRARI 640 V12)
SMR	SAN MARINO GRAND PRIX (IMOLA)	AYRTON SENNA (McLAREN MP4/5-HONDA V10)
MON	MONACO GRAND PRIX (MONTE CARLO)	AYRTON SENNA (McLAREN MP4/5-HONDA V10)
MEX	MEXICAN GRAND PRIX (MEXICO CITY)	AYRTON SENNA (McLAREN MP4/5-HONDA V10)
USA	UNITED STATES GRAND PRIX (PHOENIX)	ALAIN PROST (McLAREN MP4/5-HONDA V10)
CAN	CANADIAN GRAND PRIX (MONTRÉAL)	THIERRY BOUTSEN (WILLIAMS FW12C-RENAULT V10)
FRA	FRENCH GRAND PRIX (PAUL RICARD)	ALAIN PROST (McLAREN MP4/5-HONDA V10)
GBR	BRITISH GRAND PRIX (SILVERSTONE)	ALAIN PROST (McLAREN MP4/5-HONDA V10)
GER	GERMAN GRAND PRIX (HOCKENHEIM)	AYRTON SENNA (McLAREN MP4/5-HONDA V10)
HUN	HUNGARIAN GRAND PRIX (HUNGARORING)	NIGEL MANSELL (FERRARI 640 V12)
BEL	BELGIAN GRAND PRIX (SPA-FRANCORCHAMPS)	AYRTON SENNA (McLAREN MP4/5-HONDA V10)
ITA	ITALIAN GRAND PRIX (MONZA)	ALAIN PROST (McLAREN MP4/5-HONDA V10)
POR	PORTUGUESE GRAND PRIX (ESTORIL)	GERHARD BERGER (FERRARI 640 V12)
ESP	SPANISH GRAND PRIX (JEREZ)	AYRTON SENNA (McLAREN MP4/5-HONDA V10)
JPN	JAPANESE GRAND PRIX (SUZUKA)	ALESSANDRO NANNINI (BENETTON B189-FORD V8)
AUS	AUSTRALIAN GRAND PRIX (ADELAIDE)	THIERRY BOUTSEN (WILLIAMS FW13-RENAULT V10)

The 500th
World Championship
Grand Prix

1990s

1990

SENNA ON TOP – BUT BITTERNESS ESCALATES

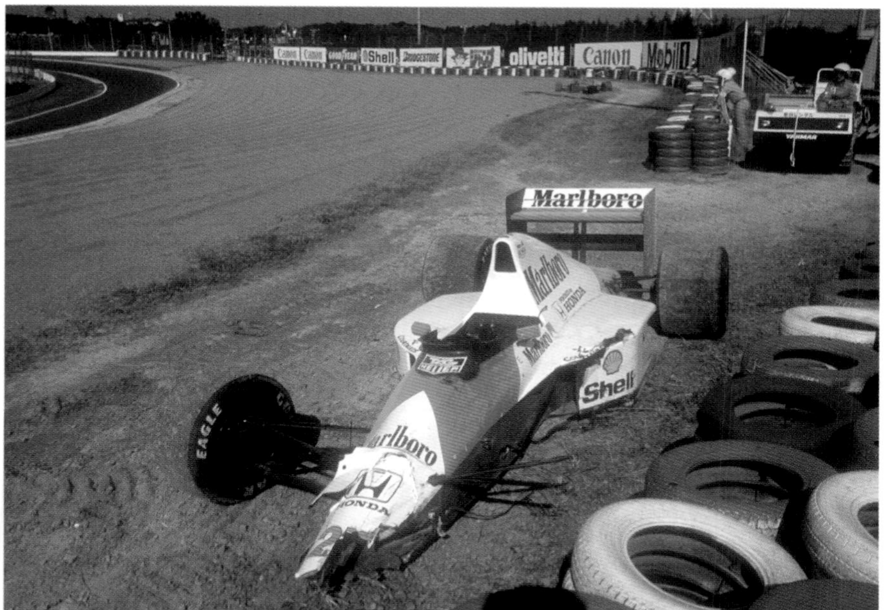

Above
Fast feud chain: Senna holds off Prost during the early stages of the Spanish GP, but the Frenchman eventually went on to win

Left
Lapse of the gods: if you can't beat them, ram them off the road at the first corner...

Far left
Life in the old dog yet: previously thought to be past it, Nelson Piquet bagged two wins at the end of a strong season with Benetton

Right
Alesi Sunday afternoon: a nudge from Berger was enough to pitch the young Tyrrell star into the gravel within yards of the start at Jerez

EUROPEAN
PIAA
PIRELLI
4

The bitter feud between Ayrton Senna and Alain Prost intensified as they went their separate ways. Senna stayed put at McLaren, but Prost quit his long-time home in favour of a switch to Ferrari.

The Italian team's chief designer John Barnard had moved on before Prost arrived, but the 641 chassis he left behind handled superbly. Its V12 engine lacked the horsepower and low-range punch of the Honda V10 in Senna's McLaren, but it was a strong enough package to ensure that the world's best two drivers were in the best two cars. A vintage season duly unfolded.

Senna won three of the opening five races, but he collided with a backmarker in Brazil and Prost capitalised. The Ferrari really began to come good in mid-season, though, and the Frenchman racked up three consecutive victories. In Spain, the 14th of 16 races, Prost took his finest win of the season, having beaten Senna fair and square even before the Brazilian retired with a punctured radiator. This brought him to within nine points of Senna and set the scene for a remarkable sequence of events in Japan.

Senna took pole position but objected strongly to being forced to start from the dirtier side of the grid. His fear that Prost would be able to outsprint him was duly realised, but Senna had a ruthless back-up plan. Prost braked at the normal place for the first corner but his nemesis didn't even lift. In a cynical move, the Brazilian drove hard into the back of his rival, taking both of them into the gravel trap. Prost could no longer overhaul his rival's points score and Senna was champion.

Their battle dwarfed the season's other stories. Prost's team-mate Nigel Mansell often showed searing speed but suffered poor reliability. After retiring his Ferrari from the lead of the British Grand Prix, the Englishman announced that he would quit racing at the end of the year. Subsequently, however, he changed his mind.

PROST BRAKED AT THE NORMAL PLACE FOR THE FIRST CORNER BUT HIS NEMESIS DIDN'T EVEN LIFT. IN A CYNICAL MOVE THE BRAZILIAN DROVE HARD INTO THE BACK OF HIS RIVAL

Far left, top
Galaxy of stars: former F1 champs gather in Australia. Top row, from left – James Hunt, Jackie Stewart, Denny Hulme; front – Nelson Piquet, Juan Manuel Fangio, Ayrton Senna, Jack Brabham

Far left, bottom
Just Williams: Thierry Boutsen keeps Gerhard Berger's McLaren at bay in Hungary, where he scored what was to be his third and final F1 success

Above
Give me a brake: Riccardo Patrese locks up on his way to sixth place in Adelaide

Left
Matter of principality: Mansell's Ferrari is dwarfed by yachts, Monaco apartment blocks and a swimming pool as he tackles the world's most recognisable grand prix circuit

1990

CHAMPIONSHIP CAR-BY-CAR

1ST AYRTON SENNA (BRA; AGE: 30) 78 PTS

McLaren MP4/5B-Honda V10
Honda Marlboro McLaren
Races: USA; BRA; SMR; MON; CAN; MEX; FRA; GBR; GER; HUN; BEL; ITA; POR; ESP; JPN; AUS (all car #27)

2ND ALAIN PROST (FRA; AGE: 35) 71(+2) PTS

Ferrari 641 V12
Scuderia Ferrari
Races: USA; BRA (both car #1)

ALAIN PROST (CONTD)

Ferrari 641/2 V12
Scuderia Ferrari
Races: SMR; MON; CAN; MEX; FRA; GBR; GER; HUN; BEL; ITA; POR; ESP; JPN; AUS (all car #1)

3RD= GERHARD BERGER (AUT; AGE: 30) 43 PTS

McLaren MP4/5B-Honda V10
Honda Marlboro McLaren
Races: USA; BRA; SMR; MON; CAN; MEX; FRA; GBR; GER; HUN; BEL; ITA; POR; ESP; JPN; AUS (all car #28)

3RD= NELSON PIQUET (BRA; AGE: 37) 43(+1) PTS

Benetton B189B-Ford V8
Benetton Formula
Races: USA; BRA (both car #20)

NELSON PIQUET (CONTD)

Benetton B190-Ford V8
Benetton Formula
Races: SMR; MON; CAN; MEX; FRA; GBR; GER; HUN; BEL; ITA; POR; ESP; JPN; AUS (all car #20)

5TH NIGEL MANSELL (GBR; AGE: 36) 37 PTS

Ferrari 641 V12
Scuderia Ferrari
Races: USA; BRA (both car #2)

NIGEL MANSELL (CONTD)

Ferrari 641/2 V12
Scuderia Ferrari
Races: SMR; MON; CAN; MEX; FRA; GBR; GER; HUN; BEL; ITA; POR; ESP; JPN; AUS (all car #2)

6TH THIERRY BOUTSEN (BEL; AGE: 33) 34 PTS

Williams FW13B-Renault V10
Canon Williams Team
Races: USA; BRA; SMR; MON; CAN; MEX; FRA; GBR; GER; HUN; BEL; ITA; POR; ESP; JPN; AUS (all car #5)

7TH RICCARDO PATRESE (ITA; AGE: 36) 23 PTS

Williams FW13B-Renault V10
Canon Williams Team
Races: USA; BRA; SMR; MON; CAN; MEX; FRA; GBR; GER; HUN; BEL; ITA; POR; ESP; JPN; AUS (all car #6)

8TH ALESSANDRO NANNINI (ITA; AGE: 31) 21 PTS

Benetton B189B-Ford V8
Benetton Formula
Races: USA; BRA (both car #19)

ALESSANDRO NANNINI (CONTD)

Benetton B190-Ford V8
Benetton Formula
Races: SMR; MON; CAN; MEX; FRA; GBR; GER; HUN; BEL; ITA; POR; ESP (all car #19)

9TH JEAN ALESI (FRA; AGE: 26) 13 PTS

Tyrrell 018-Ford V8
Tyrrell Racing Organisation
Races: USA; BRA (both car #4)

JEAN ALESI (CONTD)

Tyrrell 019-Ford V8
Tyrrell Racing Organisation
Races: SMR; MON; CAN; MEX; FRA; GBR; GER; HUN; BEL; ITA; POR; ESP; AUS (all car #4)

10TH= IVAN CAPELLI (ITA; AGE: 27) 6 PTS

Leyton House CG901-Judd V8
Leyton House Racing
Races: USA; SMR; MON; CAN; FRA; GBR; GER; HUN; BEL; ITA; POR; ESP; JPN; AUS (all car #16)

1990

CHAMPIONSHIP CAR-BY-CAR

10TH= ROBERTO MORENO (BRA; AGE: 31) 6 PTS

EuroBrun ER189-Judd V8
EuroBrun Racing
Races: USA; SMR
(both car #33)

ROBERTO MORENO (CONTD)

Benetton B190-Ford V8
Benetton Formula
Races: JPN; AUS
(both car #19)

10TH= AGURI SUZUKI (JPN; AGE: 29) 6 PTS

Lola LC89-Lamborghini V12
ESPO Larrousse F1
Races: USA; BRA
(both car #30)

AGURI SUZUKI (CONTD)

Lola 90-Lamborghini V12
ESPO Larrousse F1
Races: SMR; MON; CAN; MEX; FRA; GBR; GER; HUN; BEL; ITA; POR; ESP; JPN; AUS
(all car #30)

12TH ÉRIC BERNARD (FRA; AGE: 25) 5 PTS

Lola LC89-Lamborghini V12
ESPO Larrousse F1
Races: USA; BRA
(both car #29)

ÉRIC BERNARD (CONTD)

Lola 90-Lamborghini V12
ESPO Larrousse F1
Races: SMR; MON; CAN; MEX; FRA; GBR; GER; HUN; BEL; ITA; POR; ESP; JPN; AUS
(all car #29)

14TH= SATORU NAKAJIMA (JPN; AGE: 37) 3 PTS

Tyrrell 018-Ford V8
Tyrrell Racing Organisation
Races: USA; BRA
(both car #3)

SATORU NAKAJIMA (CONTD)

Tyrrell 019-Ford V8
Tyrrell Racing Organisation
Races: SMR; MON; CAN; MEX; FRA; GBR; GER; HUN; BEL; ITA; ESP; JPN; AUS (all car #3)

14TH= DEREK WARWICK (GBR; AGE: 35) 3 PTS

Lotus 102-Lamborghini V12
Camel Team Lotus
Races: USA; BRA; SMR; MON; CAN; MEX; FRA; GBR; GER; HUN; BEL; ITA; POR; ESP; JPN; AUS (all car #11)

16TH= ALEX CAFFI (ITA; AGE: 26) 2 PTS

Arrows A11B-Ford V8
Footwork Arrows Racing
Races: BRA; MON; CAN; FRA; GBR; GER; HUN; BEL; ITA; POR; JPN (all car #10)

16TH= STEFANO MODENA (ITA; AGE: 27) 2 PTS

Brabham BT58-Judd V8
Motor Racing Developments
Races: USA; BRA
(both car #8)

STEFANO MODENA (CONTD)

Brabham BT59-Judd V8
Motor Racing Developments
Races: SMR; MON; CAN; MEX; FRA; GBR; GER; HUN; BEL; ITA; POR; ESP; JPN; AUS
(all car #8)

18TH MAURICIO GUGELMIN (BRA; AGE: 27) 1PT

Leyton House CG901-Judd V8
Leyton House Racing
Races: USA; SMR; FRA; GER; HUN; BEL; ITA; POR; ESP; JPN; AUS (all car #15)

MICHELE ALBORETO (ITA; AGE: 33) 0 PTS

Arrows A11B-Ford V8
Footwork Arrows Racing
Races: USA; BRA; CAN; MEX; FRA; GBR; GER; HUN; BEL; ITA; POR; ESP; JPN (all car #9)

PHILIPPE ALLIOT (FRA; AGE: 36) 0 PTS

Ligier JS33B-Ford V8
Équipe Ligier Gitanes
Races: BRA; SMR; MON; CAN; MEX; FRA; GBR; GER; HUN; ITA; POR; ESP; JPN; AUS (all car #26)

1990

CHAMPIONSHIP CAR-BY-CAR

PAOLO BARILLA (ITA; AGE: 29) 0 PTS

Minardi M189-Ford V8
SCM Minardi Team
Races: USA; BRA (both car #24)

PAOLO BARILLA (CONTD)

Minardi M190-Ford V8
SCM Minardi Team
Races: SMR; MON; MEX; GBR; HUN; BEL (all car #24)

DAVID BRABHAM (AUS; AGE: 24) 0 PTS

Brabham BT59-Judd V8
Motor Racing Developments
Races: MON; MEX; FRA; GER; BEL; POR; JPN; AUS (all car #7)

ANDREA DE CESARIS (ITA; AGE: 31) 0 PTS

Dallara F190-Ford V8
Scuderia Italia
Races: USA; BRA; SMR; MON; CAN; MEX; FRA; GBR; HUN; BEL; ITA; POR; ESP; JPN; AUS (all car #22)

YANNICK DALMAS (FRA; AGE: 29) 0 PTS

AGS JH24-Ford V8
Automobiles Gonfaronaise Sportive
Races: BRA (car #18)

YANNICK DALMAS (CONTD)

AGS JH25-Ford V8
Automobiles Gonfaronaise Sportive
Races: FRA; ITA; POR; ESP (all car #18)

MARTIN DONNELLY (GBR; AGE: 26) 0 PTS

Lotus 102-Lamborghini V12
Camel Team Lotus
Races: BRA; SMR; MON; CAN; MEX; FRA; GBR; GER; HUN; BEL; ITA; POR (all car #12)

GREGOR FOITEK (SUI; AGE: 25) 0 PTS

Brabham BT58-Judd V8
Motor Racing Developments
Races: USA; BRA (both car #7)

GREGOR FOITEK (CONTD)

Onyx ORE2-Ford V8
Monteverdi Onyx Formula One
Races: SMR; MON; CAN; MEX; GER (all car #35)

OLIVIER GROUILLARD (FRA; AGE: 31) 0 PTS

Osella FA1M-Ford V8
Fondmetal Osella
Races: USA; BRA (both car #14)

OLIVIER GROUILLARD (CONTD)

Osella FA1Me-Ford V8
Fondmetal Osella
Races: SMR; CAN; MEX; BEL; ITA; ESP; AUS (all car #14)

JOHNNY HERBERT (GBR; AGE: 26) 0 PTS

Lotus 102-Lamborghini V12
Camel Team Lotus
Races: JPN; AUS (both car #12)

NICOLA LARINI (ITA; AGE: 26) 0 PTS

Ligier JS33B-Ford V8
Équipe Ligier Gitanes
Races: USA; BRA; SMR; MON; CAN; MEX; FRA; GBR; GER; HUN; BEL; ITA; POR; ESP; JPN; AUS (all car #25)

JJ LEHTO (FIN; AGE: 24) 0 PTS

Onyx ORE2-Ford V8
Monteverdi Onyx Formula One
Races: SMR; MON; CAN; MEX; GER (all car #36)

PIERLUIGI MARTINI (ITA; AGE: 29) 0 PTS

Minardi M189-Ford V8
SCM Minardi Team
Races: USA; BRA (both car #23)

1990

CHAMPIONSHIP CAR-BY-CAR

PIERLUIGI MARTINI (CONTD)

Minardi M190-Ford V8
SCM Minardi Team
Races: MON; CAN; MEX; FRA; GBR; GER; HUN; BEL; ITA; POR; ESP; JPN; AUS (all car #23)

GIANNI MORBIDELLI (ITA; AGE: 22) 0 PTS

Dallara F190-Ford V8
Scuderia Italia
Races: BRA (car #21)

GIANNI MORBIDELLI (CONTD)

Minardi M190-Ford V8
SCM Minardi Team
Races: JPN; AUS (both car #24)

EMANUELE PIRRO (ITA; AGE: 28) 0 PTS

Dallara F190-Ford V8
Scuderia Italia
Races: SMR; MON; CAN; MEX; FRA; GBR; GER; HUN; BEL; ITA; POR; ESP; JPN; AUS (all car #21)

BERND SCHNEIDER (GER; AGE: 25) 0 PTS

Arrows A11-Ford V8
Footwork Arrows Racing
Races: USA (car #10)

GABRIELE TARQUINI (ITA; AGE: 28) 0 PTS

AGS JH25-Ford V8
Automobiles Gonfaronaise Sportive
Races: GBR; HUN; ESP; AUS (all car #17)

PICTURED DURING MON PRACTICE

GRAND PRIX WINNERS 1990

	RACE (CIRCUIT)	**WINNER** (CAR)
USA	UNITED STATES GRAND PRIX (PHOENIX)	AYRTON SENNA (McLAREN MP4/5B-HONDA V10)
BRA	BRAZILIAN GRAND PRIX (INTERLAGOS)	ALAIN PROST (FERRARI 641 V12)
SMR	SAN MARINO GRAND PRIX (IMOLA)	RICCARDO PATRESE (WILLIAMS FW13B-RENAULT V10)
MON	MONACO GRAND PRIX (MONTE CARLO)	AYRTON SENNA (McLAREN MP4/5B-HONDA V10)
CAN	CANADIAN GRAND PRIX (MONTRÉAL)	AYRTON SENNA (McLAREN MP4/5B-HONDA V10)
MEX	MEXICAN GRAND PRIX (MEXICO CITY)	ALAIN PROST (FERRARI 641/2 V12)
FRA	FRENCH GRAND PRIX (PAUL RICARD)	ALAIN PROST (FERRARI 641/2 V12)
GBR	BRITISH GRAND PRIX (SILVERSTONE)	ALAIN PROST (FERRARI 641/2 V12)
GER	GERMAN GRAND PRIX (HOCKENHEIM)	AYRTON SENNA (McLAREN MP4/5B-HONDA V10)
HUN	HUNGARIAN GRAND PRIX (HUNGARORING)	THIERRY BOUTSEN (WILLIAMS FW13B-RENAULT V10)
BEL	BELGIAN GRAND PRIX (SPA-FRANCORCHAMPS)	AYRTON SENNA (McLAREN MP4/5B-HONDA V10)
ITA	ITALIAN GRAND PRIX (MONZA)	AYRTON SENNA (McLAREN MP4/5B-HONDA V10)
POR	PORTUGUESE GRAND PRIX (ESTORIL)	NIGEL MANSELL (FERRARI 641/2 V12)
ESP	SPANISH GRAND PRIX (JEREZ)	ALAIN PROST (FERRARI 641/2 V12)
JPN	JAPANESE GRAND PRIX (SUZUKA)	NELSON PIQUET (BENETTON B190-FORD V8)
AUS	AUSTRALIAN GRAND PRIX (ADELAIDE)	NELSON PIQUET (BENETTON B190-FORD V8)

1991

SENNA SEES OFF RISING THREAT OF WILLIAMS

Left
Mettle fatigue: McLaren boss Ron Dennis props up the emotionally drained Senna after his victory in Brazil

Above
Courage best: Mansell and Senna were inches apart at 190-odd mph as they tore into the first corner at Barcelona's new Circuit de Catalunya. The Englishman eventually won

Right
Mexican weave: Senna veered off and flipped while practising for the season's sixth race

Far right
You take the high road: Senna heads for Turn One at Suzuka while Mansell bounds – irretrievably – towards the gravel trap

Ayrton Senna and McLaren-Honda took a second consecutive world title together, but this time Nigel Mansell and Williams-Renault provided the stiffest opposition.

Mansell's return to Williams brought a more aggressive push to the whole tempo of the operation. By mid-season the Englishman was converting his car's pace into regular victories and he began to pose a threat to Senna's championship lead. Honda had to generate a few extra horsepower towards the end of the year to help Senna seal the title. Veteran Riccardo Patrese drove brilliantly alongside Mansell, winning in Mexico and Portugal and setting three consecutive poles mid-season. Gerhard Berger backed Senna up at McLaren and the Brazilian gifted him the Japanese Grand Prix by way of thanks.

Ferrari suffered an extraordinary implosion and failed to win a single race amid huge internal conflicts and mass firings. Not even three-time world champion Alain Prost was immune. A title contender 12 months earlier, he was sacked before the season-closing Australian GP after being publicly critical of his car.

Eddie Jordan's team graduated to F1 after many years in the junior categories. When driver Bertrand Gachot was jailed before the Belgian GP for assaulting a London cabbie, a young sports car star called Michael Schumacher took his place. The German made a huge impression by qualifying seventh although clutch failure ended his race on the opening lap. Schumacher was contracted to Benetton before Monza, a fortnight later, and went on to outpace new partner Nelson Piquet. In the twilight of a career that had brought him three world titles, the Brazilian was to retire from F1 at the season's end. Earlier in the campaign, however, he scored his 23rd grand prix win when Mansell's car cut out in the dying seconds of the Canadian GP.

Left
Easy rider: Jordan took a punt on Michael Schumacher when Bertrand Gachot was jailed before the Belgian GP. Good call...

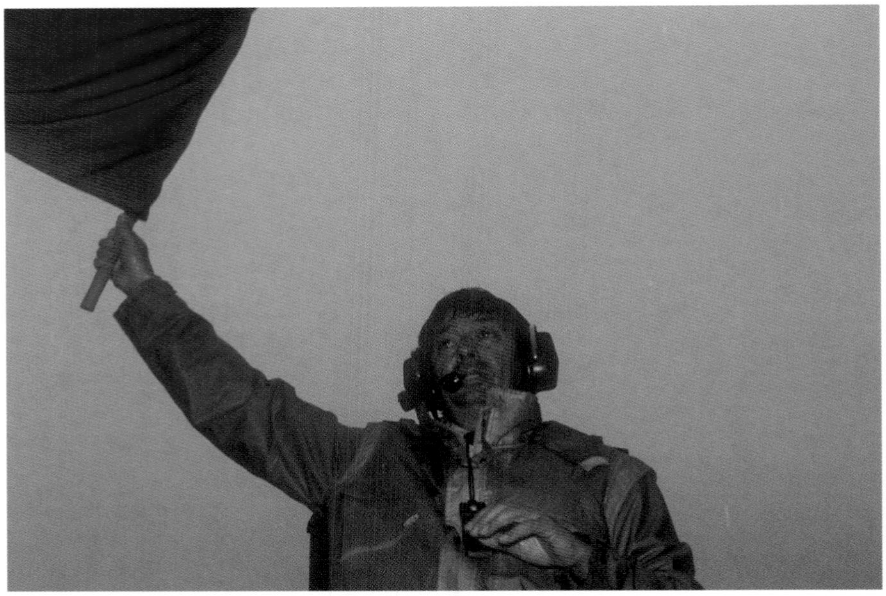

Below
Seeing red: rain brought the Australian GP to a halt after 14 laps and made it the shortest event in F1 world championship history

Bottom
Slip-slidin' away: Mansell watches Berger and Prost skate off at Imola – and this was before the race had even started

AYRTON SENNA – WORLD CHAMPION 1988, 1990 & 1991

1991

CHAMPIONSHIP CAR-BY-CAR

1ST AYRTON SENNA (BRA; AGE: 31) 96 PTS

McLaren MP4/6-Honda V12
Honda Marlboro McLaren
Races: USA; BRA; SMR; MON; CAN; MEX; FRA; GBR; GER; HUN; BEL; ITA; POR; ESP; JPN; AUS (all car #1)

2ND NIGEL MANSELL (GBR; AGE: 37) 72 PTS

Williams FW14-Renault V10
Canon Williams Team
Races: USA; BRA; SMR; MON; CAN; MEX; FRA; GBR; GER; HUN; BEL; ITA; POR; ESP; JPN; AUS (all car #5)

3RD RICCARDO PATRESE (ITA; AGE: 37) 53 PTS

Williams FW14-Renault V10
Canon Williams Team
Races: USA; BRA; SMR; MON; CAN; MEX; FRA; GBR; GER; HUN; BEL; ITA; POR; ESP; JPN; AUS (all car #6)

4TH GERHARD BERGER (AUT; AGE: 31) 43 PTS

McLaren MP4/6-Honda V12
Honda Marlboro McLaren
Races: USA; BRA; SMR; MON; CAN; MEX; FRA; GBR; GER; HUN; BEL; ITA; POR; ESP; JPN; AUS (all car #2)

5TH ALAIN PROST (FRA; AGE: 36) 34 PTS

Ferrari 642 V12
Scuderia Ferrari
Races: USA; BRA; MON; CAN; MEX (all car #27)

ALAIN PROST (CONTD)

Ferrari 643 V12
Scuderia Ferrari
Races: FRA; GBR; GER; HUN; BEL; ITA; POR; ESP; JPN (all car #27)

6TH NELSON PIQUET (BRA; AGE: 38) 26.5 PTS

Benetton B190B-Ford V8
Camel Benetton Ford
Races: USA; BRA (both car #20)

NELSON PIQUET (CONTD)

Benetton B191-Ford V8
Camel Benetton Ford
Races: SMR; MON; CAN; MEX; FRA; GBR; GER; HUN; BEL; ITA; POR; ESP; JPN; AUS (all car #20)

7TH JEAN ALESI (FRA; AGE: 27) 21 PTS

Ferrari 642 V12
Scuderia Ferrari
Races: USA; BRA; SMR; MON; CAN; MEX (all car #28)

JEAN ALESI (CONTD)

Ferrari 643 V12
Scuderia Ferrari
Races: FRA; GBR; GER; HUN; BEL; ITA; POR; ESP; JPN; AUS (all car #28)

8TH STEFANO MODENA (ITA; AGE: 28) 10 PTS

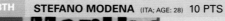

Tyrrell 020-Honda V10
Braun Tyrrell Honda
Races: USA; BRA; SMR; MON; CAN; MEX; FRA; GBR; GER; HUN; BEL; ITA; POR; ESP; JPN; AUS (all car #4)

9TH ANDREA DE CESARIS (ITA; AGE: 32) 9 PTS

Jordan 191-Ford V8
Team 7Up Jordan
Races: BRA; SMR; MON; CAN; MEX; FRA; GBR; GER; HUN; BEL; ITA; POR; ESP; JPN; AUS (all car #33)

10TH ROBERTO MORENO (BRA; AGE: 32) 8 PTS

Benetton B190B-Ford V8
Camel Benetton Ford
Races: USA; BRA (both car #19)

ROBERTO MORENO (CONTD)

Benetton B191-Ford V8
Camel Benetton Ford
Races: SMR; MON; CAN; MEX; FRA; GBR; GER; HUN; BEL (all car #19)

ROBERTO MORENO (CONTD)

Jordan 191-Ford V8
Team 7Up Jordan
Races: ITA; POR (both car #32)

1991

CHAMPIONSHIP CAR-BY-CAR

ROBERTO MORENO (CONTD)

Minardi M191-Ferrari V12
Minardi Team
Races: AUS (car #24)

11TH PIERLUIGI MARTINI (ITA; AGE: 30) 6 PTS

Minardi M191-Ferrari V12
Minardi Team
Races: USA; BRA; SMR; MON; CAN; MEX; FRA; GBR; GER; HUN; BEL; ITA; POR; ESP; JPN; AUS (all car #23)

12TH= BERTRAND GACHOT (BEL/FRA; AGE: 28) 4 PTS

Jordan 191-Ford V8
Team 7Up Jordan
Races: USA; BRA; SMR; MON; CAN; MEX; FRA; GBR; GER; HUN (all car #32)

12TH= JJ LEHTO (FIN; AGE: 25) 4 PTS

Dallara F191-Judd V10
Scuderia Italia
Races: USA; BRA; SMR; MON; CAN; MEX; FRA; GBR; GER; HUN; BEL; ITA; POR; ESP; JPN; AUS (all car #22)

12TH= MICHAEL SCHUMACHER (GER; AGE: 22) 4 PTS

Jordan 191-Ford V8
Team 7Up Jordan
Races: BEL (car #32)

MICHAEL SCHUMACHER (CONTD)

Benetton B191-Ford V8
Camel Benetton Ford
Races: ITA; POR; ESP; JPN; AUS (all car #19)

15TH= MARTIN BRUNDLE (GBR; AGE: 32) 2 PTS

Brabham BT59Y-Yamaha V12
Motor Racing Developments
Races: USA; BRA (both car #7)

MARTIN BRUNDLE (CONTD)

Brabham BT60Y-Yamaha V12
Motor Racing Developments
Races: SMR; CAN; MEX; FRA; GBR; GER; HUN; BEL; ITA; POR; ESP; JPN (all car #7)

15TH= MIKA HÄKKINEN (FIN; AGE: 22) 2 PTS

Lotus 102B-Judd V8
Team Lotus
Races: USA; BRA; SMR; MON; CAN; MEX; GBR; GER; HUN; BEL; ITA; POR; ESP; JPN; AUS (all car #11)

15TH= SATORU NAKAJIMA (JPN; AGE: 38) 2 PTS

Tyrrell 020-Honda V10
Braun Tyrrell Honda
Races: USA; BRA; SMR; MON; CAN; MEX; FRA; GBR; GER; HUN; BEL; ITA; POR; ESP; JPN; AUS (all car #3)

18TH= JULIAN BAILEY (GBR; AGE: 29) 1 PT

Lotus 102B-Judd V8
Team Lotus
Races: SMR (car#12)

PICTURED DURING MON PRACTICE

18TH= ÉRIC BERNARD (FRA; AGE: 26) 1 PT

Lola L91-Ford V8
Larrousse F1
Races: USA; BRA; SMR; MON; CAN; MEX; FRA; GBR; GER; HUN; BEL; ITA; ESP (all car #29)

18TH= MARK BLUNDELL (GBR; AGE: 25) 1 PT

Brabham BT59Y-Yamaha V12
Motor Racing Developments
Races: USA; BRA (both car #8)

MARK BLUNDELL (CONTD)

Brabham BT60Y-Yamaha V12
Motor Racing Developments
Races: SMR; MON; MEX; FRA; GBR; GER; HUN; BEL; ITA; POR; ESP; AUS (all car #8)

18TH= IVAN CAPELLI (ITA; AGE: 28) 1 PT

Leyton House CG911-Ilmor V10
Leyton House Racing
Races: USA; BRA; SMR; MON; CAN; MEX; FRA; GBR; GER; HUN; BEL; ITA; POR; ESP (all car #16)

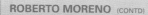

1991

CHAMPIONSHIP CAR-BY-CAR

18TH= EMANUELE PIRRO (ITA; AGE: 29) 1 PT

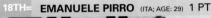

Dallara F191-Judd V10
Scuderia Italia
Races: USA; BRA; MON; CAN; GBR; GER; HUN; BEL; ITA; POR; ESP; JPN; AUS (all car #21)

18TH= AGURI SUZUKI (JPN; AGE: 30) 1 PT

Lola L91-Ford V8
Larrousse F1
Races: USA; SMR; MON; CAN; MEX; FRA; GBR; GER; HUN; POR; JPN (all car #30)

24TH GIANNI MORBIDELLI (ITA; AGE: 23) 0.5 PTS

Minardi M191-Ferrari V12
Minardi Team
Races: USA; BRA; SMR; MON; CAN; MEX; FRA; GBR; GER; HUN; BEL; ITA; POR; ESP; JPN (all car #24)

GIANNI MORBIDELLI (CONTD)

Ferrari 643 V12
Scuderia Ferrari
Races: AUS (car#27)

MICHELE ALBORETO (ITA; AGE: 34) 0 PTS

Footwork A11C-Porsche V12
Footwork Porsche
Races: USA (car#9)

MICHELE ALBORETO (CONTD)

Footwork FA12-Porsche V12
Footwork Porsche
Races: MON; CAN; MEX (all car #9)

MICHELE ALBORETO (CONTD)

Footwork FA12-Ford V8
Footwork
Races: FRA; GBR; POR; ESP; AUS (all car #9)

THIERRY BOUTSEN (BEL; AGE: 34) 0 PTS

Ligier JS35-Lamborghini V12
Équipe Ligier Gitanes
Races: USA; BRA; SMR; MON; CAN; MEX; FRA; GBR; GER; HUN; BEL; ITA; POR; ESP; JPN; AUS (all car #25)

ALEX CAFFI (ITA; AGE: 27) 0 PTS

Footwork FA12-Ford V8
Footwork
Races: JPN; AUS (both car #10)

PICTURED DURING ESP PRACTICE

ERIK COMAS (FRA; AGE: 27) 0 PTS

Ligier JS35-Lamborghini V12
Équipe Ligier Gitanes
Races: BRA; SMR; MON; CAN; FRA; GER; HUN; BEL; ITA; POR; ESP; JPN; AUS (all car #26)

OLIVIER GROUILLARD (FRA; AGE: 32) 0 PTS

Fomet F1-Ford V8
Fondmetal
Races: MEX; FRA; BEL; ITA (all car #14)

PICTURED DURING USA PRACTICE

MAURICIO GUGELMIN (BRA; AGE: 28) 0 PTS

Leyton House CG911-Ilmor V10
Leyton House Racing
Races: USA; BRA; SMR; MON; CAN; MEX; FRA; GBR; GER; HUN; BEL; ITA; POR; ESP; JPN; AUS (all car #15)

JOHNNY HERBERT (GBR; AGE: 27) 0 pts

Lotus 102B-Judd V8
Team Lotus
Races: MEX; FRA; GBR; BEL; POR; JPN; AUS (all car #12)

STEFAN JOHANSSON (SWE; AGE: 34) 0 pts

Footwork FA12-Porsche V12
Footwork Porsche
Races: CAN (car#10)

NICOLA LARINI (ITA; AGE: 27) 0 PTS

Lamborghini 291 V12
Modena Team
Races: USA; GER; HUN; ITA; AUS (all car #34)

PICTURED DURING ESP PRACTICE

1991

CHAMPIONSHIP CAR-BY-CAR

ERIC VAN DE POELE (BEL; AGE: 29) 0 PTS

Lamborghini 291 V12
Modena Team
Races: SMR (car#35)

PICTURED DURING ESP PRACTICE

GABRIELE TARQUINI (ITA; AGE: 29) 0 PTS

AGS JH25-Ford V8
Automobiles Gonfaronaise Sportive
Races: USA; BRA; MON (all car #17)

GABRIELE TARQUINI (CONTD)

Fomet F1-Ford V8
Fondmetal
Races: ESP; JPN (both car #14)

KARL WENDLINGER (AUT; AGE: 22) 0 PTS

Leyton House CG911-Ilmor V10
Leyton House Racing
Races: JPN; AUS (both car #16)

ALEX ZANARDI (ITA; AGE: 25) 0 PTS

Jordan 191-Ford V8
Team 7Up Jordan
Races: ESP; JPN; AUS (all car #32)

GRAND PRIX WINNERS 1991

	RACE (CIRCUIT)	WINNER (CAR)
USA	UNITED STATES GRAND PRIX (PHOENIX)	AYRTON SENNA (McLAREN MP4/6-HONDA V12)
BRA	BRAZILIAN GRAND PRIX (INTERLAGOS)	AYRTON SENNA (McLAREN MP4/6-HONDA V12)
SMR	SAN MARINO GRAND PRIX (IMOLA)	AYRTON SENNA (McLAREN MP4/6-HONDA V12)
MON	MONACO GRAND PRIX (MONTE CARLO)	AYRTON SENNA (McLAREN MP4/6-HONDA V12)
CAN	CANADIAN GRAND PRIX (MONTRÉAL)	NELSON PIQUET (BENETTON B191-FORD V8)
MEX	MEXICAN GRAND PRIX (MEXICO CITY)	RICCARDO PATRESE (WILLIAMS FW14-RENAULT V10)
FRA	FRENCH GRAND PRIX (MAGNY-COURS)	NIGEL MANSELL (WILLIAMS FW14-RENAULT V10)
GBR	BRITISH GRAND PRIX (SILVERSTONE)	NIGEL MANSELL (WILLIAMS FW14-RENAULT V10)
GER	GERMAN GRAND PRIX (HOCKENHEIM)	NIGEL MANSELL (WILLIAMS FW14-RENAULT V10)
HUN	HUNGARIAN GRAND PRIX (HUNGARORING)	AYRTON SENNA (McLAREN MP4/6-HONDA V12)
BEL	BELGIAN GRAND PRIX (SPA-FRANCORCHAMPS)	AYRTON SENNA (McLAREN MP4/6-HONDA V12)
ITA	ITALIAN GRAND PRIX (MONZA)	NIGEL MANSELL (WILLIAMS FW14-RENAULT V10)
POR	PORTUGUESE GRAND PRIX (ESTORIL)	RICCARDO PATRESE (WILLIAMS FW14-RENAULT V10)
ESP	SPANISH GRAND PRIX (CATALUNYA)	NIGEL MANSELL (WILLIAMS FW14-RENAULT V10)
JPN	JAPANESE GRAND PRIX (SUZUKA)	GERHARD BERGER (McLAREN MP4/6-HONDA V12)
AUS	AUSTRALIAN GRAND PRIX (ADELAIDE)	AYRTON SENNA (McLAREN MP4/6-HONDA V12)

1992

MANSELL IN A LEAGUE OF HIS OWN

Left
"Yes! I finished second": Mansell followed Senna across the line in Budapest to secure the world title almost 12 years to the day since his F1 debut

Above
French dressing: Mansell took 14 pole positions and nine victories during the season. Here at Magny-Cours he managed both

Right
Finns can only get better: Mika Häkkinen underlined his great potential during a second season with Lotus

Far right
Schuey shines: a promising young German puts Mansell under pressure at Spa en route to the first in his record-breaking tally of F1 victories. Martin Brundle gives chase

RHÔNE-POULENC
CAMEL
elf
Labatt's
5
Canon

28
KOMATSU
TOMMY
HILFIGER
FN

Canon
elf
5

After much badgering of Williams technical director Patrick Head, the team's chief aerodynamicist Adrian Newey finally got the go-ahead for the feature that transformed the Williams-Renault into an unbeatable machine – active ride.

Thus equipped, the FW14B chassis was so devastating it was often whole seconds per lap faster than the opposition. Nigel Mansell extracted the absolute maximum from it and scored a record-breaking nine victories on his way to the world championship. Team-mate Riccardo Patrese was a comfortable runner-up.

Active ride had been tried in the past but hadn't previously offered enough of a performance advantage over conventional suspension to make a case for itself. But the aerodynamic characteristics of F1 cars were now such that huge downforce gains could be made by keeping the car's pitch flat at all times.

In the final season of its partnership with Honda, McLaren was best of the rest. Ayrton Senna won three times and team-mate Gerhard Berger twice, but these were mere crumbs from the Williams-Renault table.

At Spa, on the first anniversary of his startling F1 debut, Michael Schumacher (Benetton-Ford) scored his maiden grand prix victory. Jean Alesi and Ivan Capelli struggled with Ferrari's radical 'twin-floor' chassis, which was as hopelessly off the pace as it was unreliable. Rain at Magny-Cours and Barcelona illustrated, however, that the car's traction control system worked very effectively and that Alesi was one of the world's finest wet-weather drivers.

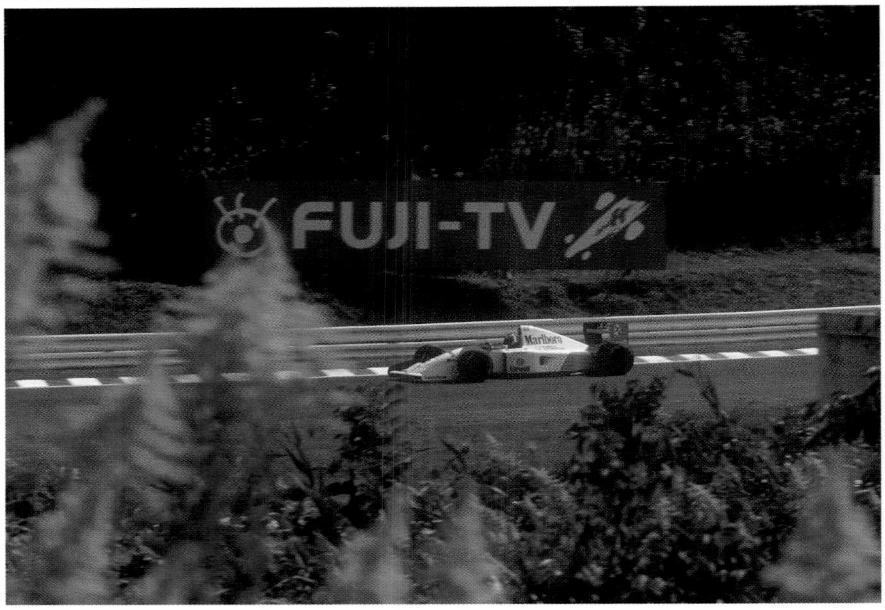

Above
Best of the rest: McLaren stars Gerhard Berger (pictured en route to second at Suzuka) and Ayrton Senna won five races between them but weren't serious title contenders

Below left
Six in the city: Senna won again in Monaco to become the most successful driver in the event's history

Bottom right
Rockin' all over the world: Mansellmania was by no means the exclusive preserve of fans at Silverstone. The difference? At Suzuka they didn't invade the track before the race had ended...

Below
Lady in waiting: Giovanna Amati tried to qualify a Brabham-Judd on three occasions but failed to make the cut

NIGEL MANSELL – WORLD CHAMPION 1992

1992

CHAMPIONSHIP CAR-BY-CAR

1ST NIGEL MANSELL (GBR; AGE: 38) 108 PTS

Williams FW14B-Renault V10
Canon Williams Team
Races: RSA; MEX; BRA; ESP; SMR; MON; CAN; FRA; GBR; GER; HUN; BEL; ITA; POR; JPN; AUS (all car #5)

2ND RICCARDO PATRESE (ITA; AGE: 38) 56 PTS

Williams FW14B-Renault V10
Canon Williams Team
Races: RSA; MEX; BRA; ESP; SMR; MON; CAN; FRA; GBR; GER; HUN; BEL; ITA; POR; JPN; AUS (all car #6)

3RD MICHAEL SCHUMACHER (GER; AGE: 23) 53 PTS

Benetton B191B-Ford V8
Camel Benetton Ford
Races: RSA; MEX; BRA (all car #19)

MICHAEL SCHUMACHER (CONTD)

Benetton B192-Ford V8
Camel Benetton Ford
Races: ESP; SMR; MON; CAN; FRA; GBR; GER; HUN; BEL; ITA; POR; JPN; AUS (all car #19)

4TH AYRTON SENNA (BRA; AGE: 32) 50 PTS

McLaren MP4/6B-Honda V12
Honda Marlboro McLaren
Races: RSA; MEX (both car #1)

AYRTON SENNA (CONTD)

McLaren MP4/7A-Honda V12
Honda Marlboro McLaren
Races: BRA; ESP; SMR; MON; CAN; FRA; GBR; GER; HUN; BEL; ITA; POR; JPN; AUS (all car #1)

5TH GERHARD BERGER (AUT; AGE: 32) 49 PTS

McLaren MP4/6B-Honda V12
Honda Marlboro McLaren
Races: RSA; MEX (both car #2)

GERHARD BERGER (CONTD)

McLaren MP4/7A-Honda V12
Honda Marlboro McLaren
Races: BRA; ESP; SMR; MON; CAN; FRA; GBR; GER; HUN; BEL; ITA; POR; JPN; AUS (all car #2)

6TH MARTIN BRUNDLE (GBR; AGE: 33) 38 PTS

Benetton B191B-Ford V8
Camel Benetton Ford
Races: RSA; MEX; BRA (all car #20)

MARTIN BRUNDLE (CONTD)

Benetton B192-Ford V8
Camel Benetton Ford
Races: ESP; SMR; MON; CAN; FRA; GBR; GER; HUN; BEL; ITA; POR; JPN; AUS (all car #20)

7TH JEAN ALESI (FRA; AGE: 28) 18 PTS

Ferrari F92A V12
Scuderia Ferrari
Races: RSA; MEX; BRA; ESP; SMR; MON; CAN; FRA; GBR; GER; HUN; BEL; ITA; POR; JPN; AUS (all car #27)

8TH MIKA HÄKKINEN (FIN; AGE: 23) 11 PTS

Lotus 102D-Ford V8
Team Lotus
Races: RSA; MEX; BRA; ESP (all car #11)

MIKA HÄKKINEN (CONTD)

Lotus 107-Ford V8
Team Lotus
Races: MON; CAN; FRA; GBR; GER; HUN; BEL; ITA; POR; JPN; AUS (all car #11)

ANDREA DE CESARIS (ITA; AGE: 33) 8 PTS

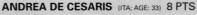

Tyrrell 020B-Ilmor V10
Tyrrell Racing Organisation
Races: RSA; MEX; BRA; ESP; SMR; MON; CAN; FRA; GBR; GER; HUN; BEL; ITA; POR; JPN; AUS (all car #4)

10TH MICHELE ALBORETO (ITA; AGE: 35) 6 PTS

Footwork FA13-Mugen V10
Footwork Mugen Honda
Races: RSA; MEX; BRA; ESP; SMR; MON; CAN; FRA; GBR; GER; HUN; BEL; ITA; POR; JPN; AUS (all car #9)

1992

CHAMPIONSHIP CAR-BY-CAR

11TH ERIK COMAS (FRA; AGE: 28) 4 PTS

Ligier JS37-Renault V10
Ligier Gitanes Blondes
Races: RSA; MEX; BRA; ESP; SMR; MON; CAN; FRA; GBR; GER; HUN; ITA; POR; JPN; AUS (all car #26)

12TH= IVAN CAPELLI (ITA; AGE: 29) 3 PTS

Ferrari F92A V12
Scuderia Ferrari
Races: RSA; MEX; BRA; ESP; SMR; MON; CAN; FRA; GBR; GER; HUN; BEL; ITA; POR (all car #28)

12TH= KARL WENDLINGER (AUT; AGE: 23) 3 PTS

March CG911-Ilmor V10
March F1
Races: RSA; MEX; BRA; ESP; SMR; MON; CAN; FRA; GBR; GER; HUN; BEL; ITA; POR (all car #16)

14TH= THIERRY BOUTSEN (BEL; AGE: 35) 2 PTS

Ligier JS37-Renault V10
Ligier Gitanes Blondes
Races: RSA; MEX; BRA; ESP; SMR; MON; CAN; FRA; GBR; GER; HUN; BEL; ITA; POR; JPN; AUS (all car #25)

14TH= JOHNNY HERBERT (GBR; AGE: 28) 2 PTS

Lotus 102D-Ford V8
Team Lotus
Races: RSA; MEX; BRA; ESP (all car #12)

JOHNNY HERBERT (CONTD)

Lotus 107-Ford V8
Team Lotus
Races: SMR; MON; CAN; FRA; GBR; GER; HUN; BEL; ITA; POR; JPN; AUS (all car #12)

14TH= PIERLUIGI MARTINI (ITA; AGE: 31) 2 PTS

Dallara F192-Ferrari V12
Scuderia Italia
Races: RSA; MEX; BRA; ESP; SMR; MON; CAN; FRA; GBR; GER; HUN; BEL; ITA; POR; JPN; AUS (all car #22)

17TH= CHRISTIAN FITTIPALDI (BRA; AGE: 21) 1 PT

Minardi M191B-Lamborghini V12
Minardi Team
Races: RSA; MEX; BRA; ESP (all car #23)

CHRISTIAN FITTIPALDI (CONTD)

Minardi M192-Lamborghini V12
Minardi Team
Races: SMR; MON; CAN; POR; JPN; AUS (all car #23)

17TH= BERTRAND GACHOT (BEL/FRA; AGE: 29) 1 PT

Larrousse LC92-Lamborghini V12
Central Park Venturi Larrousse
Races: RSA; MEX; BRA; ESP; SMR; MON; CAN; FRA; GBR; GER; HUN; BEL; ITA; POR; JPN; AUS (all car #29)

17TH= STEFANO MODENA (ITA; AGE: 29) 1 PT

Jordan 192-Yamaha V12
Sasol Jordan Yamaha
Races: MEX; BRA; SMR; MON; CAN; FRA; GBR; HUN; BEL; POR; JPN; AUS (all car #32)

PAUL BELMONDO (FRA; AGE: 29) 0 PTS

March CG911-Ilmor V10
March F1
Races: ESP; SMR; CAN; GER; HUN (all car #17)

PICTURED DURING MON PRACTICE

ANDREA CHIESA (SUI; AGE: 28) 0 PTS

Fondmetal GR01-Ford V8
Fondmetal
Races: MEX; ESP (both car #14)

PICTURED DURING RSA PRACTICE

ANDREA CHIESA (CONTD)

Fondmetal GR02-Ford V8
Fondmetal
Races: FRA (car #14)

OLIVIER GROUILLARD (FRA; AGE: 33) 0 PTS

Tyrrell 020B-Ilmor V10
Tyrrell Racing Organisation
Races: RSA; MEX; BRA; ESP; SMR; MON; CAN; FRA; GBR; GER; HUN; BEL; ITA; POR; JPN; AUS (all car #3)

1992

CHAMPIONSHIP CAR-BY-CAR

MAURICIO GUGELMIN (BRA; AGE: 29) 0 PTS

Jordan 192-Yamaha V12
Sasol Jordan Yamaha
Races: RSA; MEX; BRA; ESP; SMR; MON; CAN; FRA; GBR; GER; HUN; BEL; ITA; POR; JPN; AUS (all car #33)

DAMON HILL (GBR; AGE: 31) 0 PTS

Brabham BT60B-Judd V10
Motor Racing Developments
Races: GBR; HUN (both car #8)

UKYO KATAYAMA (JPN; AGE: 29) 0 PTS

Larrousse LC92-Lamborghini V12
Central Park Venturi Larrousse
Races: RSA; MEX; BRA; SMR; CAN; FRA; GBR; GER; HUN; BEL; ITA; POR; JPN; AUS (all car #30)

PICTURED DURING ESP PRACTICE

JAN LAMMERS (NED; AGE: 36) 0 PTS

March CG911-Ilmor V10
March F1
Races: JPN; AUS (both car #16)

NICOLA LARINI (ITA; AGE: 28) 0 PTS

Ferrari F92A V12
Scuderia Ferrari
Races: JPN; AUS (both car #28)

JJ LEHTO (FIN; AGE: 26) 0 PTS

Dallara F192-Ferrari V12
Scuderia Italia
Races: RSA; MEX; BRA; ESP; SMR; MON; CAN; FRA; GBR; GER; BEL; ITA; POR; JPN; AUS (all car #21)

GIANNI MORBIDELLI (ITA; AGE: 24) 0 PTS

Minardi M191B-Lamborghini V12
Minardi Team
Races: RSA; MEX; BRA; ESP (all car #24)

GIANNI MORBIDELLI (CONTD)

Minardi M192-Lamborghini V12
Minardi Team
Races: SMR; MON; CAN; FRA; GBR; GER; BEL; ITA; POR; JPN; AUS (all car #24)

ROBERTO MORENO (BRA; AGE: 33) 0 PTS

Andrea Moda S192-Judd V10
Andrea Moda Formula
Races: MON (car #34)

EMANUELE NASPETTI (ITA; AGE: 24) 0 PTS

March CG911-Ilmor V10
March F1
Races: BEL; ITA; POR; JPN; AUS (all car #17)

ERIC VAN DE POELE (BEL; AGE: 30) 0 PTS

Brabham BT60B-Judd V10
Motor Racing Developments
Races: RSA (car #7)

ERIC VAN DE POELE (CONTD)

Fondmetal GR02-Ford V8
Fondmetal
Races: HUN; BEL; ITA (all car #14)

AGURI SUZUKI (JPN; AGE: 31) 0 PTS

Footwork FA13-Mugen V10
Footwork Mugen Honda
Races: RSA; BRA; ESP; SMR; MON; FRA; GBR; GER; HUN; BEL; ITA; POR; JPN; AUS (all car #10)

GABRIELE TARQUINI (ITA; AGE: 30) 0 PTS

Fondmetal GR01-Ford V8
Fondmetal
Races: RSA; MEX; BRA; ESP; SMR; MON (all car #15)

GABRIELE TARQUINI (CONTD)

Fondmetal GR02-Ford V8
Fondmetal
Races: CAN; FRA; GBR; GER; HUN; BEL; ITA (all car #15)

1992

CHAMPIONSHIP CAR-BY-CAR

ALEX ZANARDI (ITA; AGE: 25) 0 PTS

Minardi M192-Lamborghini V12
Minardi Team
Races: GER (car #23)

GRAND PRIX WINNERS 1992

	RACE (CIRCUIT)	WINNER (CAR)
RSA	SOUTH AFRICAN GRAND PRIX (KYALAMI)	NIGEL MANSELL (WILLIAMS FW14B-RENAULT V10)
MEX	MEXICAN GRAND PRIX (MEXICO CITY)	NIGEL MANSELL (WILLIAMS FW14B-RENAULT V10)
BRA	BRAZILIAN GRAND PRIX (INTERLAGOS)	NIGEL MANSELL (WILLIAMS FW14B-RENAULT V10)
ESP	SPANISH GRAND PRIX (CATALUNYA)	NIGEL MANSELL (WILLIAMS FW14B-RENAULT V10)
SMR	SAN MARINO GRAND PRIX (IMOLA)	NIGEL MANSELL (WILLIAMS FW14B-RENAULT V10)
MON	MONACO GRAND PRIX (MONTE CARLO)	AYRTON SENNA (McLAREN MP4/7A-HONDA V12)
CAN	CANADIAN GRAND PRIX (MONTRÉAL)	GERHARD BERGER (McLAREN MP4/7A-HONDA V12)
FRA	FRENCH GRAND PRIX (MAGNY-COURS)	NIGEL MANSELL (WILLIAMS FW14B-RENAULT V10)
GBR	BRITISH GRAND PRIX (SILVERSTONE)	NIGEL MANSELL (WILLIAMS FW14B-RENAULT V10)
GER	GERMAN GRAND PRIX (HOCKENHEIM)	NIGEL MANSELL (WILLIAMS FW14B-RENAULT V10)
HUN	HUNGARIAN GRAND PRIX (HUNGARORING)	AYRTON SENNA (McLAREN MP4/7A-HONDA V12)
BEL	BELGIAN GRAND PRIX (SPA-FRANCORCHAMPS)	MICHAEL SCHUMACHER (BENETTON B192-FORD V8)
ITA	ITALIAN GRAND PRIX (MONZA)	AYRTON SENNA (McLAREN MP4/7A-HONDA V12)
POR	PORTUGUESE GRAND PRIX (ESTORIL)	NIGEL MANSELL (WILLIAMS FW14B-RENAULT V10)
JPN	JAPANESE GRAND PRIX (SUZUKA)	RICCARDO PATRESE (WILLIAMS FW14B-RENAULT V10)
AUS	AUSTRALIAN GRAND PRIX (ADELAIDE)	GERHARD BERGER (McLAREN MP4/7A-HONDA V12)

RICCARDO PATRESE

1993

PROST RETURNS – THEN BOWS OUT ON A HIGH

Far left
Portuguese man of warmth: Prost takes a tricolour on his lap of honour at Estoril after finishing second to Michael Schumacher and wrapping up his fourth world title

Left
Prost haste: did they make this kind of fuss about Fangio in 1956? Er, no

Below
Berger fling: Gerhard finished sixth for Ferrari in South Africa – despite his occasionally unsubtle approach. Mind you, he was three laps adrift

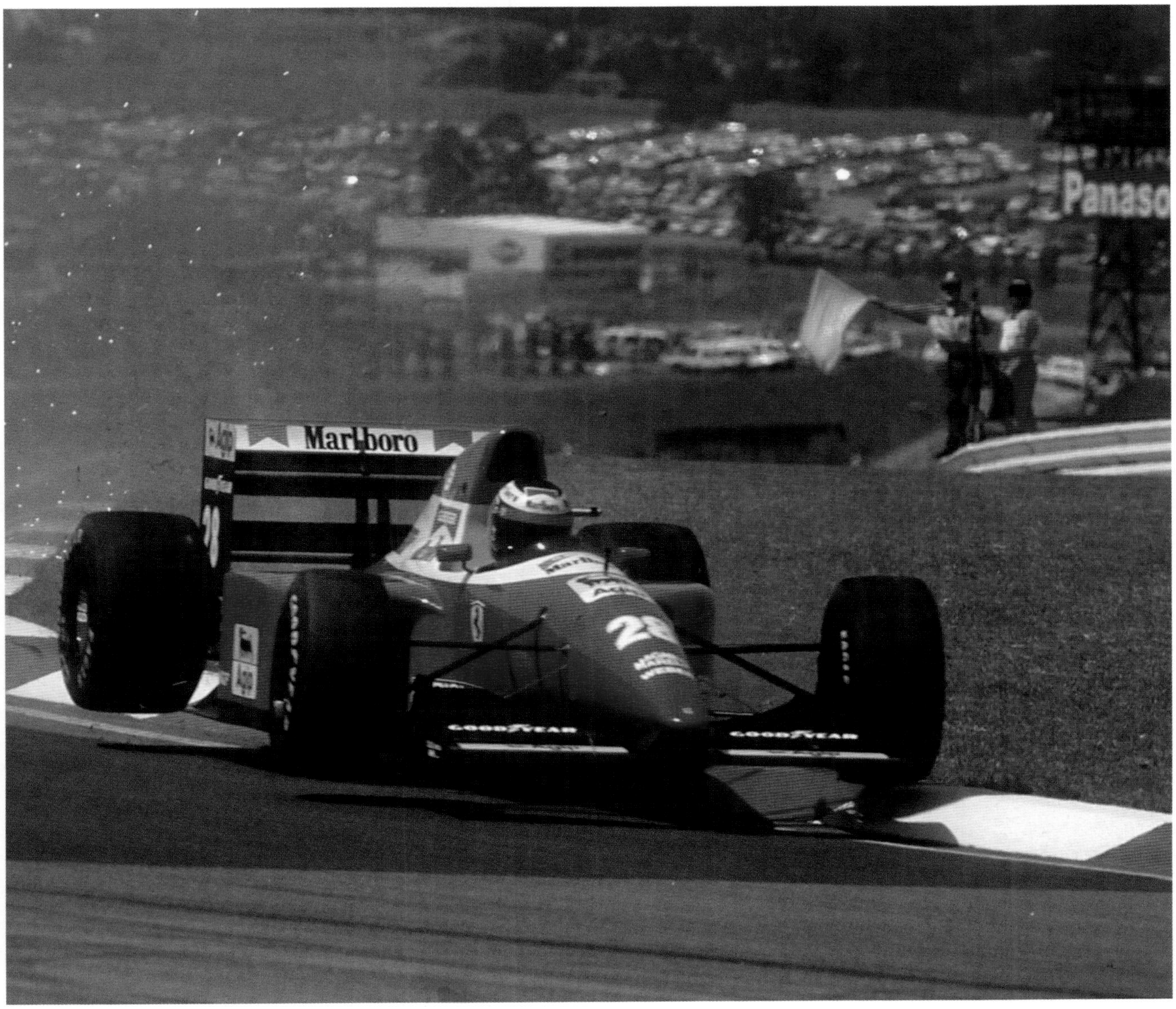

While most leading teams had caught up with Williams in terms of technical gizmos, they still had to overcome Adrian Newey's aerodynamics, Renault's horsepower and Alain Prost's driving. Result? The Frenchman went on to collect his fourth world championship and extend his tally of race wins to 51. Job done, he bowed out of the sport at the end of the year.

The all-conquering Williams team signed Prost while he was on a sabbatical in 1992. Its incumbent world champion Nigel Mansell failed to agree terms to partner the Frenchman and headed off to the US-based Champ Car series. Williams test driver Damon Hill took Mansell's place and Prost had a relatively untroubled run to the title.

There were days, though, when Ayrton Senna showed why he was still the world's number one, regardless of titles or statistics. A sequence of rain-affected races early in the season enabled him to weave his magic in a McLaren with a customer Ford-Cosworth V8 that had nothing like the horsepower of a Renault V10. Senna scored a home win in Brazil, after Prost spun out, and took an early-season championship lead. He extended this with one of the greatest victories of his career in the very wet Grand Prix of Europe at Donington Park, England. But the Williams-Renault's performance became irresistible as the season wore on. At the end of the year Senna announced that he would be replacing Prost at Williams for 1994. He signed off his McLaren career in style by winning the final two races.

Hill took his first victory in Hungary and followed it up with two more, while Michael Schumacher (Benetton-Ford) won in Portugal in a style that confirmed his standing as a future champion. American star Michael Andretti suffered a dispiriting season alongside Senna at McLaren and test driver Mika Häkkinen took his place before the end of the year. The Finn caused a sensation by outqualifying Senna first time out in Portugal.

Far left
Over the Hill: Damon prepares to land on his head in an Estoril gravel trap after clipping Irvine's Jordan during practice

Left
Bubbly bath: Ayrton Senna soaks up the plaudits after winning his home race for a second time

Below
Trouble ahead: Senna comes up to lap F1 first-timer Irvine and Hill at Suzuka. The Ulster rookie initially let the Brazilian through but subsequently repassed him. Ayrton went to remonstrate after the race – and ended up throwing a punch

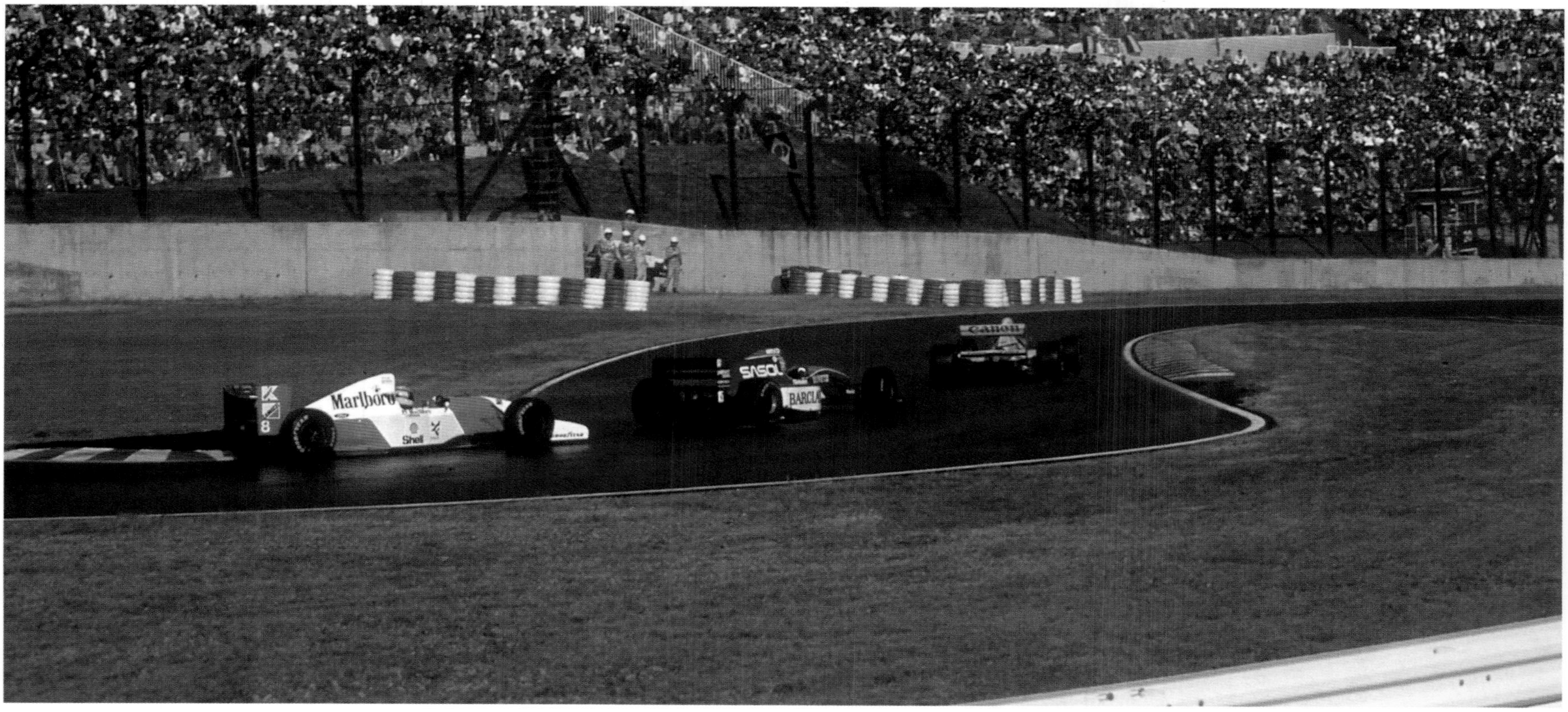

1993

CHAMPIONSHIP CAR-BY-CAR

1ST ALAIN PROST (FRA; AGE: 38) 99 PTS

Williams FW15C-Renault V10
Canon Williams Renault
Races: RSA; BRA; EUR; SMR; ESP; MON; CAN; FRA; GBR; GER; HUN; BEL; ITA; POR; JPN; AUS (all car #2)

2ND AYRTON SENNA (BRA; AGE: 33) 73 PTS

McLaren MP4/8-Ford V8
Marlboro McLaren
Races: RSA; BRA; EUR; SMR; ESP; MON; CAN; FRA; GBR; GER; HUN; BEL; ITA; POR; JPN; AUS (all car #8)

3RD DAMON HILL (GBR; AGE: 32) 69 PTS

Williams FW15C-Renault V10
Canon Williams Renault
Races: RSA; BRA; EUR; SMR; ESP; MON; CAN; FRA; GBR; GER; HUN; BEL; ITA; POR; JPN; AUS (all car #0)

4TH MICHAEL SCHUMACHER (GER; AGE: 24) 52 PTS

Benetton B193-Ford V8
Camel Benetton Ford
Races: RSA; BRA; EUR; SMR; ESP; MON; CAN; FRA; GBR; GER; HUN; BEL; ITA; POR; JPN; AUS (all car #5)

5TH RICCARDO PATRESE (ITA; AGE: 39) 20 PTS

Benetton B193-Ford V8
Camel Benetton Ford
Races: RSA; BRA; EUR; SMR; ESP; MON; CAN; FRA; GBR; GER; HUN; BEL; ITA; POR; JPN; AUS (all car #6)

6TH JEAN ALESI (FRA; AGE: 29) 16 PTS

Ferrari F93A V12
Scuderia Ferrari
Races: RSA; BRA; EUR; SMR; ESP; MON; CAN; FRA; GBR; GER; HUN; BEL; ITA; POR; JPN; AUS (all car #27)

7TH MARTIN BRUNDLE (GBR; AGE: 34) 13 PTS

Ligier JS39-Renault V10
Ligier Gitanes Blondes
Races: RSA; BRA; EUR; SMR; ESP; MON; CAN; FRA; GBR; GER; HUN; BEL; ITA; POR; JPN; AUS (all car #25)

8TH GERHARD BERGER (AUT; AGE: 33) 12 PTS

Ferrari F93A V12
Scuderia Ferrari
Races: RSA; BRA; EUR; SMR; ESP; MON; CAN; FRA; GBR; GER; HUN; BEL; ITA; POR; JPN; AUS (all car #28)

9TH JOHNNY HERBERT (GBR; AGE: 29) 11 PTS

Lotus 107B-Ford V8
Team Lotus
Races: RSA; BRA; EUR; SMR; ESP; MON; CAN; FRA; GBR; GER; HUN; BEL; ITA; POR; JPN; AUS (all car #12)

10TH MARK BLUNDELL (GBR; AGE: 27) 10 PTS

Ligier JS39-Renault V10
Ligier Gitanes Blondes
Races: RSA; BRA; EUR; SMR; ESP; MON; CAN; FRA; GBR; GER; HUN; BEL; ITA; POR; JPN; AUS (all car #26)

11TH= MICHAEL ANDRETTI (USA; AGE: 30) 7 PTS

McLaren MP4/8-Ford V8
Marlboro McLaren
Races: RSA; BRA; EUR; SMR; ESP; MON; CAN; FRA; GBR; GER; HUN; BEL; ITA (all car #7)

11TH= KARL WENDLINGER (AUT; AGE: 24) 7 PTS

Sauber C12-Ilmor V10
Sauber
Races: RSA; BRA; EUR; SMR; ESP; MON; CAN; FRA; GBR; GER; HUN; BEL; ITA; POR; JPN; AUS (all car #29)

13TH= CHRISTIAN FITTIPALDI (BRA; AGE: 22) 5 PTS

Minardi M193-Ford V8
Minardi Team
Races: RSA; BRA; EUR; SMR; ESP; MON; CAN; FRA; GBR; GER; HUN; BEL; ITA; POR (all car #23)

13TH= JJ LEHTO (FIN; AGE: 27) 5 PTS

Sauber C12-Ilmor V10
Sauber
Races: RSA; BRA; EUR; SMR; ESP; MON; CAN; FRA; GBR; GER; HUN; BEL; ITA; POR; JPN; AUS (all car #30)

15TH= MIKA HÄKKINEN (FIN; AGE: 25) 4 PTS

McLaren MP4/8-Ford V8
Marlboro McLaren
Races: POR; JPN; AUS (all car #7)

1993

CHAMPIONSHIP CAR-BY-CAR

15TH= DEREK WARWICK (GBR; AGE: 38) 4 PTS

Footwork FA13B-Mugen V10
Footwork Mugen Honda
Races: RSA; BRA (both car #9)

DEREK WARWICK (CONTD)

Footwork FA14-Mugen V10
Footwork Mugen Honda
Races: EUR; SMR; ESP; MON; CAN; FRA; GBR; GER; HUN; BEL; ITA; POR; JPN; AUS (all car #9)

17TH= PHILIPPE ALLIOT (FRA; AGE: 38) 2 PTS

Larrousse LH93-Lamborghini V12
Larrousse F1
Races: RSA; BRA; EUR; SMR; ESP; MON; CAN; FRA; GBR; GER; HUN; BEL; ITA; POR (all car #19)

17TH= FABRIZIO BARBAZZA (ITA; AGE: 30) 2 PTS

Minardi M193-Ford V8
Minardi Team
Races: RSA; BRA; EUR; SMR; ESP; MON; CAN; FRA (all car #24)

17TH= RUBENS BARRICHELLO (BRA; AGE: 21) 2 PTS

Jordan 193-Hart V10
Sasol Jordan
Races: RSA; BRA; EUR; SMR; ESP; MON; CAN; FRA; GBR; GER; HUN; BEL; ITA; POR; JPN; AUS (all car #14)

20TH= ERIK COMAS (FRA; AGE: 29) 1 PT

Larrousse LH93-Lamborghini V12
Larrousse F1
Races: RSA; BRA; EUR; SMR; ESP; MON; CAN; FRA; GBR; GER; HUN; BEL; ITA; POR; JPN; AUS (all car #20)

20TH= EDDIE IRVINE (GBR; AGE: 28) 1 PT

Jordan 193-Hart V10
Sasol Jordan
Races: JPN; AUS (both car #15)

20TH= ALEX ZANARDI (ITA; AGE: 26) 1 PT

Lotus 107B-Ford V8
Team Lotus
Races: RSA; BRA; EUR; SMR; ESP; MON; CAN; FRA; GBR; GER; HUN (all car #11)

MICHELE ALBORETO (ITA; AGE: 36) 0 PTS

Lola T93/30-Ferrari V12
Lola BMS Scuderia Italia
Races: RSA; BRA; EUR; MON; GER; HUN; BEL; ITA; POR (all car #21)

MARCO APICELLA (ITA; AGE: 27) 0 PTS

Jordan 193-Hart V10
Sasol Jordan
Races: ITA (car #15)

LUCA BADOER (ITA; AGE: 22) 0 PTS

Lola T93/30-Ferrari V12
Lola BMS Scuderia Italia
Races: RSA; BRA; SMR; ESP; CAN; FRA; GBR; GER; HUN; BEL; ITA; POR (all car #22)

THIERRY BOUTSEN (BEL; AGE: 35) 0 PTS

Jordan 193-Hart V10
Sasol Jordan
Races: EUR; SMR; ESP; MON; CAN; FRA; GBR; GER; HUN; BEL (all car #15)

IVAN CAPELLI (ITA; AGE: 29) 0 PTS

Jordan 193-Hart V10
Sasol Jordan
Races: RSA (car #15)

ANDREA DE CESARIS (ITA; AGE: 34) 0 PTS

Tyrrell 020C-Yamaha V10
Tyrrell Racing Organisation
Races: RSA; BRA; EUR; SMR; ESP; MON; CAN; FRA (all car #4)

ANDREA DE CESARIS (CONTD)

Tyrrell 021-Yamaha V10
Tyrrell Racing Organisation
Races: GBR; GER; HUN; BEL; ITA; POR; JPN; AUS (all car #4)

1993

CHAMPIONSHIP CAR-BY-CAR

JEAN-MARC GOUNON (FRA; AGE: 30) 0 PTS

Minardi M193-Ford V8
Minardi Team
Races: JPN; AUS (both car #23)

UKYO KATAYAMA (JPN; AGE: 30) 0 PTS

Tyrrell 020C-Yamaha V10
Tyrrell Racing Organisation
Races: RSA; BRA; EUR; SMR; ESP; MON; CAN; FRA; GBR (all car #3)

UKYO KATAYAMA (CONTD)

Tyrrell 021-Yamaha V10
Tyrrell Racing Organisation
Races: GER; HUN; BEL; ITA; POR; JPN; AUS (all car #3)

PEDRO LAMY (POR; AGE: 21) 0 PTS

Lotus 107B-FORD V8
Team Lotus
Races: ITA; POR; JPN; AUS (all car #11)

PIERLUIGI MARTINI (ITA; AGE: 32) 0 PTS

Minardi M193-Ford V8
Minardi Team
Races: GBR; GER; HUN; BEL; ITA; POR; JPN; AUS (all car #24)

EMANUELE NASPETTI (ITA; AGE: 25) 0 PTS

Jordan 193-Hart V10
Sasol Jordan
Races: POR (car #15)

AGURI SUZUKI (JPN; AGE: 32) 0 PTS

Footwork FA13B-Mugen V10
Footwork Mugen Honda
Races: RSA; BRA (both car #10)

AGURI SUZUKI (CONTD)

Footwork FA14-Mugen V10
Footwork Mugen Honda
Races: EUR; SMR; ESP; MON; CAN; FRA; GBR; GER; HUN; BEL; ITA; POR; JPN; AUS (all car #10)

TOSHIO SUZUKI (JPN; AGE: 38) 0 PTS

Larrousse LH93-Lamborghini V12
Larrousse F1
Races: JPN; AUS (both car #19)

GRAND PRIX WINNERS 1993

	RACE (CIRCUIT)	**WINNER** (CAR)
RSA	SOUTH AFRICAN GRAND PRIX (KYALAMI)	ALAIN PROST (WILLIAMS FW15C-RENAULT V10)
BRA	BRAZILIAN GRAND PRIX (INTERLAGOS)	AYRTON SENNA (McLAREN MP4/8-FORD V8)
EUR	EUROPEAN GRAND PRIX (DONINGTON PARK)	AYRTON SENNA (McLAREN MP4/8-FORD V8)
SMR	SAN MARINO GRAND PRIX (IMOLA)	ALAIN PROST (WILLIAMS FW15C-RENAULT V10)
ESP	SPANISH GRAND PRIX (CATALUNYA)	ALAIN PROST (WILLIAMS FW15C-RENAULT V10)
MON	MONACO GRAND PRIX (MONTE CARLO)	AYRTON SENNA (McLAREN MP4/8-FORD V8)
CAN	CANADIAN GRAND PRIX (MONTRÉAL)	ALAIN PROST (WILLIAMS FW15C-RENAULT V10)
FRA	FRENCH GRAND PRIX (MAGNY-COURS)	ALAIN PROST (WILLIAMS FW15C-RENAULT V10)
GBR	BRITISH GRAND PRIX (SILVERSTONE)	ALAIN PROST (WILLIAMS FW15C-RENAULT V10)
GER	GERMAN GRAND PRIX (HOCKENHEIM)	ALAIN PROST (WILLIAMS FW15C-RENAULT V10)
HUN	HUNGARIAN GRAND PRIX (HUNGARORING)	DAMON HILL (WILLIAMS FW15C-RENAULT V10)
BEL	BELGIAN GRAND PRIX (SPA-FRANCORCHAMPS)	DAMON HILL (WILLIAMS FW15C-RENAULT V10)
ITA	ITALIAN GRAND PRIX (MONZA)	DAMON HILL (WILLIAMS FW15C-RENAULT V10)
POR	PORTUGUESE GRAND PRIX (ESTORIL)	MICHAEL SCHUMACHER (BENETTON B193B-FORD V8)
JPN	JAPANESE GRAND PRIX (SUZUKA)	AYRTON SENNA (McLAREN MP4/8-FORD V8)
AUS	AUSTRALIAN GRAND PRIX (ADELAIDE)	AYRTON SENNA (McLAREN MP4/8-FORD V8)

1994

SCHUMACHER TRIUMPHS – BUT TRAGEDIES FORCE AN F1 RETHINK

Far left
May 1 1994, Imola: Ayrton Senna, Michael Schumacher, Gerhard Berger and Damon Hill trail the Safety Car in the wake of a first-lap pile-up. Senna crashed fatally shortly after the race resumed

Left
Crown duel: Schumacher and Hill lock horns in Adelaide

Below
Pit shock: mid-race refuelling returned to F1 – and things went badly wrong for Jos Verstappen's Benetton crew at Hockenheim. Remarkably, there were no serious injuries

This will forever be remembered as the tragic season that most changed Formula One. Triple world champion Ayrton Senna and rookie Roland Ratzenberger crashed fatally during the course of the San Marino Grand Prix meeting at Imola. They were the first F1 drivers to die at a race since 1982 and the repercussions were instant. The sporting authorities re-evaluated their whole approach to safety and rapidly devised speed-limiting rule changes, the first of which were implemented just two races after the tragedy. F1's safety crusade has been similarly intense ever since.

Senna lost his life in only his third race for Williams-Renault. At the time he was leading Michael Schumacher – the man who would come to be seen as the Brazilian's natural heir.

Schumacher and the Benetton-Ford team appeared to have resolved the issues arising from a pre-season ban on traction control and active ride better than Williams – initially, at least. Williams swiftly made effective chassis improvements, however, and Damon Hill was able to offer Schumacher a title challenge. This was intensified after the German received a two-race ban for ignoring a black flag shown at the British GP, where he was guilty of an illegal overtaking manoeuvre during the warm-up lap. Schumacher was also later stripped of victory in Belgium when it was found that his car's underfloor plank – a regulatory device introduced to slow the cars post-Imola – had worn away beyond the legal minimum after he spun over a kerb.

The upshot was a title decider between Schumacher and Hill during the Adelaide finale. After leaving the rest of the field far behind, the two clashed when Hill took a dive down the inside of the Benetton and Schumacher drove into him. Schuey retired immediately while Hill's car suffered terminal suspension damage. After one of the most controversial seasons in F1 history, Germany had its first champion.

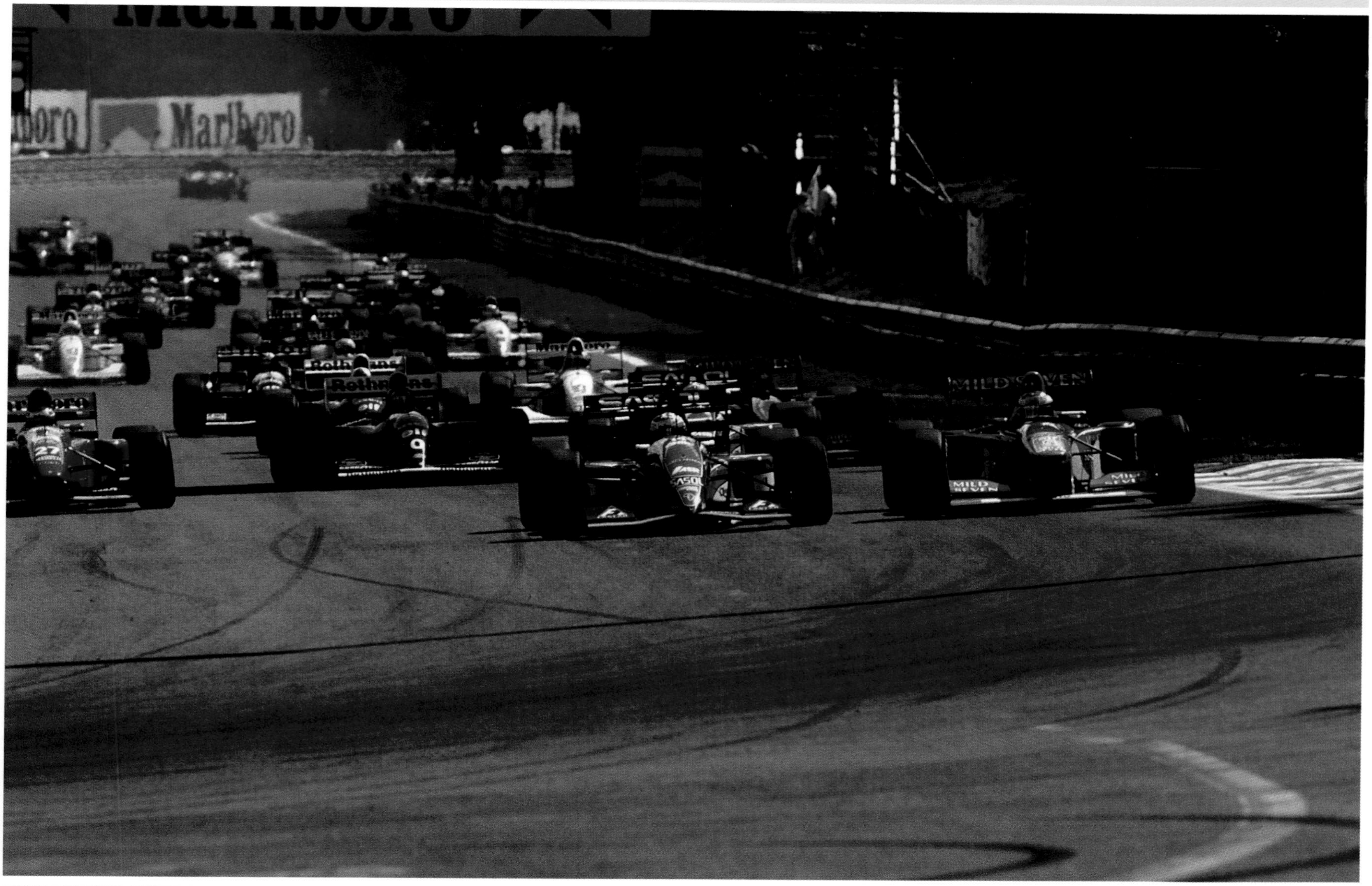

HILL TOOK A DIVE DOWN THE INSIDE AND SCHUMACHER DROVE INTO HIM. AFTER ONE OF THE MOST CONTROVERSIAL SEASONS IN F1 HISTORY, GERMANY HAD ITS FIRST CHAMPION

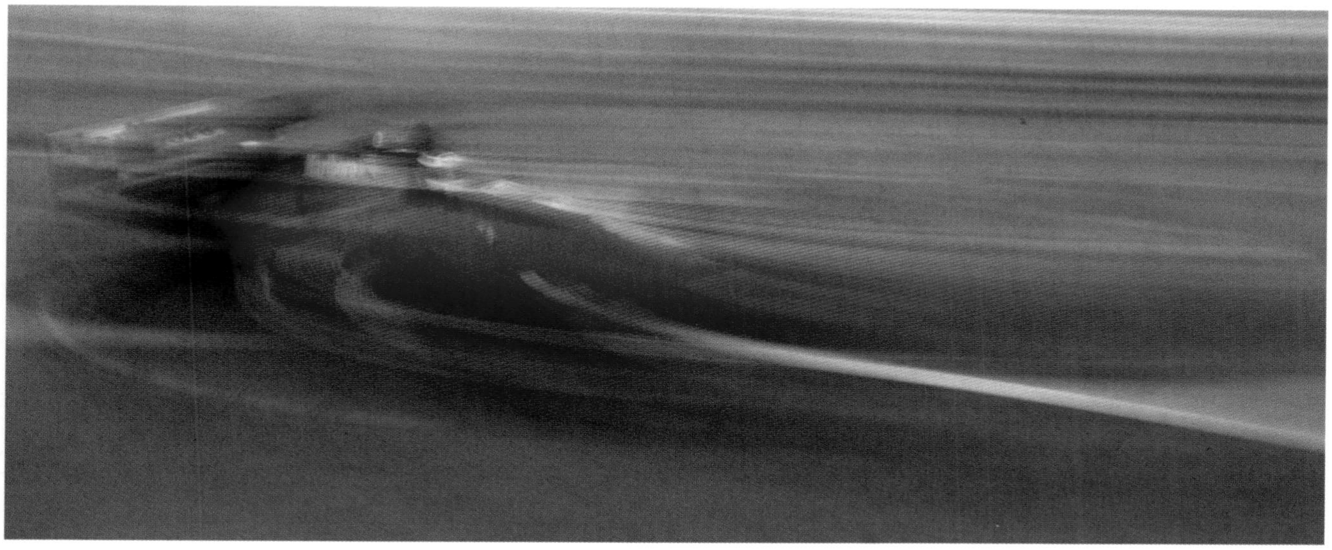

Far left, top
Sweet but short: Schuey in good humour at Spa – before he was stripped of victory for a technical infringement

Far left, bottom
Reasons to be cheerful: Nigel Mansell crosses the line in Adelaide to score the 31st and final victory of a distinguished F1 career

Above
Qualified success: Rubens Barrichello leads away at Spa after a quick-witted tyre decision allowed him to plant his Jordan on pole

Left
Red run: Jean Alesi heads for fifth place in Monaco

1994

CHAMPIONSHIP CAR-BY-CAR

1ST MICHAEL SCHUMACHER (GER; AGE: 25) 92 PTS

Benetton B194-Ford V8
Mild Seven Benetton Ford
Races: BRA; PAC; SMR; MON; ESP; CAN; FRA; GBR; GER; HUN; BEL; EUR; JPN; AUS (all car #5)

2ND DAMON HILL (GBR; AGE: 33) 91 PTS

Williams FW16-Renault V10
Rothmans Williams Renault
Races: BRA; PAC; SMR; MON; ESP; CAN; FRA; GBR; GER; HUN; BEL; ITA; POR; EUR; JPN; AUS (all car #0)

3RD GERHARD BERGER (AUT; AGE: 34) 41 PTS

Ferrari 412T1 V12
Scuderia Ferrari
Races: BRA; PAC; SMR; MON; ESP; CAN; FRA; GBR; GER; HUN; BEL; ITA; POR; EUR; JPN; AUS (all car #28)

4TH MIKA HÄKKINEN (FIN; AGE: 25) 26 PTS

McLaren MP4/9-Peugeot V10
Marlboro McLaren Peugeot
Races: BRA; PAC; SMR; MON; ESP; CAN; FRA; GBR; GER; BEL; ITA; POR; EUR; JPN; AUS (all car #7)

5TH JEAN ALESI (FRA; AGE: 30) 24 PTS

Ferrari 412T1 V12
Scuderia Ferrari
Races: BRA; MON; ESP; CAN; FRA; GBR; GER; HUN; BEL; ITA; POR; EUR; JPN; AUS (all car #27)

6TH RUBENS BARRICHELLO (BRA; AGE: 22) 19 PTS

Jordan 194-Hart V10
Sasol Jordan
Races: BRA; PAC; MON; ESP; CAN; FRA; GBR; GER; HUN; BEL; ITA; POR; EUR; JPN; AUS (all car #14)

7TH MARTIN BRUNDLE (GBR; AGE: 35) 16 PTS

McLaren MP4/9-Peugeot V10
Marlboro McLaren Peugeot
Races: BRA; PAC; SMR; MON; ESP; CAN; FRA; GBR; GER; HUN; BEL; ITA; POR; EUR; JPN; AUS (all car #8)

8TH DAVID COULTHARD (GBR; AGE: 23) 14 PTS

Williams FW16-Renault V10
Rothmans Williams Renault
Races: ESP; CAN; GBR; GER; HUN; BEL; ITA; POR (all car #2)

9TH NIGEL MANSELL (GBR; AGE: 41) 13 PTS

Williams FW16-Renault V10
Rothmans Williams Renault
Races: FRA; EUR; JPN; AUS (all car #2)

10TH JOS VERSTAPPEN (NED; AGE: 22) 10 PTS

Benetton B194-Ford V8
Mild Seven Benetton Ford
Races: BRA; PAC; FRA; GBR; GER; HUN; BEL; ITA; POR; EUR (all car #6)

11TH OLIVIER PANIS (FRA; AGE: 27) 9 PTS

Ligier JS39B-Renault V10
Ligier Gitanes Blondes
Races: BRA; PAC; SMR; MON; ESP; CAN; FRA; GBR; GER; HUN; BEL; ITA; POR; EUR; JPN; AUS (all car #26)

12TH MARK BLUNDELL (GBR; AGE: 28) 8 PTS

Tyrrell 022-Yamaha V10
Tyrrell Racing Organisation
Races: BRA; PAC; SMR; MON; ESP; CAN; FRA; GBR; GER; HUN; BEL; ITA; POR; EUR; JPN; AUS (all car #4)

13TH HEINZ-HARALD FRENTZEN (GER; AGE: 27) 7 PTS

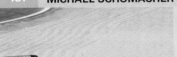

Sauber C13-Mercedes V10
Broker Sauber Mercedes
Races: BRA; PAC; SMR; ESP; CAN; FRA; GBR; GER; HUN; BEL; ITA; POR; EUR; JPN; AUS (all car #30)

14TH= CHRISTIAN FITTIPALDI (BRA; AGE: 23) 6 PTS

Footwork FA15-Ford V8
Footwork Ford
Races: BRA; PAC; SMR; MON; ESP; CAN; FRA; GBR; GER; HUN; BEL; ITA; POR; EUR; JPN; AUS (all car #9)

14TH= EDDIE IRVINE (GBR; AGE: 28) 6 PTS

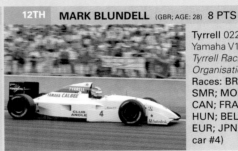

Jordan 194-Hart V10
Sasol Jordan
Races: BRA; ESP; CAN; FRA; GER; HUN; BEL; ITA; POR; EUR; JPN; AUS (all car #15)

1994

CHAMPIONSHIP CAR-BY-CAR

14TH= NICOLA LARINI (ITA; AGE: 30) 6 PTS

Ferrari 412T1 V12
Scuderia Ferrari
Races: PAC; SMR (both car #27)

17TH UKYO KATAYAMA (JPN; AGE: 31) 5 PTS

Tyrrell 022-Yamaha V10
Tyrrell Racing Organisation
Races: BRA; PAC; SMR; MON; ESP; CAN; FRA; GBR; GER; HUN; BEL; ITA; POR; EUR; JPN; AUS (all car #3)

18TH= ÉRIC BERNARD (FRA; AGE: 29) 4 PTS

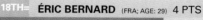

Ligier JS39B-Renault V10
Ligier Gitanes Blondes
Races: BRA; PAC; SMR; MON; ESP; CAN; FRA; GBR; GER; HUN; BEL; ITA; POR (all car #25)

ÉRIC BERNARD (CONTD)

Lotus 109-Mugen V8
Team Lotus
Races: EUR (car #12)

18TH= ANDREA DE CESARIS (ITA; AGE: 35) 4 PTS

Jordan 194-Hart V10
Sasol Jordan
Races: SMR; MON (both car #15)

ANDREA DE CESARIS (CONTD)

Sauber C13-Mercedes V10
Broker Sauber Mercedes
Races: CAN; FRA; GBR; GER; HUN; BEL; ITA; POR; EUR (all car #29)

18TH= PIERLUIGI MARTINI (ITA; AGE: 33) 4 PTS

Minardi M193B-Ford V8
Minardi Scuderia Italia
Races: BRA; PAC; SMR; MON; ESP (all car #23)

PIERLUIGI MARTINI (CONTD)

Minardi M194-Ford V8
Minardi Scuderia Italia
Races: CAN; FRA; GBR; GER; HUN; BEL; ITA; POR; EUR; JPN; AUS (all car #23)

18TH= KARL WENDLINGER (AUT; AGE: 25) 4 PTS

Sauber C13-Mercedes V10
Broker Sauber Mercedes
Races: BRA; PAC; SMR (all car #29)

22ND GIANNI MORBIDELLI (ITA; AGE: 26) 3 PTS

Footwork FA15-Ford V8
Footwork Ford
Races: BRA; PAC; SMR; MON; ESP; CAN; FRA; GBR; GER; HUN; BEL; ITA; POR; EUR; JPN; AUS (all car #10)

23RD ERIK COMAS (FRA; AGE: 30) 2 PTS

Larrousse LH94-Ford V8
Tourtel Larrousse F1
Races: BRA; PAC; SMR; MON; ESP; CAN; FRA; GBR; GER; HUN; BEL; ITA; POR; EUR; JPN (all car #20)

24TH= MICHELE ALBORETO (ITA; AGE: 37) 1 PT

Minardi M193B-Ford V8
Minardi Scuderia Italia
Races: BRA; PAC; SMR; MON; ESP (all car #24)

MICHELE ALBORETO (CONTD)

Minardi M194-Ford V8
Minardi Scuderia Italia
Races: CAN; FRA; GBR; GER; HUN; BEL; ITA; POR; EUR; JPN; AUS (all car #24)

24TH= JJ LEHTO (FIN; AGE: 28) 1 PT

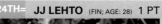

Benetton B194-Ford V8
Mild Seven Benetton Ford
Races: SMR; MON; ESP; CAN (all car #6); ITA; POR (both #5)

JJ LEHTO (CONTD)

Sauber C13-Mercedes V10
Sauber Mercedes
Races: JPN; AUS (both car #29)

1994

CHAMPIONSHIP CAR-BY-CAR

PHILIPPE ADAMS (BEL; AGE: 24) 0 PTS

Lotus 109-Mugen V8
Team Lotus
Races: BEL; POR (both car #11)

PHILIPPE ALLIOT (FRA; AGE: 40) 0 PTS

McLaren MP4/9-Peugeot V10
Marlboro McLaren Peugeot
Races: HUN (car #7)

PHILIPPE ALLIOT (CONTD)

Larrousse LH94-Ford V8
Tourtel Larrousse F1
Races: BEL (car #19)

PAUL BELMONDO (FRA; AGE: 31) 0 PTS

Pacific PR01-Ilmor V10
Pacific Grand Prix
Races: MON; ESP (both car #33)

PICTURED DURING FRA PRACTICE

OLIVIER BERETTA (MON; AGE: 24) 0 PTS

Larrousse LH94-Ford V8
Tourtel Larrousse F1
Races: BRA; PAC; SMR; MON; CAN; FRA; GBR; GER; HUN (all car #19)

DAVID BRABHAM (AUS; AGE: 28) 0 PTS

Simtek S941-Ford V8
MTV Simtek Ford
Races: BRA; PAC; SMR; MON; ESP; CAN; FRA; GBR; GER; HUN; BEL; ITA; POR; EUR; JPN; AUS (all car #31)

YANNICK DALMAS (FRA; AGE: 33) 0 PTS

Larrousse LH94-Ford V8
Tourtel Larrousse F1
Races: ITA; POR (both car #19)

JEAN-DENIS DELETRAZ (SUI; AGE: 31) 0 PTS

Larrousse LH94-Ford V8
Tourtel Larrousse F1
Races: AUS (car #20)

BERTRAND GACHOT (BEL/FRA; AGE: 31) 0 PTS

Pacific PR01-Ilmor V10
Pacific Grand Prix
Races: BRA; SMR; MON; ESP; CAN (all car #34)

PICTURED DURING ITA PRACTICE

JEAN-MARC GOUNON (FRA; AGE: 31) 0 PTS

Simtek S941-Ford V8
MTV Simtek Ford
Races: FRA; GBR; GER; HUN; BEL; ITA; POR (all car #32)

JOHNNY HERBERT (GBR; AGE: 30) 0 PTS

Lotus 107C-Mugen V10
Team Lotus
Races: BRA; PAC; SMR; MON (all car #12)

JOHNNY HERBERT (CONTD)

Lotus 109-Mugen V8
Team Lotus
Races: ESP; CAN; FRA; GBR; GER; HUN; BEL; ITA; POR (all car #12)

JOHNNY HERBERT (CONTD)

Ligier JS39B-Renault V10
Ligier Gitanes Blondes
Races: EUR (car #25)

JOHNNY HERBERT (CONTD)

Benetton B194-Ford V8
Mild Seven Benetton Ford
Races: JPN; AUS (all car #6)

TAKI INOUE (JPN; AGE: 31) 0 PTS

Simtek S941-Ford V8
MTV Simtek Ford
Races: JPN (car #32)

1994

CHAMPIONSHIP CAR-BY-CAR

FRANCK LAGORCE (FRA; AGE: 26) 0 PTS

Ligier JS39B-Renault V10
Ligier Gitanes Blondes
Races: JPN; AUS (both car #25)

PEDRO LAMY (POR; AGE: 22) 0 PTS

Lotus 107C-Mugen V10
Team Lotus
Races: BRA; PAC; SMR; MON (all car #11)

HIDEKI NODA (JPN; AGE: 25) 0 PTS

Larrousse LH94-Ford V8
Tourtel Larrousse F1
Races: EUR; JPN; AUS (all car #19)

ROLAND RATZENBERGER (AUT; AGE: 31) 0 PTS

Simtek S941-Ford V8
MTV Simtek Ford
Races: PAC (car #32)

PICTURED DURING BRA PRACTICE

MIKA SALO (FIN; AGE: 27) 0 PTS

Lotus 109-Mugen V8
Team Lotus
Races: JPN; AUS (both car #12)

MIMMO SCHIATTARELLA (ITA; AGE: 27) 0 PTS

Simtek S941-Ford V8
MTV Simtek Ford
Races: EUR; AUS (both car #32)

AYRTON SENNA (BRA; AGE: 34) 0 PTS

Williams FW16-Renault V10
Rothmans Williams Renault
Races: BRA; PAC; SMR (all car #2)

AGURI SUZUKI (JPN; AGE: 33) 0 PTS

Jordan 194-Hart V10
Sasol Jordan
Races: PAC (car #15)

ALEX ZANARDI (ITA; AGE: 27) 0 PTS

Lotus 107C-Mugen V10
Team Lotus
Races: ESP; CAN (both car #11)

ALEX ZANARDI (CONTD)

Lotus 109-Mugen V8
Team Lotus
Races: FRA; GBR; GER; HUN; ITA; EUR; JPN; AUS (all car #11)

GRAND PRIX WINNERS 1994

	RACE (CIRCUIT)	**WINNER** (CAR)
BRA	BRAZILIAN GRAND PRIX (INTERLAGOS)	MICHAEL SCHUMACHER (BENETTON B194-FORD V8)
PAC	PACIFIC GRAND PRIX (TI CIRCUIT, AIDA)	MICHAEL SCHUMACHER (BENETTON B194-FORD V8)
SMR	SAN MARINO GRAND PRIX (IMOLA)	MICHAEL SCHUMACHER (BENETTON B194-FORD V8)
MON	MONACO GRAND PRIX (MONTE CARLO)	MICHAEL SCHUMACHER (BENETTON B194-FORD V8)
ESP	SPANISH GRAND PRIX (CATALUNYA)	DAMON HILL (WILLIAMS FW16-RENAULT V10)
CAN	CANADIAN GRAND PRIX (MONTRÉAL)	MICHAEL SCHUMACHER (BENETTON B194-FORD V8)
FRA	FRENCH GRAND PRIX (MAGNY-COURS)	MICHAEL SCHUMACHER (BENETTON B194-FORD V8)
GBR	BRITISH GRAND PRIX (SILVERSTONE)	DAMON HILL (WILLIAMS FW16-RENAULT V10)
GER	GERMAN GRAND PRIX (HOCKENHEIM)	GERHARD BERGER (FERRARI 412T1B V12)
HUN	HUNGARIAN GRAND PRIX (HUNGARORING)	MICHAEL SCHUMACHER (BENETTON B194-FORD V8)
BEL	BELGIAN GRAND PRIX (SPA-FRANCORCHAMPS)	DAMON HILL (WILLIAMS FW16B-RENAULT V10)
ITA	ITALIAN GRAND PRIX (MONZA)	DAMON HILL (WILLIAMS FW16B-RENAULT V10)
POR	PORTUGUESE GRAND PRIX (ESTORIL)	DAMON HILL (WILLIAMS FW16B-RENAULT V10)
EUR	EUROPEAN GRAND PRIX (JEREZ)	MICHAEL SCHUMACHER (BENETTON B194-FORD V8)
JPN	JAPANESE GRAND PRIX (SUZUKA)	DAMON HILL (WILLIAMS FW16B-RENAULT V10)
AUS	AUSTRALIAN GRAND PRIX (ADELAIDE)	NIGEL MANSELL (WILLIAMS FW16B-RENAULT V10)

1995

MORE POWER TO SCHUMACHER'S ELBOW

Left
All the fun of the flair: Michael Schumacher piles on the opposite lock as he exits the Loews Hairpin en route to winning the Monaco GP for the second successive season

Right
Herbie goes bananas: Johnny Herbert gets to experience the sensation of winning a grand prix. He broke his F1 duck on home soil at Silverstone

Below
Delighted colours of Benetton: Schumacher needed only to finish fourth in the Pacific GP to be sure of the title. Result? He stormed to his eighth win of the season and kick-started a post-race party. Note to Flavio Briatore: the passage of time hasn't made your back-to-front cap look any more stylish

Following the previous season's controversies, Michael Schumacher and Benetton were determined to win the title in a manner that left no question marks hanging over their performance. The German hammered the point home by racking up a record-equalling nine victories – and his team-mate Johnny Herbert picked up two for good measure.

Benetton switched engine allegiance from Ford-Cosworth to Renault as Formula One's new three-litre limit came into force – and that gave the team parity with Williams. Although it was accepted that Williams had the fastest car, Schumacher and Benetton technical director Ross Brawn devised a series of consistently effective refuelling strategies that frequently made their rivals look inept in the races.

Damon Hill led the Williams offensive but his four victories couldn't paper over the cracks of a disappointing campaign. His battles with Schumacher were frequently fraught and a degree of ill feeling built up, especially when he collided with the German while trying to pass him at Silverstone and Monza. On both occasions Herbert was there to pick up the pieces.

Hill's team-mate David Coulthard completed his first full grand prix season and developed well. He scored his maiden F1 victory in Portugal and set four consecutive pole positions towards the end of the year – by which time it had been confirmed that he would be leaving to join McLaren.

Jean Alesi took an emotional first F1 win in Canada – the final flourish for the Ferrari V12, that most evocative of engines. Nigel Mansell's supposed full-time return with McLaren ended after just a few races. The former world champion missed the start of the season, while the team modified its cockpit to accommodate him, and the Mercedes-powered chassis proved uncompetitive. After spinning into a gravel trap during the Spanish GP, Mansell hopped out and walked away from F1 – this time for good.

MICHAEL SCHUMACHER AND BENETTON WERE DETERMINED TO WIN THE TITLE IN A MANNER THAT LEFT NO QUESTION MARKS HANGING OVER THEIR PERFORMANCE

Left
Hill strait blues: the Williams team leader stormed into the lead at Hockenheim, but undid his good work by spinning off on lap two

Above
Follow my lieder: Michael Schumacher's fans were in good voice after their hero's arch-rival pitched his Williams into the tyre wall

Top
The long and wounding road: Jean Alesi might have signed for Williams in 1991 and picked up a clutch of titles by the mid-1990s. Instead he opted for Ferrari and had to wait until Montreal 1995, 91 races into his F1 career, to score his first – and only – GP victory

1995

CHAMPIONSHIP CAR-BY-CAR

1ST MICHAEL SCHUMACHER (GER; AGE: 26) 102 PTS

Benetton B195-Renault V10
Mild Seven Benetton Renault
Races: BRA; ARG; SMR; ESP; MON; CAN; FRA; GBR; GER; HUN; BEL; ITA; POR; EUR; PAC; JPN; AUS (all car #1)

2ND DAMON HILL (GBR; AGE: 34) 69 PTS

Williams FW17-Renault V10
Rothmans Williams Renault
Races: BRA; ARG; SMR; ESP; MON; CAN; FRA; GBR; GER; HUN; BEL; ITA; POR; EUR; PAC; JPN; AUS (all car #5)

3RD DAVID COULTHARD (GBR; AGE: 24) 49 PTS

Williams FW17-Renault V10
Rothmans Williams Renault
Races: BRA; ARG; SMR; ESP; MON; CAN; FRA; GBR; GER; HUN; BEL; ITA; POR; EUR; PAC; JPN; AUS (all car #6)

4TH JOHNNY HERBERT (GBR; AGE: 31) 45 PTS

Benetton B195-Renault V10
Mild Seven Benetton Renault
Races: BRA; ARG; SMR; ESP; MON; CAN; FRA; GBR; GER; HUN; BEL; ITA; POR; EUR; PAC; JPN; AUS (all car #2)

5TH JEAN ALESI (FRA; AGE: 31) 42 PTS

Ferrari 412T2 V12
Scuderia Ferrari
Races: BRA; ARG; SMR; ESP; MON; CAN; FRA; GBR; GER; HUN; BEL; ITA; POR; EUR; PAC; JPN; AUS (all car #27)

6TH GERHARD BERGER (AUT; AGE: 35) 31 PTS

Ferrari 412T2 V12
Scuderia Ferrari
Races: BRA; ARG; SMR; ESP; MON; CAN; FRA; GBR; GER; HUN; BEL; ITA; POR; EUR; PAC; JPN; AUS (all car #28)

7TH MIKA HÄKKINEN (FIN; AGE: 26) 17 PTS

McLaren MP4/10-Mercedes V10
Marlboro McLaren Mercedes
Races: BRA; ARG; SMR; ESP; MON; CAN; FRA; GBR; GER; HUN; BEL; ITA; POR; EUR; JPN (all car #8)

8TH OLIVIER PANIS (FRA; AGE: 28) 16 PTS

Ligier JS41-Mugen V10
Ligier Gitanes Blondes
Races: BRA; ARG; SMR; ESP; MON; CAN; FRA; GBR; GER; HUN; BEL; ITA; POR; EUR; PAC; JPN; AUS (all car #26)

9TH HEINZ-HARALD FRENTZEN (GER; AGE: 28) 15 PTS

Sauber C14-Ford V10
Red Bull Sauber Ford
Races: BRA; ARG; SMR; ESP; MON; CAN; FRA; GBR; GER; HUN; BEL; ITA; POR; EUR; PAC; JPN; AUS (all car #30)

10TH MARK BLUNDELL (GBR; AGE: 29) 13 PTS

McLaren MP4/10-Mercedes V10
Marlboro McLaren Mercedes
Races: BRA; ARG; MON; CAN; FRA; GBR; GER; HUN; BEL; ITA; POR; EUR; PAC; JPN; AUS (all car #7)

11TH RUBENS BARRICHELLO (BRA; AGE: 23) 11 PTS

Jordan 195-Peugeot V10
Total Jordan Peugeot
Races: BRA; ARG; SMR; ESP; MON; CAN; FRA; GBR; GER; HUN; BEL; ITA; POR; EUR; PAC; JPN; AUS (all car #14)

12TH EDDIE IRVINE (GBR; AGE: 29) 10 PTS

Jordan 195-Peugeot V10
Total Jordan Peugeot
Races: BRA; ARG; SMR; ESP; MON; CAN; FRA; GBR; GER; HUN; BEL; ITA; POR; EUR; PAC; JPN; AUS (all car #15)

13TH MARTIN BRUNDLE (GBR; AGE: 36) 7 PTS

Ligier JS41-Mugen V10
Ligier Gitanes Blondes
Races: ESP; MON; CAN; FRA; GBR; HUN; BEL; ITA; POR; EUR; AUS (all car #25)

14TH= GIANNI MORBIDELLI (ITA; AGE: 27) 5 PTS

Footwork FA16-Hart V8
Footwork Hart
Races: BRA; ARG; SMR; ESP; MON; CAN; FRA; PAC; JPN; AUS (all car #9)

14TH= MIKA SALO (FIN; AGE: 28) 5 PTS

Tyrrell 023-Yamaha V10
Nokia Tyrrell Yamaha
Races: BRA; ARG; SMR; ESP; MON; CAN; FRA; GBR; GER; HUN; BEL; ITA; POR; EUR; PAC; JPN; AUS (all car #4)

1995

CHAMPIONSHIP CAR-BY-CAR

16TH JEAN-CHRISTOPHE BOULLION (FRA; AGE: 25) 3 PTS

Sauber C14-Ford V10
Red Bull Sauber Ford
Races: MON; CAN; FRA; GBR; GER; HUN; BEL; ITA; POR; EUR; PAC (all car #29)

17TH= PEDRO LAMY (POR; AGE: 23) 1 PT

Minardi M195-Ford V8
Minardi Scuderia Italia
Races: HUN; BEL; ITA; POR; EUR; PAC; JPN; AUS (all car #23)

17TH= AGURI SUZUKI (JPN; AGE: 34) 1 PT

Ligier JS41-Mugen V10
Ligier Gitanes Blondes
Races: BRA; ARG; SMR; GER; PAC (all car #25)

LUCA BADOER (ITA; AGE: 24) 0 PTS

Minardi M195-Ford V8
Minardi Scuderia Italia
Races: BRA; ARG; SMR; ESP; MON; CAN; FRA; GBR; GER; HUN; BEL; ITA; POR; EUR; PAC; JPN (all car #24)

JEAN-DENIS DELETRAZ (SUI; AGE: 32) 0 PTS

Pacific PR02-Ford V8
Pacific Grand Prix
Races: POR; EUR (both car #16)

PEDRO DINIZ (BRA; AGE: 25) 0 PTS

Forti FG01-Ford V8
Parmalat Forti Ford
Races: BRA; ARG; SMR; ESP; MON; CAN; FRA; GBR; GER; HUN; BEL; ITA; POR; EUR; PAC; JPN; AUS (all car #21)

BERTRAND GACHOT (BEL/FRA; AGE: 32) 0 PTS

Pacific PR02-Ford V8
Pacific Grand Prix
Races: BRA; ARG; SMR; ESP; MON; CAN; FRA; GBR; PAC; JPN; AUS (all car #16)

TAKI INOUE (JPN; AGE: 31) 0 PTS

Footwork FA16-Hart V8
Footwork Hart
Races: BRA; ARG; SMR; ESP; MON; CAN; FRA; GBR; GER; HUN; BEL; ITA; POR; EUR; PAC; JPN; AUS (all car #10)

UKYO KATAYAMA (JPN; AGE: 32) 0 PTS

Tyrrell 023-Yamaha V10
Nokia Tyrrell Yamaha
Races: BRA; ARG; SMR; ESP; MON; CAN; FRA; GBR; GER; HUN; BEL; ITA; POR; PAC; JPN; AUS (all car #3)

GIOVANNI LAVAGGI (ITA; AGE: 37) 0 PTS

Pacific PR02-Ford V8
Pacific Grand Prix
Races: GER; HUN; BEL; ITA (all car #16)

JAN MAGNUSSEN (DEN; AGE: 22) 0 PTS

McLaren MP4/10-Mercedes V10
Marlboro McLaren Mercedes
Races: PAC (car #8)

NIGEL MANSELL (GBR; AGE: 41) 0 PTS

McLaren MP4/10-Mercedes V10
Marlboro McLaren Mercedes
Races: SMR; ESP (both car #7)

PIERLUIGI MARTINI (ITA; AGE: 34) 0 PTS

Minardi M195-Ford V8
Minardi Scuderia Italia
Races: ARG; SMR; ESP; MON; CAN; FRA; GBR; GER (all car #23)

ANDREA MONTERMINI (ITA; AGE: 31) 0 PTS

Pacific PR02-Ford V8
Pacific Grand Prix
Races: BRA; ARG; SMR; MON; CAN; FRA; GBR; GER; HUN; BEL; ITA; POR; EUR; PAC; JPN; AUS (all car #17)

ROBERTO MORENO (BRA; AGE: 36) 0 PTS

Forti FG01-Ford V8
Parmalat Forti Ford
Races: BRA; ARG; SMR; ESP; MON; CAN; FRA; GBR; GER; HUN; BEL; ITA; POR; EUR; PAC; JPN; AUS (all car #22)

1995

CHAMPIONSHIP CAR-BY-CAR

MAX PAPIS (ITA; AGE: 25) 0 PTS

Footwork FA16-Hart V8
Footwork Hart
Races: GBR; GER; HUN; BEL; ITA; POR; EUR (all car #9)

MIMMO SCHIATTARELLA (ITA; AGE: 27) 0 PTS

Simtek S951-Ford V8
MTV Simtek Ford
Races: BRA; ARG; SMR; ESP; MON (all car #11)

GABRIELE TARQUINI (ITA; AGE: 33) 0 PTS

Tyrrell 023-Yamaha V10
Nokia Tyrrell Yamaha
Races: EUR (car #3)

JOS VERSTAPPEN (NED; AGE: 23) 0 PTS

Simtek S951-Ford V8
MTV Simtek Ford
Races: BRA; ARG; SMR; ESP; MON (all car #12)

KARL WENDLINGER (AUT; AGE: 26) 0 PTS

Sauber C14-Ford V10
Red Bull Sauber Ford
Races: BRA; ARG; SMR; ESP; JPN; AUS (all car #29)

GRAND PRIX WINNERS 1995

	RACE (CIRCUIT)	**WINNER** (CAR)
BRA	BRAZILIAN GRAND PRIX (INTERLAGOS)	MICHAEL SCHUMACHER (BENETTON B195-RENAULT V10)
ARG	ARGENTINE GRAND PRIX (BUENOS AIRES)	DAMON HILL (WILLIAMS FW17-RENAULT V10)
SMR	SAN MARINO GRAND PRIX (IMOLA)	DAMON HILL (WILLIAMS FW17-RENAULT V10)
ESP	SPANISH GRAND PRIX (CATALUNYA)	MICHAEL SCHUMACHER (BENETTON B195-RENAULT V10)
MON	MONACO GRAND PRIX (MONTE CARLO)	MICHAEL SCHUMACHER (BENETTON B195-RENAULT V10)
CAN	CANADIAN GRAND PRIX (MONTRÉAL)	JEAN ALESI (FERRARI 412T2 V12)
FRA	FRENCH GRAND PRIX (MAGNY-COURS)	MICHAEL SCHUMACHER (BENETTON B195-RENAULT V10)
GBR	BRITISH GRAND PRIX (SILVERSTONE)	JOHNNY HERBERT (BENETTON B195-RENAULT V10)
GER	GERMAN GRAND PRIX (HOCKENHEIM)	MICHAEL SCHUMACHER (BENETTON B195-RENAULT V10)
HUN	HUNGARIAN GRAND PRIX (HUNGARORING)	DAMON HILL (WILLIAMS FW17-RENAULT V10)
BEL	BELGIAN GRAND PRIX (SPA-FRANCORCHAMPS)	MICHAEL SCHUMACHER (BENETTON B195-RENAULT V10)
ITA	ITALIAN GRAND PRIX (MONZA)	JOHNNY HERBERT (BENETTON B195-RENAULT V10)
POR	PORTUGUESE GRAND PRIX (ESTORIL)	DAVID COULTHARD (WILLIAMS FW17-RENAULT V10)
EUR	EUROPEAN GRAND PRIX (NÜRBURGRING)	MICHAEL SCHUMACHER (BENETTON B195-RENAULT V10)
PAC	PACIFIC GRAND PRIX (TI CIRCUIT, AIDA)	MICHAEL SCHUMACHER (BENETTON B195-RENAULT V10)
JPN	JAPANESE GRAND PRIX (SUZUKA)	MICHAEL SCHUMACHER (BENETTON B195-RENAULT V10)
AUS	AUSTRALIAN GRAND PRIX (ADELAIDE)	DAMON HILL (WILLIAMS FW17B-RENAULT V10)

1996

HILL MAKES HISTORY – BUT VILLENEUVE RUNS HIM CLOSE

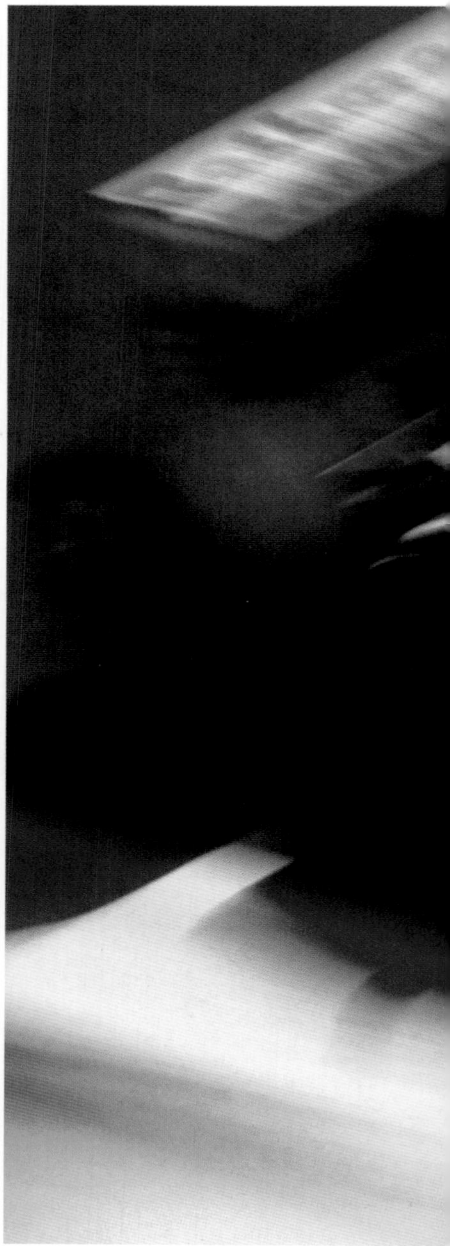

Left
Owed to joy: Damon Hill comes over all emotional after his title-clinching drive in Japan. In a nearby commentary box, meanwhile, Murray Walker was blubbing, too

Above
Pair of genes: Hill netted eight wins during the year to become the first son of a previous-generation F1 star to take the world crown

Right
In the court of the crimson king: the tifosi began their first-hand love affair with new Ferrari signing Michael Schumacher at Imola

Far Right
Talk torque: Heinz-Harald Frentzen and team boss Peter Sauber chat on the Melbourne grid ahead of an indifferent campaign but HHF would still sign for Williams by the end of the year

HILL STORMED TO EIGHT VICTORIES AND HIS ONLY REAL RIVAL WAS TEAM-MATE JACQUES VILLENEUVE. THE SON OF FORMER FERRARI LEGEND GILLES COMPLETED THE MOST SUCCESSFUL ROOKIE SEASON IN GRAND PRIX HISTORY

Top
Flair Canada: Jacques Villeneuve leaves the pits in Budapest en route to the third of his four wins

Opposite page, top
Olivier's army: marshals greet surprise Monaco victor Panis, who has just scored Ligier's first win since September 1981

Opposite page, bottom
Question time: Coulthard raced with a borrowed Schumacher helmet in Monaco and ensured himself a permanent place in future pub quiz books

Right
Herr we go, Herr we go, Herr we go: formerly an ocean of blue, Hockenheim was now officially a sea of red

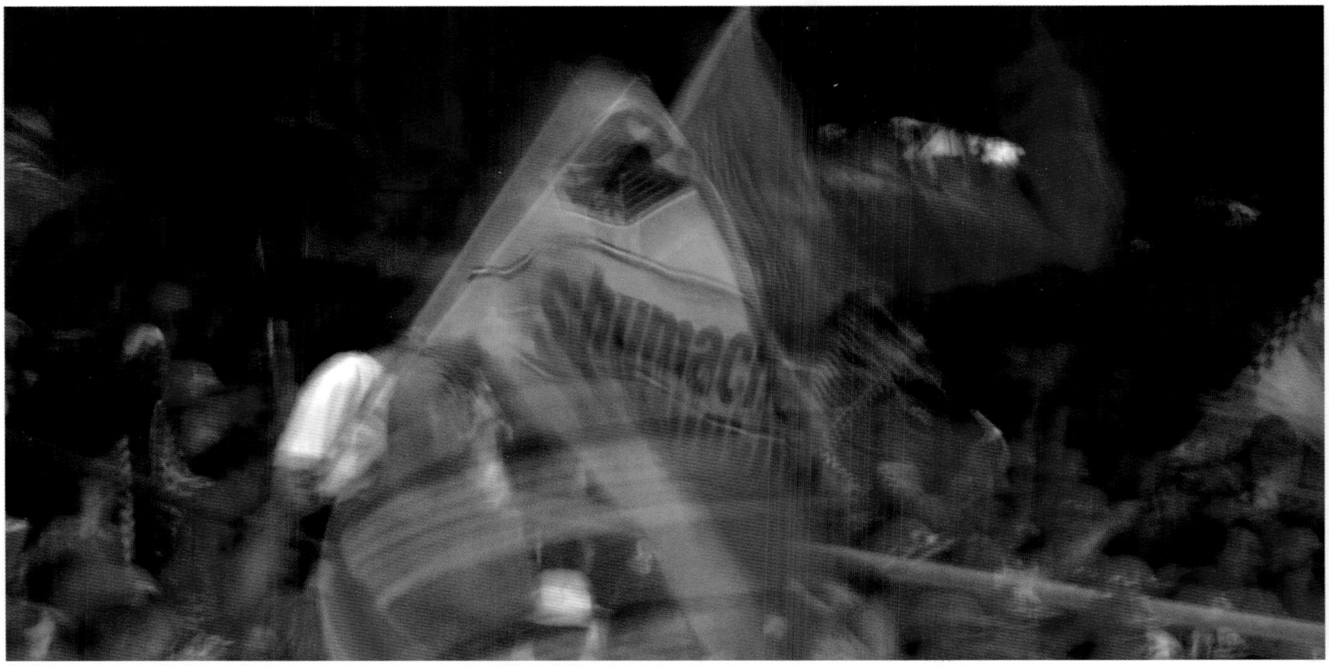

Michael Schumacher appeared to have done the unthinkable by leaving Benetton in the wake of back-to-back world titles. He transferred to Ferrari – a proud name but in many ways a bare shell of a team. He'd been encouraged when he'd tested its 1995 car but hugely disappointed when he'd subsequently tried the new F310, Ferrari's first V10-powered Formula One racer. He knew immediately he was in for a tough season – and he was right. Only his deft touch allowed him to win three races – Spain, Spa and Monza – and at no stage was he a championship threat.

All this represented the best possible chance for Damon Hill and Williams – and they capitalised superbly. At the wheel of his Renault-powered FW18, Hill stormed to eight victories and his only real rival was team-mate Jacques Villeneuve. Hill sealed the title in true champion's fashion with a dominant drive in the Japanese finale at Suzuka.

By finishing as runner-up, Villeneuve – son of former Ferrari legend Gilles – completed the most successful rookie season in grand prix history. Arriving in F1 as winner of the prestigious, US-based Champ Car series, he got off to a flying start by taking pole position in Australia. Only a damaged oil pipe, caused by a late trip across the grass, cost him victory in that first race.

He scored his maiden win at the Nürburgring after withstanding intense pressure from Schumacher – but it was in Estoril, Portugal, that he really made his mark. He passed Schumacher around the outside of the ultra-fast final corner, a move that caught the F1 world's attention and laid an exciting marker for the future.

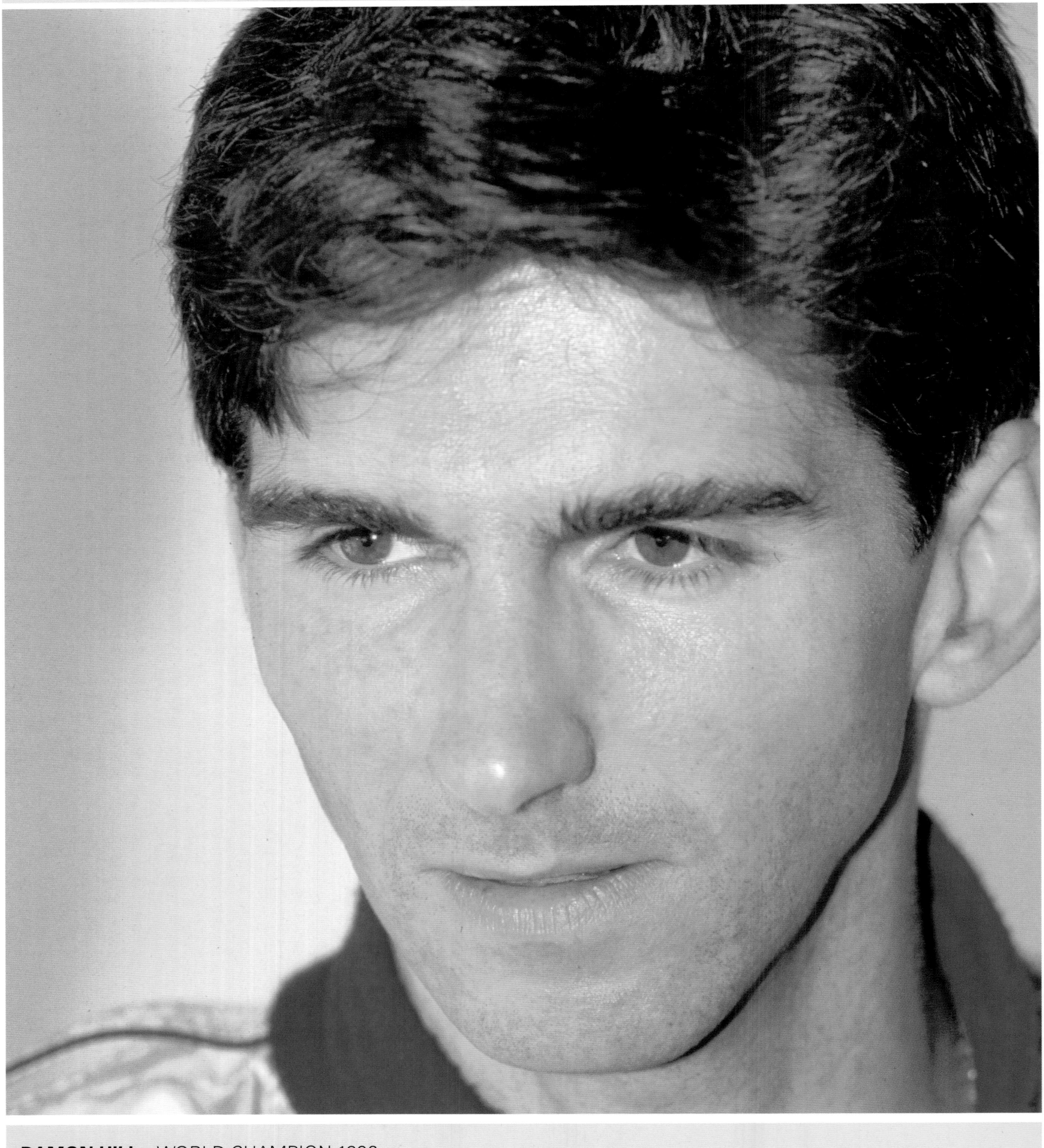

DAMON HILL – WORLD CHAMPION 1996

1996

CHAMPIONSHIP CAR-BY-CAR

1ST DAMON HILL (GBR; AGE: 35) 97 PTS

Williams FW18-Renault V10
Rothmans Williams Renault
Races: AUS; BRA; ARG; EUR; SMR; MON; ESP; CAN; FRA; GBR; GER; HUN; BEL; ITA; POR; JPN (all car #5)

2ND JACQUES VILLENEUVE (CAN; AGE: 25) 78 PTS

Williams FW18-Renault V10
Rothmans Williams Renault
Races: AUS; BRA; ARG; EUR; SMR; MON; ESP; CAN; FRA; GBR; GER; HUN; BEL; ITA; POR; JPN (all car #6)

3RD MICHAEL SCHUMACHER (GER; AGE: 27) 59 PTS

Ferrari F310 V10
Scuderia Ferrari
Races: AUS; BRA; ARG; EUR; SMR; MON; ESP; CAN; GBR; GER; HUN; BEL; ITA; POR; JPN (all car #1)

4TH JEAN ALESI (FRA; AGE: 32) 47 PTS

Benetton B196-Renault V10
Mild Seven Benetton Renault
Races: AUS; BRA; ARG; EUR; SMR; MON; ESP; CAN; FRA; GBR; GER; HUN; BEL; ITA; POR; JPN (all car #3)

5TH MIKA HÄKKINEN (FIN; AGE: 27) 31 PTS

McLaren MP4/11-Mercedes V10
Marlboro McLaren Mercedes
Races: AUS; BRA; ARG; EUR; SMR; MON; ESP; CAN; FRA; GBR; GER; HUN; BEL; ITA; POR; JPN (all car #7)

6TH GERHARD BERGER (AUT; AGE: 36) 21 PTS

Benetton B196-Renault V10
Mild Seven Benetton Renault
Races: AUS; BRA; ARG; EUR; SMR; MON; ESP; CAN; FRA; GBR; GER; HUN; BEL; ITA; POR; JPN (all car #4)

7TH DAVID COULTHARD (GBR; AGE: 25) 18 PTS

McLaren MP4/11-Mercedes V10
Marlboro McLaren Mercedes
Races: AUS; BRA; ARG; EUR; SMR; MON; ESP; CAN; FRA; GBR; GER; HUN; BEL; ITA; POR; JPN (all car #8)

8TH RUBENS BARRICHELLO (BRA; AGE: 24) 14 PTS

Jordan 196-Peugeot V10
Benson & Hedges Total Jordan Peugeot
Races: AUS; BRA; ARG; EUR; SMR; MON; ESP; CAN; FRA; GBR; GER; HUN; BEL; ITA; POR; JPN (all car #11)

9TH OLIVIER PANIS (FRA; AGE: 29) 13 PTS

Ligier JS43-Mugen V10
Ligier Gauloises Blondes
Races: AUS; BRA; ARG; EUR; SMR; MON; ESP; CAN; FRA; GBR; GER; HUN; BEL; ITA; POR; JPN (all car #9)

10TH EDDIE IRVINE (GBR; AGE: 30) 11 PTS

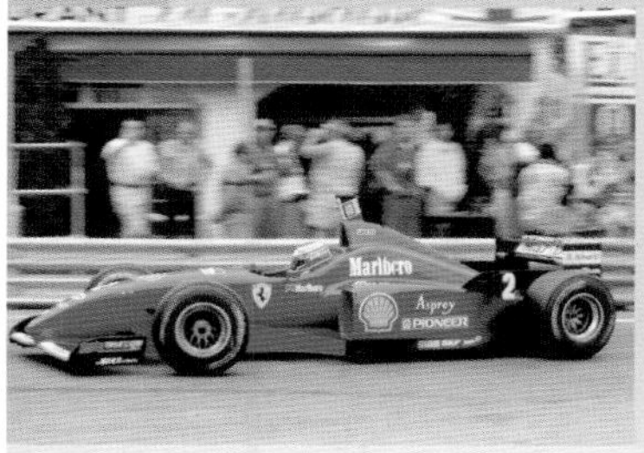

Ferrari F310 V10
Scuderia Ferrari
Races: AUS; BRA; ARG; EUR; SMR; MON; ESP; CAN; FRA; GBR; GER; HUN; BEL; ITA; POR; JPN (all car #2)

11TH MARTIN BRUNDLE (GBR; AGE: 37) 8 PTS

Jordan 196-Peugeot V10
Benson & Hedges Total Jordan Peugeot
Races: AUS; BRA; ARG; EUR; SMR; MON; ESP; CAN; FRA; GBR; GER; HUN; BEL; ITA; POR; JPN (all car #12)

12TH HEINZ-HARALD FRENTZEN (GER; AGE: 29) 7 PTS

Sauber C15-Ford V10
Red Bull Sauber Ford
Races: AUS; BRA; ARG; EUR; SMR; MON; ESP; CAN; FRA; GBR; GER; HUN; BEL; ITA; POR; JPN (all car #15)

13TH MIKA SALO (FIN; AGE: 29) 5 PTS

Tyrrell 024-Yamaha V10
Tyrrell Yamaha
Races: AUS; BRA; ARG; EUR; SMR; MON; ESP; CAN; FRA; GBR; GER; HUN; BEL; ITA; POR; JPN (all car #19)

14TH JOHNNY HERBERT (GBR; AGE: 32) 4 PTS

Sauber C15-Ford V10
Red Bull Sauber Ford
Races: AUS; BRA; ARG; EUR; SMR; MON; ESP; CAN; FRA; GBR; GER; HUN; BEL; ITA; POR; JPN (all car #14)

15TH PEDRO DINIZ (BRA; AGE: 26) 2 PTS

Ligier JS43-Mugen V10
Ligier Gauloises Blondes
Races: AUS; BRA; ARG; EUR; SMR; MON; ESP; CAN; FRA; GBR; GER; HUN; BEL; ITA; POR; JPN (all car #10)

1996

CHAMPIONSHIP CAR-BY-CAR

JOS VERSTAPPEN (NED; AGE: 24) 1 PT

Footwork FA17-Hart V8
Footwork Hart
Races: AUS; BRA; ARG; EUR; SMR; MON; ESP; CAN; FRA; GBR; GER; HUN; BEL; ITA; POR; JPN (all car #17)

LUCA BADOER (ITA; AGE: 25) 0 PTS

Forti FG01B-Ford V8
Forti Grand Prix
Races: BRA; ARG; MON (all car #22)

LUCA BADOER (CONTD)

Forti FG03-Ford V8
Forti Grand Prix
Races: SMR; CAN; FRA (all car #22)

PICTURED DURING GBR PRACTICE

GIANCARLO FISICHELLA (ITA; AGE: 23) 0 PTS

Minardi M195B-Ford V8
Minardi Team
Races: AUS; EUR; SMR; MON; ESP; CAN; FRA; GBR (all car #21)

UKYO KATAYAMA (JPN; AGE: 33) 0 PTS

Tyrrell 024-Yamaha V10
Tyrrell Yamaha
Races: AUS; BRA; ARG; EUR; SMR; MON; ESP; CAN; FRA; GBR; GER; HUN; BEL; ITA; POR; JPN (all car #18)

PEDRO LAMY (POR; AGE: 24) 0 PTS

Minardi M195B-Ford V8
Minardi Team
Races: AUS; BRA; ARG; EUR; SMR; MON; ESP; CAN; FRA; GBR; GER; HUN; BEL; ITA; POR; JPN (all car #20)

GIOVANNI LAVAGGI (ITA; AGE: 38) 0 PTS

Minardi M195B-Ford V8
Minardi Team
Races: HUN; ITA; POR (all car #21)

PICTURED DURING GER PRACTICE

TARSO MARQUES (BRA; AGE: 20) 0 PTS

Minardi M195B-Ford V8
Minardi Team
Races: BRA; ARG (both car #21)

ANDREA MONTERMINI (ITA; AGE: 32) 0 PTS

Forti FG01B-Ford V8
Forti Grand Prix
Races: BRA; ARG (both car #23)

PICTURED DURING SMR PRACTICE

ANDREA MONTERMINI (CONTD)

Forti FG03-Ford V8
Forti Grand Prix
Races: CAN; FRA (both car #23)

RICARDO ROSSET (BRA; AGE: 27) 0 PTS

Footwork FA17-Hart V8
Footwork Hart
Races: AUS; BRA; ARG; EUR; SMR; MON; ESP; CAN; FRA; GBR; GER; HUN; BEL; ITA; POR; JPN (all car #16)

1996

CHAMPIONSHIP CAR-BY-CAR

GRAND PRIX WINNERS 1996

	RACE (CIRCUIT)	WINNER (CAR)
AUS	AUSTRALIAN GRAND PRIX (ALBERT PARK)	DAMON HILL (WILLIAMS FW18-RENAULT V10)
BRA	BRAZILIAN GRAND PRIX (INTERLAGOS)	DAMON HILL (WILLIAMS FW18-RENAULT V10)
ARG	ARGENTINE GRAND PRIX (BUENOS AIRES)	DAMON HILL (WILLIAMS FW18-RENAULT V10)
EUR	EUROPEAN GRAND PRIX (NÜRBURGRING)	JACQUES VILLENEUVE (WILLIAMS FW18-RENAULT V10)
SMR	SAN MARINO GRAND PRIX (IMOLA)	DAMON HILL (WILLIAMS FW18-RENAULT V10)
MON	MONACO GRAND PRIX (MONTE CARLO)	OLIVIER PANIS (LIGIER JS43-MUGEN V10)
ESP	SPANISH GRAND PRIX (CATALUNYA)	MICHAEL SCHUMACHER (FERRARI F310 V10)
CAN	CANADIAN GRAND PRIX (MONTRÉAL)	DAMON HILL (WILLIAMS FW18-RENAULT V10)
FRA	FRENCH GRAND PRIX (MAGNY-COURS)	DAMON HILL (WILLIAMS FW18-RENAULT V10)
GBR	BRITISH GRAND PRIX (SILVERSTONE)	JACQUES VILLENEUVE (WILLIAMS FW18-RENAULT V10)
GER	GERMAN GRAND PRIX (HOCKENHEIM)	DAMON HILL (WILLIAMS FW18-RENAULT V10)
HUN	HUNGARIAN GRAND PRIX (HUNGARORING)	JACQUES VILLENEUVE (WILLIAMS FW18-RENAULT V10)
BEL	BELGIAN GRAND PRIX (SPA-FRANCORCHAMPS)	MICHAEL SCHUMACHER (FERRARI F310 V10)
ITA	ITALIAN GRAND PRIX (MONZA)	MICHAEL SCHUMACHER (FERRARI F310 V10)
POR	PORTUGUESE GRAND PRIX (ESTORIL)	JACQUES VILLENEUVE (WILLIAMS FW18-RENAULT V10)
JPN	JAPANESE GRAND PRIX (SUZUKA)	DAMON HILL (WILLIAMS FW18-RENAULT V10)

GERHARD BERGER

1997

VILLENEUVE ON TOP AS SCHUEY FINDS CRIME FAILS TO PAY

Left
Wheels meet again: Jacques Villeneuve lunges inside Michael Schumacher at Jerez. A millisecond later the German suffered the consequences of his forceful defence and slithered into the gravel, his title hopes shot

Top
Young bucks fizz: Villeneuve sprays the bubbly in Argentina with F1's latest Schumacher. Ralf made the podium in only his third GP (it took Michael eight)

Above
Tough at the top: Williams newcomer Frentzen had a difficult season and won only once, at Imola

Armed with a year's Formula One experience and the sport's fastest car in the shape of the Williams-Renault FW19, Jacques Villeneuve was ready to stage a full world championship onslaught. He was ultimately successful – but first he had to contain the savage challenge of Michael Schumacher and Ferrari.

Williams won four of the opening six races because Ferrari's new car was not quite on the pace. And Villeneuve was very much team leader following the departure of Damon Hill, whose replacement Heinz-Harald Frentzen couldn't find the consistency to challenge the French-Canadian.

Schumacher used his natural brilliance to dominate at Monaco and kept himself in the title hunt by taking full advantage when Villeneuve crashed out of his home event in Montreal. Ferrari's development then began to kick in and Schumacher's victory during the penultimate race in Japan – his fifth of the season – set up a title showdown prior to the Grand Prix of Europe in Jerez, Spain.

Schumacher was leading when Villeneuve attempted an outbraking manoeuvre from a long way back. In a split-second of desperation Schumacher tried to force his adversary off the road, but succeeded only in putting himself in the gravel. Unlike Adelaide three years earlier, his professional foul failed to come off and the Williams driver was champion. By way of punishment, the sport's authorities later stripped Schumacher of second place in the title race.

Right
Seconds away, round one: Frentzen made a flying start to his Williams career in Melbourne – until his brakes overheated. The following Villeneuve was bundled off in a multiple shunt at the first corner

Bottom left
Stop me and fry one: engine failure caused Prost driver Jarno Trulli to spin while practising at Monza. Having started the season with Minardi, the Italian rookie switched to Prost after Olivier Panis sustained leg injuries in the Canadian GP. Impressively, he led in Austria until another V10 went bang

Bottom right
No smoke without tyre: Mika Häkkinen pushes his Goodyears to the limit at the Nürburgring

Bottom centre
I'd like to teach the world champion to sing: Damon Hill was never going to be able to defend his title in an Arrows, although he came close to scoring a shock victory in Budapest. He also starred on stage at Silverstone

SCHUMACHER TRIED TO FORCE HIS ADVERSARY OFF THE ROAD, BUT SUCCEEDED ONLY IN PUTTING HIMSELF IN THE GRAVEL. UNLIKE ADELAIDE THREE YEARS EARLIER, HIS PROFESSIONAL FOUL FAILED TO COME OFF

JACQUES VILLENEUVE – WORLD CHAMPION 1997

1997

CHAMPIONSHIP CAR-BY-CAR

1ST JACQUES VILLENEUVE (CAN; AGE: 26) 81 PTS

Williams FW19-Renault V10
Rothmans Williams Renault
Races: AUS; BRA; ARG; SMR; MON; ESP; CAN; FRA; GBR; GER; HUN; BEL; ITA; AUT; LUX; JPN; EUR (all car #3)

DSQ MICHAEL SCHUMACHER (GER; AGE: 28) 0(+78) PTS

Ferrari F310B V10
Scuderia Ferrari Marlboro
Races: AUS; BRA; ARG; SMR; MON; ESP; CAN; FRA; GBR; GER; HUN; BEL; ITA; AUT; LUX; JPN; EUR (all car #5)

2ND HEINZ-HARALD FRENTZEN (GER; AGE: 30) 42 PTS

Williams FW19-Renault V10
Rothmans Williams Renault
Races: AUS; BRA; ARG; SMR; MON; ESP; CAN; FRA; GBR; GER; HUN; BEL; ITA; AUT; LUX; JPN; EUR (all car #4)

3RD DAVID COULTHARD (GBR; AGE: 26) 36 PTS

McLaren MP4/12-Mercedes V10
West McLaren Mercedes
Races: AUS; BRA; ARG; SMR; MON; ESP; CAN; FRA; GBR; GER; HUN; BEL; ITA; AUT; LUX; JPN; EUR (all car #10)

4TH JEAN ALESI (FRA; AGE: 33) 36 PTS

Benetton B197-Renault V10
Mild Seven Benetton Renault
Races: AUS; BRA; ARG; SMR; MON; ESP; CAN; FRA; GBR; GER; HUN; BEL; ITA; AUT; LUX; JPN; EUR (all car #7)

5TH GERHARD BERGER (AUT; AGE: 37) 27 PTS

Benetton B197-Renault V10
Mild Seven Benetton Renault
Races: AUS; BRA; ARG; SMR; MON; ESP; GER; HUN; BEL; ITA; AUT; LUX; JPN; EUR (all car #8)

6TH MIKA HÄKKINEN (FIN; AGE: 28) 27 PTS

McLaren MP4/12-Mercedes V10
West McLaren Mercedes
Races: AUS; BRA; ARG; SMR; MON; ESP; CAN; FRA; GBR; GER; HUN; BEL; ITA; AUT; LUX; JPN; EUR (all car #9)

7TH EDDIE IRVINE (GBR; AGE: 31) 24 PTS

Ferrari F310B V10
Scuderia Ferrari Marlboro
Races: AUS; BRA; ARG; SMR; MON; ESP; CAN; FRA; GBR; GER; HUN; BEL; ITA; AUT; LUX; JPN; EUR (all car #6)

8TH GIANCARLO FISICHELLA (ITA; AGE: 24) 20 PTS

Jordan 197-Peugeot V10
Benson & Hedges Jordan Peugeot
Races: AUS; BRA; ARG; SMR; MON; ESP; CAN; FRA; GBR; GER; HUN; BEL; ITA; AUT; LUX; JPN; EUR (all car #12)

9TH OLIVIER PANIS (FRA; AGE: 30) 16 PTS

Prost JS45-Mugen V10
Prost Gauloises Blondes
Races: AUS; BRA; ARG; SMR; MON; ESP; CAN; LUX; JPN; EUR (all car #14)

10TH JOHNNY HERBERT (GBR; AGE: 33) 15 PTS

Sauber C16-Petronas V10
Red Bull Sauber Petronas
Races: AUS; BRA; ARG; SMR; MON; ESP; CAN; FRA; GBR; GER; HUN; BEL; ITA; AUT; LUX; JPN; EUR (all car #16)

11TH RALF SCHUMACHER (GER; AGE: 22) 13 PTS

Jordan 197-Peugeot V10
Benson & Hedges Jordan Peugeot
Races: AUS; BRA; ARG; SMR; MON; ESP; CAN; FRA; GBR; GER; HUN; BEL; ITA; AUT; LUX; JPN; EUR (all car #11)

12TH DAMON HILL (GBR; AGE: 36) 7 PTS

Arrows A18-Yamaha V10
Danka Arrows Yamaha
Races: BRA; ARG; SMR; MON; ESP; CAN; FRA; GBR; GER; HUN; BEL; ITA; AUT; LUX; JPN; EUR (all car #1)

13TH RUBENS BARRICHELLO (BRA; AGE: 25) 6 PTS

Stewart SF1-Ford V10
Stewart Ford
Races: AUS; BRA; ARG; SMR; MON; ESP; CAN; FRA; GBR; GER; HUN; BEL; ITA; AUT; LUX; JPN; EUR (all car #22)

14TH ALEX WURZ (AUT; AGE: 23) 4 PTS

Benetton B197-Renault V10
Mild Seven Benetton Renault
Races: CAN; FRA; GBR (all car #8)

1997

CHAMPIONSHIP CAR-BY-CAR

15TH JARNO TRULLI (ITA; AGE: 22) 3 PTS

Minardi M197-Hart V8
Minardi Team
Races: AUS; BRA; ARG; MON; ESP; CAN (all car #21)

JARNO TRULLI (CONTD)

Prost JS45-Mugen V10
Prost Gauloises Blondes
Races: FRA; GBR; GER; HUN; BEL; ITA; AUT (all car #14)

16TH PEDRO DINIZ (BRA; AGE: 27) 2 PTS

Arrows A18-Yamaha V10
Danka Arrows Yamaha
Races: AUS; BRA; ARG; SMR; MON; ESP; CAN; FRA; GBR; GER; HUN; BEL; ITA; AUT; LUX; JPN; EUR (all car #2)

17TH MIKA SALO (FIN; AGE: 30) 2 PTS

Tyrrell 025-Ford V8
Tyrrell Racing Organisation
Races: AUS; BRA; ARG; SMR; MON; ESP; CAN; FRA; GBR; GER; HUN; BEL; ITA; AUT; LUX; JPN; EUR (all car #19)

18TH SHINJI NAKANO (JPN; AGE: 26) 2 PTS

Prost JS45-Mugen V10
Prost Gauloises Blondes
Races: AUS; BRA; ARG; SMR; MON; ESP; CAN; FRA; GBR; GER; HUN; BEL; ITA; AUT; LUX; JPN; EUR (all car #15)

19TH NICOLA LARINI (ITA; AGE: 33) 1 PT

Sauber C16-Petronas V10
Red Bull Sauber Petronas
Races: AUS; BRA; ARG; SMR; MON (all car #17)

NORBERTO FONTANA (ARG; AGE: 22) 0 PTS

Sauber C16-Petronas V10
Red Bull Sauber Petronas
Races: FRA; GBR; GER; EUR (all car #17)

UKYO KATAYAMA (JPN; AGE: 34) 0 PTS

Minardi M197-Hart V8
Minardi Team
Races: AUS; BRA; ARG; SMR; MON; ESP; CAN; FRA; GBR; GER; HUN; BEL; ITA; AUT; LUX; JPN; EUR (all car #20)

JAN MAGNUSSEN (DEN; AGE: 24) 0 PTS

Stewart SF1-Ford V10
Stewart Ford
Races: AUS; BRA; ARG; SMR; MON; ESP; CAN; FRA; GBR; GER; HUN; BEL; ITA; AUT; LUX; JPN; EUR (all car #23)

TARSO MARQUES (BRA; AGE: 21) 0 PTS

Minardi M197-Hart V8
Minardi Team
Races: FRA; GBR; GER; HUN; BEL; ITA; LUX; JPN; EUR (all car #21)

GIANNI MORBIDELLI (ITA; AGE: 29) 0 PTS

Sauber C16-Petronas V10
Red Bull Sauber Petronas
Races: ESP; CAN; HUN; BEL; ITA; AUT; LUX (all car #17)

JOS VERSTAPPEN (NED; AGE: 25) 0 PTS

Tyrrell 025-Ford V8
Tyrrell Racing Organisation
Races: AUS; BRA; ARG; SMR; MON; ESP; CAN; FRA; GBR; GER; HUN; BEL; ITA; AUT; LUX; JPN; EUR (all car #18)

1997

CHAMPIONSHIP CAR-BY-CAR

GRAND PRIX WINNERS 1997

	RACE (CIRCUIT)	WINNER (CAR)
AUS	AUSTRALIAN GRAND PRIX (ALBERT PARK)	DAVID COULTHARD (McLAREN MP4/12-MERCEDES V10)
BRA	BRAZILIAN GRAND PRIX (INTERLAGOS)	JACQUES VILLENEUVE (WILLIAMS FW19-RENAULT V10)
ARG	ARGENTINE GRAND PRIX (BUENOS AIRES)	JACQUES VILLENEUVE (WILLIAMS FW19-RENAULT V10)
SMR	SAN MARINO GRAND PRIX (IMOLA)	HEINZ-HARALD FRENTZEN (WILLIAMS FW19-RENAULT V10)
MON	MONACO GRAND PRIX (MONTE CARLO)	MICHAEL SCHUMACHER (FERRARI F310B V10)
ESP	SPANISH GRAND PRIX (CATALUNYA)	JACQUES VILLENEUVE (WILLIAMS FW19-RENAULT V10)
CAN	CANADIAN GRAND PRIX (MONTRÉAL)	MICHAEL SCHUMACHER (FERRARI F310B V10)
FRA	FRENCH GRAND PRIX (MAGNY-COURS)	MICHAEL SCHUMACHER (FERRARI F310B V10)
GBR	BRITISH GRAND PRIX (SILVERSTONE)	JACQUES VILLENEUVE (WILLIAMS FW19-RENAULT V10)
GER	GERMAN GRAND PRIX (HOCKENHEIM)	GERHARD BERGER (BENETTON B197-RENAULT V10)
HUN	HUNGARIAN GRAND PRIX (HUNGARORING)	JACQUES VILLENEUVE (WILLIAMS FW19-RENAULT V10)
BEL	BELGIAN GRAND PRIX (SPA-FRANCORCHAMPS)	MICHAEL SCHUMACHER (FERRARI F310B V10)
ITA	ITALIAN GRAND PRIX (MONZA)	DAVID COULTHARD (McLAREN MP4/12-MERCEDES V10)
AUT	AUSTRIAN GRAND PRIX (A1 RING)	JACQUES VILLENEUVE (WILLIAMS FW19-RENAULT V10)
LUX	LUXEMBOURG GRAND PRIX (NÜRBURGRING)	JACQUES VILLENEUVE (WILLIAMS FW19-RENAULT V10)
JPN	JAPANESE GRAND PRIX (SUZUKA)	MICHAEL SCHUMACHER (FERRARI F310B V10)
EUR	EUROPEAN GRAND PRIX (JEREZ)	MIKA HÄKKINEN (McLAREN MP4/12-MERCEDES V10)

DAVID COULTHARD

1998

McLAREN RETURNS TO PEAK FITNESS

Far left
Vanishing point: David Coulthard cedes the lead to team-mate Mika Häkkinen in Australia, thousands of people tear up suddenly worthless betting slips and the Finn scorches away in the general direction of a first world title

Above
Resistance is fertile: Alexander Wurz (left) gives as good as he gets while under attack from Schumacher in Monaco

Left
No parking zone: Jarno Trulli's Prost comes to rest halfway up Jean Alesi's Sauber. It took a couple of attempts to get the 1998 Canadian GP started…

In the first year of the new narrow-track/grooved-tyre regulations, McLaren finally returned from its post-Senna blues – and did so in devastating fashion. The latest rules coincided with aerodynamic genius Adrian Newey presiding over his first design for the team and the former Williams man's MP4/13 chassis set the standard. Mika Häkkinen took eight victories in the effective silver machine and team-mate David Coulthard, who often acted as the Finn's tail-gunner during the second half of the season, won once.

Ferrari was taken aback by McLaren's early-season pace on its freshly-acquired Bridgestone rubber. In partnership with tyre supplier Goodyear (destined to quit at the end of the campaign, after a 33-year stint in Formula One), the Italian team began a ferocious development programme that was soon reaping rewards and Michael Schumacher went to the last race with a chance of pinching the title. All he had to do was beat Hakkinen.

It didn't quite work out like that. Schuey stalled before the final parade lap and caused the start to be delayed – which meant he had to line up at the back rather than on pole. Häkkinen took full advantage to storm away into the lead. Schumacher clambered through the field and worked his way into third, but a puncture finally put him out of contention. Häkkinen duly took his maiden F1 title and McLaren became world champion constructor for the first time in seven years.

Bereft of a) a factory engine and b) Newey's talent, Williams struggled to look remotely like a defending champion and failed to register a win.

In contrast, Jordan Grand Prix scored its breakthrough victory at Spa, where Damon Hill led Ralf Schumacher to a team one-two.

Above
Leap of faith: Michael Schumacher shows how it feels to win for Ferrari at Monza. In another life he might have been a goalkeeper. Or a member of Steps. Or Stan Laurel

Right
Another page, another damaged Sauber: Johnny Herbert clattered into Häkkinen at Spa after Schuey tipped the Finn into a spin

Top
Once bitten, twice Sly: Hollywood star Sylvester Stallone's movie research made him a frequent grand prix visitor for a while. Here he interrupts Jacques Villeneuve's pre-race reverie in Monaco

MIKA HÄKKINEN – WORLD CHAMPION 1998 & 1999

1998

CHAMPIONSHIP CAR-BY-CAR

1ST MIKA HÄKKINEN (FIN; AGE: 29) 100 PTS

McLaren MP4/13-Mercedes V10
West McLaren Mercedes
Races: AUS; BRA; ARG; SMR; ESP; MON; CAN; FRA; GBR; AUT; GER; HUN; BEL; ITA; LUX; JPN
(all car #8)

2ND MICHAEL SCHUMACHER (GER; AGE: 29) 86 PTS

Ferrari F300 V10
Scuderia Ferrari Marlboro
Races: AUS; BRA; ARG; SMR; ESP; MON; CAN; FRA; GBR; AUT; GER; HUN; BEL; ITA; LUX; JPN
(all car #3)

3RD DAVID COULTHARD (GBR; AGE: 27) 56 PTS

McLaren MP4/13-Mercedes V10
West McLaren Mercedes
Races: AUS; BRA; ARG; SMR; ESP; MON; CAN; FRA; GBR; AUT; GER; HUN; BEL; ITA; LUX; JPN
(all car #7)

4TH EDDIE IRVINE (GBR; AGE: 32) 47 PTS

Ferrari F300 V10
Scuderia Ferrari Marlboro
Races: AUS; BRA; ARG; SMR; ESP; MON; CAN; FRA; GBR; AUT; GER; HUN; BEL; ITA; LUX; JPN
(all car #4)

5TH JACQUES VILLENEUVE (CAN; AGE: 27) 21 PTS

Williams FW20-Mecachrome V10
Winfield Williams
Races: AUS; BRA; ARG; SMR; ESP; MON; CAN; FRA; GBR; AUT; GER; HUN; BEL; ITA; LUX; JPN
(all car #1)

6TH DAMON HILL (GBR; AGE: 37) 20 PTS

Jordan 198-Mugen V10
Benson & Hedges Jordan Mugen Honda
Races: AUS; BRA; ARG; SMR; ESP; MON; CAN; FRA; GBR; AUT; GER; HUN; BEL; ITA; LUX; JPN
(all car #9)

7TH HEINZ-HARALD FRENTZEN (GER; AGE: 31) 17 PTS

Williams FW20-Mecachrome V10
Winfield Williams
Races: AUS; BRA; ARG; SMR; ESP; MON; CAN; FRA; GBR; AUT; GER; HUN; BEL; ITA; LUX; JPN
(all car #2)

6TH ALEX WURZ (AUT; AGE: 24) 17 PTS

Benetton B198-Playlife V10
Mild Seven Benetton Playlife
Races: AUS; BRA; ARG; SMR; ESP; MON; CAN; FRA; GBR; AUT; GER; HUN; BEL; ITA; LUX; JPN
(all car #6)

9TH GIANCARLO FISICHELLA (ITA; AGE: 25) 16 PTS

Benetton B198-Playlife V10
Mild Seven Benetton Playlife
Races: AUS; BRA; ARG; SMR; ESP; MON; CAN; FRA; GBR; AUT; GER; HUN; BEL; ITA; LUX; JPN
(all car #5)

10TH RALF SCHUMACHER (GER; AGE: 23) 14 PTS

Jordan 198-Mugen V10
Benson & Hedges Jordan Mugen Honda
Races: AUS; BRA; ARG; SMR; ESP; MON; CAN; FRA; GBR; AUT; GER; HUN; BEL; ITA; LUX; JPN
(all car #10)

11TH JEAN ALESI (FRA; AGE: 34) 9 PTS

Sauber C17-Petronas V10
Red Bull Sauber Petronas
Races: AUS; BRA; ARG; SMR; ESP; MON; CAN; FRA; GBR; AUT; GER; HUN; BEL; ITA; LUX; JPN
(all car #14)

12TH RUBENS BARRICHELLO (BRA; AGE: 26) 4 PTS

Stewart SF2-Ford V10
Stewart Ford
Races: AUS; BRA; ARG; SMR; ESP; MON; CAN; FRA; GBR; AUT; GER; HUN; BEL; ITA; LUX; JPN
(all car #18)

13TH MIKA SALO (FIN; AGE: 31) 3 PTS

Arrows A19 V10
Danka Zepter Arrows
Races: AUS; BRA; ARG; SMR; ESP; MON; CAN; FRA; GBR; AUT; GER; HUN; BEL; ITA; LUX; JPN
(all car #17)

14TH PEDRO DINIZ (BRA; AGE: 28) 3 PTS

Arrows A19 V10
Danka Zepter Arrows
Races: AUS; BRA; ARG; SMR; ESP; MON; CAN; FRA; GBR; AUT; GER; HUN; BEL; ITA; LUX; JPN
(all car #16)

15TH JOHNNY HERBERT (GBR; AGE: 34) 1 PT

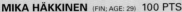

Sauber C17-Petronas V10
Red Bull Sauber Petronas
Races: AUS; BRA; ARG; SMR; ESP; MON; CAN; FRA; GBR; AUT; GER; HUN; BEL; ITA; LUX; JPN
(all car #15)

1998

CHAMPIONSHIP CAR-BY-CAR

16TH JAN MAGNUSSEN (DEN; AGE: 24) 1 PT

Stewart SF2-Ford V10
Stewart Ford
Races: AUS; BRA; ARG; SMR; ESP; MON; CAN (all car #19)

17TH JARNO TRULLI (ITA; AGE: 24) 1 PT

Prost AP01-Peugeot V10
Gauloises Prost Peugeot
Races: AUS; BRA; ARG; SMR; ESP; MON; CAN; FRA; GBR; AUT; GER; HUN; BEL; ITA; LUX; JPN (all car #12)

SHINJI NAKANO (JPN; AGE: 27) 0 PTS

Minardi M198-Ford V10
Fondmetal Minardi Ford
Races: AUS; BRA; ARG; SMR; ESP; MON; CAN; FRA; GBR; AUT; GER; HUN; BEL; ITA; LUX; JPN (all car #22)

OLIVIER PANIS (FRA; AGE: 31) 0 PTS

Prost AP01-Peugeot V10
Gauloises Prost Peugeot
Races: AUS; BRA; ARG; SMR; ESP; MON; CAN; FRA; GBR; AUT; GER; HUN; BEL; ITA; LUX; JPN (all car #11)

RICARDO ROSSET (BRA; AGE: 29) 0 PTS

Tyrrell 026-Ford V10
Tyrrell Ford
Races: AUS; BRA; ARG; SMR; CAN; FRA; GBR; AUT; BEL; ITA; LUX (all car #20)

TORANOSUKE TAKAGI (JPN; AGE: 24) 0 PTS

Tyrrell 026-Ford V10
Tyrrell Ford
Races: AUS; BRA; ARG; SMR; ESP; MON; CAN; FRA; GBR; AUT; GER; HUN; BEL; ITA; LUX; JPN (all car #21)

ESTEBAN TUERO (ARG; AGE: 20) 0 PTS

Minardi M198-Ford V10
Fondmetal Minardi Ford
Races: AUS; BRA; ARG; SMR; ESP; MON; CAN; FRA; GBR; AUT; GER; HUN; BEL; ITA; LUX; JPN (all car #23)

JOS VERSTAPPEN (NED; AGE: 26) 0 PTS

Stewart SF2-Ford V10
Stewart Ford
Races: FRA; GBR; AUT; GER; HUN; BEL; ITA; LUX; JPN (all car #19)

GRAND PRIX WINNERS 1998

	RACE (CIRCUIT)	**WINNER** (CAR)
AUS	AUSTRALIAN GRAND PRIX (ALBERT PARK)	MIKA HÄKKINEN (McLAREN MP4/13-MERCEDES V10)
BRA	BRAZILIAN GRAND PRIX (INTERLAGOS)	MIKA HÄKKINEN (McLAREN MP4/13-MERCEDES V10)
ARG	ARGENTINE GRAND PRIX (BUENOS AIRES)	MICHAEL SCHUMACHER (FERRARI F300 V10)
SMR	SAN MARINO GRAND PRIX (IMOLA)	DAVID COULTHARD (McLAREN MP4/13-MERCEDES V10)
ESP	SPANISH GRAND PRIX (CATALUNYA)	MIKA HAKKINEN (McLAREN MP4/13-MERCEDES V10)
MON	MONACO GRAND PRIX (MONTE CARLO)	MIKA HÄKKINEN (McLAREN MP4/13-MERCEDES V10)
CAN	CANADIAN GRAND PRIX (MONTRÉAL)	MICHAEL SCHUMACHER (FERRARI F300 V10)
FRA	FRENCH GRAND PRIX (MAGNY-COURS)	MICHAEL SCHUMACHER (FERRARI F300 V10)
GBR	BRITISH GRAND PRIX (SILVERSTONE)	MICHAEL SCHUMACHER (FERRARI F300 V10)
AUT	AUSTRIAN GRAND PRIX (A1 RING)	MIKA HÄKKINEN (McLAREN MP4/13-MERCEDES V10)
GER	GERMAN GRAND PRIX (HOCKENHEIM)	MIKA HÄKKINEN (McLAREN MP4/13-MERCEDES V10)
HUN	HUNGARIAN GRAND PRIX (HUNGARORING)	MICHAEL SCHUMACHER (FERRARI F300 V10)
BEL	BELGIAN GRAND PRIX (SPA-FRANCORCHAMPS)	DAMON HILL (JORDAN 198-MUGEN V10)
ITA	ITALIAN GRAND PRIX (MONZA)	MICHAEL SCHUMACHER (FERRARI F300 V10)
LUX	LUXEMBOURG GRAND PRIX (NÜRBURGRING)	MIKA HÄKKINEN (McLAREN MP4/13-MERCEDES V10)
JPN	JAPANESE GRAND PRIX (SUZUKA)	MIKA HÄKKINEN (McLAREN MP4/13-MERCEDES V10)

1999

HÄKKINEN FENDS OFF ALIEN INVASION

Far left
Grass guzzler: Mika Häkkinen flirts with the verge at Silverstone, where he led until his McLaren developed a rear-wheel problem

Above left
Canada high: Häkkinen celebrates in Montreal, scene of the third of his five wins during the season

Above
Top of the stops: Eddie Irvine comes in for a routine service in Malaysia. Excellent teamwork on and off the track paved the way to a victory that sustained his championship bid

Left
Shattered hopes: Michael Schumacher crashed on the opening lap of the British GP and broke his right leg. From then on, Irvine was Ferrari's main title contender

IT WAS THE TITLE NO ONE SEEMED TO WANT. AFTER SCHUMACHER BROKE HIS LEG THE SEASON SHOULD HAVE BEEN A RELATIVE CRUISE FOR HÄKKINEN. BUT IT WASN'T

Above
Born slippery: rain at the Nürburgring is not exactly front-page news, but it caught Giancarlo Fisichella unawares. And he'd forgotten his umbrella

Far left
Come together: David Coulthard partnered Mika Häkkinen for the fourth time in what would be a record-breaking six-season partnership

Left
Painting the town red: Eddie Irvine and Ferrari stand-in Mika Salo send a Get Well Soon (but not too soon) message to Schuey after their Hockenheim one-two

Right
Heinz full of beans: Frentzen profited from a Häkkinen error at Monza to notch up his and Jordan's second win of the campaign

It was the title no one seemed to want. After Michael Schumacher put himself out of contention by breaking a leg in an accident during the British Grand Prix, the season should have been a relative cruise for Mika Häkkinen and McLaren. But it wasn't.

Firstly, Ferrari revealed its strength in depth when number two Eddie Irvine picked up Schuey's baton and made McLaren fight. The Ulsterman might have scored a slightly fortuitous win in Australia, the opening event of the season, but he drove a stormer to beat the McLarens in Austria, Ferrari's first race without Schumacher since 1995. A few days later, Schuey's stand-in Mika Salo moved aside to hand Irvine victory at Hockenheim and breathe fresh life into the title race. Ferrari was unable, however, to maintain quite the competitive momentum it had before its talisman was sidelined.

Meanwhile, a rank outsider began to loom large. In his first season with Jordan, Williams refugee Heinz-Harald Frentzen won in the wet at Magny-Cours and scored again at Monza after Häkkinen crashed while leading comfortably. The German took pole position for the next race, the Grand Prix of Europe at the Nürburgring, but failed to finish a chaotic event (in which Johnny Herbert scored the Stewart-Ford team's maiden F1 victory) and that marked the end of his realistic title hopes.

Schumacher returned in Malaysia and stunned rivals when he annexed pole position by more than a second. In the race he played dutiful back-up to Irvine and twice handed him the lead, the second time for keeps. There was a brief flurry of post-race excitement when the Ferraris' barge boards were declared illegal, but that decision was overturned in court a few days later. Häkkinen finally sealed the title with a perfect drive to victory in Japan, leaving Ferrari with the consolation of the championship for constructors. The Suzuka finale marked former champion Damon Hill's F1 swansong. He bowed out after a desultory season with Jordan.

1999

CHAMPIONSHIP CAR-BY-CAR

1ST MIKA HÄKKINEN (FIN; AGE: 30) 76 PTS

McLaren MP4/14-Mercedes V10
West McLaren Mercedes
Races: AUS; BRA; SMR; MON; ESP; CAN; FRA; GBR; AUT; GER; HUN; BEL; ITA; EUR; MAL; JPN (all car #1)

2ND EDDIE IRVINE (GBR; AGE: 33) 74 PTS

Ferrari F399 V10
Scuderia Ferrari Marlboro
Races: AUS; BRA; SMR; MON; ESP; CAN; FRA; GBR; AUT; GER; HUN; BEL; ITA; EUR; MAL; JPN (all car #4)

3RD HEINZ-HARALD FRENTZEN (GER; AGE: 32) 54 pts

Jordan 199-Mugen V10
Benson & Hedges Jordan Mugen Honda
Races: AUS; BRA; SMR; MON; ESP; CAN; FRA; GBR; AUT; GER; HUN; BEL; ITA; EUR; MAL; JPN (all car #8)

4TH DAVID COULTHARD (GBR; AGE: 28) 48 PTS

McLaren MP4/14-Mercedes V10
West McLaren Mercedes
Races: AUS; BRA; SMR; MON; ESP; CAN; FRA; GBR; AUT; GER; HUN; BEL; ITA; EUR; MAL; JPN (all car #2)

5TH MICHAEL SCHUMACHER (GER; AGE: 30) 44 PTS

Ferrari F399 V10
Scuderia Ferrari Marlboro
Races: AUS; BRA; SMR; MON; ESP; CAN; FRA; GBR; MAL; JPN (all car #3)

6TH RALF SCHUMACHER (GER; AGE: 24) 35 PTS

Williams FW21-Supertec V10
Winfield Williams
Races: AUS; BRA; SMR; MON; ESP; CAN; FRA; GBR; AUT; GER; HUN; BEL; ITA; EUR; MAL; JPN (all car #6)

7TH RUBENS BARRICHELLO (BRA; AGE: 27) 21 PTS

Stewart SF3-Ford V10
Stewart Ford
Races: AUS; BRA; SMR; MON; ESP; CAN; FRA; GBR; AUT; GER; HUN; BEL; ITA; EUR; MAL; JPN (all car #16)

8TH JOHNNY HERBERT (GBR; AGE: 35) 15 PTS

Stewart SF3-Ford V10
Stewart Ford
Races: AUS; BRA; SMR; MON; ESP; CAN; FRA; GBR; AUT; GER; HUN; BEL; ITA; EUR; MAL; JPN (all car #17)

9TH GIANCARLO FISICHELLA (ITA; AGE: 26) 13 PTS

Benetton B199-Playlife V10
Mild Seven Benetton Playlife
Races: AUS; BRA; SMR; MON; ESP; CAN; FRA; GBR; AUT; GER; HUN; BEL; ITA; EUR; MAL; JPN (all car #9)

10TH MIKA SALO (FIN; AGE: 32) 10 PTS

BAR 001-Supertec V10
British American Racing
Races: SMR; MON; ESP (all car #23)

MIKA SALO (CONTD)

Ferrari F399 V10
Scuderia Ferrari Marlboro
Races: AUT; GER; HUN; BEL; ITA; EUR (all car #3)

11TH JARNO TRULLI (ITA; AGE: 25) 7 PTS

Prost AP02-Peugeot V10
Gauloises Prost Peugeot
Races: AUS; BRA; SMR; MON; ESP; CAN; FRA; GBR; AUT; GER; HUN; BEL; ITA; EUR; JPN (all car #19)

12TH DAMON HILL (GBR; AGE: 38) 7 PTS

Jordan 199-Mugen V10
Benson & Hedges Jordan Mugen Honda
Races: AUS; BRA; SMR; MON; ESP; CAN; FRA; GBR; AUT; GER; HUN; BEL; ITA; EUR; MAL; JPN (all car #7)

13TH ALEX WURZ (AUT; AGE: 25) 3 PTS

Benetton B199-Playlife V10
Mild Seven Benetton Playlife
Races: AUS; BRA; SMR; MON; ESP; CAN; FRA; GBR; AUT; GER; HUN; BEL; ITA; EUR; MAL; JPN (all car #10)

14TH PEDRO DINIZ (BRA; AGE: 29) 3 PTS

Sauber C18-Petronas V10
Red Bull Sauber Petronas
Races: AUS; BRA; SMR; MON; ESP; CAN; FRA; GBR; AUT; GER; HUN; BEL; ITA; EUR; MAL; JPN (all car #12)

1999

CHAMPIONSHIP CAR-BY-CAR

15TH JEAN ALESI (FRA; AGE: 35) 2 PTS

Sauber C18-Petronas V10
Red Bull Sauber Petronas
Races: AUS; BRA; SMR; MON; ESP; CAN; FRA; GBR; AUT; GER; HUN; BEL; ITA; EUR; MAL; JPN (all car #11)

16TH OLIVIER PANIS (FRA; AGE: 32) 2 PTS

Prost AP02-Peugeot V10
Gauloises Prost Peugeot
Races: AUS; BRA; SMR; MON; ESP; CAN; FRA; GBR; AUT; GER; HUN; BEL; ITA; EUR; MAL; JPN (all car #18)

17TH PEDRO DE LA ROSA (ESP; AGE: 28) 1 PT

Arrows A20 V10
Arrows
Races: AUS; BRA; SMR; MON; ESP; CAN; FRA; GBR; AUT; GER; HUN; BEL; ITA; EUR; MAL; JPN (all car #14)

18TH MARC GENÉ (ESP; AGE: 25) 1 PT

Minardi M01-Ford V10
Fondmetal Minardi Ford
Races: AUS; BRA; SMR; MON; ESP; CAN; FRA; GBR; AUT; GER; HUN; BEL; ITA; EUR; MAL; JPN (all car #21)

LUCA BADOER (ITA; AGE: 28) 0 PTS

Minardi M01-Ford V10
Fondmetal Minardi Ford
Races: AUS; SMR; MON; ESP; CAN; FRA; GBR; AUT; GER; HUN; BEL; ITA; EUR; MAL; JPN (all car #20)

STÉPHANE SARRAZIN (FRA; AGE: 24) 0 PTS

Minardi M01-Ford V10
Fondmetal Minardi Ford
Races: BRA (car #20)

TORANOSUKE TAKAGI (JPN; AGE: 25) 0 PTS

Arrows A20 V10
Arrows
Races: AUS; BRA; SMR; MON; ESP; CAN; FRA; GBR; AUT; GER; HUN; BEL; ITA; EUR; MAL; JPN (all car #15)

JACQUES VILLENEUVE (CAN; AGE: 28) 0 PTS

BAR 001-Supertec V10
British American Racing
Races: AUS; BRA; SMR; MON; ESP; CAN; FRA; GBR; AUT; GER; HUN; BEL; ITA; EUR; MAL; JPN (all car #22)

ALEX ZANARDI (ITA; AGE: 32) 0 PTS

Williams FW21-Supertec V10
Winfield Williams
Races: AUS; BRA; SMR; MON; ESP; CAN; FRA; GBR; AUT; GER; HUN; BEL; ITA; EUR; MAL; JPN (all car #5)

RICARDO ZONTA (BRA; AGE: 23) 0 PTS

BAR 001-Supertec V10
British American Racing
Races: AUS; CAN; FRA; GBR; AUT; GER; HUN; BEL; ITA; EUR; MAL; JPN (all car #23)

GRAND PRIX WINNERS 1999

	RACE (CIRCUIT)	WINNER (CAR)
AUS	AUSTRALIAN GRAND PRIX (ALBERT PARK)	EDDIE IRVINE (FERRARI F399 V10)
BRA	BRAZILIAN GRAND PRIX (INTERLAGOS)	MIKA HÄKKINEN (McLAREN MP4/14-MERCEDES V10)
SMR	SAN MARINO GRAND PRIX (IMOLA)	MICHAEL SCHUMACHER (FERRARI F399 V10)
MON	MONACO GRAND PRIX (MONTE CARLO)	MICHAEL SCHUMACHER (FERRARI F399 V10)
ESP	SPANISH GRAND PRIX (CATALUNYA)	MIKA HÄKKINEN (McLAREN MP4/14-MERCEDES V10)
CAN	CANADIAN GRAND PRIX (MONTRÉAL)	MIKA HÄKKINEN (McLAREN MP4/14-MERCEDES V10)
FRA	FRENCH GRAND PRIX (MAGNY-COURS)	HEINZ-HARALD FRENTZEN (JORDAN 199-MUGEN V10)
GBR	BRITISH GRAND PRIX (SILVERSTONE)	DAVID COULTHARD (McLAREN MP4/14-MERCEDES V10)
AUT	AUSTRIAN GRAND PRIX (A1 RING)	EDDIE IRVINE (FERRARI F399 V10)
GER	GERMAN GRAND PRIX (HOCKENHEIM)	EDDIE IRVINE (FERRARI F399 V10)
HUN	HUNGARIAN GRAND PRIX (HUNGARORING)	MIKA HÄKKINEN (McLAREN MP4/14-MERCEDES V10)
BEL	BELGIAN GRAND PRIX (SPA-FRANCORCHAMPS)	DAVID COULTHARD (McLAREN MP4/14-MERCEDES V10)
ITA	ITALIAN GRAND PRIX (MONZA)	HEINZ-HARALD FRENTZEN (JORDAN 199-MUGEN V10)
EUR	EUROPEAN GRAND PRIX (NÜRBURGRING)	JOHNNY HERBERT (STEWART SF3-FORD V10)
MAL	MALAYSIAN GRAND PRIX (SEPANG)	EDDIE IRVINE (FERRARI F399 V10)
JPN	JAPANESE GRAND PRIX (SUZUKA)	MIKA HÄKKINEN (McLAREN MP4/14-MERCEDES V10)

BRIDGESTONE

NORTEL
NETWORKS

SAP

2000s

2000

NO DROUGHT ABOUT IT – FERRARI BACK ON TOP

Left
Captain scarlet: the Imola crowd goes appropriately bonkers as Michael Schumacher soaks up his San Marino GP success – his fourth win on Italian soil since joining Ferrari in 1996

Top
Smiles per hour: how it feels to win the Monaco GP, by David Coulthard

Above
It's raining, men: Barrichello started 18th at Hockenheim, profited from a little luck (a one-man track invasion by a disgruntled fan led to a Safety Car period that worked in the Brazilian's favour) and went on to score his first F1 victory. Then he cried and made the place even wetter

THE GLADIATORIAL BATTLE BETWEEN THE ERA'S TWO GREATEST DRIVERS, SCHUMACHER AND HÄKKINEN, REACHED ITS ZENITH AT SPA. SCHUEY EASED THE FINN TOWARDS THE GRASS AT 200MPH

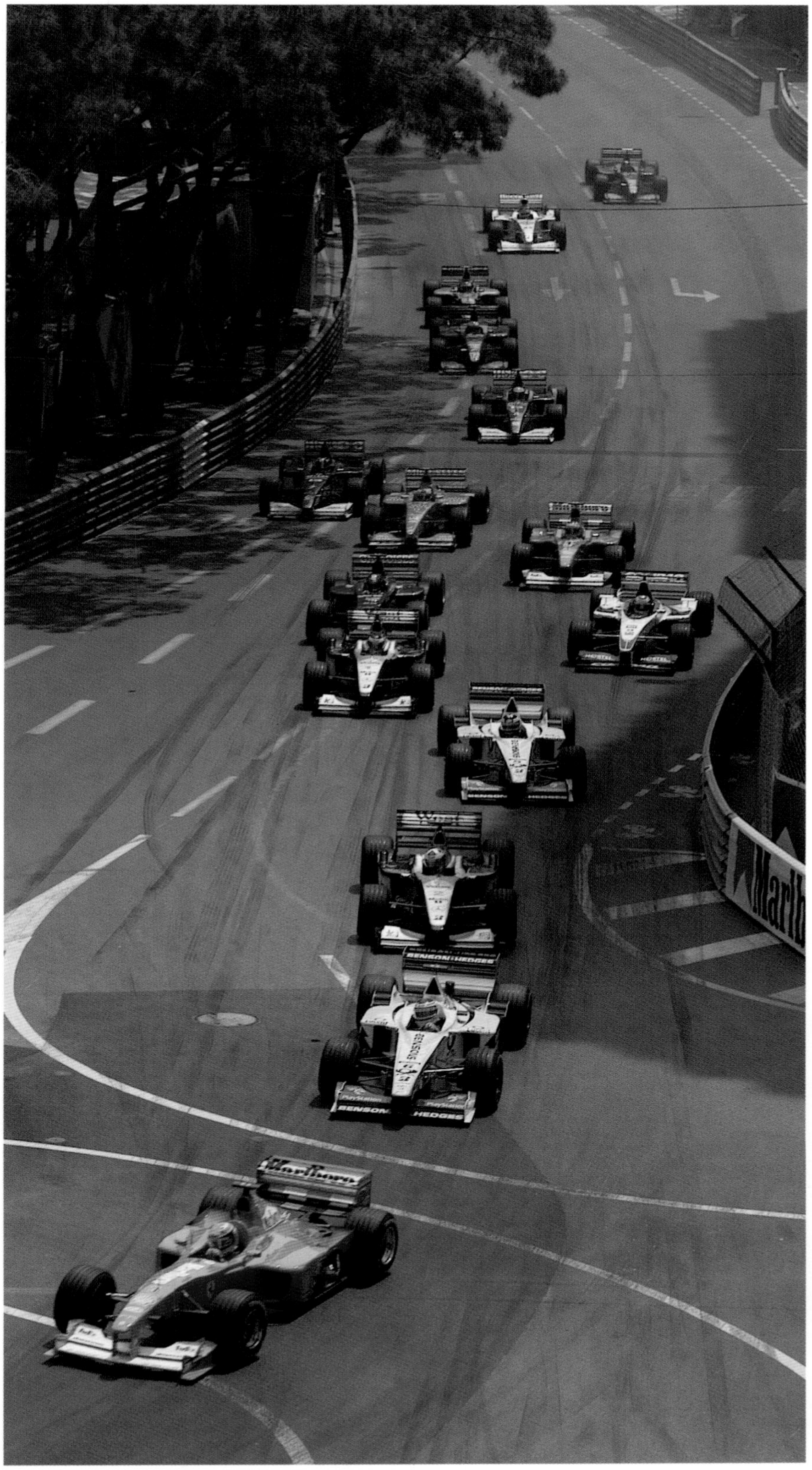

Michael Schumacher ended a 21-year drought by becoming the first Ferrari driver since Jody Scheckter to win the world championship. The F1-2000 was the first chassis conceived in the team's new on-site wind tunnel and the Scuderia set the pace from the start of the year – something it had conspicuously failed to do for the previous three seasons.

Unreliability blunted the McLaren-Mercedes challenge early in the campaign. The team came on strong mid-season, however, and Mika Hakkinen fought his way back into title contention with some vintage performances. The gladiatorial battle between the era's two greatest drivers, Schumacher and Häkkinen, reached its zenith at Spa. The Finn went on to win courtesy of a breathtaking pass in the closing laps, shortly after Schuey had eased him towards the grass at 200mph.

It wasn't enough to swing the title Häkkinen's way, but the outcome was only decided in Japan, the penultimate race, after Schumacher got the best of a tense contest.

There was clear water between Ferrari, McLaren and the rest – and nobody else so much as challenged for a race victory. In the first year of a new partnership with BMW, Williams finished third in the championship for constructors. Its star rookie Jenson Button created a big impression, but the team's first victory since 1997 still looked a sizeable step away.

In a landmark development, Formula One returned to America for the first time since 1991 – and did so in style at a new track in Indianapolis. This incorporated part of the legendary Indy 500 oval.

Far left, top
Brawn in the USA: the first grand prix at Indianapolis blasts off and Formula One cements its return to America after a nine-year absence

Above left
Streets, cars, names, desire: Michael Schumacher leads Trulli, Coulthard and the rest into Ste Dévote at the start of the Monaco GP

Sequence, left
It takes two to tangle: while Häkkinen sprints through to take the lead from fourth on the grid at Hockenheim, Fisichella dampens local spirits by snagging Schuey and causing them both to retire

Above
Cruel for cats: Irvine qualified sixth in Brazil but his Jaguar looked a touch lame long before the end of the race

2000

CHAMPIONSHIP CAR-BY-CAR

1ST MICHAEL SCHUMACHER (GER; AGE: 31) 108 PTS

Ferrari F1-2000 V10
Scuderia Ferrari Marlboro
Races: AUS; BRA; SMR; GBR; ESP; EUR; MON; CAN; FRA; AUT; GER; HUN; BEL; ITA; USA; JPN; MAL (all car #3)

2ND MIKA HÄKKINEN (FIN; AGE: 31) 89 PTS

McLaren MP4/15-Mercedes V10
West McLaren Mercedes
Races: AUS; BRA; SMR; GBR; ESP; EUR; MON; CAN; FRA; AUT; GER; HUN; BEL; ITA; USA; JPN; MAL (all car #1)

3RD DAVID COULTHARD (GBR; AGE: 29) 73 PTS

McLaren MP4/15-Mercedes V10
West McLaren Mercedes
Races: AUS; BRA; SMR; GBR; ESP; EUR; MON; CAN; FRA; AUT; GER; HUN; BEL; ITA; USA; JPN; MAL (all car #2)

4TH RUBENS BARRICHELLO (BRA; AGE: 28) 62 PTS

Ferrari F1-2000 V10
Scuderia Ferrari Marlboro
Races: AUS; BRA; SMR; GBR; ESP; EUR; MON; CAN; FRA; AUT; GER; HUN; BEL; ITA; USA; JPN; MAL (all car #4)

5TH RALF SCHUMACHER (GER; AGE: 25) 24 PTS

Williams FW22-BMW V10
BMW Williams F1
Races: AUS; BRA; SMR; GBR; ESP; EUR; MON; CAN; FRA; AUT; GER; HUN; BEL; ITA; USA; JPN; MAL (all car #9)

6TH GIANCARLO FISICHELLA (ITA; AGE: 27) 18 pts

Benetton B200-Playlife V10
Mild Seven Benetton Playlife
Races: AUS; BRA; SMR; GBR; ESP; EUR; MON; CAN; FRA; AUT; GER; HUN; BEL; ITA; USA; JPN; MAL (all car #11)

7TH JACQUES VILLENEUVE (CAN; AGE: 29) 17 PTS

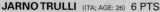

BAR 002-Honda V10
British American Racing Honda
Races: AUS; BRA; SMR; GBR; ESP; EUR; MON; CAN; FRA; AUT; GER; HUN; BEL; ITA; USA; JPN; MAL (all car #22)

8TYH JENSON BUTTON (GBR; AGE: 20) 12 PTS

Williams FW22-BMW V10
BMW Williams F1
Races: AUS; BRA; SMR; GBR; ESP; EUR; MON; CAN; FRA; AUT; GER; HUN; BEL; ITA; USA; JPN; MAL (all car #10)

9TH HEINZ-HARALD FRENTZEN (GER; AGE: 33) 11 PTS

Jordan EJ10-Mugen V10
Benson & Hedges Jordan Mugen Honda
Races: AUS; BRA; SMR; GBR; ESP; EUR; MON; CAN; FRA; AUT; GER; HUN; BEL; ITA; USA; JPN; MAL (all car #5)

10TH JARNO TRULLI (ITA; AGE: 26) 6 PTS

Jordan EJ10-Mugen V10
Benson & Hedges Jordan Mugen Honda
Races: AUS; BRA; SMR; GBR; ESP; EUR; MON; CAN; FRA; AUT; GER; HUN; BEL; ITA; USA; JPN; MAL (all car #6)

11TH MIKA SALO (FIN; AGE: 33) 6 PTS

Sauber C19-Petronas V10
Red Bull Sauber Petronas
Races: AUS; SMR; GBR; ESP; EUR; MON; CAN; FRA; AUT; GER; HUN; BEL; ITA; USA; JPN; MAL (all car #17)

12TH JOS VERSTAPPEN (NED; AGE: 28) 5 PTS

Arrows A21-Supertec V10
Orange Arrows F1 Team
Races: AUS; BRA; SMR; GBR; ESP; EUR; MON; CAN; FRA; AUT; GER; HUN; BEL; ITA; USA; JPN; MAL (all car #19)

13TH EDDIE IRVINE (GBR; AGE: 34) 4 PTS

Jaguar R1-Cosworth V10
Jaguar Racing
Races: AUS; BRA; SMR; GBR; ESP; EUR; MON; CAN; FRA; GER; HUN; BEL; ITA; USA; JPN; MAL (all car #7)

14TH RICARDO ZONTA (BRA; AGE: 24) 3 PTS

BAR 002-Honda V10
British American Racing Honda
Races: AUS; BRA; SMR; GBR; ESP; EUR; MON; CAN; FRA; AUT; GER; HUN; BEL; ITA; USA; JPN; MAL (all car #23)

15TH ALEX WURZ (AUT; AGE: 26) 2 PTS

Benetton B200-Playlife V10
Mild Seven Benetton Playlife
Races: AUS; BRA; SMR; GBR; ESP; EUR; MON; CAN; FRA; AUT; GER; HUN; BEL; ITA; USA; JPN; MAL (all car #12)

2000

CHAMPIONSHIP CAR-BY-CAR

16TH PEDRO DE LA ROSA (ESP; AGE: 29) 2 PTS

Arrows A21-Supertec V10
Orange Arrows F1 Team
Races: AUS; BRA; SMR; GBR; ESP; EUR; MON; CAN; FRA; AUT; GER; HUN; BEL; ITA; USA; JPN; MAL (all car #18)

JEAN ALESI (FRA; AGE: 36) 0 PTS

Prost AP03-Peugeot V10
Gauloises Prost Peugeot
Races: AUS; BRA; SMR; GBR; ESP; EUR; MON; CAN; FRA; AUT; GER; HUN; BEL; ITA; USA; JPN; MAL (all car #14)

LUCIANO BURTI (BRA; AGE: 25) 0 PTS

Jaguar R1-Cosworth V10
Jaguar Racing
Races: AUT (car #7)

PEDRO DINIZ (BRA; AGE: 30) 0 PTS

Sauber C19-Petronas V10
Red Bull Sauber Petronas
Races: AUS; SMR; GBR; ESP; EUR; MON; CAN; FRA; AUT; GER; HUN; BEL; ITA; USA; JPN; MAL (all car #16)

MARC GENÉ (ESP; AGE: 26) 0 PTS

Minardi M02-Fondmetal V10
Telefonica Minardi Fondmetal
Races: AUS; BRA; SMR; GBR; ESP; EUR; MON; CAN; FRA; AUT; GER; HUN; BEL; ITA; USA; JPN; MAL (all car #20)

NICK HEIDFELD (GER; AGE: 23) 0 PTS

Prost AP03-Peugeot V10
Gauloises Prost Peugeot
Races: AUS; BRA; SMR; GBR; ESP; MON; CAN; FRA; AUT; GER; HUN; BEL; ITA; USA; JPN; MAL (all car #15)

JOHNNY HERBERT (GBR; AGE: 36) 0 PTS

Jaguar R1-Cosworth V10
Jaguar Racing
Races: AUS; BRA; SMR; GBR; ESP; EUR; MON; CAN; FRA; AUT; GER; HUN; BEL; ITA; USA; JPN; MAL (all car #8)

GASTON MAZZACANE (ARG; AGE: 25) 0 PTS

Minardi M02-Fondmetal V10
Telefonica Minardi Fondmetal
Races: AUS; BRA; SMR; GBR; ESP; EUR; MON; CAN; FRA; AUT; GER; HUN; BEL; ITA; USA; JPN; MAL (all car #21)

GRAND PRIX WINNERS 2000

	RACE (CIRCUIT)	WINNER (CAR)
AUS	AUSTRALIAN GRAND PRIX (ALBERT PARK)	MICHAEL SCHUMACHER (FERRARI F1-2000 V10)
BRA	BRAZILIAN GRAND PRIX (INTERLAGOS)	MICHAEL SCHUMACHER (FERRARI F1-2000 V10)
SMR	SAN MARINO GRAND PRIX (IMOLA)	MICHAEL SCHUMACHER (FERRARI F1-2000 V10)
GBR	BRITISH GRAND PRIX (SILVERSTONE)	DAVID COULTHARD (McLAREN MP4/15-MERCEDES V10)
ESP	SPANISH GRAND PRIX (CATALUNYA)	MIKA HÄKKINEN (McLAREN MP4/15-MERCEDES V10)
EUR	EUROPEAN GRAND PRIX (NÜRBURGRING)	MICHAEL SCHUMACHER (FERRARI F1-2000 V10)
MON	MONACO GRAND PRIX (MONTE CARLO)	DAVID COULTHARD (McLAREN MP4/15-MERCEDES V10)
CAN	CANADIAN GRAND PRIX (MONTRÉAL)	MICHAEL SCHUMACHER (FERRARI F1-2000 V10)
FRA	FRENCH GRAND PRIX (MAGNY-COURS)	DAVID COULTHARD (McLAREN MP4/15-MERCEDES V10)
AUT	AUSTRIAN GRAND PRIX (A1 RING)	MIKA HÄKKINEN (McLAREN MP4/15-MERCEDES V10)
GER	GERMAN GRAND PRIX (HOCKENHEIM)	RUBENS BARRICHELLO (FERRARI F1-2000 V10)
HUN	HUNGARIAN GRAND PRIX (HUNGARORING)	MIKA HÄKKINEN (McLAREN MP4/15-MERCEDES V10)
BEL	BELGIAN GRAND PRIX (SPA-FRANCORCHAMPS)	MIKA HÄKKINEN (McLAREN MP4/15-MERCEDES V10)
ITA	ITALIAN GRAND PRIX (MONZA)	MICHAEL SCHUMACHER (FERRARI F1-2000 V10)
USA	US GRAND PRIX (INDIANAPOLIS)	MICHAEL SCHUMACHER (FERRARI F1-2000 V10)
JPN	JAPANESE GRAND PRIX (SUZUKA)	MICHAEL SCHUMACHER (FERRARI F1-2000 V10)
MAL	MALAYSIAN GRAND PRIX (SEPANG)	MICHAEL SCHUMACHER (FERRARI F1-2000 V10)

2001

SIMPLY RED – FERRARI TIGHTENS ITS GRIP

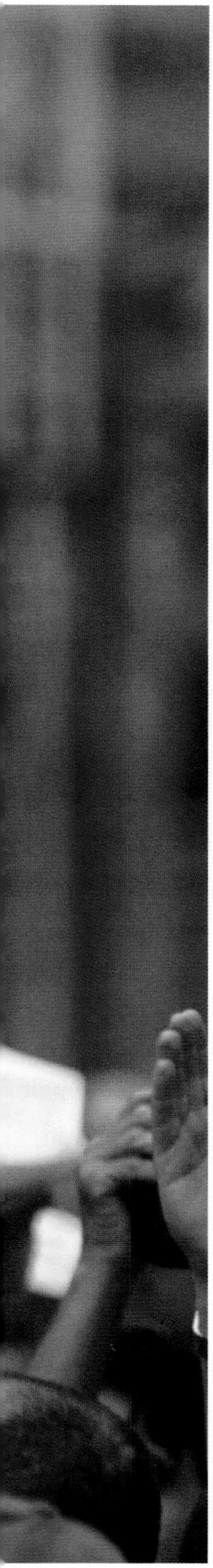

Far left
Raising the Teutonic: Ferrari mechanics give Michael Schumacher a lift after he'd done the same for them with a stirring performance in Monaco

Above
Thou shalt not pass: irresistible German force encounters immovable Colombian object. Schuey (right) and Montoya tangle during the Austrian GP

Left
Tumbling dicer: Prost driver Luciano Burti somersaults towards the first corner at Hockenheim after clipping Schumacher's slowing Ferrari. The Brazilian was unhurt

Ferrari strengthened its hold on grand prix racing with the F1-2001 – a car that proved to be brilliantly effective as an all-rounder. And team leader Michael Schumacher eclipsed Alain Prost's record of 51 victories to become the most successful Formula One driver of all time. He also picked up a fourth championship crown to equal the Frenchman's title tally.

McLaren-Mercedes was only occasionally as potent a threat as it had been during recent seasons. Its former champion Mika Häkkinen drove for much of the year in the certainty that he wanted to retire. By the end of the campaign he had confirmed that he intended to do just that, although he didn't rule out an eventual comeback. He put thoughts of winding down to one side, however, to win the United States Grand Prix, his penultimate race. Team-mate David Coulthard put in some terrific performances – notably in Spain, where he finished second only days after surviving a plane crash that killed two members of the flight crew – but his car was too inconsistent to give him a sustained run at the Ferraris.

Williams-BMW stepped up as Ferrari's strongest rival and the German manufacturer's impressive V10 set a new standard for horsepower. The team's Colombian signing Juan Pablo Montoya put together one of the most impressive rookie F1 seasons of all time. It included several moments of spine-tingling excitement – not least in Brazil, where he rubbed wheels with Michael Schumacher while wresting the lead. Although later forced out of that race, he would eventually score his maiden victory at Monza. Team-mate Ralf Schumacher broke his F1 duck at Imola earlier in the season. That was Williams's first success since 1997 and, in its F1 comeback season, tyre supplier Michelin's first since 1984.

Left
Midfield generals: former champ Jacques Villeneuve's BAR heads Jarno Trulli's Jordan at the Nürburgring

Below left
Look sharp: Sauber recruit Kimi Räikkönen poses in Melbourne with fellow F1 rookies Juan Pablo Montoya, Fernando Alonso and Enrique Bernoldi. Three of them went on to make names For themselves by driving quickly; Bernoldi created headlines (well, small ones in the corner of gossip columns) by dating tennis star Jelena Dokic

Below right
Hi ho silver leaning: BMW and Williams celebrate their first win as partners, courtesy of Ralf Schumacher at Imola. Having returned to F1 in 2000, it took BMW only 21 grands prix to re-establish itself as a winner

2001

CHAMPIONSHIP CAR-BY-CAR

1ST MICHAEL SCHUMACHER (GER; AGE: 32) 123 PTS

Ferrari F2001 V10
Scuderia Ferrari Marlboro
Races: AUS; MAL; BRA; SMR; ESP; AUT; MON; CAN; EUR; FRA; GBR; GER; HUN; BEL; ITA; USA; JPN (all car #1)

2ND DAVID COULTHARD (GBR; AGE: 30) 65 PTS

McLaren MP4/16-Mercedes **V10**
West McLaren Mercedes
Races: AUS; MAL; BRA; SMR; ESP; AUT; MON; CAN; EUR; FRA; GBR; GER; HUN; BEL; ITA; USA; JPN (all car #4)

3RD RUBENS BARRICHELLO (BRA; AGE: 29) 56 PTS

Ferrari F2001 V10
Scuderia Ferrari Marlboro
Races: AUS; MAL; BRA; SMR; ESP; AUT; MON; CAN; EUR; FRA; GBR; GER; HUN; BEL; ITA; USA; JPN (all car #2)

4TH RALF SCHUMACHER (GER; AGE: 26) 49 PTS

Williams FW23-BMW V10
BMW Williams F1
Races: AUS; MAL; BRA; SMR; ESP; AUT; MON; CAN; EUR; FRA; GBR; GER; HUN; BEL; ITA; USA; JPN (all car #5)

5TH MIKA HÄKKINEN (FIN; AGE: 32) 37 PTS

McLaren MP4/16-Mercedes V10
West McLaren Mercedes
Races: AUS; MAL; BRA; SMR; ESP; AUT; MON; CAN; EUR; GBR; GER; HUN; BEL; ITA; USA; JPN (all car #3)

6TH JUAN PABLO MONTOYA (COL; AGE: 25) 31 PTS

Williams FW23-BMW V10
BMW Williams F1
Races: AUS; MAL; BRA; SMR; ESP; AUT; MON; CAN; EUR; FRA; GBR; GER; HUN; BEL; ITA; USA; JPN (all car #6)

7TH JACQUES VILLENEUVE (CAN; AGE: 30) 12 PTS

BAR 003-Honda V10
Lucky Strike British American Racing Honda
Races: AUS; MAL; BRA; SMR; ESP; AUT; MON; CAN; EUR; FRA; GBR; GER; HUN; BEL; ITA; USA; JPN (all car #10)

8TH NICK HEIDFELD (GER; AGE: 24) 12 PTS

Sauber C20-Petronas V10
Red Bull Sauber Petronas
Races: AUS; MAL; BRA; SMR; ESP; AUT; MON; CAN; EUR; FRA; GBR; GER; HUN; BEL; ITA; USA; JPN (all car #16)

9TH JARNO TRULLI (ITA; AGE: 26) 12 PTS

Jordan EJ11-Honda V10
Benson & Hedges Jordan Honda
Races: AUS; MAL; BRA; SMR; ESP; AUT; MON; CAN; EUR; FRA; GBR; GER (all car #12); HUN; BEL; ITA; USA; JPN (all #11)

10TH KIMI RÄIKKÖNEN (FIN; AGE: 21) 9 PTS

Sauber C20-Petronas V10
Red Bull Sauber Petronas
Races: AUS; MAL; BRA; SMR; ESP; AUT; MON; CAN; EUR; FRA; GBR; GER; HUN; BEL; ITA; USA; JPN (all car #17)

11TH GIANCARLO FISICHELLA (ITA; AGE: 28) 8 PTS

Benetton B201-Renault V10
Mild Seven Benetton Renault
Races: AUS; MAL; BRA; SMR; ESP; AUT; MON; CAN; EUR; FRA; GBR; GER; HUN; BEL; ITA; USA; JPN (all car #7)

12TH EDDIE IRVINE (GBR; AGE: 35) 6 PTS

Jaguar R2-Cosworth V10
Jaguar Racing
Races: AUS; MAL; BRA; SMR; ESP; AUT; MON; CAN; EUR; FRA; GBR; GER; HUN; BEL; ITA; USA; JPN (all car #18)

13TH HEINZ-HARALD FRENTZEN (GER; AGE: 34) 6 PTS

Jordan EJ11-Honda V10
Benson & Hedges Jordan Honda
Races: AUS; MAL; BRA; SMR; ESP; AUT; MON; EUR; FRA; GBR (all car #11)

HEINZ-HARALD FRENTZEN (CONTD)

Prost AP04-Acer V10
Prost Grand Prix
Races: HUN; BEL; ITA; USA; JPN (all car #22)

14TH OLIVIER PANIS (FRA; AGE: 34) 5 PTS

BAR 003-Honda V10
Lucky Strike British American Racing Honda
Races: AUS; MAL; BRA; SMR; ESP; AUT; MON; CAN; EUR; FRA; GBR; GER; HUN; BEL; ITA; USA; JPN (all car #9)

2001

CHAMPIONSHIP CAR-BY-CAR

15TH JEAN ALESI (FRA; AGE: 37) 5 PTS

Prost AP04-Acer V10
Prost Grand Prix
Races: AUS; MAL; BRA; SMR; ESP; AUT; MON; CAN; EUR; FRA; GBR; GER (all car #22)

JEAN ALESI (CONTD)

Jordan EJ11-Honda V10
Benson & Hedges Jordan Honda
Races: HUN; BEL; ITA; USA; JPN (all car #12)

16TH PEDRO DE LA ROSA (ESP; AGE: 30) 3 PTS

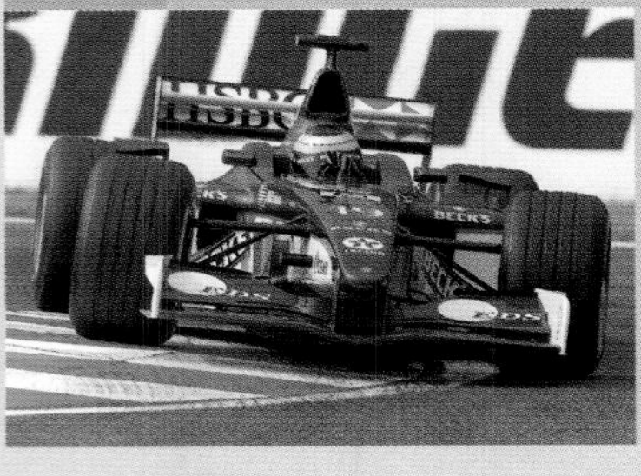

Jaguar R2-Cosworth V10
Jaguar Racing
Races: ESP; AUT; MON; CAN; EUR; FRA; GBR; GER; HUN; BEL; ITA; USA; JPN (all car #19)

17TH JENSON BUTTON (GBR; AGE: 21) 2 PTS

Benetton B201-Renault V10
Mild Seven Benetton Renault
Races: AUS; MAL; BRA; SMR; ESP; AUT; MON; CAN; EUR; FRA; GBR; GER; HUN; BEL; ITA; USA; JPN (all car #8)

18TH JOS VERSTAPPEN (NED; AGE: 29) 1 PT

Arrows A22-Asiatech V10
Orange Arrows Asiatech
Races: AUS; MAL; BRA; SMR; ESP; AUT; MON; CAN; EUR; FRA; GBR; GER; HUN; BEL; ITA; USA; JPN (all car #14)

FERNANDO ALONSO (ESP; AGE: 19) 0 PTS

Minardi PS01-European V10
European Minardi F1
Races: AUS; MAL; BRA; SMR; ESP; AUT; MON; CAN; EUR; FRA; GBR; GER; HUN; BEL; ITA; USA; JPN (all car #21)

ENRIQUE BERNOLDI (BRA; AGE: 22) 0 PTS

Arrows A22-Asiatech V10
Orange Arrows Asiatech
Races: AUS; MAL; BRA; SMR; ESP; AUT; MON; CAN; EUR; FRA; GBR; GER; HUN; BEL; ITA; USA; JPN (all car #15)

LUCIANO BURTI (BRA; AGE: 26) 0 PTS

Jaguar R2-Cosworth V10
Jaguar Racing
Races: AUS; MAL; BRA; SMR (all car #19)

LUCIANO BURTI (CONTD)

Prost AP04-Acer V10
Prost Grand Prix
Races: ESP; AUT; MON; CAN; EUR; FRA; GBR; GER; HUN; BEL (all car #23)

TOMAS ENGE (CZE; AGE: 25) 0 PTS

Prost AP04-Acer V10
Prost Grand Prix
Races: ITA; USA; JPN (all car #23)

TARSO MARQUES (BRA; AGE: 25) 0 PTS

Minardi PS01-European V10
European Minardi F1
Races: AUS; MAL; BRA; SMR; ESP; AUT; MON; CAN; EUR; FRA; GER; HUN; BEL (all car #20)

GASTON MAZZACANE (ARG; AGE: 25) 0 PTS

Prost AP04-Acer V10
Prost Grand Prix
Races: AUS; MAL; BRA; SMR (all car #23)

ALEX YOONG (MAL; AGE: 25) 0 PTS

Minardi PS01-European V10
European Minardi F1
Races: ITA; USA; JPN (all car #20)

RICARDO ZONTA (BRA; AGE: 25) 0 PTS

Jordan EJ11-Honda V10
Benson & Hedges Jordan Honda
Races: CAN; GER (both car #11)

2001

CHAMPIONSHIP CAR-BY-CAR

GRAND PRIX WINNERS 2001

	RACE (CIRCUIT)	WINNER (CAR)
AUS	AUSTRALIAN GRAND PRIX (ALBERT PARK)	MICHAEL SCHUMACHER (FERRARI F2001 V10)
MAL	MALAYSIAN GRAND PRIX (SEPANG)	MICHAEL SCHUMACHER (FERRARI F2001 V10)
BRA	BRAZILIAN GRAND PRIX (INTERLAGOS)	DAVID COULTHARD (McLAREN MP4/16-MERCEDES V10)
SMR	SAN MARINO GRAND PRIX (IMOLA)	RALF SCHUMACHER (WILLIAMS FW23-BMW V10)
ESP	SPANISH GRAND PRIX (CATALUNYA)	MICHAEL SCHUMACHER (FERRARI F2001 V10)
AUT	AUSTRIAN GRAND PRIX (A1 RING)	DAVID COULTHARD (McLAREN MP4/16-MERCEDES V10)
MON	MONACO GRAND PRIX (MONTE CARLO)	MICHAEL SCHUMACHER (FERRARI F2001 V10)
CAN	CANADIAN GRAND PRIX (MONTRÉAL)	RALF SCHUMACHER (WILLIAMS FW23-BMW V10)
EUR	EUROPEAN GRAND PRIX (NÜRBURGRING)	MICHAEL SCHUMACHER (FERRARI F2001 V10)
FRA	FRENCH GRAND PRIX (MAGNY-COURS)	MICHAEL SCHUMACHER (FERRARI F2001 V10)
GBR	BRITISH GRAND PRIX (SILVERSTONE)	MIKA HÄKKINEN (McLAREN MP4/16-MERCEDES V10)
GER	GERMAN GRAND PRIX (HOCKENHEIM)	RALF SCHUMACHER (WILLIAMS FW23-BMW V10)
HUN	HUNGARIAN GRAND PRIX (HUNGARORING)	MICHAEL SCHUMACHER (FERRARI F2001 V10)
BEL	BELGIAN GRAND PRIX (SPA-FRANCORCHAMPS)	MICHAEL SCHUMACHER (FERRARI F2001 V10)
ITA	ITALIAN GRAND PRIX (MONZA)	JUAN PABLO MONTOYA (WILLIAMS FW23-BMW V10)
USA	US GRAND PRIX (INDIANAPOLIS)	MIKA HÄKKINEN (McLAREN MP4/16-MERCEDES V10)
JPN	JAPANESE GRAND PRIX (SUZUKA)	MICHAEL SCHUMACHER (FERRARI F2001 V10)

JUAN PABLO MONTOYA

2002

A ONE PRANCING-HORSE RACE

Far left
Indiana groans: Barrichello pips Michael Schumacher to the line in America after the German backed off a bit too fiercely

Left
You got me feelin' the boos: Schuey and Barrichello face a jeering crowd after their staged finish in Austria

Bottom
I'm handy, fly me: Ralf Schumacher made a storming start to the Australian GP, but was launched over Barrichello within seconds

Below
Herr spray: the Schumacher siblings surround winner Barrichello for podium festivities in Budapest

This was the season that Ferrari's steamroller gathered its full momentum and flattened any sign of opposition. Records were hit for six as the team won all but two of 17 championship races. Michael Schumacher equalled Juan Manuel Fangio's all-time record of five world titles and finished every race on the podium. Ferrari scored more points than the rest of its rivals put together.

Such was the scale of the Italian team's domination that alarm bells rang throughout F1. TV viewing figures went down noticeably after Schumacher clinched the title at Magny-Cours (in July, with six races to go) – and that triggered all sorts of wild and wonderful ideas about the sport's future format. It was even suggested that drivers might in future swap teams from race to race, to spice up the show.

Ferrari did itself no favours early in the season. Rubens Barrichello led the Austrian Grand Prix from the start, but was instructed to pull over on the last lap and hand victory to team-mate Schumacher. Jeers from the crowd told an eloquent tale of how the team was felt to be trivialising the sport.

It wouldn't have been in a position to do so if Williams-BMW and McLaren-Mercedes had offered stronger opposition. Williams had the most potent engine in F1 but was hampered by an over-conservative chassis. Its FW24 won only once, courtesy of Ralf Schumacher in Malaysia, although it exploited its one-lap Michelin grip so well that the explosive Juan Pablo Montoya took seven pole positions. McLaren was short of horsepower for much of the campaign, but David Coulthard scored a brilliant Monaco victory in the face of sustained pressure from the season's dominant driver.

FERRARI'S STEAMROLLER GATHERED ITS FULL MOMENTUM AND FLATTENED ANY SIGN OF OPPOSITION. RECORDS WERE HIT FOR SIX AS THE TEAM WON ALL BUT TWO OF 17 CHAMPIONSHIP RACES

Above
Scot free: Coulthard gets a decisive break after outsprinting Montoya at the start of the Monaco GP

Above right
Sheer dart attack: after 382 grands prix – and no wins – the cash-strapped Arrows team packs its bags at Spa, never to be seen again

Far right
Local hero: Jordan racer Takuma Sato celebrates his career-best fifth place in the season's Suzuka finale

Right
Hungary heart: grid girl, Budapest

MICHAEL SCHUMACHER – WORLD CHAMPION 1994, 1995, 2000, 2001 & 2002

2002

CHAMPIONSHIP CAR-BY-CAR

1ST MICHAEL SCHUMACHER (GER; AGE: 33) 144 PTS

Ferrari F2001 V10
Scuderia Ferrari Marlboro
Races: AUS; MAL (both car #1)

MICHAEL SCHUMACHER (CONTD)

Ferrari F2002 V10
Scuderia Ferrari Marlboro
Races: BRA; SMR; ESP; AUT; MON; CAN; EUR; GBR; FRA; GER; HUN; BEL; ITA; USA; JPN (all car #1)

2ND RUBENS BARRICHELLO (BRA; AGE: 30) 77 PTS

Ferrari F2001 V10
Scuderia Ferrari Marlboro
Races: AUS; MAL; BRA (all car #2)

RUBENS BARRICHELLO (CONTD)

Ferrari F2002 V10
Scuderia Ferrari Marlboro
Races: SMR; AUT; MON; CAN; EUR; GBR; GER; HUN; BEL; ITA; USA; JPN (all car #2)

3RD JUAN PABLO MONTOYA (COL; AGE: 26) 50 PTS

Williams FW24-BMW V10
BMW Williams F1
Races: AUS; MAL; BRA; SMR; ESP; AUT; MON; CAN; EUR; GBR; FRA; GER; HUN; BEL; ITA; USA; JPN (all car #6)

4TH RALF SCHUMACHER (GER; AGE: 27) 42 PTS

Williams FW24-BMW V10
BMW Williams F1
Races: AUS; MAL; BRA; SMR; ESP; AUT; MON; CAN; EUR; GBR; FRA; GER; HUN; BEL; ITA; USA; JPN (all car #5)

5TH DAVID COULTHARD (GBR; AGE: 31) 41 PTS

McLaren MP4/17-Mercedes V10
West McLaren Mercedes
Races: AUS; MAL; BRA; SMR; ESP; AUT; MON; CAN; EUR; GBR; FRA; GER; HUN; BEL; ITA; USA; JPN (all car #3)

6TH KIMI RÄIKKÖNEN (FIN; AGE: 22) 24 PTS

McLaren MP4/17-Mercedes V10
West McLaren Mercedes
Races: AUS; MAL; BRA; SMR; ESP; AUT; MON; CAN; EUR; GBR; FRA; GER; HUN; BEL; ITA; USA; JPN (all car #4)

7TH JENSON BUTTON (GBR; AGE: 22) 14 PTS

Renault R202 V10
Mild Seven Renault Sport
Races: AUS; MAL; BRA; SMR; ESP; AUT; MON; CAN; EUR; GBR; FRA; GER; HUN; BEL; ITA; USA; JPN (all car #15)

8TH JARNO TRULLI (ITA; AGE: 27) 9 PTS

Renault R202 V10
Mild Seven Renault Sport
Races: AUS; MAL; BRA; SMR; ESP; AUT; MON; CAN; EUR; GBR; FRA; GER; HUN; BEL; ITA; USA; JPN (all car #14)

9TH EDDIE IRVINE (GBR; AGE: 36) 8 PTS

Jaguar R3-Cosworth V10
Jaguar Racing
Races: AUS; MAL; BRA; SMR; ESP; AUT; MON; CAN; EUR; GBR; FRA; GER; HUN; BEL; ITA; USA; JPN (all car #16)

10TH NICK HEIDFELD (GER; AGE: 25) 7 PTS

Sauber C21-Petronas V10
Sauber Petronas
Races: AUS; MAL; BRA; SMR; ESP; AUT; MON; CAN; EUR; GBR; FRA; GER; HUN; BEL; ITA; USA; JPN (all car #7)

11TH GIANCARLO FISICHELLA (ITA; AGE: 29) 7 PTS

Jordan EJ12-Honda V10
DHL Jordan Honda
Races: AUS; MAL; BRA; SMR; ESP; AUT; MON; CAN; EUR; GBR; GER; HUN; BEL; ITA; USA; JPN (all car #9)

12TH JACQUES VILLENEUVE (CAN; AGE: 31) 4 PTS

BAR 004-Honda V10
Lucky Strike British American Racing Honda
Races: AUS; MAL; BRA; SMR; ESP; AUT; MON; CAN; EUR; GBR; FRA; GER; HUN; BEL; ITA; USA; JPN (all car #11)

13TH FELIPE MASSA (BRA; AGE: 21) 4 PTS

Sauber C21-Petronas V10
Sauber Petronas
Races: AUS; MAL; BRA; SMR; ESP; AUT; MON; CAN; EUR; GBR; FRA; GER; HUN; BEL; ITA; JPN (all car #8)

2002

CHAMPIONSHIP CAR-BY-CAR

14TH OLIVIER PANIS (FRA; AGE: 35) 3 PTS

BAR 004-Honda V10
Lucky Strike British American Racing Honda
Races: AUS; MAL; BRA; SMR; ESP; AUT; MON; CAN; EUR; GBR; FRA; GER; HUN; BEL; ITA; USA; JPN (all car #12)

15TH TAKUMA SATO (JPN; AGE: 25) 2 PTS

Jordan EJ12-Honda V10
DHL Jordan Honda
Races: AUS; MAL; BRA; SMR; ESP; AUT; MON; CAN; EUR; GBR; FRA; GER; HUN; BEL; ITA; USA; JPN (all car #10)

16TH MARK WEBBER (AUS; AGE: 25) 2 PTS

Minardi PS02-Asiatech V10
Go KL Minardi Asiatech
Races: AUS; MAL; BRA; SMR; AUT; MON; CAN; EUR; GBR; FRA; GER; HUN; BEL; ITA; USA; JPN (all car #23)

17TH MIKA SALO (FIN; AGE: 35) 2 PTS

Toyota TF102 V10
Panasonic Toyota Racing
Races: AUS; MAL; BRA; SMR; ESP; AUT; MON; CAN; EUR; GBR; FRA; GER; HUN; BEL; ITA; USA; JPN (all car #24)

18TH HEINZ-HARALD FRENTZEN (GER; AGE: 35) 2 PTS

Arrows A23-Cosworth V10
Orange Arrows F1 Team
Races: AUS; MAL; BRA; SMR; ESP; AUT; MON; CAN; EUR; GBR; GER (all car #20)

HEINZ-HARALD FRENTZEN (CONTD)

Sauber C21-Petronas V10
Sauber Petronas
Races: USA (car #8)

ENRIQUE BERNOLDI (BRA; AGE: 23) 0 PTS

Arrows A23-Cosworth V10
Orange Arrows F1 Team
Races: AUS; MAL; BRA; SMR; ESP; AUT; MON; CAN; EUR; GBR; GER (all car #21)

ANTHONY DAVIDSON (GBR; AGE: 23) 0 PTS

Minardi PS02-Asiatech V10
Go KL Minardi Asiatech
Races: HUN; BEL (both car #22)

ALLAN McNISH (GBR; AGE: 32) 0 PTS

Toyota TF102 V10
Panasonic Toyota Racing
Races: AUS; MAL; BRA; SMR; ESP; AUT; MON; CAN; EUR; GBR; FRA; GER; HUN; BEL; ITA; USA (all car #25)

PEDRO DE LA ROSA (ESP; AGE: 31) 0 PTS

Jaguar R3-Cosworth V10
Jaguar Racing
Races: AUS; MAL; BRA; SMR; ESP; AUT; MON; CAN; EUR; GBR; FRA; GER; HUN; BEL; ITA; USA; JPN (all car #17)

ALEX YOONG (MAL; AGE: 25) 0 PTS

Minardi PS02-Asiatech V10
Go KL Minardi Asiatech
Races: AUS; MAL; BRA; AUT; MON; CAN; EUR; FRA; ITA; USA; JPN (all car #22)

2002

CHAMPIONSHIP CAR-BY-CAR

GRAND PRIX WINNERS 2002

	RACE (CIRCUIT)	**WINNER** (CAR)
AUS	AUSTRALIAN GRAND PRIX (ALBERT PARK)	MICHAEL SCHUMACHER (FERRARI F2001 V10)
MAL	MALAYSIAN GRAND PRIX (SEPANG)	RALF SCHUMACHER (WILLIAMS FW24-BMW V10)
BRA	BRAZILIAN GRAND PRIX (INTERLAGOS)	MICHAEL SCHUMACHER (FERRARI F2002 V10)
SMR	SAN MARINO GRAND PRIX (IMOLA)	MICHAEL SCHUMACHER (FERRARI F2002 V10)
ESP	SPANISH GRAND PRIX (CATALUNYA)	MICHAEL SCHUMACHER (FERRARI F2002 V10)
AUT	AUSTRIAN GRAND PRIX (A1 RING)	MICHAEL SCHUMACHER (FERRARI F2002 V10)
MON	MONACO GRAND PRIX (MONTE CARLO)	DAVID COULTHARD (McLAREN MP4/17-MERCEDES V10)
CAN	CANADIAN GRAND PRIX (MONTRÉAL)	MICHAEL SCHUMACHER (FERRARI F2002 V10)
EUR	EUROPEAN GRAND PRIX (NÜRBURGRING)	RUBENS BARRICHELLO (FERRARI F2002 V10)
GBR	BRITISH GRAND PRIX (SILVERSTONE)	MICHAEL SCHUMACHER (FERRARI F2002 V10)
FRA	FRENCH GRAND PRIX (MAGNY-COURS)	MICHAEL SCHUMACHER (FERRARI F2002 V10)
GER	GERMAN GRAND PRIX (HOCKENHEIM)	MICHAEL SCHUMACHER (FERRARI F2002 V10)
HUN	HUNGARIAN GRAND PRIX (HUNGARORING)	RUBENS BARRICHELLO (FERRARI F2002 V10)
BEL	BELGIAN GRAND PRIX (SPA-FRANCORCHAMPS)	MICHAEL SCHUMACHER (FERRARI F2002 V10)
ITA	ITALIAN GRAND PRIX (MONZA)	RUBENS BARRICHELLO (FERRARI F2002 V10)
USA	US GRAND PRIX (INDIANAPOLIS)	RUBENS BARRICHELLO (FERRARI F2002 V10)
JPN	JAPANESE GRAND PRIX (SUZUKA)	MICHAEL SCHUMACHER (FERRARI F2002 V10)

RUBENS BARRICHELLO

2003

CHAMPIONSHIP CAR-BY-CAR

CAR #1 MICHAEL SCHUMACHER (GER; AGE: 34)

Ferrari F2002 V10
Scuderia Ferrari Marlboro

MICHAEL SCHUMACHER (CONTD)

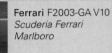

Ferrari F2003-GA V10
Scuderia Ferrari Marlboro

CAR #2 RUBENS BARRICHELLO (BRA; AGE: 31)

Ferrari F2002 V10
Scuderia Ferrari Marlboro

RUBENS BARRICHELLO (CONTD)

Ferrari F2003-GA V10
Scuderia Ferrari Marlboro

CAR #3 JUAN PABLO MONTOYA (COL; AGE: 27)

Williams FW25-BMW V10
BMW Williams F1

CAR #4 RALF SCHUMACHER (GER; AGE: 28)

Williams FW25-BMW V10
BMW Williams F1

CAR #5 DAVID COULTHARD (GBR; AGE: 32)

McLaren MP4/17D-Mercedes V10
West McLaren Mercedes

CAR #6 KIMI RÄIKKÖNEN (FIN; AGE: 23)

McLaren MP4/17D-Mercedes V10
West McLaren Mercedes

CAR #7 JARNO TRULLI (ITA; AGE: 28)

Renault R23 V10
Mild Seven Renault Sport

CAR #8 FERNANDO ALONSO (ESP; AGE: 21)

Renault R23 V10
Mild Seven Renault Sport

CAR #9 NICK HEIDFELD (GER; AGE: 26)

Sauber C22-Petronas V10
Sauber Petronas

CAR #10 HEINZ-HARALD FRENTZEN (GER; AGE: 36)

Sauber C22-Petronas V10
Sauber Petronas

CAR #11 GIANCARLO FISICHELLA (ITA; AGE: 30)

Jordan EJ13-Ford V10
Jordan Ford

CAR #12 RALPH FIRMAN (GBR; AGE: 27)

Jordan EJ13-Ford V10
Jordan Ford

CAR #14 MARK WEBBER (AUS; AGE: 26)

Jaguar R4-Cosworth V10
Jaguar Racing

2003

CHAMPIONSHIP CAR-BY-CAR

CAR #15 **ANTONIO PIZZONIA** (BRA; AGE: 22)

Jaguar R4-Cosworth V10
Jaguar Racing

CAR #16 **JACQUES VILLENEUVE** (CAN; AGE: 32)

BAR 005-Honda V10
Lucky Strike BAR Honda

CAR #17 **JENSON BUTTON** (GBR; AGE: 23)

BAR 005-Honda V10
Lucky Strike BAR Honda

CAR #18 **JUSTIN WILSON** (GBR; AGE: 24)

Minardi PS03-Cosworth V10
European Minardi Cosworth

CAR #19 **JOS VERSTAPPEN** (NED; AGE: 31)

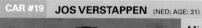

Minardi PS03-Cosworth V10
European Minardi Cosworth

CAR #20 **OLIVIER PANIS** (FRA; AGE: 36)

Toyota TF103 V10
Panasonic Toyota Racing

CAR #21 **CRISTIANO DA MATTA** (BRA; AGE: 26)

Toyota TF103 V10
Panasonic Toyota Racing

CAR #15 **JUSTIN WILSON** (GBR; AGE: 25)

Jaguar C4-Cosworth V10
Jaguar Racing

CAR #18 **NICOLAS KIESA** (DEN; AGE: 25)

Minardi PS03-Cosworth V10
European Minardi F1

A-Z

DRIVER A-Z

GEORGE ABECASSIS
Nat: GBR. Born: 21.03.1913. Died: 18.12.1991
Debut: 1951 Swiss GP. Starts: 2

KENNETH ACHESON
Nat: GBR. Born: 27.11.1957
Debut: 1983 South African GP. Starts: 3

ANDREA DE ADAMICH
Nat: ITA. Born: 3.10.1941
Debut: 1968 South African GP. Starts: 30. Points: 6

PHILIPPE ADAMS
Nat: BEL. Born: 19.11.1969
Debut: 1994 Belgian GP. Starts: 2

KURT ADOLFF
Nat: GER. Born: 5.11.1921
Debut: 1953 German GP. Starts: 1

KURT AHRENS JR
Nat: GER. Born: 19.04.1940
Debut: 1966 German GP. Starts: 4

MICHELE ALBORETO
Nat: ITA. Born: 23.12.1956. Died: 25.04.2001
Debut: 1981 San Marino GP. Starts: 194. Points: 186.5. Wins: 5. PP: 2. FL: 5

JEAN ALESI
Nat: FRA. Born: 11.06.1964
Debut: 1989 French GP. Starts: 201. Points: 241. Wins: 1. PP: 2. FL: 4

PHILIPPE ALLIOT
Nat: FRA. Born: 27.07.1954
Debut: 1984 Brazilian GP. Starts: 109. Points: 7

CLIFF ALLISON
Nat: GBR. Born: 8.02.1932
Debut: 1958 Monaco GP. Starts: 16. Points: 11

FERNANDO ALONSO
Nat: ESP. Born: 29.07.1981
Debut: 2001 Australian GP. Starts: 17

CHRIS AMON
Nat: NZ. Born: 20.07.1943
Debut: 1963 Belgian GP. Starts: 96. Points: 83. PP: 5. FL: 3

BOB ANDERSON
Nat: RHO. Born: 19.05.1931. Died: 14.08.1967
Debut: 1963 British GP. Starts: 25. Points: 8

CONNY ANDERSSON
Nat: SWE. Born: 28.12.1939
Debut: 1976 Dutch GP. Starts: 1

MARIO ANDRETTI
Nat: USA. Born: 28.02.1940
Debut: 1968 United States GP. Starts: 128. Points: 180. Wins: 12. PP: 18. FL: 10

MICHAEL ANDRETTI
Nat: USA. Born: 5.10.1962
Debut: 1993 South African GP. Starts: 13. Points: 7

ELIO DE ANGELIS
Nat: ITA. Born: 26.03.1958. Died: 15.05.1986
Debut: 1979 Argentine GP. Starts: 108. Points: 122. Wins: 2. PP: 3

MARCO APICELLA
Nat: ITA. Born: 7.10.1965
Debut: 1993 Italian GP. Starts: 1

RENÉ ARNOUX
Nat: FRA. Born: 4.07.1948
Debut: 1978 Belgian GP. Starts: 149. Points: 181. Wins: 7. PP: 18. FL: 12

PETER ARUNDELL
Nat: GBR. Born: 8.11.1933
Debut: 1964 Monaco GP. Starts: 11. Points: 12

A-Z

DRIVER A-Z

ASCARI

ASHDOWN

ASTON

ATTWOOD

BANDINI

BARBAZZA

ASHMORE

BADOER

BAILEY

BARILLA

BARBER, SKIP

ASHLEY

BAGHETTI

BALDI

BARRICHELLO

BARTH

ALBERTO ASCARI

Nat: ITA. Born: 13.07.1918. Died: 26.05.1955 Debut: 1950 Monaco GP. Starts: 31. Points: 140.64. Wins: 13. PP: 14. FL: 13

PETER ASHDOWN

Nat: GBR. Born: 16.10.1934 Debut: 1959 British GP. Starts: 1

IAN ASHLEY

Nat: GBR. Born: 26.10.1947 Debut: 1974 German GP. Starts: 4

GERRY ASHMORE

Nat: GBR. Born: 25.07.1936 Debut: 1961 British GP. Starts: 3

BILL ASTON

Nat: GBR. Born: 29.03.1900. Died: 4.03.1974 Debut: 1952 German GP. Starts: 1

RICHARD ATTWOOD

Nat: GBR. Born: 4.04.1940 Debut: 1965 Monaco GP. Starts: 17. Points: 11. FL: 1

LUCA BADOER

Nat: ITA. Born: 25.01.1971 Debut: 1993 South African GP. Starts: 49

GIANCARLO BAGHETTI

Nat: ITA. Born: 25.12.1934. Died: 27.11.1995 Debut: 1961 French GP. Starts: 21. Points: 14. Wins: 1. FL: 1

JULIAN BAILEY

Nat: GBR. Born: 9.10.1961 Debut: 1988 San Marino GP. Starts: 7. Points: 1

MAURO BALDI

Nat: ITA. Born: 31.01.1954 Debut: 1982 Brazilian GP. Starts: 36. Points: 5

MARCEL BALSA

Nat: FRA. Born: 1.01.1909. Died: 11.08.1984 Debut: 1952 German GP. Starts: 1

LORENZO BANDINI

Nat: ITA. Born: 21.12.1935. Died: 10.05.1967 Debut: 1961 Belgian GP. Starts: 42. Points: 58. Wins: 1. PP: 1. FL: 2

FABRIZIO BARBAZZA

Nat: ITA. Born: 2.04.1963 Debut: 1993 South African GP. Starts: 8. Points: 2

JOHN BARBER

Nat: GBR. Born: 22.07.1929 Debut: 1953 Argentine GP. Starts: 1

SKIP BARBER

Nat: USA. Born: 16.11.1936 Debut: 1971 Dutch GP. Starts: 5

PAOLO BARILLA

Nat: ITA. Born: 20.04.1961 Debut: 1989 Japanese GP. Starts: 9

RUBENS BARRICHELLO

Nat: BRA. Born: 23.05.1972 Debut: 1993 South African GP. Starts: 162. Points: 272. Wins: 5. PP: 6. FL: 8

EDGAR BARTH

Nat: DDR. Born: 26.01.1917. Died: 20.05.1965 Debut: 1953 German GP. Starts: 5

GIORGIO BASSI

Nat: ITA. Born: 20.01.1934 Debut: 1965 Italian GP. Starts: 1

ERWIN BAUER

Nat: GER. Born: 17.07.1912. Died: 3.06.1958 Debut: 1953 German GP. Starts: 1

A-Z

DRIVER A-Z

ÉLIE BAYOL

Nat: FRA. Born: 28.02.1914. Died: 25.05.1995
Debut: 1952 Italian GP. Starts: 7. Points: 2

CAREL GODIN DE BEAUFORT

Nat: NED. Born: 10.04.1934. Died: 3.08.1964
Debut: 1957 German GP. Starts: 28.
Points: 4

DON BEAUMAN

Nat: GBR. Born: 26.07.1928. Died: 9.07.1955
Debut: 1954 British GP. Starts: 1

GÜNTHER BECHEM

Nat: GER. Born: 21.12.1921
Debut: 1952 German GP. Starts: 2

JEAN BEHRA

Nat: FRA. Born: 16.02.1921. Died: 1.08.1959
Debut: 1952 Swiss GP. Starts: 52. Points:
51.140. FL: 1

DEREK BELL

Nat: GBR. Born: 31.10.1941
Debut: 1968 Italian GP. Starts: 9. Points: 1

STEFAN BELLOF

Nat: GER. Born: 20.11.1957. Died: 1.09.1985
Debut: 1984 Brazilian GP. Starts: 20.
Points: 4

PAUL BELMONDO

Nat: FRA. Born: 23.04.1963
Debut: 1992 Spanish GP. Starts: 7

TOM BELSO

Nat: DEN. Born: 27.08.1942
Debut: 1974 South African GP. Starts: 2

JEAN-PIERRE BELTOISE

Nat: FRA. Born: 26.04.1937
Debut: 1966 German GP. Starts: 86.
Points: 77. Wins: 1. FL: 4

OLIVIER BERETTA

Nat: MON. Born: 23.11.1969
Debut: 1994 Brazilian GP. Starts: 9

ALLEN BERG

Nat: CAN. Born: 1.08.1961
Debut: 1986 Detroit GP. Starts: 9

GEORGES BERGER

Nat: BEL. Born: 14.09.1918. Died: 23.08.1967
Debut: 1953 Belgian GP. Starts: 2

GERHARD BERGER

Nat: AUT. Born: 27.08.1959
Debut: 1984 Austrian GP. Starts: 210.
Points: 385. Wins: 10. PP: 12. FL: 21

ÉRIC BERNARD

Nat: FRA. Born: 24.08.1964
Debut: 1989 French GP. Starts: 45. Points: 10

ENRIQUE BERNOLDI

Nat: BRA. Born: 19.10.1978
Debut: 2001 Australian GP. Starts: 28

MIKE BEUTTLER

Nat: GBR. Born: 13.08.1940. Died:
29.12.1988
Debut: 1971 British GP. Starts: 28

LUCIEN BIANCHI

Nat: BEL. Born: 10.11.1934. Died: 30.03.1969
Debut: 1960 Belgian GP. Starts: 17. Points: 6

GINO BIANCO

Nat: BRA. Born: 22.07.1916. Died: 17.01.1983
Debut: 1952 British GP. Starts: 4

HANS BINDER

Nat: AUT. Born: 12.06.1948
Debut: 1976 Austrian GP. Starts: 13

A-Z

DRIVER A-Z

CLEMENTE BIONDETTI
Nat: ITA. Born: 18.08.1898. Died: 24.02.1955
Debut: 1950 Italian GP. Starts: 1

"B BIRA"
Nat: THA. Born: 15.07.1914. Died: 23.12.1985
Debut: 1950 British GP. Starts: 19. Points: 8

PABLO BIRGER
Nat: ARG. Born: 6.01.1924. Died: 9.03.1966
Debut: 1953 Argentine GP. Starts: 2

HARRY BLANCHARD
Nat: USA. Born: 30.06.1931. Died: 31.01.1960
Debut: 1959 United States GP. Starts: 1

MICHAEL BLEEKEMOLEN
Nat: NED. Born: 2.10.1949
Debut: 1978 United States GP. Starts: 1

TREVOR BLOKDYK
Nat: RSA. Born: 30.11.1935. Died: 19.03.1995
Debut: 1963 South African GP. Starts: 1

MARK BLUNDELL
Nat: GBR. Born: 8.04.1966
Debut: 1991 United States GP. Starts: 61. Points: 32

RAUL BOESEL
Nat: BRA. Born: 4.12.1957
Debut: 1982 South African GP. Starts: 23

BOB BONDURANT
Nat: USA. Born: 27.04.1933
Debut: 1965 United States GP. Starts: 9. Points: 3

FELICE BONETTO
Nat: ITA. Born: 9.06.1903. Died: 21.11.1953
Debut: 1950 Swiss GP. Starts: 15. Points: 17.5

JO BONNIER
Nat: SWE. Born: 31.01.1930. Died: 11.06.1972
Debut: 1956 Italian GP. Starts: 104. Points: 39. Wins: 1. PP: 1

ROBERTO BONOMI
Nat: ARG. Born: 30.09.1919
Debut: 1960 Argentine GP. Starts: 1

SLIM BORGUDD
Nat: SWE. Born: 25.11.1946
Debut: 1981 San Marino GP. Starts: 10. Points: 1

LUKI BOTHA
Nat: RSA. Born: 16.01.1930
Debut: 1967 South African GP. Starts: 1

JEAN-CHRISTOPHE BOULLION
Nat: FRA. Born: 27.12.1969
Debut: 1995 Monaco GP. Starts: 11. Points: 3

THIERRY BOUTSEN
Nat: BEL. Born: 13.07.1957
Debut: 1983 Belgian GP. Starts: 163. Points: 132. Wins: 3. PP: 1. FL: 1

DAVID BRABHAM
Nat: AUS. Born: 5.09.1965
Debut: 1990 Monaco GP. Starts: 24

JACK BRABHAM
Nat: AUS. Born: 2.04.1926
Debut: 1955 British GP. Starts: 126. Points: 261. Wins: 14. PP: 13. FL: 12

BILL BRACK
Nat: CAN. Born: 26.12.1935
Debut: 1968 Canadian GP. Starts: 3

VITTORIO BRAMBILLA
Nat: ITA. Born: 11.11.1937. Died: 26.05.2001
Debut: 1974 South African GP. Starts: 74. Points: 15.5. Wins: 1. PP: 1. FL: 1

A-Z

DRIVER A-Z

BRANCA

BRANDON

BROEKER

BROOKS

BRUNDLE

BURGESS

BURTI

BRIDGER
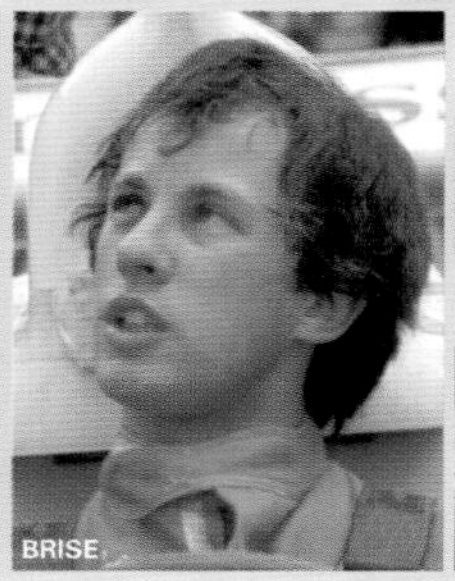
BRISE

BROWN, WARWICK

BROWN, ALAN

BUCCI

BUSSINELLO

BRISTOW

BUCKNUM

BRUDES

BUEB

BUENO

BUTTON

BYRNE

ANTONIO BRANCA
Nat: SUI. Born: 15.09.1916. Died: 10.05.1985
Debut: 1950 Swiss GP. Starts: 3

ERIC BRANDON
Nat: GBR. Born: 18.07.1920. Died: 8.08.1982
Debut: 1952 Swiss GP. Starts: 5

TOMMY BRIDGER
Nat: GBR. Born: 24.06.1934. Died: 30.07.1991
Debut: 1958 Moroccan GP. Starts: 1

TONY BRISE
Nat: GBR. Born: 28.03.1952. Died: 29.11.1975
Debut: 1975 Spanish GP. Starts: 10.
Points: 1

CHRIS BRISTOW
Nat: GBR. Born: 2.12.1937. Died: 19.06.1960
Debut: 1959 British GP. Starts: 4

PETER BROEKER
Nat: CAN. Born: 15.5.1929. Died: 1980
Debut: 1963 United States GP. Starts: 1

TONY BROOKS
Nat: GBR. Born: 25.02.1932
Debut: 1956 British GP. Starts: 38. Points: 75.
Wins: 6. PP: 3. FL: 3

ALAN BROWN
Nat: GBR. Born: 20.11.1919
Debut: 1952 Swiss GP. Starts: 8. Points: 2

WARWICK BROWN
Nat: AUS. Born: 24.12.1949
Debut: 1976 United States GP. Starts: 1

ADOLF BRUDES
Nat: GER. Born: 15.10.1899. Died: 5.11.1986
Debut: 1952 German GP. Starts: 1

MARTIN BRUNDLE
Nat: GBR. Born: 1.06.1959
Debut: 1984 Brazilian GP. Starts: 158.
Points: 98

CLEMAR BUCCI
Nat: ARG. Born: 4.09.1920
Debut: 1954 British GP. Starts: 5

RONNIE BUCKNUM
Nat: USA. Born: 5.04.1936. Died: 25.04.1992
Debut: 1964 German GP. Starts: 11.
Points: 2

IVOR BUEB
Nat: GBR. Born: 6.06.1923. Died: 1.08.1959
Debut: 1957 Monaco GP. Starts: 5

LUIZ-PEREIRA BUENO
Nat: BRA. Born: 16.01.1937
Debut: 1973 Brazilian GP. Starts: 1

IAN BURGESS
Nat: GBR. Born: 6.07.1930
Debut: 1958 British GP. Starts: 16

LUCIANO BURTI
Nat: BRA. Born: 5.03.1975
Debut: 2000 Austrian GP. Starts: 15

ROBERO BUSSINELLO
Nat: ITA. Born: 4.10.1927. Died: 24.08.1999
Debut: 1961 Italian GP. Starts: 2

JENSON BUTTON
Nat: GBR. Born: 19.01.1980
Debut: 2000 Australian GP. Starts: 51.
Points: 28

TOMMY BYRNE
Nat: IRL. Born: 6.05.1958
Debut: 1982 Austrian GP. Starts: 2

A-Z

DRIVER A-Z

GIULIO CABIANCA

Nat: ITA. Born: 19.02.1923. Died: 15.06.1961
Debut: 1958 Italian GP. Starts: 3. Points: 3

MARIO ARAUJO DE CABRAL

Nat: POR. Born: 15.01.1934
Debut: 1959 Portuguese GP. Starts: 4

ALEX CAFFI

Nat: ITA. Born: 18.03.1964
Debut: 1986 Italian GP. Starts: 56. Points: 6

JOHN CAMPBELL-JONES

Nat: GBR. Born: 21.01.1930
Debut: 1962 Belgian GP. Starts: 2

ADRIAN CAMPOS

Nat: ESP. Born: 17.06.1960
Debut: 1987 Brazilian GP. Starts: 17

JOHN CANNON

Nat: CAN. Born: 21.06.1937. Died: 18.10.1999
Debut: 1971 United States GP. Starts: 1

EITEL CANTONI

Nat: URU. Born: 4.10.1896. Died: ??.6.1997
Debut: 1952 British GP. Starts: 3

IVAN CAPELLI

Nat: ITA. Born: 24.05.1963
Debut: 1985 European GP. Starts: 93. Points: 31

PIERO CARINI

Nat: ITA. Born: 6.03.1921. Died: 30.05.1957
Debut: 1952 French GP. Starts: 3

EUGENIO CASTELLOTTI

Nat: ITA. Born: 10.10.1930. Died: 14.03.1957
Debut: 1955 Argentine GP. Starts: 14. Points: 19.5. PP: 1

ROBERT LA CAZE

Nat: MAR. Born: 26.02.1917
Debut: 1958 Moroccan GP. Starts: 1

JOHNNY CECOTTO

Nat: VEN. Born: 25.01.1956
Debut: 1983 Brazilian GP. Starts: 18. Points: 1

ANDREA DE CESARIS

Nat: ITA. Born: 31.05.1959
Debut: 1980 Canadian GP. Starts: 208. Points: 59. PP: 1. FL: 1

FRANÇOIS CEVERT

Nat: FRA. Born: 25.02.1944. Died: 6.10.1973
Debut: 1969 German GP. Starts: 47. Points: 89. Wins: 1. FL: 2

EUGÈNE CHABOUD

Nat: FRA. Born: 12.04.1907. Died: 28.12.1983
Debut: 1950 Belgian GP. Starts: 3. Points: 1

JAY CHAMBERLAIN

Nat: USA. Born: 29.12.1925. Died: 1.08.2001
Debut: 1962 British GP. Starts: 1

DAVE CHARLTON

Nat: RSA. Born: 27.10.1936
Debut: 1967 South African GP. Starts: 11

EDDIE CHEEVER

Nat: USA. Born: 10.01.1958
Debut: 1978 South African GP. Starts: 132. Points: 70

ANDREA CHIESA

Nat: SUI. Born: 6.05.1964
Debut: 1992 Mexican GP. Starts: 3

ETTORE CHIMERI

Nat: VEN. Born: 4.06.1921. Died: 27.02.1960
Debut: 1960 Argentine GP. Starts: 1

A-Z

DRIVER A-Z

CHIRON

CLAES

COLLINS

COLLOMB

COMAS

COMOTTI

CROOK

CROSSLEY

CLARK

COULTHARD

COURAGE

CORDTS

DAIGH

DALMAS

CRAFT

CRAWFORD

DALY

DANNER

LOUIS CHIRON
Nat: MON. Born: 3.08.1899. Died: 22.06.1979
Debut: 1950 British GP. Starts: 15. Points: 4

JOHNNY CLAES
Nat: BEL. Born: 11.08.1916. Died: 3.02.1956
Debut: 1950 British GP. Starts: 23

JIM CLARK
Nat: GBR. Born: 4.03.1936. Died: 7.04.1968
Debut: 1960 Dutch GP. Starts: 72. Points: 274. Wins: 25. PP: 33. FL: 28

PETER COLLINS
Nat: GBR. Born: 6.11.1931. Died: 3.08.1958
Debut: 1952 Swiss GP. Starts: 32. Points: 47. Wins: 3

BERNARD COLLOMB
Nat: FRA. Born: 7.10.1930
Debut: 1961 French GP. Starts: 4

ERIK COMAS
Nat: FRA. Born: 28.09.1963
Debut: 1991 Brazilian GP. Starts: 59. Points: 7

GIANFRANCO COMOTTI
Nat: ITA. Born: 24.07.1906. Died: 10.05.1963
Debut: 1950 Italian GP. Starts: 2

GEORGE CONSTANTINE
Nat: USA. Born: 22.02.1918. Died: 7.01.1968
Debut: 1959 United States GP. Starts: 1

JOHN CORDTS
Nat: CAN. Born: 23.07.1935
Debut: 1969 Canadian GP. Starts: 1

DAVID COULTHARD
Nat: GBR. Born: 27.03.1971
Debut: 1994 Spanish GP. Starts: 141. Points: 400. Wins: 12. PP: 12. FL: 18

PIERS COURAGE
Nat: GBR. Born: 27.05.1942. Died: 21.06.1970
Debut: 1966 German GP. Starts: 28. Points: 20

CHRIS CRAFT
Nat: GBR. Born: 17.11.1939
Debut: 1971 United States GP. Starts: 1

JIM CRAWFORD
Nat: GBR. Born: 13.02.1948. Died: 6.08.2002
Debut: 1975 British GP. Starts: 2

ANTONIO CREUS
Nat: ESP. Born: 28.10.1919. Died: 19.02.1966
Debut: 1960 Argentine GP. Starts: 1

TONY CROOK
Nat: GBR. Born: 16.02.1920
Debut: 1952 British GP. Starts: 2

GEOFFREY CROSSLEY
Nat: GBR. Born: 11.05.1921. Died: 7.01.2002
Debut: 1950 British GP. Starts: 2

CHUCK DAIGH
Nat: USA. Born: 29.11.1923
Debut: 1960 Belgian GP. Starts: 3

YANNICK DALMAS
Nat: FRA. Born: 28.07.1961
Debut: 1987 Mexican GP. Starts: 23

DEREK DALY
Nat: IRL. Born: 11.03.1953
Debut: 1978 British GP. Starts: 49. Points: 15

CHRISTIAN DANNER
Nat: GER. Born: 4.04.1958
Debut: 1985 Belgian GP. Starts: 36. Points: 4

A-Z

DRIVER A-Z

JORGE DAPONTE

Nat: ARG. Born: 5.06.1923. Died: 9.03.1963
Debut: 1954 Argentine GP. Starts: 2

ANTHONY DAVIDSON

Nat: GBR. Born: 18.04.1979
Debut: 2002 Hungarian GP. Starts: 2

COLIN DAVIS

Nat: GBR. Born: 29.07.1933
Debut: 1959 French GP. Starts: 2

JEAN-DENIS DELETRAZ

Nat: SUI. Born: 1.10.1963
Debut: 1994 Australian GP. Starts: 3

PATRICK DEPAILLER

Nat: FRA. Born: 9.08.1944. Died: 1.08.1980
Debut: 1972 French GP. Starts: 95.
Points: 141. Wins: 2. PP: 1. FL: 4

PEDRO DINIZ

Nat: BRA. Born: 22.05.1970
Debut: 1995 Brazilian GP. Starts: 98.
Points: 10

JOSÉ DOLHEM

Nat: FRA. Born: 26.04.1944. Died: 16.04.1988
Debut: 1974 United States GP. Starts: 1

MARTIN DONNELLY

Nat: GBR. Born: 26.03.1964
Debut: 1989 French GP. Starts: 13

MARK DONOHUE

Nat: USA. Born: 18.03.1937. Died: 19.08.1975
Debut: 1971 Canadian GP. Starts: 14.
Points: 8

KEN DOWNING

Nat: GBR. Born: 5.12.1917
Debut: 1952 British GP. Starts: 2

BOB DRAKE

Nat: USA. Born: 14.12.1919. Died: 18.04.1990
Debut: 1960 United States GP. Starts: 1

PADDY DRIVER

Nat: RSA. Born: 13.05.1934
Debut: 1974 South African GP. Starts: 1

PIERO DROGO

Nat: VEN. Born: 8.08.1926. Died: 28.04.1973
Debut: 1960 Italian GP. Starts: 1

JOHNNY DUMFRIES

Nat: GBR. Born: 26.04.1958
Debut: 1986 Brazilian GP. Starts: 15.
Points: 3

GEORGE EATON

Nat: CAN. Born: 12.11.1945
Debut: 1969 United States GP. Starts: 11

GUY EDWARDS

Nat: GBR. Born: 30.12.1942
Debut: 1974 Argentine GP. Starts: 11

VIC ELFORD

Nat: GBR. Born: 10.06.1935
Debut: 1968 French GP. Starts: 13.
Points: 8

PAUL EMERY

Nat: GBR. Born: 12.11.1916. Died: 3.02.1993
Debut: 1956 British GP. Starts: 1

TOMAS ENGE

Nat: CZE. Born: 11.09.1976
Debut: 2001 Italian GP. Starts: 3

PAUL ENGLAND

Nat: AUS. Born: 28.03.1929
Debut: 1957 German GP. Starts: 1

A-Z

DRIVER A-Z

HARALD ERTL
Nat: AUT. Born: 31.08.1948. Died: 7.04.1982
Debut: 1975 German GP. Starts: 19

NASIF ESTEFANO
Nat: ARG. Born: 18.11.1932. Died: 21.10.1973
Debut: 1960 Argentine GP. Starts: 1

PHILIPPE ÉTANÇELIN
Nat: FRA. Born: 28.12.1896. Died: 13.10.1981
Debut: 1950 British GP. Starts: 12. Points: 3

BOB EVANS
Nat: GBR. Born: 11.06.1947
Debut: 1975 South African GP. Starts: 10

CORRADO FABI
Nat: ITA. Born: 12.04.1961
Debut: 1983 Brazilian GP. Starts: 12

TEO FABI
Nat: ITA. Born: 9.03.1955
Debut: 1982 San Marino GP. Starts: 64. Points: 23. PP: 3. FL: 2

PASCAL FABRE
Nat: FRA. Born: 9.01.1960
Debut: 1987 Brazilian GP. Starts: 11

LUIGI FAGIOLI
Nat: ITA. Born: 9.06.1898. Died: 20.06.1952
Debut: 1950 British GP. Starts: 7. Points: 32. Wins: 1

JACK FAIRMAN
Nat: GBR. Born: 15.03.1913. Died: 7.02.2002
Debut: 1953 British GP. Starts: 12. Points: 5

JUAN MANUEL FANGIO
Nat: ARG. Born: 24.06.1911. Died: 17.07.1995
Debut: 1950 British GP. Starts: 51. Points: 278.64. Wins: 24. PP: 29. FL: 23

GIUSEPPE FARINA
Nat: ITA. Born: 30.10.1906. Died: 30.06.1966
Debut: 1950 British GP. Starts: 33. Points: 127.330. Wins: 5. PP: 5. FL: 5

MARIA TERESA DE FILIPPIS
Nat: ITA. Born: 11.11.1926
Debut: 1958 Belgian GP. Starts: 3

RALPH FIRMAN JR
Nat: GBR. Born: 20.05.1975
Debut: 2003 Australian GP

RUDOLF FISCHER
Nat: SUI. Born: 19.04.1912. Died: 30.12.1976
Debut: 1951 Swiss GP. Starts: 7. Points: 10

MIKE FISHER
Nat: USA. Born: 13.03.1943
Debut: 1967 Canadian GP. Starts: 2

GIANCARLO FISICHELLA
Nat: ITA. Born: 14.01.1973
Debut: 1996 Australian GP. Starts: 107. Points: 82. PP: 1. FL: 1

JOHN FITCH
Nat: USA. Born: 4.08.1917
Debut: 1953 Italian GP. Starts: 2

CHRISTIAN FITTIPALDI
Nat: BRA. Born: 18.01.1971
Debut: 1992 South African GP. Starts: 40. Points: 12

EMERSON FITTIPALDI
Nat: BRA. Born: 12.12.1946
Debut: 1970 British GP. Starts: 144. Points: 281. Wins: 14. PP: 6. FL: 6

WILSON FITTIPALDI
Nat: BRA. Born: 25.12.1943
Debut: 1972 Spanish GP. Starts: 35. Points: 3

A-Z

DRIVER A-Z

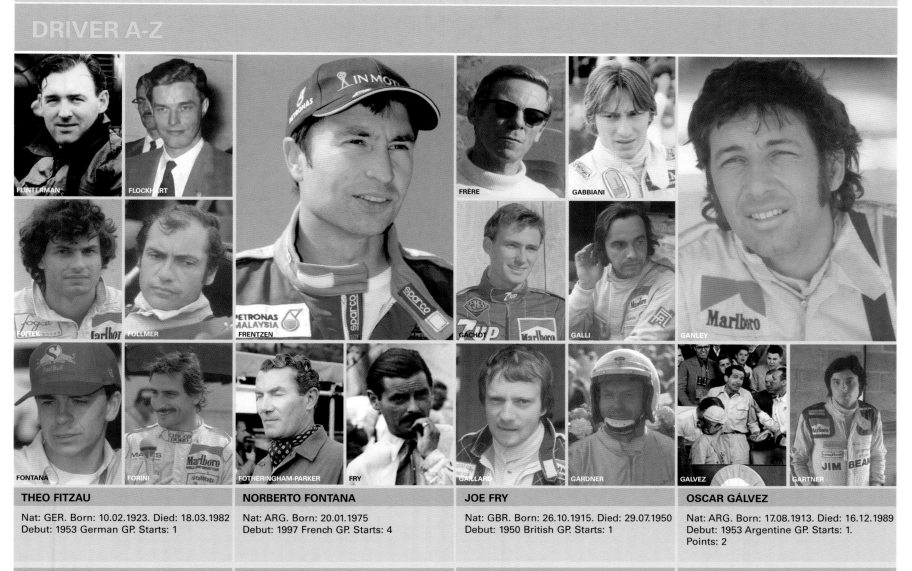

THEO FITZAU
Nat: GER. Born: 10.02.1923. Died: 18.03.1982
Debut: 1953 German GP. Starts: 1

JAN FLINTERMAN
Nat: NED. Born: 2.10.1919. Died: 26.12.1992
Debut: 1952 Dutch GP. Starts: 1

RON FLOCKHART
Nat: GBR. Born: 16.06.1923. Died: 12.04.1962
Debut: 1954 British GP. Starts: 13. Points: 5

GREGOR FOITEK
Nat: SUI. Born: 27.03.1965
Debut: 1990 United States GP. Starts: 7

GEORGE FOLLMER
Nat: USA. Born: 27.01.1934
Debut: 1973 South African GP. Starts: 12. Points: 5

NORBERTO FONTANA
Nat: ARG. Born: 20.01.1975
Debut: 1997 French GP. Starts: 4

FRANCO FORINI
Nat: SUI. Born: 22.09.1958
Debut: 1987 Italian GP. Starts: 2

PHILIP FOTHERINGHAM-PARKER
Nat: GBR. Born: 22.09.1907. Died: 15.10.1981
Debut: 1951 British GP. Starts: 1

HEINZ-HARALD FRENTZEN
Nat: GER. Born: 18.05.1967
Debut: 1994 Brazilian GP. Starts: 141. Points: 161. Wins: 3. PP: 2. FL: 6

PAUL FRÈRE
Nat: BEL. Born: 30.01.1917
Debut: 1952 Belgian GP. Starts: 11. Points: 11

JOE FRY
Nat: GBR. Born: 26.10.1915. Died: 29.07.1950
Debut: 1950 British GP. Starts: 1

BEPPE GABBIANI
Nat: ITA. Born: 2.01.1957
Debut: 1981 Long Beach GP. Starts: 3

BERTRAND GACHOT
Nat: BEL. Born: 23.12.1962
Debut: 1989 French GP. Starts: 47. Points: 5. FL: 1

PATRICK GAILLARD
Nat: FRA. Born: 12.02.1952
Debut: 1979 British GP. Starts: 2

NANNI GALLI
Nat: ITA. Born: 2.10.1940
Debut: 1971 Dutch GP. Starts: 17

OSCAR GÁLVEZ
Nat: ARG. Born: 17.08.1913. Died: 16.12.1989
Debut: 1953 Argentine GP. Starts: 1. Points: 2

FRED GAMBLE
Nat: USA. Born: 17.03.1932
Debut: 1960 Italian GP. Starts: 1

HOWDEN GANLEY
Nat: NZ. Born: 24.12.1941
Debut: 1971 South African GP. Starts: 35. Points: 10

FRANK GARDNER
Nat: AUS. Born: 1.10.1930
Debut: 1964 British GP. Starts: 8

JO GARTNER
Nat: AUT. Born: 4.01.1954. Died: 1.06.1986
Debut: 1984 San Marino GP. Starts: 8

A-Z

DRIVER A-Z

GAZE

GETHIN

GINTHER

GONZÁLEZ, JOSÉ FR

GOULD

GENE

GHINZANI

GERARD

GOUNON

GENDEBIEN

GIACOMELLI

GIRAUD-CABANTOUS

GIUNTI

GODIA-SALES

DE GRAFFE

TONY GAZE
Nat: AUS. Born: 3.02.1920
Debut: 1952 Belgian GP. Starts: 3

OLIVIER GENDEBIEN
Nat: BEL. Born: 12.01.1924. Died: 2.10.1998
Debut: 1956 Argentine GP. Starts: 14. Points: 18

MARC GENE
Nat: ESP. Born: 29.03.1974
Debut: 1999 Australian GP. Starts: 33. Points: 1

BOB GERARD
Nat: GBR. Born: 19.01.1914. Died: 26.01.1990
Debut: 1950 British GP. Starts: 8

GERINO GERINI
Nat: ITA. Born: 10.08.1928
Debut: 1956 Argentine GP. Starts: 6. Points: 1.5

PETER GETHIN
Nat: GBR. Born: 21.02.1940
Debut: 1970 Dutch GP. Starts: 30. Points: 11. Wins: 1

PIERCARLO GHINZANI
Nat: ITA. Born: 16.01.1952
Debut: 1981 Belgian GP. Starts: 76. Points: 2

BRUNO GIACOMELLI
Nat: ITA. Born: 10.09.1952
Debut: 1977 Italian GP. Starts: 69. Points: 14. PP: 1

DICK GIBSON
Nat: GBR. Born: 16.04.1918
Debut: 1957 German GP. Starts: 2

RICHIE GINTHER
Nat: USA. Born: 5.08.1930. Died: 20.09.1989
Debut: 1960 Monaco GP. Starts: 52. Points: 107. Wins: 1. FL: 3

YVES GIRAUD-CABANTOUS
Nat: FRA. Born: 8.10.1904. Died: 31.03.1973
Debut: 1950 British GP. Starts: 13. Points: 5

IGNAZIO GIUNTI
Nat: ITA. Born: 30.08.1941. Died: 10.01.1971
Debut: 1970 Belgian GP. Starts: 4. Points: 3

CHICO GODIA-SALES
Nat: ESP. Born: 21.03.1921. Died: 28.11.1990
Debut: 1951 Spanish GP. Starts: 13. Points: 6

CHRISTIAN GOETHALS
Nat: BEL. Born: 4.08.1928
Debut: 1958 German GP. Starts: 1

JOSÉ FROILÁN GONZÁLEZ
Nat: ARG. Born: 5.10.1922
Debut: 1950 Monaco GP. Starts: 26. Points: 77.64. Wins: 2. PP: 3. FL: 6

OSCAR GONZÁLEZ
Nat: URU. Born: 10.11.1923. Died: 1999
Debut: 1956 Argentine GP. Starts: 1

ALDO GORDINI
Nat: FRA. Born: 20.05.1921. Died: 28.01.1995
Debut: 1951 French GP. Starts: 1

HORACE GOULD
Nat: GBR. Born: 20.09.1921. Died: 4.11.1968
Debut: 1954 British GP. Starts: 14. Points: 2

JEAN-MARC GOUNON
Nat: FRA. Born: 1.01.1963
Debut: 1993 Japanese GP. Starts: 9

EMMANUEL DE GRAFFENRIED
Nat: SUI. Born: 18.05.1914
Debut: 1950 British GP. Starts: 22. Points: 9

A-Z

DRIVER A-Z

KEITH GREENE

Nat: GBR. Born: 5.01.1938
Debut: 1960 British GP. Starts: 3

MASTEN GREGORY

Nat: USA. Born: 29.02.1932. Died: 8.11.1985
Debut: 1957 Monaco GP. Starts: 38.
Points: 21

GEORGES GRIGNARD

Nat: FRA. Born: 25.07.1905. Died: 7.12.1977
Debut: 1951 Spanish GP. Starts: 1

OLIVIER GROUILLARD

Nat: FRA. Born: 2.09.1958
Debut: 1989 Brazilian GP. Starts: 41.
Points: 1

ANDRÉ GUELFI

Nat: FRA. Born: 6.05.1919
Debut: 1958 Moroccan GP. Starts: 1

MIGUEL ANGEL GUERRA

Nat: ARG. Born: 31.08.1953
Debut: 1981 San Marino GP. Starts: 1

ROBERTO GUERRERO

Nat: COL. Born: 16.11.1958
Debut: 1982 Long Beach GP. Starts: 21

MAURICIO GUGELMIN

Nat: BRA. Born: 20.04.1963
Debut: 1988 Brazilian GP. Starts: 74.
Points: 10. FL: 1

DAN GURNEY

Nat: USA. Born: 13.04.1931
Debut: 1959 French GP. Starts: 86.
Points: 133. Wins: 4. PP: 3. FL: 6

HUBERT HAHNE

Nat: GER. Born: 28.03.1935
Debut: 1966 German GP. Starts: 3

MIKE HAILWOOD

Nat: GBR. Born: 2.04.1940. Died: 23.03.1981
Debut: 1963 British GP. Starts: 50.
Points: 29. FL: 1

MIKA HÄKKINEN

Nat: FIN. Born: 28.09.1968
Debut: 1991 United States GP. Starts: 161.
Points: 420. Wins: 20. PP: 26. FL: 25

BRUCE HALFORD

Nat: GBR. Born: 18.05.1931. Died: 2.12.2001
Debut: 1956 British GP. Starts: 8

JIM HALL

Nat: USA. Born: 23.07.1935
Debut: 1960 United States GP. Starts: 11.
Points: 3

DUNCAN HAMILTON

Nat: GBR. Born: 30.04.1920. Died: 13.05.1994
Debut: 1951 British GP. Starts: 5

DAVID HAMPSHIRE

Nat: GBR. Born: 29.12.1917. Died: 25.08.1990
Debut: 1950 British GP. Starts: 2

WALT HANSGEN

Nat: USA. Born: 28.10.1919. Died: 7.04.1966
Debut: 1961 United States GP. Starts: 2.
Points: 2

MIKE HARRIS

Nat: RHO. Born: 25.05.1939
Debut: 1962 South African GP. Starts: 1

CUTH HARRISON

Nat: GBR. Born: 6.07.1906. Died: 21.01.1981
Debut: 1950 British GP. Starts: 3

BRIAN HART

Nat: GBR. Born: 7.09.1936
Debut: 1967 German GP. Starts: 1

A-Z

DRIVER A-Z

MASAHIRO HASEMI

Nat: JAP. Born: 13.11.1945
Debut: 1976 Japanese GP. Starts: 1. FL: 1

PAUL HAWKINS

Nat: AUS. Born: 12.10.1937. Died: 26.05.1969
Debut: 1965 South African GP. Starts: 3

MIKE HAWTHORN

Nat: GBR. Born: 10.04.1929. Died: 22.01.1959
Debut: 1952 Belgian GP. Starts: 45. Points: 127.64. Wins: 3. PP: 4. FL: 6

BOY HAYJE

Nat: NED. Born: 3.05.1949
Debut: 1976 Dutch GP. Starts: 3

WILLI HEEKS

Nat: GER. Born: 13.02.1922. Died: 13.08.1996
Debut: 1952 German GP. Starts: 2

NICK HEIDFELD

Nat: GER. Born: 10.05.1977
Debut: 2000 Australian GP. Starts: 50. Points: 19

THEO HELFRICH

Nat: GER. Born: 13.05.1913. Died: 29.04.1978
Debut: 1952 German GP. Starts: 3

BRIAN HENTON

Nat: GBR. Born: 19.09.1946
Debut: 1975 British GP. Starts: 19. FL: 1

JOHNNY HERBERT

Nat: GBR. Born: 25.06.1964
Debut: 1989 Brazilian GP. Starts: 162. Points: 98. Wins: 3

HANS HERRMANN

Nat: GER. Born: 23.02.1928
Debut: 1953 German GP. Starts: 18. Points: 10. FL: 1

FRANÇOIS HESNAULT

Nat: FRA. Born: 30.12.1956
Debut: 1984 Brazilian GP. Starts: 19

HANS HEYER

Nat: GER. Born: 16.03.1943
Debut: 1977 German GP. Starts: 1

DAMON HILL

Nat: GBR. Born: 17.09.1960
Debut: 1992 British GP. Starts: 115. Points: 360. Wins: 22. PP: 20. FL: 19

GRAHAM HILL

Nat: GBR. Born: 15.02.1929. Died: 29.11.1975
Debut: 1958 Monaco GP. Starts: 176. Points: 289. Wins: 14. PP: 13. FL: 10

PHIL HILL

Nat: USA. Born: 20.04.1927
Debut: 1958 French GP. Starts: 48. Points: 98. Wins: 3. PP: 6. FL: 6

PETER HIRT

Nat: SUI. Born: 30.03.1910. Died: 28.06.1992
Debut: 1951 Swiss GP. Starts: 5

DAVID HOBBS

Nat: GBR. Born: 9.06.1939
Debut: 1967 British GP. Starts: 7

INGO HOFFMANN

Nat: BRA. Born: 18.02.1953
Debut: 1976 Brazilian GP. Starts: 3

KAZUYOSHI HOSHINO

Nat: JAP. Born: 1.07.1947
Debut: 1976 Japanese GP. Starts: 2

DENNY HULME

Nat: NZ. Born: 18.06.1936. Died: 4.10.1992
Debut: 1965 Monaco GP. Starts: 112. Points: 248. Wins: 8. PP: 1. FL: 9

A-Z

DRIVER A-Z

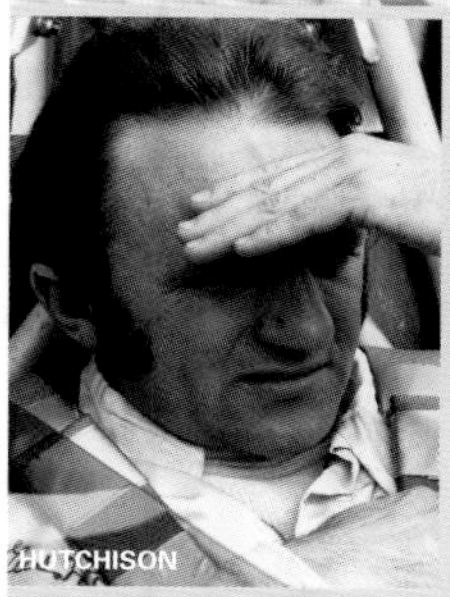

JAMES HUNT
Nat: GBR. Born: 29.08.1947. Died: 15.06.1993
Debut: 1973 Monaco GP. Starts: 92.
Points: 179. Wins: 10. PP: 14. FL: 8

GUS HUTCHISON
Nat: USA. Born: 26.04.1937
Debut: 1970 United States GP. Starts: 1

JACKY ICKX
Nat: BEL. Born: 1.01.1945
Debut: 1966 German GP. Starts: 116.
Points: 181. Wins: 8. PP: 13. FL: 14

JÉSUS IGLESIAS
Nat: ARG. Born: 22.02.1922
Debut: 1955 Argentine GP. Starts: 1

TAKI INOUE
Nat: JAP. Born: 5.09.1963
Debut: 1994 Japanese GP. Starts: 18

INNES IRELAND
Nat: GBR. Born: 12.06.1930. Died: 22.10.1993
Debut: 1959 Dutch GP. Starts: 50.
Points: 47. Wins: 1. FL: 1

EDDIE IRVINE
Nat: GBR. Born: 10.11.1965
Debut: 1993 Japanese GP. Starts: 146.
Points: 191. Wins: 4. FL: 1

CHRIS IRWIN
Nat: GBR. Born: 27.06.1942
Debut: 1966 British GP. Starts: 10. Points: 2

JEAN-PIERRE JABOUILLE
Nat: FRA. Born: 1.10.1942
Debut: 1975 French GP. Starts: 49.
Points: 21. Wins: 2. PP: 6

JOHN JAMES
Nat: GBR. Born: 10.05.1914
Debut: 1951 British GP. Starts: 1

JEAN-PIERRE JARIER
Nat: FRA. Born: 10.07.1946
Debut: 1971 Italian GP. Starts: 133.
Points: 31.5. PP: 3. FL: 3

STEFAN JOHANSSON
Nat: SWE. Born: 8.09.1956
Debut: 1983 British GP. Starts: 79.
Points: 88

LESLIE JOHNSON
Nat: GBR. Born: 22.03.1912. Died: 8.06.1959
Debut: 1950 British GP. Starts: 1

BRUCE JOHNSTONE
Nat: RSA. Born: 30.01.1937
Debut: 1962 South African GP. Starts: 1

ALAN JONES
Nat: AUS. Born: 2.11.1946
Debut: 1975 Spanish GP. Starts: 116.
Points: 206. Wins: 12. PP: 6. FL: 13

OSWALD KARCH
Nat: GER. Born: 6.03.1917
Debut: 1953 German GP. Starts: 1

UKYO KATAYAMA
Nat: JAP. Born: 29.05.1963
Debut: 1992 South African GP. Starts: 95.
Points: 5

RUPERT KEEGAN
Nat: GBR. Born: 26.02.1955
Debut: 1977 Spanish GP. Starts: 25

EDDIE KEIZAN
Nat: RSA. Born: 12.09.1944
Debut: 1973 South African GP. Starts: 3

JOE KELLY
Nat: IRL. Born: 13.03.1913. Died: 28.11.1993
Debut: 1950 British GP. Starts: 2

A-Z

DRIVER A-Z

KESSEL

KINNUNEN

LAFFITE

LAGORCE

LARINI

KLENK

DE KLERK

LAMMERS

LAMY

LARROUSSE

KLING

KOINIGG

LANDI

LANG

LARRAURI

LAUDA

LORIS KESSEL
Nat: SUI. Born: 1.04.1950
Debut: 1976 Belgian GP. Starts: 3

LEO KINNUNEN
Nat: FIN. Born: 5.08.1943
Debut: 1974 Swedish GP. Starts: 1

HANS KLENK
Nat: GER. Born: 28.10.1919
Debut: 1952 German GP. Starts: 1

PIET DE KLERK
Nat: RSA. Born: 16.03.1936
Debut: 1963 South African GP. Starts: 4

KARL KLING
Nat: GER. Born: 16.09.1910. Died: 19.03.2003
Debut: 1954 French GP. Starts: 11.
Points: 17. FL: 1

ERNST KLODWIG
Nat: DDR. Born: 23.05.1903. Died: 15.04.1973
Debut: 1952 German GP. Starts: 2

HELMUTH KOINIGG
Nat: AUT. Born: 3.11.1948. Died: 6.10.1974
Debut: 1974 Canadian GP. Starts: 2

RUDOLF KRAUSE
Nat: DDR. Born: 30.03.1907. Died: 11.04.1987
Debut: 1952 German GP. Starts: 2

JACQUES LAFFITE
Nat: FRA. Born: 21.11.1943
Debut: 1974 German GP. Starts: 176. Points: 228. Wins: 6. PP: 7. FL: 6

FRANCK LAGORCE
Nat: FRA. Born: 1.09.1968
Debut: 1994 Japanese GP. Starts: 2

JAN LAMMERS
Nat: NED. Born: 2.06.1956
Debut: 1979 Argentine GP. Starts: 23

PEDRO LAMY
Nat: POR. Born: 20.03.1972
Debut: 1993 Italian GP. Starts: 32. Points: 1

CHICO LANDI
Nat: BRA. Born: 14.07.1907. Died: 7.06.1989
Debut: 1951 Italian GP. Starts: 6. Points: 1.5

HERMANN LANG
Nat: GER. Born: 6.04.1909. Died: 19.10.1987
Debut: 1953 Swiss GP. Starts: 2. Points: 2

NICOLA LARINI
Nat: ITA. Born: 19.03.1964
Debut: 1987 Spanish GP. Starts: 49.
Points: 7

OSCAR LARRAURI
Nat: ARG. Born: 19.08.1954
Debut: 1988 Monaco GP. Starts: 7

ALBERTO RODRIGUEZ LARRETA
Nat: ARG. Born: 14.01.1934. Died: 11.03.1977
Debut: 1960 Argentine GP. Starts: 1

GÉRARD LARROUSSE
Nat: FRA. Born: 23.05.1940
Debut: 1974 Belgian GP. Starts: 1

NIKI LAUDA
Nat: AUT. Born: 22.02.1949
Debut: 1971 Austrian GP. Starts: 171.
Points: 420.5. Wins: 25. PP: 24. FL: 24

ROGER LAURENT
Nat: BEL. Born: 21.02.1913. Died: 6.02.1997
Debut: 1952 Belgian GP. Starts: 2

A-Z

DRIVER A-Z

GIOVANNI LAVAGGI

Nat: ITA. Born: 18.02.1958
Debut: 1995 German GP. Starts: 7

CHRIS LAWRENCE

Nat: GBR. Born: 27.07.1933
Debut: 1966 British GP. Starts: 2

MICHEL LECLÈRE

Nat: FRA. Born: 18.03.1946
Debut: 1975 United States GP. Starts: 7

NEVILLE LEDERLE

Nat: RSA. Born: 25.09.1938
Debut: 1962 South African GP. Starts: 1. Points: 1

GEOFF LEES

Nat: GBR. Born: 1.05.1951
Debut: 1979 German GP. Starts: 5

ARTHUR LEGAT

Nat: BEL. Born: 1.11.1898. Died: 23.02.1960
Debut: 1952 Belgian GP. Starts: 2

JJ LEHTO

Nat: FIN. Born: 31.01.1966
Debut: 1989 Spanish GP. Starts: 62. Points: 10

GIJS VAN LENNEP

Nat: NED. Born: 16.03.1942
Debut: 1971 Dutch GP. Starts: 8. Points: 2

LAMBERTO LEONI

Nat: ITA. Born: 24.05.1953
Debut: 1978 Argentine GP. Starts: 1

LES LESTON

Nat: GBR. Born: 16.12.1920
Debut: 1956 Italian GP. Starts: 2

"PIERRE LEVEGH"

Nat: FRA. Born: 22.12.1905. Died: 11.06.1955
Debut: 1950 Belgian GP. Starts: 6

JACKIE LEWIS

Nat: GBR. Born: 1.11.1936
Debut: 1961 Belgian GP. Starts: 9. Points: 3

STUART LEWIS-EVANS

Nat: GBR. Born: 20.04.1930. Died: 25.10.1958
Debut: 1957 Monaco GP. Starts: 14. Points: 16. PP: 2

GUY LIGIER

Nat: FRA. Born: 12.07.1930
Debut: 1966 Monaco GP. Starts: 12. Points: 1

ROBERTO LIPPI

Nat: ITA. Born: 17.10.1926
Debut: 1961 Italian GP. Starts: 1

DRIES VAN DER LOF

Nat: NED. Born: 23.08.1919. Died: 24.05.1990
Debut: 1952 Dutch GP. Starts: 1

LELLA LOMBARDI

Nat: ITA. Born: 26.03.1941. Died: 3.03.1992
Debut: 1975 South African GP. Starts: 12. Points: 0.5

ERNST LOOF

Nat: GER. Born: 4.07.1907. Died: 3.03.1956
Debut: 1953 German GP. Starts: 1

HENRI LOUVEAU

Nat: FRA. Born: 25.01.1910. Died: 7.01.1991
Debut: 1950 Italian GP. Starts: 2

JOHN LOVE

Nat: RHO. Born: 7.12.1924
Debut: 1962 South African GP. Starts: 9. Points: 6

A-Z

DRIVER A-Z

PETE LOVELY
Nat: USA. Born: 11.04.1926
Debut: 1960 United States GP. Starts: 7

ROGER LOYER
Nat: FRA. Born: 5.08.1907. Died: 24.03.1988
Debut: 1954 Argentine GP. Starts: 1

JEAN LUCAS
Nat: FRA. Born: 25.04.1917
Debut: 1955 Italian GP. Starts: 1

BRETT LUNGER
Nat: USA. Born: 14.11.1945
Debut: 1975 Austrian GP. Starts: 34

MIKE MACDOWEL
Nat: GBR. Born: 13.09.1932
Debut: 1957 French GP. Starts: 1

HERBERT MACKAY-FRASER
Nat: USA. Born: 23.06.1927. Died: 14.07.1957
Debut: 1957 French GP. Starts: 1

LANCE MACKLIN
Nat: GBR. Born: 2.09.1919. Died: 29.08.2002
Debut: 1952 Swiss GP. Starts: 13

DAMIEN MAGEE
Nat: GBR. Born: 17.11.1945
Debut: 1975 Swedish GP. Starts: 1

TONY MAGGS
Nat: RSA. Born: 9.02.1937
Debut: 1961 British GP. Starts: 25. Points: 26

UMBERTO MAGLIOLI
Nat: ITA. Born: 5.06.1928. Died: 6.02.1999
Debut: 1953 Italian GP. Starts: 10.
Points: 3.330

JAN MAGNUSSEN
Nat: DEN. Born: 4.07.1973
Debut: 1995 Pacific GP. Starts: 25. Points: 1

GUY MAIRESSE
Nat: FRA. Born: 10.08.1910. Died: 24.04.1954
Debut: 1950 Italian GP. Starts: 3

WILLY MAIRESSE
Nat: BEL. Born: 1.10.1928. Died: 2.09.1969
Debut: 1960 Belgian GP. Starts: 12. Points: 7

NIGEL MANSELL
Nat: GBR. Born: 8.08.1953
Debut: 1980 Austrian GP. Starts: 187.
Points: 482. Wins: 31. PP: 32. FL: 29

SERGIO MANTOVANI
Nat: ITA. Born: 22.05.1929. Died: 23.02.2001
Debut: 1953 Italian GP. Starts: 7. Points: 4

ROBERT MANZON
Nat: FRA. Born: 12.04.1917
Debut: 1950 Monaco GP. Starts: 28.
Points: 16

ONOFRÉ MARIMON
Nat: ARG. Born: 19.12.1923. Died: 31.07.1954
Debut: 1951 French GP. Starts: 11.
Points: 8.140. FL: 1

HELMUT MARKO
Nat: AUT. Born: 27.04.1943
Debut: 1971 Austrian GP. Starts: 9

TARSO MARQUES
Nat: BRA. Born: 19.01.1976
Debut: 1996 Brazilian GP. Starts: 24

LESLIE MARR
Nat: GBR. Born: 14.08.1922
Debut: 1954 British GP. Starts: 2

A-Z

DRIVER A-Z

TONY MARSH

Nat: GBR. Born: 20.07.1931
Debut: 1957 German GP. Starts: 4

EUGÈNE MARTIN

Nat: FRA. Born: 24.03.1915
Debut: 1950 British GP. Starts: 2

PIERLUIGI MARTINI

Nat: ITA. Born: 23.04.1961
Debut: 1985 Brazilian GP. Starts: 118. Points: 18

JOCHEN MASS

Nat: GER. Born: 30.09.1946
Debut: 1973 British GP. Starts: 105. Points: 71. Wins: 1. FL: 2

FELIPE MASSA

Nat: BRA. Born: 25.04.1981
Debut: 2002 Australian GP. Starts: 16. Points: 4

CRISTIANO DA MATTA

Nat: BRA. Born: 19.09.1973
Debut: 2003 Australian GP

JEAN MAX

Nat: FRA. Born: 27.07.1943
Debut: 1971 French GP. Starts: 1

MICHEL MAY

Nat: SUI. Born: 18.08.1934
Debut: 1961 Monaco GP. Starts: 2

TIMMY MAYER

Nat: USA. Born: 22.02.1938. Died: 28.02.1964
Debut: 1962 United States GP. Starts: 1

FRANÇOIS MAZET

Nat: FRA. Born: 26.02.1943
Debut: 1971 French GP. Starts: 1

GASTON MAZZACANE

Nat: ARG. Born: 8.05.1975
Debut: 2000 Australian GP. Starts: 21

KENNETH McALPINE

Nat: GBR. Born: 21.09.1920
Debut: 1952 British GP. Starts: 7

BRUCE McLAREN

Nat: NZ. Born: 30.08.1937. Died: 2.06.1970
Debut: 1958 German GP. Starts: 100. Points: 196.5. Wins: 4. FL: 3

ALLAN McNISH

Nat: GBR. Born: 29.12.1969
Debut: 2002 Australian GP. Starts: 16

GRAHAM McRAE

Nat: NZ. Born: 5.03.1940
Debut: 1973 British GP. Starts: 1

CARLOS MENDITÉGUY

Nat: ARG. Born: 10.08.1915. Died: 28.04.1973
Debut: 1953 Argentine GP. Starts: 10. Points: 9

ARTURO MERZARIO

Nat: ITA. Born: 11.03.1943
Debut: 1972 British GP. Starts: 57. Points: 11

ROBERTO MIÈRES

Nat: ARG. Born: 3.12.1924
Debut: 1953 Dutch GP. Starts: 17. Points: 13. FL: 1

FRANÇOIS MIGAULT

Nat: FRA. Born: 4.12.1944
Debut: 1972 Austrian GP. Starts: 13

JOHN MILES

Nat: GBR. Born: 14.06.1943
Debut: 1969 French GP. Starts: 12. Points: 2

A-Z

DRIVER A-Z

ANDRÉ MILHOUX

Nat: BEL. Born: 9.12.1928
Debut: 1956 German GP. Starts: 1

GERHARD MITTER

Nat: GER. Born: 30.08.1935. Died: 1.08.1969
Debut: 1963 Dutch GP. Starts: 5. Points: 3

STEFANO MODENA

Nat: ITA. Born: 12.05.1963
Debut: 1987 Australian GP. Starts: 70. Points: 17

ANDREA MONTERMINI

Nat: ITA. Born: 30.05.1964
Debut: 1995 Brazilian GP. Starts: 20

ROBIN MONTGOMERIE-CHARRINGTON

Nat: USA. Born: 22.06.1915
Debut: 1952 Belgian GP. Starts: 1

JUAN PABLO MONTOYA

Nat: COL. Born: 20.09.1975
Debut: 2001 Australian GP. Starts: 34. Points: 81. Wins: 1. PP: 10. FL: 6

GIANNI MORBIDELLI

Nat: ITA. Born: 13.01.1968
Debut: 1990 Brazilian GP. Starts: 67. Points: 8.5

ROBERTO MORENO

Nat: BRA. Born: 11.02.1959
Debut: 1987 Japanese GP. Starts: 42. Points: 15. FL: 1

DAVE MORGAN

Nat: GBR. Born: 7.08.1944
Debut: 1975 British GP. Starts: 1

SILVIO MOSER

Nat: SUI. Born: 24.04.1941. Died: 26.05.1974
Debut: 1967 British GP. Starts: 12. Points: 3

STIRLING MOSS

Nat: GBR. Born: 17.09.1929
Debut: 1951 Swiss GP. Starts: 66. Points: 186.64. Wins: 16. PP: 16. FL: 19

GINO MUNARON

Nat: ITA. Born: 2.04.1928
Debut: 1960 Argentine GP. Starts: 4

DAVID MURRAY

Nat: GBR. Born: 28.12.1909. Died: 5.04.1973
Debut: 1950 British GP. Starts: 4

LUIGI MUSSO

Nat: ITA. Born: 29.07.1924. Died: 6.07.1958
Debut: 1953 Italian GP. Starts: 24. Points: 44. Wins: 1. FL: 1

SATORU NAKAJIMA

Nat: JAP. Born: 23.02.1953
Debut: 1987 Brazilian GP. Starts: 74. Points: 16. FL: 1

SHINJI NAKANO

Nat: JAP. Born: 4.04.1971
Debut: 1997 Australian GP. Starts: 33. Points: 2

ALESSANDRO NANNINI

Nat: ITA. Born: 7.07.1959
Debut: 1986 Brazilian GP. Starts: 76. Points: 65. Wins: 1. FL: 2

EMANUELE NASPETTI

Nat: ITA. Born: 24.02.1968
Debut: 1992 Belgian GP. Starts: 6

MASSIMO NATILI

Nat: ITA. Born: 28.07.1935
Debut: 1961 British GP. Starts: 1

BRIAN NAYLOR

Nat: GBR. Born: 24.03.1923. Died: 8.08.1989
Debut: 1957 German GP. Starts: 7

DRIVER A-Z

NILSSON · NEEDELL · ONGAIS · OLIVER · PALM · PALMER · NEVE · NICHOLSON · NODA · OWEN · VON OPEL · PACE · PAGANI · PALETTI · PANIS

TIFF NEEDELL

Nat: GBR. Born: 29.10.1951
Debut: 1980 Belgian GP. Starts: 1

PATRICK NEVE

Nat: BEL. Born: 13.10.1949
Debut: 1976 Belgian GP. Starts: 10

JOHN NICHOLSON

Nat: NZ. Born: 6.10.1941
Debut: 1975 British GP. Starts: 1

HELMUT NIEDERMAYR

Nat: GER. Born: 29.11.1915. Died: 3.04.1985
Debut: 1952 German GP. Starts: 1

BRAUSCH NIEMANN

Nat: RSA. Born: 7.01.1939
Debut: 1963 South African GP. Starts: 1

GUNNAR NILSSON

Nat: SWE. Born: 20.11.1948. Died: 20.10.1978
Debut: 1976 South African GP. Starts: 31.
Points: 31. Wins: 1. FL: 1

HIDEKI NODA

Nat: JAP. Born: 7.03.1969
Debut: 1994 European GP. Starts: 3

RODNEY NUCKEY

Nat: GBR. Born: 26.06.1929. Died: 29.06.2000
Debut: 1953 German GP. Starts: 1

ROBERT O'BRIEN

Nat: USA. Born: 30.03.1922. Died:
30.05.1997
Debut: 1952 Belgian GP. Starts: 1

JACKIE OLIVER

Nat: GBR. Born: 14.08.1942
Debut: 1967 German GP. Starts: 50.
Points: 13. FL: 1

DANNY ONGAIS

Nat: USA. Born: 21.05.1942
Debut: 1977 United States GP. Starts: 4

RIKKY VON OPEL

Nat: LIE. Born: 14.10.1947
Debut: 1973 French GP. Starts: 10

FRITZ D'OREY

Nat: BRA. Born: 25.3.1938. Died: 1961
Debut: 1959 French GP. Starts: 3

ARTHUR OWEN

Nat: GBR. Born: 23.03.1915
Debut: 1960 Italian GP. Starts: 1

CARLOS PACE

Nat: BRA. Born: 6.10.1944. Died: 18.03.1977
Debut: 1972 South African GP. Starts: 72.
Points: 58. Wins: 1. PP: 1. FL: 5

NELLO PAGANI

Nat: ITA. Born: 11.10.1911
Debut: 1950 Swiss GP. Starts: 1

RICCARDO PALETTI

Nat: ITA. Born: 15.06.1958. Died: 13.06.1982
Debut: 1982 San Marino GP. Starts: 2

TORSTEN PALM

Nat: SWE. Born: 23.07.1947
Debut: 1975 Swedish GP. Starts: 1

JONATHAN PALMER

Nat: GBR. Born: 7.11.1956
Debut: 1983 European GP. Starts: 83.
Points: 14. FL: 1

OLIVIER PANIS

Nat: FRA. Born: 2.09.1966
Debut: 1994 Brazilian GP. Starts: 125.
Points: 64. Wins: 1

A-Z

DRIVER A-Z

MASSIMILIANO PAPIS

Nat: ITA. Born: 3.10.1969
Debut: 1995 British GP. Starts: 7

MICHAEL PARKES

Nat: GBR. Born: 24.09.1931. Died: 28.08.1977
Debut: 1966 French GP. Starts: 6. Points: 14. PP: 1

REG PARNELL

Nat: GBR. Born: 2.07.1911. Died: 7.01.1964
Debut: 1950 British GP. Starts: 6. Points: 9

TIM PARNELL

Nat: GBR. Born: 25.06.1932
Debut: 1961 British GP. Starts: 2

RICCARDO PATRESE

Nat: ITA. Born: 17.04.1954
Debut: 1977 Monaco GP. Starts: 256. Points: 281. Wins: 6. PP: 8. FL: 15

AL PEASE

Nat: CAN. Born: 15.10.1921
Debut: 1967 Canadian GP. Starts: 2

ROGER PENSKE

Nat: USA. Born: 20.02.1937
Debut: 1961 United States GP. Starts: 2

CESARE PERDISA

Nat: ITA. Born: 21.10.1932. Died: 10.05.1998
Debut: 1955 Monaco GP. Starts: 7. Points: 5

LARRY PERKINS

Nat: AUS. Born: 18.03.1950
Debut: 1976 Spanish GP. Starts: 11

XAVIER PERROT

Nat: SUI. Born: 1.02.1942
Debut: 1969 German GP. Starts: 1

HENRI PESCAROLO

Nat: FRA. Born: 25.09.1942
Debut: 1968 Canadian GP. Starts: 57. Points: 12. FL: 1

ALESSANDRO PESENTI-ROSSI

Nat: ITA. Born: 31.08.1942
Debut: 1976 German GP. Starts: 3

JOSEF PETERS

Nat: GER. Born: 16.09.1914. Died: 24.04.2001
Debut: 1952 German GP. Starts: 1

RONNIE PETERSON

Nat: SWE. Born: 14.02.1944. Died: 11.09.1978
Debut: 1970 Monaco GP. Starts: 123. Points: 206. Wins: 10. PP: 14. FL: 9

FRANÇOIS PICARD

Nat: FRA. Born: 26.04.1921. Died: 29.04.1996
Debut: 1958 Moroccan GP. Starts: 1

ERNEST PIETERSE

Nat: RSA. Born: 4.07.1938
Debut: 1962 South African GP. Starts: 2

PAUL PIETSCH

Nat: GER. Born: 20.06.1911
Debut: 1950 Italian GP. Starts: 3

ANDRÉ PILETTE

Nat: BEL. Born: 6.10.1918. Died: 27.12.1993
Debut: 1951 Belgian GP. Starts: 9. Points: 2

TEDDY PILETTE

Nat: BEL. Born: 26.07.1942
Debut: 1974 Belgian GP. Starts: 1

LUIGI PIOTTI

Nat: ITA. Born: 27.10.1913. Died: 19.04.1971
Debut: 1956 Argentine GP. Starts: 6

A-Z

DRIVER A-Z

DAVID PIPER

Nat: GBR. Born: 2.12.1930
Debut: 1959 British GP. Starts: 2

NELSON PIQUET

Nat: BRA. Born: 17.08.1952
Debut: 1978 German GP. Starts: 204. Points: 485.5. Wins: 23. PP: 24. FL: 23

RENATO PIROCCHI

Nat: ITA. Born: 23.06.1933
Debut: 1961 Italian GP. Starts: 1

DIDIER PIRONI

Nat: FRA. Born: 26.03.1952. Died: 23.08.1987
Debut: 1978 Argentine GP. Starts: 70. Points: 101. Wins: 3. PP: 4. FL: 5

EMANUELE PIRRO

Nat: ITA. Born: 12.01.1962
Debut: 1989 French GP. Starts: 37. Points: 3

ANTONIO PIZZONIA

Nat: BRA. Born: 11.09.1980
Debut: 2003 Australian GP

ÉRIC VAN DE POELE

Nat: BEL. Born: 30.09.1961
Debut: 1991 San Marino GP. Starts: 5

JACQUES POLLET

Nat: FRA. Born: 28.07.1922. Died: 16.08.1997
Debut: 1954 French GP. Starts: 5

BEN PON

Nat: NED. Born: 9.12.1936
Debut: 1962 Dutch GP. Starts: 1

DENNIS POORE

Nat: GBR. Born: 19.08.1916. Died: 12.02.1987
Debut: 1952 British GP. Starts: 2. Points: 3

ALFONSO DE PORTAGO

Nat: ESP. Born: 11.10.1928. Died: 12.05.1957
Debut: 1956 French GP. Starts: 5. Points: 4

SAM POSEY

Nat: USA. Born: 26.05.1944
Debut: 1971 United States GP. Starts: 2

CHARLES POZZI

Nat: FRA. Born: 27.08.1909. Died: 28.02.2001
Debut: 1950 French GP. Starts: 1

JACKIE PRETORIUS

Nat: RSA. Born: 22.11.1934
Debut: 1968 South African GP. Starts: 3

DAVID PROPHET

Nat: GBR. Born: 9.10.1937. Died: 29.03.1981
Debut: 1963 South African GP. Starts: 2

ALAIN PROST

Nat: FRA. Born: 24.02.1955
Debut: 1980 Argentine GP. Starts: 199. Points: 798.5. Wins: 51. PP: 33. FL: 41

TOM PRYCE

Nat: GBR. Born: 11.06.1949. Died: 5.03.1977
Debut: 1974 Belgian GP. Starts: 42. Points: 19. PP: 1

DAVID PURLEY

Nat: GBR. Born: 26.01.1945. Died: 2.07.1985
Debut: 1973 Monaco GP. Starts: 7

DIETER QUESTER

Nat: AUT. Born: 30.05.1939
Debut: 1974 Austrian GP. Starts: 1

IAN RABY

Nat: GBR. Born: 22.09.1921. Died: 7.11.1967
Debut: 1963 British GP. Starts: 3

A-Z

DRIVER A-Z

BOBBY RAHAL

Nat: USA. Born: 10.01.1953
Debut: 1978 United States GP. Starts: 2

KIMI RÄIKKÖNEN

Nat: FIN. Born: 17.10.1979
Debut: 2001 Australian GP. Starts: 34.
Points: 33. FL: 1

PIERRE-HENRI RAPHANEL

Nat: FRA. Born: 27.05.1961
Debut: 1989 Monaco GP. Starts: 1

ROLAND RATZENBERGER

Nat: AUT. Born: 4.07.1962. Died: 30.04.1994
Debut: 1994 Pacific GP. Starts: 1

HECTOR REBAQUE

Nat: MEX. Born: 5.02.1956
Debut: 1977 German GP. Starts: 41.
Points: 13

BRIAN REDMAN

Nat: GBR. Born: 9.03.1937
Debut: 1968 South African GP. Starts: 12.
Points: 8

ALAN REES

Nat: GBR. Born: 12.01.1938
Debut: 1966 German GP. Starts: 3

CLAY REGAZZONI

Nat: SUI. Born: 5.09.1939
Debut: 1970 Dutch GP. Starts: 132.
Points: 212. Wins: 5. PP: 5. FL: 15

CARLOS REUTEMANN

Nat: ARG. Born: 12.04.1942
Debut: 1972 Argentine GP. Starts: 146.
Points: 310. Wins: 12. PP: 6. FL: 5

LANCE REVENTLOW

Nat: USA. Born: 24.02.1936. Died: 24.07.1972
Debut: 1960 Belgian GP. Starts: 1

PETER REVSON

Nat: USA. Born: 27.02.1939. Died: 22.03.1974
Debut: 1964 Belgian GP. Starts: 30.
Points: 61. Wins: 2. PP: 1

JOHN RHODES

Nat: GBR. Born: 18.08.1927
Debut: 1965 British GP. Starts: 1

ALEX RIBEIRO

Nat: BRA. Born: 7.11.1948
Debut: 1976 United States GP. Starts: 10

FRITZ RIESS

Nat: GER. Born: 11.07.1922. Died: 15.05.1991
Debut: 1952 German GP. Starts: 1

JOCHEN RINDT

Nat: AUT. Born: 18.04.1942. Died: 5.09.1970
Debut: 1964 Austrian GP. Starts: 60.
Points: 109. Wins: 6. PP: 10. FL: 3

JOHN RISELEY-PRICHARD

Nat: GBR. Born: 17.01.1924. Died: 8.07.1993
Debut: 1954 British GP. Starts: 1

RICHARD ROBARTS

Nat: GBR. Born: 22.09.1944
Debut: 1974 Argentine GP. Starts: 3

PEDRO RODRIGUEZ

Nat: MEX. Born: 18.01.1940. Died: 11.07.1971
Debut: 1963 United States GP. Starts: 55.
Points: 71. Wins: 2. FL: 1

RICARDO RODRIGUEZ

Nat: MEX. Born: 14.02.1942. Died: 1.11.1962
Debut: 1961 Italian GP. Starts: 5. Points: 4

FRANCO ROL

Nat: ITA. Born: 5.06.1908. Died: 18.06.1977
Debut: 1950 Monaco GP. Starts: 5

A-Z

DRIVER A-Z

TONY ROLT

Nat: GBR. Born: 16.10.1918
Debut: 1950 British GP. Starts: 3

BERTIL ROOS

Nat: SWE. Born: 12.10.1943
Debut: 1974 Swedish GP. Starts: 1

BASIL VAN ROOYEN

Nat: RSA. Born: 19.04.1939
Debut: 1968 South African GP. Starts: 2

PEDRO DE LA ROSA

Nat: ESP. Born: 24.02.1971
Debut: 1999 Australian GP. Starts: 63.
Points: 6

KEKE ROSBERG

Nat: FIN. Born: 6.12.1948
Debut: 1978 South African GP. Starts: 114.
Points: 159.5. Wins: 5. PP: 5. FL: 3

LOUIS ROSIER

Nat: FRA. Born: 5.11.1905. Died: 29.10.1956
Debut: 1950 British GP. Starts: 38.
Points: 18

RICARDO ROSSET

Nat: BRA. Born: 27.07.1968
Debut: 1996 Australian GP. Starts: 27

HUUB ROTHENGATTER

Nat: NED. Born: 8.10.1954
Debut: 1984 Canadian GP. Starts: 25

LLOYD RUBY

Nat: USA. Born: 12.01.1928
Debut: 1961 United States GP. Starts: 1

"GEKI" RUSSO

Nat: ITA. Born: 23.10.1937. Died: 18.06.1967
Debut: 1965 Italian GP. Starts: 2

TROY RUTTMAN

Nat: USA. Born: 11.03.1930. Died: 19.05.1997
Debut: 1958 French GP. Starts: 1

PETER RYAN

Nat: CAN. Born: 10.06.1940. Died: 2.07.1962
Debut: 1961 United States GP. Starts: 1

BOB SAID

Nat: USA. Born: 5.05.1932. Died: 24.03.2002
Debut: 1959 United States GP. Starts: 1

LUIS PEREZ SALA

Nat: ESP. Born: 15.05.1959
Debut: 1988 Brazilian GP. Starts: 26.
Points: 1

ELISEO SALAZAR

Nat: RCH. Born: 14.11.1954
Debut: 1981 San Marino GP. Starts: 24.
Points: 3

MIKA SALO

Nat: FIN. Born: 30.11.1966
Debut: 1994 Japanese GP. Starts: 110.
Points: 33

ROY SALVADORI

Nat: GBR. Born: 12.05.1922
Debut: 1952 British GP. Starts: 47. Points: 19

CONSALVO SANESI

Nat: ITA. Born: 28.03.1911. Died: 28.07.1998
Debut: 1950 Italian GP. Starts: 5. Points: 3

STEPHANE SARRAZIN

Nat: FRA. Born: 2.11.1974
Debut: 1999 Brazilian GP. Starts: 1

TAKUMA SATO

Nat: JAP. Born: 28.01.1977
Debut: 2002 Australian GP. Starts: 17.
Points: 2

A-Z

DRIVER A-Z

SCARFIOTTI

SCARLATTI

SCHECKTER, JODY

SCHUMACHER, MICHAEL

SCHUPPAN

SCHECKTER, IAN

SCHELL

SCHWELM CRUZ

SCHENKEN

SCHIATTARELLA

SCHLESSER, JEAN-LOUIS

SCHLESSER

SCHNEIDER

SCHUMACHER, RALF

SCOTT-BROWN

LUDOVICO SCARFIOTTI
Nat: ITA. Born: 18.10.1933. Died: 8.06.1968
Debut: 1963 Dutch GP. Starts: 10. Points: 17. Wins: 1. FL: 1

GIORGIO SCARLATTI
Nat: ITA. Born: 2.10.1921. Died: 26.07.1990
Debut: 1956 German GP. Starts: 12. Points: 1

IAN SCHECKTER
Nat: RSA. Born: 22.08.1947
Debut: 1974 South African GP. Starts: 18

JODY SCHECKTER
Nat: RSA. Born: 29.01.1950
Debut: 1972 United States GP. Starts: 112. Points: 255. Wins: 10. PP: 3. FL: 5

HARRY SCHELL
Nat: USA. Born: 29.06.1921. Died: 13.05.1960
Debut: 1950 Monaco GP. Starts: 56. Points: 32

TIM SCHENKEN
Nat: AUS. Born: 26.09.1943
Debut: 1970 Austrian GP. Starts: 34. Points: 7

ALBERT SCHERRER
Nat: SUI. Born: 28.02.1908. Died: 5.07.1986
Debut: 1953 Swiss GP. Starts: 1

DOMENICO SCHIATTARELLA
Nat: ITA. Born: 17.11.1967
Debut: 1994 European GP. Starts: 7

HEINZ SCHILLER
Nat: SUI. Born: 25.01.1930
Debut: 1962 German GP. Starts: 1

JEAN-LOUIS SCHLESSER
Nat: FRA. Born: 12.09.1948
Debut: 1988 Italian GP. Starts: 1

JO SCHLESSER
Nat: FRA. Born: 18.05.1928. Died: 7.07.1968
Debut: 1966 German GP. Starts: 3

BERND SCHNEIDER
Nat: GER. Born: 20.07.1964
Debut: 1988 Mexican GP. Starts: 9

RUDOLF SCHOELLER
Nat: SUI. Born: 27.04.1902. Died: 7.03.1978
Debut: 1952 German GP. Starts: 1

ROB SCHROEDER
Nat: USA. Born: 11.05.1926
Debut: 1962 United States GP. Starts: 1

MICHAEL SCHUMACHER
Nat: GER. Born: 3.01.1969
Debut: 1991 Belgian GP. Starts: 178. Points: 945. Wins: 64. PP: 50. FL: 51

RALF SCHUMACHER
Nat: GER. Born: 30.06.1975
Debut: 1997 Australian GP. Starts: 100. Points: 177. Wins: 4. PP: 1. FL: 6

VERN SCHUPPAN
Nat: AUS. Born: 19.03.1943
Debut: 1974 Belgian GP. Starts: 9

ADOLFO SCHWELM CRUZ
Nat: ARG. Born: 28.06.1923
Debut: 1953 Argentine GP. Starts: 1

ARCHIE SCOTT-BROWN
Nat: GBR. Born: 13.05.1927. Died: 19.05.1958
Debut: 1956 British GP. Starts: 1

PIERO SCOTTI
Nat: ITA. Born: 11.11.1909. Died: 14.02.1976
Debut: 1956 Belgian GP. Starts: 1

A-Z

DRIVER A-Z

WOLFGANG SEIDEL

Nat: GER. Born: 4.07.1926. Died: 1.03.1987
Debut: 1953 German GP. Starts: 10

AYRTON SENNA

Nat: BRA. Born: 21.03.1960. Died: 1.05.1994
Debut: 1984 Brazilian GP. Starts: 161.
Points: 614. Wins: 41. PP: 65. FL: 19

DORINO SERAFINI

Nat: ITA. Born: 22.07.1909. Died: 5.07.2000
Debut: 1950 Italian GP. Starts: 1. Points: 3

CHICO SERRA

Nat: BRA. Born: 3.02.1957
Debut: 1981 Long Beach GP. Starts: 18.
Points: 1

DOUG SERRURIER

Nat: RSA. Born: 9.12.1920
Debut: 1962 South African GP. Starts: 2

JOHNNY SERVOZ-GAVIN

Nat: FRA. Born: 18.01.1942
Debut: 1967 Monaco GP. Starts: 12.
Points: 9

TONY SETTEMBER

Nat: USA. Born: 10.07.1926
Debut: 1962 British GP. Starts: 6

HAP SHARP

Nat: USA. Born: 1.01.1928. Died: 11.05.1992
Debut: 1961 United States GP. Starts: 6

BRIAN SHAWE-TAYLOR

Nat: GBR. Born: 28.01.1915. Died: 1.05.1999
Debut: 1950 British GP. Starts: 2

CARROLL SHELBY

Nat: USA. Born: 11.01.1923
Debut: 1958 French GP. Starts: 8

TONY SHELLY

Nat: NZ. Born: 2.02.1937. Died: 4.10.1998
Debut: 1962 British GP. Starts: 1

JO SIFFERT

Nat: SUI. Born: 7.07.1936. Died: 24.10.1971
Debut: 1962 Belgian GP. Starts: 96.
Points: 68. Wins: 2. PP: 2. FL: 4

HERMANO DA SILVA RAMOS

Nat: BRA. Born: 7.12.1925
Debut: 1955 Dutch GP. Starts: 7. Points: 2

ANDRÉ SIMON

Nat: FRA. Born: 5.01.1920
Debut: 1951 French GP. Starts: 11

MOISES SOLANA

Nat: MEX. Born: 26.12.1935. Died: 27.07.1969
Debut: 1963 Mexican GP. Starts: 8

ALEX SOLER-ROIG

Nat: ESP. Born: 29.10.1932
Debut: 1971 South African GP. Starts: 6

RAYMOND SOMMER

Nat: FRA. Born: 31.08.1906. Died: 10.09.1950
Debut: 1950 Monaco GP. Starts: 5. Points: 3

MIKE SPARKEN

Nat: FRA. Born: 16.06.1930
Debut: 1955 British GP. Starts: 1

MIKE SPENCE

Nat: GBR. Born: 30.12.1936. Died: 7.05.1968
Debut: 1963 Italian GP. Starts: 36. Points: 27

ALAN STACEY

Nat: GBR. Born: 29.08.1933. Died:
19.06.1960
Debut: 1958 British GP. Starts: 7

A-Z

DRIVER A-Z

STEWART, IAN

STEWART, JACKIE

STUCK, HANS

STUCK, HANS-JOACHIM

SWATERS

TAKAGI

STEWART, JIMMY

SULLIVAN

SURER

SUZUKI, AGURI

TAKAHARA

TAKAHASHI

STOHR

STOMMELEN

STREIFF

SURTEES

SUZUKI, TOSHIO

TAMBAY

TARQUINI

GAETANO STARRABBA

Nat: ITA. Born: 3.12.1932
Debut: 1961 Italian GP. Starts: 1

IAN STEWART

Nat: GBR. Born: 15.07.1929
Debut: 1953 British GP. Starts: 1

JACKIE STEWART

Nat: GBR. Born: 11.06.1939
Debut: 1965 South African GP. Starts: 99.
Points: 360. Wins: 27. PP: 17. FL: 15

JIMMY STEWART

Nat: GBR. Born: 6.03.1931
Debut: 1953 British GP. Starts: 1

SIEGFRIED STOHR

Nat: ITA. Born: 10.10.1952
Debut: 1981 Brazilian GP. Starts: 9

ROLF STOMMELEN

Nat: GER. Born: 11.07.1943. Died: 24.04.1983
Debut: 1969 German GP. Starts: 54.
Points: 14

PHILIPPE STREIFF

Nat: FRA. Born: 26.06.1955
Debut: 1984 Portuguese GP. Starts: 53.
Points: 11

HANS STUCK

Nat: GER. Born: 27.12.1900. Died: 8.02.1978
Debut: 1952 Swiss GP. Starts: 3

HANS-JOACHIM STUCK

Nat: GER. Born: 1.01.1951
Debut: 1974 Argentine GP. Starts: 74. Points: 29

DANNY SULLIVAN

Nat: USA. Born: 9.03.1950
Debut: 1983 Brazilian GP. Starts: 15.
Points: 2

MARC SURER

Nat: SUI. Born: 18.09.1951
Debut: 1979 United States GP. Starts: 81.
Points: 17. FL: 1

JOHN SURTEES

Nat: GBR. Born: 11.02.1934
Debut: 1960 Monaco GP. Starts: 111.
Points: 180. Wins: 6. PP: 8. FL: 11

AGURI SUZUKI

Nat: JAP. Born: 8.09.1960
Debut: 1988 Japanese GP. Starts: 64.
Points: 8

TOSHIO SUZUKI

Nat: JAP. Born: 10.03.1955
Debut: 1993 Japanese GP. Starts: 2

JACQUES SWATERS

Nat: BEL. Born: 30.10.1926
Debut: 1951 German GP. Starts: 7

TORANOSUKE TAKAGI

Nat: JAP. Born: 12.02.1974
Debut: 1998 Australian GP. Starts: 32

NORITAKE TAKAHARA

Nat: JAP. Born: 6.06.1951
Debut: 1976 Japanese GP. Starts: 2

KUNIMITSU TAKAHASHI

Nat: JAP. Born: 29.01.1940
Debut: 1977 Japanese GP. Starts: 1

PATRICK TAMBAY

Nat: FRA. Born: 25.06.1949
Debut: 1977 British GP. Starts: 114.
Points: 103. Wins: 2. PP: 5. FL: 2

GABRIELE TARQUINI

Nat: ITA. Born: 2.03.1962
Debut: 1987 San Marino GP. Starts: 38.
Points: 1

A-Z

DRIVER A-Z

TARUFFI

TAYLOR, HENRY

THOMPSON

TINGLE

DE TORNACO

VON TRIPS

TUERO

TAYLOR, JOHN

TAYLOR, MIKE

TITTERINGTON

THACKWELL

DE TOMASO

TUNMER

TAYLOR, TREVOR

TRINTIGNANT

TRULLI

ULMEN

PIERO TARUFFI
Nat: ITA. Born: 12.10.1906. Died: 12.01.1988
Debut: 1950 Italian GP. Starts: 18.
Points: 41. Wins: 1. FL: 1

HENRY TAYLOR
Nat: GBR. Born: 16.12.1932
Debut: 1959 British GP. Starts: 8. Points: 3

JOHN TAYLOR
Nat: GBR. Born: 23.03.1933. Died: 6.09.1966
Debut: 1964 British GP. Starts: 5. Points: 1

MIKE TAYLOR
Nat: GBR. Born: 24.04.1934
Debut: 1959 British GP. Starts: 1

TREVOR TAYLOR
Nat: GBR. Born: 26.12.1936
Debut: 1961 Dutch GP. Starts: 27. Points: 8

MAX DE TERRA
Nat: SUI. Born: 6.10.1918. Died: 29.12.1982
Debut: 1952 Swiss GP. Starts: 2

MIKE THACKWELL
Nat: NZ. Born: 30.03.1961
Debut: 1980 Canadian GP. Starts: 2

ALFONSO THIELE
Nat: USA. Born: 5.4.1922. Died: 1986
Debut: 1960 Italian GP. Starts: 1

ERIC THOMPSON
Nat: GBR. Born: 4.11.1919
Debut: 1952 British GP. Starts: 1. Points: 2

LESLIE THORNE
Nat: GBR. Born: 23.06.1916. Died: 13.07.1993
Debut: 1954 British GP. Starts: 1

SAM TINGLE
Nat: RHO. Born: 24.08.1921
Debut: 1963 South African GP. Starts: 5

DESMOND TITTERINGTON
Nat: GBR. Born: 1.05.1928. Died: 13.04.2002
Debut: 1956 British GP. Starts: 1

ALEJANDRO DE TOMASO
Nat: ARG. Born: 10.07.1928. Died: 21.05.2003
Debut: 1957 Argentine GP. Starts: 2

CHARLES DE TORNACO
Nat: BEL. Born: 7.06.1927. Died: 18.09.1953
Debut: 1952 Belgian GP. Starts: 2

MAURICE TRINTIGNANT
Nat: FRA. Born: 30.10.1917
Debut: 1950 Monaco GP. Starts: 82. Points: 72.330. Wins: 2. FL: 1

WOLFGANG VON TRIPS
Nat: GER. Born: 4.05.1928. Died: 10.09.1961
Debut: 1957 Argentine GP. Starts: 27. Points: 56. Wins: 2. PP: 1

JARNO TRULLI
Nat: ITA. Born: 13.07.1974
Debut: 1997 Australian GP. Starts: 95.
Points: 38

ESTEBAN TUERO
Nat: ARG. Born: 22.04.1978
Debut: 1998 Australian GP. Starts: 16

GUY TUNMER
Nat: RSA. Born: 1.12.1948. Died: 22.06.1999
Debut: 1975 South African GP. Starts: 1

TONI ULMEN
Nat: GER. Born: 25.01.1906. Died: 4.11.1976
Debut: 1952 Swiss GP. Starts: 2

A-Z

DRIVER A-Z

UNSER

VACCARELLA

VILLENEUVE, JACQUES

VERSTAPPEN

DE VILLOTA

WARD

WEBBER

VILLENEUVE, GILLES

VONLANTHEN

WALKER, DAVE

WATSON

VILLORESI

WARWICK

WALKER, PETER

WENDLINGER

WESTBURY

BOBBY UNSER
Nat: USA. Born: 20.02.1934
Debut: 1968 United States GP. Starts: 1

ALBERTO URIA
Nat: URU. Born: 11.07.1924. Died: 4.12.1988
Debut: 1955 Argentine GP. Starts: 2

NINO VACCARELLA
Nat: ITA. Born: 4.03.1933
Debut: 1961 Italian GP. Starts: 4

JOS VERSTAPPEN
Nat: NED. Born: 4.03.1972
Debut: 1994 Brazilian GP. Starts: 91.
Points: 17

GILLES VILLENEUVE
Nat: CAN. Born: 18.01.1950. Died: 8.05.1982
Debut: 1977 British GP. Starts: 67.
Points: 107. Wins: 6. PP: 2. FL: 8

JACQUES VILLENEUVE
Nat: CAN. Born: 9.04.1971
Debut: 1996 Australian GP. Starts: 116.
Points: 213. Wins: 11. PP: 13. FL: 9

LUIGI VILLORESI
Nat: ITA. Born: 16.05.1909. Died: 24.08.1997
Debut: 1950 Monaco GP. Starts: 31.
Points: 49. FL: 1

EMILIO DE VILLOTA
Nat: ESP. Born: 26.07.1946
Debut: 1977 Spanish GP. Starts: 2

OTTORINO VOLONTERIO
Nat: SUI. Born: 7.12.1917
Debut: 1954 Spanish GP. Starts: 3

JOSEPH VONLANTHEN
Nat: SUI. Born: 31.05.1942
Debut: 1975 Austrian GP. Starts: 1

FRED WACKER
Nat: USA. Born: 10.07.1918. Died: 16.06.1998
Debut: 1953 Belgian GP. Starts: 3

DAVE WALKER
Nat: AUS. Born: 10.06.1941
Debut: 1971 Dutch GP. Starts: 11

PETER WALKER
Nat: GBR. Born: 7.10.1912. Died: 1.03.1984
Debut: 1950 British GP. Starts: 4

HEINI WALTER
Nat: SUI. Born: 28.07.1927
Debut: 1962 German GP. Starts: 1

RODGER WARD
Nat: USA. Born: 10.01.1921
Debut: 1959 United States GP. Starts: 2

DEREK WARWICK
Nat: GBR. Born: 27.08.1954
Debut: 1981 Las Vegas GP. Starts: 146.
Points: 71. FL: 2

JOHN WATSON
Nat: GBR. Born: 4.05.1946
Debut: 1973 British GP. Starts: 152.
Points: 169. Wins: 5. PP: 2. FL: 5

MARK WEBBER
Nat: AUS. Born: 27.08.1976
Debut: 2002 Australian GP. Starts: 16.
Points: 2

KARL WENDLINGER
Nat: AUT. Born: 20.12.1968
Debut: 1991 Japanese GP. Starts: 41.
Points: 14

PETER WESTBURY
Nat: GBR. Born: 26.05.1938
Debut: 1969 German GP. Starts: 1

A-Z

DRIVER A-Z

KEN WHARTON

Nat: GBR. Born: 21.03.1916. Died: 12.01.1957
Debut: 1952 Swiss GP. Starts: 15.
Points: 3

GRAHAM WHITEHEAD

Nat: GBR. Born: 15.04.1922. Died: 15.01.1981
Debut: 1952 British GP. Starts: 1

PETER WHITEHEAD

Nat: GBR. Born: 12.11.1914. Died: 20.09.1958
Debut: 1950 French GP. Starts: 10.
Points: 4

BILL WHITEHOUSE

Nat: GBR. Born: 1.04.1909. Died: 14.07.1957
Debut: 1954 British GP. Starts: 1

ROBIN WIDDOWS

Nat: GBR. Born: 27.05.1942
Debut: 1968 British GP. Starts: 1

EPPIE WIETZES

Nat: CAN. Born: 28.05.1938
Debut: 1967 Canadian GP. Starts: 2

MIKE WILDS

Nat: GBR. Born: 7.01.1946
Debut: 1974 United States GP. Starts: 3

JONATHAN WILLIAMS

Nat: GBR. Born: 26.10.1942
Debut: 1967 Mexican GP. Starts: 1

ROGER WILLIAMSON

Nat: GBR. Born: 4.02.1948. Died: 29.07.1973
Debut: 1973 British GP. Starts: 2

JUSTIN WILSON

Nat: GBR. Born: 31.07.1978
Debut: 2003 Australian GP

VIC WILSON

Nat: GBR. Born: 14.4.1931. Died: 2002
Debut: 1960 Italian GP. Starts: 1

MANFRED WINKELHOCK

Nat: GER. Born: 6.10.1951. Died: 12.08.1985
Debut: 1982 South African GP. Starts: 47.
Points: 2

REINE WISELL

Nat: SWE. Born: 30.09.1941
Debut: 1970 United States GP. Starts: 22.
Points: 13

ROELOF WUNDERINK

Nat: NED. Born: 12.12.1948
Debut: 1975 Spanish GP. Starts: 3

ALEXANDER WURZ

Nat: AUT. Born: 15.02.1974
Debut: 1997 Canadian GP. Starts: 52.
Points: 26. FL: 1

ALEX YOONG

Nat: MAL. Born: 20.07.1976
Debut: 2001 Italian GP. Starts: 14

ALESSANDRO ZANARDI

Nat: ITA. Born: 23.10.1966
Debut: 1991 Spanish GP. Starts: 41.
Points: 1

RICARDO ZONTA

Nat: BRA. Born: 23.03.1976
Debut: 1999 Australian GP. Starts: 31.
Points: 3

RENZO ZORZI

Nat: ITA. Born: 12.12.1946
Debut: 1975 Italian GP. Starts: 7. Points: 1

RICARDO ZUNINO

Nat: ARG. Born: 13.04.1949
Debut: 1979 Canadian GP. Starts: 10

Note: All statistics up to 2002

ACKNOWLEDGEMENTS

WRITTEN BY:	SIMON ARRON, MARK HUGHES
STATISTICS:	PETER HIGHAM
PICTURE RESEARCH:	KATHY AGER, TIM WRIGHT, KEVIN WOOD, PETER HIGHAM
BLACK & WHITE PRINTING:	CHARLOTTE GILHOOLY, EMMA CHAMPION
SCANNING:	MARK LEADER, MATT JENNINGS, JOHNNY TINGLE, JENNY CULLIS (ALL LAT), DAN TAYLOR (F1 COLOUR)

Thank you to Paul Fearnley, Steve Small, Henry Hope-Frost, the GP Library (Matt and Diane Spitzley, Doug Nye and Paul Vestey), the Klemantaski Collection (Peter Sachs), Iacona & Bertschi Collection (Cris Bertschi), Archives Serge Pozzoli (Flavien Marcais), National Motor Museum (Jonathan Day, Tom Wood), William Green, F1 Colour (Jamie Robinson, Dan Taylor, Iain Bell, Ken Harrison)

PICTURE CREDITS

All photographs LAT Photographic except: GP Library – p18 (Ascari 2), p18 (Parnell 2), p19 (Sommer 2), p19 (Bonetto), p19 (Chaboud), p19 (Branca), p20 (Levegh), p20 (Louveau), p20 (Pagani), p20 (Pietsch), p26 (De Graffenried 1), p27 (Abecassis), p35 (Abecassis), p36 (Heeks), p37 (Helfrich), p37 (Klenk), p37 (Klodwig), p37 (Laurent 2), p37 (Moss 1), p38 (Stuck), p39 (De Tornaco), p46 (Giraud-Cabantous), p46 (Heeks), p47 (Krause), p47 (Pilette), p48 (Seidel), p87 (Goethals), p458 (Galvez), p466 (Mieres); Klemantaski Collection – p20 (Martin), p26 (Gonzalez 1), p27 (Fischer), p28 (Hamilton), p37 (Laurent 1), p38 (O'Brien), p54 (Maglioli 2), p55 (Berger), p55 (Flockhart), p63 (Gonzalez), p63 (Herrmann), p63 (Bucci), p65 (Schell 1), p71 (Gonzalez 2), p79 (England), p88 (Guelfi), p88 (Herrmann), p95 (De Beaufort 2), p105 (Cabianca), p106 (Drogo), p108 (Thiele), p108 (Wilson), p117 (Collomb), p117 (Fairman), p126 (Seidel 1), p142 (Taylor 3), p142 (Gardner); Archives Serge Pozzoli – p20 (Rol); National Motor Museum – p35 (Frere 2), p36 (Flinterman), p37 (Van Der Lof); Iacona & Bertacchi Collection – p44 (Galvez), p44 (Barber), p45 (Birger), p47 (Manzon), p47 (Menditeguy), p48 (Schwelm Cruz), p53 (Farina 1), p54 (Bayol), p55 (Loyer), p56 (Rosier 1), p63 (Birger), p64 (Iglesias), p64 (Mantovani), p79 (De Portago), p85 (Schell 1), p88 (Gould), p88 (Menditeguy), p105 (Menditeguy), p106 (Bonomi), p106 (Creus), p106 (Estefano), p107 (Gonzalez), p107 (Gregory), p107 (Rodriguez Larreta), p108 (Scarlatti), p108 (Stacey), p455 (Cantoni), p464 (Landi), p474 (Schwelm Cruz), p475 (Serafini); Motor Presse – p83 (Gibson); William Green Motor Racing Library – p126 (Mayer); Grand Prix Photo – p466 (Manzon), p470 (Perdisa), p471 (Raby), p474 (Scarlatti), p474 (Jo Schlesser).

Every effort has been made to contact all copyright holders and any omissions will be rectified in any subsequent editions